History of Education in America

Eighth Edition

John D. Pulliam
Professor Emeritus
University of Montana

James J. Van Patten
University of Arkansas–Fayetteville

Merrill
Prentice Hall

Upper Saddle River, New Jersey
Columbus, Ohio

Library of Congress Cataloging in Publication Data

Pulliam, John D.
    History of education in America / John D. Pulliam, James J. Van Patten.—8th ed.
        p. cm.
    Includes bibliographical references and index.
    ISBN 0-13-061894-2
        1. Education—United States—History. I. Van Patten, James J. II. Title.
    LA205 .P84 2003
    370'973—dc21

2001056839

Vice President and Publisher: Jeffery W. Johnston
Executive Editor: Debra A. Stollenwerk
Editorial Assistant: Mary Morrill
Production Editor: Kimberly J. Lundy
Assistant Editor: Daniel J. Parker
Production Coordination: Lea Baranowski, Carlisle Publishers Services
Design Coordinator: Diane C. Lorenzo
Photo Coordinator: Kathleen Kirtland
Cover Designer: Bryan Huber
Cover Image: Corbis Stock Market
Production Manager: Pamela D. Bennett
Director of Marketing: Ann Castel Davis
Marketing Manager: Krista Groshong
Marketing Coordinator: Tyra Cooper

This book was set in Garamond by Carlisle Communications, Ltd. It was printed and bound by R. R. Donnelley & Sons Company. The cover was printed by The Lehigh Press, Inc.

Photo Credits:
H. M. Herget/National Geographic Image Collection, p. 1; Will Rapport/B. F. Skinner Foundation, Courtesy of B. F. Skinner, p. 29; New England Dame School, 1713 (engraving)/Corbis, p. 79; Corporate Digital Archive, p. 103; Land Grant College, University of Arkansas–Fayetteville, Old Main, p. 127; Laimute E. Druskis/PH College, p. 155; Scott Cunningham/Merrill, pp. 185, 289; Stan Wakefield/PH College, p. 229; Anthony Magnacca/Merrill, p. 337.

Pearson Education Ltd.
Pearson Education Australia Pty. Limited
Pearson Education Singapore Pte. Ltd.
Pearson Education North Asia Ltd.
Pearson Education Canada, Ltd.
Pearson Educación de Mexico, S.A. de C.V.
Pearson Education—Japan
Pearson Education Malaysia Pte. Ltd.
Pearson Education, Upper Saddle River, New Jersey

Merrill
Prentice Hall

10 9 8 7 6 5 4 3
ISBN: 0-13-061894-2

PREFACE

The Importance of Gaining Perspective

As we pass through the portal of a new millennium, the times are changing so rapidly that keeping pace with any field is extremely difficult. This knowledge explosion affects all scholars as they seek to find and synthesize the latest research. Many educators discover that they must reduce the scope of their reading in order to concentrate on their own special areas. At the same time, only knowledge of the entire field can provide a strong foundation for understanding the profession, thereby enabling educators to gain perspective on their personal roles.

As we place current events in historical perspective, cycles of both proactive and reactive thinking and action are revealed. Educators continue to revisit concepts previously discarded and, by putting new wine in an old bottle, proclaim innovations and new frontiers for education without being aware that this knowledge is already part of educational history. As historian Christopher Lasch pointed out in *The Culture of Narcissism,* people with no understanding of their history are lost in the present and unable to plan for the future.

In *War and Anti-War,* Alvin Toffler notes that we are living at a fantastic moment of human history. He finds the world system taking on Prigoginian characteristics—looking more like the physical, chemical, and social systems described by Ilya Prigogine, the Nobel prize-winning scientist who identified what he called "dissipative-structures." In these structures, all parts of the system are in constant fluctuation. Parts of each system become extremely vulnerable to external influences. This idea is also the basis of chaos theory. How does this apply to education? Educators and their institutions are facing flux and instability as attempts are made to respond to myriad new external and internal pressures and influences. Educational historians have an opportunity to place these changes in proper perspective.

The Purpose of This Textbook

The purpose of this book is to provide an overview of the history of American education and to serve as a quick reference to the most important persons, dates, events, and movements that shaped the nation's system of education. The basic concepts and theories that underlie educational practice are presented in compact form. In order to pack as much information as possible into a succinct volume, interpretation is left largely to the reader or to professors who use the book as a text. Certainly the raging controversy between the traditionalists and revisionists is important. The differences between Michael Katz and H. Giroux (radical revisionists) and David Tyack (interpreter of social forces) are pronounced. Before readers can make judgments of interpretation, they must read and retain a great deal of factual information, and that is provided in this book. Comprehensive coverage is presented in the same compact, readable format of earlier editions. Quotes from leading authors of the period introduce each chapter.

New to the Eighth Edition

- ❑ Reorganization into three major divisions for ease in reading and finding information. The first deals with the historical, philosophical, psychological, and social foundations upon which all education is based. The second is a chronological treatment of American education from colonial beginnings to the modern era. The third covers laws, court cases, issues, political changes, and conflicts in education today with a view toward future events.
- ❑ Graphs, photographs, and time lines depicting events, people, and significant milestones in American education.
- ❑ A Companion Website (www.prenhall.com/pulliam) accompanying this text includes topic overviews, web links, readings, and resources. With the Electronic Bluebook feature, students can send answers to end-of-chapter activities, homework assignments, or essays directly to their instructor's e-mail. "Increasing Understanding Through Online Research" articles provide avenues to research pertinent topics via the Internet.
- ❑ Expanded treatment of new educational delivery systems such as distance learning, online resources, computer-based research, and emerging educational technologies.
- ❑ Integration of activities and study guides at the end of each chapter with expanded and updated sources, including the glossary and annotated bibliography.
- ❑ Inclusion of the development of educational technology and the influence of technology on schooling throughout the book.
- ❑ Update of laws, litigation, and current educational issues both in the chapters and in the "Then to Now" sections.
- ❑ New emphasis on special education, the education of women and minorities, the impact of political conflict on educational theory and practice, and an overview of modern assessment and educational testing.
- ❑ Treatment throughout of the social and psychological influence on schools caused by dramatic events such as school violence and the war on terrorism following September 11, 2001.

Other Text Features

- ❑ The end of each chapter provides sections for engaging students in higher order thinking and "hands-on" learning experiences. "Gaining Perspective Through Critical Analysis" presents discussion questions that review significant content areas. "History in Action in Today's Classrooms" suggests activities to get students out of the classroom and engaging in meaningful learning experiences.

❑ This edition includes the most recent legislation, court decisions, and governmental policies and programs initiated by the current Congress and the George W. Bush administration to improve student access and achievement at all educational levels. Also included is information about universal public school access to the Internet and the World Wide Web with proper safeguards (such as Cyberpatrol).

❑ A chapter on educational trends integrates past and future and reflects the work of such popular authors as Arthur Wirth, John Naisbitt, Alvin Toffler, Joseph Coates, Paul Kennedy, Wendell Bell, Bill Gates, and C. Owen Paepke. Changing demographics and new delivery systems are included in this edition.

❑ Selective chapter bibliographies and a general annotated bibliography have been updated and are provided as guides for more detailed study. The reader is also urged to pursue original documents as well as interpretative histories.

ACKNOWLEDGMENTS

We are indebted to Debra A. Stollenwerk for her support and encouragement to produce an eighth edition, to Lea Baranowski and Kimberly J. Lundy for production guidance, to copy editor Leslie Weber for excellent editing, to assistant editor Daniel J. Parker, whose constant support for our work was invaluable, and to Carol Sykes and Kathy Kirtland for their work in securing photos. Their readiness to answer our many questions during the writing process made it a valuable experience for us. In addition, Timothy J. Bergen Jr., Fred Kierstead, Joseph Coates, and Marcia Imbeau made invaluable suggestions about material to be included in this edition.

Also invaluable was the work of Brenda Luper with her computer expertise, cheerful disposition, and readiness to assist in manuscript completion. Also invaluable was the support and computer, proofreading, and research skills of Elizabeth C. McKee (University of Arkansas librarian), Dean Reed Greenwood, Chris Lucas, Bart Cohen, Brandi Holt, Gina and Sonja Bennett, and Tommie Astin. Special thanks go to Florida Atlantic University doctoral candidate Susan B. Korb for her assistance with the project

Last, but certainly not least, we want to thank the reviewers for this edition: Richard Farber, The College of New Jersey; John Georgeoff, Purdue University; Anne M. Knupfer, Purdue University; and Sheryl McGlamery, University of Nebraska at Omaha.

DISCOVER THE COMPANION WEBSITE ACCOMPANYING THIS BOOK

The Prentice Hall Companion Website: A Virtual Learning Environment

Technology is a constantly growing and changing aspect of our field that is creating a need for content and resources. To address this emerging need, Prentice Hall has developed an online learning environment for students and professors alike—Companion Websites—to support our textbooks.

In creating a Companion Website, our goal is to build on and enhance what the textbook already offers. For this reason, the content for each user-friendly website is organized by topic and provides the professor and student with a variety of meaningful resources. Common features of a Companion Website include:

For the Professor—

Every Companion Website integrates **Syllabus Manager**™, an online syllabus creation and management utility.

- ❑ **Syllabus Manager**™ provides you, the instructor, with an easy, step-by-step process to create and revise syllabi, with direct links into the Companion Website and other online content without having to learn HTML.
- ❑ Students may log on to your syllabus during any study session. All they need to know is the web address for the Companion Website and the password you've assigned to your syllabus.
- ❑ After you have created a syllabus using **Syllabus Manager**™, students may enter the syllabus for their course section from any point in the Companion Website.
- ❑ Clicking on a date, the student is shown the list of activities for the assignment. The activities for each assignment are linked directly to actual content, saving time for students.
- ❑ Adding assignments consists of clicking on the desired due date, then filling in the details of the assignment—name of the assignment, instructions, and whether it is a one-time or repeating assignment.

- In addition, links to other activities can be created easily. If the activity is online, a URL can be entered in the space provided, and it will be linked automatically in the final syllabus.
- Your completed syllabus is hosted on our servers, allowing convenient updates from any computer on the Internet. Changes you make to your syllabus are immediately available to your students at their next logon.

For the Student—

- **Topic Overviews**—outline key concepts in topic areas
- **Web Links**—a wide range of websites that provide useful and current information related to each topic area
- **Readings**—suggested readings or further study of certain aspects of the topic areas
- **Resources**—a listing of links to more general resources within each topic area
- **Organizations**—lists of links to organizations pertinent to certain topic areas
- **Electronic Bluebook**—send homework or essays directly to your instructor's e-mail with this paperless form
- **Message Board**—serves as a virtual bulletin board to post—or respond to—questions or comments to/from a national audience
- **Chat**—real-time chat with anyone who is using the text anywhere in the country—ideal for discussion and study groups, class projects, etc.

To take advantage of these and other resources, please visit the *History of Education in America,* Eighth Edition, Companion Website at

www.prenhall.com/pulliam

CONTENTS

Chapter 1   Introduction: Applying History to Education Today   1

Society and Education: Schools and the Communities They Serve   8
Accelerating Rate of Change   11
History and Purposes of Educational History   16
Intellectual Background   20
Then to Now   23
Gaining Perspective Through Critical Analysis   26
History in Action in Today's Classrooms   27
Increased Understanding Through Online Research   27
Bibliography   27

Chapter 2   Shaping the Schools: Philosophical and Psychological Foundations   29

Introduction to Educational Philosophy   30
Schools of Educational Philosophy   32
Psychology and Education   59
Child Study and Measurement   70
Then to Now   73
Gaining Perspective Through Critical Analysis   76
History in Action in Today's Classrooms   76
Increased Understanding Through Online Research   76
Bibliography   76

Chapter 3   American Education: Our European Heritage and the Colonial Influence   79

Colonial Melting Pot   82
Religious Sectarianism   83

Social Class in the Colonial Environment   84
The Southern Colonies   85
The Middle Colonies   89
The New England Colonies   92
Then to Now   97
Gaining Perspective Through Critical Analysis   101
History in Action in Today's Classrooms   101
Increased Understanding Through Online Research   102
Bibliography   102

Chapter 4   American Education: The American Revolution   103

Democratic Ideals   104
Changes in Colonial Culture   105
The Shift in the Colonial Mind   106
Colonial Liberalism   108
Educational Changes in the Later Colonial Period   109
The War and After   110
Efforts of Educational Founders   111
Revolutionary Period Educational Leadership   112
Early Government Proposals   114
Other Educational Movements   115
School Ideas and the Curriculum   116
Then to Now   117
Gaining Perspective Through Critical Analysis   123
History in Action in Today's Classrooms   124
Increased Understanding Through Online Research   124
Bibliography   124

Chapter 5   American Education: 1812–1865   127

Social, Political, and Economic Trends   128
The Age of the Common School Revival   133
Birth of the American High School   135
Higher Education Before the Civil War   136
American Educational Leadership   139
European Influences   142
Then to Now   148
Gaining Perspective Through Critical Analysis   152
History in Action in Today's Classrooms   153
Increased Understanding Through Online Research   153
Bibliography   153

Chapter 6 American Education: 1865–1918 155

Inhibited Development of Education in the South   158
National Affairs and Progress   161
The Public School Ideal   163
The American Public High School   163
Vocational and Industrial Education   167
Parochial and Private Education   169
Higher Education   170
Schools and Colleges for Minority Groups   172
Teacher Education   173
Development of Educational Philosophy   176
Then to Now   179
Gaining Perspective Through Critical Analysis   183
History in Action in Today's Classrooms   183
Increased Understanding Through Online Research   184
Bibliography   184

Chapter 7 American Education: 1918 to the Present   185

Major Educational Changes   187
Evolution of the Modern Institutional Structure   190
School Finance and Control   202
Federal Participation in Education   204
Experiments and Innovations in the Twentieth Century   209
Progressive Educators and Their Critics   212
Academic Freedom and the Educational Profession   214
Teacher Education   215
A New Century—The Twenty-First   220
Then to Now   222
Gaining Perspective Through Critical Analysis   225
History in Action in Today's Classrooms   225
Increased Understanding Through Online Research   226
Bibliography   226

Chapter 8 Issues in Modern American Education   229

Litigation: The Courts and Problems of Education   232
More Recent Educational Critics   249
Assessment and Accountability   259
Taking Sides Today and Tomorrow   280
Gaining Perspective Through Critical Analysis   284
History in Action in Today's Classroom   284

Increased Understanding Through Online Research   284
Bibliography   285

Chapter 9   *Educational Reform: 1980s, 1990s, 2000s, and the Search for Excellence   289*

The Great American Educational Reform Movement   290
Achieving Excellence in Teacher Education   316
Reform in Educational Administration   326
The Search for Excellence Continues   330
Gaining Perspective Through Critical Analysis   331
History in Action in Today's Classrooms   331
Increased Understanding Through Online Research   332
Bibliography   332

Chapter 10   *Education in the Future: From Now to Then   337*

Trends in Education in the Twenty-First Century   345
The Futures Movement   347
Methods of Futures Research   350
Schools of Futuristic Thought   352
Implications for Educational Theory   356
Characteristics of Futuristic Education   359
Futures Curriculum   364
Future Trends   367
Gaining Perspective Through Critical Analysis   372
History in Action in Today's Classrooms   372
Increased Understanding Through Online Research   373
Bibliography   373

General Annotated Bibliography   376

Glossary   381

Index   387

CHAPTER ONE

INTRODUCTION: APPLYING HISTORY TO EDUCATION TODAY

Lycurgus would never reduce his laws into writing . . . for he thought that the most material points . . . such as . . . the public welfare, being imprinted on the hearts of their youth by a good discipline . . . would find a stronger security, than any compulsion would be, in the principles of action formed in them by their best lawgiver, education.

Plutarch

Being a form of social action, education . . . is rooted in some actual culture and expresses the philosophy and recognized needs of that culture.

Alexis de Tocqueville

Greek City States	Roman Republic	BC	AD	Roman Empire	Dark Ages
c 900 Homer	Cato		First Century Hebrew elementary schools		
	Cicero		Quintilian Tacitus		
Athens Sparta					
		University of Alexandria		360 Julian revived classical learning	
Fifth and Fourth Centuries Socrates Plato Aristotle Isocrates				529 Justinian closed pagan universities	

Figure 1.1   Selected Historical Figures and Events That Influenced American Education

As part of the celebration of the close of the second millennium, a group of world-famous scientists met in New York to identify the most profound invention or discovery of the past 1,000 years. There were advocates of the voyages of discovery, the internal combustion engine, space exploration, and the splitting of the atom. Others suggested the big bang theory of the creation of the universe, DNA, or the development of the microchip computer. But in the final analysis these experts agreed that no invention was more significant than Gutenberg's use of movable type in a printing press in the year 1440. Thus the most salient invention in terms of its impact on human life and culture was one in educational technology. Printing and the spread of knowledge did more to alter civilization than anything else. This illustrates just how powerful a force education and the dissemination of information can be.

This is a book in the field of social foundations of education with a major focus on the history of education in the United States. It is not confined to tracing events specific to one aspect of the culture, such as the schools, but also deals with the underlying social and philosophical conditions that support those schools. Purposes and goals of educational institutions in a simple agricultural village in colonial or early national America were vastly different from those found in a modern, urban, diverse, multicultural community. Contemporary institutions are best understood by studying the history of how they evolved. Sociology of the community, different concepts of the psychology of learning, conflicting ideas about what values are most important, and issues about how schools should be controlled and supported are fundamental to comprehending education now.

Superimposed upon this is the accelerating rate of change and the vast increase in available information, which alter the learning environment and the curriculum for the future. Most adult Americans matriculated before personal computers and the

Middle Ages		Renaissance		Reformation
569–632 Mohammed	776–804 Alcuin	1158 University of Paris	1466–1536 Erasmus and humanism	
800 Learning revived by Charlemagne	Chivalry	1225–1274 Thomas Aquinas		1517 Luther's 95 Theses
Monasticism		Scholasticism		1509–1565 Calvin
		Growth of universities		1550 Knox and English Puritans

Internet were universally available, and certainly before there was a global market-place or an information economy. Therefore history cannot ignore the social, philo-sophical, and psychological foundations of education. It must also treat themes such as the rapid rate of social change, new vocational and informational skills, educational issues and reform, and the shifting economy (agricultural–industrial–informational). The reader may find additional sources for these themes at the Merrill Teaching Foundations Website *http://www.prenhall.com/foundations-cluster.*

In this chapter we will examine a few of the most important social forces that govern the relationship between educational institutions and the communities they serve. We will also treat educational history as a discipline and survey the intellectual forces that have had a major influence on American schools. Chapter 2 deals with the philosophical and psychological foundations of education.

No educational system is created in a vacuum. Schools exist now to serve the needs of contemporary American society, but these needs are changing rapidly as is the society itself. There is a good deal of confusion and conflict now about the goals of education and about what alterations should be made. This is easier to compre-hend when we examine cultures less complicated than ours is now. Examples are found in colonial villages and nineteenth-century rural communities where agree-ment about the aims of education and the structure of institutions was easily reached. We will also briefly look at pedagogical models from societies antecedent to ours for comparison.

The authors assume that readers of this volume have some familiarity with mod-ern American education, probably from having passed through the public schools. Firsthand experience is critical, and its great value in teacher preparation is widely recognized. This is why almost all colleges and departments of education require field experience prior to student teaching. But attending or working in a given school may create the false impression that there is universal agreement about the function, philosophy, curriculum, and learning styles. It may not reveal the deep divisions over educational policy found in many communities. This is why a broader historical study of educational institutions and the foundations upon which they rest is necessary for understanding as well as for participating in making changes in the future.

The fundamental link between any educational theory and the historical context in which it developed can never be ignored. No one in contemporary America would deny sexual, class, or racial equality so far as educational opportunity is concerned. Yet, we need look only back to the 1880s for a time when women had no control over their own property and acquired schooling only with permission of their husbands or fathers. Racially segregated schools were commonplace in the United States until the 1950s while in parts of colonial America only boys from upper classes received formal education.

Today we try to provide schooling for every child, including those so severely handicapped or disabled that special education teachers must be sent to their homes, while those able to attend school are mainstreamed into regular classrooms in order to provide the least restrictive environment. Efforts are made to accommodate children who are not proficient in the use of English through bilingual programs, while the children of aliens not legally living and working in the United States are admitted to schools under the child benefit theory. Equality of educational opportunity is a core value, but there is much concern over the cost of programs that benefit only a small part of the population.

Obviously the ability to succeed in a multicultural society, to work in a global economy, to access the Internet, or to find employment in a foreign business environment were not goals of the founding fathers. While we must constantly alter the schools to meet current and future needs, we are never free from the influence of the past. Social history shows why French, German, and Spanish are widely taught in American schools while Chinese, Russian, and Swahili are not. Should this be so? The fact that a fifth of the world's people speak Chinese is certainly an argument for teaching that language. Yet, if Chinese were to be taught to all American students, something else in the curriculum would have to be eliminated or time in school would have to be extended. The choice is a philosophic one, closely related to social theory and influenced by history.

As Alvin Toffler demonstrated in *Future Shock*, the pace of change and the creation of new information are the most significant characteristics of modern society. Schools were established for the express purpose of inducting the young into the culture of the society into which they were born and in which they must learn to live as responsible and useful members of the community. This is not so easily accomplished in an age of accelerating change. Schools are major social institutions. As such, they are constantly bombarded with new demands and challenged with alternative ideas about how goals might be achieved. Historical traditions and entrenched values conflict with preparation for an unknown future. American culture has long provided for opposing viewpoints to be passionately expressed, but debate is more intense today because basic values and the public philosophy are at stake.

Presently, the United States is enjoying a period of relative prosperity. Threats of Communist domination and nuclear war have vastly diminished. Nevertheless the world suffers from poverty, pollution, underemployment, starvation, ethnic strife, and the violation of basic human rights. That terrorism exists was clearly demonstrated by the attack on September 11, 2001. The appearance of safety and economic well-being does not guarantee that today's students will be free to meet all of their future needs. Education must anticipate the knowledge, skills, and attitudes required for future success. Modern teachers are likely to be overwhelmed by the number and variety of demands made and by conflicting ideas about how these should be met. In this age of information overload—when the number of words electronically stored exceeds the total number in print—it is especially important for educators to have a theoretical base to serve as a guide through the labyrinth of opinions and facts. Misconceptions and misunderstandings can be avoided if teachers have the social, philosophical, and psychological foundations well in hand.

Our present culture has been built over time. The schools have always reflected the dominant ideology of a given period of history. In colonial times, the orientation was toward Europe, building character for salvation, and the preservation of values. There was no distinction between philosophy and theology. It was assumed that the future would be just like the past. Today, we must expect that the current rate of change will continue to accelerate. Our students must "learn" a living, build a foundation for continuing education throughout life, and contribute to solving the problems of the world. An understanding of how we evolved to this stage and a study of the sociology, psychology, and theory of education will aid in building a bridge to the future.

The age of electronic communications, cybernation, the Internet, and mushrooming scientific discovery is upon us. Astronomers ponder an expanding universe filled with quasars, visible galaxies no longer in existence, rapidly spinning neutron stars, supernova explosions, and elusive black holes. At the opposite end of reality, quantum physicists study subatomic quarks, which are only virtual because they can never be seen or directly measured. Artificial intelligence and human cloning are on the horizon while superconductors are grown from organic crystal. In history, exact dates are fixed by comparing the decay of radioactive carbon-14 in living tissues with the more stable and common carbon-12.

To understand schooling in this age of exponential change, teachers must know how educational institutions developed, their relationship to society, what dangers and opportunities are linked to them, what future developments can be predicted, and the philosophical implications. In short, the theory and practice of education now are best revealed through the historical, social, philosophical, and psychological foundations. The relationship between these foundations and the schools is more easily seen in societies less complex than ours. The five following historical models illustrate efforts to educate prior to the evolution of many contemporary issues:

In 490 B.C. the first marathon runner arrived in the city-state of Athens to announce victory over the Persians. Were we to reconstruct a school of the time, it would be located in one of the temples or public buildings, perhaps on the *stoa* (open porch). Students would be adolescent boys of the citizenship class. Their status would be apparent from their short woolen tunics with classic designs embroidered around the skirt hems. The teacher is a young man from a leading family, chosen for his dignified bearing and knowledge of the culture. It would be beneath his dignity to accept pay for the civic duty and privilege of teaching, although pleased fathers might sometimes give him a present. Responsibility for the education of sons rests with the fathers, who would have taught them basic reading before entering the school. Military training only is a function of the state, and these students will spend their afternoons practicing martial arts and athletics. The curriculum this morning is based on the *Iliad,* a copy of which, on rolled parchment, is in the hands of the instructor. Each boy in turn recites a previously learned passage from the familiar poem. The pupils are evaluated for accuracy, attitude, clarity of speech, posture, and enthusiasm. Passing citizens pause to listen to the presentations and to praise good work. The boys understand the importance of learning their culture, which they believe to be the superior one not only in Greece but in the world. Language, literature, manners, customs, skill in debate, and national defense are vital to these boys, who will later proudly take their seats in the assembly of free citizens.

Half a century after the death of Julius Caesar and the dawn of the Christian era, M. F. Quintilian has opened his school of oratory in a room of his spacious Roman home. His fame and success enable him to charge high fees, and graduates of his school find high places in the governmental bureaucracy. Quintilian has written several books on education and invented pedagogical devices such as carved ivory blocks over which children move their fingers to learn Latin letters. The dozen well-dressed and well-groomed students obviously are from wealthy patrician families. They have learned to read Latin and a little Greek at home from their fathers or hired tutors. Now in the Institution of Oratory, they seek skills needed for clerks, legal advisers, and business managers in the service of the wealthy and politically powerful. Quintilian's model is a "good man skilled in speaking." By this he means one able to present logical arguments and to persuade, but also a person of character and integrity. The classroom is light, and one side is open to a fountain in the atrium. On a raised platform, a boy wearing a white toga as befits one running for public office is making a speech in favor of invading Gaul. His speech is judged for logic, clarity, and power to persuade. When finished, the whole class offers a critique, supervised by the master. Students here are motivated because they know upward mobility in the vast empire depends upon skill in speaking and forensics.

In the year 1636 when Harvard College was founded in the American colonies, the Moravian educator J. A. Comenius received permission from the city fathers of Amsterdam to open a school. Like most European cities at the time, Amsterdam had no system of public education, but the town council was anxious to promote learning and had raised a modest fund to help support the famous teacher. Comenius agreed to teach thirty boys and girls from Protestant families in the community who could not afford private schooling and to furnish each with an illustrated textbook of eighteen pages. Published in German, the text could be used by pupils not prepared in Latin grammar.

Located in a loft above a grain merchant's warehouse, the school is furnished with stools, maps, scientific drawings, and objects designed to arouse the interest of students. Comenius is a fatherly figure with a long flowing beard and gowns appropriate to his office as bishop of the Moravian sect. There is an atmosphere of love and kindness here with no corporal punishment or harsh discipline. Believing that all children including females should be able to read the Bible for themselves, the parents encourage these youngsters to learn. Everything is made easy by moving from the simple to the complex and from the familiar to the unfamiliar. Comenius believes in a curriculum as broad as life itself, but concentrates here on what each pupil is able to master at a given age. The students are clean and neatly dressed. The teacher has made a real effort to explain why the lessons are important and to create a family-like environment. Students feel fortunate to attend and will be sorry to see the school close in a few months. Civic leaders wish that there were more teachers like Comenius and that similar schools could be provided for all children.

At the dawn of the eighteenth century, a primary school is operating in the town of Deham in Massachusetts Bay Colony. Here, a plain clapboard building has been built by the town and furnished with benches, a fireplace, a board for writing sums with chalk, and an imposing desk on a raised platform for the master. Twenty-five pupils in attendance range in age from six to fourteen. Both sexes are represented, but there are no blacks or Indians or children from non-Puritan families. The teacher is proud of his three years of higher education at Harvard College, which gives him status in the community almost equal to that of the local preacher. This is a school of reading with a little writing and simple sums in addition. The *New England Primer*, the *Psalter*, and the Bible are in evidence, while younger children carry hornbooks. Students read and recite aloud. The schoolmaster maintains a stern and severe atmosphere and is ready to use his hickory stick at any sign of inattention or mischief. Learning here is considered a serious matter and a duty for every child. Today the opening exercise is a lecture on the behavior God expects from good children and the consequences of failure to meet those expectations.

Two years after the stock market crash in 1929, thirty pupils are seated in small chairs in a circle around their teacher. This is a fourth grade class in a public school in Springfield, Missouri. The sixteen girls and fourteen boys are much alike in that they all come from middle-class homes. While most are Protestant, there are four Catholic children and one who is Jewish. The teacher is pleased that two of the girls are black because most Negro children attend a school on the other side of town and she believes in integration. A graduate of the Normal school in Warrensburg, she has been steeped in the theory of progressive education and Gestalt psychology. She tries to implement principles such as interest as the guide to all work, scientific study of child development, and freedom to choose styles of learning. The teacher very much admires John Dewey, whom she once heard speak in St. Louis. Before the students arrived this morning, she "seeded" the classroom with potted tulips, wooden shoes, cheeses, and pictures of windmills. The teacher expects that this will lead to spontaneous interest on the part of the children in studying the culture of Holland.

The atmosphere here is open and friendly, and the teacher hopes that a better understanding of other societies will improve relations among and between her classroom charges.

SOCIETY AND EDUCATION:
SCHOOLS AND THE COMMUNITIES THEY SERVE

Unexpected, dramatic, and unwanted events may have a shocking impact which destroys the tranquil nature of a culture and upsets the stable balance between society and education. Incidents of school violence create turmoil and fear with which teachers must deal before normal instruction can be resumed. Other prime examples of disruption include the Civil War, the Great Depression, the Japanese attack on Pearl Harbor and the terrorist bombing of the World Trade Center in New York. Such happenings alter the world as we know it, and this is especially significant when the causes and true nature of the occurrence are poorly understood. American adults and pupils in schools could not easily comprehend the reasons why innocent civilians would be attacked or disease-laden letters would be sent. Few incidents like the September 11, 2001 attack have had a major impact on American society, but those few had profound and lasting consequences. Consider these examples:

Following the election of Abraham Lincoln in 1860, Southern states confidently expected that after a few military setbacks the federal government would allow their secession. No one anticipated a destructive war lasting nearly five years, the impact of the emancipation of slaves, the bitterness of the fighting, or the sacrifices that would be made by every community. Whole academies of young men and their teachers went off to join both armies, and public education in the South suffered for generations following the war. At the end, the Union was preserved, sectionalism and states rights declined, a new nation emerged, and the old South was indeed gone with the wind. The Civil War had a major and lasting effect on all aspects of American culture, education included.

America escaped almost unscathed from World War I. There followed a period of prosperity and optimism which was suddenly shattered by the stock market crash of 1929. Most Americans could not comprehend the reasons for the economic collapse and the resulting unemployment, poverty, soup kitchens, and loss of confidence. New Deal efforts to stimulate the economy were not entirely successful and the depression only ended with the wartime economy of 1941. No aspect of the culture escaped the shattering of the American dream which permeated the society in the 1930's, but education was especially hard hit. Teachers had to work with students from families which had lost faith in the system and who had little hope for gainful employment in the future.

The ravaging surprise attack on Pearl Harbor in December, 1941, affected all Americans as much as the destruction of the World Trade Center in 2001. Neither attack was anticipated, and both electrified the people and brought about a unified response. With Pearl Harbor, the enemy was known and the appropriate reaction was clear. Certainly there was fear, but at no other time in American history has the solidarity and resolve of the people been so clearly demonstrated. The educational system geared up with the rest of the nation to defeat the empire of Japan. Yet in both World War II and the recent terrorist attacks, there were aspects that passed the understanding of most Americans. When Japanese military power had been largely destroyed, why would thousands of young men volunteer to train for suicide missions as pilots of kamikaze aircraft? The vast majority of these planes were shot out of the air but those that got through killed many sailors and sank numerous American Navy ships. Following September 11, 2001, many asked why the terrorists hated us enough to commit these hideous acts, and why they would commit suicide to kill Americans. The restoration of order after chaotic events take place requires an effort to understand what happened so that teachers may help students comprehend the nature of the tragedy. History is the best tool we have for making sense out of otherwise incomprehensible events. From feudal times, Japanese society was dominated by the Samurai class of warriors with their strict code called Bushido. This required unquestioning loyalty and obedience and placed honor before life. Superimposed upon this was the divine status of the emperor and his god-like authority. Military leaders in Japan used this tradition as a basis of training generations of soldiers, including kamikaze pilots. Since they had complete control over the media and the schools, information about military defeats was suppressed while stress on fanatic patriotism and loyalty to the emperor continued to the end.

On the opposite side of the world, Islamic people developed a tradition quite different from the Japanese Bushido but with similar results. From 1090, an order of Muslim fanatics known as Assassins emerged in Persia and Syria. They believed it was the will of Allah that they kill Crusaders and other infidels. They interpreted the Koran to say that if they were killed while fighting nonbelievers, they would go at once to heaven and be given wonderful rewards forever. The Assassin tradition has been revived many times in history, especially during times of fundamentalist revolution such as occurred recently in Iraq and Iran. It has been used in training camps for Islamic warriors and fits easily into the mind-set for terrorists, especially those who believe the United States is the great evil. Historical analysis should help in the discussion of outrageous events that must be part of the healing process before normal schooling can continue. Understanding is just as important as restoring a sense of safety.

Obviously the learning process needs safe and stable conditions and a feeling of wellbeing. During the cold war, teachers had to deal with the very real threat of a nuclear attack. Students in schools that have experienced acts of violence by other students need to be calmed and reassured. American society has been vastly altered by the events of September 11, 2001, and the subsequent hunt for the culprits in Afghanistan. The changes brought about by the terrorism directed at the World Trade Center and the Pentagon cannot be ignored by educators. As the famous educational philosopher John Dewey held, schools must simplify, purify, and order the environment so that learning may proceed. All American teachers must now shoulder the difficult task of making students feel safe and comfortable in an age of terrorist fear.

History of American education has its primary focus on the creation and evolution of schools in the United States. It also requires careful examination of the antecedents, especially those of European and Western civilization. This is not to imply that what happened in Inca, Chinese, or Egyptian culture, among others, is less important but only that the direct historical roots of our modern system are found in ancient Greece, Rome, and the nations of Europe. As these cultures evolved, many practices and assumptions about schools became traditional. Schools have not existed in all cultures. They were not found in hunting and gathering societies prior to the agricultural revolution. Formal efforts to teach came with civilization, writing, literature, and distinct cultural values. Different answers to fundamental questions emerged quite early.

Upper-class Athenian fathers assumed responsibility for teaching their sons the unique parts of their culture that they believed vital for the good life and the preservation of their city. No provision was made for girls, slaves, lower-class Athenian boys, or foreigners. Sparta, with its warlike traditions, opted for a state-controlled military academy for both boys and girls of the citizenship class. Neither Athens nor Sparta believed in vocational education. Making a living was left to the servile class in Athens and to the Helot slaves in Sparta. Educational theory remained simple until Plato developed his sophisticated system (see Chapter 2). Basic questions such as who would be taught, qualifications of teachers, the curriculum, and how schools would be supported were answered by the ancients in ways not now acceptable. Some things do persist over long periods of time. The *Iliad* was studied in ancient Athens, Rome, eighteenth-century British public schools, colonial America, and frontier colleges in the United States. Even with all the new subjects added and all the programs now required in contemporary schools, it is likely that all students will have some familiarity with Homer's classic poem, although perhaps not for the reasons it was studied in the ancient world.

To understand just how important is the relationship between a culture and its education, we must trace the most salient forces that have shaped and continue to influence communities. Insight may be gained by considering the most uncomplicated culture we can imagine.

A familiar example before the American Revolution is found in Longfellow's classic poem *Evangeline.* Here, the Acadian farmers who make up the tiny village of Grand Pré, Nova Scotia, are all on a first name basis with one another. Their forefathers are all from Normandy, they speak French, and they belong to the Catholic church. No extremes of wealth and poverty exist. Everyone lives in a thatched-roof house of wood with similar outbuildings and gardens. All live by farming except Basil the blacksmith, Michael the fiddler, René the notary, and Father Felician. They all share the same customs, beliefs, taboos, and faith. For example, it is universally held that a fever may be cured by enclosing a spider in a nutshell. Decisions are made by mutual agreement with no need for formal government or law enforcement. The Church is the only institution in Grand Pré. Father Felician is both priest and pedagogue, teaching letters to Evangeline, Gabriel, and other village children. Nothing else is necessary since the notary writes the letters, mathematics is confined to measures of grain, and vocational training is by example. Grand Pré has no strife or conflict. It might have remained so had not a distant English king ordered the village burned. It is unlikely that any actual society as ideal as Grand Pré ever existed, but there were many in early America that were almost as simple. Clearly in such places there would be no issues over the curriculum, the qualifications of teachers, who should be taught, or support and control of education.

Since the development of sociology as a discipline by Auguste Comte, Emile Durkheim, and Max Weber early in the twentieth century, systematic efforts have been made to study social change. Space does not permit a full discussion here, but some themes must be treated in order to understand the history of education as it relates to the culture. Among these are the accelerating rate of change, the concept of cultural lag, and the shrinking of core values.

ACCELERATING RATE OF CHANGE

For most of human history, women and men lived out their lives in periods of slow, evolutionary change. As Toffler argues in *The Third Wave*, past sweeping revolutions have been few and there has been time to adjust. The first major revolution came with the domestication of animals and the deliberate cultivation of crops. Before this, everyone had been engaged in hunting and gathering. There were no social classes, no division of labor, no cities, and no stable food supply. Agriculture allowed for civilization to develop, with rulers, priests, soldiers, and artisans living from the surplus farmers could produce. The population expanded, cities were built, and inventions like irrigation, architecture, philosophy, law, and organized religion flourished. The revolution did not, however, lead to rapid improvement in agricultural methods or technology. It is estimated that in Plato's time seven full-time farmers could produce only enough food for one nonfarmer. Roman farmers tilled the soil by means of a noose around the neck of a horse or ox. The horse collar, which increased the land one man could break by a factor of four, was not invented until the ninth century. Indeed, many centuries were known for only one major technological change, such as the chimney in the eleventh century, which altered architecture. Long after the Industrial Revolution had started, most Americans lived by farming and saw little need for schools to prepare for anything else.

Breakthroughs in science and technology triggered an acceleration of invention in the eighteenth century known as the Industrial Revolution. This time the change was far more rapid, and almost every life was affected. From it we got factories, mass production, automobiles, electricity, labor-saving devices, and great wealth. It also brought pollution, slums, environmental destruction, crowded urban areas, and social unrest. It is misleading to conceive of the Industrial Revolution as an event in history—something that had an end. On the contrary, the changes this great transition brought continue to accumulate at an exponential rate. While we are still adjusting to the huge impact of the Industrial Revolution, the third wave is upon us. This is a revolution marked by the space age, automation, cyberspace, genetic engineering, computers, and the global information economy. It is a revolution of the magnitude of the agricultural or the industrial age, but this time we must adjust to the change in a single generation.

Most futurists anticipate that we will experience changes as great as this each decade into the future. It is this vastly accelerating rate of change that makes it difficult to plan for and anticipate the future or to get social agreement on what needs to be done with education. As you read these words, think of the new things you have experienced so far in your life. A child born today has a reasonable chance to see the dawn of the twenty-second century. Try to imagine what the world will be like then. More to the point, what must we do to prepare the child for survival and success in that world?

In sociology, the most famous treatment of social change was made by William F. Ogburn. He applied statistical methods to social change caused by advances in technology. Ogburn divided the culture into three parts—the material, the adaptive nonmaterial, and the nonadaptive nonmaterial. Material change is the dynamic and accumulative phase of the culture. Over time, the adaptive nonmaterial adjusts to technological change. For example, automobiles were invented and mass produced before there were licenses, traffic laws, or companies offering insurance, but these adjustments were made. However, the motor car also had an impact on personal freedom, houses built in suburbs, and the value system of adolescents—the nonadaptive nonmaterial culture.

The first four historical models presented were not subject to the stresses of rapid change, but the progressive school of the 1930s certainly was. Since the Great Depression, technological invention steadily gained momentum and became increasingly difficult to fathom. Those currently holding positions on school boards or making decisions about federal aid to education may still think in terms of an economy driven by industrial production rather than one based on computer software and microchips. Ogburn was correct in saying that it is difficult for the nonmaterial culture to adapt. This is reflected also in the work of other sociologists like Gunnar Myrdal, Karl Mannheim, and William Sumner. It is a major theme in Merle Curti's *The Social Ideas of American Educators* and underpins almost all futures theory.

There are other interpretations of the impact of technological invention as a driving social force. Sumner was a social Darwinist who applied natural selection and survival of the fittest to social change. In his view, schools should be used as sorting and selecting agencies to pick out those of highest ability and to discard the rest. Social Darwinism is no longer widely accepted in the United States, but its influence can still be seen. An example is the familiar comparison of achievement levels in the American comprehensive secondary school, which admits and attempts to retain all students, with European or Japanese schools, which are highly selective in admission. Karl Marx saw materialistic invention as the basis of class struggle, which is the driving force for all human culture. No longer dominant in eastern Europe, versions of Marxism still control educational theory in China and Cuba. The explanation of just how accelerating change and the creation of new information alter society may continue to be a subject of debate, but there can be no question about its impact upon all social institutions including education.

Cultural Lag.   The crisis facing those who shape education today cannot be explained entirely by the tempo of innovation in the material culture. Ogburn pointed out that scarcity of invention in the adaptive culture along with factors such as conservatism in social habits causes widespread maladjustment in society. He called this "cultural lag" and argued that it is most severe during periods of basic transformation such as the Industrial Revolution. This seems so obviously true that it has become a building block for modern sociology and is fundamental to the work of Pitirim Sorokin, Thorstein Veblen, and most futurists. Lag theory was quickly applied to economics, demography, and social psychology. It clearly shows how failure to adjust to material change causes devastation. An infamous example occurred in World War I when generals and political leaders insisted on following outdated Napoleonic tactics while their armies were killed by machine guns, tanks, poison gas, and airplanes. Culture lag in education happens when communities fall behind a transformation that is taking place. In 1954 the Supreme Court ruled that blacks could no longer be segregated in public schools, but many local districts did everything in their power to block the rule, even closing schools in Prince Edward County, Virginia.

Unequal rates of change create pervasive maladjustments when a series of industrial and technological revolutions occur within a short span of time. Common patterns of thinking and acting upon which collective action is based are disrupted during such periods. Sociologist Robert MacIver argues that serious and numerous lags in the nonmaterial culture can only be resolved by fundamental alteration in normative principles and institutional arrangements. No institutions, not even governments, are more fundamental to the success of society than educational institutions. In our dynamic and fluid world, education must not be allowed to lag behind. What is taught may be vital or useless to the student depending upon the current state of the culture. Skill in using typewriters and adding machines is obsolete, but keyboard skills apply to using computers and accessing the World Wide Web. Library research may teach students to compare numerous sources to verify the validity of a statement. The truth of statements found on the Internet is not so easy to verify. The problem of culture lag is revealed in the history of education, especially the most current history. It is also a problem all teachers face in the future.

Errors and misconceptions in the mass culture are another form of lag that poses a special problem for teachers. For example, in 1911, British physicist Ernest Rutherford developed his model of the atom. He said that the atom resembles a tiny solar system in which electrons orbit the nucleus just as Earth rotates around the sun. So simple and clear was this model that it became the standard conception of atomic structure for generations of Americans. It persisted even though Niels Bohr had proved two years earlier that it could not be true. Today, science teachers trying to communicate the difficult notion that electrons are both waves and particles that make quantum jumps and appear to be in two places at once must combat the planetary model of the atom. The only part of Rutherford's model still accepted is that atomic structure is largely empty space, but many adults still think of an electron as a miniscule planet.

Core Values.   Defining the final objectives of education is not in the hands of professional educators but rests with the wider community. Obviously there are conflicting ideas about the kind of social philosophy schools should encourage, character they should try to develop, subjects they should teach, and methods they should use. These issues are even more fundamental than arguments about support and control of education. Achieving consensus depends upon finding common ground—values upon which the whole community can agree. In a Greek city-state or a colonial village, the community was homogeneous and a core of common values was easily found. In the sophisticated, complex, multicultural, multiracial, and diverse modern society, the task is much more difficult. Some sociologists suggest that the core values in modern America may be breaking up, a condition leading to social chaos. Anthropologist Ralph Linton is credited with the clearest statement about the relationship between core and alternative values. Since decisions about the basic standards and norms (called mores by Sumner) are based on the cultural core, so are the most fundamental choices concerning education.

Linton held that all cultures have a solid, well-integrated, and fairly stable core of fundamental values and a fluid, constantly changing, and mostly unintegrated set of alternative values not shared by all members. In a simple agricultural village like Grand Pré, the core would be very large in comparison to the alternatives. Choices in such societies are limited to occupation and avocation. The community tolerates no choice in religion, moral values, lifestyles, or expressed opinion. The tyranny of nineteenth-century communities has been well documented in history and literature. There was insistence upon rigid moral standards, customary modes of behavior, and even standard dress. There were certainly positive factors such as kinship, sympathy, and shared joys, but public opinion was almost irresistible. Arguments between members of the community existed, but they did not extend to differences in the core values.

By contrast, modern society contains so many alternatives that the core of shared values is relatively small. Our society has minute division of labor, extreme heterogeneity, profound conflict of interests, and significantly different conceptions of the good life. In the twentieth century, new forces such as industrialization, specialization, urbanization, and improved communications contributed to the decline of the local community. Organized interest groups began to pay a more important role because their members shared interests not common to everyone. Our century is a transitional era. It is a peculiarly strategic time in which rapid change has destroyed the old basis of an ordered society. Synthesis of core values, however, may still be found in some parts of the democratic tradition. Values such as equality of educational opportunity still form a core from which decisions may be made.

While we must not overlook the fact that millions of people, all over the world, have been sincerely and passionately devoted to totalitarian ideology in Fascist or Communist form, our society is committed to the democratic ideal. As closely contested as was the presidential election of 2000, everyone agreed that once George W. Bush was declared the winner, that decision would be binding. In some cultures, the loser of a close election might form an army and head for the hills, but the American core value of political stability and government by the people prevails here. It

Early or simple society with a large
core and few alternative values

Contemporary American society with a
small core and many alternative values

Large well-
integrated core of
common values

Few alternatives

Small core
of common
values

Many alternatives not
shared by all

Linton's Concept of Core Values

is very important for education that a core of common values still exists, for otherwise there could be no social consensus concerning essential action. Americans differ sharply about how the school needs of students can best be served. But not that
they must be served. Nevertheless, the search for pedagogical authority is more complicated in our fluid, dynamic, and rapidly changing culture than it was in our earlier history. Schooling in this nation is primarily a state function, but significant roles
also are played by the local school boards and the federal government. A core of
common values may be larger and more easily agreed upon at the local than at the
national level.

Social forces are reflected in the relationship between philosophy and history.
Parents in the early national period wanted their children to learn the three Rs and
values such as patriotism and responsibility but demanded little more. In the present multicultural nation with its myriad of conflicting religions, ideals, values, and
ethnic cultures, much is expected of schools. Even so, some modern adults are primarily interested in seeing that their children learn the skills and information
needed for success in the global marketplace. Others place more value on equality of opportunity, a violence- and drug-free environment, or the chance to participate in varsity sports. Whatever happens in the wider culture influences education as well. Controversy over gays in the military causes school boards to review
policies, although few schools would knowingly hire homosexual teachers. Litigation brought by parents seeking admission for their daughters to all-male football
teams led to the creation of new opportunities in sports such as women's basket-
ball and volleyball in high schools and colleges. School violence, especially instances of the shooting of students by students, so profoundly impacted the public mind that demands for security became the number one educational concern
in many communities.

Even in our modern society with its many cultural differences, we may be unprepared for customs and rules in less open environments. For example, a few years

ago one author of this book was teaching a short course to teachers of the American School in Dhahran, on the Persian Gulf.

> While there, the Saudi Ministry of Education asked me to address a group of teacher candidates in training at a seminary in Riyadh. When I arrived, imagine my shock to find a heavy cloth screen suspended around the podium from which I was to speak. At the time, I was dean of an American college of education and respected by the Saudi's as a scholar. Nevertheless, as a man, a foreigner and a non-Moslem, I was not allowed to look upon the young ladies to whom I spoke!

A complete history of American education is not possible in a book of this length. Many excellent treatments with more detail are available, and reference is made to most of them. The object of this work is to provide an outline of the most significant educational events, movements, and theories that shaped the American schools. It is designed to provide a sound historical base from which to evaluate modern educational practice and to plan for the future.

The level of information provided is sufficient for candidates preparing to teach and is about what most universities require of graduate students not majoring in educational foundations. This book should therefore prove useful for passing the National Teacher's Examination or preparing for graduate record examinations. It is hoped that you will go beyond this volume for greater breadth and detail, but we believe that a sound foundation is provided within these pages. The broad chronological organization and time lines are designed to help you find topics and organize facts. Information about recent events is as current as possible.

HISTORY AND PURPOSES OF EDUCATIONAL HISTORY

On February 23, 1987, the Canadian astronomer Ian Shelton photographed the Large Magellanic Cloud from an observatory in Chile and noted a bright spot that had not been there the night before. He quickly ran outside and became the first person in a century to view a supernova. This one was the brightest seen since Johannes Kelper recorded one in 1604, which was also noted in China. The discovery by Shelton duly entered the history books as fact in the manner that with the date noted, humans measure time. But the maelstrom exploding with the energy of 200 million suns was not there when Shelton viewed it. Traveling at 196,000 miles per second, light from the supernova required 167,000 years to reach Earth. Our ordinary conception of time in increments of hours, days, and centuries must be recast to accommodate space time.

To be accurate, we must constantly rethink history. Consider the 5,200-year-old "ice man" recently found in a glacier in the European Alps. Tests on his hair made possible by new forensic technology revealed traces of arsenic. This shows that the ancient fellow was probably involved in smelting the bronze for the head of the ax he carried. Prior to this discovery, it was not known that the smelting of metals took place in this region at this early date. History does not change, but our techniques for understanding and interpreting it do.

New evidence forces us to reconsider history at all stages. This becomes more difficult as we approach the present. As futurists like Daniel Bell, Joseph Coats, and Robert Heilbroner are fond of pointing out, the rate of change is so rapid that it becomes ever more difficult to understand the forces that shape society. It is easier to demonstrate something in an objective way for times long past where vested interests no longer apply. Educational historians are more comfortable in explaining the role of the Freedmen's Bureau in serving the educational needs of blacks after the Civil War than in explaining why the gap between white and black school achievement did not decline in the 1990s as it did in the 1980s. The authors will provide as much guidance as possible, but ultimate interpretation of history must be left to the reader. The more independent sources consulted, the better the chances of being right.

Another difficulty with history is the multiplication of records as we move from the past to the future. Significant events were less numerous in former times. Few records and fewer artifacts survive from schools on the American frontier. By contrast, almost every county in the nation has a detailed history that traces local development of public schools. It is easy to enumerate early educational court cases such as the Dartmouth College Case, but the sheer volume of litigation in the past half century is overwhelming. One could spend a lifetime just reading the briefs pertaining to educational judicial decision since 1995. By 1947 in the United States, 98.6 percent of all children through the age of thirteen attended public or private schools. Since modern American education is such an enormous enterprise, its history is also mammoth.

Some long-standing decisions such as that schools should be public, state controlled, tax supported, and open to all are unlikely to be challenged now, but cultural events always demand educational responses. In 1842, the Citadel was founded in South Carolina as a military college for men. With women in military careers and female cadets at West Point the Citadel found it necessary to admit females. It was soon caught up in the accusations and incidents of sexual harassment that plagued other military training centers. Such events force public schools to look again at sexual equality, bias in programs, and possible discrimination.

As subjects of study or "disciplines" go, the history of education is relatively new. In a general way, it has been included as part of the field of history, but intellectual and cultural history (of which the history of education is a segment) is much more recent than military and political history. Systematic study of the history of education has developed in America largely within the past century, although there were many earlier accounts of the training of particular individuals or unique groups. Thus, literature contains some history of education, as in the case of the life of Lycurgus in Plutarch's *The Lives of the Noble Grecians and Romans*, which provides considerable information about the training of boys in the ancient Greek city-state of Sparta. Biography is obviously a rich source of information about educational practices in times past, because authors nearly always attempt to account for character development by describing childhood experiences, schooling included. Historians have also been attracted by customs or practices that they considered rare or bizarre, so that atypical educational systems often have been described in some detail.

Modern history of education received its greatest stimulation from the theory that teachers should have, as a part of their professional program, knowledge of the development of at least their own national school system. Obviously, this belief was dependent upon some sort of formal training for teachers—training that did not occur in the United States until after 1825 and then only to a limited degree.

The common assumption that educational historiography started in the nineteenth century is largely true, even though one may point to numerous efforts to trace school development in earlier times. Quintilian, a Roman educator of the first century, included some history of education in his *Institutio Oratoria;* and Robert Goulet's book, *Compendium on the Magnificence, Dignity, and Excellence of the University of Paris in the Year of Grace 1517,* helps us understand the origins of our modern university as well as linkages with our present secondary educational system. Similarly, Goulet's *On the Origins of the University of Paris,* published in 1517, could be considered educational history. Professor Harry Good identifies Claude Fleury's *Treatise on the Selection and Methods of Studies* (France, circa 1700) as the oldest systematic history of education. There were numerous histories of institutions of higher learning and some efforts to describe higher education generally, such as that of the Puritan minister Cotton Mather, who wrote about New England college programs around the year 1700.

Nevertheless, the history of American education was hardly a field for systematic study until Ellwood P. Cubberley of Stanford University published his *Public Education in the United States*, followed by books of readings in the history of education and critically annotated bibliographies on the subject. Cubberley, who produced his books just after 1900, was a widely respected educator and scholar who had considerable influence upon the inclusion of the history of American education among standard subjects in teacher-training programs. Since normal school education had become common by the beginning of the twentieth century and education departments were by then established in many of the nation's leading universities, courses dealing with history of education in the United States sprang up all over the country. Historians who were not also educators continued to avoid the field. But scholars such as Paul Monroe, with his *Founding of the American Public School Systems,* 1940, and I. L. Kandel, with his *International Yearbook of the International Institute of Teachers College* (1st to 21st editions), 1942–1944 (which explored adult education in other countries), contributed vastly to our knowledge.

History of education was identified by its broad area of coverage compared with other kinds of history. The emphasis of historians who were also interested in teacher preparation and school improvement was not simply on the development of the public system of education but also on the social factors that gave rise to the system. In this sense, the history of education may be called the earliest systematic treatment of cultural and intellectual factors affecting the American people. No full understanding of the current educational situation in any nation is possible without knowledge of the evolution of its school system, together with the practices and theories that contributed to its growth. Thus, the educational historians do not limit themselves to a single field of knowledge but draw upon information from such disciplines as economics, sociology, anthropology, and psychology in an effort to get a true conception of educational development. For this reason, their approach should be considered interdisciplinary.

Differing Points of View.

Leading historians of education have been more interested in the application of their studies to professional improvement of teaching than to the study of "pure" history for its own sake. This fact and the educators' point of view have led to disagreements between modern historians of education and professors of history who are interested in studying education. Both groups add to the existing body of knowledge about education. The historian contributes special skill in the detailed study of limited periods, geographical areas, and special topics. Educational historians are usually interested in interpreting broad cultural trends in order to clarify the goals and aims of education, as well as in intensive work on specific topics related to schooling.

Historians of education have differed on the interpretation of the facts, especially since scholars entered the field with a strong interest in sociology. Bernard Bailyn (1962) is an example of an author who feels the schools have generally supported educational equality; but Michael Katz, Peter McLaren, and Joel Spring argue that they have served the special interests of the dominant middle-class whites. Much of the current historical literature in education aligns itself with one of these interpretations of the role of education in American culture.

Influence of Recent Changes.

During the past few years, a number of changes have taken place in education that have had a marked influence upon the study of the history of education. Among the more important developments are the following: (a) rapid increase in scientific activity and the accumulation of knowledge, together with an extension of average time spent in school and a major increase in adult education and training by private industries; (b) substantial involvement of the federal government in educational matters, especially after the success of the Soviet space effort in 1957; (c) growth of graduate work in education due to a much larger demand for teachers with advanced degrees, bringing many more scholars to the field of history of education; (d) an increased interest in foreign school systems, the role of education in emerging nations, and the problems of social class, racial integration, gender equality, and poverty in America; and (e) the work of critics of the school system in the United States who have taken issue with the organization, methods, and especially the curriculum of our public schools.

The history of education is therefore a developing rather than a finished area of study. It is concerned with building a full understanding of the current educational situation through the study of the evolution of educational practices, ideas, and institutions in social context. In a 1964 lecture to the Department of Education of Johns Hopkins University, William W. Brickman described educational history as that branch of history that deals with the development of thought, practice, materials, personnel, administration, organization, and problems of schools. Educational history also includes institutions and organizations that instruct the young and the mature, the mass media, and other learning experiences.

INTELLECTUAL BACKGROUND

American education is Western education, and therefore the intellectual roots for it extend back to ancient Greece and Rome. Socrates, Plato, and Aristotle formed the basis of the school curriculum and also laid the foundation for educational theory. Classical studies especially stressed Latin and the culture of the Greeks and Romans. Humanism in the age of Erasmus (sixteenth century) looked back to Cicero and Quintilian for models of literary style. Leaders of the American Revolution were familiar with writings of classical antiquity and often quoted the ancient writers. (See Chapter 2 for a philosophic discussion of early writers.)

Force of Medieval Tradition.   With the decline and fall of the Roman Empire, an intellectual and social stagnation began in Europe that continued until the several revivals of learning known collectively as the Renaissance. During this era, feudal patterns of social structure and economics developed, and philosophy and learning were handmaidens of the Church. Education was at a low ebb; the monasteries and a few cathedral schools were the chief instruments of instruction. Charlemagne made an effort to revive learning at the end of the eighth century, but theological questions continued to occupy the minds of the learned elite while the great bulk of the people remained ignorant in an "otherworldly" society.

A reintroduction of ancient classical learning, especially the Arabic translations of Aristotle in the thirteenth century, gave rise to the higher level scholarship of Albert the Great and Thomas Aquinas. Medieval universities and the scholasticism of Thomas Aquinas eventually provided a basis for moving beyond the traditions of the Middle Ages. Nevertheless, medieval influences were still very strong at the time of American colonization. They are to be found in the social structure, the dominance of religion, superstitions, and other beliefs widely held by settlers from all parts of Europe.

Impact of the Renaissance.   The Renaissance, or rebirth of learning, began in the 1200s and lasted through the Reformation of the 1500s. Many aspects of this movement had some influence on American development. The Renaissance replaced a religious point of view with a secular one, making man rather than God the focal point with reference to art, literature, and the government. This emphasis on secular concerns, or humanism, was based partly on the transfer of wealth and political power from the Church to laymen and nation-states. The Renaissance also included a revival of interest in the classical culture of ancient Greece and Rome.

Humanists studied and imitated the manuscripts of the great writers of the past. They also examined the ancient social order (especially of Rome) and made critical comparisons with their own time. Classicism protested against the narrow religious nature of education in the Middle Ages. Erasmus made editions of the New Testament in Latin and Greek and also criticized the ignorance of the clergy and the injustice of society. Renaissance emphasis on the development of the individual helped to purge ignorance and encourage education.

Significant and new inventions made rapid progress in learning possible. As the Renaissance swept through Europe, a great desire for books developed that hand copying or block printing could not satisfy. By about 1440, Johannes Gutenberg had developed his technique for using separate pieces of raised metal type in a press. The resulting revolution in the production and availability of printed information had a profound impact on education in the Western world. The availability of books at a low cost allowed many more members of society to read and think for themselves, instead of accepting everything on the authority of scholars. Growth of cities, revival of trade, exploration, and increased mobility of scholars helped to spread information and expedited the exchange of ideas.

Impact of Scientific Thinking.

From 1500 to 1700, significant changes were taking place in Europe, such as geographic exploration, religious revolution, the growth of nationalism, and the development of science. While the classical humanism of the Renaissance period continued to be the dominant educational force, commercial interests and cultural diversity gave rise to the growth of scientific facts and methods.

Around 1500, Leonardo da Vinci called attention to the importance of observation and experimentation in learning. Francis Bacon (1561–1626) popularized the scientific technique in *Novum Organum*. The astronomical discoveries of Copernicus, Kepler, Galileo, and Bruno challenged traditional conceptions of the universe. William Gilbert made studies of electricity, Robert Boyle examined the chemical properties of gases, and Isaac Newton published basic laws of physics and mechanics. Mathematical support for science was found in the contributions made to calculus and analytical geometry by Leibniz, Descartes, and Newton.

Science was still suspect when the American colonies were founded. Very few learned people accepted the materialism and the concept of a machine universe expounded by Thomas Hobbes or Pierre Gassendi. Nevertheless, the scientific method of thinking did provide a challenge to established beliefs and laid a foundation for the enlightenment of the eighteenth century. William Harvey's theory of the circulation of the blood was discussed at Harvard while that institution remained a theological college strongly opposed to science.

Significance of Religious Revolutions.

Probably no single movement so greatly affected colonial America as the Protestant Reformation and the Catholic Counter-Reformation. The tremendous impact of the Reformation on social, economic, and political life was of paramount importance in the formation of the United States, and some of the influences are still felt today.

In 1517, when Martin Luther posted his Ninety-five Theses on the Church door in Wittenberg, Germany, the Catholic church was the most important educational agency in the world. At the close of the Thirty Years War, all institutions and every aspect of the culture had been affected. Most of the Europeans who came to America were Protestants, but there were many denominations. Lutherans from Germany and Scandinavia settled in the middle colonies, especially Pennsylvania. Puritans, Presbyterians, Huguenots, and several smaller sects represented followers of John Calvin. Anabaptists (followers of Huldreich Zwingli [1484–1531]) were persecuted by both Catholic and Protestant authorities, and therefore sought freedom in the New World. Much of the struggle known as the Reformation centered upon efforts to capture the minds of men, and therefore great emphasis was placed upon the written word. Obviously, schools were needed by both sides to foster the growth of each denomination or sect.

Luther's doctrine of the "priesthood of all believers" made it necessary for boys and girls to learn to read the Scriptures. Educational programs that were intended to give the masses the ability to read the Bible in the vernacular were started by Protestant groups in Germany and wherever Luther's concepts spread. Although the schools were often rudimentary, they offered universal education for all children, regardless of wealth, and were supported by both church and state. Protestants also provided secondary education of higher quality for the elite destined to enter positions in the government or the Church. Although Catholics played a substantially smaller role in colonial America, they were very much part of the Counter-Reformation. Leaders such as Jean Baptiste de la Salle and St. Ignatius of Loyola influenced Catholics in Maryland.

In England, the break with the Catholic church came when Clement VII refused to annul Henry VIII's marriage to Catherine of Aragon. By the Act of Supremacy in 1534, Henry became head of the church in England and proceeded to break up the monasteries. The English church remained very much the same during Henry's time, with the Reformation really starting under Edward VI. Mary I briefly restored Catholicism, but during the long reign of Elizabeth, Anglicanism was firmly established. Anglicanism is a moderate form of Protestantism, which preserves most of the organizational structure of the Catholic church. English Calvinists who wanted to change or purify the Anglican church became known as Puritans and were very important in the settlement of New England. Other dissenters from the Anglican faith included some called Separatists, who denied the establishment of religion and held that each man must be free to worship as he thought fit. Followers of John Knox (1505–1572) in Scotland (Presbyterians), Quakers, and Catholics tended to move to America when the political tide was against them in England. For example, the great Puritan migrations in the 1630s took place because of the persecution directed by Anglican Archbishop Laud.

Conservative Traditions.   Students sometimes get the idea that the Renaissance and the Reformation were entirely progressive movements. In fact, they were often reactionary. Humanism looked to the past rather than the future for its model. The Reformation had a tendency to make religion once again the dominant intellectual interest of mankind. Other forces, however, tended to counteract the importance of the Reformation and the Renaissance. The American colonies were an integral part of a great English colonial empire. They were not isolated outposts or temporary communities but a portion of a larger capitalistic scheme brought about by a strong middle class for the purpose of material gain. The rise of capitalism was one of the strongest factors in the development of this nation. Economic motives and interests profoundly affected American civilization from the first. Even the New England Puritan, who came to a "stern and rockbound coast" in order to escape religious oppression, was not without economic concern. The soil in New England was shallow and unproductive. In order to make a living, Pilgrims and Puritans soon turned to timber cutting, ship building, fishing for cod, manufacturing, and trade.

In addition to capitalism, the colonists brought the parliamentary form of government to America. The New Englanders especially supported Parliament against the King. They wished to substitute their own body politic for the authority that had been vested in the crown. Thus, the effort of the Pilgrim fathers in drawing up the Mayflower Compact, which served as a constitution and defined the responsibilities of the people as well as centering authority in the people, could hardly have occurred without the struggle for parliamentary supremacy that had taken place in the mother country.

Many other potent forces played a part in the intellectual climate out of which American educational institutions developed. The rise of science, British empiricism, the forces of rationalism, and the movement toward greater intellectual discovery all had their effect on the birth of American schools. The point to be made is that American educational and intellectual foundations have roots that run very deep into the European past. While many of the most conservative ideas, such as the evil nature of man, were preserved in America, there were also factors tending to develop an attitude of change.

THEN TO NOW

The casual student of history may not immediately see the relationship of the remote past to the age in which we live. Nevertheless, connections do exist between the world of today and those past traditions that were once dominant. A better understanding of modern attitudes and ideas can be gleaned from an analysis of historical forces. Consider, for example, the curriculum of present schools and colleges. Medieval universities offered studies derived from ancient educational interests reaching back to Aristotle. These were the seven liberal arts that scholars believed to be essential to the life of the mind and the education of men. The basic or tool subjects were grammar, logic, and rhetoric. Advanced studies consisted of arithmetic, geometry, astronomy, and harmony. Although the names have sometimes changed (music for harmony and language arts for grammar), it is obvious that these medieval curriculum offerings are still found in the schools. It is also true that modern groupings into the natural sciences, the social sciences, and the humanities are based on these early subjects and that we still speak of a liberal arts curriculum in reference to such studies. There have been many modifications and additions, but the curriculum of the universities of the Middle Ages has not disappeared. The whole idea of a university stems from the medieval organization of a guild of teachers and a guild of students. The modern master's degree is named after the guild practice of awarding master craftsman status for those who had demonstrated excellence in their work. Our most modern research universities still have deans, lecture halls, graduation rites, student organizations, and rectors (presidents), all of which were part of the early universities.

The rebirth of learning known as the Renaissance has never really ceased. Ideas from the classical past together with the humanism of scholars like Erasmus produced a new desire to understand the forces that shape human society. When modern sociologists attempt to analyze the actions of groups of people, they are involved in the spirit of inquiry that was the heart of the Renaissance. Educators today still debate the role of humanistic studies in an age of scientific research and specialization. Likewise the invention of the printing press led to improved production and distribution of information that is still accelerating. Modern telecommunications, information superhighways, electronic media, and computer-based research are current aspects of the revolution started by Gutenberg. It should be obvious also that the secular scientific thinking started by Bacon, Galileo, Gilbert, and others has continued to grow and expand at a rapid rate. The study of the history of science in many universities and popular television programs like *Connections* illustrate the need for understanding the past in order to cope with the present. Current issues over tax support for religious schools may be linked to the struggles of the Protestant Reformation and the Catholic Counter-Reformation.

Although we are able to get a better picture of the forces that shaped values and attitudes of historical times than we can of the forces that shaped the values and attitudes of today, currents of opinion and climates of thought are difficult to isolate in any age. It is easy enough to mark the founding of the English settlement on the American seaboard with Jamestown in 1607 and to mark the first major school law with the Old Deluder Satan Act of 1647, but it is another matter to trace the cultural forces that shaped the minds and deeds of the colonists. Nevertheless, whatever light can be cast on the intellectual, social, ethical, and philosophic forces that created colonial culture will be useful in helping to gain a better understanding of our own times. Just as the Puritan ethic of early America still casts its shadow over modern educational theory and practice (as in the case of Bible reading and prayer in public schools), so the Puritans themselves were influenced by mainstreams of thought going back at least to medieval times. As difficult as the task may be, cultural and intellectual history must try to identify main currents of thought and influential values that set the parameters of basic cultural beliefs. In this way, history can be a most useful tool in helping us to understand ourselves and the times in which we live.

Because we tend to think in a contemporary time frame, it is important to recall that many of the movements considered in this book occurred over a period of years. The Protestant Reformation and the Catholic Counter-Reformation were not single events like those reported every day on the CBS News. They were revolutions of many facets of society that took centuries to develop and decades to complete, and their aftermath continues to be felt in contemporary society. Due to the brief treatment given to colonial history in the common school history courses, it is easy to make the error of thinking of the colonial period as brief. Actually, the years between the settlement of Jamestown and the American Revolution cover almost half of the time that has elapsed since 1607. In the passing of nearly two centuries, the changes that occurred in colonial America were dramatic and vast, even though they took place at a slower rate than modern transformations. The revolt against England and the birth of a new nation could hardly have taken place in the conservative climate of opinion that existed in the beginning of the seventeenth century.

Educational development in colonial America and its influence on the schools of later times can only be appreciated against the backdrop of an earlier Old World culture. What is happening in education today must also be evaluated in terms of changing world conditions. For the first time in history, all of the school-age children in mainland China actually attend school. Mass starvation and continuing ethnic conflicts in East and Central Africa make it impossible for children there to reach their full potential or to achieve educational goals. Currently, nations of the former Soviet Union are in the throes of trying to reconcile Western capitalism with citizens' demands for jobs and the sustenance protection offered by the old Communist regime. The Bosnian conflict also reflects a return to the balance of power system so prevalent in history. Russia has emerged as a power broker, influencing competing interests in Bosnia as well as in the Middle East. The continuing pressures of an interdependent global community will influence our economic system. All people are affected by the ways in which natural resources are used, and all are demanding more human services, including education. An airport or a computer is much the same whether it is found in New York, Manila, or Buenos Aires. Our educational history began with influences from many areas and traditions; the future of education also depends on events and developments that are global in nature.

Many causes were at work in the settlement of the American colonies. Adventure, money, love of God, and a desire to convert the Native Americans gave rise to the colonies. Many wished to escape oppressive governments and the hard times in Europe such as the English depression of 1595. The first settlers were Europeans, dominated by English traditions. Modern society in the United States has been greatly modified by the influx of other people and ideas, but the Protestant religions and the English language remain dominant today although Hispanic culture and language are expanding. This dominance, like that of middle-class values in schools, creates a major educational problem in equal treatment of students whose first language is other than English or who represent religious backgrounds other than Protestant Christian.

Most of the time and effort of teachers and administrators in schools is spent dealing with contemporary needs and problems. It is all too easy for us to think of events in the remote past as having no relevance for modern educators, if we think of such events at all. This is a fundamental mistake that may prevent us from making the best decisions for the well-being of our students and their communities. Religious conflicts starting with the protests of Martin Luther are still evident in current arguments over prayer in public schools. Attacks by the "ultra right wing" on "secular humanism," as well as by various other special interest groups including advocates of home schooling, can be clarified by an understanding of conservative theology, Renaissance humanism, and *laissez-faire* politics. Several states have passed or are considering passage of a law requiring schools to give equal time to the biblical theory of creation and the theory of evolution. It is not enough to link this matter with the work of Darwin or with the Scopes trial in 1925. The educator needs also to consider it in the light of the opposition to scientific knowledge in the time of Copernicus and Bruno. Historical knowledge is vital for placing current issues into perspective and making decisions that will stand critical analysis.

Sources of educational history include deeds, contracts, oral history, archival records, newspaper morgues, personal correspondence, archaeological discoveries, museums, art, tools, garments, flyers, government documents, artifacts, charters, journals, texts, and diaries of the period, all of which provide avenues to understanding our past. Formal sources for educational theory consist of the formal writings of philosophers and treatments of schools of philosophy from idealism to postmodernism. Educational theory can also be gleaned from values, attitudes, curriculum choices, and criticism of schools, whether or not they are linked to an articulated philosophy.

How Does the History of Education Apply to Teachers/Educators Today?   As one examines our educational history, cycles of change indicate that everything old is rediscovered by putting new wine in old bottles. New terminology often covers age-old educational concepts and innovations. Plutarch's Lycurgus sought critical thinking, discipline, and ethical conduct through education. Today people emphasize these concepts and the importance of character building. Although we have witnessed increased educational and employment opportunities for women, minorities, culturally diverse populations, those who are physically or mentally challenged, and senior citizens, debate over curriculum content, public and private education, and what is ultimately worth knowing continues now as in the past.

GAINING PERSPECTIVE THROUGH CRITICAL ANALYSIS

1. Evaluate the process of making educational decisions in a culture with a large core of common values as compared to doing so in contemporary American society.
2. Describe the significance of each of the following forces on education:

   ❑ Medieval tradition
   ❑ The Renaissance
   ❑ Scientific thinking
   ❑ Religious revolutions

3. Identify three reasons why teachers and other educators can benefit from studying the history of education.

4. Give two examples of modern educators "reinventing the wheel" because they lack historical knowledge and perspective.

5. Compare and contrast the contributions of the Protestant Reformation and the Catholic Counter-Reformation on the development of education in colonial America. Identify some current religious influences on current educational practice.

HISTORY IN ACTION IN TODAY'S CLASSROOMS

1. Interview a retired teacher or administrator. Ask him or her to discuss educational reform cycles and trends during his or her career. Does he or she remember one-room schools? Keep a journal of your findings to share in class.

2. What are some current forces that have shaped educational history as a discipline in recent years? Cite a journal or Internet article to support your opinion.

INCREASED UNDERSTANDING THROUGH ONLINE RESEARCH

Visit the Prentice Hall Foundations Web site (*http://www.prenhall.com/foundations-cluster*) and select Topic 4—Historical Foundations—from the menu. Using the resources available in this topic of the site, write a detailed essay comparing the impact of book printing on education in the Renaissance and colonial period with electronic publishing and the Internet. Write and submit your response to your instructor using the Electronic Bluebook module also found in the Web site.

BIBLIOGRAPHY

Bailyn, Bernard. *Education in the Forming of American Society: Needs and Opportunities for Study*. New York: W. W. Norton, 1962.

Barrow, Robin. *Plato and Education*. Boston: Routledge & Kegan Paul, 1976.

Brann, Eva. *Paradoxes of Education in a Republic*. Chicago: The University of Chicago Press, 1979.

Cahn, Steven M. *Classic and Contemporary Readings in the Philosophy of Education*. New York: McGraw, 1997.

Church, Robert L. *Education in the United States*. New York: The Free Press, 1976.

Clough, A. H. *Plutarch's Lives*. New York: Bigelow, Smith and Co., 1911.

Cremin, Lawrence A. *American Education, The Colonial Experience*. New York: Harper & Row, 1970.

Cruickshank, Donald R., and Associates. *Preparing America's Teachers*. Bloomington, IN: Phi Delta Kappa, 1996.

Curtis, Stanley, and M. E. A. Boultwood. *A Short History of Educational Ideas*. 3d ed. London: University Tutorial Press, 1964.

Grant, Gerald, ed. *Review of Research in Education: Section 11 History and Philosophy*. Washington, DC: American Educational Research Association, 1992.

Gross, Richard, ed. *Heritage of American Education*. Boston: Allyn & Bacon, 1962.

Gwynn, Aubrey. *Roman Education from Cicero to Quintilian*. rev. ed. New York: Teachers College Press, 1966.

Holley, Raymond. *Religious Education and Religious Understanding*. Boston: Routledge & Kegan Paul, 1978.

Katz, Michael B. *Class, Bureaucracy and the School*. New York: Praeger, 1971.

Labaree, David F. "Public Goods, Private Goods: The American Struggle Over Educational Goals." *American Educational Research Association Journal* (Spring 1997) 34(1): 39–82.

McLaren, Peter. *Critical Pedagogy and Predatory Culture*. New York: Routledge, 1995.

McMillan, James H., and Sally Schumacher. *Research in Education: A Conceptual Introduction*. New York: Harper Collins, College Publishers, 1993.

Meyer, Adolphe. *Grandmasters of Educational Thought*. New York: McGraw-Hill, 1975.

Mulhern, James. *A History of Education*. 2d ed. New York: Ronald, 1959.

Perkinson, Harry. *Two Hundred Years of American Educational Thought*. New York: David McKay Company, Inc., 1976.

Pounds, Ralph. *The Development of Education in Western Culture*. New York: Appleton-Century-Crofts, 1968.

Ravitch, Diane. *The Revisionists Revisited: A Critique of the Radical Attack on the Schools*. New York: Basic Books, 1978.

Reed, Ronald F. *Philosophical Documents in Education*. New York: Longman, 1996.

Rusk, Robert. *The Doctrines of the Great Educators*. rev. ed. New York: Macmillan, 1969.

Sherman, Robert, ed. *Understanding History of Education*. rev. ed. Cambridge, MA: Schenkaman Publishing Company, Inc., 1984.

Spring, Joel. *The American School: 1642–1990*. New York: Longman, 1990.

———. *Images of American Life*. Albany, NY: State University of New York Press, 1992.

Wood, Norman. *The Reformation and English Education*. London: University Tutorial Press, 1931.

CHAPTER TWO

SHAPING THE SCHOOLS: PHILOSOPHICAL AND PSYCHOLOGICAL FOUNDATIONS

Only in education, never in the life of farmer, sailor, merchant, physician, or laboratory experimenter, does knowledge mean primarily a store of information aloof from doing.

John Dewey

BC	AD	1200–1800	1800–1900
427–347 Plato		Aquinas (1225–1274)	Kierkegaard (1813–1855)
		Locke (1632–1704)	Spencer (1820–1903)
		Berkeley (1685–1753)	Peirce (1839–1914)
384–322 Aristotle		Rousseau (1712–1778)	Whitehead (1861–1947)
		Herbart (1776–1841)	Russell (1872–1970)

Figure 2.1   Time Line for Philosopies of Education

John Dewey, the best known American educational philosopher and the intellectual founder of the progressive movement, wanted to make schools practical, experience based, and a mirror of life. To do so, he had to combat long-standing educational traditions and the entrenched theories of education grounded in idealism and realism. Shaping any school system requires knowledge of the historical forces in play, a clear understanding of goals determined by philosophy, and consideration of anticipated change. For example, modern China is approaching a population of a billion and a half people. This is largely due to political and economic changes that have almost doubled life expectancy. For the first time in history, all the children in China receive state-supported schooling and, although opportunities are still limited, an increasing number of students go on to higher education. Although communism is in decline in the rest of the world, one cannot hope to understand modern Chinese educational theory without knowledge of the philosophy of Marx and Mao. This knowledge is also critical to American education as the Chinese move into the global marketplace. See Figure 2.1.

Because contemporary American schools look very much the same in organization, structure, and curriculum, it is easy to assume that there is agreement on their philosophic foundations. In fact, as educational issues occur and recur, so do underlying philosophical contentions. A shared public philosophy may support universal schooling with tax support for all American children, but it does not extend to cover what subjects are most important in the curriculum, whether compulsory education is justified, or what ethical training should be included in schools. Shaping schools requires an exploration of alternative views of what is ultimately worth knowing and the various aims, policies, and ideologies expressed in school and society throughout history as well as in the contemporary period. There can be no educational program without clarity of its aims and theory. It is of vital importance for a teacher, a staff member, or an administrator to know what theory underlies his or her school policy and also to understand philosophically the basis for criticism or disagreement from parents or the public.

INTRODUCTION TO EDUCATIONAL PHILOSOPHY

Webster defines philosophy as the "love of wisdom," which is a literal rendering of the Greek word. Philosophy deals with ultimate questions such as the nature of truth, what is real, and what is of value. Speculative, reflective, and theoretical attempts to

Modern	
James (1842–1910)	Skinner (1904–1990)
Dewey (1859–1952)	Foucault (1926–1984)
Buber (1878–1965)	Habermas (1929–)
Thorndike (1874–1949)	Rorty (1931–)
Wittgenstein (1889–1951)	

answer questions about the basic purposes, goals, and outcomes of formal education are philosophical in nature. Those questions dealing with the nature of knowledge, the characteristics of the educated person, or the structure of the curriculum are the broadest issues for philosophy of education. Those dealing with methods of teaching or the length of the school year have a somewhat less abstract nature. Although the terms are sometimes used interchangeably, educational theory is more focused and narrow in scope than educational philosophy. Before the twentieth century, most American educational philosophy was derived from the great systems or schools of philosophy, especially idealism and realism. Although these positions are still supported with vigor by many policy makers in education, they have been challenged recently by contrasting views expressed by pragmatists, existentialists, futurists, and analytic philosophers, among others.

Traditional philosophy, like other fields of discipline inquiry, is divided into categories. These categories are important because they focus the arguments between schools and illustrate what is most important to individual philosophers. Idealism and realism deal equally with all divisions, pragmatists have little to say on questions of ultimate reality, and analytic philosophers concentrate on rules of valid thinking. The basic divisions are metaphysics, epistemology, axiology, and logic.

Metaphysics is concerned with reality and existence. For education, the conception of reality reflected in the curriculum and the experiences of the student are paramount. Formal education describes and defines reality as it is understood by those in control of the learning environment. Obviously, reality would appear differently to an Athenian citizen in the age of Pericles, to a Puritan minister in colonial New England, or to an astronomer gathering X-ray data on a distant galaxy.

Epistemology is the theory of knowledge and includes the study of how we know. Does knowledge begin with sensations from objects, as realists think? Are pragmatists correct in their belief that we create knowledge by interaction with our environment? Are idealists correct in saying that knowing is the recall of absolute ideas that have an independent existence of their own? The answers imply stimulating questions about the learner, problem solving, and the utilization of sensory stimuli. Clearly, knowing and knowledge are critical to any theory of education.

The division known as axiology includes ethics, aesthetics, and the formation of values. Ethics examines moral values; aesthetics deals with the values of beauty and art. All teachers must be concerned with the formation of values by children and the encouragement of behaviors that conform to some conception of that which is true, good, or beautiful. Many educational theories such as idealism and realism hold that values are valid in all times and places (objective theory of value); however, pragmatists and social theorists say that they are culturally or ethically relative. Many of the major conflicts over the impact of the school in the formation of character and in guiding behavior are grounded in axiology.

The final division, logic, is concerned with the rules of valid thinking. The study of logic was once required of all university students. Logic is now limited to the discipline of formal philosophy, but it is still basic to the rules of correct argument. Analytical philosophy relies on logic; existentialism subsumes it under personal feeling and individual freedom. Inductive logic is associated with empiricism and pragmatism; realism and perennialism rely on deduction from first principles. A very good way to understand philosophers or schools of philosophy is to study their positions on metaphysics, epistemology, axiology, and logic. Questions about ultimate reality, the nature of knowledge, values, and rules of thinking (even when a given theory is silent on the topic) reveal a great deal about any philosopher or philosophy.

SCHOOLS OF EDUCATIONAL PHILOSOPHY

Neither educational philosophy nor philosophy itself divides automatically into neat categories. The discrete schools, or "isms" as they are often called, have no validity apart from the thinkers whose systems of thought they represent. Just as Aristotle found it helpful to group plants and animals into classes according to their similarities, students of philosophy find that classifying is a good tool for understanding theoretical positions. We must remember, however, that individual members of a school or "ism" do not always agree on every point. There is no substitute for a biographical approach in which the lives and major works of intellectual giants are individually studied. Still, the schools of thought may be useful as a beginning point, because they illustrate common ground between members and are easily contrasted with opposing philosophical views (see Tables 2.1, 2.2, and 2.3).

Most everyone agrees that Plato, Hegel, Kant, Berkeley, and Horne are representatives of idealism, whereas Bacon, Locke, and Hume are British empiricists. On the other hand, Albert Camus is called both a logical positivist and an existentialist, and some philosophers defy classification altogether. Names may also be confusing. For example, John Dewey only slightly modified his position during his long career but is classified by different authors as a pragmatist, an instrumentalist, and a progressive. Most commonly used categories provide a foundation for the study of educational practice grounded in philosophy, but classification schemes may vary. For example, J. Donald Butler in *Four Philosophies and Their Practice in Education and Religion* (1957) includes naturalism as a school, and J. Arthur Cooper in *Exemplars in Educational Philosophy* (1988) created a division called "eternalism." Most of the authors included under naturalism or eternalism are identified in other standard categories.

As we examine the schools, one other disclaimer should be kept in mind. Some famous philosophers such as Rousseau and Whitehead devoted much of their attention

Table 2.1   Alternative Philosophies of Education and Their Exponents

Educational Philosophy	Influences	Rationale	Curriculum
Perennialism (Neo-Thomism)	St. Thomas Aquinas Jacques Maritain Robert M. Hutchins Stringfellow Barr Max Rafferty Mortimer Adler	Stresses intellectual attainment and the search for truth	The Great Books The Classics Liberal Arts
Idealism (Essentialism)	Plato Josiah Royce Immanuel Kant Ralph Waldo Emerson Herman Horne	All material things are explainable	History Biography Humanities
Realism (Essentialism)	Alfred N. Whitehead Aristotle John Amos Comenius Johann F. Herbart John Locke Harry Broudy	Propositions are true only if they correspond with known facts	Science Mathematics Quantitative subjects Foreign language
Pragmatism	Boyd Bode John Dewey William James Charles Peirce William Kilpatrick	Search for things that work Experimental Democratic	Core curriculum Student centered Revolves around the interest of the student
Reconstructionism	Theodore Brameld George Counts Harold Rugg Ivan Illich John Holt Paul Goodman	Seeks to reconstruct society through education	Current events Social problems Futures research Sociology Political Science
Protest Philosophy (Behaviorism, Existentialism, and Postmodernism)	John Paul Sartre Soren Kierkegaard Martin Buber Albert Camus Martin Heidegger A. S. Neill Carl Rogers B. F. Skinnner Richard Rorty	Importance of the individual Subjectivity Discover the inner nature of things and people Rejection of logic and reason	Individual preference Psychology Human Relations

Developed by Timothy J. Bergen Jr., University of South Carolina, and modified by the authors.

Table 2.2 Educational Implications of Alternative Philosophies of Education

Educational Philosophy	Teacher	Method of Teaching	Examinations
Perennialism (Neo-Thomism)	A taskmaster— philosophically oriented and knowledgeable about the Great Books	Lectures Discussions Seminars	Essay
Idealism (Perennialism)	Serves as the ideal A good role model	Lectures Discussions Imitation	Essay
Realism (Essentialism)	Presents subject in a highly organized and very exact manner	Lectures Demonstrations Sensory experiences Teaching machines	Objective
Pragmatism	A guide One who can present meaningful knowledge with skill	Discussions Projects	Gauge how well people can problem solve
Reconstructionism	Social activist	Real-life projects	Student select, administer, and evaluate Gauge ability as an activist
Protest Philosophy (Behaviorism, Existentialism, and Postmodernism)	Very committed individual Person who is both teacher and learner One who provides a free environment to learn	Learner is encouraged to discover the best method for him/herself	Student should learn to examine him/herself Learner should be aware of sexism, racism, and social control

Developed by Timothy J. Bergen Jr., University of South Carolina, and modified by the authors.

to education; others such as Hegel and Bergson did not write on the subject. There are major educational theorists, Comenius and Pestalozzi, for example, who are not recognized as important in general philosophy. Sometimes educational ideas from a variety of nonphilosophical sources are incorporated into a theoretical school. Educational futurism draws from sociology, economics, communications theory, and cybernetics as much as from philosophy. Postmodernism tends to defy analysis in terms of the models used by classical philosophers.

American educational philosophy developed slowly. Colonial and early national schools were simple in curriculum, goals, and organization. So long as the general public (consisting largely of farmers and factory workers) was satisfied with the three "Rs"—history, spelling, and religion—conflict was minimal. Common values could be identified in a fairly homogeneous population keenly interested in a better standard of living but less concerned with social and intellectual issues. Before the vast expansion of the high school following the Kalamazoo decision, secondary education was confined to the college-bound elite. Colleges dictated both the educational

Table 2.3 Educational Outcomes of Alternative Philosophies of Education

Educational Philosophy	Preferred Architecture	Criticism	Educational Outcome
Perennialism (Neo-Thomism)	Classical	Very elite and aristocratic Must be accepted on faith and absolute truth	An intellectual scholar
Idealism (Perennialism)	Traditional	Elite	An intellectual scholar
Realism (Essentialism)	Efficient Functional	Often fails to deal with social change	Technician Scientist
Pragmatism	Flexible Natural	Permissive Very democratic Replace history with social studies	Good problem solver
Reconstructionism	Non-school setting "Schools without walls"	Very utopian Very impatient	Social activist
Protest Philosophy (Behaviorism, Existentialism, and Postmodernism)	Individual preference	Unsystematic Rejects all authority Opposes discipline, order, and logic	Inner-directed Authentic person Committed, involved, cares Independent thinking and nonconformist

Developed by Timothy J. Bergen Jr., University of South Carolina, and modified by the authors.

theory and the curriculum of the high schools. In turn, colleges and universities reflected the beliefs of their boards, presidents, and faculties. Religious idealism was strong in denominational colleges, Scottish realism dominated state universities, and Thomism governed the Catholic institutions. Science was not in vogue, and no alternative values were tolerated in high schools or colleges.

Not only was philosophic conflict rare in American education prior to this century, but the most important educational ideas were imported from Europe. Comenius, Locke, Rousseau, Pestalozzi, Froebel, and Herbart were the respected leaders in educational theory until the twentieth-century American philosophers emerged. Even today, foreign thinkers contribute to many educational theories. With the collapse of the Soviet Union, Russian Communism is in decline, but at least a fourth of the world's children are in schools that follow some form of Marxism. Only a handful of Americans accept or contribute to the contemporary school of Marxist education, but it is a vital philosophy in Europe, Africa, and Asia. Existentialism is largely European with some American support, and analytic philosophy of education is about evenly split between British and American authors. On the other hand, pragmatism, behaviorism, and social reconstructionism are unique to the United States. Postmodernism as well as social and futures philosophy are still emerging;

thus, the major contributors to these educational theories are still emerging. It is useful to examine the various schools in order to understand the basis of contemporary education.

Idealism.   Idealism is a very old traditional philosophy, and Plato (427–347 B.C.) is credited with providing the philosophic principles upon which it rests. The term refers to the reality of ideas, or mind, spirit, and reason. Idealism is in opposition to materialism and realism. Plato held that only mental or spiritual aspects of experience are ultimately real. He used the myth of the cave and the allegory of the divided line to convince his followers that ordinary commonsense objects exist only as copies of absolute ideas or "forms." In the cave, a person held captive from birth experiences only the dim light and shadows on the wall made by his captors and the objects they manipulate. Eventually he breaks loose and emerges from the cave where he experiences the "real" world of sunshine, other people, farms, and the sea. Having once "seen the light" he can never again believe in the reality of the cave.

In the allegory of the divided line, Plato shows that dreams, shadows, mirages, and the like, often fool our senses. These dreams, shadows, and mirages are related to sense objects, which have a higher order of reality. By the same argument, Plato claims that sense objects are related to constructs and concepts that are more real than the objects and that the concepts and constructs refer to pure ideas or forms. Thus, the order for water would be first a mirage of water on a dry road, then water in a glass, then H_2O, and finally the form *water*.

If only ideas are real, then pure ideas should be the objects of education. For example, once the pure idea "justice" is understood, the learner has a basis for judging all human acts as just or unjust. Plato also placed all human beings into a hierarchy of categories according to aspects of their souls. The largest and lowest group is dominated by appetite, and those in it should be the workers in society. The middle group is dominated by spirit, and those in it should make good soldiers. The top group is dominated by reason, and those in it should be the philosopher–kings who rule the state. Education is intended to sort out those who have rational souls and to enable them to "remember" the forms that represent ultimate truth. A mathematical concept such as a point or a line cannot be found in the sense world but must be described in theory. Constructs of plane geometry are, therefore, excellent studies for philosopher–kings. Plato's *Republic* is the first full statement of a philosophy of education. It describes the organization and the curriculum of ideal education in detail, and its scope is from early childhood through adult life.

Since the universal mind is real for idealists and the individual's spiritual essence, or soul, is permanent, the philosophy is compatible with organized religion. St. Augustine (354–430) had been a teacher of rhetoric as a young man. He employed many of the ideas of Plato in the Church and made idealism a Christian theology. The seven liberal arts consisting of the trivium (logic, grammar, and rhetoric) and the quadrivium (music, arithmetic, geometry, and astronomy) were Platonic subjects, modified by the fathers of the Church. They persisted into the medieval universities and are still found in the modern curriculum.

Other famous idealists include René Descartes (1596–1650), George Berkeley (1685–1753), Immanuel Kant (1724–1804), and George W. F. Hegel (1770–1831). Berkeley took the extreme position that physical objects cannot exist on their own but depend on some mind for their reality. Kant's transcendental idealism stated that an object consisted of ideas in our mind but that a thing observed might exist "in itself" independent of the knowing mind. For Hegel's "absolute idealism," both the object itself and the object known to us are ideas of the universal mind. If the universal mind is defined as God, it is easy to see why this philosophy dominated religious institutions and influenced American transcendentalists such as Emerson and Thoreau. American education in the nineteenth century was greatly influenced by Friedrich Froebel and William Torrey Harris, both idealists. Josiah Royce (1855–1916) and Herman Horne (1874–1946), contemporaries of John Dewey, were idealists in America. And J. Donald Butler was an ardent spokesman for American educational idealism.

Idealists think that only the spiritual is ultimately real and that the universe is the expression of a universal mind or a generalized intelligence. This mind is permanent, regular, orderly, and eternal; the truth it represents is absolute and universal. Through education, the individual mind or soul may come to understand and appreciate these unalterable truths. Plato argued that ideas do not come into the mind from an outside source but are always present as a manifestation of the universal mind and may be recalled through the intellectual process of working with ideas. For idealists, teaching is bringing forth the latent knowledge so that a general awareness of universal truths will emerge.

Intellectual disciplines or conceptional systems—such as mathematics, language, ethical studies, history, and the sciences—represent a synthesis of the universal mind. The liberal arts and all other formal intellectual disciplines lead to the highest order of knowledge about reality. Integration of all subjects is important to idealistic pedagogy. Logic and mathematics are powerful tools that cultivate the ability of the student to deal with abstractions and the most sophisticated aspects of the cultural heritage. Vocational subjects, or those that have a practical outcome, are not valued highly. Natural and physical sciences are useful because they deal with cause and effect. History and literature hold a higher place in the curriculum because they provide cultural models. At the top of the hierarchy are the general disciplines of philosophy and theology, which are the most abstract and which transcend time and space. Clearly an idealist school or college would lean heavily toward the arts and sciences and would stress general or what is called "liberal" education of the arts. Idealists will not tolerate an elective system by which students may choose to boycott general education and concentrate on job preparation.

Although idealism as a philosophy of education is still found among educators in the United States, it is no longer a dominant theory, as was the case in the nineteenth century. The vast expansion of science and technology has also contributed to the decline of idealism, so it is now more of a protest philosophy than a mainstream one. Idealism still finds its advocates, however, as in Mortimer Adler's call for universal knowledge that all individuals ought to have as members of the human race.

Friedrich Froebel, founder of the kindergarten, followed the tenets of idealism in both theory and practice in his work with childhood education. William Van Til, in *Education: A Beginning,* noted that Froebel's own childhood experiences of loneliness led to his deep religious faith and emphasis on a home united by love, which was reflected in his educational philosophy (Val Til, 1974: 391).

Educational aims of seventeenth- and eighteenth-century American colleges included moral and ethical conduct, universal truths and knowledge, and expounding the best ideals of humankind. Although often honored more in the breach than the observance, these idealistic values were taught in colonial colleges as well as in their European models. Religion and idealism were often interrelated in schools and colleges of the period.

Realism.   Realism is a school of philosophy that stresses objective knowledge and information that comes from the senses. These philosophers hold that there is a real world not constructed by human minds that can be known by the mind. Knowledge of reality is the only reliable means of guiding individual and social conduct. Reality is found in the realm of objects and perceptions about objects, and these objects are matter. According to realists, division between object and form does not exist. Human beings can know reality through examination of objects and through reason.

Plato's student, Aristotle (384–322 B.C.), is considered to be the father of philosophic realism. Although he did not reject the existence of ideas or forms, Aristotle found it impossible to separate the study of sense objects from their blueprints or forms. Plato would consider the idea of a rectangular solid in the abstract. Aristotle insisted on examining the object itself. For example, a brick takes the form of a rectangular solid, and that is its basic plan or idea. The brick is made of straw, sand, and clay, and that is its materialistic nature. Aristotle was also interested in the force that made the object (the brick maker) and the purpose for which it was intended, such as a brick wall (final cause). He invented many of the standard ways of looking at things, such as classification into categories and the examination of individuals within a class. We can know objects directly through sensation and indirectly through contemplation or abstraction. When a number of individual objects have the same characteristics, we can generalize about them. This is a spectator epistemology in that the learner is an onlooker who sorts and classifies objects in his or her environment. Spectators may verify conceptions by correspondence with objects in the sense world. This is the empirical principle of John Locke (1632–1704).

Just as Plato's ideas were adapted to the Church by St. Augustine, those of Aristotle were brought into harmony with Christian doctrine by St. Thomas Aquinas (1225–1274). He held that God is pure reason, and by use of reason, we could come to know the truth of reality. Proofs of the existence of God rely heavily upon observation so that scientific activity, while subordinate to reason, is justified. Aquinas saw philosophy as the handmaiden of theology and, therefore, a tool for reaching God. Knowledge can be gained from sense experience, and reason may be applied to sense data, revealing the divine plan. A proper education recognizes both the material and the spiritual nature of man. Thomism is still the philosophy of education for Roman Catholic institutions and has greatly influenced other branches of Christianity as well.

The term **sense realism** refers to the process of sorting objects in the environment and gaining an understanding of reality through observation and classification. In this sense, Bacon, Locke, Comenius, Rousseau, and Pestalozzi were realists. Sense realism, as in the case of Comenius, may be combined with religious or rational realism. For the sense realist, the learning environment must be rich in objects against which conceptions can be tested. A field trip to a farm for kindergarten children or a chemistry laboratory for secondary students meets this requirement. Objects have characteristics that may be used to classify or categorize them, and realism stresses placing everything into an objective order according to shared characteristics or similarities. Thus, realists feel that zoological criteria for listing animals in groups should be learned and practiced early in the educational process. The curriculum should be organized into separate subjects in order to create an efficient and effective means of learning about the real world.

The school then becomes a reflection of the systematic way in which the intellectual disciplines are organized in the university, and those, in turn, reflect the universal order of the world. For the realist, knowledge comes through pursuit of the ordered and disciplined inquiry of bodies of knowledge and subject matters. Realists also value prescriptions to govern intelligent behavior. Such behavior is rational when it conforms to the way objects behave in reality as they follow natural laws or physical laws. The educated person must live according to the rules of civilized social organization and must exhibit rational characteristics.

Modern Realism.   Modern realism has flourished in the scientific era. Herbart combined sense realism with psychology to produce an influential theory of education that dominated professional education in the 1890s. Contemporary realism has benefited from the work of Alfred North Whitehead (1861–1947) and Bertrand Russell (1872–1970). They made their reputations in the field of mathematics, coauthoring the famous *Principia Mathematica*. Whitehead was very much interested in education and produced a book called *The Aims of Education and Other Essays* (1929). He was concerned about process and what he called "living ideas." Such ideas are connected with the experience of learners and are capable of being articulated and communicated to others. He saw this organic process pattern of education as different from the learning of "inert" ideas of the past.

An excellent statement of Whitehead's position is found in Harry Broudy's *Building a Philosophy of Education.* Russell (1932) urged a temperate approach to science and said that education held the key to a better world. He conducted some practical experiments in private education with his Beacon Hill School in Massachusetts and was active in a number of social movements against the atom bomb and all wars. Modern realism has many faces, depending on point of view. All realists agree that sense objects exist, that instruction should be organized according to intellectual disciplines, and that the role of the teacher who presents the curriculum is crucial.

Perennialism.   Realists and idealists are in fundamental opposition on the nature of reality, but their educational theories are much more similar than different. Both want a subject matter curriculum and see the school as an institution designed for the cultivation of human intelligence. Education ought to concentrate on basic moral, ethical, aesthetic, and religious principles drawn from the collective experience of culture, especially Western culture. These ideals have recently been expressed under a new rubric—perennialism. Although the term is of recent origin, perennialism presents a conservative, traditional view of human nature and education. It would not be amiss to say that the founding fathers held perennialist views, since they grounded their beliefs in religious idealism and made the basic assumption that certain ethical principles apply to all people at all times. This is so for the eternal truth from God that was the foundation for Harvard College and for Franklin's nondenominational academy in Philadelphia. The idea of universal and unchanging truth was not foreign to those who advocated the separation of church and state in the Bill of Rights or to Horace Mann in his struggle to keep schools free of sectarian control. Assuming the rational nature of human beings, realists held that education should stress the recurrent theme of human life as well as knowledge about the objective world.

The metaphysics (and epistemology) of perennialism is basically that of realism with its scientific/humanistic orientation and its belief that knowledge is relatively stable. Perennialists want a subject-matter curriculum that includes history, language, mathematics, logic, literature, the humanities, and the sciences. Such a program of study reflects the most important aspects of the learned disciplines as they have developed over the centuries, and classical literature or the great books of the Western world best represent it.

The most articulate spokespersons for the perennialist position were Robert Hutchins (1899–1986) and Mortimer Adler (1902–2001). Hutchins and Adler established the Great Books Program in 1946 and devised an index by which the answers of classical authors to the great questions could be compared. Hutchins, who was chosen dean of the Yale law school at a very early age, became the president of the University of Chicago in 1929, at the age of thirty. There, he stressed cultivation of the intellect and held that only educational institutions have the power to do so. He opposed specialized or vocational education but favored those subjects designed to develop the mind. Adler had recently reentered the field as a voice for perennialism with his book *The Paideia Proposal* (see Chapter 8). He had the support of former education secretary William Bennett, who shares the basic tenets of perennialism. Another major statement of perennialism, very popular with the intellectual community, is found in Allan Bloom's *The Closing of the American Mind*, which was published in 1987.

Pragmatism.   Pragmatism (from the Greek word meaning a thing well done) emerged as a uniquely American philosophy just before the end of the nineteenth century. Educational theories such as progressivism, John Dewey's experimentalism, and social reconstructionism are branches of pragmatism. Founded upon modern science and evolution, pragmatism developed a distinctive empirical epistemology opposed to idealism and rationalism. Its themes were practicality, change, growth, and uncertainty as opposed to the order, finality, and fixed truth dominant in older systems. Pragmatists stressed incompleteness, contingency, the consequences of human experience, and a wide-open universe. George H. Mead contributed to the movement with his social concept of the human mind as expressed in his *Mind, Self and Society*, but the major figures in pragmatism were Charles S. Peirce (1839–1914), William James (1843–1910), and John Dewey (1859–1952).

A classic statement of the philosophy by Peirce appeared in an article called "How to Make Our Ideas Clear" in the *Popular Science Quarterly* for January 1878. Peirce said that if we consider the practical effects that an object of our conception might have for our lives, these practical effects define the object. That is, an object only exists "for us" to the degree that it has practical bearings on our life space—our own existence. Since objects far distant in space called quasars have only recently been discovered, they did not exist for Peirce, but they have important practical bearings (and therefore are real) for modern astronomers and for all of us who have altered our conception of the universe on the basis of their discovery.

Peirce argued that the only genuine road to knowledge is the scientific method that is based on human experience and subject to empirical testing. An infinite community of informed observers and knowers must base the truth of an idea upon agreement. Such truth may be relatively stable because of continuing agreement by competent observers, but it can never be fixed or final. Just because learned men once thought Earth to be the center of the solar system does not make that concept true. We must live today by the best "truth" we can get but be ready to call it falsehood when new information or new techniques improve our powers of observation. Most Americans accept this theory as it is applied to science or medicine, but many object to its use in ethics, the rules of social behavior, or religion. It is not widely supported in nonscientific cultures such as those of the Third World. Peirce was never a popular writer, and many of his concepts were complex; still, his principle of verification in actual experience became the foundation for pragmatic philosophy.

William James was a major contributor to educational psychology. Like his brother, Henry, he was a famous author with a national reputation and enormous influence in intellectual circles. In *Pragmatism: A New Name for Some Old Ways of Thinking* (1907), James agreed with Peirce that truth is not absolute but depends on the "workability" or consequences of an idea in actual life. Human experience is of paramount importance for James, and he often spoke of the "stream of experience" or the serial course of events that make up our individual concrete reality. James was not such a "hardheaded" experimental scientist as Peirce and believed that truth is not always objective but that meaning is sometimes found in personal experience that is nonverifiable.

Thus, there is an existential strain in James that is reflected in his keen interest in extrasensory perception. James called upon philosophers to abandon universals, abstractions, and essences in favor of studying human experience (in the laboratory) and reflecting on personal experience (introspection). Peirce was a more systematic thinker than James and soon became upset over what he considered the "bastardization" of pragmatism (even inventing the term *pragmaticism* to distance himself from James), but James remained popular, and his theories were closely related to those of Dewey.

By any measure, John Dewey was the most important educational philosopher ever produced in the United States, as well as a major founder of pragmatism. Born in Burlington, Vermont, in 1859, the year *On the Origin of Species* was published, Dewey had an average boyhood dominated by New England Puritan values and Protestant Christianity. At the University of Vermont, an edge was put on his intellectual appetite by a course in physiology in which the theory of evolution was taught. Dewey turned to philosophy as a means of bridging the gap between the new science and his belief that the world was shaped by God's moral will. After graduation, Dewey taught school in rural Vermont and Oiltown, Pennsylvania, before entering Johns Hopkins University as a graduate student in philosophy. There, he studied under the idealists, George Morris, G. Stanley Hall, and Charles Peirce. Morris introduced Dewey to a system of thought that declared that matter was only illusion. Dewey took his Ph.D. and for ten years taught philosophy at the universities of Michigan and Minnesota. During this time, he became interested in the vigorous rate of change in technology and society, the growth of democracy, and the economic and social changes caused by industrial expansion and urban development. He became disenchanted with a system of unchanging spiritual reality and began to reject Hegelian idealism for what William James called the "wide open universe."

By 1890, Dewey was converted to pragmatism and started his own version of the philosophy, called instrumentalism or experimentalism. Dewey made pragmatism a comprehensive system of thought dealing with all problems generated by conflicts within the culture. Instrumentalism served to restore integration and cooperation between beliefs about the world in which we live and beliefs about the values and purposes that guide conduct. As much a method as a philosophy, instrumentalism concentrates on the scientific, experimental tools for clarification of ideas about social issues and moral conduct.

Dewey saw the task of philosophy not to know the nature of ultimate reality but to understand and control the world. The human mind is an instrument that must be sharpened by experience for use in problem solving and adjustment to the practical situations of human life. Experience, especially collective human experience, provides the best means for coping with a world always in flux. Anticipating Alvin Toffler and the futurists of today, Dewey held that problems cannot be solved with any degree of finality because of constant change and the unknown. Human intelligence and knowledge enable us to adapt our environment to our needs and to adapt philosophic goals to the reality of the situation of life-space in which we exist.

Like Locke, Dewey was concerned about the origin of ideas and the problem of how the mind functions. The first of his many books dealt with functional psychology. He accepted the empirical principle that ideas come from experience and are verified by comparison with objective reality. Since action must precede knowledge, there are no *a priori* ideas. Dewey drew upon the naturalistic theories of Rousseau and Froebel but also upon the biological sciences, sociology, and Darwinian evolution. He saw human survival and the progress of the race tied to the means available for solving essential problems. Natural intelligence combined with reconstruction of past experience can be the means only if antecedent action is able to trigger a scientific, rational approach to solutions. Past beliefs, grounded in tradition or drawn from authority, may actually inhibit the survival of humankind. For this reason, Dewey wanted to submit every tradition, attitude, or belief to the experimental test with its corollary of verification by experience.

As a psychological functionalist, Dewey understood that the mind is set in motion by the organism's desire to meet its needs and solve its problems. Although the human organism is of infinite complexity, intelligence may be defined as the use of experience in solving problems. Using the mind is an organic function by which humans reduce drives and satisfy needs in interaction with the environment. People are not naturally passive, and the experiences they undergo become the building blocks of meaning. Dewey understood that what people think about is related to what they do and the totality of environmental influence. Intelligence and learning must be equated with the scientific method of problem solving. Since the individual is not isolated, intelligence must be directed toward social efficiency or community issues as well as individual needs.

A central theme in Dewey's educational theory is "the complete act of thought." Although described in many of his writings, his little book *How We Think* (1910) gives the most detailed analysis of the problem-solving process. Dewey held that learning grows out of ongoing activity that must be meaningful to the learner. Activity involves the individual in the relationship between an act and its consequences. This implies that schools must foster purposeful activity by building on the common interests of children, such as communication, inquiry, construction, and artistic expression. Although activity is required for learning, no progress will be made so long as it is a routine activity and the student operates on the basis of habit.

Learning actually begins when a difficulty or problem creates a barrier and prevents an activity from continuing. The problem must be genuine (not imposed from outside by the teacher) and must be defined by the learner, so that he or she knows exactly what blocks the activity. The problem provides motivation, the driving force or interest required for thinking. At this point, information or data concerning a possible solution are gathered. This may be done merely by remembering prior experience or by more sophisticated means such as consulting an expert or using a library. The next step is forming a hypothesis—an educated guess as to how the problem may be resolved. The learner does not jump at once to any hypothesis but first reflects upon the probable outcomes and the possibility of undesirable consequences if the hypothesis is accepted. Finally, the learner chooses the most likely hypothesis to solve the problem and puts it to the empirical test of experience. If it works, the barrier to the activity is removed; if not, the learner has gained further data upon which to operate and may continue the process. Dewey's complete act of thought (activity, problem, data, hypothesis, testing) was taken directly from the scientific research model and is the basis for his pedagogy.

In *Experience and Education* (1938), Dewey defined education as the process of continuous reconstruction of experience with the purpose of widening and deepening its social content while helping the individual to gain control of the methods involved. In *Democracy and Education* (1916), he called education a process of living and not merely preparation for future living. Dewey also claimed that education is growth and that as long as growth continues, education must continue as a social process. As the title suggests, *Democracy and Education* argues that the social process of education is best served if the school is a democratic community. Dewey once said that if we are willing to conceive of education as the process of forming fundamental dispositions, philosophy might be defined as the general theory of education.

Dewey's critics often point to the contradictions and inconsistencies in his work. However, few have studied all of his books and articles, and he continued to be a prolific writer and to develop his philosophy until his death in 1952. On becoming chairperson of the Department of Philosophy at the University of Chicago, Dewey gave equal attention to the teacher education unit of which he was also in charge. He became a critic of rugged individualism, free enterprise without controls, outmoded social institutions, and a narrow definition of democracy as a form of government. His educational experiments at the laboratory school in the University of Chicago were used as models by many of his progressive followers, but he became very critical of progressives when he felt their activities were not philosophically sound. In 1916, his *Democracy and Education* was published, making him a national figure in both fields.

After leaving Chicago for Columbia University in 1904, Dewey devoted more of his attention to social and moral issues. Rejecting the idea that philosophy defines ends and education provides means, he held that ends must always be kept in view and adjusted as progress is made. Ends never justify means. Dewey was the enemy of philosophic dualisms. He saw no conflict between the school and society, the student and the curriculum, or interest and effort in education. Although vitally interested in the concepts of community and democracy, Dewey insisted upon leaving open the possibility that better social relationships might be invented in the future. To view the democratic society as an end or a goal would have violated his principle of continuous reconstruction of experience and constant adjustment to the conditions of life.

Dewey supported child-centered schools without stiff authoritarianism, but he also stressed the importance of integrated subjects in the curriculum and saw the school as a place where experiences could be simplified, purified, and ordered. His open-ended universe and pluralistic reality would not allow him to place limits on what might be studied, but he did think people could be educated so that they could control their own affairs and attain a more satisfactory collective life. Scientific method and experimental thinking can help us improve life and invent better social institutions. Although he rejected supernatural beliefs, as well as militant atheism, Dewey supported a humanistic religious position in books like *A Common Faith*. He also gave considerable attention to aesthetic development, especially in *Art as Experience*.

Dewey was not only the most articulate spokesman for pragmatism and the theoretical founder of progressivism but also the most influential American philosopher of education. He had legions of followers, and many may still be found in schools and institutions of higher education. Many colleges of education such as Teachers College of Columbia University, the University of Illinois at Urbana-Champaign, the University of Texas at Austin, Ohio State University, and Stanford remained centers of Dewey's theory long after his death. Several of his followers like Boyd Bode, Gordon Hullfish, William Kilpatrick, and Bruce Raup became well known in their own right. Criticisms were also numerous, ranging from the serious philosophical issues raised by idealist Herman Horne and the attack on relativism voiced by Allan Bloom to the unfounded political rhetoric expressed by Max Rafferty and Albert Lynd.

Social Reconstructionism.

From ancient times, educational institutions have had the function of transmitting cherished values and preserving the culture. Schools have rarely been the focus of radical social change, but they have been an instrument for social improvement, especially economic improvement. Horace Mann and other early national leaders fostered utopian ideals in education, such as equality of opportunity and ending poverty. Interest in this utopian theme accelerated during the progressive era in American history and the rise of populist parties. The women's suffrage movement, the civil rights movement, the attack on graft, and the work of muckraking authors who exposed corruption and inequality also influenced the utopian theme. Progressive education was also a force in social reconstruction as illustrated by the appearance in 1932 of George Counts' *Dare the Schools Build a New Social Order?* This book called for complete social revolution and was considered radical even by most members of the Progressive Education Society, but it did raise the question of the role of the school in changing society.

Dewey's belief in education as an instrument for the continuous reconstruction of experience, his championship of democracy as a way of life, and the pragmatic theme of understanding and controlling the world contributed to this position. In 1935, W. H. Kilpatrick, John Childs, Bruce Raup, and Harold Rugg joined Counts in founding the John Dewey Society for the Study of Education and Culture. The Society began publishing the journal *Social Frontier,* which attacked the evils of capitalism and called for active participation of educators in social change. This journal was responsible for much conservative criticism of progressive education, but it was also the focal point of those progressives who felt that schools should be active in altering society.

The most important figure in social reconstruction is Theodore Brameld (1904–1987). Brameld saw a crisis in modern society, with many contradictions and mass confusion regarding goals. He agreed with Isaac Kandel that setting up a utopian model is dangerous because there is no empirical way to define an ideal society. Still, he felt that we must take a holistic approach to alternative possibilities. Brameld's arguments are expressed in books like *Toward a Reconstructed Philosophy of Education, Education as Power,* and *Patterns of Educational Philosophy*. If the crisis—illustrated by wars, the rich–poor gap, pollution, international terrorism, the population explosion, resource depletion, and accelerating technological advance—is real, then merely transmitting dominant social values in traditional schools will not suffice. Brameld wanted to solve the pervasive problems of humankind and direct us toward a global government.

He agreed with Karl Mannheim and Robert Heilbroner that we are about to witness the very end of civilization unless we can quickly and drastically reconstruct our priorities and patterns of behavior. He saw mass confusion about goals and inadequate responses to the world crisis. He thought that nationalism is no longer adequate and that we must create a world government to control nuclear arms and stop environmental destruction. In *Education as Power*, he argues that knowledge is power and that the reconstructionist theory of value might be transmitted through schooling to produce a utopian "civilized civilization." Since values are man-made, it is possible to define ends through social consensus. It is assumed that world peace and economic cooperation are such goals, but no one wants them to be imposed by an outside authority such as a national government. In *Toward a Reconstructed Philosophy of Education*, Brameld says that education is a means for guaranteeing sufficient income to all families; meeting reasonable standards of nutrition, medical care, shelter, dress, and schooling; and utilizing all of the world's natural resources in the interests of the majority of people. Many social theorists and most futurists share this position.

Although many agree that the world crisis is real and cannot be resolved by the United States alone, a global civilization and a world government do not seem realistic. Schools under the direction of local or national governments lack the power to engage in global reconstruction. They can, as futurists argue, provide information on what is happening in our world and prepare students for problem solving and better communication in an age of rapid change.

From a practical standpoint, social reconstructionism has waxed and waned depending upon the political climate. Progressives in the '30s and '40s were successful in persuading school authorities that children learn best when they are safe, healthy, properly nourished, and enjoying a pleasant physical environment. This "whole child" philosophy led to hot lunches, health care, counseling services, and the like. The civil rights movement of the Martin Luther King era, the war on poverty, and the liberal social policies of the Kennedy and Johnson administrations fostered social engineering through schools. Racial integration, bilingual programs, special education, Head Start, Educational Talent Search, and Upward Bound are examples of such efforts at the federal level.

At one time, it appeared that Congress might pass a national equalization law that would provide the same financial support for every American child regardless of the state or district in which the student lived. Because American education is a state function with limited federal support and control, it is less subject to national politics than is the case in many other nations. Nevertheless, social engineering efforts such as busing to achieve racial integration, project Head Start, and Educational Talent Search have been more popular with a Democrat in the White House; Republicans have favored local control and less national legislation. Reconstructionist theory had little support in the administrations of Reagan and George Bush. President Clinton urged congressional action on a variety of social issues in his first term, including child care, universal health care, and the College Student Assistance program. Failure of these programs to receive adequate funding indicates the divided nature of the federal government. President George W. Bush urged more educational testing, the implementation of higher standards in all states, greater local control and more parental involvement. With a narrowly divided Congress, it remains to be seen what programs will actually become law.

Essentialism.   Essentialism is a conservative educational theory that emphasizes the value of certain "basic" subjects and the authority of the teacher. Educators have always attempted to identify what is essential to the knowledge of a learned person. Ancient Athenians thought it essential for boys of the citizenship class to learn the *Iliad*, but they did not think it good for slaves or women to study Homer. Most Americans now think computer literacy is basic, but this was not the case two decades ago. Educational history is filled with debate over what constitutes basic knowledge, which people should receive it, and how it should be transmitted. The essentialist movement in America began as a response to what was considered "soft pedagogy" or "permissive" education supported by progressives. It was recently reflected in the charge of former education secretary William Bennett that schools emphasize process and not content.

In 1938, a group of prominent educators led by William C. Bagley (1874–1946) started a movement that called for intellectual training in schools instead of "child growth and development." They said the essential skills of reading, writing, and arithmetic should be found in every elementary curriculum together with history, literature, and geography. For the secondary school, the curriculum was the Western cultural heritage, including the academic subjects in the arts and sciences. Bagley favored observed data over a strictly rational approach and, like the realists, supported scientific examination of physical phenomena. Michael Demiashkevich, Robert Ulich, and W. E. Hocking soon joined him. By this time, progressive education was on the decline, and essentialism attracted a great deal of public support.

Bagley was an articulate spokesman for the essentialist theory. He served as editor of *School and Society* from 1939 to 1946, and his position at Teachers College gave him status with educators. In "An Essentialist's Platform for the Advancement of Education" (1938), he claimed that schooling requires hard work and attention as well as respect for genuine authority. He stressed the logical sequence of subjects and called for a "back to basics" movement to combat the lowering of academic standards. There is no question that some progressives had ignored content in favor of process (although those who did were not following Dewey) and that some students were weak in factual information. Although the Eight-Year Study showed that students from progressive high schools did well in college, Bagley's argument had merit, and the political climate was right, due to the conservatism of the World War II era.

Many authors with quite different views who were determined to attack not only progressives but also those they labeled "educationists" soon supported essentialism. Arthur Bestor Jr. in *Educational Wastelands* (1953), Albert Lynd in *Quackery in the Public Schools* (1953), and Max Rafferty in *Suffer Little Children* (1962) were especially shrill in their condemnation of all educators. Although their motivation was largely political, they attracted a great deal of public support and caused essentialism to become the focal point for all criticism of public schools and teacher education programs. In discussing the "diminished mind," Mortimer Smith accused John

Dewey of destroying the ability of Americans to think. Some of the arguments were no more grounded in fact than the anti-Communist "witch hunts" of Joseph McCarthy. However, they got a similar response from the mass media, and by 1960 "education bashing" became popular.

More serious, if less colorful, were the arguments for more rigor in curriculum; these arguments came after the formation of the Council for Basic Education in 1946. Indeed, modern educational history describes a pattern of back to basics movements followed by liberal responses like team teaching and nongraded schools, followed again by back to basics. Sometimes the cycle is fostered by comparison with foreign schools, as was the case with Admiral Hyman Rickover and James B. Conant, following the Soviet success with Sputnik in 1957. More recently, the cycle was initiated by education secretary T. H. Bell and his National Commission on Excellence in Education, which produced *A Nation at Risk* in 1983.

Essentialism in education has recently been encouraged by demands of governing bodies for new requirements for high school graduation, higher College Board scores, assessment, and accountability. It has always been possible to illustrate that some students do poorly on a test of essential knowledge. In 1989, a widely televised Barbara Walters' special called attention to the lack of geographic knowledge on the part of American secondary students. Public reaction to such media events brings pressure for the elimination of "nonessential" subjects, concentration on basics, and more testing. Ultraconservative groups, such as the fundamentalist Christian "new right," use the same arguments to get rid of subjects they dislike, such as sex education and environmental studies.

Humanism.   Humanism is not so much a philosophy of education as it is a point of view based on literary studies and the assumption that the proper study of mankind is man. All systems of philosophy give some attention to human values and the human condition. The roots of humanism go back to ancient Greece, where the sophists claimed that "man is the measure of all things." In Europe, during the fourteenth and fifteenth centuries, it flourished as the intellectual core of the Renaissance. Desiderius Erasmus (1466–1536) contributed to humanism by trying to move the Church away from ceremonies and toward ideal Christian living. Early American literary humanists rejected the Puritan belief that man is sinful by nature and agreed with Comenius that the human condition could be improved through education. Franklin, Jefferson, Emerson, and Thoreau are counted among American humanists, as are all Deists.

Literary and classical humanism flourished after World War I and was represented by such advocates as Nicholas Murray Butler, Abraham Flexner, and Mark Van Doren. Drawing from the newer disciplines of psychology, political science, anthropology, and sociology, they spoke less to the supernatural nature of man than they did to his distinctively human faculties as a guide for moral conduct. Humanists support the utilitarian concept of the greatest good for the greatest number but oppose the dominance of science, materialism, and values drawn from mass behavior. Humanistic educators find too great an emphasis on vocationalism and technology in schools and urge more attention to literature and the classics.

There is a strong tie between humanists and perennialists. Indeed, Robert Hutchins and Mortimer Adler may be classified as both perennialists and humanists. Humanists say that people have distinctive qualities—such as reason, moral conscience, aesthetic taste, and religious instinct—that are quite different from those of animals. While giving priority to the literary and linguistic arts, humanists stress the heritage of Western culture, especially the classics of Greece and Rome. Such subjects lead to a well-rounded development of the intellectual, moral, aesthetic, and religious capabilities of humankind.

Neo-Thomists and mainline Protestants support humanism; fundamentalist Christians do not. Using the powerful tool of the television ministry, many "born again" Christians have launched a particularly vicious attack on what they call "secular humanism." Although the term seems to have been invented for atheistic humanists, as used by Jimmy Swaggart and Jerry Falwell, it includes liberal Christian ministers and all professors in secular universities. This blanket definition, which includes such strange bedfellows as scientists and biblical scholars under the rubric "secular humanism," has confused the issues. Falwell has claimed that "secular humanism" is a religion, something that all humanists would deny. Literary humanists have suffered from the conservative attacks, and their influence in education has been weakened. A curriculum example is the support for giving creationism equal space with the theory of evolution in school textbooks.

Analytic Philosophy of Education.

The analysis of concepts in philosophy is as old as the formal study of ideas; logic can be traced back to Aristotle. Certainly the meaning of various concepts and arguments is central to building any philosophy or educational theory. Pragmatists such as Peirce wanted to make ideas clear, but Dewey used terms like **democracy**, **interests**, and **growth** without giving them precise meaning. With the decline in emphasis on formal logic in universities and the rise of political and media slogans, the use of logic and the analysis of language gained in importance. Analytic professors now dominate many departments of educational philosophy in universities. They point out the absurdity of taking a phrase such as "self-actualization" from Maslow and making it an educational goal without understanding what Maslow really meant or how hard it would be for all students to attain such a goal. They challenge political statements of the "Lake Wobegon" sort that say all students should be better than average.

Although the roots of analytic philosophy are found in logic, British empiricism, and nineteenth-century efforts to clarify meaning in literature, its major foundation is contemporary realism and logical positivism. An Englishman, George E. Moore (1873–1958), developed the analytic branch of realism with emphasis on ordinary language. His colleague Bertrand Russell leaned toward formal language and the precise terms used in the sciences and mathematics. Moore's *A Defense of Common Sense* dealt with the meaning of propositions found in common language and pointed out that many issues in philosophy are due to misunderstanding because of abstract and technical language. Russell's formalistic approach became popular with scientific Americans, especially after he began lecturing at Harvard in 1914.

The logical positivist roots of analytic philosophy originated with a group of European scientists and mathematicians known as the "Vienna Circle." Ludwig Wittgenstein (1889–1951) was an Austrian philosopher who contributed to positivism and greatly influenced the Vienna Circle. He studied with Russell at Cambridge and became a British subject after World War I. Wittgenstein held that the job of philosophy is not to discover truth but to resolve problems and clarify ideas obtained from other fields. He wanted to deal with the language about data as opposed to the study of metaphysical statements from the great philosophical systems. Vienna Circle members Rudolph Carnap and A. J. Ayer interpreted Wittgenstein to mean that all propositions must be publicly verifiable and capable of replication.

With the growth of modern science and new disciplines, experts have used special language. An example would be computer language terms such as **BASIC** or **COBOL**. Analysts foster communication by dealing with the real meaning of terms, their truthfulness, and their reliability. They translate specialized language into ordinary meaning that can be used for educational policies.

Because of increased specialization and advanced technology, communication between experts in different fields has become more difficult. Information that comes through the mass media shows a vast range of truthfulness, reliability, and validity. Clearly, an analysis of knowing, such as that developed by Gilbert Ryle in *The Concept of Mind,* has value now.

Modern analytic professors of education like Israel Scheffler, R. S. Peters, Jonas Soltis, Henry Perkinson, and Richard Pring offer no metaphysical statements or models of schools. Instead, they clarify meaning so that those who make policy or develop curriculum may understand exactly the theories upon which they build and the consequences of their own position statements. Analytic philosophy is not a speculative system, but it provides a means for making educational ideas clear, precise, and meaningful.

Protest Philosophies.   The philosophical foundations upon which schools rest that we have so far examined assume an ordered universe, the validity of reason, logic in the curriculum, and an individual governed by ethical rules in an intelligible world. Plato believed that a person with a rational soul could not choose to do wrong if he or she clearly understood what action was right. Yet, it is obvious that a child may misbehave knowing the behavior is wrong and that an adult may act for psychological rather than logical reasons. Many theories hold that the social order is not fair or reasonable, and some say the universe is not subject to rational analysis. Such thinking leads to protest against the schools, the society, customs, moral rules, and the assumption that truth corresponds to reality. Behaviorism, existentialism, and postmodern philosophy are treated as protest positions. They are seldom the foundations for schools, but they raise troubling questions with which all educators must deal.

Behaviorism.   Psychology and education are closely related. Dewey and James were psychologists, as well as philosophers and progressives, and adopted Gestalt psychology as their own. A few modern psychologists have developed a position sufficiently broad and with enough followers, so that it is meaningful to speak of their educational philosophies. Among these are Jerome Bruner, Abraham Maslow, Carl Rogers, and especially Burrhus Frederick Skinner (1904–1990). Although best known for his programmed instruction derived from the principles of operant conditioning based on laboratory experiments with animals, Skinner has moved behavioral engineering into the realm of utopian planning, the nature of humankind, social values, and a definition of the good life.

Born in Susquehanna, Pennsylvania, Skinner taught psychology at the University of Minnesota and Indiana University before returning to Harvard, where he had taken his Ph.D. Earning a reputation as one of the most important contemporary psychologists, his work on animal behavior is a major contribution to knowledge. Building on the foundation of Ivan Pavlov (1849–1946), who began experimentation on conditioned reflexes in Russia, and the American behaviorists Edward Lee Thorndike (1874–1949) and John B. Watson (1878–1958), he developed laws of behavior and created teaching machines. Had he confined his work to "rat in a box" psychology, as it is sometimes called, there would be no behavioristic theory of education; but he went beyond the experimental laboratory in his books *Walden II* (1976) and *Beyond Freedom and Dignity* (1971).

Behaviorism is grounded in realism, especially the materialistic branch, which maintains that behavior is caused by environmental conditions. Instead of concentration on mind or consciousness, behaviorists look at observable facts, capable of empirical verification. Skinner thought philosophers who attempted to deduce a concept of human nature from a priori generalizations or introspection had made errors. Although he did not deny genetic influence, he opposed the traditional views of humankind that assume there are internal drives and hidden forces that define humans. Humanists argued that human beings possess distinctive qualities that are absolutely different from animals and that are not the product of evolution. Skinner treats humans as animals subject to the same environmental controls and evolutionary forces as any other living organism, different only in degree not kind.

Increasingly in contemporary society, environmental forces control our behavior. Some of these, such as inflation and population growth, may be accidental; others, such as advertising to make us want particular products, are intentional and manipulative. Skinner argues that since we understand the power of such forces to modify behavior, we ought to use them deliberately to construct a society of the most benefit to all. This was the theme of the utopian new Walden, where everything was done with cooperation but according to plan. Few are neutral about Skinner's theories. A common charge is that he abolished "mankind" through scientific analysis. He is interested in the complexity and uniqueness of people, but he sees people as mechanical and animal in nature. Critics suggest that the same behavioral engineering techniques he advocates might produce a nightmare society such as Orwell's *1984*. Skinner replies that we are likely to get such a society by *not* planning or attempting to control and modify human behavior.

Skinner believes in a sophisticated science of human behavior and maintains that value judgments are just as much a part of science as any other field, including philosophy. Behavior (including aggressive behavior) is explained by positive reinforcement. It is not helpful to condemn the culprit in crime or the extermination of Jews in World War II. Rather, we should look for ways to remove the positive reinforcement of such behavior. Knowing is not just a cognitive process; it is environmental, behavioral, and psychological as well. The "good" for Skinner is merely that which is rewarded; if we want to shape cultural evolution, we must find ways to reinforce that behavior that the culture defines as desirable. He points out that, historically, cultural change has been blind, accidental, or random. He holds that though we may not have a blueprint for the perfect society, we can develop better social arrangements, and education is one of the best ways to design a better culture. Again, positive reinforcement (not punishment) is the most effective way to alter institutions, because human action is shaped by rewards.

Obviously, behavior depends upon actual possibilities. In ancient Athens, the automobile was not a possibility, and it had no part of shaping the culture. For modern American adolescents, driving an automobile is rewarding. It gives a feeling of power and freedom, and the teenage subculture regards "wheels" as one of the most important status symbols. For contemporary culture, the automobile is very important, and our behavior of driving and prizing cars is reinforced.

Behaviorists view the child as a highly conditioned organism even before entering school. Whatever has gone on before, including contradiction in the values exhibited by parents or the environmental control of institutions such as churches, will have an impact on the school environment. Since teachers must engage in the modification of behavior, it is important that they know what goals they wish to achieve and how to reach them with efficiency. Skinner does not see this process as evil but as a means for expanding possibilities and developing a preference for a better kind of civilization.

Behaviorists can demonstrate that operant conditioning actually works. Successful techniques for classroom management and control are grounded in the theory, as well as instructional methods such as those of Madeline Hunter. Skinner's influence is enormous in spite of strong opposition to his ideas. Nevertheless, behaviorism is a growing educational philosophy, especially in the United States.

Existentialism.   Not a systematic philosophy, existentialism (and its psychological counterpart, phenomenology) is a protest against institutional controls, formalism, and social norms. Existentialism provides a means for examining life in a personal way, reflecting on commitments and choices, and considering the temporary nature of human life. Existentialists do not believe that we inhabit a meaningful or explainable world. The philosophy includes a theme of hope, but there is also a theme of desperation and anguish. One cannot find a model of a school based upon existentialism. The closest thing might be the schools of the American Summerhill Association (based on the work of A. S. Neill in England), which stress freedom of choice, authenticity, and personal development. Martin Buber (1878–1965) offered some existential-based suggestions about education in *I and Thou*; and critics like Holt, Leonard, and Illich reflect an existentialistic point of view. The philosophy forms a foundation for taking issue with almost all of the activities that take place in public and private schools.

Roots of existentialism go back to the admonition of Socrates to "know thyself" and the sophists, who said that "man is the measure of all things." Descartes, Pascal, and Dostoevsky stressed the idea of personal freedom and responsibility. Albert Camus, Gabriel Marcel, Friedrich Nietzsche, and Edmund Husserl, who founded phenomenology, developed the modern theme. The influence on American education has come since World War II and is largely based on Soren Kierkegaard (1813–1855), Martin Heidegger (1889–1976), Jean Paul Sartre (1905–1980), and Martin Buber.

Existentialism's primary focus has been on the nature of human existence. According to Sartre, existence precedes essence and we are "condemned" to be free. Unlike realists or idealists, existentialists think people create their own essence by choosing what they will be. This is quite different from Kant's charge that we have a duty to be moral or Mill's belief that we must act in the best interests of the greatest number. We must choose to conform, rebel, commit suicide, live independent from social norms, love, hate, or be directed by peer values. Although others seek to impinge upon our freedom to make choices, we are totally responsible. The authentic person is one who is aware of his or her freedom and is willing to take the responsibility for self-direction and self-definition.

Choices and the manner in which they are made determine what human beings we will become. Each person's situation is unique; the world is only temporary, and each of us must carry the burden of his or her own upcoming death. Existentialists will not tell us that our choices are right or wrong, only that our freedom is total, that our existence is determined by the choices we make, and that the universe is indifferent to human wishes and desires. We may choose to keep up with the Joneses, take our values from the mass media, or work only for money in a meaningless job; but such choices lead to an unfulfilled life of desperation and anguish and cut off possibilities of loving, creating, and being.

The very nature of existence poses a metaphysical question of central interest to existentialists, and their theory of value is important; but the philosophy is not concerned with logic or epistemology. Some aspects of phenomenology relate to the formation of values and ethical questions in education. Examples would be Abraham Maslow's stages of development and the theory of moral development in the work of Lawrence Kohlberg. Since schools operate on rules, conformity, acceptance of the curriculum, homework, following directions, teacher authority, and the like, students who insist on individual choice and challenge regulations are hard to manage.

Some existentialists think that schools should not exist. Others like George Leonard object to the "hidden curriculum" of social expectations and peer values that are transmitted by the school environment. They think that once the veneer of civilization is stripped away, the savage nature of man and the misery of the human condition will be revealed. No set of values or established body of knowledge can replace individual experience with its personal motives, choices, and responsibilities. To accept a philosophy or religion from others denies our right to create our own values and imposes a barrier to answering the question of what we have chosen to be. These views are also reflected in the criticism of Ivan Illich (see Chapter 7).

Existentialism is very troublesome for educators because it attacks the fundamental assumptions of systematic philosophies upon which schools rest. The themes of desperation, alienation, death, and despair are not compatible with schooling. Absolute freedom to choose is a challenge to all social organizations and the institutions of civilization. Yet the awful price we pay for giving over our choices to others and allowing them to determine our fate is the basis for a critical examination of all philosophies. Examples include the mass suicide in Jonestown, Guyana, and the Heaven's Gate group suicide in Rancho Mirage, California; in both cases, many lost their lives because they put their trust totally in others. The influence of existentialistic writers is increasing and can hardly be dismissed by policy builders or those who create educational theory, even though it is a difficult matter to deal with in schools.

Postmodernism.   The postmodern writers form less of a school of philosophy than a complex set of reactions to modern philosophy and its presuppositions, models, logic, and analytic methods. Some themes such as the nonrational character of existence and the inclusion of all types of experience as reality are related to the existentialism of Sartre, the nihilism of Nietzsche, and the phenomenology of Husserl. Postmodernists oppose essentialism, idealism, and all forms of realism including Marxism. Jean Francois Lyotard claims that his position precedes modern philosophy because it does not assume that knowledge provides an accurate picture of reality and rejects all philosophical assumptions since Plato. Reason is not sovereign for Lyotard, and no grand scheme such as democracy or economic determinism is valid. Postmodern thought also includes feminist challenges to social norms as found in the work of Judith Butler, Helene Cixous, and Martha Nussbaum. Feminist authors say that the schools reflect a society that is sexist and patriarchal, even extending to the language and the curriculum.

Leading postmodern writers include Michael Apple, Michel Foucault, Henry Giroux, Jurgen Habermas, Barry Kanpol, and Richard Rorty. Rorty's ideology of postmodernism is an extension of some of the basic philosophical premises of John Dewey. The other authors offer alternatives to the philosophical ideas of the enlightenment era. Concepts of structure, dogmatism, rationalism, modernism, positivism, and any other preconceived notion of knowledge are replaced in postmodernism by ideas of ambiguity, questioning, unsystematic narration of perceptions, and freedom from any superimposed knowledge systems. Even language and its structure are under intense scrutiny because of the limitations on truly knowing. Postmodernism is a blend of the liberating message of existentialism, with the humanism of pragmatism and the critical theory of Marxism.

Postmodernists criticize any universalistic explanations of the cosmos, replacing them with a transformation of liberation that includes concerns of "marginalized" people (those who have not always been heeded by mainstream thinkers). This celebration of diversity focuses on liberating individuals from age, class, gender, and race-based prejudices. Reaching the feelings, attitudes, and aspirations of individuals through exploration of their own account of educational politics and struggles within their school settings is achieved through micronarratives (or present-oriented dialogue). These insights into the attitudes of educators about their individual struggles and triumphs within schools provide meaningful structures that can be interwoven in metanarratives of school research findings.

As with pragmatism, postmodernism finds democracy and its institutions always in flux, change, and modification. As Dewey noted, change is always prevalent in a democracy. Change gives democracy its uniqueness and ability to meet conditions requiring innovation in theory and practice. As in existentialism, postmodernism seeks meaning in situational context, texture, and consciousness raising. The Marxist call for liberation from forms of modernism or industrialism that encroach on human freedom is found in postmodernists' attunement to an age of postindustrialism or global communication/information networks.

Postmodernists seek to build a more humane society through reaching all levels, gender, ages, and races. They seek to re-create and reinvent democracy to achieve more economic and social justice. Susan Hekman, Kate Campbell, and other feminist authors find postmodernism helpful in delineating alternatives to masculine oriented theories from the Enlightenment forward. Kai Erikson's account (1982) suggests that this is a necessary liberating approach, as can be seen from the 1637 trial of Ann Hutchinson, whose banishment from Massachusetts Colony was due in no small part to Governor Winthrop's view:

> For if she had attended her household affairs, and such things as belong to
> women, and had not gone out of her way and calling to meddle in such things as
> are proper for men, she had kept her wits, and might have improved them use-
> fully and honorably in the place that God set her. (p. 82)

The feminist struggle for liberation continues through postmodern literature as we approach the twenty-first century.

Social and Futures Philosophy.   Strongly related to social reconstructionism and the theories of John Dewey, social and futures philosophies are emerging as important bodies of thought aimed at understanding a world of accelerating change. Joel Feinberg tells us that social philosophy is less well defined than most of the other conventional branches and that social philosophy of education is even more elliptical, since it embraces philosophical matters from political science, sociology, and anthropology while including skills of analysis and critical thinking. Although the theory has roots in the Enlightenment and in the works of Comenius, Locke, and Rousseau, it is mainly a twentieth-century development.

Social and futures philosophy is especially concerned with the study of the school as a social institution and concepts like freedom, human rights, leadership, ideology, power, equity, and justice. Social and futures thinkers rely equally on work from philosophy and work from other disciplines. For example, they rely on William F. Ogburn's

Social Change, Marshall McLuhan's *Understanding Media*, Arnold Toynbee's *A Study of History*, and Kenneth Boulding's *The Meaning of the Twentieth Century*. This interdisciplinary basis means that these theorists are interested in all social issues. General statements of the futures philosophy are found in the works of Alvin Toffler and Edward Cornish. Jim Bowman, Christopher Dede, Draper Kauffmann, Fred Kierstead, and Harold Shane have developed the educational theory.

Insofar as social philosophers deal with ultimate reality, they accept the metaphysics of realism. Logic is of little interest to them, although many accept the urge to clarify language as voiced by analytical thinkers. The real thrust of the movement is epistemology and axiology. These philosophers have historically criticized "received" notions such as the accepted social role of the school, the end of preparing to enter the job market, and the notion that existing bodies of knowledge define the path to the good life. They look to the kind of information a learner must have for survival in the future, and they consider how the society might be reconstructed through education to meet new technical, social, and environmental needs. This aspect of the social philosophy has, in the current century, taken on a strong normative component, as it attempts to set forth new designs and scenarios of teaching and learning, research and study, knowledge and values, and the theoretical dimensions of special institutions. Spencer Maxcy of Louisiana State University has developed a statement of social philosophy of education, as has Harold Hodgkinson.

As the name implies, social philosophers of education are concerned with the deeper, more theoretical dimensions of social issues as they are related to education. They have criticized the accepted social role of the school. Futurists are interested in those social arrangements that will allow us to survive with a maximum realization of the human potential. They see education as a means of inventing the future and restructuring society so as to resolve the most pressing human problems and to take advantage of new opportunities provided by technological invention. This aspect of social philosophy of education has a strong value orientation as it attempts to set forth new designs and scenarios of teaching, learning, research, and study. Values and ethics, freedom, human rights, equity, justice, ideology, leadership, and the proper use of power are major areas of interest for futurists and social philosophers.

Qualitative methods of educational inquiry are increasingly used in research. Eliot Eisner, James Swartz, and others address the utility of qualitative research. William Pinar talks of the need to reconceptualize education, to move from traditional means of telling the truth about schooling to a better understanding through psychological/biographical/literary techniques and the adoption of more naturalistic methods. Philosophy, social science, and futurism join hands to provide a more workable set of solutions to the social problems facing human society. A branch of social philosophy called hermeneutics argues that the primary function of thought is seeking an understanding of the conditions we face as humans. The business of social and futures philosophy is edifying rather than providing data or statistical analysis of present conditions and interpreting social change.

These philosophers hold that in our swift technological transformation into the information age and the postindustrial society characterized by computers and cybernation, we have failed to address matters of value and ethics. They argue that industrial-age schools and materialistic/individualistic values are not appropriate for the future. In *The Minimal Self* (1984), Christopher Lasch is critical of personalistic and individualistic theories. Wendell Bell, in a 1996 discussion at the Eighth General Assembly of the World Future Society, questioned the premises of postmodernism and the consequences of social fragmentation. A philosophy of self for the future should stress survival, protecting the environment, collective needs, and the global nature of society.

In the last half-century, Americans have seen major changes that require new ethical standards. Husband and wife both work; children are sent to day-care centers; television illustrates sex, violence, and greed; gangs create havoc in cities; drug use is epidemic; child and spouse abuse as well as children against children violence is increasing; and children are having children. These things point to a need for a major shift in the teaching and formation of values, but many schools behave as if the world has not changed since 1950. Teachers and principals working toward a futures social philosophy must be sensitive to the ethical dimension of preparing citizens for a world filled with significant human problems. As Wendell Bell (1997) points out, we need to constantly question, re-examine, and judge consequences of our actions to contribute toward effective strategies for social action.

Ultimately, social philosophy is pledged to the idea that education is a flawed enterprise that may be improved through reflective thinking and "unpacking" the curriculum. Cleo Cherryholmes tells us that textbooks have rarely been scrutinized for what they leave out and that American school textbooks are bland and uniform in their treatment of critical social issues that we must face as a nation. As Robert C. Holland and Rushworth Kidder noted in an address at the Eighth General Assembly of the World Future Society (Washington, D.C., 1966), everyone has an interest in developing tolerance for and celebration of individual and cultural differences for the twenty-first century. Schools for tomorrow must take up this challenge. According to Peter Wagschal, the future studies program at the University of Massachusetts concentrates on social change and the most equalitarian educational arrangements for preparing tomorrow's citizens.

Social philosophers since the Enlightenment have focused upon the issue of freedom and liberty. Huston Smith has proposed that the traditional binary distinction between freedom and authority must be examined again in the light of new developments. He thinks that genuine freedom is not respondent to "ceiling authorities" but rests on certain "floor authorities" that make it possible to respond to change. A social theory of educational futurism is similarly concerned with the notion of freedom that will underwrite the future in a global community. There is an equal interest by both groups in the relationship of freedom to human rights. Of course, the matter of human rights and their status in a state has puzzled social philosophers for centuries. Supporting six billion people in the world, protecting the global environment, providing economic opportunity, fighting terrorism, and addressing the AIDS epidemic are examples of problems that make the issue more critical. There is also keen interest in what values need to be taught or developed in order to provide a reasonable foundation for the future. Clearly, the Puritan ethic, materialistic values of the marketplace, competition, or exploitation of resources for economic gain are not satisfactory.

Futurists and social theorists are interested in the complex problem of leadership. Jurgen Habermas has argued that one of the problems of the modern industrial/capitalistic society is that administrators concentrate on achieving goals but never question the worthiness of these ends. Since the process–product equation has come into vogue in school administration, principals see children as "products" rather than as people. Futurists find this model appalling, especially when we are moving out of the industrial era and into the global information superhighway age, or the age of cybernation. Both theories support democratic participation in running the schools and the empowerment of teachers and students to participate in the decision-making process.

Perhaps the most important theme facing social and futures philosophers concerns the kinds of social arrangements most conducive to human survival and maximum realization of the human potential. Ought we to live under a monarchy, an oligarchy, a democracy, or in anarchy with no government at all? Can existing arrangements be modified for the future, or will we need to invent quite different arrangements? Dewey suggested that this might be necessary when he argued that democracy was the best social arrangement yet developed but that it might be improved upon in the future. The search for terrorists in Afghanistan following September 11, 2001 illustrates how different is the Islamic view of social arrangements.

Philosophy and Technology.   Upon first examination it would seem that technology and philosophy are mutually exclusive fields of human inquiry, but this is not strictly true. From ancient times, it was noted that the sun and moon followed precise paths across the sky and their movement could be predicted without exception. At the beginning of the nineteenth century, the Marquis de Laplace developed the theory of scientific determinism. Most philosophers and scientists, including Samuel Johnson and Benjamin Franklin, accepted the idea that a set of precise laws governed the universe and that once these were known, everything would be within the power of human minds to know. Determinism extended Isaac Newton's laws of physics, which so well predicted the behavior of planets and objects on Earth, to cover all that exists. Metaphysics was therefore subsumed under a set of absolute natural laws, and ultimate reality depended only on finding all of these.

In 1900 the German scientist Max Planck found that X rays and other forms of light could only be emitted in certain groups that he called quanta. This was followed in 1926 by Werner Heisenberg's famous uncertainty principle. Heisenberg found that in order to predict the future position and velocity of a particle, one has to be able to measure the present position and velocity accurately. This cannot be done because the more accurately one measures the position, the shorter the wavelength of the light and therefore the higher the energy, which alters the velocity. This uncertainty principle had profound implications for the way we view the universe and was the death blow for scientific determinism. It led to the development of quantum mechanics.

Quantum mechanics cannot predict a single definite result for an observation. It does tell us how many possible outcomes there are and gives the probability of each one of these. Quantum mechanics has turned out to be very useful for dealing with subatomic particles like electrons, photons, and quarks. It underlies all modern science and is fundamental to the technology of transistors, integrated circuits, and computers. It is a method of dealing with the behavior of the smallest parts of matter we can identify when these sometimes appear to be waves and other times to be particles. The large-scale structure of the universe and the force of gravity seem to be governed by Einstein's general theory of relativity, which does not take into account the uncertainty principle, but the basic building blocks of matter must.

Philosophers have had difficulty in keeping up with new scientific theories especially since one must specialize in physics and mathematics to understand them. Ludwig Wittgenstein, one of the most famous philosophers of the twentieth century, gave up on ultimate reality and held that the only remaining field for philosophy was the analysis of language. But the fact remains that with all the scientific and technological advances, we still do not know the ultimate nature of reality. Even if we had certain proof of the big bang theory of the creation of the universe or absolute knowledge of the structure and behavior of subatomic particles, the philosophic questions still remain. The "what" of the universe does not tell us the "why." One function of education for the future might be to give students enough background in fields like astronomy and physics so that they can understand the discoveries that are being made and contribute to the ongoing philosophic inquiry.

PSYCHOLOGY AND EDUCATION

Psychology has a dual role in education because it is both a fundamental tool for the teacher and the foundation for all of learning. Basic psychology deals with the nature of the mind and learning theory while applied psychology has its focus on problems such as the emotionally disturbed child, reducing intergroup tensions, improving teaching procedures, and discipline. Specializations important to education include developmental (changes with growing older), cognitive (higher mental processes), and clinical (problems of emotional disturbance). Methods of teaching, motivation, classroom control, and self-concept of pupils are so important to the field that a course in general psychology followed by one in educational psychology is required for the preparation of all teachers. Experimental psychology is a product of the twentieth century. It is changing today because of improved techniques and a database that is always expanding. Basic psychology is now influenced by experiments on the genetic code and the creation of computers capable of mindlike functions like playing chess or writing simple stories. Work on artificial intelligence may tell us much about how the human mind operates.

Assumptions about the nature of mind and learning underpin all educational efforts. As we have seen, Plato wrote about the three divisions of the soul and the need to make reason paramount. Since he believed that only a small part of the population is ruled by the faculty of reason, his schools were set up to identify and educate only those able to become philosopher–kings. The curriculum focused on pure ideas and abstract sciences like geometry. Both sexes were admitted to the schools described in the *Republic*, but any child lacking either interest or ability was encouraged to drop out. Those who did so (the vast majority) were relegated to lower positions in society. Plato's highly elitist system has had vast influence, causing many to believe schools should sort out the best and the brightest and concentrate on subjects designed to strengthen the faculties of the mind. Aristotle studied with Plato in the Academy. While he did not reject Plato's notion of pure ideas or forms, he held that the mind is undivided and independent of the body. This dualism of mind and body was dominant throughout the Middle Ages and was reinforced by René Descartes in the sixteenth century.

A major revolution in psychological thinking came with the empirical principle and the origin of ideas from experience in John Locke's *Essay Concerning the Human Understanding* (1690). Locke's epistemology holds that there are no innate ideas, that everything in the mind comes from experience through the sense organs. Since the mind has no content at birth, it is like a blank tablet upon which experience writes. The measure of the validity of an idea comes from the experimental process of comparing it with sensory data from the real world, not from logical analysis. Locke and other empiricists such as David Hume (1711–1776) restricted human knowledge to the experience of ideas and impressions, making the flow of ideas through perception paramount. Since the rise of empiricism and sense realism, there has been a debate over what part of the understanding is genetic and how much depends upon the environment. The education profession leaned toward the environment in the nature–nurture controversy, in part because it had no control over anything else. Today, work on DNA and genetic engineering casts new light on this debate.

While philosophy still ruled psychology as it did until scientific laboratories were developed, several efforts to improve the understanding of mental activity and learning were made by leading educational theorists. John A. Comenius (Komensky), the seventeenth-century Moravian educational reformer, created lessons in graded order to accommodate stages of learning. By working from the simple to the complex and the familiar to the unfamiliar, he made teaching easier and was one of the first to propose a science of pedagogy. Together with his illustrated textbooks written in the native language of the pupil (as opposed to Latin) Comenius brought sense realism to bear directly on the improvement of learning.

In 1762 the French philosopher Jean-Jacques Rousseau published his educational book *Emile.* Advocating freedom for the child, this work called for relying on the natural interests of youngsters through a series of developmental stages. Rousseau saw no need for external rewards or punishment to be used in education. Instead he suggested altering the environment and using activities such as field trips to stimulate the natural curiosity and inquisitiveness of the learner. These ideas were quickly applied to schools by Johann H. Pestalozzi in Swiss villages and to early childhood education by Friedrich Froebel in Germany. Both Pestalozzi and Froebel saw education as the natural harmonious development of all the child's natural faculties and powers. Both had tremendous influence in Europe and later in America (see Chapter 5).

Words like *intelligence, consciousness,* and *mind* were still vague and mystical at the end of the nineteenth century. The German physician Franz Joseph Gall ascribed cerebral functions to various areas of the brain and claimed that the shape of the skull could determine mental abilities. This "phrenology" was popular for a time and drew the support of the American educator Horace Mann. The major theory for educational leaders continued to be faculty psychology, or the belief that the mind is divided into separate powers. This fosters mental discipline and the idea of transfer of training. In 1892 the Committee of Ten of the NEA based its recommendations on faculty psychology. A protest against this psychology was led by the German philosopher Johann F. Herbart. Toward the middle of the nineteenth century, he became interested in Pestalozzi's methods and developed a metaphysical theory of pluralistic realism that rejected faculty psychology. Herbart refused to believe in innate ideas but developed a theory of learning from sensory experience that formed the basis of pedagogical method for his many followers. See Figure 2.2.

The mind is divided into two parts, the conscious and the subconscious. Ideas enter the conscious mind as perceptions delivered by a sense organ (the eye). The

Figure 2.2   Herbart's Conception of the Human Mind

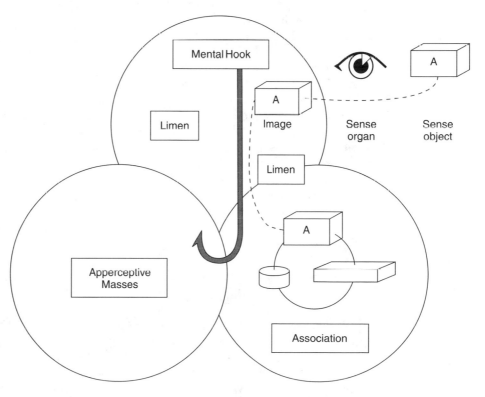

conscious mind associates the perception with others that are similar (a child's block, a box, an ice cube) and then pushes the perception through the division between the parts of the mind (the limen). Associations create an "apperceptive mass." An idea thrust into the subconscious for storage may be remembered by fishing for the associations with which it is identified. Thus, to remember some-one's name you fish for associations such as with whom you last saw the person. When dreaming, the limen is open and ideas flow from the subconscious to the conscious without order. Education must concentrate on association and apper-ceptions. We expand our knowledge by making connections between old ideas and each new one.

Psychology as a science developed in Europe and to some degree in America be-fore the beginning of the twentieth century. Herbart sought clues to mental devel-opment in the facts of physiology. Darwin's work on evolution stimulated others to study the nature of the child from a biological standpoint. Pavlov's conditioned re-flex experiments on animals in Russia created a new wave of interest in psychology. Of even more significance was the founding of the first experimental psychology lab-oratory by Wilhelm Max Wundt at Leipzig in 1878. Wundt trained a great many Amer-ican psychologists, and he is often regarded as the father of structural psychology. Other European leaders included Ebbinghaus, who worked with nonsense syllables to measure memory, and Freud, who developed psychoanalysis from the dynamics of motivation in personality formation.

Although not strictly an experimental psychologist, William James (1842–1910) did much to create a link between education and psychology. His *Principles of Psychology* (1890) was an outstanding contribution that made him internationally known and that helped to develop psychology as an independent area of study. James extracted some of the more practical ideas from his major work in psychol-ogy and published them under the title *Talks to Teachers*. This was the first attempt to provide psychological guidance for practical educators. Although his work was partly philosophical and introspection was his method, James helped to make psy-chology a valid field of educational inquiry.

American psychologists, heavily influenced by Europeans, attacked formal disci-pline and formulated new concepts of mind. Among the first were Edward Titch-ener, G. Stanley Hall, James M. Cattell, John Dewey, and Edward L. Thorndike. The history of educational psychology is best approached through the various types or schools of psychology.

Structuralism.   Titchener was a student of Wundt and a leading psychologist at Cornell University for thirty years. Concerned with the study of consciousness, Titch-ener treated psychology as an impersonal science and approached it atomistically. That is, Titchener and the structuralists attempted to isolate and analyze the basic el-ements of mental processes. He believed that a microscopic examination of the ba-sic blocks of the nervous system and psychic elements would lead to a complete science of the mind. Since structuralism did not concern itself with the living organ-ism, its relationship with education was indirect. Members of this psychological school dominated many college departments of psychology for years.

Functionalism.   William James and John Dewey were the first to identify functionalism as a division of psychology. For them, a study of consciousness could not be isolated from feelings, sensations, thoughts, and activities of the living organism. In 1900, as president of the newly formed American Psychological Association, Dewey called for the application of psychology to social and educational practice. For Dewey, the complete act of thought is the same for a child in school as it is for a scientist working on a problem in a laboratory. Both go through the same five-step process:

1. Engaging in an activity
2. Discovering a problem
3. Gathering data
4. Forming a hypothesis
5. Testing

Learning can only occur when students are engaged in genuine activities rather than in artificial ones imposed by the teacher. Problems occur when activity is blocked. Children learn how to gather data from simple sources such as their own memories or from more complicated sources such as libraries. Hypothesis formation is merely the posing of a possible solution to a problem, and the learner must examine what consequences might occur if the hypothesis is accepted. Only by testing the proposed solution against empirical evidence can learning be completed. Dewey's *Psychology* and *How We Think* (1901) described his functional theories. His *Human Nature and Conduct* (1922) is a statement of the interaction between the individual and his environment.

Other functional psychologists include Harvey Carr and James R. Angell, who established laboratories for studying the adjustment of animals to various environments. Functionalism contributed both to education and to other schools such as associationism, connectionism, and behaviorism.

Connectionist Psychology or Associationism.   Edward Lee Thorndike (1874–1949) was a student of William James and James McKeen Cattell. Building on Herman Ebbinghaus' curve of learning and forgetting and on studies of animal learning made by Lloyd Morgan in England, using puzzle boxes or a maze, Thorndike began a series of learning experiments with animals. After a series of trial and error activities, the animal would chance upon the "solution" that released food. Further trials in the same puzzle box resulted in the animal's making the proper response more rapidly than at first. This led Thorndike to his "law of effect," which he also extended to human activity. He found a very strong effect from rewards but also discovered that punishment was a less effective means for the control of behavior. Following Pavlov's lead, Thorndike assumed a connection between stimuli and responses. He developed this into S–R bond psychology using the equation Learning = Stimulus–Response. If stimulus A is known to be associated with response B, repeat A until B is produced without hesitation whenever A occurs. Teachers rapidly accepted

Thorndike's laws of learning, which they found to be highly useful devices for class-room instruction.

Since Thorndike had an impeccable reputation as a scientist, his pioneering experiments opened new fields of psychological research at the time when modern conceptions of pedagogy were being born. He was one of the first to understand that education and psychology were closely linked. Psychology forms the foundation for the science of education, and schools furnish subjects and data sources for psychological research. At Teachers College, Columbia University, Thorndike stimulated hundreds of students to esteem scientific research. Although his psychology was highly statistical and mechanical, connectionism became the leading educational psychology of the 1920s.

Behaviorism.   Associationism or connectionism gave rise to the psychological school known as behaviorism (the logical extreme). John B. Watson (1878–1958) is generally regarded as the founder, but his student Karl Lashley also contributed to this strictly objective division of psychology. One of the best known scholars in the field of behaviorism was B. F. Skinner (1904–1990) of Harvard.

Although he had studied with Dewey, Watson believed that psychology should be confined to those activities that could be verified by an outside observer. Behaviorism discarded consciousness as a subject of investigation and refused to use the method of introspection. It limited its findings to laboratory experiments that could be controlled and dealt only with those factors capable of analysis. Behaviorists believe that we have no right to project our feelings or ideas onto the subjects that we investigate. For example, if a person gives a piece of meat to a dog, it is legitimate to describe the dog's behavior (i.e., the animal jumps up, drools, opens its mouth, and eats the meat). However, it is not legitimate to say that the dog "likes" the meat since that projects the attitudes or feelings of the human onto the dog, and there is no evidence to support the statement.

Watson held that environment is far more important than heredity in the determination of human behavior. He rejected innate ideas and most instincts. His experiments with infants caused him to conclude that almost all emotional responses are learned. Watson held that if the environment could be strictly controlled, any normal child could be raised to be a mechanic, an athlete, a professional person, or a thief. Lashley was able to demonstrate that even human glands could be conditioned.

The early work of the behaviorists helped to discredit many theories about learning that were held by other psychologists. They did a great deal to foster objective evaluations of experiments. Sometimes their claims were extravagant, and certainly many educators objected to what they described as "rat in a box" psychology and the restriction of investigation to a fractional part of human behavior. Nevertheless, behaviorism won the respect of scientists in other fields, and its rigorous techniques helped to support objective educational research.

B. F. Skinner's work spans the period from early behaviorism to the present. In the late 1930s, he began a series of animal learning experiments in which he taught animals to perform complex tasks. He accomplished this by giving the subject a reward after each step of the task was successfully accomplished. Out of this grew the idea of programmed instruction and teaching machines. During World War II, new programs for using electronic devices in teaching were developed by Skinner and his students. Computer-assisted instruction, now used in numerous aspects of education, was adapted from the work of behaviorists. Skinner's books—*Science and Human Behavior, Walden II*, and *Beyond Freedom and Dignity*—have had a profound effect upon educators in modern America. Few of the findings of Skinner and other behaviorists have been scientifically rejected. The criticism of behaviorism normally comes from those who say it is too narrow, mechanical, and nonhumanistic.

Gestalt.   At about the same time that behaviorism began to influence education in America, German Gestalt psychology also became important. *Gestalt* is a German word meaning form or pattern, and it refers to the whole configuration or sum of integrated experiences present at any one time. The apparent motion created by flashing a series of photographs in the cinema is not explained by examining individual still pictures, nor can music be understood merely through the study of notes. Max Wertheimer, Kurt Koffka, and Wolfgang Kohler started Gestalt psychology in Germany. Beginning in 1914, Kohler began a series of experiments on the island of Tenerife using apes as subjects. He concluded that learning takes place as sudden insight rather than by simple trial and error. This led to the examination of the pattern perceived by the learner in his or her total environment, rather than to an atomistic consideration of essential elements in the learning process.

American Gestalt psychologists such as R. M. Ogden and Raymond Wheeler made important contributions to learning theory. Their stress on total understanding of the problem to be solved and the consequences of acting was acceptable to Dewey and the functionalists. Most members of the progressive movement adopted Gestalt psychology because it dealt with the whole child in context.

Kurt Lewin (1890–1947) was a German Gestalt psychologist who migrated to the United States when Hitler came to power. He believed that behavior is the result of energy derived from the needs or wants of the individual and the organism's efforts to meet those needs. Lewin's psychology is called field theory because of the emphasis of the life-space or field of the individual as he or she perceives it. Lewin used the term *vector* to describe the attractive or repulsive forces that motivate the organism to act.

Learning theories and psychological ideas associated with field theory are still popular in the United States. Most studies of motivation, needs, personality, feelings, and attitudes have been carried on in the light of field theory. Another group of psychologists with similar views of the child and his or her environment are called holistic. Holistic psychology emphasizes the child as a whole and insists that the individual can never be studied and understood except as he or she relates to the forces present in his or her entire environment. Modern humanistic psychologists such as Abraham Maslow and Carl Rogers have been highly influenced by Gestalt, field, and holistic psychological theories. Members of these schools have had at least as much impact on American education as behaviorists.

Psychoanalysis.   Although not strictly an educational or learning psychology, psychoanalysis has contributed to an understanding of childhood experiences and to programs for those with learning disabilities or who need therapy. Sigmund Freud, Carl Jung, Alfred Adler, and Karen Horney were major leaders in this movement. Freud's stress on the sexual attraction of infants and children to the parent of the opposite sex (Oedipus/Electra Complex) and his discussion of the animal nature of human beings (id) that must be governed by social norms (superego) have had great educational influence. Modern concerns for the impact of conflict and stress on the development of personality as found in the work of Erik Erikson are linked to Freudian concepts. A body of educational literature supporting freedom of choice for students and attacking barriers to personality development is based upon psychoanalytic theory. Dewey viewed personality development and freedom of choice as important in education.

Modern Developmental Psychology and Stage Theory.   A major thrust of educational psychology in recent years has been directed toward the relationship of curriculum and methods to stages of development in children. Conflict exists between various theories of development, but there is agreement that poor pedagogy results from attempting to teach information or concepts before the learner has reached the stage at which such information and concepts can be understood.

David Ausubel distinguishes between learning by reception and learning by discovery. Reception learning requires the student to internalize material in order to recall it at a later date (as on a test). Discovery learning does not present material in finished form but sets up an environment in which something has to be discovered or invented by the student before it can be assimilated. Discovery learning emphasizes the process; reception learning concentrates on the product. Ausubel contends that discovery learning enables the student to understand how new knowledge is generated and stimulates the learner; however, it is an inefficient method for delivering large amounts of information. Ausubel therefore believes that a balance must exist between process and product and that schools that do not offer discovery learning inhibit the progress of children and make education uninteresting.

Jerome Bruner is recognized for his efforts to apply scientific methods to teaching and for his research on the formation of concepts in children. Bruner is interested in the structure of subject matter. He believes that the teaching of particular subjects can be integrated into the way the students see the world so as to permit learners to discover the basic principles of the discipline under study. Motivation therefore should be stimulated by the subject matter itself and not from external appeals to interest or the arrangement of consequent events. Obviously, this idea differs from Skinner's operant conditioning. Bruner believes that it is possible to teach any subject in some intellectually honest way to any child at any developmental stage.

Child psychologist Robert Gagné is well known for his contributions to programmed instruction. He believes that children pass through developmental stages of learning that are determined by what is to be learned. Gagné identifies eight conditions for learning:

1. Signal learning occurs when infants learn responses to a general cue.
2. Stimulus–response learning is more precise and voluntary.
3. Chaining is the result of putting together previous responses.
4. Verbal discrimination is the association of names with objects.
5. Multiple discrimination is identifying and classifying groups of stimuli.
6. Concept learning is the ability to identify important differences and similarities between sets of stimuli.
7. Principle learning is relating one complete concept to others.
8. Problem solving is using several principles for dealing with a new situation.

Gagné urges educators to give more attention to the way in which instruction is sequenced because he holds that no learning stage can be skipped. Because Gagné believes that it is the nature of the skills to be learned that determines the sequence of stages, the curriculum must be ordered accordingly. Ausubel, Bruner, and Gagné all see the subject matter or the learning tasks as central to learning stages. On the other hand, Piaget holds that stages are related to the maturation and development of children.

Jean Piaget was born in Neuchatel, Switzerland, in 1896. He began his career as a zoology assistant at the age of eleven and published papers on mollusks at the age of fifteen. Piaget worked with Alfred Binet in Paris on standardizing tests of intelligence and became interested in the levels of logic used by children taking such tests. Building on Rousseau and Pestalozzi, Piaget attempted to establish a body of psychology to give support for educational techniques truly adapted to the laws of mental development. For many years, he carried out experiments on learning tasks with children in the J. J. Rousseau Institute. He was active in the field until he died in 1980.

Piaget believed that the two fundamental characteristics of a child's learning and cognitive development are organization and adaptation. Organization is described as the systematizing of information into meaningful patterns. These patterns are used to structure new information so that it does not seem random or chaotic to the learner. Adaptation is the process of coping, or integrating new information into existing perceptions and patterns. Intelligence for Piaget must follow from our ability to organize and adapt. Like Dewey, Piaget saw human beings as born active, curious, interested in communication, and with a need to assimilate information. His principles of organization and adaptation are in basic agreement with the theories of Bruner and Gagné. Piaget parted company with other developmental psychologists on the matter of specific stages of growth and development. His stages are determined by genetic development in connection with experience. The stages or levels are related, but they are determined by a combination of age and experience.

The sensorimotor stage covers the period from birth to about the age of two. This stage consists mostly of reflexes; however, during this time, foundations are laid for later mental growth and development. Trial and error is used for mastering the environment, and oral language develops. At about the age of two, the preoperational stage begins. From two to four, the child is preconceptual and in an intuitive stage of development but experiences vast growth in language use. Judgments are incomplete, and modeling is a basis for learning. From three to seven, children reach a symbolic stage in which drawing, role playing, size, number, and distance begin to follow some semblance of order. From seven to twelve, the child begins to think logically and not in the impressionistic way associated with the preoperational stage. The span of attention expands, and a clear sense of time emerges. Children at this level can count, weigh, test solutions, and conserve. They are not, however, able to think abstractly; nor are they motivated by delayed rewards. At the stage of formal operations, learners can think hypothetically. They do not require visible concrete cues for each stage of the thinking process. Abstract or ideal concepts are used, and the child has a clear concept of time.

Piaget and his followers urge educators to be realistic about what children can accomplish at each stage. Tests have shown that many freshmen entering universities still think on a concrete level. Even after a person has reached the formal level of operations, it is common to revert back to earlier stages under stress. Teachers, in the view of Piaget, must avoid abstract and theoretical tasks if any of the learners in their classrooms are still operating in a nonformal way.

Jerome Kagan challenges the belief that early experiences are crucial to later development. For Kagan and his associates, the most recent experiences are more important than the earliest ones. His research shows dramatic improvement when children from deprived backgrounds are exposed to an enriched environment. Rather than dealing with stages of development, Kagan urges teachers to create a stable and positive learning situation. Past experiences of the teacher and of the student are less significant to Kagan than a sense of involvement and experiences that are supportive of intellectual growth. Kagan believes that the environment is all important, and he is optimistic about programs like Head Start. His cognitive interpretation of child development states that learners do best in an environment characterized by moderate discrepancy from their existing worldview. Uncertainty and challenge are emotionally satisfying, but the shock of something totally new may create resistance in the learner.

In *Thought and Language,* Vygotsky noted that thought and speech are the key to the nature of human consciousness. Thus, understanding child development entails a totality of understanding words, thoughts, and motivations. He finds four developmental states:

1. Primitive or preverbal thought
2. Experience with physical properties (self and objects around the child)
3. Use of external and internal signs as aids in solving internal problems
4. Ingrowth of constant interaction between inner and outer operations

Vygotsky, like Dewey, placed emphasis on the cultural ingredients in human development.

Other Contributions to Educational Psychology.

Benjamin Bloom's mastery learning concept has had considerable influence on the theory and practice of teaching in modern America. Mastery learning calls for individualized instruction, with each student going at his or her own pace. Students must demonstrate that each level and condition of learning has been mastered before going on to the next level. Bloom is also known for his two taxonomies, the cognitive and the affective. Values and attitudes in the affective domain must be understood as being different from the intellectual tasks of cognition. Split-brain research and its implications for educators have supported this distinction. Neurologists like J. E. Bogen and Michael Gazzaniga claim that education has stressed verbal skills to a fault and that both language and nonlanguage techniques are needed.

Cognitive psychology contrasts sharply with the behaviorism of B. F. Skinner. It emphasizes complex intellectual processes that cannot be explained by the analysis of simple stimulus–response situations. Since 1970, cognitive psychology has become the dominant theoretical force, but most schools still reflect the behaviorist approach. Cognitive psychologists like Robert Glaser thought this would change before the end of the twentieth century. Other psychologists such as Albert Bandura and Richard Walters concern themselves with the way people acquire behavior appropriate to social circumstances. Loud expressions and slang language may be appreciated in an informal meeting of peers but is not appropriate in a classroom setting. These psychologists build on the principles of Skinner to form a theory of social learning.

Noam Chomsky of MIT has criticized Skinner on quite different grounds. He sees Skinner's learner as a robot responding to external stimuli only. Chomsky believes that all human beings have an inborn inclination to master language, regardless of the environment. His theory of transformational grammar states that learners respond not only to the environment but also to internal events.

Another area of psychology that has created considerable educational interest in recent years is described as humanistic and phenomenological. Carl Rogers is known for client-centered or nondirective therapy. He feels that psychology has focused on the experimental laboratory and Freudian theory instead of human growth and the potential of humankind. In books like *On Becoming a Person*, Rogers concerns himself with the infinite possibilities of human development, creativity, and how people can help each other to become more fully human.

Abraham Maslow is one of the best-known humanistic psychologists. He has focused on counseling and identified the needs that are basic to the educational environment. Maslow's hierarchy of needs is included in the basic preparation of many American teachers. Basic needs such as food and shelter always take priority over other needs. This is not different from the position of the progressives, who believed that before a student can be taught, the school must see that he or she is properly fed and physically well. Safety and security needs come next in Maslow's scheme. Beyond security, we all have needs for affection and love. A desire for self-esteem and the respect of others takes the next place on the hierarchy. The final need is for self-actualization. Teachers will do well to consider these needs in the light of recent events such as school violence and terrorist attacks.

For Maslow, the best education is one that deals with the real and serious problems of life. In order to understand the wider world, it is necessary to have self-knowledge and to become an authentic individual. Teachers should have deep concern for children, but teachers cannot be effective unless their own needs are met and they have healthy mental attitudes. Teachers must understand that growth has two components. The learner needs to venture out, to stretch, and to be challenged, but the learner also needs to remain safe and in familiar territory. Optimum learning occurs somewhere between absolute safety (with no risk at all) and maximum risk (which causes the learner to feel threatened and under stress). Compassionate and caring persons are good teachers. To help a child become a better person requires an atmosphere of acceptance in the classroom and a balance between objective and subjective learning experiences. A hungry or abused child may lack energy and motivation for learning. Basic needs for nourishment and a caring environment must be met for learning motivation to take place (Hohn, 1995).

CHILD STUDY AND MEASUREMENT

Education as a science or discipline is grounded in psychology, but child study and the measurement movement also provide instruments for research and development. Most of the efforts to measure ability or study children prior to 1900 were not objective. Demands for understanding the nature of the child were made as early as the first century by the Roman educator Quintilian and were repeated by Rousseau, Pestalozzi, and Froebel. However, nothing more sophisticated than the common diary existed as a tool for measuring the ability or characteristics of the child until Francis Galton (1822–1911) developed the mathematics of Karl Pearson into a means of measuring the deviation from the mean between and within groups of children. Galton was a cousin of Charles Darwin, and it was Darwin's research that caused him to become interested in measuring the deviation of characteristics within and between groups of people. Both Galton and Darwin invented tests to measure the abilities or capacities of individuals. The subject of James Cattell's *Mental Tests and Measurement* (1890) was methods for measuring and analyzing quantitative data. Galton was the first to use curves to express the distribution of individuals in terms of characteristics such as age, height, and intelligence.

While Cattell and Charles Judd were pioneering the measurement movement in America, French psychologists Alfred Binet and Theophile Simon were creating an instrument to measure intelligence. The Simon-Binet test was published in 1906, and ten years later, Lewis Terman produced the Stanford revision of that test. Millions of soldiers were given the Stanford test of intelligence during World War I; the practice resulted in the first massive data on the subject and created a model for later intelligence tests for use in public schools. The significance of both group and individual testing of intelligence can hardly be overemphasized in the modern history of American education. Test results became the basis for new programs, curriculum changes, ability grouping, and a host of other educational alternatives that are still hotly debated in professional circles.

Another contribution to the statistical measurement of learning began with the work of Dr. Joseph Rice. As editor of the *Forum,* Rice undertook a study of the achievement of students studying spelling in elementary schools. Having tested

30,000 pupils, he concluded that those who spent only fifteen minutes a day on the study of the subject learned to spell just as well as those who devoted an hour or more to the task. Naturally, there was a negative reaction from those who still supported mental discipline, but in 1912 the National Education Association (NEA) went on record as favoring candid investigation of schools and methods. The "Measurement of Educational Products" was part of the *Seventeenth Yearbook of the National Society for the Study of Education,* published in 1918. It contained eighty-four standard tests for use in elementary schools and twenty-five for high schools and covered virtually every subject of the curriculum. Thus, Thorndike's scales for measuring academic achievement and Cliff Stone's objective test of arithmetic reasoning (1908) had developed into a set of standardized achievement tests that were published and adopted by schools throughout the United States. Current emphasis on national standards for content areas has led some scholars to question who determines what is to be included and excluded in a knowledge base and why.

A firm foundation for the quantitative approach to measuring academic achievement had been laid. William McCall, one of Thorndike's students, is credited with the statement, "Whatever exists at all, exists in some amount and can be measured." Although educational investigation continued to revise and refine both tests of achievement and of intelligence, mere comparison between students soon gave way to the study of groups. Homogeneous grouping, the effects of social class, studies of educational age, and attempts to diagnose defects of underachieving students became areas of investigation between the world wars. A great many modern issues in education are related to measuring intelligence and achievement. Such measures seldom account for the cultural background of the child. Students with low scores may be discriminated against with regard to future activities such as entering college. Insofar as test scores reflect social or cultural differences, they are unfair measures of comparison between individuals, and this has been the subject of a major debate in recent years. The abuse of individual intelligence testing has also been widespread.

If IQ scores are made available to teachers, there is often a tendency to classify the student as "bright" or "slow," on the basis of that evidence alone. Cultural bias in intelligence testing has become a major target of educational research. There is considerable concern today that achievement scores used for meeting accountability requirements (now a legal obligation in most states) may create excessive emphasis on basic skills and information to the detriment of personality development or "affective" learning. Tests for general intelligence had other problems in addition to cultural bias. The Stanford-Binet scales were devised for children fifteen and under. In 1944, David Wechsler, a clinical psychologist at New York's Bellevue Hospital, designed tests of specific mental abilities in adults. These tests measured both verbal ability and performance at tasks. Later the Wechsler Scales were adapted for children and the Stanford-Binet was extended for adults.

Child Study. Quite a different approach to the study of children and learning came out of the work of G. Stanley Hall (1844–1924). Hall established a center for applied psychology at Johns Hopkins in 1884 and founded the *American Journal of Psychology.* He asked trained kindergarten teachers to test children for their understanding of about 100 words ranging from common objects to general concepts. From this study he published *The Contents of Children's Minds on Entering School.* In reporting the results of tests on children, Hall included information on social background and sex and remarked on the high degree of emotion and superstition shown by the young. Later, as president of Clark University, Hall brought together the first group of scholars interested in scientific child study. Among his students were Arnold Gesell and Lewis Terman.

Making a formal study of the adolescent child, Hall concluded that emotional development and personality growth were just as important as cognitive learning. As an evolutionist, he sought to combine the culture epoch theory of the Herbartians with the recapitulation theory of biology. He saw childhood play as the recapitulation of man's primitive stage and believed that inhibition of play might result in the expression of violent tendencies.

Child study through the observation of youngsters at play or school, efforts to measure the interests of preschool children, and the stage theory of modern learning theorists like Jean Piaget follow logically from the pioneering work of G. Stanley Hall. The specialties of child and adolescent psychology as well as developmental psychology and the study of exceptional children owe their beginning to his work.

Arnold Gesell's Clinic for Child Development at Yale, A. B. Hollingshead's *Elmtown's Youth* (1949), and James S. Coleman's *The Adolescent Society* (1961) represent efforts to understand youth in a cultural setting. Dealing with the personality of the whole child, the efficiency of the school and teacher, or the sociology of education requires methods of evaluation different from those used in the measurement of intelligence or achievement. Interest in human relations and the clarification of values grew out of the realization that the needs of youth are different from those of adults and that existing educational programs sometimes fail to meet these needs.

In 1935, the American Council on Education formed the American Youth Commission, which studied problems of youngsters. It found that economic factors, shattered homes, discrimination, and social stratification played major roles in the attitudes of young people and their school achievement. Similar commissions founded by the Progressive Education Association in the 1930s called attention to the fact that schools were subject oriented and not interested in the personal lives of students. Caroline Zachery, chairperson for one of the commissions, insisted that the personality of the individual is formed only through positive functioning relationships with others. She went on to found the mental hygiene movement in American schools. A considerable interest also developed in the area of research on the dynamics of instructional groups and the interactions between students and teachers in a classroom situation.

By 1950, the scientific measurement of groups had developed into a major interest of educational research. European sociologists such as Durkheim and Weber joined psychology and sociology in an effort to understand the psychodynamics of group interaction. Since World War II, there has been a vast increase in the research and literature dealing with the effects of teacher behavior on the student. Some of this has centered on T-groups, group encounter, and sensitivity training. Some has been concerned with the dynamics of instructional groups and is represented by the work of Ned Flanders and Henry Nelson. Sociologists interested in bureaucracies and systems functioning have also contributed to this field of study.

Tests for measuring personality, such as the Rorschach, are also commonly used in education. Temperament, aptitudes, and attitudes of students are understood to have a profound effect upon what they are able to learn and what program best fits their needs. Guidance especially has depended upon aptitudes and job analysis in an effort to fit students into a meaningful curriculum.

Educational testing and measurement now occupies a large share of the time and effort of professionals at all levels in education. Research skills are regarded as important for college and public school teachers alike, and almost all educational programs depend upon research for their support. The literature relating to measurement and testing is now so vast that considerable skill is needed just to find material that relates directly to a given problem or issue. A neglected area of measurement has been creativity and means for identifying the gifted. High IQ scores as used by Terman are not adequate for finding all students who might benefit from programs for the gifted and talented. Julian Stanley of MIT has worked out a way to find and help mathematically talented college students, but many gifted youngsters go undetected.

THEN TO NOW

The philosophies of education discussed in this chapter are certainly the major ones in contemporary America, but many educational decisions are made without any obvious link to a theoretical foundation. As Dewey once put it, philosophers may argue with one another, but "burly sinners" run the world. It is certainly true that many of the people who make decisions about education do so without a philosophic foundation or one that is pragmatic in the narrow sense of the word.

An example is former North Carolina governor James Hunt's article "Education for Economic Growth." The article appeared in the *Kappan* in April 1984. Hunt probably reflected the opinion of many Americans when he argued that the real function of schooling is to make technologically and scientifically literate citizens able to compete for jobs in the world market. As chairperson of the Task Force on Education for Economic Growth, Hunt saw education as the means for improving the economy and believed that the measure of good schools is that students get good jobs. He favored minimum competency tests for all potential high school graduates and identified the purpose of education as higher productivity, higher profits, and a better life based on income and spending power. He also thought that governments at all levels have a right to expect the outcome of better competition in the economic sector, because they provide the funds to support schools. Hunt's views are shared by many, but they represent an extremely narrow and nontheoretical concept of educational goals. Job preparation, economic growth, and competition in the marketplace have always been among the purposes of American schools, but they are seldom the major or only goal. Hunt, as chairperson of the National Commission on Teaching and America's Future, in *What Matters Most: Teaching for America's Future* (September 1996), again stressed high academic standards both for teachers and for students as well as reinventing teacher preparation and professional development to achieve success at all educational levels.

Nell Noddings, in the *Kappan* (December 1996), calls for a broader goal of education. Students should learn to become good neighbors, concerned guardians of the natural world, and honest colleagues in whatever activities they pursue. The Clinton administration called for connecting every classroom and library to the Internet by the year 2000 and for helping all students become technologically literate. This continues to be a national priority.

A few philosophical positions such as existentialism would be in total opposition to Hunt's "Education for Economic Growth," but most would think his views myopic to the extreme. Idealists and perennialists would argue that job preparation is secondary to character building, value formation, citizenship training, and a broad understanding of Western civilization. Social and futures theorists would say that Hunt's position is counterproductive to meeting even his narrow objective, because future economic growth depends on solving social problems, protecting the environment, and creating a stable world order.

It is reasonable to expect that a child born today will be a functioning member of society in the middle of the twenty-first century. If conditions change at the rate of present experience (and there is good reason to think they will alter even more rapidly), the world of 2050 will be a different one indeed. Some philosophic systems are based on the assumption of unchanging reality and the permanence of forces that shape human life. They offer less illumination for the future of education than do those that focus more directly on the problems of today and the possibilities of tomorrow.

There is a seeming contradiction between the support for individual freedom found in Rousseau's *Emile* and his effort to develop for the inhabitants of Poland a social contract that had mechanisms of social control and public schools. Futurist Fred Kierstead has expanded this conflict in order to define the meaning of the "general will" as the authority for making educational decisions. For Rousseau, the will of the people, expressed through popularity polls or single votes, was not as trustworthy as the general will. The general will was the true belief of the people as a body over time. If there is validity in the theory, we still have the problem of how to find the general will now and in the future. Politics, media campaigns, personalities of leaders, and current events may cloud our perception of what the people really want.

Philosophy may be the best tool we have for clearing away the barriers and reaching agreement on educational policy. It is unlikely that we will ever get total agreement from everyone. The comet that appeared in the sky during the spring of 1997 was an object of beauty and scientific significance for most of us. We accepted the astronomers' explanation of its existence. Yet a handful of members of the cult called Heaven's Gate believed the comet was a ship from outer space sent to take them away. Their belief was so strong that they took their own lives in order to speed the process of leaving Earth. Clearly, there are those who passionately believe what most of us consider to be nonsense.

In his *Education and Work for the Year 2000: Choices We Face* (1992), Arthur Wirth argued that we must give ourselves freedom and flexibility to explore alternatives and opinions. As educational philosopher Maxine Greene noted, Wirth's book dealt with the continuing tension between our democratic tradition and demands for technological revolution. John Dewey's concept of continuous reconstruction of experience as the basis for solving problems and planning action is compatible with Wirth. So are the ideas of futurists Kenneth Boulding, Alvin Toffler, Wendell Bell, Daniel Bell, or John R. Platt. As John Dewey put it, democracy is the form of social organization most conducive to problem solving because only in a democracy are people free to inquire. Through freedom of inquiry, the mechanisms of democracy may be used to shape the schools and resolve conflicts over such issues as teaching methods and curriculum. Democratic education may also be the means by which people can secure the civil and political freedoms necessary for the good life. This goal is obviously much broader than Governor Hunt's job preparation. Can we achieve both?

As we enter a new century, movement toward a more democratic and free market society in Russia and China has encouraged optimism among futurists that a global democratic educational system might be possible. Already there is worldwide competition for the best jobs; American children must learn how to speak foreign languages, how to access the Internet, and how to use multicultural interpersonal skills if they are to be successful. Concerns over human rights violations in China, ethnic conflict in Bosnia, or the peace efforts between Arabs and Israelis clearly indicate an unstable world culture. The great fear of nuclear war no longer threatens the globe, but philosophical differences over educational goals are even greater in the international scene than in the United States. President Clinton spoke of building an educational bridge to the future. President George W. Bush had to deal with international terrorism in the global society early in his administration.

Unlike the West Germans or the Japanese, ordinary Americans are directly involved with the governance of their schools. Americans are also inconsistent in the way they choose or represent values and philosophies. Thus, school board members often share a vague belief in an idealistic world order or universal mind while spending their time on such mundane matters as buying buses, reviewing complaints about "lax" discipline, or trying to head off the demands of teachers for better pay. Parents and community citizens may exhibit keen interest in the success of the local high school's varsity football team and very little interest in the school curriculum, although they would not list varsity sports as the purpose of secondary education.

After serving as the leader of the war on drugs and as the secretary of education, William Bennett became an articulate spokesperson for traditional values in education and the philosophy of perennialism. He is also a critic of professional educators and has made caustic remarks about the public schools. His position is almost exactly opposed to that of the Clinton administration but finds support in the administration of George W. Bush. Clinton's agenda reflected social reconstructionism and futurism while Bush's aims at high standards and family values. This conflict among leaders is certainly evident in local arguments about shaping schools. It is curious that many Americans have a negative attitude toward the "educational establishment" or public schools in general but good feelings about the schooling their children receive. Many surveys conducted in the 1990s revealed high praise for local teachers and schools but disdain for education at the state and national levels. Consistency is not a characteristic trait of Americans. Obviously, better understanding of the theoretical basis of education is required to clarify issues and meet future needs. Historical trends reflected in alternative philosophies of education enable students to assess current issues and policies more effectively.

GAINING PERSPECTIVE THROUGH CRITICAL ANALYSIS

1. How do proponents of idealism, realism, and pragmatism differ in terms of educational practice? Which philosophy is most appealing to you? Why?
2. Describe the effects the protest philosophies have had on educational policy in terms of the curriculum and the roles of the teacher, administrator, staff, and student.
3. Name two social reconstructionists, and discuss their contributions to educational policy and practice.

4. Analyze the contribution of existential thought to today's education practices and policies.
5. How does the quote that opens the chapter reflect Dewey's belief that theory and practice should always inform each other and not exist in isolation?
6. Give examples of psychological theories in educational practice.
7. Identify the dual role of psychology.
8. What were the major contributions of American psychologists to education?

HISTORY IN ACTION IN TODAY'S CLASSROOMS

1. Describe your philosophy of education and how it applies (or will apply) to your educational practice.
2. After observing a teacher or administrator, attempt to determine that person's philosophy of education. Factors to consider include classroom organization, teaching methods, and lesson planning. Make an appointment to discuss your observations and validate your findings.

3. Obtain permission to audiotape or videotape an interview with an experienced teacher or administrator. Find out how his or her philosophy of education has evolved through the years. Share your findings with your class.
4. Using the Internet, find one site that would be useful in obtaining information on or ideas about educational philosophy.

INCREASED UNDERSTANDING THROUGH ONLINE RESEARCH

Visit the Prentice Hall Foundations Web site (*http://www.prenhall.com/foundations-cluster*) and examine Topics 2 and 3. Using the resources available in these topics, identify and define at least three alternative philosophies of education and three psychological theories. Write and submit your response to your instructor using the Electronic Bluebook module also in either of these two topics of the Web site.

BIBLIOGRAPHY

Apple, Michael. *Ideology and Curriculum*. London: Routledge & Kegan Paul, 1979.

Bagley, William C. "An Essentialist's Platform for the Advancement of American Education." *Educational Administration and Supervision* (1938) 26:241–56.

Bell, Daniel. *The Coming of the Post-Industrial Society: A Venture into Social Forecasting*. New York: 1976.

Bell, Wendell. "How I Became a Futurist." *The Futurist* 64 (May–June 1997). (*Foundations of Future Studies:*

Human Science for a New Era, Volumes 1 and 2. New York: Transaction Publishers, 1996.)

Bestor, Arthur. *Educational Wastelands*. Urbana: University of Illinois Press, 1953.

———. *The Restoration of Learning*. New York: Knopf, 1955.

Brameld, Theodore. *Patterns of Educational Philosophy*. New York: Holt, Rinehart and Winston, 1971.

Butler, Donald. *Four Philosophies and Their Practice in Religion*. New York: Harper and Row, 1957.

Campbell, Kate, ed. *A Critical Feminism: Argument in the Disciplines*. Philadelphia: Open University Press, 1992.

Cherryholmes, Cleo. *Power and Criticism*: Poststructural Investigations in Education. New York: Teacher's College Press, 1988.

Cooper, J. Arthur. *Exemplars in Educational Philosophy*. Minneapolis, MN: Alphia Editions, 1988.

Cornish, Edward. *The Study of the Future*. Washington, DC: World Future Society, 1977.

Cuban, Larry. *How Teachers Taught: Constancy and Change in American Classrooms, 1890–1980*. New York: Longman, 1984.

Dewey, John. *Democracy and Education*. New York: Macmillan, 1916.

———. *Experience and Education*. Toronto: Macmillan, 1938.

Eggen, Paul D., and Donald Kauchak. *Educational Psychology: Windows on Classrooms*. New York: Prentice Hall, 2000.

Eisner, Elliot W. *The Enlightened Eye: Qualitative Inquiry and the Enhancement of Educational Practice*. New York: Macmillan, 1991.

Erickson, Kai. *Wayward Puritans: A Study in the Sociology of Deviance*. New York: Wiley and Sons, 1982.

Fineberg, Joel. *Social Philosophy*. Englewood Cliffs, NJ: Prentice-Hall, 1973.

Giroux, H. A. *Postmodernism, Feminism, and Cultural Politics*. New York: State University of New York, 1991.

Giroux, Henry. *Theory and Resistance in Education: A Pedagogy for the Opposition*. Boston: Bergin & Garvey, 1983.

Griffin, David Ray, and Huston Smith. *Primordial Truth and Postmodern Theology*. Suny Series in Constructive Postmodern Thought, 1990.

Gutek, Gerald. *Philosophical and Ideological Perspectives on Education*. Englewood Cliffs, NJ: Prentice-Hall, 1988.

Habermas, J. *The Philosophical Discourse of Modernity*. Cambridge, MA: MIT Press, 1987.

Hekman, Susan J. *Gender and Knowledge: Elements of a Postmodern Feminism*. Boston: Northeastern University Press, 1990.

Hohn, Robert L. *Classroom Learning and Teaching*. New York: Longman, 1995, 275–76.

Horne, Herman. *The Democratic Philosophy of Education*. New York: Macmillan, 1935.

Hunt, James B. Jr. *What Matters Most: Teaching for America's Future*. New York: National Commission on Teaching & America's Future, 1996.

Hutchins, Robert. *Great Books: The Foundation of a Liberal Education*. New York: Simon and Schuster, 1954.

James, William. *Pragmatism: A New Name for Some Old Ways of Thinking*. New York: Longman, Green, 1981.

Johanningmeier, Erwin. *Americans and Their Schools*. Chicago: Rand McNally, 1980.

Kanpol, Barry. *Towards a Theory and Practice of Teacher Cultural Politics: Continuing the Post Modern Debate*. Norwood, NJ: Norwood Publishing Co., 1992.

Kidder, Rushworth. *Shared Values for a Troubled World*. San Francisco: Jossey-Bass, 1994.

Kierstead, Fred D., and Paul A. Wagner Jr. *The Ethical, Legal and Multicultural Foundations of Teaching*. Madison, WI: WCB Brown and Benchmark, 1993.

Kliebard, Herbert. *The Struggle for the American Curriculum*. Boston: Routledge and Kegan Paul, 1986.

———. *Forging the American Curriculum: Essays in Curriculum History and Theory*. New York: Routledge, 1992.

Kneller, George. *Existentialism and Education*. New York: John Wiley, 1958.

Kohlberg, Lawrence. *The Philosophy of Moral Development: Moral Stages and the Idea of Justice*. San Francisco: Harper and Row, 1981.

Lasch, Christopher. *The Minimal Self: Psychic Survival in Troubled Times*. New York: W. W. Norton, 1984.

Lather, Patti. *Getting Smart*. New York: Routledge, 1991.

Lynd, Albert. *Quackery in the Public Schools*. Boston: Little Brown, 1953.

Lefrancois, Guy R. *Theories of Learning: What the Old Man Said*. New York: Thomson Learning, 2000.

Lefrancois, Guy R. *Psychology for Teaching: A Bear Is Not a Cowboy*. New York: Thomson Learning, 1999.

Lyotard, J. *The Postmodern Condition: A Report on Knowledge*. Minneapolis: University of Minnesota Press, 1984.

———. *Toward the Post Modern*. Atlantic Highlands, NJ: Humanities Press, 1991.

———. *Post Modern Explained*. Minneapolis: University of Minnesota Press, 1993.

Meadows, Donela, and Dennis Meadows. *The Limits to Growth*. New York: Universe Books, 1972.

Morris, Van Cleve. *Existentialism in Education*. New York: Harper and Row, 1966.

Neill, A. S. *Summerhill*. New York: Hart, 1960.

Noddings, Nel. "Rethinking the Benefits of the College Bound Curriculum." *The Kappan* (December 1996):285–89.

Ormrod, Jeanne Ellis. *Human Learning*. New York: Prentice Hall, 1998.

Ozmon, Howard, and Samuel Craver. *Philosophic Foundations of Education,* 6th ed. Upper Saddle River, NJ: Merrill/Prentice Hall, 1999.

Park, Joe, ed. *Selected Readings in the Philosophy of Education*. New York: Macmillan Co., 1958.

Perkinson, Henry. *Since Socrates: Studies in the History of Western Educational Thought*. New York: Longman, 1980.

Pinar, William, and William M. Reynolds, eds. *Understanding Curriculum as Phenomenological and Deconstructed Text*. New York: Teachers College Press, 1992.

Rafferty, Max. *Suffer, Little Children*. New York: Devin-Adair Co., 1962.

Rorty, Richard. *Philosophy and the Mirror of Nature*. Princeton, NJ: Princeton University Press, 1987.

———. *Objectivity, Relativism and Truth*. New York: Cambridge Press, 1991.

Russell, Bertrand. *Education and the Modern World*. New York: W. W. Norton, 1932.

Sartre, Jean Paul. *Being and Nothingness: An Essay on Phenomenological Ontology*. New York: Philosophical Library, 1956.

Sarup, Madan. *Marxism and Education*. London: Routledge & Kegan Paul, 1978.

Simpson, Douglas, and Michael Jackson. *The Teacher as Philosopher*. New York: Methuen, 1984.

Skinner, B. F. *Beyond Freedom and Dignity*. New York: Alfred A. Knopf, 1971.

Slavin, Robert E. *Educational Psychology: Theory and Practice*. New York: Pearson Publications, 2000.

Strike, Kenneth, and Jonas Soltis. *The Ethics of Teaching*. New York: Teachers College Press, 1985.

Toffler, Alvin. *Future Shock*. New York: Random House, 1970.

Van Til, William. *Education: A Beginning*. Boston: Houghton Mifflin, 1971: 391.

Wagschal, Peter H., ed. *Learning Tomorrows: Commentaries on the Future of Education*. New York: Praeger Publishers, 1979.

Whitehead, Alfred. *The Aims of Education and Other Essays*. New York: Macmillan, 1929.

Woolfolk, Anita E. *Educational Psychology*. New York: Prentice Hall, 2000.

Chapter THREE

American Education: Our European Heritage and the Colonial Influence

It being one chief object of that old deluder, Satan, to keep men from the knowledge of the scriptures, . . . it is therefore ordered, that every township . . . after the Lord hath increased them to the number of fifty householders, . . . shall . . . appoint one within their town to teach all children as shall resort to him to read and write. It is further ordered, that where any town shall increase to the number of one hundred families . . . they shall set up a grammar school, the master thereof being able to instruct youth so far as they may be fitted for the university.

Old Deluder Satan Act—Massachusetts Laws of 1647

Protestant Reformation			Glorious Revolution
1601 English Poor Law	1620 Plymouth Colony		1664 New Amsterdam became New York
1607 Jamestown	1636 Harvard College		1688 William and Mary
1619 Black slaves in Virginia	1642 Massachusetts compulsory school law	1647 Old Deluder Satan Act	1689 English Act of Toleration

Figure 3.1　　Time Line for European Heritage and Colonial Influence

Modern conceptions of reality are highly influenced by images gleaned from the mass media and systems of electronic communication. Indeed, a recent Associated Press release stated that 56 percent of American adults use the Internet while three-fourths of the children aged twelve to seventeen have Internet access. Added to film and television, this constitutes a media saturation that determines perception. It is therefore not surprising that most Americans think of the colonial era in history in terms of Benjamin Franklin toying with a kite in an electrical storm, the witch trials in Salem, or Mel Gibson playing the title role in *The Patriot*. Such images provide useful glimpses of history, but they hardly reveal the century and a half during which England ruled its American colonies.

Before the American Revolution, the colonies were more isolated from one another than from Europe and only the larger cities on the Atlantic seaboard had good means of communication with each other. School accounts of events in the last decades of the eighteenth century emphasize the unfairness of British policies and paint a grim picture of George III. Furthermore, where kings exist today, they are regarded as mere heads of state and not as superhuman. Yet even those who emigrated from England seeking religious freedom regarded the king and the royal family as belonging to a special class and did not question his divine right to rule.

The idea that all men are created equal was revolutionary indeed and did not emerge in the earlier colonial period where British social classes and social stratification dominated. America differed from England only in that it was easier here to break away to start a new life on the frontier and there was a chance of economic improvement through ability or hard work. Otherwise, the social system and its prejudices remained in vogue in the American colonies. Women were universally considered inferior beings who could not hold property or engage in politics and who had no rights beyond those given by their fathers or husbands. Native Americans, although often respected, were thought inferior to whites, while the mentality of children was ascribed to Black slaves. Others were simply ignored by the culture.

French and Indian War		Boston Massacre	
1690 *New England Primer*	1751 Franklin's Academy in Philadelphia		1763 Treaty of Paris ended the French and Indian War
1693 William and Mary College in Virginia		1762 Rousseau's *Emile* published in France	1765 Stamp Act

Persons with disabilities or physical handicaps were sometimes the object of pity and sometimes believed to be God's punishment for the sins of parents. Colonial literature does not acknowledge the existence of gays except through some vague reference to Sodom and Gomorrah. Figure 3.1

Accustomed as we are to rapid change, it is difficult to imagine the colonial culture in which everything remained very much the same for generations. Except for an increase in population, farms in New England and plantations in the South looked very much the same from the mid-1600s to the mid-1700s. The Industrial Revolution had hardly started in England by 1776 and did not reach America until the following century. Every village had its smithy and there was trade in timber, but manufacturing was not encouraged by British rulers and only the central colonies developed brisk commerce. Colonial life was theocratic with the presence of God assumed in everything. In December 2000, Irwin Victoria reported in the *Christian Science Monitor* that a number of states have implemented "a moment of silence" for prayer, meditation, or other silent activity. There are supporters and dissenters over the moment of silence in public schools, but our colonial forefathers could have never understood what the fuss is about.

The first American educational theory and practice tended to reflect European patterns, but the instances of transplantation without modification were few. The settlements of the Spanish in Florida and the French in the Mississippi Valley copied European institutions, including schools, as closely as the new environment would allow. This was true in St. Augustine, which was founded by Pedro Menendez in 1565, and in the French settlements at Montreal, Quebec, Kaskaskia, and New Orleans. Spanish monasteries were educational as well as religious institutions, and the duty of teaching Native Americans the Spanish language was required by royal order in 1643. Convents and schools founded by French and Spanish Catholics reached much of North America, including California, where Father Junipero Serra was active.

British colonials, on the other hand, began to incorporate distinctive new features in the models they took from their homeland. The apprenticeship system, elementary reading schools, the Latin grammar school, and even Harvard College were not exact duplicates of their English counterparts. The Reformation had suggested the principle of universal education, but in England it had also allowed church property to be used for secular purposes, nearly destroying elementary schools. Philanthropists, therefore, began endowing British charity schools, whereas the upper middle-class children attended schools taught by private masters for fees. In America, charity education provided by such agencies as the Society for the Propagation of the Gospel in Foreign Parts (SPG) became popular. The SPG, an agency of the Anglican church, provided money, books, teachers, and physical facilities for American children who otherwise would have had no opportunity to attend school. Of course, philanthropic education usually had special interests attached, such as furthering the cause of a particular religion or fostering a set of values esteemed by those who contributed funds.

The English pattern of high-quality private schools catering to the children of the well to do and supported by tuition was not followed to a great extent in the colonies. Secondary educational institutions modeled on Westminster, Eton, or other English "public" schools were uncommon in America. Private venture schools tended to offer practical courses such as surveying, navigation, or bookkeeping. In those areas where religion was the driving force of a community, education became an instrument for social control through transmitting and preserving the beliefs of the sect. The authorities in England had often discouraged such efforts. All schools underwent changes as a result of cultural forces in the colonies and the experience of coping with the American wilderness. Apprenticeship and the tutorial system remained dominant educational practices in the colonies, as was the case in England.

Generally the educational aims of colonial schools and teachers represented stability, tradition, authority, discipline, and preordained value systems that were marks of idealism and classical realism. Many of the European educators (discussed in Chapter 4) reflected the ideology of idealism and classical realism; Friedrich Froebel's educational writings reflected idealism, and the others reflected various forms of realism.

COLONIAL MELTING POT

Theories of educational idealism and realism were modified in theory and practice in colonial America. Modifications may be attributed to environmental difficulties, such as the struggle to produce food, the communication problem, disease, isolation, and hostile natives. Economic stresses and strains have always played a part in education.

Other changes were caused by the new intellectual climate illustrated by the many nonconformist or religiously dissenting settlers and the shift of the center of civil authority represented by the signing of the Mayflower Compact. Of course, the colonists remained Englishmen and the crown retained sovereignty until the American Revolution, but local control and some degree of political independence began to emerge quite early. Dissatisfaction with conditions in the homeland caused the migration of thousands of individuals who were not anxious to restore the agencies of their grief and oppression. The availability of free land and the desire of the English to encourage settlement made it possible for almost every group of people to find a place where they could practice their own religion and follow their own lifestyle. For example, Quakers sought freedom from restrictions on their religious activities, and indentured servants wanted freedom from bondage and the opportunity for social advancement. Many colonial communities were similar to Longfellow's Grand Pré (described in Chapter 1).

However, the European school itself was not the object of attack by dissatisfied groups. The fact that educational facilities in the homelands were often decadent and offered very limited opportunity for the children of many who stayed behind did little to harm their reputation in America or undermine the attempt to imitate them. In an effort to preserve the European civilization of which they were a part, the colonists tried to copy the educational institutions they knew best. English textbooks and school methods were widely accepted in all the American colonies. Nevertheless, schools in the colonies were not merely transplanted but also revolutionized in spirit and sometimes in form. Although the colonies were never a melting pot in the sense of mixing all the people together into one homogeneous mass, cultural diversity and the presence of many different religious denominations had a considerable influence on colonial schools.

Colonial legislatures, royal governors, proprietors, and stock companies were delegated educational authority along with political powers by the British crown. However, the degree to which civil governments took an interest in education differed greatly from one colony to another. Established churches and European governments exchanged mutual support in seventeenth-century culture. This alliance was also found throughout the colonies, although the nature of established churches differed considerably from Puritan New England to Anglican Virginia. Some degree of religious toleration developed in Rhode Island, Pennsylvania, New York, and Maryland.

RELIGIOUS SECTARIANISM

Religion played a very important part in colonial schools and colleges, both in the conduct of the institutions and in the curriculum. Although Bible reading and prayer continued to be a major part of common school practice well into the national period, control of education gradually shifted away from sectarian authorities. Just as the states in modern America delegate authority to local school boards, so the colonial governments allowed private individuals and religious groups to establish schools of their own. This practice was due, in part, to the failure of governments to support schools with tax revenues and, in part, to the rise of numerous religious sects that demanded the freedom to educate children in their own way. As a general rule, the central civil government did not engage in close supervision of schools that were built and financed by local or church agencies. This was true throughout the colonies in the eighteenth century and was especially obvious in frontier settlements.

In a very real sense, the desire for greater religious freedom contributed to the doctrine of separation of church and state. Roger Williams was driven from Massachusetts partly for supporting such separation, and he made it a policy in his Rhode Island settlement. The various sects eventually obtained freedom of worship, and since there was no consensus concerning religious principles to be taught in schools founded by civil authorities, the various denominations conducted and controlled their own schools. In New England, the selectmen of a town, the general court of the colony, or the ministers constituted ultimate educational authority. Royal governors and towns gave charters for schools in the Middle colonies. In the Anglican South, the Bishop of London was responsible for licensing teachers.

SOCIAL CLASS IN THE COLONIAL ENVIRONMENT

English feudal structure was not equally superimposed on all parts of the American colonial culture, but social class stratification was marked. Southern plantations usually contained every social class from slaves to owners of estates. Virginia reflected British class divisions almost exactly, and even feudal practices such as primogeniture (passing an estate to the eldest son) and entail (making sale or exchange of real property unlawful) were found in that colony. Indentured servants and at least a few slaves lived in all of the colonies. New England had no gentlemen–planter class; however, ministers and magistrates had great prestige, and Puritan emphasis on work and frugality soon produced wealthy merchants. Middle colonies like Maryland had a well-developed middle class consisting of artisans and skilled workers, but the middle classes grew everywhere as trade developed and the population increased. Scarcity of labor, and especially of skilled labor, made it easy for the ambitious man to improve his social status through hard work. It was difficult to prevent a servant from becoming an independent frontier farmer.

Although social-class mobility was a feature of colonial society, the schools remained class centered. Latin preparatory schools and theological colleges favored the upper classes. For many years, Harvard College class roles were arranged by social rank. Public demand for new skills resulted in a special school—the academy—that catered to the practical requirements of the commercial class. Nevertheless, many students obtained only rudimentary education, and many of the earlier settlers of the lower classes could not read or write. Even in New England, where schools were in operation by 1636, the level of instruction was low and not all children could attend. Individuals who did not adhere to acceptable religious beliefs were excluded from economic and educational opportunities. Before American independence, there were trends toward a more flexible and democratic school pattern, but the rigid class system and the strong religious atmosphere continued to influence education until comparatively recent times. Opportunities for success were limited for those who were not in the religious mainstream of the day.

Few experiences in England fitted colonists for the difficulties of sustaining life in a wilderness, and the colonies were not similar in climate, landforms, or population. Thus, quite different lifestyles emerged. The South concentrated on agriculture and created great plantations with a social system resembling that of England, and economic complexity in New England led to towns and villages sufficiently dense in population for the maintenance of schools.

Each colony also had different community patterns. Land was too cheap to sustain the feudal privileges of Southern planters, and soon a new breed of small farmers and hunters emerged. These rough-and-ready pioneers were not at all like the gentlemen who owned large estates planted in indigo, rice, or tobacco. They were not cultured or highly educated, and they had little leisure time to pursue the intellectual graces commonly acquired by wealthy slaveholders. But they soon became a political and economic force. This new class of independent people had little use for the classics or the Latin grammar schools, but they wanted their children to have the basic skills of reading and writing. In England, the sons of working men and farmers seldom had an opportunity for formal schooling. In America, the possibility for a better life in the future for children of all classes created a demand for some sort of schooling in every community. The most common practice among working and middle-class parents was to apprentice their sons to skilled tradesmen or shopkeepers.

THE SOUTHERN COLONIES

Of the English colonies on the eastern seaboard, Maryland, Virginia, the Carolinas, and Georgia most closely resembled the British homeland in cultural and social patterns. Economic factors were responsible for most of the migration of English gentlemen to the South. They were not dissatisfied with conditions in the homeland and, therefore, expected to replicate English institutions in America without substantial change. Southern planters devoted their energy to business and the development of their estates. They remained loyal to the Anglican church and the values of the British landed gentry. Plantation owners emphasized the enjoyment of the cultured life, which included gambling, dancing, literature, music, art, books, and the breeding of fine horses.

Religion was reverently practiced through prayer and church attendance, but it did not become the dominating force of life as in New England. There was no Puritan zeal for having every person taught to read the Bible. The clergy was responsible for interpreting scripture, and clerical authority was vested in the Anglican hierarchy. Educational matters also rested with the decisions of the Archbishop of Canterbury or the Bishop of London. Since both church and state favored the landed gentry and large estates were the rule, social equality did not develop in the South. Those not favored by conditions of birth and wealth were expected to be satisfied with their station in life and the decisions made for them by their "betters." In 1671, Governor Sir William Berkeley of Virginia held that every man should instruct his own children according to his means:

> I thank God, *there are no free schools nor printing*, and I hope we shall not have them these hundred years, for *learning* has brought disobedience, and heresy, and sects into the world, and *printing* has divulged them, and libels against the best government. God keeps us from them both. (Mill, 1859)

Berkeley no doubt spoke for many Virginians, but some free schools did develop in spite of the opposition. Occasionally a parish built and maintained a school that was open to children who could not pay tuition. There were numerous endowments for schools such as those provided in the wills of Benjamin Syms (1634) and Thomas Eaton (1659), both of whom gave land and goods for the maintenance of an "able schoolmaster" to teach poor children. Nevertheless, free schools remained rare in Virginia, and large areas of the South had no formal education of any kind.

The planters did devote a good deal of time to intellectual pursuits beyond the instruction of their children. The art of writing letters was highly developed, and many newspapers were circulated. Even the remote plantations usually had a good collection of books from England and other European nations. Some private libraries were excellent: That of William Byrd contained some 4,000 volumes. An excellent account of the intellectual and social life of the colonial South is found in the diary of Philip Fithian. Fithian was a graduate of Princeton and served as tutor to the Carter family of northern Virginia. Tutorial education was common practice in the South.

Leading elements of the social order attempted to copy the customs and mores of wealthy Englishmen in everything, including schools. Southern educational institutions reflected more English ideals than schools in other parts of the colonies, and every planter who could afford it wished to send his son to Oxford or Cambridge Universities or the Inns of Court (London law schools) for training.

Rigid Southern social-class distinctions allowed few opportunities for the indentured servants, the slaves, and the poverty-stricken freedmen to engage in cultural pursuits or to improve their minds. The persons lowest in social rank were entirely dependent upon the wealthy and powerful for what little education they received. Skills needed to operate farms and plantations were not taught in schools, nor was education received very clearly related to success.

Gentlemen thought of themselves as natural political leaders, as well as guardians of refined manners, learning, justice, hospitality, and religion. No effort was spared to initiate sons of the planter class into the intellectual pursuits of their fathers. They were given generalized readings in the Greek and Roman classics, French was widely taught along with English literature and the Bible, and studies such as painting and architecture were commonly included.

No single educational pattern developed in the Southern colonies, making it difficult to generalize. Although diversity of educational practice was at a maximum in the South, public interest in education was at a minimum. Virginia had money earmarked for education as early as 1618, but the revocation of the charter for the Virginia Company seven years later stopped these funds. From that time until 1660, Virginia passed laws that required children to be taught religion, although public financial support was lacking. Since Southern leaders came from the upper classes of England, the Anglican church dominated—and exercised considerable influence over the existing educational programs. Law or the church, however, only indirectly controlled schools, because education was considered a private matter left in the hands of individual citizens. Exceptions were apprenticeship education, which was carefully regulated by law, and efforts of philanthropic or religious societies in behalf of the poor, the Native Americans, and the slaves. Attempts to save souls of Native Americans met with slight success; however, continuous appeals were made for giving slaves the rudiments of a religious education, especially the entreaty that Christianity would make them more content and harder working.

Schools for those not favored by birth were limited in the Southern colonies. Early efforts to provide endowed schools for all children, including Native Americans, failed. Some laws required education for pauper children, but little was actually done. Like England, the Southern governments made an effort to keep the poor from starving and to see that children of paupers learned a trade, but the Virginia law requiring training of "bound" boys was not passed until 1705. Virginians saw nothing odd in imposing requirements upon parents and ministers for religious instruction without giving financial aid to education. Teachers in private schools were seldom examined on their qualifications beyond the ability to read and write but were expected to prove their orthodoxy in religion.

Meager efforts were made to establish chartered or publicly aided schools in the Carolinas. Maryland fared a little better with a provision in 1671 for a "School or College" and a system of secondary county schools founded in 1728. Duties on tobacco and fines for crimes were used to support such schools, but only a small proportion of the population had access to them. Maryland had a quasi-public corporation made up of church and government officials to make policy and secure funds for schools in each county. Georgia was the last Southern colony to be settled, and little progress toward an educational program was made there before the Revolution.

Tutorial Schools.   Tutorial schools existed throughout the South, although they varied widely in form. Very wealthy planters hired learned tutors to train their sons and frequently their daughters as well. When there was time and interest, a similar tutorial system was also used by others attached to the plantation, such as the sons of foremen or managers. Teachers were often Anglican ministers who served churches in the proximity of the estate, but private schoolmasters were also employed to teach. Sometimes it proved cheaper or more expedient to buy the teaching services of an indentured servant. Many well-trained Scots who knew Latin and Greek were included in the shiploads of indentured persons entering Southern ports, and their time could be purchased at a lower rate than that of skilled labor. Private tutorial schools were sometimes sufficient to prepare boys for college in England. The curriculum was usually classical, but practical subjects such as surveying and mathematics were by no means excluded. Girls were instructed in

French, music, dancing, and polite manners by their tutors, and for them the instruction was terminal. Boys who had mastered Lilly's *Latin Grammar* were often sent to one of the private preparatory schools (great public schools) in England.

Travel was considered to be a major part of education, even for boys who did not attend Latin grammar schools or colleges in England. Such educational leaders as James Blair and the Reverend Thomas Bray of Virginia maintained high standards of scholarship. The universal employment of tutors indicated a greater interest in education by American planters than by their English counterparts.

Old Field Schools.

One Southern innovation was the old field school. This was a local elementary school built by members of a community on one of the fallow "old" fields that had lost its productivity through overuse. Sometimes Anglican ministers taught in these schools as they did on the plantations, but the masters were often persons with very little education. Old field schools were usually maintained by private subscriptions with some sort of scholarship or other provision for impoverished scholars. Control of the schools, including the securing of teacher and materials, was in the hands of the local community. These schools were similar to later ones established in frontier towns during the national period. They commonly were in operation for only a few months each year.

Dame Schools.

In most colonies, including those in the South, dame schools could be found. These were not really schools at all but consisted of rudimentary instruction given by a woman in her own home, usually while she carried on household duties. The lessons were limited to the alphabet, counting, prayers, the catechism, and perhaps reading a few sentences from the Bible. A standard instrument in the dame school was the hornbook, which consisted of a single printed page that was attached to a wooden paddle and covered with a transparent film made by boiling down the horns of cows. Hornbooks often were inscribed with the alphabet, numerals from one to nine, and the Lord's Prayer. They were a means of keeping "letters faire from fingers damp" and were used throughout the colonies. Dames who offered instruction were often barely literate themselves. One is recorded as saying, "T'is little they pays me and little I learns em."

Secondary and Higher Education.

Plans for a Latin grammar school were made in Virginia before 1630. Property bequeathed by Syms and Eaton apparently was used for such classical schools. Thomas Jefferson graduated from a Latin school before entering William and Mary College. Nevertheless, due to preference for sending sons to preparatory schools in England and the sparse early population, few secondary schools developed. Some towns were able to maintain academies. Those in Charleston were supported by a combination of fees and grants. Some academies were classical schools for college preparation, and others taught only practical or commercial subjects. William and Mary was the only institution of higher learning in the southern region during the colonial period. It began granting degrees in 1700.

Charity Education.

Other educational measures were taken by philanthropic societies, most of which were organized by religious institutions. The Anglican church encouraged slaveholders to teach their charges Christianity. Charity schools were operated in England, and this idea soon spread to America, for the training of orphans and paupers. The SPG of the Anglican church was, by far, the most active group; it raised funds in England and used the money to send out teachers and to buy textbooks for the colonies. Many able instructors (often young ministers) brought their knowledge and missionary zeal to the colonial schools for the poor. The best charity schools and also the most numerous ones in the Southern and Middle colonies were provided by this Anglican society. It printed and distributed books on history, agriculture, and mathematics, as well as religious tracts.

Perhaps the most conspicuous thing about education in the South before the American Revolution was the lack of public interest in schools. Several factors contributed to this attitude, some of which continued to affect public schools in the national period. It was strongly believed by the dominant planter class that each man was responsible for the education of his own children. Further, it was against the prevailing custom to tax one person for the education of the sons of others. Southern colonies had widely scattered populations not concentrated in cities and towns.

Even if the people had wanted an educational system, physical remoteness made one almost impossible. Secondary schools of either the Latin grammar or practical academy type did not develop. The classes most interested in education could afford to hire tutors or to send their sons to England; many of the smaller landowners and pioneer hunters were more concerned with the practical skills necessary for survival than with formal schooling. Also, the Southern attitude toward religion failed to bring about the New England emphasis on education as a means of salvation. Southern colonial education remained very much like education in England. Nevertheless, many of the most learned and able leaders in the revolutionary period were from the South.

THE MIDDLE COLONIES

Diversity and **parochialism** are perhaps the words that best describe the colonial settlements of Delaware, New Jersey, New York, and Pennsylvania. Settlers from Holland, Germany, Sweden, England, Wales, and Scotland came to the Middle colonies in large numbers. Disparity in religion was even more pronounced than differences in nationality; thus, the colonies became a potpourri of faiths, languages, and ethnic cultures. It is said that thirteen languages were spoken in Dutch New Amsterdam before it became New York in 1664. So many different religious denominations were represented in the region that toleration soon became a necessity. The Quakers of Pennsylvania were theoretically opposed to persecution.

Commerce and trade worked better in an open society, and no single religious sect had the numerical power to force its will on the others. Although the Catholics in Maryland had been protected in Lord Baltimore's time, religious freedom was limited there after 1654. Rhode Island as well as other Middle colonies then became the haven for all persons escaping from any form of religious persecution. It was this freedom that attracted the Pietist scholar Francis Daniel Pastorius (1651–1720), who was the best-educated man in America at the time. Pastorius wrote a primer called

The True Reading, Spelling, and Writing of English, published in New York in 1697. New York, like Philadelphia (the largest British city in America during the eighteenth century), was a center for intellectual activity.

Mennonites, Quakers, Lutherans, Calvinists, Moravians, Huguenots, Separate Baptists, and Episcopalians established educational practices of their own. Small numbers of Dunkards, Jews, disciples of John Hus, and other minor sects emigrated to America and set up schools. In short, the Middle colonies were the ones with the largest number of national and religious groups; therefore, they tended to develop many kinds of schools. There was also a considerable urban growth in this area and constant communication with the most sophisticated centers of Europe. Intellectual freedom (and tolerance) was possible in the central coastal cities to a degree unheard of in New England or the South. Black, Native Americans, or other minority pupils were sometimes admitted to middle colony schools.

From its very beginning, the Dutch West India Company accepted its obligation to provide schools, and it demanded careful records showing every expenditure down to and including paper and ink. All nine villages chartered in New Netherlands probably had schools. The schoolmaster was not only a teacher but also a minor church official. He was picked for his orthodoxy and had other duties such as reading Scriptures on Sunday, digging graves, and acting as church sexton. When the English became dominant, Dutch schools continued to exist very much as they had before, but they became parochial institutions supported by local church congregations or private schools supported by towns.

Except for insisting on the right to license teachers, practically no laws were made concerning schools. The SPG of the Anglican church was responsible for the majority of the common schools in New York, which were intended for the poor and thus were charitable institutions. These enjoyed the favor and support of the governor and his offices but were seldom entirely free, each student paying what his family could afford. This system of charging different amounts was known as the "rate bill" and was widely adopted. Private instruction was sometimes similar to the plantation schools of the South, but individual tutors were rare.

Private venture schools in towns sometimes taught such practical subjects as bookkeeping, geography, and navigation. Each denomination was permitted to set up its own school system, and therefore schools were nonpublic in nature and intolerant of individuals representing other views. Nevertheless, religious differences kept the schools out of the hands of the central civil government and made them the responsibility of the churches. It was common in the Middle colonies, therefore, to have many sectarian schools together with a considerable number of charitable institutions for education.

In areas where the Quaker faith was strong, there was much support for primary education. Pennsylvania, with its Quaker commonwealth, had many laws regulating morality, including punishment for such offenses as drunkenness, dancing, gambling, and profanity. Nevertheless, jailing for debts was abolished, and a great deal of freedom of speech and religion was allowed. Since the colony was open to all creeds, Pennsylvania attracted Mennonites, Moravians, Lutherans, and Anglicans, in addition to the large numbers of Quakers.

Denominational Influence.

Dissenting factions in Pennsylvania caused many Quakers to fear for the unity of their church and to be suspicious of college education, but they remained active in their support for elementary schools. Quaker schools were excellent in quality. They taught reading, writing, arithmetic, and probably bookkeeping as well as religion; and they were not closed either to the poor or to girls. Quaker teachers received apprenticeship training, the first teacher education in America. The record shows that some control was used: The Council of Philadelphia rebuked Thomas Meking for teaching in a Friends public school without a license. Quaker schools provided the first American education for freed blacks. Smaller religious sects known as "dissenters" also established schools and colleges. The "log college" opened by Presbyterians in 1726 trained boys for the ministry. In Philadelphia, the William Penn Charter School taught both the classics and an English curriculum. The German scholar Francis Pastorius taught there. Baptists and Moravians set up denominational schools that were also open to the public. Governor Nicholson set aside land for a free Catholic school in Maryland.

Academies.

Vocational education was more significant in the Middle colonies than elsewhere in colonial America. English poor laws of 1562 and 1601 proposed the establishment of working schools; they also forced apprenticeship for the poor. William Penn was influential in bringing the idea of trade training for pauper children to Pennsylvania, and John Locke's concern for practical subjects was well known in the colonies. The academy, a terminal secondary school that prepared students for a vocation, did not become highly significant until the national period. Nevertheless, both elementary and secondary schools in the Middle colonies offered such practical subjects as merchandising, navigation, trade, and mechanics. Benjamin Franklin's academy in Philadelphia opened in 1751 and became a model for others Although it was organized in part as a Latin school, the academy was intended for the heterogeneous population of Pennsylvania. Franklin was particularly interested in training teachers for rural schools and in training officials for the government. The seeds of the American comprehensive high school, which offered vocational subjects, were planted in the private and parochial schools of the Middle colonies.

Latin Grammar Schools.

Secondary schools of the Latin grammar type were necessary for college preparation. New York, Pennsylvania, New Jersey, and Maryland had such schools. Higher English schools and Latin schools existed together in Quaker Pennsylvania, and denominational support for both was common.

The teachers were usually ministers who had no church to serve; the purpose was college preparation, leading eventually to political or church positions. Latin secondary schools and colleges were strictly for men. The curriculum often included Juvenal, Ovid, Virgil, Caesar, Cicero, and Horace, with perhaps some Greek grammar.

Religious sectarianism was a major force in Middle colony education, even though freedom of choice was respected. Schools were used for propaganda, and there was often bitter condemnation of other groups, especially Catholics.

Common Schools.   Private education in Pennsylvania was largely the prerogative of the upper classes. However, there were some accommodations for sons of
workmen and artisans of the middle class. A night school teaching writing, arithmetic, and some mathematics was opened in Philadelphia in 1731. Navigation, surveying, and mathematics were taught in another night school in the same city. Later
in the eighteenth century, private evening schools for accounting, mathematics, and
modern languages were advertised in many cities. Public lectures on natural science,
astronomy, and mechanics attracted large crowds. Private circulating libraries were
available for a fee. Journals, books, and newspapers were numerous in larger cities.
Philadelphia continued to be a major center for learning throughout the colonial era.
Although New England led in universal education during the colonial period, there
was a great deal of school activity on the elementary level in the Middle colonies.

Higher Education.   The Middle colonies also had their share of denominational
colleges as well as the College of Philadelphia (established in 1755), which was the
only nonsectarian institution of higher learning. The College of New Jersey (Princeton) was established by Presbyterians in 1746. King's College (Columbia) was an Anglican effort of 1754. And the Dutch Reformed church founded Queen's College
(Rutgers) in 1766. The College of Rhode Island (Brown) was created by the Baptists
in 1764. Of the nine colonial colleges in America, five were in the Middle colonies.
Early graduates of American colleges often found work as tutors to well-off children
in the Middle colonies and the South.

   The cultural variety that characterized the Middle colonies made education quite
different from that of both the North and the South. Particularly significant were the
early influences of settlers from Holland and the later emigration of large numbers
of Germans. There was no one single powerful ruling church, and therefore no establishment of religion. Tolerance was greater than in New England or in the South,
and many more sectarian schools developed. Class differences in the Middle colonies
were less distinct than in the South, and the central colonies became a melting pot
for many nationalities and many social positions. But by and large, less interest was
shown in educational development in the Middle colonies than in New England.

THE NEW ENGLAND COLONIES

In many ways, education in New England was most significant for the growth of later
American schools. The influence of parliamentary rule and the Christian duty of educating each child caused the theocratic governments in New England to take great
interest in schools. The Puritans wanted a state church ruled by congregations rather
than by bishops and a government that substituted the authority of the people for
the divine right of a king. New England colonies made laws requiring education of
the children but left details to local communities—thereby creating the traditions of
local autonomy and the district system. These colonies provided both for universal
elementary education and for the training of ministers, a practice that tended to per-

petuate the English dual system of education. But it is wrong to assume that Puritan efforts fostered religious freedom or democracy.

Puritan Philosophy.   Part of their educational interest stemmed from a concept of the nature of man that is found in the Calvinistic creed. The Puritans assumed that man is by nature evil, having fallen in the sin of Adam. Man is not only bad, but he also has an active nature that must be controlled to prevent the devil from becoming his master. This notion of man's being bad and active gave rise to the establishment of schools in order to prevent idleness and show mankind the way to overcome the evil in his nature. Assuming that man is depraved, there must be an effort to bring him to salvation. This, together with the Protestant notion of the priesthood of all believers, made it mandatory that the New England Puritans establish elementary schools.

In Massachusetts, New Hampshire, and Connecticut, Puritans were determined to build their own religious orthodoxy in the way Calvin had suggested. They established theocracies in which the church and state ruled by means of public disapproval, whipping, banishment, and fines. It was common for them to use the general court and the authority of the minister to enforce conformity both in behavior and in belief. Such positive support of religion required not only the creation of schools but also that every child be able to read and understand both the Scriptures and the capital laws.

Numerous Puritan ministers wrote works in theology and philosophy that reinforced this educational theory. In his book, *A Family Well-Ordered*, Cotton Mather dwelt upon the duties of parents and the obligations of children. John Cotton reflected the same view. And even the learned Jonathan Edwards (1703–1758) made his idealism the servant of a narrow Calvinistic theology. The views of these Puritan theorists are clearly seen in the religious nature of textbooks like the *New England Primer* of 1690. This textbook includes the following verses:

> *In Adam's Fall*
> *We Sinned all*
> *. . . Thy Life to Mend*
> *This Book Attend*
> *. . . The Idle Fool*
> *Is Whipt at School*

As previously stated, in New England the farm land was not especially fertile, and people turned early to such occupations as shipbuilding, manufacturing, and trade. A merchant class developed that had need of people who could take care of business accounts and work with all sorts of business documents. It was therefore an economic necessity to have large numbers of people able not only to read and write but also to cast accounts. Even so, the New England schools were primarily established for the propagation of the Gospel and the control of new generations. It was usual for children to spend only a few years in the common school. However, Latin grammar schools were established for the elite.

The Pilgrims insisted that the parents take care of education. As early as 1642, however, the General Court of Massachusetts came to the conclusion that many parents were neglecting the training of their children. Therefore, the court ordered that the selectmen of every town should require that all parents and masters undertake the education of their children. After a short time, it was found that this provision was not working well. In 1647, therefore, the General Court passed its famous Old Deluder Satan Act. This law required every town to set up a school or to pay a sum of money to the next larger town for the support of education. A precedent was thus made for requiring the towns (or townships) to take the responsibility for establishing and maintaining schools. The theocracy not only required education but also set both the curriculum and the standard procedures for operation. These early efforts of Massachusetts were soon picked up by other parts of New England.

The first tax on property for local schools was in Dedham, Massachusetts, in 1648. New Hampshire required towns to support elementary schools as early as 1693. Taxes were used to pay the wages of teachers and to build school buildings, but tuition fees were universally charged in the New England colonies. The curriculum of the early New England schools was almost entirely religious, for these institutions were viewed officially as being indispensable to the stability of Puritan society. Such books as the Bible, the *New England Primer*, and the catechism were widely used in schools. Education was for salvation as well as for getting along in life. It was a primary duty of parents to bring their children up according to the orthodox religious beliefs of Puritan society.

The Puritans feared leaving an illiterate ministry to the people. For this reason they established Harvard College (1636) almost as early as the town schools. The college was primarily for the education of ministers of the Gospel, though after a few years students preparing for professions such as law attended as well.

Once the college had been established, it was necessary that Latin grammar schools be provided so that the boys wishing to enter Harvard could get the necessary preparatory studies. The first of these schools was established in Boston. A famous teacher, Ezekiel Cheever, taught for over fifty years in the Ipswich Grammar School and in the Boston Latin Grammar School; his teaching had considerable influence on the prestige of the teaching profession in the New England area. Almost no curriculum choice was offered in any of the colonial schools, and the methods were both fixed and harsh. It was ordained that schoolmasters be examined and certified by the minister of the town or the adjoining towns where the school was to be held. Education was generally narrow, limited, elementary, and moral in character. In Massachusetts it was common for masters who failed to carry out their responsibilities adequately to be fined and sometimes even thrown out of their jobs.

Educational Conditions.

In the lower schools, there was normally one master for a room full of children of various ages. The local minister and the "selectmen" of the town provided supervision of the school. Buildings were of the log cabin or clapboard variety, furnished with benches, a fireplace, shelves around the walls for writing, and a few small windows. The master usually had a chair and lectern, but the meager equipment seldom included blackboards or maps. A whipping post was commonly erected by the school door. Severe floggings were administered for misbehavior or breaking the rules, since Puritan philosophy called for literally beating the devil out of the child. According to the law in Massachusetts, children could be confined in stocks for some offenses, and fathers had the right to execute their children if they could not be controlled, although this extreme was never practiced. There are records of pupils who were tortured by having a stick of flat wood (whispering stick) placed like a bit between their teeth, pupils made to kneel on hard pebbles, and pupils made to wear heavy wooden yokes. The school in colonial New England was not a pleasant place, either physically or psychologically. Great emphasis was placed on the shortness of life, the torments of hell, and the fear that one's behavior might not be acceptable for salvation. Children in dull and grim schools memorized passages such as:

> *I in the Burying Place may see*
> *Graves shorter there than I;*
> *From Death's Arrest no Age is free,*
> *Young Children too must die.*
>
> *Oh God may such an Awful Sight*
> *Awakening to Me be,*
> *That by Early Grace I shall,*
> *For Death Prepared be. (Ford, 1987)*

The elementary curriculum consisted of the four R's: religion, reading, writing, and arithmetic. Boys and girls entered the school at the age of six or seven. They began with the hornbook or a similar instrument printed on stiff paper called a battledore. Next they were given the *New England Primer;* a crudely illustrated reading text that included the *Westminster Shorter Catechism;* a picture of the martyr John Rogers being burned at the stake in England; a dialogue between Christ, a youth, and the devil; and John Cotton's *Spiritual Milk for American Babes drawn from Both Brests of the Testements for their Souls' Nourshment*. Many children remained in school only three or four years and did not progress beyond the primer. For those who remained longer, there was the *Psalter* (Book of Psalms) and the Bible. Paper was scarce and of very poor quality. It came in large unlined sheets and had to be folded, sewn together, and marked with pieces of lead in order to make a tablet for the children. Students provided hornbooks, crude slates, and quill pens. Often the masters would canvass the community to determine the availability of books, and whatever they found would be used as reading material for older pupils.

The school normally operated six days each week, except in the summer. There were long periods of prayer and Bible reading both morning and evening. Most of the subject matter was memorized by the student and tested in a cue and recitation session before the master. There were no group activities or mass assignments. Students were not encouraged to express opinions or to ask questions. The word of the master and the text were regarded as absolute authorities. Teachers had no pedagogical training as such, but in New England the schoolmasters were often among the best-educated members of the community. The pay was extremely low, and many communities required masters to "board around" in order to save money.

Latin Schools and College Programs.

Boston had a free Latin grammar school, and many other New England towns developed secondary schools supported by tuition. These "higher track" schools for the social and intellectual elite were intended to prepare boys for college and were always taught by college graduates—often ministers. Boys usually entered the Latin school at the age of eight after having learned to read English at home or in a lower school. The curriculum consisted of three years of Latin grammar "accidence" and practice in parsing Latin sentences. Thereafter, the scholars began to "make Latin" and to translate Latin literature into English. The program continued from six to eight years and included some Greek and Hebrew in the last two years. All the students in the Latin grammar school hoped to be admitted to a college, for that was the entire purpose of such schools. Entrance requirements for Harvard College indicated the curriculum of that institution:

> When any Schollar is able to understand Tully, or such like classical Latine Author extempore, and make and speake true Latine Verse and Prose, . . . and decline perfectly the Paradigm's of Nounes and Verbes in the Greek toungue: Let him then and not before be capable of admission into the College.

Since the first Puritan ministers were graduates of Oxford and Cambridge, colleges in New England closely copied those English institutions. Until 1653, Harvard was a three-year college with a fixed course offering one subject at a time, so that the president could teach all classes. Classical and theological studies were the mainstay of the program. Aristotelian logic and physics, arithmetic, geometry, astronomy, grammar, rhetoric, dialectic, etymology, syntax, and prosody were taught for the purpose of disciplining the mind. Upperclassmen studied Greek and Hebrew grammar, and there were occasional lectures in history and natural science. Students were expected to declaim once a month, and great stress was placed on study of the Bible. For a degree, the student had to present evidence of his ability to read the Scriptures in Latin and to resolve them logically, "withall being of godly life and conversation."

Yale College was founded in 1701 and Dartmouth in 1769. All three New England colleges were Congregationalist and similar in curriculum. They were theological seminaries, not schools for professional men in other fields such as law, medicine, or science.

Religious Cycles.

Education in New England during the colonial period was highly influenced by religion, but the degree of religious activity varied greatly. Harvard and the early town schools of Massachusetts were established during the time of religious enthusiasm of the great Puritan migration. Economic interests and secular views soon created apathy, which caused a decline of educational zeal. Between 1661 and 1681, enrollment at Harvard dropped steadily, and the district schools had difficulty obtaining support. But in the first half of the eighteenth century, there occurred a fervent religious revival known as the Great Awakening. Although the movement was largely evangelistic, it sparked renewed interest in schools at all levels. Yale

College opened at the beginning of that period of new religious enthusiasm and produced the most famous preacher of the time, Jonathan Edwards. Edwards was an eloquent speaker, well known for his fiery "Hell and Damnation" sermons. He was also a learned scholar and the author of many pamphlets widely used in schools and colleges. The Great Awakening and the efforts of Edwards caused numerous conflicts, such as the issue over predestination that split the "Old Lights" from the "New Lights"; but it also caused a major revival of educational activity. The new demand for ministers led Eleazar Wheelock to found a school in Connecticut in 1754; it was later moved to New Hampshire and renamed Dartmouth College. The College of Rhode Island, founded by the Baptists, was also a product of the Great Awakening.

New England schools were crude in form, narrow in curriculum, and poorly supported; but the significant fact remains that they existed in quantity. Long before the United States became a nation, traditions of education, including the ideas of universal schooling and public support, had been formed. Americans had already started to demand what was to become standard—better education for children than their parents had enjoyed.

THEN TO NOW

Life in pre-Revolutionary colonial American culture seems to bear very little direct relationship to present conditions, at least at first glance. Educational institutions such as dame schools, academies, old field schools, and Latin grammar schools have long since disappeared. Of course, the New England pattern of district schools, compulsory education, taxation, and distinct educational levels continues to exist in highly modified form. More important than the schools, however, is the vast heritage of beliefs, values, and attitudes inherited from the Puritans. Modern citizens are more highly influenced by the colonial past than they might imagine, because systems of value tend to persist over generations. As the theory of culture lag suggests, materialistic and technological inventions occur rapidly, and concepts of proper conduct and ideas about the good life change so slowly that they appear to remain constant. Alteration of values is likely to be slow and evolutionary, while changes in material aspects of the culture are quick and revolutionary. This is obviously important, because schools have a major role in transmitting the core values from one generation to the next.

Teaching values or value clarification is always difficult, but it is even more complicated in a multicultural society in which some children come from families more influenced by the Puritan ethic than others. Choosing and reinforcing values for survival and maximum realization of the human potential in the present and the future are central to the socialization function of education. Socialization can hardly be accomplished without a basic understanding of the Puritan ethic of the old Massachusetts Bay colony. Puritan beliefs about the evil nature of the children and their support for corporal punishment are no longer popular, but the basic values are found in the "pioneer spirit," the work ethic, and middle-class values.

Puritan Values.   Since the Puritans held that God allowed his elect to prosper and that idle hands did the work of the devil, they stressed productive work and striving for economic improvement. Today, schools support justification of one's existence through hard work and social service. Puritans were not supposed to display their wealth; therefore, they invested in land and various commercial enterprises. Living a frugal lifestyle, saving money, preparing for the future, and investing were New England values that proved useful to business and commercial interests. These values are not limited to the Puritan tradition (they are practiced also in Japan), but they are central to the American cultural core. One should not overlook the fact that Puritans were intolerant to dissenters in their time. Social ostracism was often used to gain conformity to their values. The credit card economy has tended to undermine values of thrift and frugality.

Socialization requires that the most important aspects of the dominant culture be taught. Using models of accepted behavior and sanctions, schools attempt to get students to accept and internalize values cherished by the institutions and the leaders of the dominant culture. Following are some of these values that can be traced to the Puritan heritage:

- Respect for authority
- Postponing immediate gratification
- Neatness
- Punctuality
- Responsibility for one's own work
- Honesty
- Patriotism and loyalty
- Striving for personal achievement
- Competition
- Repression of aggression and overt sexual expression
- Respect for the rights and property of others
- Obeying rules and regulations

Without making a judgment about these values, it may be pointed out that teaching them creates certain problems. Ours is a multicultural society in which minority and ethnic groups differ in the emphasis they place on traditional values of the majority culture. Contemporary American society is also stratified, and the various social classes do not exhibit the same esteem for all behaviors prized by schools. For example, American Indian and Hispanic cultures have had a more casual attitude toward time than the middle-class Caucasian society. As a result, they cherish punctuality less, and their children may not understand the school's demand that homework be turned in on time.

Economically and socially challenged at-risk youngsters seldom have the future orientation that is the ordinary time frame of the middle class. Living for the immediate moment and letting tomorrow take care of itself is an attitude sure to be in conflict with schools that require planning and a postponement of rewards. Some ethnic groups may discourage competition, even when schools encourage it. Urban African-American youngsters are not apt to appear neat to white teachers, even when their appearance is quite acceptable to their parents and peers. The "macho" image many socially and economically challenged boys need to create for peer acceptance makes them seem rude and loud in school. Expression of sexual interest may be tolerated and encouraged within some communities in ways likely to be unacceptable and punished in middle-class schools. Extreme concern about respect for property and the need to be still while others speak may be more difficult for students with no experience in valuing such behavior.

Puritans were not tolerant of any violation of their social norms. They were quick to condemn and punish any who dared to challenge the authority of the institutions or to break the rules. Middle-class teachers may insist upon modern versions of the Puritan ethic, but many students find that ethic incompatible with their own cultural backgrounds. The critical literature on contemporary education indicates that children of ethnic groups and minorities are more likely to fail in school if the school attempts to teach values foreign to them. This is the message of Ebonics supporters.

Of course, Puritans did not believe in democracy; however, modern education must attempt to promote democratic values in order to deal constructively and creatively with the confusions and conflicts of the modern world. Puritans also had the church, the family, and the local community in absolute support of their educational efforts, while contemporary schools exist in an environment of special interests and conflicting beliefs.

Multidimensional Values. Not all middle-class people from the dominant culture support the traditional values of the schools. Sociologists say that there are emerging values in American culture that are in conflict with the traditional ones. The family as a socialization agent often needs additional support, and as that duty is passed to schools, the schools need support. Single-parent households often struggle to make ends meet, relying on schools to pick up some of the child-care duties. These are examples of emergent values in conflict with traditional ones. The peer subculture of American adolescents is unconcerned with older traditional belief systems. Rock and roll, rap, punk, freaking, grinding, booty dancing, the nasty, hip hop and funk music; experimentation with drugs; and permissive attitudes toward sex often reflect the interests of teenagers. Educators strive to encourage healthy lifestyles through sex and drug education. Some parents find these efforts in conflict with their values systems.

Another potent force in value formation is the mass media. Television and the Internet may foster values in conflict with those of traditional schools and the Puritan ethic. A few television programs may urge people to immediately gratify their every desire, to "buy now and pay later," and to enjoy life without concern for future consequences. Many members of the modern society have little faith that honesty really is the best policy or that patriotism is a higher value than individual gratification. Computer software such as "cyberpatrol" is designed to block student access to offensive material, and educators are working to assist students in developing critical and selective viewing skills.

Dissolution of the traditional family unit with its support network, single-parent families, multiple partner parents, the challenges of AIDS (HIV), teenage suicide, teenage pregnancy, an increase in crime (on and off school campuses), random violence, children killing or maiming other children, children whose health has been affected by parental use of drugs, and inner-city riots that wipe out a lifetime of savings in a matter of minutes are part of the American culture of the twenty-first century. Reports of child abuse grew exponentially in the early 2000s, and there are few solutions in sight. The harsh youth discipline of Puritan days, acceptable then, would be classified and reported as child abuse today. Whatever the causes of these challenges to the social fabric—whether increased unemployment, lack of skills to cope with an increasingly complex society, emotional instability, or uncontrollable drug use—there are ever growing numbers of families and children at risk. These challenges lead to social fragmentation that conflicts with the goals of consensus and social unity in democracy. To deal with these issues, there are increasingly strident calls for character, values, and moral education in our schools.

Minority, single-parent, and nontraditional families are less likely to agree with the Puritan ethic than middle-class, majority culture parents. If they do agree with the ethic, they are less able to reinforce the values of schools at home. Some Americans reflect the fierce independence shown by the early colonists. An example is the litigation known as *Wisconsin v. Yoder* (1972), in which Amish families won exemption for children from the compulsory education laws of the state. Like early colonists, the Amish were willing to challenge secular authority on religious grounds and to define their own values. Another example is the home-school movement. Some parents wish to teach their children at home in order to "protect" them from values taught at school. Vouchers and charter schools are available in many states to increase parental school choice and to cut down on local, state, and federal regulations.

Some educators also believe the school should work for diversity, tolerance, open-mindedness, and the development of self-concept. They do not agree with the function of transmitting an authoritative body of knowledge, and they do not want the school to impose values on children. Nevertheless, modern American schools still reflect many Puritan values, as seen in current reform reports calling for effort, work, and discipline.

It remains to be seen just how effective the schools will be in supporting traditional values or in teaching emerging ones. It may be that some of the Puritan values are not at all appropriate for a future learning society in which leisure and cooperation are envisioned. Schools tend to be quite conservative, but there are many other institutions that carry cultural values. In Puritan America, the family and the church supported values taught in schools. Contemporary society finds the schools often in conflict with such agents as the mass media and advertising.

At present, the Moral Majority, the Christian Coalition, and other fundamentalist conservative religious groups support some of the values of the Puritan ethic; other groups push for diversity, free choice, and multiculturalism. President George W. Bush stressed family values during his election campaign. Laurel Walters, in his article "Religious Right Win Seats on School Boards Across the US," noted that religious right candidates won school board elections in twelve states in 1992–1993. People for the American Way also are working to elect school board candidates to represent their point of view. These groups represent increased public interest in education decision making. Both groups are active as we enter a new millennium. Tolerance and an appreciation of the energy and contributions of a diverse population are essential in our democratic society. Kansas school authorities recently reinstated the teaching of evolution after it had been replaced by creation science by conservative interest groups. This demonstrates the continual pendulum swinging between conservative and liberal interest groups and its effect on public schools.

Historical Perspective.   Educators need to understand the historical link with the colonial past. Although the Puritan heritage can be overemphasized, its contributions are important in understanding the present culture and preparing for a viable future. Beliefs of the early settlers of colonial New England still cast a shadow over values in the modern American society. Those who do not appreciate this historical fact are ill prepared to understand the value conflicts that are central to so many modern educational issues.

GAINING PERSPECTIVE THROUGH CRITICAL ANALYSIS

1. What does the Old Deluder Satan Act of 1647 demonstrate about the relationship between religion and education? (A review of the chapter opening quotation will help you with your answer.)
2. Compare and contrast the roles of religion and social class on colonial education and on education today.
3. How did the culture and history of the Southern colonies make educational practice different from education in the New England and Middle colonies?
4. Identify the goals of the tutorial, old field, dame, and charity schools. Compare the goals of these colonial schools with the goals of public schools today.
5. What reasons can you give for the differences between school discipline in colonial times and discipline in public schools today?
6. Compare educational facilities, instruction method, and curriculum content in colonial days with the current state of education.

HISTORY IN ACTION IN TODAY'S CLASSROOMS

1. Find an example of multicultural literature that "fits" the melting pot theory. Share the book with your class and describe why you chose it. (See Glossary)
2. Interview a teacher or an administrator. Ask him or her about school discipline in the past and present. What are his or her opinions about civility, responsibility, and character education in the past and present? Add these findings to your journal.
3. Define core values, alternative values and culture lag (covered in Chapter 1). Show how these terms apply to colonial education and to a modern multicultural school setting.
4. Define the theory of cultural lag. Write a brief dialogue or drama that exemplifies this theory in practice.

INCREASED UNDERSTANDING THROUGH ONLINE RESEARCH

Visit the Prentice Hall Foundations Web site (*http://www.prenhall.com/foundations-cluster*) and examine Topics 4 and 10. Using the resources available in these topics, find examples of multicultural literature that reflect the melting pot, salad bowl, and mosaic theories. Write and submit your response to your instructor using the Electronic Bluebook module also in either of these two topics of the Web site.

BIBLIOGRAPHY

Butts, R. Freeman, and Lawrence A. Cremin. *A History of Education in American Culture.* New York: Rinehart and Winston, 1953.

Church, Robert. *Education in the United States: An Interpretive History.* New York: The Free Press, 1977.

Cohen, Sheldon. *A History of Colonial Education, 1607–1776.* New York: Wiley, 1974.

Curti, Merle. *The Social Ideas of American Educators.* Patterson, NJ: Littlefield, Adams, 1959.

Edwards, Newton, and Herman G. Richey. *The School in the American Social Order.* Boston: Houghton Mifflin, 1963.

Eggen, Paul D., and Donald Kauchak. *Educational Psychology.* New York: Prentice Hall, 2000.

Ford, Paul Leicester, ed. *The New England Primer.* New York: Dodd, Mead and Co., 1987, 22, 123.

Gay, Geneva. *At the Essence of Learning: Multicultural Education.* West Lafayette, IN: Kappa Delta Pi, 1994.

Good, Harry, and James Teller. *A History of American Education.* 2d ed. New York: Macmillan, 1973.

Havinghurst, Robert, and Daniel Levine. *Society and Education.* 5th ed. Boston: Allyn and Bacon, 1975.

Jernegan, Marcus. *Laboring and Dependent Classes in Colonial America, 1607–1783.* New York: Frederick Ungar, 1960.

Knight, Edgar W. *Education in the United States.* Boston: Ginn and Co., 1951.

Lefrancois, Guy R. *Theories of Learning: What the Old Man Said.* New York: Thomson Learning, 2000.

Mill, J. S. *On Liberty.* London: J. S. Parker and Son, 1859, 190–91.

Miller, Perry, ed. *The American Puritans: Their Prose and Poetry.* Garden City, NY: Doubleday, 1956.

Morrison, Samuel Eliot. *The Intellectual Life of Colonial New England.* New York: New York University Press, 1956.

Potter, Robert. *The Stream of American Education.* New York: American Book Company, 1967.

Rippa, S. Alexander. *Education in a Free Society: An American History.* 7th ed. New York: Longman, 1992.

Rippa, S. Alexander, ed. *Educational Ideas in America: A Documentary History.* New York: David McKay, 1969.

Van Til, William. *Education: A Beginning.* Boston: Houghton Mifflin, 1974.

Victoria, Irwin. "Prayer and Giggles During 'Silent Moment.'" *Christian Science Monitor* (December 11, 2000): 1, 9.

Walters, Laurel. "Religious Right Win Seats on School Boards Across the US." *Christian Science Monitor* (August 9, 1993):1, 20.

Warren, Donald, ed. *History, Education, and Public Policy.* Berkeley, CA: McCutchan, 1978.

Woolfolk, Anita E. *Educational Psychology.* New York: Allyn and Bacon, 2000.

CHAPTER FOUR

AMERICAN EDUCATION:
THE AMERICAN REVOLUTION

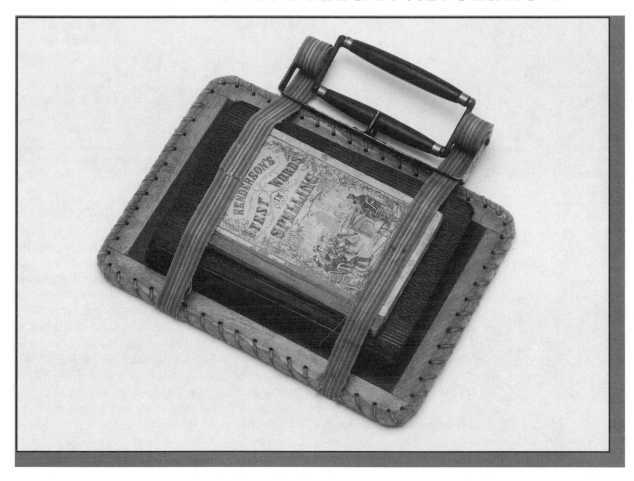

Although I do not, with some enthusiasts, believe that the human condition will ever advance to such a state of perfection as that there shall no longer be pain or vice in the world, yet I believe it susceptible of much improvement, and most of all, in matters of government and religion, and that the diffusion of knowledge among the people is to be the instrument by which it is to be effected.

Thomas Jefferson

American Revolution		
1776 Declaration of Independence	1780 English Sunday school founded by Robert Raikes	1785 Northwest Ordinance Land Grant
Thomas Paine's *Common Sense*	1781 Battle of Yorktown	1787 Constitutional Convention
Adam Smith's *Wealth of Nations*	1783 Treaty of Paris ended war with England	1789 Constitution accepted without mentioning education

Figure 4.1   Time Line from the American Revolution to the War of 1812

Before the time of the Revolutionary War, the population of the American colonies had grown to more than 2.5 million people. An expanding frontier fostered perseverance, ingenuity, self-confidence, and a defiant individualism among the Western settlers. This frontier character was unique to America, as was the mixture of nationalities and religions found in the Middle colonies. The district system with its decentralization and local control continued to dominate New England schools before and after the Revolution, and the idea of free, compulsory, universal education was central to the ideal of self-government there. Although schools varied widely in number and quality in the New England colonies and later in the New England states, America looked to Massachusetts, Rhode Island, and Connecticut for educational leadership. Religious denominational or parochial schools remained common in the Middle colonies until the country became independent, but such sectarian schools were weakened by the withdrawal of English financial support and by the separation of church and state. Please refer to Figure 4.1 for a time line from the American Revolution to the War of 1812.

DEMOCRATIC IDEALS

The rising tide of democracy threatened a dual system of education in which the elite enjoyed good schools and the masses were largely ignored. This factor accounts for the shrinking influence of Latin grammar schools and the vast growth of the academy. The revolutionary period saw academies—with their emphasis on practical subjects such as bookkeeping, navigation, and surveying—increase in popularity. Town schools in the most populated areas and even crude schools of the remote frontier settlements became more numerous as the eighteenth century closed, and

French Revolution		War of 1812
1791 Bill of Rights ratified	1798 Joseph Lancaster and Andrew Bell start Monitorial Schools	1805 New York Free School Society
Philadelphia Sunday School Society	1802 West Point	1806 New York Monitorial Schools
	1803 Louisiana Purchase	1812 State Superintendent appointed in New York

such educational institutions did not cater to an aristocracy. Southern educational patterns altered little during the revolutionary era, except that students did not study in England and many of the charity schools were closed.

CHANGES IN COLONIAL CULTURE

American capitalism provided general growth and prosperity in the economic order and in intercolonial trade before the Revolution. New York, Boston, Philadelphia, and Charleston became large cities with sophisticated populations interested in all sorts of European ideas. There was a diffusion of culture between the various parts of the colonies, as well as much travel and correspondence. Newspapers like the *Boston News Letter* and other periodicals such as *Poor Richard's Almanac*, published by Benjamin Franklin, stimulated colonial intellectual life. At the outbreak of hostilities in 1775, there were thirty-seven newspapers in regular publication.

College, private, and city libraries were found throughout the colonies, although many did not permit the free circulation of books. Subscription libraries were available at a small fee. Only a few Americans published books before the Revolution, but British volumes were for sale in most large towns. Bookstalls had the works of Bacon, Locke, Boyle, Newton, Swift, Milton, Hume, Voltaire, and Addison, among others. Learned professions like law and medicine made progress in the late eighteenth century and gained in respect. Experiments in science and medicine were as popular as speculation in philosophy. The American Philosophical Society, which developed from a proposal by Franklin, brought Americans into contact with the learned world of Europe. Not many colonial minds were on a par with the cosmopolitan Benjamin Franklin or the theologian–philosopher Jonathan Edwards, but there were well educated, widely read, cultured Americans before the Revolution. Leaders in public life like Patrick Henry, John Adams, and Thomas Jefferson were much influenced by intellectual changes in Europe.

THE SHIFT IN THE COLONIAL MIND

Dissatisfaction with conditions in Europe was one reason for the first American settlements, but this feeling shifted to dissatisfaction with English colonial policies such as mercantile capitalism. The American Revolution was a combination of native efforts and contributions from foreign thinkers and movements. Political philosophers like John Locke and Jean Jacques Rousseau, whose effect on education was both direct and indirect, provided the rationale for the American experiment in self-government.

Locke's Influence.   The English philosopher John Locke (1632–1704) not only provided a theoretical basis for the Declaration of Independence but also contributed to American educational thought. Locke's political ideas concerning the inalienable rights of humanity and the contract relationship between a people and its government were accepted almost without qualification by Thomas Jefferson and other leaders in the movement for independence. The high reputation Locke enjoyed among Americans caused his philosophical writings to be widely circulated in the colonies and later in the United States. Locke had severely altered the direction of educational thought through his denial of the existence of innate ideas and his insistence that the mind at birth is passive and like a blank tablet (tabula rasa) upon which experience writes. He believed that all our ideas come from experience and that the measure of the truth of an idea is its correspondence with concrete, objective, commonsense reality (empirical principle). Emphasis on experience, good study habits, a utilitarian curriculum, and sense-realism aided the scientific and practical elements in American education.

Franklin's belief in self-education for practical utility, his broad interest in empirical science, and his desire to provide educational opportunity for anyone who wanted to learn were all in keeping with Locke's theories. The emergence of a strong middle class with large numbers of lawyers and merchants was an event of the late colonial period that helped to support the ideas of Locke. Franklin and Locke emphasized the secular aspects of education as opposed to the ecclesiasticism of the schools supported by religious organizations. Although sectionalism, a lack of money, disunity, and religious sectarianism prevented any common educational program in colonial America, the theoretical foundation for free, universal, and public schools was laid.

Comenius.   (Komenski) An outstanding spokesperson for the power of education in improving the human condition was John Amos Comenius (1592–1671). Born in the village of Nivnitz in Moravia, Comenius became bishop of the Moravian Brethren, a Hussite religious sect persecuted by both Lutherans and Catholics. In spite of exile, the murder of his family, and the destruction of his library, Comenius managed to develop a philosophy of education and to write some of the most influential schoolbooks produced in Europe. His *Great Didactic* and *Door of the Languages Unlocked* (an introduction to Latin grammar) were produced while he was rector of the Gymnasium at Lissa, Poland. Influential Englishmen invited Comenius to present his plan for universal knowledge and a world university to Parliament, but the English Civil War of 1642 prevented his appearance. For six years he wrote textbooks for Latin schools in Sweden and later established a school at Sanosptak, Hungary. There, Comenius developed his idea of schools in graded order from "the school at the mother's knee" to the university. In 1658, while living in Amsterdam, he published his *Orbis Sensualism Pictus*, the first popular illustrated textbook for children. Cotton Mather claimed that Comenius was invited to become president of Harvard in 1654. He was a highly respected educator whose ideas fell on fertile soil in America.

Although the religious background of Comenius caused him to accept the doctrine of original sin, he agreed with Locke that ideas come from experience and that our sense organs are our teachers. This sense-realism lent support to empirical investigation, practical education, and the potential of science. Comenius believed that war could be prevented if scholars were brought together to work out solutions to international problems. To this end he proposed a pansophic university with functions faintly similar to those of the United Nations. He felt that universal education could improve civilization through the discovery and dissemination of practical information on subjects such as economics, medicine, agriculture, and sanitation.

Although a linguist himself, Comenius believed that primary instruction should be given in the vernacular. He encouraged the publication of dictionaries, textbooks, and encyclopedias in order to simplify instruction. He thought that a science of education was possible and that teachers could be trained to practice it. Comenius influenced American education through his textbooks, his support for science, and his belief that education must be practical. The growth of the academy and the concept of self-education made popular by Franklin were also part of the educational theory of Comenius.

Impact of European Movements.

The sense-realism of Comenius, the empiricism of Locke, and the scientific movement in Europe paved the way for new conceptions of people and society. The verbal or humanistic realism of John Milton advocated encyclopedic studies and general education. In place of the narrow religious view and conservatism of the New England Puritans, Englishmen were substituting a secular, realistic, liberal worldview.

The life of the mind in the American colonies varied from theological arguments in the early Puritan settlements to broad scientific and secular issues addressed by men like Franklin in the urban centers of the Middle colonies. The scientific revolution of seventeenth-century Europe reached America by degrees and had a major impact after 1750. Findings of the Royal Society of London for Improving Natural Knowledge excited American interests and stimulated discussion, especially of the physical sciences. Empiricism, sense-realism, and scientific discovery foreshadowed the movement of the late seventeenth and early eighteenth centuries known as the Enlightenment.

The Enlightenment was a rational, liberal, humanistic, and scientific trend in thought that vastly altered the climate of opinion in Europe. It was grounded in the natural and social theories of Comenius and Locke but found new expression in the works of Diderot, Voltaire, Rousseau, Hume, Paine, and Kant. Kant described the Enlightenment as the liberation of man from his self-caused state of minority. The Enlightenment was a protest against authority that insisted upon man's ability to understand the universe without divine revelation. It held that men as individuals have worth and dignity and that they are able to judge truth for themselves. It fostered belief in a universe governed by natural law that reason could penetrate. The Enlightenment was a protest against both the authority of Christian dogma and absolute monarchs. Its leaders sought a balanced social order free from the control of a single powerful class.

Enlightenment thought favored autonomous economic enterprise and parliamentary forms of government. It created an attitude of distrust for despotic monarchs and all other forms of strong centralized government. British mercantile capitalism, which exploited colonies as sources of raw materials and dumping grounds for surplus manufactured goods, was attacked by the theorists of the Enlightenment. Scottish economist Adam Smith, with his ideas of value placed on labor, *laissez-faire,* and a free market, appealed to leaders of the Enlightenment.

Humanism looked to the past, through a study of classics, for solutions to problems of the world. Great interest was shown in the social and governmental arrangements of ancient Greece and Rome. Men like Jefferson used classical models for the new republic and for institutions such as the University of Virginia. Sense-realism placed humankind (not God) at the focal point and sought knowledge through ordinary experience or scientific observation. American revolutionary leaders were much influenced by books written by liberals like the humanitarian Montesquieu. Cultural changes of the Enlightenment helped to plant the ideas that grew in the fertile soil of a comparatively free society and that became the timber of revolution. It should also be remembered that more than 150 years of colonial growth and development before the Revolution provided ample time for a major alteration of values and beliefs. The intellectual climate of 1776 was far different from that of 1620.

COLONIAL LIBERALISM

By no means were all of the colonial settlers conservative and narrow in their beliefs, in spite of restrictions imposed by Puritan and Anglican authorities. James Oglethorpe proposed colonization of Georgia as an experiment in humanitarianism after he had visited English prisons. The Quakers of Pennsylvania were not only tolerant of other religious beliefs but also concerned about the dignity and worth of all persons without regard to color, creed, or social position. Catholics in Maryland brought a different tradition to America, and they were hardly in a position to resist religious freedom.

The Puritans were outspoken in their opposition to secular authority that overran the "just bounds" that they defined as God's word and the common interest, although they were not willing to grant religious freedom. Even so, Roger Williams, Thomas Hooker, Jonathan Mayhew, and John Wise were Puritans who dissented from church authority with considerable success. Puritan schools were dominated by orthodox teachers like Ezekiel Cheever, who was praised by Cotton Mather as much for his preaching as for his pedagogy; but tolerance and liberalism became widespread ideals before the Revolution.

Other systems of thought had considerable influence on the cultural climate before the United States emerged as a nation. The Puritan theologian Jonathan Edwards was hard pressed to defend his religion against science. Samuel Johnson was attracted to the idealism of Bishop Berkeley, while deism (the belief that God created the world and then withdrew to let it operate according to natural law) was popular with many intellectuals. The naturalism of Rousseau and his concept of government were known in America, although his influence on education was severely curtailed by the conservative reaction that followed the war for independence. Adam Smith's *Wealth of Nations* appeared in 1776 and became the basic economic theory of the new nation. Thomas Paine was one of the great champions of the American Revolution because of such writings as *Common Sense,* which had an enormous circulation and which proclaimed independence. However, Paine's *Age of Reason* was considered radical in the conservative period that followed the Revolution, and its author lost his influence in the United States.

EDUCATIONAL CHANGES IN THE LATER COLONIAL PERIOD

Several of the colonial colleges were founded in what could be called the revolutionary era. Harvard College, William and Mary College, Yale College, and the College of New Jersey were founded between 1636 and 1746. King's College, the College of Philadelphia, the College of Rhode Island, Queen's College, and Dartmouth College were all founded between 1750 and 1776. Some of the political leaders in the movement for freedom from England were products of the colonial colleges, which were basically conservative institutions. The total enrollment of the nine colonial colleges operating on the eve of the Revolution was about 750 students.

On the secondary level, Latin grammar schools declined in importance with respect to the academy. Academies were more democratic in organization and far more geared to the needs of an expanding economy. Franklin's first effort at Philadelphia in 1751 was secular, practical, and widely copied. Courses in Latin and Greek were included in some academies, but modern languages, including French and German, were more popular. Gauging, drawing in perspective, merchant's accounts, logic, chronology, astronomy, and rhetoric were added to the older subjects of history, geography, bookkeeping, writing, surveying, and navigation.

Academies and some private venture secondary schools flourished in the larger towns in the decades before the war. As colonial interest shifted from religion to shipping, commerce, and agriculture, civil town governments became more important in education. Many efforts were made to obtain town schools in which children without means could receive rudimentary training, and town schools often had secondary departments for those who could pay.

Elementary schools continued to operate with crude instruction and equipment. Several factors led to the decline of certain kinds of schools, but the educational tradition continued. The early New England writing school, which had never been in great demand, expired before the Revolution. In Pennsylvania, the SPG gave up in disgust after 1763, and the decline of New England theocracies made schools more difficult to support. Massachusetts, Connecticut, and Rhode Island did not abandon efforts to educate all the children. But some towns were without schools, and many provided them for only a few winter months. Denominational efforts such as the Reverend William Tennant's Log College (a classical secondary school for training Presbyterian preachers) declined after 1742. Nevertheless, elementary education was provided for most colonial children who could pay a small fee. A larger and more prosperous population gave rise to more schools in the Middle colonies than had been the case earlier.

THE WAR AND AFTER

The Revolutionary War directed men's energies away from education and science, as De Witt Clinton observed years later. Illiteracy increased because rural schools had to close their doors and because even the larger town Latin grammar schools were crippled. British occupation of New York caused schools to be abandoned there. New England schools continued to operate, but they suffered from a lack of funds and teachers.

Higher education was restricted in part because many talented teachers were Loyalists. Books were scarce because many of them came from England and because colonial printers could not maintain their presses without outside English supplies. Yale College was broken up into groups centered in different towns, and Harvard's buildings and those of the College of Rhode Island housed provincial troops. Dartmouth had neither money nor books, and classes had to be discontinued at the College of Philadelphia. The Colleges of New Jersey and William and Mary also suffered but were not closed.

British support, as in the case of the Anglican SPG, was cut off and never revived. Lack of money and the interruption of the normal economic process made the operation of educational institutions almost impossible. Teachers and scholars joined the fighting forces, and school buildings were converted into barracks. Tory or Loyalist teachers were turned out of their schools. Sometimes the schools were burned and libraries were scattered or destroyed. Nevertheless, the conflict was restricted to certain parts of the colonial territory, and areas that escaped destruction continued with education. Peace allowed for a restoration of many schools, even though the money was scarce and authority uncertain.

Sway of Independence.

The Revolution dealt harsh blows to intellectual life in America, but it also provided the seeds for intellectual activity independent of Europe. As long as the colonists were tied to the value system of the mother country, it was almost impossible for the native culture to rival the established and sophisticated English life of the mind. But the Revolution broke those ties and stimulated considerable literary activity, expressed in antimonarchical and pro-democratic pamphlets and books. Further, the heroes of the Revolution were elevated to a dignified and popular social and political status in the new nation. Their ideas gained immediate support. Many revolutionary leaders attempted to put ideas central to the struggle for liberty—such as natural rights, freedom, equality, patriotism, and resistance to tyranny—into the laws. A free press and freedom of speech called attention to the need for schools if the new government of the people was to be successful.

EFFORTS OF EDUCATIONAL FOUNDERS

Many of the men who contributed to the birth of the new nation had plans for schools or other educational institutions. For a variety of reasons, including the national debt of $75 million (which seemed a staggering sum at the time) and Federalist conservatism, few of these plans were actually realized.

Freedom of Religion.

Patrick Henry first became involved in the struggle for religious freedom in 1763, when he defended a group of Virginia farmers against Anglican ministers who were suing for their back pay. He lost the suit, but the jury fixed the pay of the ministers at one penny, which was a victory for the opponents of established religion. James Madison and Thomas Jefferson carried the banner of freedom of religion during the war. They offered a bill in 1776 to exempt dissenters from paying the church tax. In 1779 Jefferson sponsored a bill establishing religious freedom, but it was unsuccessful. Patrick Henry proposed a law in the Virginia legislature that would have provided tax support for Teachers of the Christian Religion, without regard to denomination. Madison feared the creation of a "multiple establishment of religion," and in 1785 he managed to push through Jefferson's earlier proposal. Virginia became the first state to have a law guaranteeing freedom of religion. Jefferson returned from his mission in France in 1787. Finding no constitutional guarantees for individual rights, he refused to support ratification of the Constitution without the series of amendments known as the Bill of Rights.

The First Amendment specifically prevented Congress from making any law respecting the establishment of religion or prohibiting religious practice. Connecticut, Maryland, Massachusetts, and New Hampshire did have constitutional provisions for tax-supported religion, but they abolished these provisions by 1833. Although the long-range effects of disestablishment and religious freedom were beneficial to public schools, the immediate result was to take away public funds that had been used to support church-related schools. Separation of church and state also gave rise to educational problems that persist today, such as the issue over prayer and Bible reading in public schools. Nevertheless, sectarian control over public education was broken by the provision for religious freedom.

National University.   James Madison and Charles Pinckney attempted to include in the Constitution a provision for a national university. Although it failed, several national leaders including Washington expressed interest in the idea. His farewell speech to the army emphasized the need for the promotion and diffusion of knowledge. Several times Washington attempted to get Congress to establish a national university, and he left part of his estate to the proposed institution. John Jay, James Monroe, and John Quincy Adams shared the desire for a national university with Washington, Jefferson, and Madison. The university was never built, partly because Congress failed to act and partly because of legal and financial arguments.

Plans for a National System.   Despite the omission of education from the Constitution, revolutionary statesmen made a number of proposals for a national school system. In 1795, the American Philosophical Society offered a prize for the best essay on the subject of a national system of education. Many plans were submitted including those of Benjamin Rush, Noah Webster, Samuel Smith, Samuel Knox, and Pierre DuPont de Nemours. Knox and Rush shared the prize. All these plans were founded on the theory that a public system of education is necessary for a free and self-governing republic. Consideration was given in the plans for public control, public support, a practical curriculum, compulsory attendance, and all levels of schools including a national university. The plans differed; however, one in particular, designed by Rush, offered a very extensive system with supervision of schools and academies for teacher training. Support for an American school system also came from essayists such as Robert Coram of Delaware and Revolutionary War officer Nathaniel Chipman. In spite of the interest, Congress rejected all plans for a national system.

REVOLUTIONARY PERIOD EDUCATIONAL LEADERSHIP

Many men aided the cause of schools during the period of the American Revolution. Benjamin Franklin lent his great prestige to all intellectual and cultural causes, although he supported practical self-education more than public schools. Benjamin Rush, a signer of the Declaration of Independence, wrote numerous essays on education, in addition to his plan for a national system. Perhaps the most important influence of the era came from Noah Webster and Thomas Jefferson.

Noah Webster.   Known as the "Schoolmaster to America" because of the popularity of his textbooks, Noah Webster (1758–1843) was a major educational force for many years. His *Compendious Dictionary* (1806) was the first of a series of dictionaries and lexicons that made his name a household word in the United States. While keeping a classical school in New York, Webster began his *Grammatical Institute of the English Language,* of which the first section, often revised, became the famous "blue-backed speller." It is estimated that this book had sold 19 million copies by the time of Webster's death, and by all measures it was the most successful textbook ever produced in America. He also wrote books on grammar, reading, and history, all with a strong patriotic and nationalistic flavor. As a young man, Webster was caught up in the liberal ideas of the Enlightenment and the Revolution. He supported free schools, a national language as a band of union, and separation of church and state.

The French Revolution shocked Webster, and he repudiated his earlier republican principles in favor of conservative federalism. His later works stressed religious morality, respect for government, and a patriotism that sometimes bordered upon the fanatic. He believed that all books, schools, masters, and programs for the schools of the republic should be strictly American and even suggested that the first word taught to an infant should be *Washington.* Webster called for strict teaching and supported traditional methods of instruction, but he was against corporal punishment. He wanted education for girls because they would be the mothers of future citizens and the teachers of youth. Webster felt that no legislature should ignore the need for free schools in which all American children could learn the virtues of liberty, just laws, morality, hard work, and patriotism.

Thomas Jefferson.   Jefferson's contribution to education would constitute ample material for an entire book. He provided the ideology for extending educational opportunity to all citizens and argued that no democratic society is safe without an educated population. For more than fifty years, Jefferson was personally active in efforts to put his educational theory into actual practice. As a young man he worked to reform the schools of Virginia, while much of his old age was devoted to building the University of Virginia. The basic theme of Jefferson's educational policy was academic excellence with equality of opportunity for all. He was not, like Hamilton, a supporter of strong federal government, and therefore his efforts to improve schools were on a local and state level. Jefferson did not agree with the schemes for a national system of education, although he did not oppose a national university.

Jefferson's *Bill for More General Diffusion of Knowledge* in Virginia was widely circulated and used as a model. The plan called for a state system of free elementary schools with local control. Secondary schools were to be tuition institutions, with a provision for scholarships to meet the needs of poor but gifted boys. A state university was to crown the educational system. Jefferson submitted three bills to the Virginia Assembly, but he was not successful in passing any of his proposals except that for the University of Virginia. His effort to overcome the danger of an ignorant populace was very modest; the bill called for only three years of public schooling. His organizational pattern with decentralized control and localization of financial responsibility became popular even though Virginia failed to adopt the plan. For example, Edward Coles became governor of Illinois in 1818 and promptly submitted a plan for a school system in that state that borrowed many of Jefferson's ideas.

After attempting to reform the College of William and Mary, Jefferson became convinced that an entirely new university was required. Few institutions have reflected one person's views as closely as the University of Virginia reflected those of Thomas Jefferson. Not only was he the driving force for the creation of the university, but he organized the curriculum, hired the faculty, planned many of the buildings, purchased and catalogued the books for the library, and generally supervised the entire operation. In 1825, Jefferson saw his creation open with forty students. The University of Virginia became the first state university and the first one with a "modern" curriculum.

EARLY GOVERNMENT PROPOSALS

It was the prevailing view of the founding fathers that while knowledge was the best guardian of liberty, education did not belong in federal hands. James Madison wanted a general tax for schools, and Samuel Knox argued that private schools were subversive in a republic. But such reasoning did not convince the Constitutional Convention. The Constitution, therefore, contains no reference to education, although the First Amendment and the Tenth Amendment ensure state control and nonsectarian public schools. Other measures significant in the development of education came out of the early national period.

Early National Legislation.   In 1785, Congress outlined regulations for the national territory west of the Alleghenies, north of the Ohio River, and east of the Mississippi River. This Northwest Territory was to be laid out in townships consisting of thirty-six sections. By the Ordinance of 1785 (also called the Northwest Ordinance), the sixteenth section (one square mile) in each township in the territory was reserved for the support of schools within the township. A second Ordinance two years later authorized not more than two full townships in each new state to be reserved for a university. The act contained a statement that schools and education should forever be encouraged for the benefit of human happiness and good government. These acts became a precedent for land grants to the states for public schools and colleges. By later acts, most new states entering the Union received federal land for educational purposes.

In 1802, Congress established the national military academy at West Point. This was the first of many federal acts that created special educational institutions with specialized functions. West Point had the first American training center for engineers.

State Efforts.   Seven of the state constitutions adopted before 1800 mentioned education. Those of Pennsylvania, North Carolina, and Vermont called for the establishment of schools in each county, with some public financial support. The Pennsylvania Constitution, accepted in 1776, became a model for several others. It required that the state pay salaries of teachers in public schools. New Hampshire and Massachusetts stressed the need for wisdom and knowledge as a means of preserving liberty, but their constitutions did not require schools. Massachusetts legalized its traditional local district school system and in 1789 admitted girls to district schools. New York made public lands and certain other funds available to free schools.

Before 1812, the Union had grown considerably with the purchase of the Louisiana Territory in 1803 and the admission of the new states of Vermont, Kentucky, Tennessee, Ohio, and Louisiana. The constitutions for these states all indicated some concern about education, and several set up a system of schools that was enacted into law. As the nation grew, each new state adopted a constitution modeled after those that were admitted earlier. Having educational provisions in the state constitutions became a tradition.

OTHER EDUCATIONAL MOVEMENTS

Lacking public school systems and the ability to obtain laws for education, a number of leaders tried to support schools by other means. Many church-related institutions continued to offer charity education as they had in the colonial period.

Monitorial Schools.   Monitorial schools originated in England through the work of Joseph Lancaster and Andrew Bell. This type of school provided for inexpensive education that could be given to the masses by a minimum teaching staff. Students of ability were selected as monitors or student teachers, and the master instructed these monitors. The monitors, in turn, taught the lessons they had learned to small groups of pupils. Simple lessons were memorized, and slates or chalkboards were used. The Lancasterian monitorial system allowed one teacher to instruct hundreds of children. One of these schools appeared in New York City in 1806, and the idea spread. Lancaster himself came to America in 1818; while in America, he promoted his mass education program until 1830. After 1830, complaints of "factory" type schools, excessive uniformity, and inability of monitors to maintain discipline led to the eventual demise of the monitorial school.

Sunday Schools.   Another English educational plan introduced in America was the Sunday school. Not a church school in the modern sense, the purpose of the Sunday school was to provide basic education to the poor. Its champion was Robert Raikes of Gloucester. Raikes wanted to rescue children of factory workers from their filth, ignorance, and sin. Since the children worked in the mills all week, schools could be provided only on Sundays. Several religious groups, especially Methodists, supported the Sunday school with money and teachers. Children were supervised and given instruction in rudimentary principles during their free time on the Sabbath.

In 1791, a Sunday School Society was organized in Philadelphia. American Sunday schools developed in most of the major cities. They were primarily for the poor but were not confined to factory or mill workers. Generally, the schools operated from six to ten o'clock on Sunday morning and again from two to six in the afternoon, leaving time for worship. Although they could hardly have provided more than the bare fundamentals of education, these institutions taught many children to read.

Free School Societies.   School societies were organized to develop monitorial schools, Sunday schools, and free public schools in certain areas. The Connecticut school societies were authorized to be district school authorities, while the New York

Free School Society promoted several types of education. The New York group founded schools for girls and for the poor; the group later became the Public School Society of New York. It was assumed in this period that students who could afford private schools would attend them, and indeed they did. Public schools and free schools carried the stigma of poverty because they were charity institutions.

SCHOOL IDEAS AND THE CURRICULUM

Independence brought about the development of a native American culture and a set of national institutions. Education was a reflection of this new spirit, as were self-reliance, optimism, individualism, and democracy. Farmers wanted more education for their children because education was a mark of achievement and a step up the social ladder. The population of the new nation grew rapidly, increasing more than tenfold in a single century after the Revolution. Much of this growth came through immigration from European nations other than England. For these new citizens, education was the means of becoming "real Americans."

Improvements in transportation brought about social consciousness that was lacking in isolated colonies. This social consciousness fostered an exchange of ideas and a national feeling that aided schooling. The start of the American Industrial Revolution shifted many people from rural to city areas, especially in the Northeast. Factory workers created special needs for free elementary education on a much larger scale. Doctrines of freedom and equality gave rise to free speech and a free press, which in turn fostered democracy.

But there was also a conservative reaction to the War for Independence. Those who feared the education of the masses and federal control opposed liberals who fought for a free public system on the national level. Lack of money and opposition to direct taxation prevented the building even of a national university. However, there was keen interest in the building of state universities, and these universities became a unique American cornerstone of higher education. Educational interest was also expressed in state constitutions, land grants, school societies, and philanthropy. The start of free public schools for all the people can be found in the period before the War of 1812.

Separation of church and state did not take religion out of the schools. Both sectarian and public schools of the revolutionary era continued to use textbooks that were religiously centered. The Bible and the *New England Primer* were by no means expelled. Use of Cheever's *Accidence*, the *Westminster Catechism*, and the *Psalter* continued in New England schools after independence.

New Materials.   Changes did occur, however, in fields like mathematics, commerce, history, geography, and English grammar. Lindley Murray's *English Grammar* and the *Universal Geography* of Jedidiah Morse appeared before 1800. Samuel Goodrich wrote texts in reading under the pen name of Peter Parley, and Nicholas Pike's *A New and Complete System of Arithmetic* appeared in 1788. Noah Webster entered the field with his *Grammatical Institute of the English Language* in 1783.

In 1812, New York provided for a superintendent of common schools but later abolished the office. Supervision was almost nonexistent in the revolutionary period, except in monitorial schools and in those operated by school societies. There was little effort to train teachers. Methods remained as crude as they had been earlier, with memorization the central concern. Liberal ideas from Europe and the frontier brought about changes in textbooks but not in the conduct of the schools, for it was still believed necessary to keep strict discipline by means of corporal punishment. Difficult subjects were learned for their value as a "discipline" to exercise the faculties of the mind. A more enlightened theory of learning was not to develop for more than fifty years.

THEN TO NOW

Anyone interested in describing an educational system must look for answers to several fundamental questions. The following are among the most important: Who will be educated? What institution will control education? Who will provide the financial support? Why do certain groups get different quality education? The colonial era was a period of transition from European educational patterns to ones more appropriate for life in the American environment. As we have seen, Southern planters retained the English family-supported tutorial system, and New England towns adopted a district system with some tax support. By the time of the rebellion against the British, no uniform educational policies had been established. Sectional differences in attitudes toward public schooling continued in the states as in the colonies.

The great liberal leader Thomas Jefferson understood the need for citizens of a republic to be educated, but he did not believe in a federal system of schools. His *Bill for the More General Diffusion of Knowledge* proposed to the Virginia legislature in 1779 was a very modest plan that combined elements of an aristocratic attitude with a desire to broaden the educational opportunities of poor but able students. Even so, Jefferson's ideas were too liberal to gain the support of his colleagues from the South. Far-reaching plans for a national system of education such as those designed by Robert Coram, Benjamin Rush, and Noah Webster met with even more opposition. Yet whether education should be public or private, supported centrally or locally, and managed by parents or governmental agencies are issues that are still debated.

Although the fifty state systems of public schools have been operational for many years, Americans are still divided on numerous educational issues. An example is the argument over tuition tax credits for parents who send their children to private schools. These credits and the debate over the various voucher plans constitute significant support and control disputes about which many modern Americans obviously disagree. Another public concern is a disparity in school finance between rich and poor school districts. Many states are under federal court orders to equalize school funding. Other points of disagreement include the use of standardized test scores for ranking and placing students as opposed to authentic assessment or the use of a balance of evaluation measures and evaluating progress on a continuing basis utilizing portfolios in which students narrate their backgrounds and goals. While some educators advocate alternative forms of assessment that do not rely on a competitive evaluation system with a percentage of students bound to fail, others including major urban political leaders use standardized test results to have students with low scores repeat grade levels.

Another example is the rejection by a growing number of parents of educational *outcomes* movements in which children are assessed on standards of performance that include values of tolerance and cooperation. Pennsylvania and other states are modifying outcomes assessment programs due in part to parental complaints that their children had to learn about and accept diversity in American culture. The philosophy of outcomes continues to be practiced but under different terminology.

In a November 1993 election, Californians voted on a school-voucher system to expand parental choice of schools. Under the proposal parents would receive half the amount spent on each public school student or about $2,500. Parents could choose private, parochial, or public schools. Although the voucher proposal was rejected by a large margin of Californians, several states have implemented a voucher system, and others are considering the concept. California has a number of charter schools, but the populace again rejected vouchers in 1997. A small New Jersey school district has proposed vouchers that will enable parents, regardless of their income, to send their children to any public or private secondary school, including religious schools. In November 2000, voters in Michigan and California rejected ballot voucher plans. The Bush administration plans to offer federal money for vouchers to students in public schools that fail to meet standards. Some 4,000 children attended church-related schools in Cleveland through a voucher program in 2000. A federal appeals court ruled against Ohio's voucher plans on the basis of government support of religion. The voucher case will be decided by the U.S. Supreme Court, which has ordered a stay in the federal appeals court Ohio order, allowing the voucher plan to continue in the fall. There is strong opposition to the voucher proposal by several civil rights groups, and the Bush administration's voucher plans may face intense opposition.

Many of the founding fathers of the United States feared that leaving education in the hands of private families, churches, local communities, or philanthropic societies would not guarantee the survival of a democracy. Nevertheless, they were unable to promote a national system of education at any level. Considerable effort was made to obtain a national university, but even that modest proposal was finally defeated. Education was not mentioned in the Constitution. Under the Tenth Amendment, the power to create, maintain, and govern schools fell to the states by default. Today there is continued conflict over what powers rightfully belong to the federal government, to the states, and to local school boards.

One of the major current issues in American education centers on the influence of political and governmental forces on community educational practices. The states were very slow in passing educational laws, even though the right was stated in the enabling acts incorporated in the several state constitutions. Responsibility for public education was assumed by the states in the 1830s, modified by federal aid to education in the Kennedy–Johnson era, and restored to the states under the administrations of Reagan and Bush. The Clinton administration moved toward national models for educational standards, curricula, and assessment to meet the need for achievement equity among schools. After one of the narrowest election margins in history, George W. Bush's presidency sought bipartisan legislation and governance. An education bill establishing national standards and testing passed through Congress and became law in January, 2002.

Early national practices allowed religious organizations, free school societies, and monitorial schools to fill the void before state systems were developed. Laws provided for a great deal of autonomy to be delegated to local school boards, while funding came largely from local property taxes. Under these conditions, it was natural for the district school authorities to consider themselves all-powerful and beyond much control by the state. In the early national period, leaders like Horace Mann and Henry Barnard built their respective state school systems without taking away the policy-making power of boards of education. Since World War II, the tradition of local autonomy has resulted in considerable conflict with state legislatures. State governments and state departments of education now take a more active role in teacher certification, establishing lists of approved course materials and even mandating the curriculum. Many states now have a provision for *academic bankruptcy,* whereby the state department of education takes over school districts when school achievement standards are not met.

Federal pressure on local schools comes through court-ordered plans of desegregation, laws for equal educational opportunity—including opportunities for disabled, disadvantaged, and limited English proficient children—and regulation of programs supported by federal taxes. There exists a great deal of resentment over the involvement of the central government in matters many consider to be the business of local boards. School boards and parents often feel that the bureaucrats in Washington have no understanding of local conditions and needs. Public sentiment for getting the federal government out of the schools and restoring local control was clearly demonstrated in the Reagan victory in the election of 1980. Although there is increasing federal school funding together with a movement toward national standards for education, some parental rights groups are seeking passage of a *Parental Rights and Responsibilities Act.* Parental rights and school choice remain a goal of some citizens in the early 2000s.

Much of the criticism of modern education from sources like *A Nation at Risk* is federal or national in origin; however, the reforms mandated are to be carried out at state or local levels. The Clinton administration explored the use of federal funds to ensure that every school had the facilities, computers, Internet access, and funding to enable all of its students to reach high performance levels. Encouraged by the George W. Bush administration, there is currently widespread public approval of a move toward testing and accountability for student performance.

In his State of the Union address, Clinton proposed a ten-point plan for education that included (1) promotion of national standards, (2) provisions for funding a National Board of Professional Teaching Standards to certify 100,000 master teachers, (3) volunteer assistance for reading improvement, (4) early learning assistance, (5) creating 3,000 charter schools by the year 2000, (6) character education, (7) building improvement, (8) college incentives, (9) skills training, and (10) connecting every classroom and library in America to the Internet by the year 2000. With few exceptions, both political parties and the public place education improvement high on their agendas although funding may limit implementation of the ten-point program. In December 2000, Congress passed a record $42 billion education budget. Funds for reducing class size, upgrading teacher skills and quality, improving reading and math, school facilities renovation, special education grants to states, Pell grants and Gear Up and Trio programs, together with comprehensive school reform, accountability, and twenty-first-century after-school programs were included. This funding record at the end of the Clinton administration and with a bipartisan Republican-Democratic coalition reflected education as a national priority and commitment.

Two points need to be made here. First, the history of the early national period clearly indicates that education is a state function even though the states have traditionally permitted a high degree of local control. Second, although the federal Constitution did not deal with education, there has been a long tradition of federal aid to the states and to local schools as well. People who are trying to understand the current issue over local, state, and federal control of education should remember that all three levels have had input into educational policy since the founding of the nation. Granting federal land to the states for educational purposes began with the Northwest Ordinance of 1785. During the Civil War era, this practice continued with the Morrill Act, which used federal land grants to create universities.

Congress also established a number of schools for specific purposes and encouraged vocational education through legislation such as the Smith-Hughes Act. Recent federal acts such as the National Defense Education Act, the Elementary and Secondary Education Acts of 1965, the Equal Opportunity Act, the National Service Legislation of 1993 (the National and Community Trust Act), and the Education of All Handicapped Children Act of 1975 (better known as Public Law 94-142) are merely current extensions of federal involvement in education that reaches back to American historical beginnings. The 1990 Individuals with Disabilities Education Act (IDEA) and the Education Amendments of 1997 extended provisions of Public Law 94-142 to all citizens from ages two to twenty-one. Provisions of both acts are under continuing review by congressional committees to clarify various provisions. The acts require inclusion, or placing students with physical and emotional challenges in regular classrooms.

The mood of the nation has often been reflected in political activity that has a direct bearing on education. The history of the United States Department of Education is an example. As we have seen, many of the founding fathers wanted to establish a federal system of education. In 1829, Congressman Joseph Richardson proposed a federal committee on education to coordinate the state programs. Congress squelched this proposal, but the idea kept emerging. Charles Brooks of Massachusetts (a Unitarian minister and school reformer) devoted thirty years to efforts at getting a national system. Although he failed, he stimulated educators to form communications networks to gather data and influenced Congress to consider federal aid to the South after the Civil War. Following the war, the National Association of School Superintendents proposed a bureau of education.

In somewhat reduced form, the bill creating a department of education was passed and signed into law by President Andrew Johnson in 1867. Henry Barnard, who had also lobbied for such a department, became the first commissioner. Barnard was not popular in Washington, and the department was soon reduced to a bureau in the political turmoil following Johnson's near impeachment. General John Eaton, Barnard's successor, toned down the office and made its function mainly one of collecting information. For almost a century after its creation, the United States Office of Education kept a low profile and concentrated on statistics. Then, in the 1950s, with the black revolution and the civil rights movement, latter-day reformers found the Office of Education to be a useful instrument for implementing the reforms of the Great Society.

In the Kennedy–Johnson years, the Office of Education gained great power and status. It was authorized to distribute vast sums of money to compensate for the inequality of educational opportunity and to stimulate plans for school integration. The Office of Education was placed in the Department of Health, Education, and Welfare; and its staff grew to enormous size. Under President Carter, it became a separate cabinet-level Department of Education.

The administration of President Reagan, however, took a very dim view of social engineering through federal spending and reduced both the budget and the influence of the department. The Clinton administration sought to reverse the Reagan and Bush educational spending programs by utilizing every avenue of the federal government to focus on updating and upgrading the educational effort nationwide. The George W. Bush administration is focusing on local control and accountability to parents in an attempt to improve the education of children, with an especially strong emphasis on parental involvement. All through history, the progress of education has been linked to the whims of politics and public attitudes. It should be remembered that the reason we do not have a federal system of public schools in the United States is because of the political climate at the time of the writing of the Constitution.

Another example of politics and education is shown by the attempts of politicians to control higher education. During the American Revolution, criticism and attacks were directed at conservative colleges because they were considered to be insufficiently patriotic. William Smith, the president of the College of Philadelphia, was an Anglican minister accused of Tory sentiments. In 1776, the legislature investigated the college, dissolved the board of trustees, and dismissed the faculty. The legislature created a new board and a new institution called the University of the State of Pennsylvania. The old college continued to function without legal status, and finally, in 1789, the two institutions joined to form the University of Pennsylvania. The case of the College of Philadelphia is similar to that of Dartmouth College (discussed in Chapter 5). The point is that political influence over education is nothing new in American history.

Periods of political unrest foster attacks on institutions of education. Notable modern examples include the investigations by Senator Joseph McCarthy following World War II and the controversy over loyalty oaths for teachers (*Wieman v. Updegraff*) in the 1950s. While education is legally a state function, all levels of government are involved in educational matters. The arguments over control and support of education that began in the period of the Revolution are very much alive today and may be expected to continue into the future.

Inventions and discoveries that have dramatically altered the human condition have no steady or evolutionary history but consist of dramatic breakthroughs commonly followed by periods of inactivity. Thus, ancient Romans invested in aqueducts and sophisticated plumbing for baths and fountains while later Europeans living in the Middle Ages not only lost the technology but attributed the ruins to a race of magical super beings.

A parallel situation is found in contributions to education and learning. In today's world of mass media and electronic communications it seems strange that so much of human history passed with few developments in education and that some of the important inventions were not passed on to other cultures. Nevertheless, progress before modern times was slow and sporadic.

Consider writing, the ultimate foundation for educational progress and schools in all cultures. Pictographs or symbols representing specific things such as heavenly bodies, men, or animals are found in cultures as diverse as the Chinese, Egyptian, and Inca, so we may assume independent invention. It was, however, the Sumerians who developed true writing in the third millennium B.C. The Sumerians of Mesopotamia developed a strong sense of personal property, creating a need to mark objects for ownership, especially when artifacts were presented to the gods. Names or identification marks scratched in the wet clay soon gave way to individual cylinder seals that could be rolled into the damp tablets. This evolved into cylinders for special purposes such as contracts for business or marriage, with names and dates added on the clay tablet with a wedge-shaped stylus made of wood or bone. Some seals may have been made of wood, but many were cut into bronze. Numerous examples have been recovered by archaeologists. Unlike Egyptian papyrus pith paper or Roman velum, clay tablets do not disintegrate in dry climates, so many thousands have been recovered from ancient sites in the Fertile Crescent. Legal documents are sometimes found encased in their own envelopes or sheaths with identification marking on the outside clay layer. These Sumerian written records are the oldest form of writing anywhere, and some words such as *crocus*, *myrrh*, and *saffron* are still in use. These early people created symbols for syllables as well as words and developed lexicons and grammars. A thousand years passed before the next major change came in writing with the true alphabet, invented by the Phoenicians.

In addition to the keyboards on our computers, everyone today has access to a vast array of pens, pencils, crayons, and markers. Oddly, the Egyptians, Greeks, and Romans failed to develop a pen or pencil and relied on reeds with frayed ends for writing. Marking fluids were made from various combinations of oils, soot, berry juices, and vegetable dyes until the Greeks learned to extract ink from marine animals. The quill pen was an invention of the Middle Ages and was the mainstay of handwriting for a thousand years. Not until 1828 did a metal point fitted into a wooden pen come into common use. Fountain pens were early twentieth-century inventions while the ballpoint instrument appeared in 1948.

Limestone, charcoal, lead, and chalk have always been used for temporary marking when available. In early America chalk was scarce, and so soft stone was used for doing sums on slates and blackboards. Sometimes blackboards were "whiteboards" painted or whitewashed and written upon with charcoal. The story of young Abraham Lincoln doing mathematical exercises with charcoal on the back of a shovel reflects common conditions on the American frontier. Graphite was discovered near Keswick, England, about A.D. 1500. First used as a mold for cannonballs, graphite was cut into small slabs for marking in the days of Elizabeth I. The earliest pencils were wrapped in sheepskin, but the wooden holder developed in Italy became standard. Pencil making was a cottage industry until the French learned to mix ground graphite with clay and fire it in a furnace to make a thin pencil filler. Thereafter cheap manufactured pencils became standard tools for writing practice in schools everywhere.

Educational technologies often follow those of manufacturing and industry. Everyone is familiar with the standard school desk and seat made of wood with cast-iron side supports. Rows of such desks were bolted to the floors of American schools for generations, and some are in use today. Iron and steel production in America were not well developed until the coming of the railroads. In 1829 with George Stephenson's locomotive *Rocket* and a year later with Peter Cooper's locomotive *Tom Thumb*, the steam rail industry was born. The need for strong, cheap metal rails stimulated the iron and steel industry, which revolutionized American manufacturing. At the time, Horace Mann was calling for improved, standardized public schools. He drew plans for cast-iron school desk supports that could be made at little expense as a by-product of the railroad rail manufacturing, and thus began the common school basic furniture industry.

The Role of History of Education. Educational issues and the visions of Webster, Jefferson, Locke, and Comenius are often reflected in current educational debates. Bilingualism versus English immersion, the relation of the government and its citizens, experience and learning, the role of the church and state in education, international and global education, controversies over economic globalization, collective bargaining, academic freedom, decisions on what is ultimately worth knowing, and professional versus general education remain issues for schools and society. Governmental gridlock occurs when narrow margins between the political parties lead to conflicts as single special interest groups seek to promote their ends through the law and political power. This leads to social fragmentation as these single interest groups push legislation often for interests detrimental or not beneficial for the larger population.

GAINING PERSPECTIVE THROUGH CRITICAL ANALYSIS

1. Name three European philosophers who helped to shape colonial thought before the Revolutionary War. How did each of them influence American educational practice?

2. What was the significance of the thinking and writing of Noah Webster and Thomas Jefferson on education? (A review of the chapter opening quotation will help you with your answer.)

3. How did societal changes lead to curriculum modifications during the American Revolution?

4. Do you think you would have had more effect on American education as a member of Congress in colonial times or today? Give three reasons for your answer. Identify *governmental gridlock* and *social fragmentation.*

5. What were the primary differences between monitorial schools, Sunday schools, and free school societies established during the period of the American Revolution? Give examples of similar efforts to expand educational access and opportunity today.

6. Examine the literature on the Northwest Ordinance, and relate the content of the ordinance to school finance issues then and now.

HISTORY IN ACTION IN TODAY'S CLASSROOMS

1. Interview a retired teacher or administrator. Discuss his or her perceptions of the changing role of women and curriculum changes throughout his or her career. Add the findings of your interview to your journal, and share them with your class.

2. Using the library, the media, or the Internet, review current legislation that supports either national control or state/local control of education in your area. Use your journal to record the results of your search.

INCREASED UNDERSTANDING THROUGH ONLINE RESEARCH

Visit the Prentice Hall Foundations Web site (*http://www.prenhall.com/foundations-cluster*) and select Topic 16—Trends and Issues—from the menu. Using the resources available in this topic of the site, identify three pros and cons for the use of vouchers for parental choice of schools. Write and submit your response to your instructor using the Electronic Bluebook module also in this topic of the Web site.

BIBLIOGRAPHY

Arrowood, Charles Flinn. *Thomas Jefferson and Education in a Republic.* New York: McGraw-Hill, 1930.

Bergen, Tim. *Foundations of American Public Education.* New York: McGraw-Hill, 1994.

Best, John Hardin, ed. *Benjamin Franklin on Education.* Teachers College, Columbia University Bureau of Publications, no. 14. New York: Columbia University Press, 1962.

Butts, R. Freeman, and Lawrence A. Cremin. *A History of Education in American Culture.* New York: Holt, Rinehart and Winston, 1953.

Church, Robert, and Michael Sedlak. *Education in the United States: An Interpretive History.* New York: Free Press, 1976.

Clinton, Bill, and Al Gore. *Putting People First.* New York: Random House-Time Books, 1992.

Davis, David. *The Problem of Slavery in the Age of Revolution, 1770–1823.* Ithaca, NY: Cornell University Press, 1975.

French, William M. *American's Educational Tradition, an Interpretive History.* Boston: D. C. Heath, 1964.

Gay, Peter. *John Locke on Education.* New York: Teachers College Press, Columbia University, 1964.

Gutek, Gerald. *An Historical Introduction to American Education.* New York: Thomas Crowell, 1970.

Hansen, Allen O. *Liberalism and American Education in the Eighteenth Century.* New York: Macmillan, 1926.

Hoff, David J. "Clinton Gives Top Billing to Education Plan." *Education Week* (February 12, 1997):1, 34.

Hofstadter, Richard, and Wilson Smith. *American Higher Education: A Documentary History.* Chicago: The University of Chicago Press, 1961.

Homstad, Wayne. *Anatomy of a Book Controversy.* Bloomington, IN: Phi Delta Kappa, 1995.

Jefferson, Thomas. "Letter to Pierre DuPont de Nemours, April 24, 1816." In *Jefferson on Religion in Public Education,* by Robert M. Healey, 181. New Haven, CT: Yale University Press, 1962.

Ketcham, Ralph. *From Colony to Country: The Revolution in American Thought, 1750–1820.* New York: Macmillan, 1974.

Meyer, Adolphe. *Grandmasters of Educational Thought.* New York: McGraw-Hill, 1975.

Perkinson, Henry J. *Since Socrates: Studies in the History of Educational Thought.* New York: Longman, 1980.

Ravitch, Diane. *National Standards in American Education: A Citizens Guide.* Washington, DC: Brookings, 1995.

Thayer, V. T. *Formative Ideas in American Education.* New York: Dodd, Mead, 1965.

Travers, Paul, and Ronald Rebore. *Foundations of Education: Becoming a Teacher.* Englewood Cliffs, NJ: Prentice-Hall, 1987.

Ulich, Robert, ed. *Three Thousand Years of Educational Wisdom.* 2d ed. Cambridge: Harvard University Press, 1963.

Walsh, Mark. "New Jersey District Proposes Vouchers for High Schoolers." *Education Week* (February 12, 1997):6.

Woody, Thomas. *Educational Views of Benjamin Franklin.* New York: McGraw-Hill, 1931.

Chapter FIVE

American Education: 1812–1865

I believe in the existence of a great, immutable principle of natural law, or natural ethics— which provides the absolute right of every human being that comes into the world to an education; and which, of course, proves the correlative duty of every government to see that the means of that education are provided for all.

Horace Mann

Jacksonian Democracy		
1817 Thomas Gallaudet established school for the deaf in Boston	1821 First American high school, Boston	1827 Massachusetts required high schools
1818 Robert Owen's infant school	Emma Willard's school for girls	1832 New York school for the blind
1819 Dartmouth College case	1825 Friedrich Froebel published *Education of Man*	1837 Calvin Stowe's report on Prussian schools
University of Virginia	Henry Barnard visits Prussian schools	Horace Mann made secretary of Massachusetts school board

Figure 5.1   Time Line of American Education 1812–1865

Before the War of 1812, education was virtually a religious enterprise, with the exception of some academies and free school societies. The period from 1812 to the Civil War was a transitional one during which educational leaders such as Horace Mann, James C. Carter, and Henry Barnard forged the first links in what has evolved as a free, public school system, supported and controlled by the state. The rise of nationalism and Jacksonian Democracy, the Industrial Revolution, and the forces of westward expansion, immigration, and population growth provided impetus to the concept of universal education. There was a rebirth in the growth of the elementary or common schools. Academies supplanted the elite-oriented Latin grammar schools, which flourished until their peak in 1850.

More important in this era was the birth of the American high school, an institution that would, in time, become the vital force of secondary education. This period saw the passing of the Morrill Act and the subsequent establishment of land grant colleges. European ideas were transplanted by innovations such as those of Victor Cousin, Joseph Lancaster, and Margarethe Meyer Schurz. The curriculum was expanded. The sectarian stronghold gave way to a more secular orientation, and the concept of teacher training was realized in the establishment of the first normal school in 1839.

SOCIAL, POLITICAL, AND ECONOMIC TRENDS

The period of time from the War of 1812 through the Civil War is often referred to as the age of the common man. This is true in part because of the impact of Jacksonian Democracy and the social, political, and economic developments of the nation.

Missouri Compromise		Civil War
1839 First American normal school, Lexington, Massachusetts	1848 Attempt to teach the profoundly retarded Boston	1855 German-speaking kindergarten
1840 Rhode Island compulsory education	1849 New York general tax for schools	1860 English kindergarten in Boston 1861 M.I.T. founded
1846 Laboratory sciences in colleges	1852 Massachusetts attendance law	1861 Civil War begins 1862 Morrill Land Grant College Act

Throughout the land, the advancement of the common man carried the banner of education as a basic right and opportunity that should not be denied any citizen.

Common School Ideal.   The doctrine of equality of all citizens demanded mass education and made a system of separate schools for the elite social classes unacceptable. Equality led to the belief that all should read in order to participate in government and to have the opportunity to improve. The idea that schools could provide a ladder by which one might climb socially and economically was widespread. There was a demand for general education and for vocational skills as well. The attitude supported local control with no federal regulations. It was felt that common schools should be public in curriculum and tax supported. In limited resource communities, the poor—including minorities, whites, and women—were often excluded from political, social, and economic equality. Separation of church and state was upheld, but no restrictions were placed on nondenominational religious instruction in public schools.

Impact of the Industrial Revolution.   The Industrial Revolution began in Europe before the American Revolution and slowly spread to other nations including the United States. British inventions including Watt's steam engine, Arkwright's spinning frame, and Cartwright's power loom were instrumental in moving toward an industrial economy for which Adam Smith supplied the economic theory. Machines made of wood and driven by water or wind evolved into factories with iron mechanical devices powered by steam.

At the opening of the nineteenth century, agriculture dominated the American economy. This was still the case in the South and West at the opening of the Civil War but not in the Northeast and Midwest where textile mills, coal mining, iron and steel plants, commercial enterprises, food packing companies, and railroads became dominant. The steam engine was the catalyst of change, and railroads transformed agrarian communities into mill towns with job opportunities for expanding populations. Major cities on the Atlantic coast became nerve centers for short rail lines, but soon distant inland points like Cleveland, Chicago, and Atlanta were connected. Railroads were not so numerous in the South, but lines were built to carry cotton to market after Eli Whitney invented the gin in 1793. The open hearth and Bessemer process made malleable iron and steel available for rails and engines, creating yet another industry.

As always is the case, material invention precedes social adjustment so that no provision was made for the vast changes created by the new economic order. Slums, crowded conditions, pollution, abuse of labor, poverty, and social unrest were also caused by the Industrial Revolution. The greatest impact of this technological change occurred after the Civil War, but it altered American society long before that.

Not only was the Industrial Revolution uneven in its spread across the nation, but it also contributed to extreme sectional differences. It is often pointed out that the United States lacked a sense of nationalism before 1865 and that loyalty was centered in various regions instead of in the nation as a whole. The Whiskey Rebellion of 1794 established the federal government's power to tax, but it created vast resentment among local farmers who lived by converting corn into liquor. High tariffs could not be equally good for farmers and factory owners. Black slaves were considered an economic necessity in the South, but their use violated a growing sense of human rights elsewhere. An illustration of the power of sectionalism is found in the life of Robert E. Lee. Except for the aged Winfield Scott, Lee was the best known American soldier at the time of the attack on Fort Sumter. As such, he was offered the command of the Union Army. But while Lee was a dedicated career officer and opposed secession, he could not lift his sword against his neighbors and fellow Southerners. He therefore resigned his commission and offered his services to Virginia.

One effect of the change from an agricultural to an industrial economy was a demand for a terminal secondary school to prepare boys for the work for which they were destined. After 1830, considerable pressure was generated for the expansion and improvement of public schools. The industrial working class became a political factor. Workers in urban areas could not afford to send their children to private schools. They wanted a better opportunity for their sons and daughters than they had enjoyed. Factory labor was often recruited from the vast numbers of foreign born people who crowded into cities. These immigrants joined forces with others supporting public education. Today, Arizona and California are moving away from bilingual programs in favor of one year of English immersion before students are integrated in all-English classrooms. This follows years of the practice of primary instruction in the native language of the student, especially Spanish. Foreigners entering the United States in the nineteenth century made no demand for instruction in anything but English. Their demand was for universal free schools, but they expected their children to learn the national language. Indeed, they saw English usage as a requirement for entering the job market.

In the industrial East, the growth of cities and factories tended to increase the desire for schools and to decrease the opportunity many children had to attend them. Factories often employed entire families. Some youngsters began working twelve-hour shifts at the age of eight. The severity of the problem is illustrated by the fact that in the 1830s, two-fifths of New England's workforce was made up of children under sixteen years of age. Child labor, the lack of safety devices or worker's rights, extreme poverty, and crowded slums added to social problems of the day. Many reformers hoped to use education as a means of overcoming the difficulties produced by the Industrial Revolution. Women and girls in urban factories worked under sweatshop conditions with little opportunity for a better life. Under a *laissez-faire* philosophy, employers saw no requirement to improve the conditions of work. This led to greater demands for reform by workers and social leaders, and public education for all children.

Public School Support.

Throughout this period, there was an increase in the political power of the ordinary man, and aristocratic birth came to be a political handicap. Private philanthropy, even by such a popular organization as the Public School Society of New York, could not really provide the answer, and increased agitation for tax-supported schools became commonplace. Bands of factory workers in cities formed working men's societies; these organizations tended to give their support to public education. Because they were important politically, the working men's societies had considerable effect.

The theory behind the taxation of every person for the education of all children was eventually accepted in most parts of the country, and the belief that schools must be both free and tax supported developed into general public policy before the Civil War. This did not mean that all states had established their school systems before 1865 or that all resentment of tax support for education had disappeared. However, the American people had generally accepted the notion of public support for common school education.

There was some feeling, particularly expressed by the *New York Working Men's Advocate*, that the public schools ought to board children so that those from poor families would not feel inferior to the sons and daughters of the rich; they felt that by doing so, equal educational opportunity would be a reality. This argument of 1830 serves as a reminder of some of the present controversy over civil rights legislation. It was also held that the curriculum ought to be the same for all students and that, rather than the classics, a practical education including the rudiments of the English language should be the basis.

Today the population explosion has manifest implications for education, but even in the early national period demographic changes had their educational impact. From 1820 to 1850 the centers of commerce, especially cities like Boston and New York, jumped vastly in population. Rapid growth of the cities and the subsequent surge of poverty and slums made reform and public concern with educational matters much more important. By 1845, the flow of people from foreign countries was so pronounced that cities like Boston had as many as one-third foreign-born residents. The nation's population exceeded 30 million in 1860.

Nationalization.   Many immigrants had customs and languages different from those of the native-born population; therefore, the schools became a major instrument in the transfer of the American culture to the foreigners. One aspect of this "Americanization" was not limited to the newcomers. The two wars with England and the rapid growth of America had nurtured a growing nationalism. This nationalism resulted in the educational principle that schools should pursue the inculcation of patriotism—love and respect for America, its ideals, its history, and its potential. Frontier equality aided public education through the belief that people ought to have equal educational opportunity without the stigma of charity. Hence, the new states with large frontier communities tended to provide for education as they provided for universal suffrage. Many ethnic groups including Germans, Italians, Irish, and Dutch maintained their cultural identity while their children mainstreamed into the American culture through the public schools.

Frontier Impact.   Frederick Jackson Turner (1861–1932) was an American historian who became famous for his theory of the significance of the frontier in the development of the United States. He thought that an abundance of free land strengthened the democratic ideals and that western expansion provided a safety valve that prevented social revolution caused by economic stress. His view of the impact of western expansion and the moving frontier dominated American historical thinking for decades.

Other historians challenged Turner's ideas, but it is certainly true that free land, westward expansion, and the constant development of new outposts of civilization were significant factors in the creation of the United States. Although it is true that there was a certain amount of anti-intellectualism on the frontier, it is also the case that most pioneer farmers wanted their children to have the rudiments of an education. The frontier towns were raw and unsophisticated but never dominated by only one class of people. Doctors, lawyers, and well-educated ministers were present along with farmers, ranchers, prospectors, and scouts. Pioneer virtues of thrift, hard work, self-reliance, and independence were often reflected in attitudes toward social institutions such as schools. The theory of minimum public education for every child found wide acceptance on the frontier, but getting tax money for schools often met with a good deal of opposition. The egalitarian view that one man was just as good as any other without regard to wealth, family, or social status became commonplace on the frontier and in American schools. The frontier fostered individual freedom and lack of governmental restraint—values that often made it difficult to support and regulate schools. There was also a general distrust of classical or "foreign" education on the American frontier, reliance being placed on practical wisdom and basic skills like reading.

The first quarter of the nineteenth century was remarkable in many ways; it brought about, in the various states of the country, the beginning of the school systems that still exist in one form or another today. During this time of common school revival, the older colonial educational programs that had developed in Massachusetts and the other New England states were re-established. Of course, there was widespread opposition. Many newspapers were against taxes for the support of schools, and it was not possible to raise revenues with the speed necessary to develop a genuinely good school system. But well before the Civil War, all the states had given at least some attention to the question of developing a system of public schools for the children of all the people.

First State Programs. It was not thought necessary by the founders of the American common schools to guarantee a democratic system of education for all the people. The earliest state provisions usually created an ex officio superintendent of schools, whose other duties might include, for example, serving as secretary of state. It was also common to empower local groups interested in education to establish an educational corporation for the purpose of building school buildings, hiring teachers, and whatever else seemed necessary to the making of a school. But the states moved slowly in the passage of laws that set up their various educational systems. The state superintendent of free schools or common schools, or the state superintendent of public instruction, as the officer was sometimes called, often had very feeble powers. Even when the states passed laws necessary for a real school system, they tended to be very slow in the enforcement of those laws. For a long time it was difficult to collect school taxes and nearly impossible to ensure compulsory attendance, even when such attendance was a legal requirement. Hence, the development of the state school systems varied as the interest of the people tended to wax and wane. Educational progress was hindered by the old tradition that children should be educated first by their parents and second by the church. However, in the long run, frontier democracy overcame the prejudices against public schools.

THE AGE OF THE COMMON SCHOOL REVIVAL

Educational historians often refer to this period, 1812 to 1865, as the age of common school revival. It was during this time that the old New England demand for universal common education became an ideal for the American people. The common elementary school was established in the North and West; it had the task of building social, political, and moral character needed in a democracy. In addition, it was concerned with the teaching of basic skills. The battle for free public education, supported and controlled by the state, was centered on the common school.

As the curtain rose on the nineteenth century, the condition of elementary school education was most depressing. The SPG withdrew its efforts after the split with England, and there were few schools that were for the benefit of the masses. Most existing schools required tuition, although some scholarships were available. Education was traditional, and discipline was harsh. In the few public schools, most of which were in New England, the teachers' workloads were heavy, and only the fundamentals were taught. For the most part, school buildings and equipment were very poor, even in the private schools and academies. Textbooks, blackboards, and all working materials were in extremely short supply. Buildings were not kept up, lighting was not adequate, and quite often one poorly trained teacher was in charge not only of one school but also of an entire district.

Teachers who possessed only an elementary school education were frequently hired. Of course, teachers in the Latin grammar schools and academies were educated, but there was certainly no formal teacher training system. There were some teachers of ability, but frequently men who were dreamers or who could not succeed in other professions became schoolmasters. Perhaps people of better quality and training would have been attracted to teaching if the pay and conditions could have been improved, but this was beyond the capability of the settlers in most of the newer areas of the country. It is true that even on the frontier some well-educated and excellent teachers could be found, but in most cases the quality of teaching was extremely low and the children could expect to gain little learning in return for the brief time and small fees that were required of them.

State Funds and State Laws.   Permanent school funds had been set up by a number of states during the early national period. Connecticut used the money from the sale of its Western Reserve for this purpose in 1795. New York and Virginia also had provisions for standing school funds before the passage of laws that set up their state systems. Although much educational support came from these funds, the tendency to rely on them probably retarded efforts to get real tax support.

One of the first acts commonly passed by states for education was a provision that local districts might tax themselves to support schools if the people in the district agreed. Such a law was passed in Pennsylvania in 1834. Although no district was required to provide schools, more than half of the Pennsylvania districts did so. There was a great deal of opposition to school taxes in Pennsylvania, especially among Catholics and German-speaking farmers. Accordingly, the state senate voted repeal of the 1834 law, and it was expected that the house would agree. At this point, one of the most unusual developments in the history of American education took place. An appeal was made to Thaddeus Stevens to support the repeal. Instead, Stevens made one of the most eloquent appeals known for free public schools. He offered a substitute law that would strengthen the public schools rather than repeal their support. Stevens used the common man ideal, the need for equality, and the argument that public schools cost less than jails or welfare programs. Stevens was able to carry the day, and Pennsylvania accepted his substitute bill. Three years later, Massachusetts passed a school law that established the right to use tax money for public schools. Other states soon passed similar legislation.

Curriculum Improvement.   Changes in the curriculum came gradually. Development was slow partly because most states could not afford teacher education or schools that offered much beyond the basic "R's." English grammar and spelling gained a place in school programs in the early national period. In western frontier towns, spelling sometimes was stressed more than reading and writing. American history was offered in some form to boys and girls who remained in school beyond three years. Geography was introduced into many of the elementary schools before 1825. Arithmetic was much improved by the addition of new texts and materials, but many pupils were taught only addition and simple multiplication "to the rule of three." As in colonial schools, reading, grammar, spelling, and (later) history and geography were taught by the recitation method. In 1836, William Holmes McGuffey began to publish his readers; they sold over 120 million copies by 1920. These readers stressed individual virtue, literacy, hard work, and moral development. The readers—with the theme of "rugged individualism" and *"laissez-faire"* important to industrialists during the period—were used to indoctrinate pupils into a middle- and upper-class value system.

Graded Primary Schools.

It had been the custom for parents to teach their children to read and write before sending them to school; therefore, primary education was not considered the responsibility of the state. In Boston in 1818, primary schools were set up to take over this function. The schools were taught by women and eventually were consolidated with grammar and writing schools; this union led to the formation of the eight-year elementary school, a structure that is still prevalent in many areas today.

The start of a graded elementary school, though not uniform throughout, can be traced to 1818, when the Boston Primary School was organized into six classes with the grammar or secondary school forming the seventh. In 1823, the grammar school was also divided into reading and writing sections. Many of the town schools had two rooms. Children were placed in the primary or the advanced room according to age. The person in charge of the older students was called the "principal teacher"—a title that eventually led to an administrative distinction. The introduction of *McGuffey's Eclectic Readers* contributed to the grading movement as did the work of John D. Philbrick as principal of the Quincy Grammar School in Boston after 1848. Of course, many schools remained with no grades or divisions, especially in rural areas.

In 1850, 45 percent of the nation's youngsters attended school, and half of the states had established their school systems before the Civil War. Quality remained poor in most schools. The typical common elementary school of 1860 was a crowded one-room institution with poor lighting, bad ventilation, inadequate furniture, and no special equipment. The poorly educated and untrained teachers did not have a program to follow, and much of the time was spent in individual recitations. Severe discipline and corporal punishment stifled creativity and imagination. Nevertheless, schools were growing in number, and the principle of direct tax support for elementary education had been generally accepted.

BIRTH OF THE AMERICAN HIGH SCHOOL

Secondary education in the early national period consisted of the Latin grammar school, the academy, and the high school. Latin grammar schools were strictly for the preparation of the college-bound elite, and high fees were charged. Academies also charged tuition, though some had scholarships for poor students. A booming economy and the religious revival known as the Second Great Awakening contributed to the development of academies. Many were boarding schools that provided a protected moral environment for students. By 1860, there were 250,000 students enrolled in 6,000 academies. However, the middle class and many workers made a growing demand for terminal secondary education with free tax support. Increasing urban growth and industrial expansion also contributed to the birth of the public high school.

In 1821, Boston opened the English Classical School and renamed it the English High School in 1824. This first American high school was established to meet the needs of boys who did not plan to attend college. Boys as young as age twelve were admitted by examination; however, very few poor or working-class youngsters were involved. English, mathematics, history, science, geography, philosophy, bookkeeping, and surveying were taught. Massachusetts passed a law in 1827 that required towns of 4,000 or more to create a high school, but not all towns complied.

At first, high schools grew slowly. There was competition from well-established academies and opposition to taxation for secondary schools. Still, the idea of a free secondary school or a "college for all the people" appealed to the middle class and grew in popularity. In 1826, Boston opened a female high school under the direction of Ebenezer Bailey. So many girls applied for admission that the school was closed for lack of funds. In 1855, Boston established another school for girls that included teacher training in a "normal" department.

There were no electives in these high schools. Students were expected to take all of the courses offered; however, there was a choice between an English, a classical, or a commercial curriculum. Entrance requirements and standardization of courses varied. There were arguments over whether high schools should be terminal institutions only. When the Civil War began, there were over 300 high schools, of which one-third were in Massachusetts.

HIGHER EDUCATION BEFORE THE CIVIL WAR

Except for the College of Philadelphia, all the colonial institutions of higher learning had been church related. In spite of efforts to make them democratic, most colleges remained sectarian and aristocratic. Classics, theology, and mathematics dominated their curricula. Control was vested with religious leaders and with the wealthy. Although it was possible to prepare for college in a low-cost academy and some students worked their way through college by teaching school during vacation periods, only a small fraction of the population attended college. A majority of the students were preparing for the ministry or for a life of leisure that their families could provide.

Dartmouth College Case.   The struggle over the question of public or private control of colleges came to a head with the Dartmouth College issue. Dartmouth had been founded through the efforts of Eleazar Wheelock, who was succeeded by his son John. A dominant figure, John Wheelock came into conflict with the trustees of the college. In 1815, the board removed Wheelock from the presidency of Dartmouth; however, in 1816, the successful Jeffersonian Democrats converted Dartmouth into a state university and restored Wheelock. As a result, the students and faculty rebelled, and the trustees filed suit to recover the college. In 1818, the case reached the Supreme Court of the United States. John Marshall wrote the decision; it held that a private educational institution could not be taken over by a state against its will. This decision clearly established the right of private as well as state colleges to exist and to solicit gifts or grants for support.

State Universities.

State universities were chartered first where no institution of higher learning existed. They reflected the theory of the Enlightenment that education should promote social improvement and individual happiness. Georgia chartered its university in 1785 and opened it in 1800. North Carolina chartered its university in 1789, Vermont in 1791, and South Carolina in 1801. There was also Blount College in 1794; it later became the University of Tennessee. None of these colleges grew rapidly. They were state universities in name; however, all were under the control of a private board, and the curriculum included a large measure of classical studies.

The best known of the early state universities was that of Virginia; Thomas Jefferson dominated it. There was a degree of academic freedom there: Professors could select their own textbooks, and they held tenure. The curriculum was also much more liberal than at other colleges. Jefferson called for professors of ancient languages, modern languages, mathematics, natural philosophy, natural history, medicine, moral philosophy, and law. This was the first attempt to include such professional studies as law and medicine in a university program, and the students could select (or elect) the program they wished to follow. In September 1825, there were over 100 students attending the University of Virginia.

While the new program at Virginia was getting under way, an effort was made to reform Harvard. George Ticknor, a professor of modern languages, proposed a series of changes based upon European universities that he had visited. Among his reforms were the departmentalization of the university, strict examinations, teaching by the lecture method, and student election of some subjects. These reforms would have created a university similar to those of Germany, which had very high standards of scholarship. The reforms were unpopular with faculty members, and Ticknor was forced to resign in 1835.

Resistance to change was also demonstrated by the Yale Report of 1828. This report placed stress on the status quo, emphasizing classical languages and theology as a means of gaining discipline over the mind. It put little faith in science and held that the foundation of a superior education is grounded in traditional subjects. The Yale Report called for recitations rather than lectures and placed stress on the "superintendence" of the faculty over all student activities. It supported the idea that traditional studies are a good foundation for all vocations including the learned professions. The Yale Report was a clear statement of the conservatism that continued to dominate most colleges until after the Civil War.

In addition to Harvard and Virginia, Union College in New York and Brown University began using the elective system. The major growth in higher education before 1860 was in the private and denominational colleges. Private and church-related colleges accepted the principles of the Yale Report and rejected the elective system. In 1810, there were about thirty private colleges and more than fifty in 1830. Eastern missionaries were especially active, founding colleges in western states like Ohio, Indiana, and Illinois. After the sponsorship of the Society for Promotion of Collegiate and Theological Education in the West, which united Presbyterian and Congregationalist efforts, even more western denominational colleges were established. Methodists were also active. Many graduates of Princeton and Yale believed that creating new colleges was a way of reforming society and expressing religious beliefs. There were 182 American colleges in operation before the Civil War, although some of these offered only secondary instruction. Many of them ceased to exist before 1900.

State universities were also set up in the areas of westward expansion before 1861. In 1837, the University of Michigan was authorized to begin offering literary, scientific, and practical courses; there was also a branch for the education of primary school teachers. Indiana, Kentucky, Missouri, Mississippi, Iowa, Wisconsin, Minnesota, Louisiana, and California chartered their state universities prior to 1860. Many of these institutions did not reach university status until later.

Technical and scientific education began to increase with the foundation of Rensselaer Polytechnic Institute in 1824. The Lawrence Scientific School at Harvard opened in 1847, and Yale created the Sheffield Scientific School in 1852. There was a great demand for people trained in scientific and engineering skills long before most universities developed professional schools. West Point–educated engineers were too few to meet the need, and there were no universities where one could study agriculture. By 1850, there was considerable pressure for the establishment of scientific, agricultural, and engineering colleges.

An adult education movement developing during the early part of the nineteenth century gave considerable attention to public schools as well as the educational improvement of older citizens. In 1826, Josiah Holbrook of Massachusetts organized the first lyceum, or association of men and women for cultural advancement. By 1832, a national lyceum movement had been organized for the improvement of useful knowledge and the advancement of public schools. Lyceums especially encouraged female teachers and invited them to participate in local educational movements for better support of and higher quality in common schools. Lyceum meetings were similar to county institutes. The nonsectarian character of the lyceum provided common ground for persons of divergent religious persuasion to discuss educational matters.

Other literary and cultural activities helped to give indirect leadership to the school cause. Ralph Waldo Emerson and Walt Whitman idealized the common man. Transcendentalism supported raising the educational level of the whole people as a means of social improvement. Newspaper editorials and publications of workingmen's societies, such as the *Mechanics' Free Press,* continued to urge free schools throughout the nation.

Morrill Act.   In 1857, Justin Morrill, a congressman from Vermont, offered a bill for the grant of public lands to the states for colleges that would offer agriculture and the mechanical arts. The precedent of federal land grants of large size for schools and colleges had been established by the Ordinance of 1785. Morrill had the support of the farm interests in the South and West, but there was fear concerning the federal control of education. The Senate passed the bill, but President Buchanan vetoed it. Congress passed it again when Lincoln became president, and it became law in 1862.

The Morrill Act granted each state 30,000 acres of public land for each senator and representative it had in Congress. The land was to be used for the endowment and maintenance of at least one college in each state for the teaching of agriculture and the mechanical arts. Military science and tactics were also required, but the states retained control of the administration of the colleges and the remainder of the curriculum. Some states used the money to develop existing colleges; others created new agricultural and mechanical universities. The actual building of these state institutions did not occur until after the war years. Congress made a number of supplementary cash grants to these colleges in later years (Figure 5.2).

AMERICAN EDUCATIONAL LEADERSHIP

Political Leaders.　　　Political support for educational reform came from many parts of society. De Witt Clinton of New York was a political leader who showed great interest in educational matters. He often urged that the legislature establish tax-supported common schools and institutions for teacher training. In 1827, Clinton was largely responsible for creating a fund for aiding academies and promoting teacher education. He promoted the creation of the first office of superintendent of schools in New York, to which Gideon Hawley was appointed in 1812.

Governor Wolf of Pennsylvania charged in 1833 that his state had failed to meet the constitutional requirement that required the legislature to provide poor children with free education. Thaddeus Stevens helped put Pennsylvania at the forefront of the fight for common schools. Archibald Murphy in North Carolina, Calvin Stowe in Ohio, and Edward Coles in Illinois called for complete educational programs in their states. Governors and influential political leaders in all parts of the nation attempted to persuade the various legislatures to pass school laws and provide tax support. Of course, there was opposition and not many political figures had the success of Horace Mann and Henry Barnard, but many were trying.

Literary Support.　　　Barnard's *Connecticut Common School Journal*, William Russell's *American Journal of Education*, and the *Academician,* all of which appeared in 1818, are examples of early educational journals that aided the common school cause. The mission of the Western Literary Institute was to create favorable public opinion for free schools, according to John Prickett, who founded the organization in 1831.

Professional Educators.　　　Cyrus Peirce, Samuel Hall, Edward Sheldon, and Henry Barnard pioneered the normal school movement. Sheldon, school superintendent in Oswego, New York, implemented Pestalozzi's educational concepts in the United

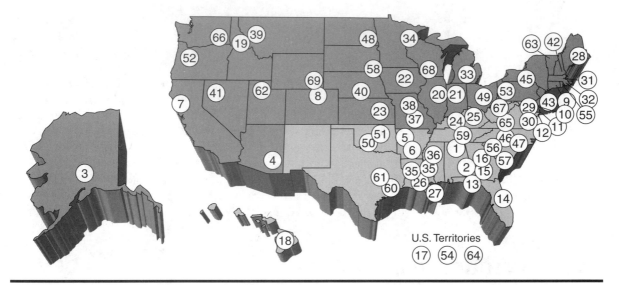

1. Alabama A&M University
2. Auburn University
3. University of Alaska
4. Arizona State University
5. University of Arkansas, Fayetteville
6. University of Arkansas, Pine Bluff
7. University of California
8. Colorado State University
9. University of Connecticut
10. University of Delaware
11. Delaware State College
12. University of the District of Columbia
13. Florida A&M University
14. University of Florida
15. Fort Valley State College
16. University of Georgia
17. University of Guam
18. University of Hawaii
19. University of Idaho
20. University of Illinois
21. Purdue University
22. Iowa State University
23. Kansas State University
24. Kentucky State University

25. University of Kentucky
26. Louisiana State University
27. Southern University
28. University of Maine
29. University of Maryland
30. University or Maryland, Eastern Shore
31. Massachusetts Institute of Technology
32. University of Massachusetts
33. Michigan State University
34. University of Minnesota
35. Alcorn State University
36. Mississippi State University
37. Lincoln University
38. University of Missouri
39. Montana State University
40. University of Nebraska
41. University of Nevada, Reno
42. University of New Hampshire
43. Rutgers, The State University of New Jersey
44. New Mexico State University
45. Cornell University
46. North Carolina A&T State University

47. North Carolina State University
48. North Dakota State University
49. Ohio State University
50. Langston University
51. Oklahoma State University
52. Oregon State University
53. Pennsylvania State University
54. University of Puerto Rico
55. University of Rhode Island
56. Clemson University
57. South Carolina State College
58. South Dakota State University
59. Tennessee State University
60. Prairie View A&M University
61. Texas A&M University
62. Utah State University
63. University of Vermont
64. University of the Virgin Islands
65. Virginia Polytechnic Institute & State University
66. Washington State University
67. West Virginia University
68. University of Wisconsin-Madison
69. University of Wyoming

Figure 5.2 Land Grant Universities as Designated by State Legislatures

Source: Robert O'Neil, Chairman. *Factbook.* Washington, DC: National Association of Land Grant Colleges, 1989, 39–41.

States. Catherine Beecher, Emma Hart Willard (founder of the Troy Female Seminary), and Mary Lyon were among the promoters of education for women. In 1962, Frederick Rudolph, in *The American College and University,* identified challenges to women's education. He wrote of fears of men, such as Reverend John Todd, who dreaded coeducation:

> Must we crowd education on our daughters, and for the sake of having them "intellectuals" make them puny, nervous, and their whole earthly existence a struggle between life and death.
>
> Early female college buildings were often only two stories, since there were fears that any more stair climbing would completely unsex women!

Caleb Mills in Indiana, John D. Pierce in Michigan, Calvin Wiley in North Carolina, and John Swett in California were important early educators. Probably James Carter, Horace Mann, and Henry Barnard exerted the greatest influence.

Carter.   James G. Carter (1795–1845) was a pioneer educational reformer who worked his way through Harvard University by teaching in the Massachusetts district schools. He is often called the "father" of the Massachusetts school system and of normal schools. Carter was largely responsible for the passage of the Massachusetts school law of 1827; the law provided for public secondary schools in that state. He made an effort to influence Massachusetts to establish public normal schools for the training of common school teachers, and he helped to set up the state board of education in 1837. Carter wrote essays on popular education in which he attacked the antidemocratic character of the private schools that existed in the early national period. He feared that private education, and especially private academies, would give rise to a differentiation between the classes of citizens, a differentiation that would be detrimental to America. Hence, in addition to his direct work with the schools—work that included not only his efforts to pass school laws but also some personal experiments with private schools—Carter contributed vastly to the belief in democratic education for all people without regard for social class or wealth.

Mann.   Horace Mann (1796–1859) was perhaps the best known of the important leaders in developing the American public school system. Mann worked with Carter to persuade the Commonwealth of Massachusetts to establish a board of education; then he resigned from the legislature in order to become secretary of that board. During his twelve years as secretary, he was the most active leader of the movement for common school education in the country. *The Common School Journal,* of which Mann was editor, was circulated throughout the nation and in foreign lands as well. Mann often received letters from educational reformers and others interested in schools beyond their own states, and he gave many lectures and made public appearances in the cause of education. Mann became the acknowledged leader in American school organization, and he created a revival in Massachusetts that spread throughout the land.

The twelve annual reports published during his period as secretary of the board contained much information about how the schools could be improved. Mann was an enemy of the old district schools of Massachusetts, and he believed that education should be little influenced by private or religious societies. He succeeded in obtaining the support of the state legislature for liberal taxation, which increased educational opportunities through new buildings and better salaries for teachers. From 1839 to 1840, Mann organized three of the first normal schools in the country. He also created fifty new high schools and had a marked effect on increased attendance in public schools at all levels. He worked, too, for improvement of teaching methods and for a better curriculum for the common schools. He attempted to use the schools to improve social conditions as well as to provide an opportunity for those who were on the bottom of the economic order.

Mann's work was so respected that his influence was very great throughout the United States. His system for Massachusetts was widely copied as the development of common schools and high schools progressed in the rest of the nation.

Barnard.   Henry Barnard (1811–1900) played a role in Connecticut and Rhode Island that was similar to the role played by Mann in Massachusetts. He was secretary of the board of education in Connecticut, principal of a normal school there, and, beginning in 1845, the state superintendent of Rhode Island. Barnard's major contribution came through his editorship of educational publications, particularly the *American Journal of Education,* published between 1855 and 1881. Barnard initiated the teacher's institute movement in 1839 and became a popular disseminator of information about better schools. A member of the Connecticut legislature, in 1838 he sponsored successful legislation similar to the Massachusetts bill of 1837, which created a state school board. He became the first secretary of the board of education and stirred much interest in education, although the legislature soon abolished his office.

Next, Barnard moved to Rhode Island. There, after a two-year campaign to awaken the citizens to the problems of the schools, he managed to get a law passed creating public schools and served as commissioner until 1849. Connecticut made some efforts to reverse its previous error in firing Barnard by setting up a normal school and inviting him to be its principal. He held both positions for a number of years, and during this time he also produced many letters, articles, and educational studies. Barnard was also chancellor at the University of Wisconsin, president of St. John's College at Annapolis, and the first U.S. commissioner of education from 1867 to 1870. His greatest success lay in democratic philosophy and his ability to rouse public interest through the dissemination of information about education. Barnard is sometimes called the "father of American school administration," as well as the founder of American educational journalism.

EUROPEAN INFLUENCES

Although it is true that American education was formed and molded by many factors that were uniquely American, the importance of transplanted European movements should not be underestimated. In the period from 1810 to 1865, the influence of European ideas was quite evident in the evolution of American preschool institutions.

Infant Schools.　　The infant school of England, originated by Robert Owen and modified by Samuel Wilderspin, ministered to toddlers from the age of three. Owen's version encompassed a sort of informal education centered around health, physical training, and spontaneous activity. Wilderspin defined the school's function in more traditional terms, and his schools have been described as "intellectual packing-houses." In 1818, Boston made provisions for the first American infant school, with an allocation of $5,000. Dubbed the "primary school," this institution catered to children who had attained their fourth birthday. Within a decade, similar schools had sprouted in New York, Philadelphia, and Providence. Both originators influenced the American infant school, or primary school, but the Wilderspin format enjoyed the greatest development.

By mid-century, the primary school had been absorbed into the common elementary schools. Infant schools were started to help the children of poor factory workers, but they did not satisfy the demand for free public schools.

Kindergartens.　　European educators instituted the kindergarten as the proper foundation for education. The "garden of children" nurtured growth with the concept of activity, accenting the importance of play, songs, and stories. Froebel's educational ideas formed a complex and sophisticated philosophical position, but the kindergarten movement in America only encompassed the outward manifestations of his theory. Strangely enough, the kindergarten met with stern resistance in Froebel's homeland of Germany; its greatest development was in the United States.

In the midst of a wave of German immigration following the Prussian Revolution in 1848, Margarethe Meyer Schurz, a former pupil of Froebel, established the first American kindergarten. Formed in Watertown, Wisconsin, in 1856, Mrs. Schurz' school was really a German kindergarten on American soil, with German language as the means of communication. Elizabeth Peabody, who in 1860 established in Boston the first English-speaking kindergarten, considerably fostered the growth of American kindergartens. In 1873, the kindergarten was brought into the realm of the public schools, due to the efforts of Superintendent William T. Harris in St. Louis, with the assistance of Susan E. Blow, who published *Educational Issues in the Kindergarten* in 1908. The movement was expanded in the private arena with contributions of philanthropic societies. In the early years, kindergartens served children from ages three to seven. By the 1970s, they served ages three to five and were found throughout America.

The kindergarten has become a stable part of the modern educational system, with more than 90 percent of America's five-year-olds enrolled. Many of the ideas made operational by the progressives in the twentieth century trace their roots to Froebel and the kindergarten.

European School Model.　　If the American schools were not altogether adequate, there was at least an awareness that better programs for education were available in other parts of the world. The influence of reports on European education can hardly be overemphasized, and the most influential of the lot was by Victor Cousin. His detailed monograph on Prussian schools was first published in 1831 and translated into English in 1834. It was widely circulated in America, and its impact can be judged from the fact that shortly after it gained prominence, a number of important educators journeyed to Europe with the intent of studying the European systems and Prussia's in particular. Calvin Stowe's visit resulted in his treatise, *Elementary Education in Europe* (1837). Mann made the trip in 1843 and gathered material for his famous *Seventh Annual Report to the Massachusetts Board of Education.* Although he disapproved of Prussian purposes, Mann found great merit in their efficient methods, universality, high-quality buildings, broad curriculum, and significantly effective teacher training. Almost all the American educators who had an opportunity to visit schools on the European mainland returned with favorable impressions. They used German or Prussian schools as a model for making the American educational program more uniform and efficient.

European Educational Theory.   Although some of the advances made in European schools were the result of national or political forces, there was also a new philosophic basis for change. In addition to Comenius and Locke (discussed in Chapter 4), major educational concepts were developed by Jean Jacques Rousseau (1712–1778), Johann Basedow (1734–1790), Johann H. Pestalozzi (1746–1827), Johann Herbart (1776–1841), and Friedrich Froebel (1782–1852).

Rousseau.   Rousseau was a critic of conventional civilization, which he viewed as depraved and artificial. Rejecting the doctrine of original sin, he held that the basic nature of man is good and only social institutions—such as governments, churches, and schools—cause evil. Rousseau demanded a return to nature and an opportunity for the child to pass through natural stages of development without being molded by degenerate social forces.

Although better known for his *Social Contract,* Rousseau's *Émile* became a major educational classic. In it, he advocated emotional, intellectual, and educational freedom for children. Distrusting books and standard pedagogical techniques of his day, Rousseau believed that children should learn directly from experience. Thus, physical activity, field trips, learning by doing (including manual or vocational experiences), freedom to pursue natural interests, and play were advocated as means for developing the latent potentialities of the child. Rousseau suggested that people be aware of "negative education," by which he meant protecting the student from the influences of superficial social institutions. Rousseau's attack on formalism and support for natural interests had little direct influence on American education until the period of John Dewey and the progressive educators. However, his effect on European educators and schools had an indirect bearing on American schools at an earlier date.

Basedow.   The German educator Johann Basedow attempted to put many of Rousseau's ideas into operation in his Philanthropinum. This school was open to all students, regardless of wealth or class. It stressed natural development, teaching through conversation and sense experience, play, physical activity, and object lessons. Basedow included health, sex education, vocational training, and "world citizenship" in his curriculum. He wrote *Elementary Work,* a book on his theories; and he advocated teacher training. One of the teachers at the Philanthropinum, Christian Salzmann, later created his own school. Salzmann required his students to learn gardening, pursue gymnastics, and develop vocational skills; but there was also time for play, nature study, and formal classes. Other disciples of Basedow, such as J. H. Campe and Johann Guts-Muths, developed German children's literature and the physical education program for the German states.

Pestalozzi.   The Swiss educator Johann H. Pestalozzi experimented with some of the more practical ideas of Rousseau's *Émile* and applied many of his own theories as well. Pestalozzi's major books included *Leonard and Gertrude, How Gertrude Teaches Her Children, Book for Mothers*, and the *Evening Hours of the Hermit*. Pestalozzi conducted schools at Neuhof, Stanz, Burgdorf, Hofwyl, and Yverdon. Starting with his own son's education, about which he kept a careful diary of observations, Pestalozzi developed educational programs for impoverished children and methods that were useful for teaching the children of the common people.

Pestalozzi looked upon the child's mind as a union of separate moral, physical, and intellectual faculties. He believed that education was the natural, progressive, and harmonious development of the natural faculties and powers. He trusted children's natural instincts and thought they should provide the motives for learning. Instead of threats and corporal punishment, Pestalozzi believed that cooperation and sympathy could produce discipline in a homelike atmosphere. He saw education as a mutual effort by the student and the teacher, an effort that produced mutual respect. Like Rousseau, Pestalozzi believed that the child unfolds or develops through various natural stages, according to the principle of growth. He thought that sense impressions were the foundation of all knowledge. Pestalozzi wanted to develop each child's potential to the maximum and, therefore, spoke of educating the "hand and the heart," as well as the "head." Moral education and vocational training were just as important to Pestalozzi as intellectual subjects.

For Pestalozzi, education was based on actual observations rather than on books and theories. He relied on object lessons to develop the child's senses of sight, touch, and sound. Plants, animals, music, tools, and the natural environment were important in his education. Unlike the earliest sense realists, he did not view the mind as a passive receptor of sense impressions. He insisted that the mind is active in perceiving, analyzing, and selecting. Pestalozzi believed that society could be improved through adequate educational opportunity for all. Teachers from all over Europe came to observe his methods, and Pestalozzi offered them training. He believed that the basis for teaching should be close observation of the attitudes and activities of children.

In England, Charles Mayo made the ideas of Pestalozzi popular. American followers included Joseph Neef, who wrote *Methods of Instruction*, and Edward Sheldon, who created the Oswego movement (see Chapter 6).

Froebel.   Since the advent of the kindergarten, educational leaders have been much influenced by Friedrich Froebel's theories concerning education of the very young. Froebel became a follower of Pestalozzi while teaching at a small private school at Frankfurt, Germany. In 1816, he opened a school of his own, and six years later published *The Education of Man*. At Blankenburg, Froebel finally was able to establish his educational institution offering programs for children between the ages of three and eight. (The German term for his school was *Kleinkinderbeschaftingungsanstalt;* that term was later reduced to *kindergarten.*)

Froebel was basically an idealist who looked upon the child as the agency for the realization of God's will in human nature. A mystic, Froebel believed that the spirit of the child could be linked with the absolute through the unity of experience and divine nature. From a practical standpoint, the significance of Froebel was in his conception of the educative process as something that must begin with a child of three or four years of age. Early childhood educational activities centering on play, music, and physical activity made him famous. Froebel created new respect for children, especially for their individuality and for the dynamic and active qualities of their nature. Froebel's program supported constructive use of objects, storytelling, and cooperative social activities. Children were free to express themselves and to build good relationships with others in the kindergarten. Although later educators often disagreed with Froebel's mystical concepts, his efforts to create early childhood education had a profound effect. Froebel greatly influenced both Maria Montessori and John Dewey.

Growth of Academies.

The age of the common school revival was also a time of expansion for academies. Those that developed in colonial times were terminal private venture schools with practical programs. Many of those in operation before the Civil War offered college preparatory courses. Some were denominational; a local board or city government governed others. Most academies charged tuition, but several enjoyed some sort of private endowment as well. Various schemes for public support of academies were tried, and a large number did benefit from some degree of public finance. The curriculum of the academy was never fixed; many offered a wide range of courses. Reading, writing, grammar, arithmetic, and higher mathematics were usually offered. Chemistry, botany, mineralogy, logic, moral philosophy, and natural science were sometimes in the program. Many academies offered modern languages and music. Some claimed to prepare students for teaching and other professions. A large number of academies admitted girls, and some were designated as "female seminaries" or schools for girls only.

After 1860, academies declined in number, due largely to the vast increase in public high schools. The census of 1850 numbered 6,085 private schools and academies in the United States. New York had over 800 incorporated academies. Both Ohio and Virginia chartered more than 200 before 1860. The majority were located in eastern states, but there were frontier academies in newly settled regions as well. Many academies closed after a few months because of lack of support. Some were only elementary schools, and others were largely vocational. However, most American communities had access to some sort of academy for those who could afford tuition.

Normal Schools and Institutes.

Private academies for the training of teachers did not satisfy educational leaders like Mann, Barnard, and the Reverend Charles Brooks. Brooks began a campaign for state normal schools in Massachusetts in 1835, using the Prussian model of teacher education as a guide. Brooks had some influence on the school board; and in 1838, when Edmund Dwight offered $10,000 for educational improvement, three normal schools were founded. The state matched Dwight's grant and used the funds for salaries and operating expenses of the teacher-training institutions. In 1846, the normal school at Bridgewater got its own building. The name "normal" school came from the model or practice school in which the standard or normal curriculum and methods were observed. Cyrus Peirce, the first principal of the normal school at Lexington, stressed the review of common subjects and practice teaching under his own observation.

New York created a state normal school at Albany in 1844, but state money was also used to subsidize private academies for teachers. David Page, a principal at Albany, wrote *Theory and Practice of Teaching;* the book became a standard text for teacher education. Only twelve normal schools were created in the United States before the Civil War. Many districts were satisfied with the untrained young ladies they hired as elementary teachers.

Henry Barnard started the teacher's institute. This was a meeting of a group of teachers for instruction; it usually lasted only a few weeks. County superintendents of schools often conducted institutes for teachers in summer months. A similar effort was made by the NEA Teacher Center, popular in the 1870s.

Educational Opportunity for Women.

The growth of academies provided a much greater opportunity for secondary and higher education for women. A few girls' schools in colonial times offered courses in ornamental needlework, polite manners, music, French, and other subjects deemed proper for females. Many of the academies that were in operation before 1860 expanded the curriculum. There was some opposition to teaching girls Latin, logic, and the sciences; but all other courses were offered in at least some of the schools for girls. Coeducation was rare; most academies admitted one sex or the other, but not both. Employment of male teachers only, except in the dame schools, ended during the early national period. Horace Mann and other educational leaders encouraged women to teach in elementary schools. It became common for many academies to offer courses in "schoolkeeping" for girls. Preparation of common school teachers was largely confined to a review of the common branches and a series of highly moralistic lectures on the "duties" of teachers; however, it was often the only teacher training available. Samuel Hall's *Lectures on Schoolkeeping* was the basic text for teacher training until normal schools such as Edward Sheldon's opened in 1853 in Oswego, New York.

Catherine Beecher, Mary Lyon, Almira Phelps, and Emma Willard were leaders in the movement for girls' secondary education. In 1821, Mrs. Willard opened the Troy Female Seminary, and Mary Lyon founded Mt. Holyoke Female Seminary in 1837. Catherine Beecher founded the American Women's Education Association, and Almira Phelps wrote a series of *Lectures to Young Ladies.* The efforts of these women educators helped to establish the first coeducational college program at Oberlin in 1838.

Polly Welts Kaufman, in *Women Teachers on the Frontier,* wrote about women sent by the National Board of Popular Education in the decades before the Civil War to teach in the South and West. Some 600 women were sent to teach in Missouri, Ohio, Indiana, and other Western and Southern states. Many remained and settled in the West. The board accepted only those women who could prove membership in an evangelical church as well as tell about their conversion experiences. Reasons for women choosing to leave their homes in the East included better job opportunities, adventure, and missionary zeal. Bible readings, singing programs as advocated by Horace Mann, and instilling high ideals in their pupils were part of their curriculum. Although teachers' salaries have improved in recent years, one may still find a gap in teacher salaries between men and women. The perception of women teachers' worth was expressed in the early 1800s in an 1855 Annual Report of the School Committee of Concord, Massachusetts. According to the report, town officials found that students improved more when women teachers rather than men teachers taught them.

> Sure, this being the fact, it is not good economy to employ a man to teach those Schools, when the services of a woman of the best qualifications, can be obtained for two-thirds or three-fourths the expense. (Kaufman, 1984)

Minority Education.   Very little progress was made in providing educational opportunity for minority children before 1861. Early schools that had been established for Native-American children by missionaries were largely unsuccessful because the teachers misunderstood Native-American culture and attitudes. An occasional student learned to read English, but formal schooling was almost nonexistent for the Native-American population.

In the colonial period, many slave owners permitted blacks to read. Some felt it was their duty to teach slaves something about the Bible and the tenets of religion. A few free blacks made their way into Quaker schools in the North, which were open to all. In 1833, a Quaker teacher named Prudence Crandall was criticized for admitting black girls to her school in Connecticut. In 1846, Benjamin Roberts of Boston filed suit because his son was forced to attend a segregated school for black boys. The Massachusetts Supreme Court held that the school committees had a right to keep schools segregated. However, by 1857, Massachusetts passed a law preventing discrimination. The school laws in most states before the Civil War did not provide for black scholars. Those of Indiana and Illinois specifically required schools for white children.

Even in the South, blacks were occasionally educated. John Chavis was a teacher and a licensed Presbyterian minister before North Carolina passed a law against black preachers in 1832. Most Southern states prohibited the teaching of blacks after Nat Turner's rebellion of 1831.

THEN TO NOW

The age of the common school revival was a period in which equality of educational opportunity was stressed. Horace Mann was a great champion of education for all. He and Henry Barnard believed that the schools had the power to unite the United States into an integrated national community. Economic, social, racial, ethnic, and religious diversity were to be subsumed under one democratic system of education that would unite all the people into a single indivisible nation. Education was to be used as the chief instrument for assimilating the foreign born into the mainstream of American life and culture.

Schools did have a considerable measure of success in creating a single culture. Some 35 million immigrants came to America in the nineteenth century, and they were Americanized largely by the public schools. Still, the aim of Mann and Barnard to achieve equality and social integration was not fully realized. Many persons living in the United States today are excluded from full participation in the social and economic life of the nation. Contemporary concerns about equality for ethnic groups and blacks are clear indications that the melting pot ideal has not been fulfilled. Mann also wanted to move away from the extreme differences between rich and poor. He believed that a strong nation must provide opportunity for all and that differences between the haves and the have-nots must be reduced. Although many Americans have achieved affluence in the modern era, there are still many who are poor or the victims of discrimination.

Black education in the South was almost nonexistent before the Civil War and very limited in Northern states. President Lincoln liberated about 4 million slaves, almost all of them illiterate. The Fourteenth Amendment (ratified in 1868) specified that states should not deprive any person of life, liberty, or property without due process of law. Nevertheless, blacks remained second-class citizens. Jim Crow laws of the 1880s were passed to "keep the Colored in their place" (Sandifer, 1969), and discrimination was universally practiced. The separate but equal doctrine of *Plessy v. Ferguson* in 1896 legalized racial segregation until 1954. Private black colleges and those created by the Second Morrill Act helped to improve the quality of teachers; however, black schools lacked funds, and the extreme poverty of the people made progress very slow. States claimed to provide equal support for black and white schools, but many actually put more dollars into education for the majority race (Figure 5.3).

This difficulty has not been resolved in the modern era. An end to legal segregation and plans for achieving racial balance in school systems have had an impact, but problems remain. Many American cities are still segregated de facto. This situation is not improving in many areas that are becoming almost totally populated by one race or ethnic group. Affluent blacks (and other minorities) who represent the professions or the middle class have little difficulty in assimilating with white society. Integration in schools works well when all the students come from a similar socioeconomic background. However, there are major problems when black children from urban slums are placed in classrooms with students from more affluent families. The issue is especially clear when busing is used as a means of bringing together students from different races, ethnic groups, and socioeconomic backgrounds. Demographic patterns in many large cities are shifting so rapidly that efforts to integrate schools are frustrated. Atlanta, Houston, Washington, D.C., and Newark are cities that experienced dramatic increases in the number of minority students just when they began to implement plans for desegregation.

Desegregation efforts are illustrated by the Little Rock, Arkansas, school districts, which are under a Federal Court Order to desegregate. Ann S. Marshall, Federal

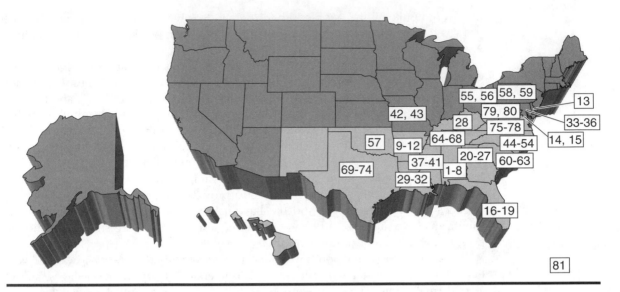

1. Alabama A&M University
2. Alabama State University
3. Concordia College
4. Miles College
5. Oakwood College
6. Stillman College
7. Talladega College
8. Tuskegee University
9. Arkansas Baptist College
10. Philander Smith College
11. Shorter College
12. University of Arkansas, Pine Bluff
13. Delaware State University
14. Howard University
15. University of the District of Columbia
16. Bethune-Cookman College
17. Edward Waters College
18. Florida A&M University
19. Florida Memorial College
20. Albany State College
21. Clark Atlanta University
22. Fort Valley State College
23. Morehouse College
24. Morris Brown College
25. Paine College
26. Savannah State College
27. Spelman College
28. Kentucky State University

29. Dillard University
30. Grambling State University
31. Southern University
32. Xavier University of Louisiana
33. Bowie State University
34. Coppin State College
35. Morgan State University
36. University of Maryland: Eastern Shore
37. Alcorn State University
38. Jackson State University
39. Mississippi Valley State University
40. Rust College
41. Tougaloo College
42. Harris Stowe State College
43. Lincoln University
44. Barber-Scotia College
45. Bennett College
46. Elizabeth City State University
47. Fayetteville State University
48. Johnson C. Smith University
49. Livingstone College
50. North Carolina A&T State University
51. North Carolina Central University
52. St. Augustine's College
53. Shaw University
54. Winston-Salem State College

55. Central State University
56. Wilberforce University
57. Langston University
58. Cheyney University of Pennsylvania
59. Lincoln University
60. Benedict College
61. Chaflin College
62. South Carolina State University
63. Voorhees Collge
64. Fisk University
65. Knoxville College
66. Lane College
67. LeMoyne-Owen College
68. Tennessee State University
69. Huston-Tillotson College
70. Paul Quinn College
71. Prairieview A&M University
72. Texas College
73. Texas Southern University
74. Wiley College
75. Hampton University
76. Norfolk State University
77. St. Paul's College
78. Virginia State University
79. Bluefield State College
80. West Virginia State College
81. University of the Virgin Islands

Figure 5.3 Colleges and Universities with Large Black Enrollment (60% to 98%)

Source: Editors of the Chronicle of Higher Education, the Almanac of Higher Education. IL: University of Chicago Press, 1995, 321–90. (Figures compiled by the U.S. Department of Education.)

Monitor to the Office of Desegregation Monitoring, reported that in 1993 the three districts of the system—Little Rock, North Little Rock, and Pulaski County—had a racial black–white enrollment of approximately 60–40, 50–50, and 30–70, respectively. The districts created magnet schools that sought to draw more students from throughout the district, but the end result was the proportion as noted. In 1999–2000 there were five racially identifiable schools. These were schools with such a high black enrollment that they were designated double-funded incentive schools. The double funding was designed to compensate for the racially isolated environment and to provide an incentive for white students to transfer to these schools. By 1999–2000 the racial black—white balance of the districts was 68–32, 58–42, and 34–66, with five incentive schools in operation.

In 1995 the District Court withdrew its monitoring and supervision of North Little Rock School District in the area of student assignments, but enrollment trends continue to be published because enrollment and racial balance in the district remain a factor in majority-to-minority transfers and in the proportion of students eligible for magnet school enrollment. A 2000 Pulaski County Special School District plan included requiring yearly reporting on one–race classes, as well as studying disciplinary practices with African-American students, particularly male students at the secondary level. Efforts are under way to explore unification status for Little Rock in which case the school district would no longer be under control of court supervision.

With an increasing number of immigrants, ethnic minorities by or before 2050 may dominate some states such as California. The dominant groups in the state may be Hispanics and Asian Americans, with Caucasians in a minority group. Penny Loeb and colleagues, in an article entitled "To Make a Nation," noted that in the 1980s over 8.6 million newcomers mainly from Asia, Latin America, and the Caribbean—the greatest influx since the 1920s—came to the United States. Although all parts of the country were influenced by an increase of 63 percent in 1980 and 1990 over the previous decade, most foreign–born arrivals settled in five states—California, New York, Texas, Florida, and New Jersey.

According to Bouvier's *Shaping Florida: The Effects of Immigration* (1995) and *Florida in the 21st Century* (1992), the Orlando School District in Orange County has an enrollment of 50.1 percent minorities. Although the county's overall population is 67 percent white, "blacks (28.6%), Hispanics (17.7%), Asians and other minorities (3.8%)" constitute the majority of the school district's enrollment. Projections indicate that Florida's population by 2020 will become a "majority-minority."

By late 1997, federal legislation restricting immigrant inflows and benefits such as food stamps, aid to families with dependent children, supplemental security income, and Medicaid was being explored for both illegal and legal immigrants. However, rather than restrict immigration, a leading futures think tank, the Hudson Institute, issued a report entitled *Workforce 2020* that suggested increasing immigration of skilled workers to compensate for an aging workforce. Striving for tolerance and appreciation of diversity in our population is a continuing goal of educators now as it has been in the past.

Much effort has been devoted to creating and expanding public schools, including high schools. Educational leaders like James Carter did their best to make schools available to all and to improve their quality. The goal of providing equal educational opportunity to everyone and also of having excellent programs is still a difficult one to reach.

Even before Thurgood Marshall (as lawyer for the NAACP in 1954) argued that segregated schools are inherently unequal, there was general agreement that minority schools had lower standards. It could have hardly been otherwise, for those schools enrolled many children who were poor and culturally deprived. Black schools had less equipment, worse buildings, and teachers with very limited training. Beyond question, minority students have gained a great deal since desegregation. It stands to reason that placing children in better schools will be of some benefit to them. Still, many schools have not been integrated, and critics say that progress in those that have been is not satisfactory. Lower overall achievement sometimes occurs when children with a poor educational background are placed in the same classrooms with those who have done better. Historically, labeling students on the basis of preconceived biases has prevented some minority students and women from acquiring access and equity in education. Mainstreaming of special needs students has often enhanced self-esteem, increased life skills, and improved achievement levels. The current attacks on remediation, social promotion, and soft pedagogy reflect public dissatisfaction with students' academic achievement levels and with educational standards.

In addition, there are many current issues over attempts to teach the same values in all schools and to Americanize all youth. Ethnic and minority groups often argue that this practice takes away from the unique characteristics of children who are not of the white, middle-class, dominant culture. Teachers in some school districts with large black populations are being encouraged to communicate and instruct in Ebonics, or the subculture language of inner cities and other centers of minority populations. Supporters believe educators should understand the dialogue of minorities in order to effectively bridge racial divides and improve communication between teachers and pupils. Others believe, as did Noah Webster, that pupils need to be taught English language skills for common values and citizenship in the nation. The struggle for equality and for excellence is far from over in American education.

History reveals the continued efforts to achieve Horace Mann's call for an absolute right of all citizens to an education. Exploring alternative methods of teaching students from different language backgrounds contributes to universal education.

GAINING PERSPECTIVE THROUGH CRITICAL ANALYSIS

1. Name the similarities and differences between the impact of the Industrial Revolution on historical educational policies and practices and the impact of technology on today's policies and practices.

2. Give your interpretation of the purpose and contribution of the common school revival to educational theory and practice.

3. Name three educational leaders who contributed to the development of public school systems. What policies and practices initiated by these leaders are still utilized today?

4. Compare and contrast the educational opportunities available for minorities and women in early America with opportunities for those groups today.

5. What examples of English, classical, and commercial curriculum are still found in today's high school curricula?

HISTORY IN ACTION IN TODAY'S CLASSROOMS

1. Contact people, organizations, and institutions in your community to determine the educational and employment opportunities available for women and minorities.

2. Interview a staff member or community leader of one of the organizations or institutions that try to create educational opportunities for women and minorities. Explore his or her perceptions of equality and excellence available to the populations he or she serves. Add the findings to your journal.

3. How has federal legislation attempted to increase access to educational opportunities and employment since World War I?

INCREASED UNDERSTANDING THROUGH ONLINE RESEARCH

Visit the Prentice Hall Foundations Web site (*http://www.prenhall.com/foundations-cluster*) and examine Topics 7 and 16. Using the resources available in these topics, complete an essay on challenges faced by public education that are similar to and different from those experienced by our nation's founders. Write and submit your response to your instructor using the Electronic Bluebook module also in either of these two topics of the Web site.

BIBLIOGRAPHY

Bailyn, Bernard. *Education in the Forming of American Society.* New York: Random House, 1960.

Binder, Frederick. *The Age of the Common School, 1830–1865.* New York: Wiley, 1974.

Bouvier, Leon. *Florida in the 21st Century.* Washington, DC: The Center for Immigration Studies, 1992.

———. *Shaping Florida: The Effects of Immigration.* Washington, DC: The Center for Immigration Studies, 1995, 3–15.

Brown, Ann. *Federal Monitor to the Office of Desegregation Monitoring.* Little Rock: U.S. Government Printing Office, 1993. (*1999-00 Enrollment and Racial Balance in the Little Rock School District and Pulaski County Special School District* report filed with U.S. Eastern District Court, Arkansas, March 29, 2000.)

Brubacher, John. *Henry Barnard on Education.* New York: McGraw-Hill, 1931.

Burton, Warren. *The District School as It Was.* Boston: Lee & Shepard, 1897.

Butts, Freeman. *The American Tradition in Religion and Education.* Boston: Beacon Press, 1950.

Bystydzienski, Jill M. *Women in Cross-Cultural Transitions.* Bloomington, IN: Phi Delta Kappa: 1994.

Cremin, Lawrence, ed. *The Republic and the School: Horace Mann on the Education of Free Man.* New York: Teachers College Press, 1957.

Curti, Merle. *The Social Ideas of American Educators.* New York: Littlefield Adams, 1966.

"The First Kindergarten in the United States," Available: *http://www.russkelly.com/myhometown/00002bl.html*

or *http://www.exploremilwaukee.com/lcattractl.html* (Mrs. Carl Schurz, 1856).

Good, Harry G., and James D. Teller. *A History of American Education*. New York: Macmillan, 1973.

Gutek, Gerald L. *American Education in a Global Society*. New York: Longman, 1993. Westview, 1997.

Kaufman, Polly Welts. *Women Teachers on the Frontier*. New Haven, CT: Yale University Press, 1984, xvii–xxiii, 6, 22. (*Annual Report of the School Committee of the Town of Concord, Year Ending April 1, 1855*, Concord, Massachusetts, 1855, p. 15.)

Loeb, Penny, Dorian Friedman, Mary C. Lord, Dan McGraw, and Kukula Glastris. "To Make a Nation." *U.S. News and World Report* (October 4, 1993):47–54.

MacMullen, Edith Nye. *In the Cause of True Education: Henry Barnard and Nineteenth Century Educational Reform*. New Haven, CT: Yale University Press, 1991.

Mann, Horace. *Lectures and Annual Reports on Education*, Cambridge, MA: Cornhill Press of Boston, 1867.

———. "Tenth Annual Report (1846)," in *The Republic and the School: Horace Mann*, Lawrence A. Cremin, ed., 63. New York: Teachers College Press, Columbia University, 1957.

Pratte, Richard. *Ideology and Education*. New York: Wiley, 1977.

Rudolph, Frederick. *The American College and University*. Athens, GA: University of Georgia Press, 1990, 360. Original printing 1962.

Rusk, Robert, and James Scotland. *Doctrines of the Great Educators*. New York: St. Martin's Press, 1979.

Sandifer, Jawn A., ed. *The Afro-American in United States History*. New York: Globe Book Company, 1969, 214.

Silver, Harold, ed. *Robert Owen on Education*. Cambridge, MA: Harvard University Press, 1969.

Veblen, Thorstein. *The Higher Learning in America*. New York: B. W. Huebsch, 1918.

Woody, Thomas. *A History of Women's Education in the United States*. New York: Farrar Strauss, Octagon Books, 1966.

CHAPTER SIX

AMERICAN EDUCATION: 1865–1918

We want education for ourselves . . . adequate, expertly taught, and continuing through the elementary grades, through high school and as far beyond that as proven gift and desert show is clearly for human welfare, no matter what the race, sex or religion of the recipient. This education is a public duty and should be at public expense. It should continue beyond school years, and in the form of adult education for all.

W. E. B. Du Bois

Reconstruction	Herbartian Movement	Progressive Era
1865 Slavery abolished by Thirteenth Amendment	1870 School superintendents in 28 American cities	1890 Second Morrill Act provided black A. M. and N. colleges
1868 Fourteenth Amendment protects life and property	1874 Kalamazoo case made tax support legal for high schools	1893 Rhode Island begins special education programs
1869 Fifteenth Amendment guarantees civil rights	1890 National Herbart Society	

Figure 6.1   Time Line of American Education 1865–1918

Because historical interpretation is influenced by personal experiences, it is some-times difficult to understand the conditions of times past. Twenty-first-century teach-ers, administrators, and law enforcement officers find it difficult to enforce compulsory attendance laws. Almost every school has at least a few students who do not want to attend and who will not cooperate. Oftentimes, these children are from dysfunctional homes or are involved in drug or alcohol abuse. Sometimes they are so socially maladjusted that they threaten others with violence. Apart from coun-seling and disciplinary action, there is very little that educational authorities can do to keep such students in school, but every state requires attendance at public or pri-vate school, normally through the age of sixteen. These laws were enacted in the late nineteenth and early twentieth century throughout the United States. Their his-torical purpose, however, was not to force children to attend but to prevent others from keeping them out of school. As America became one of the great industrial economies of the world, labor organizations brought great pressure to end child la-bor. Political leaders and social reformers attacked the parental practice of putting children to work and taking their wages. When public schools became the norm, it was widely accepted that every child should have the opportunity to attend, and this was the reason for compulsory attendance laws. Today, some believe that compul-sory attendance is obsolete, but it is a firmly grounded tradition and the laws are likely to persist.

All of us tend to think of schooling in terms of our own educational experience. Just how much computer-assisted instruction one received and how sophisticated the electronic information was depends on how long ago the education took place and where one went to school. Virtual high schools, e-mail photos, online courses, videoconferencing, powerpoint presentations, and new delivery systems are part of

Urban and Industrial Growth		Social and Political Reform
1909 Junior high school in Berkeley, California	1913 Thorndike published his *Educational Psychology*	1916 Dewey published *Democracy and* *Education*
1910 Junior college in Fresno, California	1914 Smith-Lever Act encouraged agriculture	1917 Smith-Hughes Act encouraged vocational schools
Vast growth of high schools		

our education culture. If this new image-morphing computer technology is not familiar, neither is the lack of technological support suffered by teachers in history.

The recitation method used before the Civil War was inefficient and crude. It devoted the attention of the teacher to one student at a time and ignored the rest. One reason for the slow development of group methods was that there was no way to duplicate or copy materials. Tests were given orally or questions were written on the blackboard, but copying a test by hand for each student was just too much labor for teachers. By 1875, the hectograph appeared. This crude instrument allowed for ink transfer on a shallow pan or box filled with gelatin. Several copies could be made from a prepared master. Eventually, a flexible master was placed on a drum so that copies could be cranked out on a machine. Such duplicating or other copying devices were in common use until electronic copiers such as photocopying machines were developed. The first typewriters were for the use of the blind, but L. C. Scholes made a commercial model in 1867. Most schools had manual typewriters available to teachers by 1900, and an electric model was invented in 1935. Making carbon copies on typewriters was tedious at best, but eventually typed duplication masters were made available.

Making copies of materials for students is only one of many examples of the very slow growth of educational technology before the modern period. Maps, laboratory equipment, vocational training devices, and mathematical calculators underwent a similar evolution. So also did school libraries and reference materials for research. Computers, electronic copies, desktop printing, and the Internet make conditions of teaching altogether different from those of past historical periods. It is easier to understand history and to anticipate future change when the slow rate of past invention is compared with the accelerating rate today.

Wars are by no means the most significant checkpoints in educational chronology, but the period between the Civil War and World War I was the era for the development of the modern American school system. Westward expansion and the growth of industry, agriculture, and population put vastly increased demands upon existing schools and required the building not only of new schools but also of whole new educational systems. By 1890, the frontier had almost ceased to be, and with the addition of New Mexico and Arizona to the Union in 1912, the continental United States was formed. Industrial growth carried with it the new problem of educating children in the urban slums and the need for Americanizing immigrants on a grand scale. Natural increase and immigration swelled the population from just over 30 million in 1860 to more than 100 million by 1920.

Before 1860, the Northern states had largely developed the outlines of their educational systems, and some had made substantial progress in bringing state education to all the people. States were not uniform in their growth; those first to be settled usually developed their systems earlier. By 1873, laws for the organization of a state school system, including the school tax and some form of state control, were to be found all over the nation. Before World War I, public school education in America typically included an eight-year elementary school and an expansion of the four-year high school. State universities capped the systems, although only a small percentage of the people could take advantage of them. Public kindergartens, junior high schools, and junior colleges were found in only a few areas before 1920 and were not yet a significant part of the public school organization.

Educational theory passed through a series of stages that included sectarian dominance, *laissez-faire,* slavish copying of European models, and the scientific-progressive movement. Professional training for teachers and administrators became firmly established as an ideal with the growth of normal schools and colleges or departments of education in the universities. Compulsory attendance, expanded curriculum, fully graded common schools, public high schools, and large increases in spending for buildings and equipment marked the period. However, the late nineteenth century witnessed extreme sectional differences in educational structure and quality.

INHIBITED DEVELOPMENT OF EDUCATION IN THE SOUTH

The Civil War interfered with education all over the nation, causing schools to be closed and governmental revenues to be directed to the immediate expenses of the conflict. But Northern states were able to continue their school programs in spite of the reduction in available money and the loss of many teachers. Sometimes an entire student body and faculty went off to join the army, as in the case of Illinois College at Jacksonville, Illinois; but elementary schools in the Union states continued to operate through the wartime years. It was not so in the South; there the battle devastation and increased sacrifice to support the war severely crippled the embryonic school systems. Southern states spent many years recovering even the low educational level they had enjoyed before the national strife, and some of the scars are still visible in the slower school development of the rural South.

Southern Collapse.   The war left Southern states in physical and economic ruin—with crops destroyed, buildings burned, livestock slaughtered, and the labor force demoralized. Civil authority broke down, courts were nonexistent, and 4 million black citizens were without economic resources or leadership. Presidents Lincoln and Johnson hoped to enlist the cooperation of former Confederate leaders in rebuilding the South, but the radical Republicans in Congress wanted to punish the Southern states. In the struggle, Andrew Johnson was nearly impeached, and a military reconstruction government dominated by Northern interests was imposed. These governments—consisting of "carpetbaggers," former slaves, and fortune seekers— failed to obtain the support of the Southern white majority.

Very little real progress had been made by 1876, when the radical reconstruction government finally ended and the Union army of the occupation was removed. Southerners, bitter about their treatment after the conflict and fearful of black power, set about to undo the acts of the reconstruction era. Measures providing for public education, especially where racially mixed schools were concerned, were either ignored or removed from the books. Sectional hatred and opposition to black schools might have paralyzed education even if money had been available, but the war and the waste of the first postwar governments left the South bankrupt.

Newfound freedom did nothing to improve the living standards of the Southern blacks. Most of them were as economically dependent and as subject to exploitation as they had been in slavery. Economic expansion was slow to develop, and both races remained poor, especially small farmers and sharecroppers. Industry received a boost in the 1880s with the founding of textile mills. Tobacco products, lumber, and even steel mills in Alabama contributed to a stronger economy. But agriculture continued to be the mainstay of the Southern economy, and very little tax money was available for school purposes until the twentieth century. Many Southern statesmen deplored the low level and retarded growth of public schools but were powerless to provide adequate support.

African-American Education.   Some money for educating the newly freed citizens came from private and church associations that sent teachers to the South in considerable numbers. The Peabody and other philanthropic funds provided some assistance, but control remained in the hands of whites. In 1869, there were about 9,000 such teachers, working mostly in schools for freedmen. Several societies for the aid of freed slaves were formed, the most important of which were the American Freedman's Union (secular) and the American Missionary Association (religious). Congress established the Freedmen's Bureau in 1865. Its head, General O. O. Howard, considered education to be the most pressing need of blacks in the South.

There was considerable enthusiasm for schooling among former slaves in the period immediately following the war, but adults soon learned that education was something for which they had neither the time nor the preparation. The economic support was often sporadic, and it appears that many of the schools were very ill equipped and of poor quality. Social liberals and political propagandists among the teachers from the North were unpopular. Like all things "Yankee," the freedmen's schools became objects of attack once the power of reconstruction government was broken after 1873. Although the South was still organized as a series of military provinces, new constitutions were adopted that included provisions for education. But for all practical purposes, the states of the South were bankrupt, so that little more than a paper system of education existed in 1870.

Hoar Bill.   In 1870, a bill was introduced in Congress by George F. Hoar of Massachusetts; the bill would have established a federal school system in Southern states. The measure was designed to compel the establishment of a system of instruction and the appointment of a federal superintendent in all states where a minimum standard was not met. Textbooks were to be prescribed by the United States Commissioner of Education, and the schools were to be supported by a centrally collected direct tax. The bill was defeated partly because of the opposition of the National Education Association (NEA) and Superintendent Wickersham of Pennsylvania. They felt that national control over part of the nation's schools could not be tolerated, although gifts of federal money with local autonomy could be. Roots of the modern day issue over federal aid to education can be seen in the arguments over the Hoar Bill.

Blair Bill.   A second effort to get national aid for states unable to maintain schools came in the form of a proposed national school fund from the sale of public land in the tradition of the Ordinance of 1785. When it appeared that this plan would not be adopted, Senator Henry Blair of New Hampshire introduced a bill in 1882 to help states with the greatest educational need. The Blair Bill (in final form) provided for $77 million to be divided among the states in proportion to the number of illiterates in each. The money was to be used as each state saw fit, provided that it was used only for education. This measure passed the Senate three times but was never successful in the House of Representatives. No further bills of this nature were proposed until recent times, although the federal government continued to aid colleges through the Morrill Act of 1890.

Philanthropy.   Private agencies made an effort to fill the educational void in the South and to stimulate greater local effort. George Peabody gave $2 million for this purpose. A board of trustees headed in turn by Barnas Sears, Horace Mann, and J. L. M. Curry administered the Peabody Fund. Under the direction of Curry, a Southerner, the money was used to develop a limited number of high-quality schools as models. Part of the Peabody Fund went to normal schools for women teachers of both races and also to what became the George Peabody College for Teachers in Nashville. Agents who supervised private funds also visited schools and opened lines of communication between groups interested in school improvement.

Southern Associations.   Thirty years after the Civil War, a Conference for Education in the South was organized, and numerous meetings were held for the purpose of improving education. Out of this grew the Southern Education Board and the General Education Board (1903). A Southern Association of Colleges and Schools was established, as well as many private boards that were connected with philanthropic societies, such as the Carnegie Foundation and the Rosenwald Fund. Although stimulation and information were given, the public systems tended to make only limited progress before 1920. Only meager tax support was available in agricultural areas, and even Southern cities were poor by Northern standards.

The educational conservatism of the prewar period and hostility toward schools introduced in the reconstruction era dampened interest in public schools. The most negative factor of all was insistence on separation of white and black schools. This segregation required the building and maintenance of a dual system with duplication of buildings and teachers in states that could least afford them. Because schools for white children were given significantly more support due to a stronger community tax base together with segregation, funds were distributed unevenly leading to lower levels of education for African Americans. This was a major factor in keeping the educational level of Southern states lower than that of the rest of the nation for several decades.

In the early 1900s, the South was still marked by short school terms (seventy days in North Carolina), high illiteracy, ineffective administration, poorly trained teachers, and meager tax support. Salaries of Southern teachers in 1900 averaged about half that of Northern teachers, and black teachers were paid lowest of all.

NATIONAL AFFAIRS AND PROGRESS

If progress was slow in the Southern states between the Civil War and World War I, those years also marked the transition from an old agrarian to a modern, industrial America. In less than half a century, wounds of the Civil War were largely healed, and America entered the era of industrial world powers. Territorial expansion had given way to a greater and faster development of Northern industrial capacities. The growth and development of industry was at least as important a factor in the population growth figure as immigration. Due to a favorable attitude by the government, untapped industrial resources, and cheap labor, this was the period in which it was possible for the Goulds, the Carnegies, and the Rockefellers to build vast industrial empires and accumulate great fortunes. Many of the industrial barons were interested in education and helped to found colleges, universities, and better public schools.

Industrial Exploitation. The other side of the Industrial Revolution had a negative effect on education. Exploitation of children and working men was widespread, and it was not uncommon for immigrants in the cities to labor sixteen hours a day. The growth of great industry swallowed up the small businessman, and there was much corruption in government at all levels. City slums also presented a different kind of educational problem. The need for reform was seen, but many of the people in power sought to make more severe laws and to develop additional penitentiaries, rather than to cure the problem through education.

The Republican Party dominated politics and held control of the presidency between the end of the Civil War and the election of Woodrow Wilson in 1913, with the single exception of the two terms of Grover Cleveland. Distinctly the party of business, industrial, and commercial interests, it did not promote mass educational reform supported by federal and state governments. What was done for the education of the masses in the cities was done largely through private enterprise and with the interests of individuals who saw most clearly the need for reform. The dissatisfaction of the laboring masses began to show itself in the latter part of the nineteenth century. Numerous labor reform parties came into being in the 1870s, and the agrarian and labor groups organized the Independent or Greenback Party in 1874. Later, several independent groups organized the Populist Party, which became part of the Democratic Party in 1896 and came very close to electing William Jennings Bryan over William McKinley.

The tremendous increase in industrial growth in the urban areas of the United States—especially obvious in the northern and eastern sections—together with the growth of large corporations controlling vast amounts of wealth, changed the nature of American society considerably. There was a strong belief in a hands-off, or *laissez-faire,* governmental policy. This was the period of change of the basic nature of American society from rural to urban. The great cities were beginning to take present-day shape, and the idea of the independent farmer class as the dominant one in America was beginning to fade.

Agricultural, Population, and Vocational Changes.

There was also a revolution in farming due to such inventions as McCormick's reaper and the new scientific knowledge about agriculture that had been greatly advanced by the agricultural colleges set up under the Morrill acts. However, the farmer did not immediately benefit from the better technology, because the increase in production caused prices to fall. Hence, the period from 1865 to 1900 saw the rise of many farm organizations designed to aid the plight of the farmer with his decreasing income. This, too, was the beginning of the period of organized labor in America. The Knights of Labor gave way to the American Federation of Labor, and the union movement was well under way by 1900.

The character of the population changed at this time. Immigrants coming to the United States had previously been largely from northwestern Europe, especially England, Ireland, Germany, and Scandinavia. But the people who arrived after the Civil War came from other parts of Europe such as Spain, Russia, Austria, Hungary, and Italy. There were also a few from non-European nations such as China, Japan, and Mexico. Chinese workers helped build the transcontinental railroad. Due to economic and labor problems in the 1870s, some Americans in Western states sought to restrict Chinese immigration; this restriction led to the 1882 Chinese Exclusion Act.

Immigration laws were relaxed in the following decades. However, discrimination has occurred against minorities and newcomers throughout our history. Societies and individuals are prisoners of the intolerance of the ages in which they live. Butts and Cremin (1953) noted that after the Civil War, groups that had been excluded from public elementary schools—Negroes, Indians, Chinese, and Mexicans, as well as those with mental or physical handicaps—were increasingly provided access as a matter of right rather than as charity. The immigrant population became radically different during this period of time; Eastern Europeans and non-Europeans arrived, making the educational task considerably more difficult. Tremendous growth in communication and the transportation system, together with an increased centralization in American life, also had an effect on the educational needs of the people.

THE PUBLIC SCHOOL IDEAL

A major principle of education put into practice after the Civil War was that public education should be free to all. In contrast with the European dual system in which elementary education was for the lower classes and secondary reserved for the elite, the United States established a ladder system by which one might advance from the first grade through college in a series of yearly steps. In theory at least, each child was free to begin at the lowest level and progress as fast as his or her abilities would allow. It was an American belief that the schools could be used for advancement up the social ladder, and the person of ability could qualify for a high-paying job by acquiring education.

This was an age of social revolution in which the industrial and financial leaders accumulated great wealth as industrial and technological expansion increased. With the commercial production of petroleum starting in 1859, the opening of the West to farmers and ranchers, and the joining of the Union Pacific with the Central Pacific to make the first transcontinental railroad line in 1869, growth of wealth and commerce accelerated. Although wealthy families seldom sent their children to public schools before 1900, class distinctions were foreign to the educational ideal. Laboring and middle-class families demanded high-quality public schools for their sons and daughters. Training for making a good living was important, but so too was education for citizenship, morality, and self-improvement. The common elementary school for all citizens was established in theory before the Civil War. It became a reality between 1865 and 1900 for the majority of Americans. Before World War I, the theory was extended upward to include secondary education. The standard American high school became a major part of the educational program and cultural experience of the nation. Dewey's *Democracy and Education,* published in 1916, addressed the role of education in a pluralistic society.

THE AMERICAN PUBLIC HIGH SCHOOL

The academy reached its zenith of popularity by the middle of the nineteenth century and declined rapidly after that time. Growth of high schools in the United States was slow at first. In 1875, there were fewer than 25,000 students enrolled in public high schools. In the 1880s, more students attended high schools than academies, and by 1890, some 2,500 high schools enrolled more than 200,000 students. By 1900, there were more than 6,000 high schools and over 500,000 students.

Kalamazoo Case. Although the age of the common school revival clearly established the principle of free, tax-supported elementary schools, considerable controversy continued over taxation for high schools. Public secondary schools in some states were financed from common school funds; others charged tuition. Since one major function of high schools was to prepare students for college and since high schools were not patronized by all children, some citizens felt the states had no right to tax the public for support of these schools. Others, led by such spokesmen as California superintendent Ezra Carr, argued that high schools were an important part of the basic public educational system.

The best-known case dealing with tax support for high schools came after the town of Kalamazoo, Michigan, created a public secondary school in 1858. Three taxpayers brought suit to restrain the school board from collecting and using taxes to support the high school. The case reached the state supreme court, which decided in favor of the school authorities in 1874. The opinion, written by Justice Cooley, held that high schools are common schools and that they constitute a vital link between elementary schools and the state university. He pointed out that the absence of public secondary schools would discriminate in favor of the rich and, thus, prevent others from entering college. Although other cases were tried, the Kalamazoo decision became a precedent that established the right of the several states to levy taxes for public high schools. This precedent contributed to the vast growth of high schools in the period before World War I.

Curriculum.   High schools offered both traditional and practical programs, but the emphasis was usually placed on the college preparatory curriculum. In spite of the fact that only about a tenth of the students in high schools in 1900 expected to enter college, the "classical" course was taken by a majority of youngsters. Latin and algebra were the subjects that had the highest enrollment. Sometimes the college course was divided so that a student could elect an English or a scientific major, but there was no free choice of subjects. Many schools had whole programs or courses such as the manual or commercial training courses for the terminal student (not college bound); many studied the English classical course, even if they had no plans for higher education.

The English classical school, established in Boston in 1821, was modified over time, changing its focus from foreign languages (as in the Latin grammar school) to English literature and practical and vocational studies. The change in focus was designed to meet the needs of an emerging middle commercial class (Butts and Cremin, 1953; Meyer, 1957). A few high schools offered specialized vocational courses, and some offered preparation for teaching. The comprehensive high school curriculum contained a wider variety of subjects including vocational and business education. Vocational education included training in the trades, agriculture, carpentry, mechanics, and technical job skills. Business or commercial curricula included keyboard typing skills, accountancy, and bookkeeping. There were private trade and venture schools meeting increased demands for job skills in both vocational and business education. Physical education, art, music, and religion were included in the subjects offered by many high schools at the end of the nineteenth century. There was very little standardization. Some high schools offered as a four-year course what others gave in one semester or one year.

Standardizing Associations and National Education Association.   The
United States had developed a large number of secondary schools. Many difficulties
arose concerning the subjects of the curriculum, the length of time spent on each
subject, and the quality of the instruction. Associations of standardization were created to deal with these issues. They also considered the preparation of teachers, the
length of the school year, libraries, physical facilities, and graduation requirements.
The New England Association of Colleges and Secondary Schools was founded in
1789. Next came the Middle Atlantic States Association (1892), the North Central Association (1894), the Association of College and Preparatory Schools of the Southern
States (1895), and the Northwest Association of Secondary and Higher Schools
(1918). All of these organizations had the purpose of improving and making standard the offerings of various secondary schools and some colleges.

   In 1857, forty-three leaders from ten state teachers' associations organized the National Teachers' Association in Philadelphia. In 1870, this organization merged with
the National Association of School Superintendents and the American Normal School
Association to form the National Education Association (NEA). The NEA held an annual convention and published reports dealing with all aspects of education. Later,
it became involved in defining the functions and standards for schools at all levels.
Congress granted a charter to the NEA in 1905.

Committee of Ten.   Confusion over standards in secondary schools, curriculum
issues, and the argument between "modernists" and "traditionalists" caused the NEA
to take action in 1892. In that year, the NEA appointed a Committee of Ten to examine the high school curriculum and to make recommendations about methods,
standards, and programs. Commissioner W. T. Harris and Harvard's President Charles
W. Eliot were well-known members of the committee. There were four other college
presidents, two headmasters, one professor, and one high school administrator, but
no high school teachers. College interests dominated in the Committee of Ten, and
the report was a bastion of educational conservatism.

   One of the major weaknesses of the report of the committee was that it based its
findings on the psychology of mental discipline. The assumption was made that all
subjects for general education had equal value for training the powers of the mind,
such as expression, memory, reasoning, and observation. At a time when faculty psychology (which listed active powers—each of which could be strengthened through
use of the mind—such as hunger, and intellectual powers such as memory) and mental discipline were already under attack, the Committee of Ten held that all its recommended subjects were of equal value for building sound mental habits in
children. There were subcommittees on Latin, Greek, English, the modern languages, mathematics, the physical sciences, the biological sciences, history, and geography. These subjects represented vested interests and were given support by the
committee, but vocational and commercial courses were largely ignored. In every
case, the purpose of studying a subject was held to be mental discipline and exercise of the powers of the mind. It was also held that any recommended subject that

was studied for one period each day for five days each week for a year was equal to any other recommended subject studied for the same length of time.

The Committee of Ten influenced the Committee on College Entrance Requirements (established in 1895) and the subsequent work of the Carnegie Foundation for the Advancement of Teaching. The result was the establishment of the standard unit of credit for high school subjects (Carnegie unit), the support of traditional subjects and faculty psychology, and the limitation of any new or innovative high school programs. The Committee of Ten recommended intensive study in high schools of a few subjects for long periods of time. It supported an eight-year elementary school followed by a four-year high school. No special subjects or methods were recommended for students who expected to terminate their formal education with high school graduation.

Accreditation.   The NEA Committee on College Entrance Requirements not only defined units of study in secondary schools but also recommended a set of constant or core subjects to be taken by all students. In 1902, the North Central Association set up a Committee on Unit Courses. The committee required fifteen units for high school graduation and recommended at least three units of English and two of mathematics for college entrance. Those recommendations became standard requirements in accreditation for all high schools. A College Entrance Examination Board was also established.

Cardinal Principles.   In 1918, the NEA appointed a Commission on the Reorganization of Secondary Education. This commission recognized the high schools as instruments for social integration and building values. It warned against specialized schools that would divide the population of students and supported the idea of a comprehensive secondary school offering a variety of subjects and courses.

The commission provided some theoretical basis for the later development of a truly comprehensive secondary school. However, it is best known for issuing its seven Cardinal Principles of Secondary Education, which became standard objectives for teachers, school boards, and administrators. Following are the seven principles:

1. Health
2. Command of fundamental processes
3. Worthy home membership
4. Vocation
5. Citizenship
6. Worthy use of leisure time
7. Ethical character

Obviously, these principles could serve as a guide for curriculum and methodology, but they did not fill the need for a carefully articulated educational philosophy. The meaning of each principle may be interpreted in a variety of ways.

Rapid growth of high schools continued even though most of them, before 1920, were noncomprehensive and strictly college preparatory in curriculum. By 1900, the public high schools were almost all coeducational, and more than half of the students were girls. In the early decades of the twentieth century, high schools doubled in enrollment every ten years, until they became common schools in fact as well as name.

Reorganization.   Public high schools retained the same general characteristics and organizational structure well into the twentieth century. In addition to a principal and his or her staff, the schools usually had departmental divisions with a chairperson or "head" for each major program area or department.

Charles W. Eliot was an enthusiastic supporter of both college and high school electives. He was one of the first to suggest a new school organization that would provide more choice for high school students. Basically, Eliot wanted to extend the high school courses downward into elementary education. G. Stanley Hall, author of the first book on adolescents and no friend of Eliot's proposal, felt that reorganization was necessary to meet the needs of older elementary pupils who were no longer children. Others believed that the elementary and high schools did not provide a smooth transition from childhood to young adult life. It was felt that the opportunity for advanced elementary education of a general sort as well as some industrial and commercial training should be provided outside the senior high school. The Committee on College Entrance Requirements had recommended the division of elementary and secondary schools into six-year blocks, and the Committee of Ten had considered reorganization of some type.

As a result of these and other suggestions, junior high schools were created in Columbus, Ohio, and Berkeley, California, in 1909. Other cities soon followed, and the junior high school became a common institution in the United States after 1930. Typically, the elementary school was reduced to six years, with junior and senior high schools requiring six years together. This 6–3–3 plan was not always used; some schools retained a four-year high school and used a 6–2–4 system. Reorganization is still in process today, with many schools experimenting with a 4–4–4 or other "middle school" plan. The junior high school stressed socialization, guidance, individual differences, and survey or exploratory courses of a general nature.

VOCATIONAL AND INDUSTRIAL EDUCATION

The history of vocational education spans a long period of time in America. Apprenticeship was first used for vocational training when literary and religious education was the only prerogative of the school. However, by 1820, Eastern cities saw the establishment of a few mechanics' institutes for technical instruction. Worcester Polytechnic Institute was opened in 1868, and there were some manual labor schools built along lines suggested by the European educators Pestalozzi and Fellenberg. Manual training demonstrations were given in Philadelphia in 1876. Some cities had manual and vocational courses in high schools by 1890.

Shop work of various kinds replaced manual training in many high schools, but some secondary schools were designated as manual training high schools with no college preparatory courses. The vocational value of shop work was considered part of general education, and special trade training was avoided in favor of mechanical principles. Students learned general skills on the transfer-of-training theory rather than how to make specific articles. The need for skilled workers and the desire for high school education for those not bound for college caused the manual training movement to gain speed after 1880. Columbia University began training teachers for manual training classes, and an industrial education association was organized in 1884.

Gradually the movement for training teachers of manual arts spread through the universities. Some labor leaders feared that industrial education would develop a surplus of cheap trained labor, but labor generally approved of industrial and vocational education. In general, manufacturers were also in support of this movement, but the opposition from traditional educators with classical backgrounds was more difficult to overcome.

Smith-Hughes Act.   The vocational school movement continued to grow from 1907 to 1917, receiving its greatest boost in 1917 when the federal Smith-Hughes Act was passed. This law provided federal aid for the states by paying vocational teachers' salaries in the high schools and aiding teacher training institutions in the education of such teachers. The states were required to match the federal grant on a dollar-for-dollar basis. In an effort to provide aid for the child trying to make a choice between vocational subjects, the Vocation Bureau and Breadwinner's Institute was established in 1909.

Vocational and manual training also received support from new experiments and theories in education. John Dewey attracted attention by insisting that children learn through activities. His book *School and Society* (1989) made this point. New interest in psychology led to the beginning of professional guidance for students in industrial and vocational schools. Guidance developed slowly, and vocational high schools were the first to offer counseling services.

Demand for practical vocational skills and scientific information was especially great among the farmers of the nation. Farmers' Institutes started in 1854 and led to an interest in agricultural education on both the high school and the college levels. Colleges that resulted from the Morrill acts of 1862 and 1890 gave college status to agriculture and the mechanical arts. Demonstration farms, agricultural experiment stations, and training for improvement of agricultural techniques were provided by these colleges and by the Department of Agriculture, which was established in 1862. The Hatch Act of 1887 provided federal funds for agricultural experiments. In 1914, Congress passed the Smith-Lever Act, which created agricultural extension programs for farmers and led to vocational agriculture courses and 4-H clubs. Many high school students took advantage of federally funded vocational work, but often vocational agriculture was the only practical course offered in rural secondary schools. There was no attempt to offer general federal aid to public schools until after World War II.

PAROCHIAL AND PRIVATE EDUCATION

Obtaining exact figures on school enrollments before 1900 is difficult because neither schools nor reporting techniques were standardized. Statistics on public and private sectarian schools were often reported together as late as 1870. Although the states of the West and South were behind those of the North and East in percentages of children enrolled in public schools, it is clear that very rapid growth in all states took place between 1860 and 1900. In 1900, about 90 percent of the American secondary school students attended public high schools.

Catholic doctrine has always insisted the state should have only a secondary role in education while the parents and the church have primary responsibility. Catholic schools existed in such areas as New Mexico, California, and Louisiana early in American history, but intolerance and discrimination by the states prevented rapid growth on the eastern seaboard. In colonial America, only Pennsylvania allowed Catholics to conduct schools. However, the appointment of Father John Carroll as Superior of Missions in the United States and the guarantee of religious freedom in the Bill of Rights provided a foundation for Catholic education in America. With the large influx of Irish Catholics during the first half of the nineteenth century, interest in parochial schools increased. By 1840, Catholics had created seventy-five elementary parochial schools, twenty-five high schools, and six colleges. Many Catholic children attended public schools, but there was great controversy over Protestant creeds and the use of the King James Version of the Bible in public schools. Catholic children were often punished if they objected to non-Catholic religious practices. In 1854, the Maine Supreme Court rejected a Catholic plea to exclude the Bible from the public school curriculum, although the Ohio Supreme Court upheld a similar Catholic plea in 1872.

The Third Plenary Council of Baltimore in 1884 required all parishes to provide schools for Catholic youngsters. As a result, Catholic parochial schools increased in number to about 3,000 in 1884. Secondary Catholic schools were developed through Jesuit leadership partly in an effort to train boys for the priesthood. Parish high schools were largely an extension of the parochial school. They emphasized Latin, literature, grammar, and religion. Few if any vocational courses were offered. By 1910, there were more than 300 Catholic high schools in operation in the United States.

The Lutheran church founded the largest number of non-Catholic parochial schools. There were also schools created by Quakers, Jews, and other religious groups. Much smaller in numbers than the Catholic schools, these sectarian efforts, nevertheless, provided alternative educational opportunities for students in many parts of the nation. An interesting discussion of these issues appears in *Great School Wars* by Diane Ravitch.

Oregon Case. Bitter public reaction against parochial schools has existed in the United States for many years. Discrimination has been expressed in many ways, and direct efforts have been made to outlaw parochial schools. The most famous case occurred in the state of Oregon in 1925 and has remained unchallenged. The Oregon legislature passed a law that required all children to attend public schools through the eighth grade. The Society of Sisters of the Holy Names of Jesus and Mary and the Hill Academy brought suit against Governor Pierce in an effort to keep their schools. Although the state supreme court upheld the state law, the Supreme Court of the United States declared the action unconstitutional. It held that the state has a right to inspect and regulate private and parochial schools but that the state does not have a monopoly on education.

In addition to religious schools, a number of private schools and academies continued to operate. These were sometimes military schools or elite college preparatory institutions for wealthy children. Military academies declined after World War II, but other kinds of private schools grew rapidly in number.

HIGHER EDUCATION

Colleges and Universities.   Higher education had a steady growth during this period, and as a result of the Morrill Act of 1862 almost every state created a land grant college. Industry and scientific agriculture were emphasized by these institutions, but they were by no means confined to such subjects. The land grant schools grew slowly at first because they lacked the prestige of liberal arts colleges. However, they had the support of science and were powerful as a democratizing influence. Nine of these colleges developed into state universities, and many added colleges of engineering, home economics, and education. The Morrill Act of 1890 made $15,000 annually available to each of the original institutions, resulting in vast expansion. By 1918, many state universities became major institutions of higher education. Efforts to develop private colleges met with limited success. A high percentage of the sectarian colleges founded before the Civil War closed by World War I, but others were created. Some degree-granting colleges were really only secondary schools, although there were high-quality denominational colleges as well as good secular universities.

New University Model.   The most significant development in higher education during this period was the establishment of graduate programs based on the German example. Early supporters of this idea included Henry P. Tappan (later president of the University of Michigan) and Louis Agassiz, who developed science programs at Harvard. It was not, however, until Johns Hopkins University opened in 1876 that a real scientific research university existed in America.

Johns Hopkins was a wealthy Baltimore businessman who provided a large endowment for a university that would include a medical school and hospital. Much of the credit for the success of Johns Hopkins University goes to its first president, Daniel Coit Gilman (1831–1908). Gilman was a Yale graduate who became president of the University of California before being selected for Johns Hopkins. He was a keen administrator and a careful judge of talent. Gilman selected professors who had not yet reached national status but who had demonstrated their potential ability. The new institution had a graduate school aimed at creating new knowledge and supporting scientific investigation rather than merely transferring information and skills. It required graduate students to do research as a regular part of the program and provided the necessary laboratory equipment and other support. Inquiry, observation, freedom to seek truth without institutional restrictions, and high-quality scholarship became standard at Johns Hopkins. The idea that faculty members should do research and publish the results of their work also found favor there.

Professional Schools.

Johns Hopkins was the first American university to have a medical college with full-time professors. In the post–Civil War period, professional schools rapidly replaced the private practices of "reading law," apprentice doctors, and self-education for ministers. In 1899, there were 532 reported professional schools operating in the nation, about half of which were departments in colleges and universities. The practice at Johns Hopkins of requiring college graduation for admission to the medical school was rare, and numerous professional programs were offered for short periods of time. Low standards due to a lack of state supervision were common until after 1900 when regulations began to increase. The growth of graduate schools had a major effect on professional schools because of the training they offered to college and professional schoolteachers. Graduate departments and professional schools began to differentiate between universities and liberal arts colleges, even when such colleges referred to themselves as universities.

Curriculum Changes.

Because traditions in education are very strong, change normally meets with great resistance. College faculties have always been very conservative with regard to altering the curriculum. Nevertheless, colleges did begin to expand their offerings in the period under consideration, in spite of great faculty reluctance. Science and research made the addition of many courses necessary, although most colleges merely added the new programs without altering or eliminating the old. Agriculture, mechanical arts, and military science gained a foothold in higher education because of the Morrill acts. The sixty-five colleges and universities established under these acts by 1900 obviously had a profound effect on the curriculum. Massachusetts Institute of Technology began instruction in 1865, with theoretical support for scientific and practical subjects provided by Herbert Spencer and T. H. Huxley. Darwin's *On the Origin of Species* (1859) caused a great deal of interest in the intellectual world, and such scholars as John Fiske at Harvard soon discussed evolution. The tycoons of the "gilded age" gave substantial gifts to higher education, and in return, they influenced the curriculum. Practical, utilitarian, and business courses often had the support of philanthropists, as did conservative views of social change and classical economics.

Before the Civil War, it was unusual to allow students free selection of courses or programs in colleges. Although George Ticknor had experimented with electives, the real development of the college elective system came when Charles W. Eliot was president of Harvard. By 1894, Harvard required only French or German, English composition, and some work in physics and chemistry; all other courses could be selected by the students. Educational conservatives bitterly opposed the elective system, but leading universities soon adopted it to some degree, although a core of "disciplinary" courses was often required. The major effect of the elective system was to break the hold classics had on higher education and to allow the introduction of popular modern subjects such as history, sociology, psychology, economics, and the sciences. Breadth of the curriculum and the freedom to examine various theories or ideas became part of the university ideal.

Although coeducational colleges existed before the Civil War (Oberlin 1833, Antioch 1852, and Iowa 1856), their major development came between 1860 and 1920. By 1880, about half of the colleges and universities admitted women. Vassar, Smith, Wellesley, and Bryn Mawr were women's colleges that offered programs equivalent to colleges for men. Affiliated or "coordinate" colleges for women also were established, such as Radcliffe at Harvard. At the turn of the century, there were still some doubts about higher education for women. Frederick Rudolph wrote, in *The American College and University,* that as late as 1895 the faculty at the University of Virginia believed that women students were often physically unsexed by the strain of study. He also wrote that a Vanderbilt student stated that no man wants to come home at night and find his wife testing some new manufacturing process for oleomargarine or in the observatory sweeping the heavens for a comet. Rudolph also noted that a foreign visitor to Wellesley opined that this is all very well but how would it affect their chances for marriage. In addition, Rudolph noted that the suspicion would long linger that coeducation deprived women of some of their infinite charm and gentleness and robbed men of some of the sternness and ruggedness on which society depended for its protection. A wide curriculum was offered for women, but teaching was still the only career generally open to females in 1918.

SCHOOLS AND COLLEGES FOR MINORITY GROUPS

The adoption of the Fourteenth Amendment in 1868 gave black Americans citizenship, but few opportunities for higher education existed then. In 1826, the first college degree granted to a black student went to John Russwurm; only twenty-eight black college graduates were recorded before the Civil War. Northern colleges open to African Americans after 1860 found many ill prepared for college work because of the inadequate segregated public schools from which they came. Progress in literacy rates is clear, however, in the increase in the literacy of black Americans from 10 percent in 1866 to over 90 percent in 1936. According to Edward Knight, 132 blacks received Ph.D. degrees in this same time period.

Black schools and colleges in the South developed through the efforts of educators like Booker T. Washington. Hampton Institute for Negro Higher Education had been established in Virginia in 1870 under the sponsorship of the American Missionary Association. Washington became a student there, arriving on foot and with only fifty cents to his name. When Washington graduated in 1875, he was recommended by Principal Samuel C. Armstrong as a teacher for a proposed black normal school at Tuskegee, Alabama. Under Washington, Tuskegee Normal and Industrial

Institute became a model of black education and its director a national figure. Washington received an honorary degree from Harvard University and became the recognized leader of black education. Realizing the attitudes of white Americans in the South, Washington agreed to a subservient role for blacks in return for practical and vocational education. His Atlanta compromise speech is a classic political concession. At Tuskegee, Washington stressed hard work, vocational skills, and economic advancement. He won wide support among whites in the South, and although his institute became a model for black colleges, his willingness to accept social discrimination has drawn much criticism. Washington always avoided the demand for social and political equality made by W. E. B. Du Bois and his followers. Washington sought to improve the status of African Americans within the social and economic system; Du Bois sought social, economic, and political reforms to expand equity and access for minorities.

Minority education outside the South grew slowly but steadily during the period between the Civil War and World War I. A few liberal colleges like Antioch admitted black students early, but discrimination was practiced in most areas of the nation. Numerous black agricultural, military, and normal colleges were established with funds from the second Morrill Act, and these colleges always included programs for teachers. Federal money was badly needed, and the black agricultural, military, and normal schools soon became as important as Tuskegee and various church-related black colleges. These colleges admitted Native Americans, Asian Americans, and other minority students. Numerous Northern state universities were open to minorities, but the number actually admitted was small, due in part to entrance requirements that screened out graduates from the poor public schools. Public school segregation was maintained either legally or de facto almost everywhere (please see Figure 5.3 for more information).

Native-American Schools. Most of the formal education provided for Native Americans was through philanthropy or missionary efforts until the Office of Indian Affairs was opened in 1819. Thereafter, schools of various kinds were supported by government grants, although religious organizations continued to operate the majority of mission schools for Native Americans. A number of Native-American scholars attended Hampton Institute, and in 1879, a Native-American training school was authorized for Carlisle, Pennsylvania. Except for boarding schools on reservations and a few specific programs aimed at training for vocations, very little was done by federal or local government to meet the needs of education for Native Americans.

TEACHER EDUCATION

Although colonial teachers were sometimes college graduates, there was nothing available to them that might be considered professional training. Academies and female seminaries in the early national period often advertised pedagogical programs that consisted of a review of basic elementary subjects and some lectures on keeping school. It was long considered adequate for secondary teachers to have only a

Figure 6.2   Phenomenal
Growth of Normal Schools

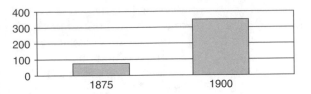

sound knowledge of their subject field, without any training in psychology or methods of teaching.

The first normal schools were academically low-level institutions, a problem that continued to exist until they were made into four-year colleges in the twentieth century. Early normal schools usually had some sort of practice teaching and a course in mental philosophy, but there was no sound theoretical foundation. Some private normal schools and academies for teachers offered programs with higher academic standards, but they also lacked a professional basis. Nevertheless, the growth of teacher education was rapid in the latter part of the nineteenth century (see Figure 6.2). In 1871, 114 schools for teachers replied to an inquiry about programs and enrollments made by the United States Bureau of Education. At least seventy normal schools were receiving some state support in 1875. By 1900, there were 345 normal schools reported in the United States (see Figure 6.2).

Women outnumbered men in the state normal schools; the sexes were about evenly divided in private schools for teachers. A great many students in normal schools already held teaching certificates, and most had some teaching experience before entering the program. Large numbers of teachers attended normal schools for short periods, but only about a third of the public school teachers were normal school graduates. Many normal school programs were offered for two years or less and usually were on the secondary school level. Most had meager equipment, insufficient support, poor facilities, and an underpaid staff.

Before World War I, however, these institutions began enlarging their curricula and requiring high school graduation for admission. Some, such as Illinois State Normal, were able to erect expensive modern buildings and to develop college-level courses. Both the number and quality of normal schools improved very rapidly in the last decades of the nineteenth century and the first decades of the twentieth. Nevertheless, normal schools, high school normal departments, academies, or college departments provided fewer than half of the trained teachers that were needed to staff public schools. Underpaid young women with little or no education beyond elementary school and perhaps a summer institute continued to teach in district schools.

Sheldon and the Oswego Movement.
A much better conceptual framework for the professional training of teachers was provided by Edward Sheldon. Sheldon became secretary of the Board of Education of Oswego, New York, in 1853. He visited a number of cities in order to find ways of improving the schools, and in 1859 in Toronto, Sheldon came across a Pestalozzian program produced by the Home and Colonial Training Institution of London. Instruction there was based on charts, pic-

tures, manuals, and objects developed by Charles and Elizabeth Mayo, who had been teachers in schools conducted by Pestalozzi.

Having purchased materials worth $300 and secured the services of Margaret E. M. Jones to demonstrate them, Sheldon proceeded to reform the Oswego schools along lines developed by Pestalozzi. The success was impressive, and in 1866, the New York legislature made Oswego a state normal school. Teachers flocked to the new program, and Oswego soon became the most famous teacher-training institution in the United States. Graduates of the school found jobs in various parts of the nation, and thus the Oswego movement influenced regions far beyond New York.

Some of the improvement attributed to the Oswego movement came from the enthusiasm of Sheldon himself, but new techniques of learning and respect for the unique personality of the child were also important. Object teaching began with something familiar to the environment of the child and moved to an abstract description of the object. Geography was taught from the local community outward, until the whole nation and the world could be understood. Study and discipline through mutual understanding and respect were also stressed. Unfortunately, the term *object lesson* was also used by textbook companies who merely wanted to sell books, and some other normal schools made highly formalized lesson plans out of what the Oswego movement had intended to be flexible. Nevertheless, Oswego provided a new model of teacher education that included new principles, better psychology, creative methods, and an effort to understand how children learn.

University Departments of Education.

For many years, pedagogy and teacher training were excluded from universities. Faculty members in the academic disciplines held all professional education in low esteem, and many had contempt for teacher training programs. In 1879, W. H. Payne, spurred on by the Kalamazoo case, was able to fill the first successful, permanent chair of pedagogy in the nation at the University of Michigan. The trustees turned down President Barnard of Columbia when he proposed a department of education in 1882. Instead, he assigned Nicholas Murray Butler to offer Saturday lectures for teachers. The interest was so great that over 2,000 teachers applied for Butler's lectures, but the trustees again refused to authorize a department of education or even a senior elective in pedagogy. Finally, Butler organized the New York College for the Training of Teachers. In 1892, under strong opposition, that college was accepted as an affiliate of Columbia University. Faculty and administration traditionalists feared that a move toward a professional college would be detrimental to the historical general education and liberal arts tradition of the university. Vocationalism and specialization were not viewed as part of the university mission.

Teacher education at the college level began at Washington College in Pennsylvania in 1831 and at New York University in 1832. The University of Iowa had a chair for didactics (education) in 1873. By 1900, professors of pedagogy were to be found in many universities, although sometimes only one professor constituted the whole department. New York University offered graduate work in education in 1887. Starting about 1890, teacher training institutions tended to become degree-granting colleges that required secondary school graduation for admission. The scientific study of education and psychology came to be linked with certification. A body of educational theory slowly developed out of work done in education at universities and graduate schools. Nevertheless, the normal school stigma continued to plague departments of education. In a 1992 article in *Change,* Harvard President Derek Bok argued that good teachers would not be produced so long as pedagogy is restricted to the fringes of the universities. Bok has worked to stress and improve teaching, and in 1991, the Harvard Center for Teaching Learning, founded in 1976, was named after him.

DEVELOPMENT OF EDUCATIONAL PHILOSOPHY

Theology and philosophical idealism dominated American educational theory before 1900. Before World War I, William James, Charles Peirce, and John Dewey made contributions to pragmatism; but their influence was much greater during the progressive era of the 1930s. It was so difficult even to provide the rudiments of education to the whole population that little effort was made to define educational goals, to equate theory with psychological principles, or to work out the logical educational positions. Once schools were established, a host of new educational demands were made, and many began to debate the proper role of education. The early influence of Rousseau, Pestalozzi, Froebel, and other European philosophers continued to be felt; but American educational theory also began to develop (see Figure 6.3).

Harris.   William T. Harris, who developed a public kindergarten in 1873 as part of the school system in St. Louis, Missouri, was superintendent of schools there from 1867 to 1880 and United States Commissioner of Education from 1889 to 1906. He was one of the best-known school administrators in America, and his ideas had wide influence throughout the nation. Harris was philosophically an idealist, a follower of the German philosopher Hegel, and a traditionalist in education. As an idealist, Harris believed education should emphasize the cultural subjects and prepare children for harmony with the absolute order of the universe as well as for life in an indus-

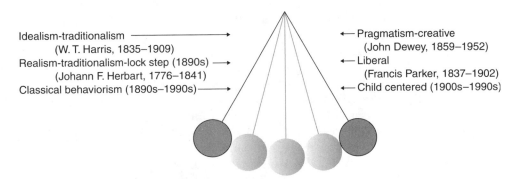

Idealism-traditionalism
    (W. T. Harris, 1835–1909)
Realism-traditionalism-lock step (1890s)
    (Johann F. Herbart, 1776–1841)
Classical behaviorism (1890s–1990s)

Pragmatism-creative
    (John Dewey, 1859–1952)
Liberal
    (Francis Parker, 1837–1902)
Child centered (1900s–1990s)

Figure 6.3   Cycles of Educational Trends

trial nation. As a traditionalist, Harris would stress universal values of right and wrong. Teachers should teach and represent the best ideals of humankind while instilling moral and ethical values in their students. He accepted some of the methods of Pestalozzi but was basically opposed to the manual training movement, science, and materialism. As U.S. Commissioner of Education, a member of the major committees of the NEA, and a leader in the National Herbart Society, his influence was very great. Harris was the great spokesman for the idealistic-traditional theory of education.

Parker.   Quite a different educational position was taken by Francis W. Parker, who was principal of schools in Carrollton, Illinois, before the Civil War. His school career was interrupted by the conflict, in which he served as a colonel in the Union forces. Parker studied in Germany, becoming familiar with the practices of Pestalozzi and Froebel. He returned to America to become superintendent of schools in Quincy, Massachusetts, and later was head of the Cook County Normal School in Chicago. Parker was a democratic individualist with a practical outlook. He followed Pestalozzi closely with regard to and respect for the creative activity of the child. Parker experimented with many kinds of school programs, including the core curriculum that attempted to relate subjects of the curriculum through such interrelated studies as history and geography. Parker provided the background for the work of John Dewey and the progressives.

The total impact of Pestalozzi and Froebel was relatively light, although kindergartens did develop and university scholars began to study the child as an individual. Public education changed very little before the American Herbartian movement started around 1890.

Herbart.   Johann F. Herbart (discussed in Chapter 2) was responsible for a much greater revolution in American education than any previous European thinker had been. Herbart held that the aim of education was attainment of good moral character and that such character could be acquired only through the process of analyzing the social interests of man to discover ideals appropriate for education. The first step in character realization was the "many sidedness of interest." Although he used the word *interest,* Herbart was really referring to a stimulus to learning. He once said that the person who lays hold of information, and because of that information reaches out for more, takes "interest" in it. In the study of history and literature, Herbart saw a core for the curriculum that could encompass or could be co-related with all other subjects. His principles of co-relation and concentration, by which he meant relation with emphasis at the core, became central to his doctrine. Despite Herbart's insistence on the social and moral aims of education, he took an intellectual approach to the learning process. He also developed a psychology that is still of some value today.

Herbart was an associationist; that is, he believed that we have to account for every new idea on the basis of ideas already in the mind, and hence we must consciously relate or associate new ideas with previous experiences. For Herbart, there could never be a totally new idea. He believed that we receive impressions to the conscious mind (presentation). These presentations are then associated with other ideas that lie together in masses in the subconscious part of the mind. When a new idea in the mind is related, it is transferred from the conscious to the subconscious mind and becomes part of an "apperceptive mass." The idea will not appear in the conscious mind again until it is needed to clarify some new presentation. Herbart's own psychology was not rigid, and his insistence upon the mind as a unity tended to break down the older faculty psychology, which understood the mind to be divided into separate faculties or abilities or powers.

American Herbartianism.   Herbart's followers in America used his insistence upon association and interests to develop a very rigid educational program. This program came to be known as the Five Formal Steps of Teaching and Learning. Following are the five formal steps:

1. Preparation, in which old ideas useful in learning new materials are called to the learner's mind
2. Presentation, or the actual giving of the new material
3. Association, in which new material is compared with and related to the old
4. Generalization, in which rules, definitions, or general principles are drawn from specific cases
5. Application, in which general principles are given meaning by reference to specific examples and practical situations

These Herbartian steps were made popular by Charles De Garmo, Charles McMurry, and Frank McMurry, who were among the early leaders of the American Herbartian Association. It must be remembered that during the late 1800s most teachers were largely without training, and there was no rational philosophy of education. The formal steps of the American Herbartianists filled a void in educational theory, and hence the influence of Herbart through his American followers became dominant in this country in the 1890s. Unfortunately, the set methods of the followers of Herbart led to a "lock-step" in American education; the same subjects were taught in the same way using the same methods and the same textbooks in every public school from Boston to Berkeley. The beneficial part of this uniformity was that it became possible for children to transfer from one school to another without a change in curriculum or loss of time; however, the respect for individuality, new ideas, and creativity, which had been so much in the theories of Froebel and Pestalozzi, was largely lost. Although difficult to identify philosophically, Herbart tended to be a realist and a traditionalist—a realist in his emphasis on fact-centered knowledge and a traditionalist in his focus on uniformity and conformity within educational systems.

Protest Against Rigid Systems.   One of the first to raise a cry against the rigid lock-step school was John Dewey. His influence was first felt in the closing years of the nineteenth century, and his importance increased considerably during the first three decades of the twentieth century. Dewey continued to write until the 1950s. However, his greatest amount of influence on education came in the 1930s, when the Progressive Education Association was at the height of its popularity. Dewey felt that Herbart and his followers had emphasized formal methods to the extreme and that they failed to account for natural growth and individual differences. He attacked schools for being antidemocratic and the curriculum for being subject-centered. For Dewey, education had to be part of life itself.

Other developments also contributed to the changing climate of opinion out of which new educational theories evolved. In 1859, Charles Darwin published his *On the Origin of Species,* a book that set off the explosive theory of evolution. The theories of scientific evolution and social Darwinism challenged the conceptions of man and the universe held by conservative educators. Evolutionary principles contributed to the formation of the philosophy of pragmatism by Charles Peirce and William James. Pragmatism emphasized the practical questions of how we can understand and control the world instead of the metaphysical question of how we can know reality. Herbert Spencer and others applied the theory of evolution to society in order to explain the existence of social classes and social institutions. Resulting studies in sociology altered traditional conceptions of humanity and opened new windows through which to view education. Evolutionary science became part of the curriculum in universities, but it created an issue in public schools, where it was often banned. The conflict of religion and science culminated in the Scopes trial, a trial that involved the teaching of evolution in Dayton, Tennessee, in 1925.

Schools continued to grow in number before World War I. Children tended to remain in school longer, teachers received more training, and education became a subject for university study. New scientific subjects were added to the high schools, and public high schools became the standard American secondary schools. Child study and psychology led to new concepts of method and new interest in the individual child.

THEN TO NOW

Events leading up to the American Civil War and the conflict itself bear a strong relationship to numerous conditions in the modern era. Extremely bitter sectional and ideological arguments not only caused the Civil War but also altered the attitudes of people for generations. Although the Union survived, negative feelings about Civil War issues continued to dominate political life into the twenty-first century. Social and educational problems created by the freeing of slaves plagued the nation, and the burden carried by the impoverished South caused a very low level of public schooling for both races. Black struggles for equality, reflected by the militant self-help and return-to-Africa movement of Marcus Garvey in 1917 or the civil rights activism of Dr. Martin Luther King Jr. in the 1960s, may be traced to this era. No struggle divided and alienated the American people like the Civil War until the outbreak of the conflict in Vietnam.

American involvement in Southeast Asia during the 1960s and 1970s caused caustic criticism of national policy, especially on university campuses. Like the Civil War, Vietnam raised ugly moral issues, created an erosion of patriotism, and shook the very foundations of the national culture. Just as the Civil War closed schools, promoted illiteracy in most of the South, and led to a system of schools segregated by race, Vietnam also created a major educational crisis. The war caused violence in colleges, alienation of students from the values of their parents, and the withdrawal of financial support to educational institutions. Although the two world wars and the Korean action had significant educational influences, only the Civil War and the conflict in Vietnam caused fundamental rifts in the very core of American culture. Tracing the modern issues over desegregation of schools to the Civil War period is easy, but the total impact of the Vietnam era on education and the American culture may not be known for generations to come.

The quick victory in the Persian Gulf War of 1990–1991 provided some counterbalance to the Vietnam episode, although determining America's role in foreign conflicts—such as those involving the Congo, Somalia, Bosnia, Kosovo, Israel, Palestine, and Haiti—continues to be a challenge. And the United States continues to face challenges such as the war on terrorism sparked by the bombing of the World Trade Center in 2001.

Intellectual and cultural historians argue that life conditions have major effects on the attitudes, values, and beliefs of all people. Thus, it is necessary to identify the most significant forces that shape values and concepts about the good life for each generation.

Those who grew up in the 1920s held establishment values. World War I, prohibition, and the Model T Ford influenced them. Young people were interested in gin and jazz, but close family ties and patriotism dominated the nation. Although the Scopes trial created a major issue, education remained conservative. By the 1930s, the economic crash had taken place, and the nation was in the Great Depression. There was mass unemployment, soup lines, and social unrest. Radical economic solutions including socialism were suggested, and Franklin Roosevelt became popular with his New Deal. Great emphasis was placed on the value of the dollar, and those who grew up in the 1930s are still very security minded. This was the age of progressive education and radical school reform.

At the beginning of the 1940s, the dominant interest was keeping America safe from the Germans and the Japanese. World War II touched every family, and patriotism permeated the culture. This was an age of working women, geographic mobility, rationing, and support for the armed forces. People became used to the idea of scarcity and waited for better times when peace would be restored. Education turned back to the basics, and the GI Bill increased enrollment in colleges. When the war ended, Americans bought all the things they could not obtain in a wartime economy. Some 50 million TV sets were sold in America, and children began growing up with Howdy Doody and Captain Kangaroo. Crew cuts gave way to longer hair, children were materialistically indulged, and Elvis Presley personified the rock and roll age. School desegregation began in the 1950s, and Martin Luther King Jr. gained a great following. The Korean conflict was considered a great tragedy, but it did not draw the patriotic support common in World War II. Hedonism, materialism, affluence, and the mass media influenced people growing up at this time.

The 1960s saw rapid economic growth, the space program, computers, and Vietnam. Alternative lifestyles were manifest in the hippie subculture, and campus rebellion shocked conservative Americans. Those who grew up in this period recall the bitterness over the Vietnam War and the conflict between generations. It was an age of assassination but also of continued financial growth and affluence. Education focused on school integration, equal opportunity, and the needs of the culturally different child. By the end of the decade, deep-rooted value conflicts had divided Americans to a degree quite similar to the era of the Civil War.

By 1970, inflation and a weaker economy were evident. Many people began to fear a return of the conditions of the Great Depression of the 1930s. Some 20 million mothers entered the workforce in order to improve family income. The energy crisis was taken seriously, and there were concerns about environmental deterioration. Richard Nixon and Watergate caused the erosion of respect for government, while the people began to distrust motives of oil companies and other industrial corporations. Music, the mass media, fast foods, and automobiles were major interests of the young. Drug abuse and alcoholism became widespread among students. Educators concentrated on computer-assisted instruction, a relevant curriculum, and compensatory education for the culturally deprived.

History shows that following wars and periods of social conflict there is often a conservative reaction. At the beginning of the 1980s, such a movement developed throughout American society. There was a demand for an end to social reconstruction through legislation, relaxation of regulations on industry, and opposition to spending for welfare. Education moved back to basics with major interest focused on tests of accountability and training for jobs. Declining economic strength, continued inflation, competition for jobs, scarcity of energy and natural resources, and concern about world peace were major interests. Meanwhile, rapid advances in technological invention, especially in communications, altered the environment and created new life conditions, and they continue to do so.

In the final years of the 1990s, economic cycles continued to bedevil America as an accumulation of the national debt took an ever-greater share of the national wealth. Working toward reducing the national debt and seeking a balanced budget while maintaining and augmenting important social programs for the young and old was a major focus of Congress and President Bill Clinton. In an effort to reduce the heavy debt load of the 1980s, business and industry downsized, merged, re-engineered, focused on their growth components, and worked to find ways to become more productive and efficient. Also, a major shift from defense spending caused dislocation in employment. The goals of the second Clinton administration, following an economic cycle of low inflation and low unemployment, included expanding educational access and opportunities at all educational levels. Some of the initiatives were education for employment, increasing job opportunities, exploring national education standards to raise student achievement levels, funding for at-risk students and students with financial needs, welfare to work programs, and child-care assistance for single parents.

During the early 2000s, the economy took a nosedive. President George W. Bush stressed tax reduction. Federal Reserve Chairman Alan Greenspan and the board lowered federal reserve fund rates as efforts were made to deal with a cyclical downturn. Bush's educational plans included grants to the states, increased assessment, accountability, and testing, as well as vouchers and charter schools for parents with children in failing public schools. "Leave no child behind" became the mantra of Rod Paige, education secretary.

Scott Baldauf, in an article entitled "Single Education Standard? States Are All Over the Map," noted that national education standards were at the core of the most ambitious White House initiative to improve American education in a generation. Baldauf found that the drive for national standards was basically an economic issue. International marketplace competitiveness requires raising educational achievement levels.

There is a strong tendency in America for each new generation to reject the ideas and the values of the generation just past. John Dewey and the progressives rebelled against the lock-step schools and the rigid systems of the followers of Herbart. The counterculture did not accept the materialism and the need of security so characteristic of the depression era and the period of affluence following World War II. Such beliefs were scorned in turn by the youth of the 1970s and early 1980s. It is also probably true that change in basic value orientation takes place more rapidly in an age of accelerating economic and technological invention than in a more stable environment. If this is the case, present conservative trends in American culture cannot be expected to continue for very many years.

The 1990s saw increasing social, political, and economic fragmentation as individuals, communities, business, and industry sought either to maintain or expand their share of an ever-smaller state and federal budget. Litigation increased in all economic, social, political, religious, and educational institutions during the period. Because performance accountability required ranking and rating of faculty in terms of publication, research, teaching, and fund acquisition, collegiality gave way to adversarial relationships in higher education. In the early 1900s, muckrakers exposed corrupt business and ethical issues in individual and institutional life; in the 1990s, corruption and lapses in morality and ethics were exposed. Upton Sinclair's 1906 *The Jungle* and *The Teapot Dome Scandal* provided an impetus for the reforms of the progressive era. In our twenty-first century, television and newspaper reporters uncover similar ethical and moral lapses among political, military, and business-industrial institutions and their personnel. And the nation faces the challenge of increasing numbers of children living in poverty. Edelman, Feldmann, Kozol, and Francis report on the need for educational and governmental assistance for the working poor.

The Civil War was a time of social and ethical conflict. When it ended, the old South had disappeared, and the whole of American society was altered. The black revolution and the demand for civil rights evolved slowly from the Civil War to the 1950s, but certainly they began in the aftermath of that conflict. Likewise, the whole of American society was changed by the turmoil of the Vietnam era. Changes of this magnitude necessarily have an impact on education and the socialization of the next generation. Periods of revolutionary conflict and social change may be followed by conservative reactions, but the culture is never restored to what it was before the conflict. Rapid, though uneven, transformation of American society has been evident since the 1860s. American values and the culture of the people can never again be what they were in the antebellum South or the period before the Vietnam conflict.

This is also the case in the rest of the world. The student rebellion in China and the struggle to achieve human rights altered the values of that nation for the future. Events in Eastern Europe and the former Soviet Union vastly changed perceptions of the Communist Bloc and the concept of the cold war. By 1990, the social and political revolutions in nations like Poland, Hungary, and Romania had altered the nature of Europe and changed global social relationships. NATO was expanded to include Eastern Europe, and Russia became involved in the organization. Regional trade organizations in Asia, Europe, and the Americas as well as proponents and opponents of globalization will affect our future. These events will continue to have great impact on the world. Education must always prepare students for change if it is to be successful.

Educators and politicians of the 1990s and early 2000s addressed growing value conflicts through conflict resolution, sensitivity training programs, and a commitment to moral, ethical, and character education at all levels of the educational system. Programs in multiculturalism, cultural diversity, and English Limited Proficiency reflect a continuing expansion of the nation's social consciousness. At the same time, home and private schooling are expanding, in part due to the many religious and secular value conflicts in society. History of education continues to show that W. E. B. Du Bois' call for universal education as a public duty and at public expense is as timely in the twenty-first century as in the twentieth.

GAINING PERSPECTIVE THROUGH CRITICAL ANALYSIS

1. Name two actions by the federal government that impacted the education in the Southern states after the Civil War. How are these actions affecting educational practices today?
2. Discuss the discrepancy between W. E. B. Du Bois' call for universal and free education and the actual funds allocated for it. (A review of the chapter opening quotation will help you with your answer.)
3. Analyze the contribution of the Kalamazoo case ruling to public schools.

4. What impact did the Smith-Hughes Act have on early educational practices, and what effects do we still see on today's vocational education?
5. What current philosophy of education is the closest equivalent to the philosophy of the Oswego movement? Give reasons for your choice.
6. Why was there so much opposition to the founding of Teacher's College at Columbia University?

HISTORY IN ACTION IN TODAY'S CLASSROOMS

1. How do the Cardinal Principles apply to today's educational system? List at least three applications in your journal.
2. Make a time line in your journal that shows the significance of the National Education Association (NEA) between 1857 and 1998 in regard to educational equity and access for women and minorities.

3. Did the NEA leadership exercise its organizational power to change traditional views of women and minorities or did the Association's actions reflect public attitudes during various historical periods? Give examples of positive action, inaction, or evasive action of the NEA concerning improving the lot of women and minorities. Add the findings to your journal.

4. Use your journal to record a sample budget for a classroom using a $300 limit. List the philosophical or historical ideas that influenced your decisions. Compare your purchases with those of Edward Sheldon.

INCREASED UNDERSTANDING THROUGH ONLINE RESEARCH

Visit the Prentice Hall Foundations Web site (*http://www.prenhall.com/foundations-cluster*) and select Topic 10—Societal Influence on Schools and Curriculum—from the menu. Using the resources available in this topic of the site, identify educators' and students' response to terrorism and bioterrorism in the United States. Write and submit your response to your instructor using the Electronic Bluebook module also in this topic of the Web site. Share your findings with your class.

BIBLIOGRAPHY

Baldauf, Scott. "Single Education Standard? States Are All Over the Map." *Christian Science Monitor* (March 7, 1997):1, 4.

Beale, Howard. *A History of Freedom of Teaching in American Schools*. New York: Octagon Books, 1974.

Bok, Derek. "Reclaiming the Public Trust." *Change* (July/August 1992) 24(4):19. *The State of the Nation*. Cambridge: Harvard Press, 1996.

Boring, Edwin G. *A History of Experimental Psychology*. New York: Appleton-Century-Crofts, 1957, 203–05.

Butts, Freeman. *The Education of the West: A Formative Chapter in the History of Civilization*. New York: McGraw-Hill, 1973.

Butts, R. Freeman, and Lawrence A. Cremin. *A History of Education in American Culture*. New York: Holt, Rinehart and Winston, 1953, 124, 404.

Counts, George. *Secondary Education and Industrialism*. Cambridge, MA: Harvard University Press, 1929.

Cubberley, Ellwood. *Readings in Public Education in the United States*. Boston: Houghton Mifflin, 1934.

Edelman, Marion Wright. "We've Got More Wallet Than Will Says Children's March Leader." *Arkansas Democrat Gazette* (May 27, 1996):6A.

Feldmann, Linda. "More Children of Working Parents Now Live in Poverty." *The Christian Science Monitor* (June 4, 1996):3.

Francis, David R. "Despite Growth, Families Suffer to Prosper in the U.S." *The Christian Science Monitor* (August 7, 1996):1, 8.

Herbart, John Frederick. *Outlines of Educational Doctrine*. New York: Macmillan Co., 1909, 62.

Kandel, Isaac. *History of Secondary Education*. Boston: Houghton Mifflin, 1930.

Karier, Clarence J. *Shaping the American Educational Experience: 1990 to the Present*. New York: Free Press, Macmillan, 1975.

Knight, Edgar, and Clifton Hall. *Readings in American Educational History*. New York: Appleton-Century-Crofts, 1951.

Mayer, Frederick. *A History of Educational Thought*. 3d ed. New York: Merrill/Macmillan, 1974.

Meyer, Adolphe E. *An Educational History of the American People*. New York: McGraw-Hill, 1957, 190.

Nassaw, David. *Schooled to Order*. New York: Oxford University Press, 1979.

Reavis, George H., and Carter V. Good. *An Educational Platform for the Public Schools*. Bloomington, IN: Phi Delta Kappa, 1996.

Rudolph, Frederick. *The American College and University: A History*. New York: Vintage Books, 1962, 326–27.

Sheldon, Edward. *Autobiography*. New York: Ives-Butler, 1911.

Vaughn, Preston. *Schools for All: The Blacks and Public Education in the South, 1865–1877*. Lexington, KY: University of Kentucky Press, 1974.

Warren, Donald. *To Enforce Education: A History of the Founding Years of the United States Office of Education*. Detroit, MI: Wayne State University Press, 1974.

Washington, Booker T. *Up from Slavery: An Autobiography*. New York: Doubleday, 1938.

Weinberg, Meyer. *W. E. B. Du Bois: A Reader*. New York: Harper and Row, 1970, 147.

Westerhoff, John. *McGuffey and His Readers: Piety, Morality, and Education in Nineteenth Century America*. Nashville, TN: Abingdon Press, 1978.

CHAPTER SEVEN

AMERICAN EDUCATION: 1918 TO THE PRESENT

Quantification, mechanization and standardization: these are then the marks of the Americanization that is conquering the world. They have their good side; external conditions and the standard of living are undoubtedly improved. But their effects are not limited to these matters; they have invaded the mind and character, and subdued the soul to their own dye.

John Dewey

World War I	Great Depression	World War II
1919 Progressive Education Association	1930 School year became 172 days and all states had compulsory attendance	1941 Military training for national defense
1923 Daytona-Cookman Collegiate Institute (Bethune-Cookman College)	1932 New Deal educational programs	1944 G.I. Bill for college tuition
1925 Oregon case guaranteed right of private schools	1930–38 Eight-Year Study confirmed value of progressive schools	1945 UNESCO 1954 *Brown v. Board of Education* in Topeka

Figure 7.1   Time Line for American Education from 1918 to the Present

Several volumes could be written on the subject of educational expansion, change, and controversy since World War I. The most obvious feature has been the tremendous growth at all levels in the numbers of students, teachers, and facilities. Secondary education grew during this period until it became standard for almost all children, just as the elementary school had done in the previous century. Higher education expanded, especially in the years following World War II, so that some kind of college or university experience was enjoyed by more than two-thirds of all American high school graduates. Many modern cities in the United States now contain more individuals engaged in formal schooling than could have been found in the entire colonial area at any one time. Sophisticated training offered by industry, early childhood education (both public and private), the federal government, expanded school choice (vouchers and charter schools), assessment, cultural diversity, and the mass media are illustrative of agencies and techniques now active in education that were not so significant in earlier times. Education is now big business in terms of money spent on training teachers, using physical plants, developing materials, and serving students.

This magnification of the educational enterprise raised new issues concerning the relationship of the school and the society. Advances in technology, the fluid social order, economic depressions, recessions and recovery, wars both hot and cold, and conflict over the meaning of democracy led to demands for a re-evaluation of educational aims.

Cold War		Vietnam Conflict
1957 *Sputnik*	1965 Head Start	1979 Secretary of Education as a cabinet position
1958 NDEA	Higher Education Act	
	Rebellion on college campuses	1981 Education Consolidation and Improvement Act
1964 Economic Opportunity Act	1967 Bilingual Education Act	1983 *A Nation at Risk*
1965 Elementary and Secondary Education Act	1975 Public Law 94-142 provided education for those with disabilities	1990s Massive educational reforms in most states

MAJOR EDUCATIONAL CHANGES

Integration of all Americans into a national community was a goal of early leaders such as Mann and Barnard. Schools were viewed as social ladders for individual and group improvement and as the means for Americanizing immigrants. Since World War II, the civil rights movement, and the black revolution, much more attention has been given to the educational problems of children from various social, economic, religious, ethnic, and racial backgrounds. Desegregating schools, helping the culturally disadvantaged, and meeting social needs in urban centers have become major goals of American education. Schools have made great strides. However, large numbers of children are still excluded from equal educational opportunity, and national unity though social integration has not been realized. Much current educational theory centers on the role of the school in solving major problems of the culture and on the kind of education that will be required to prepare the young for meeting the challenges of an uncertain future.

Among the more significant changes in education during the last half century were the following:

❑ A broader educational philosophy with social as well as individual objectives, illustrated by progressive education, deconstruction, postmodernism, social equity, aggression control, inclusion, and social reconstruction movements.

- ❑ New areas of educational concern such as vocational guidance, standardized testing, tech-prep programs for employability, and special education for the physically and mentally challenged and the gifted.
- ❑ Reorganization of schools to include junior/middle high schools, junior/community colleges, night schools, correspondence courses, as well as an explosion of graduate education, changes in graduate and undergraduate delivery systems to include Saturday and weekend classes, on-site classes in industry and business, external degree programs for individuals not able to take time off from work for further education, home study television classes with proposals for three-year bachelor's degree programs, compressed video and distance learning degree programs, and college credit for work experience.
- ❑ New emphasis on health, welfare, violence prevention, improved buildings and equipment, and the partnerships between schools/businesses/community and service learning (giving credit to students for civic participation such as helping the elderly, and participation in a wide variety of community projects).
- ❑ Enormous increase in attendance at all levels and an extension of the years of formal schooling for the average student including adult education and lifelong learning. Elderhostels are an example of continuing education efforts.
- ❑ An extension and improvement of teacher training, Master of Arts in Teaching Programs (often five-year programs), and the scientific study of education through research.
- ❑ The impact of cultural changes such as the mass media of communications; research conducted by private organizations; development of the Internet and World Wide Web with search engines such as Netscape, Alta Vista, AskJeeves, Looksmart, Microsoft MSN, AOL, Yahoo, Google; growth in distance learning programs at all educational levels; cell phones, wireless systems, Palm VII organizers, location tracking, and multimedia systems that combine telephone, computer, entertainment services, and research queries into superinformation highways; and the increased role of the federal government in educational affairs.

Historically, many famous Americans including Benjamin Franklin and Abraham Lincoln were self-educated. This required a high degree of motivation and self-sacrifice. Franklin subsisted on potatoes and used his wages to buy books while Lincoln borrowed all the reading material he could find in his frontier settlement. The availability of educational materials expanded vastly in the modern period with resources such as school, university, and public libraries.

With the onset of World War II, men prepared for work in business and industry were quickly trained to fly aircraft, drive tanks, or manage military logistics. Hundreds of thousands of women were removed from homemaking and trained to produce wartime material in the industrial plants of the nation.

With peace, almost everyone had to be educated again for different jobs with the help of the GI Bill and other governmental programs. Adult education, retraining for new jobs, and lifelong learning became a reality. No one today expects to learn nothing more after leaving school, for skills and information quickly become obsolete.

The computer and the Internet have so vastly altered the learning environment that all levels of schooling have changed. It is not now uncommon for a preadolescent child to write a sophisticated story or produce a well-researched paper that would have passed for college work a decade ago. Most homes now have Internet access, and devices such as the Connected Touch Pad provide access in places too small for PCs. Schools will certainly continue to function as the electronic age advances, but their role will no longer be to provide or transfer information that can be found elsewhere. Change continues to accelerate with Spintronics (a whole new class of electronics based on the spin of the electron), Quantum Information science and technology, virtual online external degree programs, and electronic publishing (Jeffry, 2000).

These changes are not without problems. Vast quantities of online materials are of questionable value or just plain wrong. Plagiarism is easy via the Internet, and there are few controls. Cyberlaw is out of date as soon as it is written, and accessing information does not mean that it is always well evaluated or properly applied. Nevertheless, the electronic information age will continue to govern future educational theory and practice. Inventions in this field come rapidly, and education must adjust. It is difficult to understand the impact just as it is hard to realize that the economic value of software is now greater than that of manufactured goods in America.

Perhaps the most difficult problem for educators in the United States today is how to provide varied, realistic, general, and individual education for all children and produce the experts necessary for an industrial/technology-oriented democracy at the same time. Can we really be equal and excellent too?

Social, Political, and Economic Influence.
Many of these changes, and others less dramatic, began in the nineteenth century and were developed in recent decades; but there were also innovations that came about as a result of economic and social changes during the two world wars. Older concerns with physical expansion gave way to new problems of technological discovery and scientific development. Reforms in government pursued legal measures to prevent the waste and exploitation of dwindling natural resources. Contact with the sophisticated culture of Europe during World War I and the economic crisis that followed the conflict altered many of America's basic conceptions. Woodrow Wilson's failure to persuade America to join the League of Nations and the isolationism, fatalism, and inflation of the postwar era did not destroy European influences.

However, the decade-long depression that started in 1929 shook American optimism and altered the role of government in economic affairs. When Franklin Roosevelt became president in 1932, the immense task of economic rebuilding began. The New

Deal program attempted to place 11 million unemployed persons in various types of meaningful jobs and to establish emergency measures to solve the economic crisis. It was not, however, until the beginning of World War II that the United States found its way out of the depression and into a new era of war boom and postwar prosperity.

World War II caused a rapid increase in the rate of technological advancement and stimulated American interest in the international situation, thus leading to an ideological struggle against communism that culminated in the cold war of the 1950s. The impact of space achievements resulted not only in federal support for the advancement of science, mathematics, and foreign languages in the schools but also in efforts to locate and train the exceptional pupil who could be a leader in scientific and military development. Under Truman and Eisenhower, programs developed that provided a greater amount of social security and a higher rate of employment, but the nation was faced again with a need for protection against external aggression. America became involved in the United Nations (chartered in 1945), and the need to develop peaceful co-existence with Communistic countries dominated American foreign policy. American efforts to limit Communist expansion led to commitments in Korea, Berlin, and Vietnam.

The leadership of John F. Kennedy brought new reforms and policies to the internal social development of the country, including economic stimulation and programs of health and medical care for the aged. Vast increases in federal aid to education, the war on poverty, and greater federal expenditure for education marked the presidency of Lyndon Johnson. It is important to remember that the United States contained a population of about 100 million in 1918 compared with nearly 300 million today and an increasing number of Hispanic, Asian, and other immigrants entering the country each year. Social mobility and new industry gave rise to teeming cities with very different educational problems from those of agrarian communities. Americans became the most affluent people in history (with persistent pockets of inner-city and rural poverty), and an increase of wealth produced demands for amenities, more education, and solutions to new kinds of problems.

Today, more than 50 percent of our high school students express interest in attending a college or university. Although education is still the road to economic advancement, the role of the schools in social change, education for leisure, and the evaluation of major institutions now takes on new significance. The trend to begin school earlier and to stay in school longer has by no means reached its zenith. A major educational problem of the twenty-first century centers on the need for both general education (common school experiences for all children) and increased specialization. Adult education and lifelong learning are requisites for students and workers in order to keep up with rapid changes in technology and a mobile social structure. Special efforts to improve at-risk student achievement levels are under way at all educational levels.

EVOLUTION OF THE MODERN INSTITUTIONAL STRUCTURE

A serious argument rages among educators over the adequacy of the current educational system in meeting the needs of our young people. Many studies show that children are capable of learning such skills as reading at a younger age than we had previously supposed. However, children mature at different rates so that starting all six-year-olds in the first grade is psychologically unsatisfactory.

Many students seem to benefit from early childhood education, such as a structured nursery school or a Montessori school. Most American communities now offer some kind of preschool educational experience of a formal kind. Although some people became interested in the educational ideas of Maria Montessori as early as 1911, the rapid growth of Montessori programs for young children has taken place only in the last decade. A major problem for Montessori and other preschool programs is that most are supported by private tuition. A notable exception is the federally funded Head Start program operating in all fifty states. The program provides comprehensive developmental services for America's low-income at-risk children from three to five.

Many children who could benefit from formal educational experience prior to entering kindergarten are from families unable to pay the fees, and Head Start is not available to all. Since 1970, kindergartens have been publicly supported as part of the public school system in almost all American communities. Before that date, some kindergartens were private and some cities had none at all. Some schools now offer developmental programs for kindergarten-age children who are found through testing to be immature. By 2001, a large number of American pre-kindergarten children were in day-care centers. Day-care centers often have educational programs, and most of them teach social skills.

Currently day-care centers, most privately owned, are widely available for children at risk. They vary in effectiveness. Some nonprofit centers supported by a combination of private, community, and federal funding and volunteers—such as the Community Child Care Center of Delray Beach, Florida, nationally accredited by the National Academy of Early Childhood programs—offer expanded services from the age at which children can walk through age five. Among the clientele are abused, neglected, at-risk children from low-income working poor, refugees, teen parents in school, and those in job training. Parents are also assisted in dealing with drug use, AIDS, aggressive/dysfunctional behavior, and inadequate job skills. Immigrant and minority communities with a large number of single parents with transient partners are given special assistance for employability in conjunction with some day-care centers like the Community Child Care Center. Many day-care centers offer services to families.

Elementary Programs. Before the beginning of the twentieth century, the modern school system had emerged as a single track from the elementary grades through college. American schools are still divided into fifty different state systems, with a great deal of control vested in local boards and state departments of education. However, the past fifty years have clearly demonstrated a trend to build larger units, to standardize programs, and to put more schools under the jurisdiction of centralized administrative units.

In 1893, the NEA appointed a Committee of Fifteen on the organization and program of primary and grammar schools. The committee stressed good English usage including literature, United States history, geography, writing, arithmetic, physical science, and music. It suggested manual training for boys and cooking or sewing for girls, along with Latin for children in the eighth grade. The effect of the recommendations was to standardize the curriculum of elementary schools throughout the nation.

Most modern elementary schools do not extend beyond the sixth grade. Although curriculum changes have taken place, most elementary students still devote the majority of their time to skill subjects such as reading, writing, grammar, and mathematics. These schools have combined history and geography into "social studies," have added biological sciences, and have replaced arithmetic with the "new math" of the 1960s (which focuses on formal math structure).

Art, music, and physical education are often the first courses to be cut during budget shortfalls, even though research has shown that achievement in mathematics and music is interrelated. However, social studies now receive more attention than spelling. Physical education might consist of organized sports, calisthenics, or merely free play at recess or noon, although efforts are made to employ full- or part-time instructors in the field. Many subjects such as sex education, aggression control, multicultural studies, and health education have been added to the curriculum. And sometimes state legislatures have taken it upon themselves to pass laws requiring the teaching of additional subjects such as drug education and, more recently, character and aggression control education. Educators have experimented with the curriculum, and much new information has been added. However, there have been more changes in attitudes and methods than in basic subjects.

Innovations.   Innovations now found in many elementary schools include team teaching, nongraded schools, block scheduling, aggression-control programs, tokenism (food, games, money, tickets, and a variety of other reinforcers for learning), school uniforms, cultural diversity and sensitivity programs, assistive technology, individualized instruction, open classrooms, looping (the same teacher stays with students through first and second grades and the cycle repeats with a new group of students), portfolios, frameworks (teachers draw up their own tests, using state guidelines), and programmed learning. Although traditional methods are still dominant, a great many districts are experimenting with innovative plans and programs.

In contrast with the self-contained classroom, team teaching provides for the cooperation of a group of teachers working together with children. A team of teachers with a leader might be responsible for all the instruction of children who normally would be assigned to the primary grades (first, second, and third grades). Teams normally use some large-group, some small-group, and some individual instruction. Advantages include more time for planning, better evaluation of the progress of pupils, the opportunity for teachers to help one another improve practice, and flexibility in meeting the needs of students.

It is difficult to have team teaching in a building designed for self-contained rooms. Success also depends upon the degree to which teachers are able to work together effectively. Many European elementary schools are now organized so that a team of teachers stays with the same students for several years, thus getting to know them well. This model is becoming more attractive in America.

Nongraded schools allow children to progress at their own rate without locking them into the content of a given grade. A student in a graded school who is unable to satisfy the requirements of a given area (say third grade reading) must be either retained or promoted at the end of the year. In nongraded schools, students who need a year and a half to master third grade reading are neither punished by failing the grade nor promoted beyond their ability to cope.

Children mature at different rates, have different interests, and are not motivated in the same way. Experiments in individualized instruction are designed to meet needs through a flexible program that allows each student to participate in planning his or her own program of instruction. Some individual instruction plans operate by providing a large number of groups at different levels for various subjects. A low teacher-pupil ratio and adequate support (including a high-quality instructional materials center) are needed for successful individualized instruction.

Herbert Kohl and others who advocate the open classroom say that the standard curriculum prevents creativity and good communication. By Kohl's standards, not many American elementary schools are "open." However, many schools now offer the pupil a wide choice of activities and provide numerous opportunities for self-expression, the development of interests, and creative activities. Open classrooms provide for greater student interaction and scheduling and instructional flexibility; self-contained traditional classrooms provide for a more structured teaching and learning environment. Both the open and traditional classroom models are frequently modified to incorporate the best practices in each method.

Programmed learning, including computer-assisted instruction, is used in connection with other innovative programs. These programs are often found in the media centers of schools with open or individualized plans for instruction. Various forms of technology—including closed-circuit television, microfilm, VCRs, tape recorders, Powerpoint presentations, CD-RW burners, interactive video systems, computer video networks, virtual reality systems, computer–slide–overhead projector combinations, and projectors for slides and films—are also used in traditional schools. In our twenty-first century, powerful desktop computers—including new high-speed chip systems with ever more RAM; prototypes with over ten-gigahertz speed; two-gigahertz chips that can provide for voice recognition, fingerprint authentication, and wireless video in computers and cell phones; and increased amounts of hard drive with multimedia capacities—are becoming more common and less expensive.

The Pew Internet and American Life Project, which tracks Internet usage, found that over half (56 percent) of the U.S. population and three-quarters of children ages twelve to seventeen were using the Internet while only 38 percent of the poorest Americans (earning less than $38,000) and 15 percent of sixty-five and older groups were online in 2001. New powerful modems with networking capabilities are now bringing services from financial reports to shopping, travel, and banking into schools, homes, and offices.

The World Wide Web and the Internet accessed by network browsers such as Netscape and Microsoft Explorer are changing the way students gain access to knowledge bases. Students can contact experts in fields of interest through computer networking using a variety of search engines including Google, Alta Vista, Yahoo, Lycos, Excite, Web Crawler, and Infoseek. As costs decrease and computers are simplified, more classrooms and homes will have minicomputers with mainframe computer power.

Public schools and universities now have e-mail, Internet (originally called ARPANET, or Advanced Research Projects Administration, and limited to Pentagon use), and Telnet highways that allow students and faculty to gain ready access to worldwide library and research facilities, as well as political, social, religious, and economic information. The Integrated Services Digital Network technology provides for rapid access to national and international multiple information channels. New search engines provide the widest access to information in the world. Philanthropic groups have provided new computers and software for public schools, libraries, and universities. The Bill and Melinda Gates Foundation is one of the major philanthropic organizations committed to improving access to technology. IBM has developed software that gives individuals a broad menu of personalized Web pages for use virtually anywhere, from desk to handheld devices.

Citizens can contact government officials through e-mail and glean information from Web sites. Government computer systems have been updated to enhance government communications systems. Efforts have been made to connect all public and private educational systems in the country with the Internet. The speed with which computer technology changes makes it difficult to keep up with the advances. High-definition television, thin picture frame–type television screens and computer monitors, and multimedia and information centers utilizing a combination of computers, wireless communication, and television are on the market.

Elementary schoolchildren in the 2000s find it hard to imagine a world without computer technology. Few inventions in history have been able to cross boundaries, borders, cultures, and languages as easily and effectively as our World Wide Web. One can frequently find Chinese, Iranian, European, African, South American, and other international students spending hours at the twenty-four-hour university computer centers. Sitting side by side, they use chat lines with intensity and spend hours exchanging messages with other students throughout the world. Portable laptop computers with desktop power make access to information universal. Zip drives and CD-RW burners provide a way of carrying massive amounts of information from one location to another with ease. Internet providers such as earthlink, MSN, and AOL assist individuals in accessing and disseminating information rapidly.

It seems safe to predict that multimedia systems will have increased utilization as America moves into a lifelong learning society and the information age. The rapidity of technological change requires constant adjustment to new challenges, from copyrighting material found in cyberspace and intellectual property rights to monitoring students who can easily complete class assignments by downloading information or copying complete research papers from the Internet.

The School Survey.   Educational leaders as early as the period of James Carter and Horace Mann looked hard at the adequacy of schools in various states, but it was not until 1910 that a formal survey of schools took place. In that year, Superintendent William Kendall of Indianapolis was invited to visit and make a report on

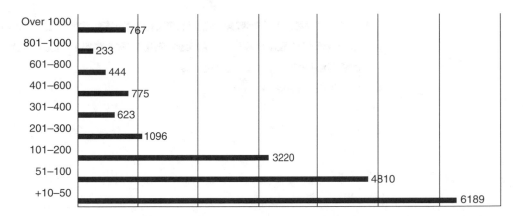

Figure 7.2   Distribution of U.S. Public High Schools by Enrollment for 1926

Note: The average number enrolled in the 18,157 schools was 211.4. De Witt Clinton High School of New York City was the largest school with an enrollment of 8,611.

Source: From the U.S. Bureau of Education *Bulletin,* 1927, No. 3, Statistics of Public High Schools. Cited in Department of Superintendence *Seventh Yearbook* (p. 208), 1929, Washington, DC: Department of Superintendence of the National Education Association.

the schools of Boise, Idaho. His survey covered teachers, the curriculum, the organization of schools and buildings, and the attitude of citizens toward their educational system. By 1914, the school survey was an established practice, but not many were as detailed as the three-year $100,000 survey conducted in New York City.

Early surveys utilized the services of well-known educators and ranked the subject system against others that were regarded as comparable. Nothing more sophisticated than observation was used as a tool for measurement. Criticism of the large numbers of changes recommended and failure to consider the limitations of resources caused surveys by teams of experts to be unpopular. The Thirteenth Yearbook of the National Society for the Study of Education offered suggestions about how surveys might be conducted by local educators with only slight assistance from experts. Data from a 1926 survey of secondary school units with "regular" and "reorganized" (refers to various types of junior-senior combinations) high school enrollments (see Figure 7.2) showed that over 60 percent of the 18,157 high schools in the United States had an enrollment of 100 pupils or less.

Detailed surveys are still conducted in the United States. They serve a variety of purposes such as planning for consolidation, desegregation, new building, curriculum change, and administrative reorganization. Surveys are also used by organizations for accrediting schools and evaluating programs. Laurie Lewis and her colleagues conducted "The Condition of America's Public School Facilities," a 1999 National Center for Educational Statistics survey. The survey reported that although a majority of the nation's schools are at least in adequate condition, over half of all school respondents noted that roofs, electrical systems, heating, ventilation, and air conditioning were less than adequate. An estimated $127 billion, or $2.2 million per school, would be needed for school repair and update.

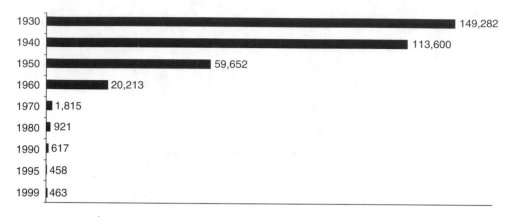

Figure 7.3   Decline of One-Room Schools

Source: From *Digest of Educational Statistics 1996*, 1996 (p. 96) by Thomas Snyder, Washington, DC: U.S. Office of Education, National Center for Educational Statistics.

Consolidation.   One of the earlier shifts in design resulted from the consolidation of one-room district schools in rural areas. Local elementary schools were first built just far enough apart to permit scholars to walk from their homes. Concentrations of population, the wide use of automobiles, and a reduction of the number of farm families made it possible to build united schools that were larger and more efficient. Just after World War I, about 70 percent of the public school buildings in the United States were of the one-room variety. Such schools were expensive to maintain, lacking in equipment, poorly supervised, and without specialization. Consolidation has reduced the number of one-room schools to less than 5 percent of the total. Today, even sparsely populated communities often have modern multiroom physical plants, complete with gymnasium, cafeteria, and modern equipment. Bus service is normally provided by consolidated school districts. The *Digest of Educational Statistics 1999* gives a picture of the dramatic decline of one-teacher, one-room schools (see Figure 7.3). The report found some 463 one-room, one-teacher schools with the majority in Montana (82) and Nebraska (97). The others are in rural areas throughout the country. We may expect them all to disappear in the near future.

The modern elementary school has changed in both consolidated and urban school districts. Elementary schools are not as directly linked to colleges (although there are more cooperative programs between universities and elementary schools) as are high schools. This has allowed more flexibility in the curriculum and in scheduling. Team teaching, block scheduling, programmed instruction, and minicourses for student electives—such as introduction to foreign languages, vocational education, keyboarding, computer literacy, teaching machines, and computer-assisted instruction—are used in connection with other innovative programs in instructional technology. The organization, administration, structures, and curriculums of schools in America are not fixed or final. Further evolution of schools and programs may be expected in the future. Many schools have specially trained

Elementary	Middle	High School
6		3
6		6
6	2	4
4	4	4

Table 7.1 Combinations of Organizational Plans for Public Schools

teachers for art, speech correction, guidance counseling, and so forth. Extracurricular activities, such as team sports, and a federally subsidized lunch program are commonly found in elementary schools.

Junior High and Middle Schools.

Eight-year elementary schools and four-year high schools are still found in the United States, but other organizational plans are more common. Junior high schools increased slowly in number during the first half of the twentieth century, but their number increased markedly in the past thirty years. Middle schools or mid–high schools are now found in many communities. Since the middle of this century, the 6–3–3 or 6–6 plan of organization has become more common than the traditional eight-year elementary school followed by a four-year high school. Some cities have experimented with a 6–2–4 or a 4–4–4 organizational plan (see Table 7.1). And the two-year community college has sometimes been added as an extension of the common school system.

The typical junior high school consists of seventh, eighth, and ninth grades. Part of the theory behind junior high schools relates to a need for vocational or terminal secondary education. Their success and popularity can be attributed in part to an exploratory curriculum with general courses in science and introductory work in various fields. The students receive guidance concerning their abilities and limitations. They study fewer subjects (with a different teacher for each course), but greater detail is given than for elementary subjects. It is assumed that junior/middle high school students no longer need the security of belonging to one classroom with one teacher. And they are expected to have a longer attention span than younger children.

Perhaps the most important reason for the popularity of the three-year junior high school is that it separates youngsters just starting the adolescent period of life from both older and younger students. This separation contributes to the development of social skills. Children of all ages are not crammed together into a matrix of social and intellectual competition. Some middle schools have innovative multiage-teaming child-centered philosophy programs. Junior high schools may be attached to an elementary or high school or may be completely separated.

High Schools.

The most important thing about the American high school in the past fifty years is its phenomenal growth. In the sense that it caters to a range of abilities, interests, and goals, the secondary school has become a school of all the people, just as the elementary school was in an earlier period. In 1920, there were about 2.5 million secondary school students—approximately a third of the population between the ages of fourteen and seventeen—in the United States. In 1965, there were more than 15 million secondary school students—approximately 85 percent of the high school age group. There are a number of vocational or technical high schools, especially in large cities, but the typical American secondary school has become the "comprehensive" public high school.

Comprehensive is a term used by scholars such as James B. Conant who have studied the program of the high schools in detail. Basically, it refers to a secondary school that has a program designed to meet the various needs and interests of students, regardless of whether or not they expect to attend college. Vocational courses have long been offered by high schools, but the major emphasis is still on college preparation. With the increasing affluence of the American people and the growing scarcity of jobs for which little training is required, college preparation is not likely to lose ground as the major purpose of the high school. According to the *Digest of Educational Statistics 1996* and the *Statistical Abstract of the United States 1996*, college enrollment increased 41 percent between 1970 and 1980 and 20 percent from 1980 to 1992, or from 12.1 million to 14.6 million, a record level. Over 15 million students were enrolled in higher education institutions in 1994. Nevertheless, the purpose of secondary education and the program of the high schools continue to be the most hotly debated issues in American education.

Shortly after the Kalamazoo decision ensured tax support, the public high school took on qualities of both the academy and the classical school. It offered courses that were practical and cultural, on the one hand, and college preparatory, on the other. Training of the mind became equated with preparation for life, and the college preparatory course was considered to be the best mental training. Electives were offered in high schools, but the curriculum was shaped by what colleges would accept for entrance. The report of the Committee of Ten of the NEA in 1892 emphasized that high schools were for the elite.

The twentieth century gave rise to an increase in national wealth, an improved living standard, and a need for a better trained labor force. High schools were forced to cater to the needs of the entire population in a growing industrial democracy. An NEA Commission on the Reorganization of Secondary Education, meeting in 1918, developed the Cardinal Principles of Secondary Education. In contrast with the college-centered and mental-discipline-oriented Committee of Ten, these principles stressed guidance, a wide range of subjects, adaptation of content and methods to the abilities and interest of students, and flexibility of organization and administration. In addition to fundamental processes and academic subjects, high schools began to stress health, citizenship, vocational preparation, ethical development, and the worthy use of leisure time. In short, they became comprehensive.

A demand for experts to improve industry and to help win the cold war resulted in more science courses; and new subjects such as driver training, mental hygiene, and personal relations reflected the needs of individuals in a complex society. The American comprehensive high school has received harsh criticism, especially from those who emphasize traditional subject matter and academic excellence. There is still a question of whether or not the high school should be specialized and, if so, how specialized and how early in the student's career. In 1946, a Harvard committee published *General Education in a Free Society;* the book suggests that specialization on the secondary level is unsound. Others have joined the battle to extend general education through the high school on the grounds that modern society demands generalized knowledge of many areas for true human fulfillment and good citizenship.

The American high school has provided universal education for the nation's youth. Regardless of the variation in school facilities and achievement levels, few other nations have an institution serving such a broad-based student body. Record levels of enrollment are occurring in our twenty-first century. Public elementary school enrollment (K–8) is projected to be 38.8 million, with 17 million secondary school students enrolled by 2003. Education expenditures rose to $371 billion in the 1998–1999 school year. Some 7.3 percent of the gross domestic product is spent on public education at all levels (*Digest of Educational Statistics 1999, National Center for Education Statistics 2000*).

Higher Education.   Due to the phenomenal growth of colleges and universities, high schools in the United States have never entirely lost their college preparatory function. With the exception of the period of the Great Depression, college enrollments have had a steady increase throughout this century, but the great explosion in size and number of colleges has taken place since World War II. Colleges have become more utilitarian and scientific in nature, although the liberal arts college is still a major American institution. With the addition of colleges and universities of a professional nature (education, agriculture, engineering, commerce, architecture, computer information systems and quantitative analysis, criminal justice institutes, food science, dentistry, and veterinary medicine) and the creation of separate departments within colleges, higher education has become very specialized. Practical and scientific courses were in demand before World War I, but the expansion of industry and the explosion of knowledge have made college training indispensable to many occupations that previously needed little formal schooling.

Mary McLeod Bethune (1875–1955) recognized the need for advanced education for minority women. She had a lifelong commitment to the improvement of education and the socioeconomic status of African-American women. Bethune was born in Mayesville, South Carolina, and was educated in a mission school (Scotia Seminary) and in the Moody Bible Institute. Bethune taught in Florida and Georgia from 1897 to 1903. She founded the Daytona Educational and Industrial Training School for Negro Girls in 1904. The curriculum included reading, writing, spelling, arithmetic, cooking, cleaning, sewing, and religion. With financial support from white liberal tourists from the North and blacks and whites in the community, the school was maintained. Bethune often had her students sing in tourist hotels to raise funds for the school. In 1923, the school was merged with Cookman Institute of Jacksonville, Florida. Daytona-Cookman Collegiate Institute became Bethune-Cookman College. Bethune was president of the college from 1904 to 1942 and from 1946 to 1947.

She used a variety of prestigious national positions to advance the cause of African-American education. Bethune held leadership positions in the National Association for Colored Women and its Florida Sunshine State Affiliate. Bethune was a consultant to the United States contingent at the founding conference of the United

Nations in San Francisco. Appointed director of the Negro Affairs Division of the National Youth Administration (1936–1944) by President Franklin Roosevelt, she served as a powerful advocate for civil rights of African Americans. During this period, Bethune was a consultant to the United States Secretary of War in the selection of the first female officer candidates for the armed forces. Her energy, persuasive skills, and ability to build bridges between the races served as a model in her time.

She utilized the differences in the philosophies of Booker T. Washington, who stressed working within the system, and W. E. B. Du Bois, who sought political change, to advance the cause of African-American women. Bethune used the ideas of Washington and Du Bois as engines for social change while working within the arena of political reality. Through work and an iron will, she raised a national awareness of the lack of social, educational, and economic opportunities for black women. She raised social consciousness and was a model for future minority change agents. Her contributions to higher education remain not only in the hearts, minds, and lives of those she influenced but also in the college that carries her name (McKissack, 1987; Smith, 1995).

Hundreds of new special occupations resulted from the changes brought about by scientific research in the universities. Veterans returning from World War II demanded and got practical courses from colleges and universities that had previously offered only liberal education. Governmental support of veterans' education through the GI Bill stimulated a trend toward considerable federal interest in higher education. Large numbers of students attended colleges and graduate schools through grants made by the National Defense Education Act of 1958 or other scholarships. The 500,000 students enrolled in college in 1918 seems a very small amount compared with today's figure, which exceeds 16 million students. It seems fair to predict that college enrollments in America will follow the same general growth trend as that of high school enrollments fifty years ago. Already, graduate schools are growing more rapidly than colleges did in the nineteenth century. Between 1984 and 1994, full-time male graduate student enrollment increased by 25 percent compared with 62 percent for women. Part-time graduate student enrollment shows the same trend. Enrollment of men during the period increased by 8 percent compared with a 30 percent increase for women.

The *Digest of Educational Statistics* and *Projections of Educational Statistics to 2008* further reveal an increase in Hispanic and Asian graduate student enrollment from 1976 to 1994. There are projections that 9.2 million women may be enrolled in higher education by 2008. They will constitute 57 percent of college enrollment while an estimated 6.2 to 6.9 million men will be enrolled in higher education by 2008. In the 1998–1999 school year, some $247 billion was spent on higher education.

In the 2000s, we face many new challenges in higher education. Among them are demands for more information, including graduate and retention rates especially for minorities, faculty workload, staff and administration evaluation, class size, and other measures of accountability. Higher education institution audits are being explored in many states, such as Oklahoma, to ensure maximum effectiveness in cost control. In addition, Congress passed a Students Right to Know and Crime Awareness and Campus Security Act in 1990 with an expanded list of crimes to be disclosed in The Higher Education Amendments of 1998. The legislation requires higher education institutions to publish graduation and crime rates on each campus including "hate crimes" to be reported by "category of prejudice."

Higher education institutions are facing a new form of competitiveness in alternative degree programs. Distance learning through accredited degree programs— such as that offered via e-mail by Phoenix University—is leading traditional colleges and universities to explore Saturday, weekend, compressed video and other forms of flexible delivery systems, as well as other options.

Junior/Community Colleges.

A direct result of the expansion in higher education that could not be accommodated by existing colleges was the junior college movement. Two-year terminal colleges, often staffed by senior high school teachers, began to appear before World War I. There have been both private and public junior colleges, but those with public control and tax support have increased most rapidly in recent years. The government established some junior colleges during the depression years, but city or state junior college boards have developed the greatest number. Municipal junior colleges have often provided the first two years of standard college education, thus taking some of the pressure off colleges and universities. Public junior/community colleges are either free or charge a very low tuition, and students usually live at home while attending them.

The junior/community college therefore offers an extension of educational opportunity to students who could not otherwise afford higher education. There is a vastly increased demand for more junior/community colleges of both the terminal (associate degree) and the nonterminal type (entry-level job skills/transfer courses for senior colleges). Financing is a serious problem in communities that direct a major portion of school taxes to the lower public schools. By 1997, more than 1,473 junior and community colleges were operating with a combined enrollment of over 5 million students (see Figure 7.4). National efforts are under way to expand opportunities for education through the fourteenth grade or the community college level. These efforts revive the Truman Commission's 1947 report recommending expanding universal education through the community college.

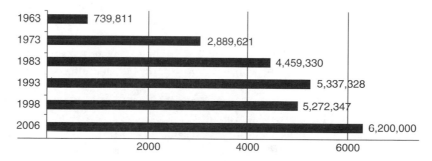

Figure 7.4   Growth of Public Two-Year Community Colleges

Source: From *Digest of Educational Statistics, 2000* (p. 228) (Table 199). Thomas Snyder, Washington, DC: U.S. Office of Education, National Center for Educational Statistics.

The average length of time spent in school has expanded at both ends of the continuum. Many students now have the opportunity to attend kindergarten before starting public school at the age of six. Quite a large number of school systems have public kindergartens, with the K–6–3–3 or K–4–4–4 plans being most common. Public kindergartens are found in all but the smaller rural schools. Day-care centers and Montessori schools for pre-kindergarten youngsters are available in most cities, but they usually require tuition. Head Start programs make an effort to give underprivileged children some of the preschool experiences enjoyed by middle-class youngsters.

SCHOOL FINANCE AND CONTROL

An issue that is developing into a major educational argument in America concerns the location of authority and the source of support for public schools. Although this has always been an issue in education, the voucher and charter school movement is bringing it to the forefront. As the federal government becomes more active in providing money through such measures as the Elementary and Secondary Education Act of 1965 and the 1999 Reauthorization Act, the role of the central government in education becomes larger. Many leaders feel that the schools ought to remain in local hands, and they fear that federal aid to education will eventually lead to complete federal control of schools. On the other hand, national authorities have allowed a good deal of local administration of federal funds when local and state governments have been unable to raise sufficient money for high-quality schools. We can predict that the argument over federal control of schools will continue, although it also seems likely that a larger share of future school finance will be handled by the national government.

Local and State Control.   Educational support and control in the United States has been a curious composite of local, state, and national functions. Because education was not considered a federal responsibility by the founding fathers, each state set up its own unique educational system. Many of the states have similar laws, but each is autonomous with regard to public schools and educational requirements within its own borders. Although the states have guarded their authority over schools and generally opposed federal financial aid, local school boards have been granted a considerable degree of freedom in managing the schools. State boards of education have served largely for making policy, and state superintendents or commissioners have been responsible for administration and general supervision. States differ widely in their method of selecting boards and executive school officers. Sometimes they are elected, sometimes appointed by the governor, and sometimes appointed by the state legislature.

Most states have well-organized educational offices with specialists for inspecting schools, certifying teachers, and allocating funds that are distributed by the state. There are normally smaller administrative units presided over by township, county, or district superintendents. Cities often have independent school districts with superintendents who work directly for the locally elected board of education and who perform the functions otherwise delegated to county superintendents. There is no uniformity with regard to the size and type of school districts in the United States. One superintendent and board of education in a metropolitan area may be responsible for hundreds of schools at all levels. At the other end of the extreme is the school board and executive officer governing only one small school building, although with increased focus on cost effectiveness through consolidation, this is becoming rare.

Although teachers' salaries are uniform in some states, it is still common to find adjacent school districts that differ in money paid to teachers and otherwise expended for the education of children. The inequality of educational opportunity in various districts has encouraged state and federal participation in education.

School Finance. In the twentieth century, states began to play a much more important role in school finance. State funds originated as early as 1795, when Connecticut sold its vast Western Reserve lands and put the money in permanent school funds. Most states have such funds, drawing money from public land sales, taxes, special appropriations, and so forth. Historically, the states have used their meager allotments for giving state aid to local districts that agreed to tax themselves for schools and for making payments to districts unable to obtain sufficient local revenues for a minimum standard. By and large, the concentrated wealth and population of cities, as compared with that of rural communities, has made it relatively easy for urban areas to levy taxes and support schools. Local taxes have paid the lion's share of public school costs, and the states have confined their administration to a minimum. However, state funds have encouraged the keeping of accurate records of attendance, school inspection, and the establishment of accepted minimum standards. Between 1930 and 1970, the percentage of locally raised public school funds dropped from about 83 percent to 51 percent.

As the proportion of local support has fallen, state and federal support has increased. Quite naturally, the larger governmental units have begun to place more restrictions on the money that they have collected and distributed. Such restrictions have usually been confined to general rules for the use of money, but there is no question that centralized control is increasing. Throughout the nation there is increased litigation over school funding as low-income school districts seek additional funds. Over twenty states have had their school funding systems declared unconstitutional by state and federal courts. George W. Bush supports having dollars follow the child by giving parents more choice through vouchers, charter schools, and opportunities to select public schools.

States use a variety of means for funding public schools including sales tax, state income tax, lotteries, state property tax, fees, and licenses on items such as automobiles. According to a National Conference of State Legislatures report, in 1992 at least fourteen states earmarked a percentage of their lottery money for education. Other states are considering lotteries to fund a portion of their education budget. Manzo (2000) reported that there were lotteries in thirty-eight states (including the District of Columbia). Twenty states earmark a portion of the proceeds for public education. However, funds are often inadequate, and the relationship between local and state sources creates a political problem. School districts have the power to raise only ad valorem property taxes within district boundaries. If the wealth of the district is low, it may not be possible to meet school funding needs even if the voters in the district support the levy. When this occurs, schools can turn to the courts to force the states to fund a larger part of the school budget. For example, more than 100 school districts in Montana sued the state in 1988 on the grounds that they did not have the power to raise enough taxes to meet state-mandated requirements for a basic education. The state supreme court agreed with the schools and required the legislature to provide a means for additional state funding for all public schools in Montana.

There is increasing litigation in the states over equity in school district financing. Federal and state court rulings continue to address the need for adjusting the balance between rich and poor districts as well as expanding educational opportunities for all children. There is an increase in class action lawsuits to roll back tax increases, which has affected public school financing. The Fayetteville, Arkansas, school district faced such a rollback in 2000. The National Council of State Legislatures has created an information clearinghouse on school finance. The center will track information on funding formulas in the fifty states and keep a Web site on all aspects of school finance.

Historically, the federal government has been interested in the improvement of higher education and in specialized training in such subjects as agriculture. Local property taxes are still widely used for school finance, but they are neither sufficiently flexible nor adequate to care for the changing population distribution. Knowledge of the emergence of the federal government as a major educational agency is vital to an understanding of the current issue over support and control of the schools.

FEDERAL PARTICIPATION IN EDUCATION

(The amount of involvement of the United States government has increased so much in the past few years that only major areas of activity are discussed here.) The United States Office of Education has grown rapidly in size and influence, due largely to the need for administering federal funds and advising participants in federal projects. The office has had a varied history, having been moved from the Department of the Interior and given separate status in 1930, moved again to the Federal Security Agency in 1939, and made part of the Department of Health, Education, and Welfare (HEW) in 1953. Large grants made through HEW to schools and universities contributed to the importance of the Office of Education, and it was made a separate cabinet level position under the Carter administration over the objection of now Vice President Dick Cheney. Cutbacks in federal spending in the Reagan administration created some loss of prestige, and some members of Congress suggested that it should be abolished. The future of the office of Secretary of Education will depend upon politics and federal policy concerning finance.

The American Association of School Administrators reported that outgoing President Bill Clinton signed a bill with an 18 percent increase in federal funding for education, a record education increase. President George W. Bush made educational reform, higher standards, assessment of student achievement, and school improvement a centerpiece of his administration. By the spring of 2002 the Bush administration's educational bill passed Congress with bipartisan support. The challenge will be implementation of the educational reform measures in the states. A Republican control of Congress by the mid term election of 2002 may further the Bush educational agenda

Support for Industrial and Vocational Education.   Among the earlier efforts of Congress to aid education were acts designed to fill a need for industrial and vocational education. Through the Smith-Hughes Act (1917), the George-Reed Act (1929), and the George-Dean Act (1937), Congress attempted to promote vocational education in public schools. A Federal Board of Vocational Education was created in 1917 and, after 1919, was given the additional task of supervising training of people with disabilities.

Ten years later, the Capper-Ketcham Act extended the previous Smith-Lever Act to cover education in home economics and agriculture. During World War I, the government found it necessary to train many technicians, but industrial inactivity during the depression resulted in a great shortage of trained technicians and engineers. The National Defense Training Program of 1940 provided courses for more than 7 million workers during World War II. The Rural War Production Training Program trained farm youth for industry and for jobs in food production. Vocational training also benefited from the National Defense Education Act (1958), but the Vocational Education Act extended previous legislation to cover any skilled, technical, or semi-skilled occupation and included provisions for keeping potential dropouts in school.

The original purpose of federal efforts to promote vocational and industrial education was to provide the nation with skilled workers and technicians when other agencies had failed to do so. Clearly, this was the same rationale that fostered the agricultural and mechanical colleges developed from the Morrill acts. However, Congress has increasingly turned its attention to vocational education that may serve social needs by improving the economy, keeping children in school longer, fighting poverty, and creating new jobs for the unemployed. The *Digest of Educational Statistics 1999* identified the 1998 Workforce Investment Act for adult and family literacy as receiving increased funding in the 2001 appropriations and budget bill. Other federal funding focuses were the Carl D. Perkins Vocational and Applied Technology Education 1998 Amendments and the Assistive Technology Act of 1998 designed to address needs of at-risk individuals and those with disabilities. Funding authorization was provided through 2003, reflecting continuing federal investments in vocational and disabilities education. Further legislation to strengthen vocational education in order to fight against unemployment and provide employable skills seems almost certain.

New Deal Acts.   Attempts to improve the national welfare and increase equality of opportunity were made through the so-called New Deal legislation passed during the administration of Franklin D. Roosevelt. The Civilian Conservation Corps employed young men and gave them vocational training, especially in conservation and building trades; and small grants were given to needy students through the National Youth Administration. The Works Progress Administration subsidized teachers' salaries for programs in job training for adults and aliens and for nursery schools. The Public Works Administration provided loans for communities to use in building schools and libraries. In 1935, the Secretary of Agriculture was authorized to distribute surplus foods to schools, and this led directly to the National School Lunch Act of 1946 (an act that continues to make both food and money available to school lunch programs). Loss of tax funds for schools during the depression led to loans to school boards through the Reconstruction Finance Corporation. This trend led to legislation such as the Economic Opportunity Act (EOA) of 1964. The 106th Congress passed a 2001 appropriations bill with provisions for a variety of youth support services including safe schools/healthy students community-wide programs to prevent youth violence and drug abuse.

Title I of the EOA set up the Job Corps to train youth between the ages of sixteen and twenty-one for useful employment and citizenship. Job Corps training centers were built around the nation. Students were given training in basic skills as well as in vocational subjects. There continues to be a work-study program for high school students who need to earn money and one for college students with financial need. Title II of the EOA authorized aid for adult education and cultural enrichment programs for children from disadvantaged families. The Head Start program was aimed at children from three to five years of age who would not normally have had the advantage of nursery schools or kindergartens.

Wartime Measures.   Wartime activity has also contributed to the involvement of the federal government in education. During World War I, the government trained technicians, and troops drilled on college campuses. In World War II, loans were made to students majoring in fields such as medicine, fields in which there was a critical need. Congress began giving assistance to those school districts that absorbed large numbers of children of military or defense personnel. Laws aiding such affected areas were extended in 1950 and 1966. In addition, equipment purchased by the government for special war training was later turned over to schools, and surplus property was made available to all nonprofit educational institutions.

During World War II, women were called upon to enter the workforce. Thousands of "Rosie the Riveters" helped build aircraft, ships, and tanks for the military. Their wartime contributions proved that women workers were dependable, efficient, productive, and capable. Since that time, women have increasingly entered the workforce. They constitute 60 million or over 48 percent of our nation's workforce as we move toward the twenty-first century.

In an effort to meet the needs of veterans whose schooling had been interrupted by military duty, the Servicemen's Readjustment Act of 1944 (the GI Bill) was passed. This measure has provided subsistence and school cost allowances for veterans who have continued their education, and it has resulted in the expansion of colleges to accommodate them. The effort to assist returning veterans through government support had its critics. One university president said the GI Bill would open higher education to a flood of unqualified students and depress academic standards, while another saw the bill as a threat to higher learning and said that education was not a device to prevent mass unemployment. Veterans, many from poor families, many at-risk minority students, flooded the nation's colleges. In 1947, a peak year, some 1,150,000 veterans attended school. A report by the Syracuse University Research Institute found a far greater percentage of the population could benefit from higher education than previously thought possible. The Syracuse report found veterans were more serious, contributed more to society on graduation, and received higher grades than nonveteran classmates. The GI Bill was revived for veterans of the Korean War, and the benefits were increased for Vietnam veterans in 1972, Desert Storm veterans in 1991, and provisions will be made for those who served in Afghanistan.

National Defense Education Act.
A new period of federal activity in education started with the cold war and with the Soviet success in launching *Sputnik*, the first space satellite. The National Defense Education Act (NDEA) of 1958 was designed for the purpose of giving aid to education as a means of strengthening the nation. NDEA loans have been made to prospective teachers in amounts up to $5,000, and half of the loan has been cancelable through service as a public school teacher after graduation. Funds have been made available for laboratory equipment and other materials to improve instruction in science, and fellowships have been offered to persons training to be college professors. State testing and guidance to find and encourage able students, an extension of vocational education, and research on new educational media have also been financed by NDEA funds. Out of the administrations of John F. Kennedy and Lyndon B. Johnson came a host of federal measures designed to promote equality of educational opportunity, to fight poverty, and to strengthen defense. The Higher Education Facilities Act of 1963 made funds available for the construction of college buildings, with matching sums provided by the college or state.

Elementary and Secondary Education Act.
Federal aid to education took another big step with the Elementary and Secondary Education Act of 1965. This measure provided funds for textbooks and other instructional materials and services in public and private elementary and secondary schools. The primary purpose was to ensure that children from low-income families had access to adequate materials. State and local governments, rather than federal agencies, had control of the funds. The act also included $100 million for research in the field of education to be administered by the United States Office of Education. This act was extended for four more years in 1966, at a cost of about $12 billion. In 1981, the Education Consolidation and Improvement Act provided funds for better quality programs and the encouragement of consolidation efforts. Federal block grants also targeted low-income and minority areas for special funding.

In the fall of 1993, Secretary of Education Richard W. Riley, reflecting the Clinton administration theme of re-inventing government to make it more effective, proposed retooling the Elementary and Secondary Education Act to improve the lot of poor children. Chapter I funding would be directed to schools with high concentrations of poor, neglected, migrant, delinquent, and at-risk children. In addition, states would be encouraged to adopt standards and ways to measure student progress. In December 2000, President Clinton signed a fiscal 2001 Labor, Health and Education Bill, which provided an 18 percent federal funding boost that included funds for school facilities update and construction, class-size reduction, Head Start, college-prep GEAR UP, and Pell grants among other initiatives to improve education and assist students at risk and with special needs. President George W. Bush made education a centerpiece of his administration.

In 1965, the Higher Education Act (which includes the Education Professions Development Act of 1967) was enacted. Since its enactment, it has provided large sums of money for the acquisition of books and other library materials in colleges, for improving and extending teacher education programs, for strengthening programs related to community problems like housing and poverty, for supporting developing institutions of higher education, for giving financial assistance to students through grants and loans, and for developing the National Teachers Corps.

Teacher Corps employed specially trained teachers and college students to supplement instruction in schools with numerous low-income students. The education given Teacher Corps trainees included living in the neighborhoods near the schools and studying ethnic and minority culture. In 1980, Teacher Corps shifted from teacher training to in-service education. Congress has not always appropriated funds for Teacher Corps, and many of the training centers were closed during the Reagan administration. The Higher Education Act provided about 25,000 graduate fellowships for teacher trainees yearly, supported research and development in colleges of education, and established a National Advisory Council on Quality Teacher Education.

Although the federal government entered the educational arena in a big way in the 1960s, new legislation dropped off after the Johnson administration. One reason is that the shortage of teachers at the time of the National Defense Education Act changed into an oversupply of teachers by 1970. Another reason is the fear of federal control over local schools. In the early 1980s, the mood of the nation favored reduced federal spending and a cut in bureaucracy. Nevertheless, educators now predict a shortage of teachers in the future because of low pay and the impact of inflation. Equality of educational opportunity can hardly be guaranteed with local taxes alone. Central tax collection and distribution by the national government appears to be the only way of ensuring equal education for the mobile American population. A number of educators have suggested some sort of federal equalization fund to make up for differences in economic support between states. Of course, fear of federal control has also caused many of the states to take steps for the reformation of their own tax laws. Inequality exists within school districts or cities, such as that demonstrated in the Rodriguez case of San Antonio, Texas. Although Rodriguez did not win, pressure was put on state legislatures to make taxation more equitable.

Congressional efforts to aid education have not been uniform over the past several years. Funding of bills passed during the Kennedy and Johnson administrations was not always continued during the presidency of Richard Nixon. Few new federal education measures were proposed during the Nixon administration, but President Ford signed a new elementary and secondary education act into law as one of his first official acts. In spite of the economic recession of the 1970s, efforts to provide federal help for schools and local educational programs have not ended. Less money was provided in the 1970s than in the 1960s, but the impact of federal aid continued. The Department of Health, Education, and Welfare used the withholding of funds (or the threat of such withholding) as an instrument for enforcing plans for racial integration. This was continued under President Carter, but President Reagan voiced strong opposition to using the power of the federal government to control local action. The courts have also taken a less vigorous stand. In the 1981 Los Angeles case, for example, busing to achieve racial balance in schools was not supported. Federal courts re-installed court control over several school districts including Kansas City in 2000 to ensure that state standards are being met in inner cities for students at risk.

One of the burning issues in American education is the control and support of schools. Public opposition to national educational policy is illustrated by the controversy surrounding the integration of South High School in Boston in 1974. On the one hand, many laypeople want less federal government in educational affairs and fear that local school boards are vanishing. On the other hand, many believe that federal funds and programs are necessary for the success of many schools.

EXPERIMENTS AND INNOVATIONS IN THE TWENTIETH CENTURY

Francis W. Parker tried out many new ideas in school organization and curricula in the late nineteenth century and built the foundations for an experimental program in the Cook County Normal School. John Dewey expanded Parker's ideas into his experimental school—which was truly a laboratory for testing educational innovations—at the University of Chicago. The laboratory school lasted only seven years, but it was a child-centered school that experimented with democratic organization, nontraditional methods and equipment, and a curriculum based on the natural needs and interests of children (activity curriculum). Many of the ideas that appeared in Dewey's 1916 educational classic, *Democracy and Education*, were tried in the laboratory school, and the Dewey school gave rise to new educational experiments by the progressive educators.

Progressive Education.   Even before the organization of the Progressive Education Association in 1919, schools were being organized according to the liberal ideas of Rousseau, Pestalozzi, Froebel, Parker, and Dewey. In 1907, Marietta Johnson pioneered a School of Organic Education at Fairhope, Alabama. Teachers did not assign tasks in her school, so students were free to follow their own interests. Natural growth and development according to nature replaced early emphasis on reading and accumulating knowledge. Johnson's program followed Rousseau's *Emile*. The curriculum included nature study, physical education, music, handicrafts, field geography, drama, storytelling, games, and number concepts.

Professor Junius L. Meriam established a similar school under the supervision of the University of Missouri. Meriam's school had a flexible time schedule with no rigid periods for drills, exercises, or formal lessons. Others soon followed the lead of Meriam and Johnson. The Cottage School of Riverside, Illinois, and the Little School in the Woods at Greenwich, Connecticut, were activity-centered institutions. John and Evelyn Dewey reported on a number of these efforts in *Schools of Tomorrow* in 1915.

Within a few years of the beginning of progressive education as a movement, the number of private experimental schools increased rapidly. The founders undertook few sound statistical studies of their programs, but they and others who were critical of traditional schools did highly publicize them.

Progressive Education Association (PEA).   Although the PEA existed as an organization only from 1919 until 1955, its influence on American education was profound. Marietta Johnson joined with Eugene R. Smith of the Park School in Baltimore and Stanwood Cobb (a Naval Academy instructor) to organize the society. Aimed at the coordination of educational reform among private school leaders, the group was highly influenced by the theories of John Dewey. At an organizational meeting of the association held in Washington, D.C., on March 15, 1919, the eighty-five charter members adopted the following seven principles:

1. Freedom to develop naturally
2. Interest as the motive for all work
3. The teacher as guide, not as taskmaster
4. Scientific study of pupil development
5. Greater attention to all that affects the child's physical development
6. Cooperation between school and home to meet the needs of child life
7. The progressive school as leader in educational movements

Charles W. Eliot agreed to become the first honorary president of the PEA, lending his prestige to the organization. The journal *Progressive Education* appeared in 1924 and continued to be a major publication until 1957.

In the early 1920s, the membership of PEA consisted largely of teachers and parents in private schools, but by the late 1930s there were more than 10,000 members. Most of the professional educators in colleges and universities joined, as did the superintendents and administrators of many public school systems. In addition to the experimental schools supported by the organization, there were annual public conferences devoted to educational reform. Scientific study of pupil development and strong cooperation between schools and the society were major beliefs of PEA. William H. Kilpatrick, developer of the project method, was a major spokesman for progressive education and made the views of John Dewey popular among many educators at all levels. With Ellsworth Collings, Kilpatrick recommended that the school organize its work through a series of activities that would develop the student's purposeful effort. His projects included drills, problems, appreciation activities, and creative or construction projects.

The PEA soon broke into camps with quite different interests. The Social Frontier group, led by George S. Counts, wanted to use education as a means for social revolution and reform. Dewey and his followers were interested in a sophisticated educational theory and careful research. Other progressive educators merely developed new methods or supported freedom for children.

Extended School Use.

Not all the early innovations were aimed at the individual development of the child. In Gary, Indiana, William Wirt tried intensive use of the school facilities to relieve social problems caused by unexpected urban growth. In an effort to meet the failure of the culture to provide for the needs of city children, the school offered a longer day with constantly open and supervised workshops, gymnasiums, laboratories, auditoriums, and playgrounds. To give all children the opportunity for extended school participation, schools were kept open on Saturday and during vacation periods. Adult night classes were offered, and pupils did their own repair and maintenance work. Costs were kept low by the platoon system, by which work in classrooms, laboratories, and workshops alternated with activities scheduled in auditoriums, playgrounds, and gymnasiums, so as to keep all facilities continuously occupied. This plan for maximum school use spread widely in the United States; by 1929, more than a thousand schools were using a platoon organization. Today, scheduling one school day early in the morning and another beginning in the afternoon relieves crowding in some schools.

Other important efforts to relate the schools to the needs of the society were made by Carleton Washburne in Winnetka, Illinois, and by Helen Parkhurst in Dalton, Massachusetts. The Winnetka plan divided school offerings into creative and group activities and common essentials such as science and basic skills. Work in the essentials was by units and given at the student's own rate of learning, a practice now common in schools using programmed instruction. The Dalton laboratory plan incorporated Dewey's educational principles and many of the methods suggested by the Italian educator Maria Montessori. Both the Dalton and the Winnetka plans sought to develop the whole child and were concerned with physical and social as well as intellectual education.

Influence of Experimental Programs.

Although the early experimental schools did not become standard in America, they served as models for a different approach to basic educational questions. Ideas put into practice in laboratory or innovated schools were often adopted, with modifications, into the programs of the more traditional institutions. Sometimes new schools were created in response to criticisms of existing conditions and were intended to serve as contrasts with older plans.

Charles W. Eliot prepared a report for the General Education Board in 1916, in which he called for changes in American high schools. Partly at the urging of Eliot, the Lincoln School was established as an experimental arm of Teachers College, Columbia University, and it continued to operate until 1948. Today, many of the leading teachers' colleges and universities that have departments of education maintain laboratory schools. Research and development centers for testing all sorts of educational innovations are appearing in teaching-training institutions. Sophisticated statistical processes and refined methods of testing have given a new dimension to educational testing, and the growth of graduate programs has created an explosion in research. Doctoral dissertations in the area of educational psychology alone now provide us with a vast body of knowledge concerning the effectiveness of various pedagogical techniques.

PROGRESSIVE EDUCATORS AND THEIR CRITICS

By 1928, Dewey had become critical of the Progressive Education Association for its lack of sound social philosophy. His arguments against experiments lacking in theory were expressed well in *Experience and Education*, which appeared in 1938. By the 1930s, interest of the progressives shifted from a reaction against formal subject matter and harsh discipline to the social and economic problems of the whole culture. Many of the members continued with their experiments in natural development, the activity curriculum, and the child-centered school; however, the possibility of the schools as leaders in improving or reconstructing society became the theme of progressives like George Counts.

Although the progressives continued to meet until 1955, their organization was divided into factions with different points of view, and their efforts provoked a growing amount of controversy. Meanwhile, significant projects were being carried on that were to alter major educational concepts. The *Eight-Year Study* of the Progressive Education Association involved thirty high schools interested in experimentation and exploration. They altered the secondary curriculum and made it conform to known laws of learning and the various social environments. The report, published in 1942, showed that students in the progressive high schools did at least as well in college as their counterparts in traditional secondary schools and that they were better oriented to adult life.

Life Adjustment Education.   In 1945, a group of educators launched the life adjustment movement. This group was theoretically related to the progressive education movement, and its concern was mostly with those students who were not preparing for college. The life adjustment movement was aimed at a greater equalization of educational opportunity and was critical of any program that was not suitable for the majority of young Americans. The movement was short-lived because of the bitter attacks from many segments of the American people. The life adjustment movement had the support of several educational organizations and the United States Office of Education but was bitterly condemned by many college professors and by those interested in the subject-matter curriculum.

Dr. Charles Prosser pointed out that high schools failed to meet the needs of the 60 percent of the students who were not being trained for a vocational skill. In 1947, Commissioner of Education John Studebaker called attention to the 20 percent of the children who did not enter secondary schools and to the 40 percent who dropped out before graduation. Attention was also given to the wide range of individual differences among secondary school students and the effect of family or cultural background on achievement. Twenty-nine states developed some kind of curriculum revision associated with life adjustment by 1954. Many school systems became interested in how to meet the needs of those who seemed not to benefit from standard courses. Studies were made of the holding power of secondary schools (dropout rate) and of the relevance of programs in the view of students.

Because of the heavy criticism by those interested only in intellectual development and a great public fear that academic standards were being lowered by life adjustment, the program was terminated in the late 1950s. Nevertheless, life adjustment gave attention to the concern for equal educational opportunities and the problems of cultural deprivation; this development later brought about programs such as Head Start and the Job Corps. A basic issue remains in American education over whether we should concentrate on educating the whole child or whether intellectual excellence has priority. Many believe that neither meeting the psychological needs of the child nor developing the mind is enough. Few would argue that mastery of the essential subjects—particularly those that can be called tool subjects—is not important, but the great challenge is one of relating the experiences of the child to the cultural environment. American schools continue to have large numbers of students who leave school because they are bored, poorly adjusted, unable to compete, or merely uninterested in the programs offered. Today, numerous school systems are attempting to offer alternative high schools, work-study programs, storefront schools, or "schools without walls" in an effort to meet the needs of students for whom the regular educational program is unsatisfactory. This is exactly what the life adjustment plan intended to accomplish.

Another progressive innovation, which seemed to offer a possible solution to some of the social problems in modern America, was the community school. Based on such books as John Dewey's *Schools of Tomorrow,* the concept centered upon organizing the curriculum around the lives of students and involving members of the community as resources. The school was to be used for all sorts of community projects such as recreational activities and as a local center for communications. It was also expected that students and adults would work together on problems that involved the whole community. With grants from the Sloan Foundation in the 1940s, several universities established experimental community schools, but only a few remain in operation. George Leonard's *Education and Ecstasy* describes a future school of this kind.

Critics of Progressive Influence.

Idealists, realists, essentialists, and others with a philosophy opposed to pragmatism were critical of progressive education from the beginning. Dewey himself believed that many of the members of the progressive movement had been too quick to adopt new programs or methods without a proper theoretical base. Boyd Bode, one of the outstanding leaders of progressive education, criticized the determination of educational needs by looking at the individual child, rather than the society and the child together. Bode insisted that the meanings of liberty and democracy are linked and that people must make a moral commitment to the kind of society they want before content and authority in education can be established.

In addition to philosophic criticisms, a number of studies of academic achievement revealed certain weaknesses in the students who had attended progressive schools. These studies were not conclusive and most were less impressive than the *Eight-Year Study,* which was favorable to progressive schools, but they provided support for those who disagreed with progressive theory. It should be remembered that although the progressive movement had great influence on public elementary schools and colleges of education, the effect on secondary schools was slight and practically nonexistent on the academic disciplines in the universities. Some of those who blame Dewey and the progressives for the ills of education and society attribute more influence to the progressive movement than the historical evidence supports.

In the 1950s, equality of educational opportunity took on a new aspect. Life adjustment had been concerned with the terminal student, but during the cold war years, the great cry was for the academically talented student to receive adequate training. Arthur Bestor, James Conant, John Gardner, and Hyman Rickover were among prominent critics making new demands on education. They claimed that equality of opportunity did not mean the same education for everyone and that the national welfare demanded special provisions for the gifted. The success of the former Soviet Union in launching *Sputnik* in 1957 shifted emphasis from life adjustment to excellence and led to the National Defense Education Act. This law greatly increased technical and scientific offerings in American high schools and colleges. Not all educators were enthusiastic about the narrow emphasis on quality for the elite or the stress placed on mathematics, science, and foreign languages.

The 1960s were dominated by concerns for equality of opportunity. In the wake of the black revolution following the Brown case and a new concern for civil rights, efforts were made to meet the needs of all children. Ethnic and multicultural studies became popular, and bilingual programs were started in schools with many non-English-speaking students. Efforts at reorganizing schools to bring about desegregation and the use of busing to create integrated schools dominated the 1960s and 1970s. Efforts were made to help the lower-class youngster compete in middle-class schools through programs like project Head Start. Critics felt that integration and equality efforts took away from the drive toward excellence, and public support for education was in decline by 1980. Others expressed concern about the lack of literary and humanistic emphasis in school programs. Renewed focus on working to raise school standards nationwide became an issue in the William Clinton and the George W. Bush administrations. (These issues are discussed in detail in Chapter 9.)

ACADEMIC FREEDOM AND THE EDUCATIONAL PROFESSION

Early in this century, American schoolteachers could not smoke, drink alcoholic beverages, or express political preferences without fear of losing their jobs. Although this situation has improved, public school staff members are still attacked for what they teach and for their personal activities. Thus, a teacher who asks children to read Huxley's *Brave New World,* or advocates adding fluoride to water, or supports racial integration might be branded a "Communist" by those who fear such ideas. Nor are the schools themselves free from attack. Frequently, a school board, a superintendent, or even an entire school system will find itself under violent fire from organized groups or powerful individuals. During the Joseph McCarthy era, mere accusation of "red influence" was sufficient to frighten many school officials into firing teachers or removing books from the school libraries. In some cases, however, school boards have been willing to stand up to criticism and to make their assailants prove their case, if they have one.

In the 1980s, public school teachers came increasingly under attack from the religious "new right," which accused them of teaching values clarification or secular humanism. Teachers have often been unable to fight due to the lack of support from a strong professional organization, a scarcity of financial backing, or the reluctance of some school administrators to take a stand. Thus, a teacher who has a controversial point of view or who refuses to sign a loyalty oath could be asked to resign quietly in return for "keeping his or her record clean." Significant increases in the quantity and quality of teacher training have been made in the last few years, but teachers still lack autonomy to control the admission requirements to their own profession. Teachers find it difficult to identify an agreed upon and enforceable professional code of ethics or to develop an organization that represents them all. American public school teachers still lack the academic freedom enjoyed by most university professors. Tenure has been dropped for faculty and administrators in most public schools and some colleges.

Although tenure was under attack in the 2000s, major research universities continue to support it in order to recruit topflight faculty.

TEACHER EDUCATION

Divergent educational practices in the United States have been reflected in teacher education; today this diversity is becoming less pronounced, but it still exists. Many normal schools early in the twentieth century were more like secondary schools than colleges. For years, a shortage of teachers created a reluctance to enforce general standards of certification. Large numbers of rural teachers were given certificates on the basis of passing examinations or on the strength of a year or two of college work. Although temporary or emergency certificates are no longer issued except under unusual circumstances, state requirements differ with regard to the number and type of professional courses demanded.

Without exception, normal schools did become four-year colleges, and most state universities developed departments, schools, and colleges of education. The forty-five colleges for teachers in 1920 had grown to four times that number by 1940. Depression years caused the first oversupply of teachers, a condition that gave rise to higher minimum standards. After World War II, most teachers were prepared with a general or liberal college education, specialized knowledge of the field to be taught, professional courses including methods and psychology, and practice teaching. Beyond question, American teachers are better qualified to practice their profession than ever before in history. Nevertheless, there is considerable criticism of teacher education.

The education of American teachers is a persistent national problem. Parents complain about the performance of teachers, university professors question their subject matter competence, administrators feel the universities certify people who cannot cope with school problems, and teachers themselves often feel ill prepared to work with children, especially those from diverse cultures. Numerous studies of teacher education have been published in recent years, most of which give a negative evaluation. Scholars report that teacher training appears to make little difference in the ability of teachers to affect student achievement. Radical critics such as Ivan Illich question having teachers trained and certified at all.

Formal and informal surveys and studies reveal that seasoned teachers rate field experience as the most relevant and beneficial part of their training. In 1972, the Commission of Public School Personnel Policies in Ohio reported that 78 percent of the teachers who had graduated from the fifty-three teacher education institutions in the state thought student teaching was the most valuable part of their preparation. This study also indicated that educational practice or student teaching is insufficient, poorly supervised, and comes too late in the course sequence. In-service training for teachers already certified and working is also criticized for being of little use to the teacher in actually improving methods, classroom management, communication skills, and techniques for motivation of students.

Alternative programs are being developed each year by colleges and other institutions in an effort to build more relevance and skill into teacher education. Teacher Corps required interns to live and work in school communities (often lower economic areas with large numbers of minority students) while receiving instruction in theory. Colleges of education now offer programs to help middle-class teacher candidates understand the problems of lower-class students. Many colleges of education offer special courses and degree programs for English as a second language students.

The major problem of teacher education is providing sufficient field experiences and practice teaching. Institutions of teacher education now usually require many hours of observation and work in schools or with children in other settings prior to practice teaching. There is general agreement that at least one year of internship would be a vast improvement over a semester of practice teaching with one cooperating teacher. By 1980, Florida and Oklahoma had passed laws requiring teacher candidates to spend a fifth year in schools as teacher interns before granting full certification. One problem is that teachers are not paid well enough to justify the extra year of entry-level training. Nevertheless, many colleges of education continue to move toward a five-year plan, with some instituting a Master of Teaching in Education degree. Because on-site experience has proved to be beneficial for entry-level teachers, university–public school partnerships are increasing.

Competency-based teacher education, commonly referred to as CBTE or performance-based teacher education, is now used in many university-based colleges of education. CBTE is directed toward the development of specific skills or categories of behavior that have a direct connection to meaningful and observable learning on the part of the student. Instead of merely having students accumulate credits in various courses, CBTE attempts to offer methods and content selected for their ability to accomplish the goals of professional training effectively and expediently.

Some colleges are now cooperating with urban school districts to provide experiences for teacher interns designed to prepare them for work with the special educational problems of children in the ghettos of large cities. Others have developed teaching centers where professional teachers, practice teachers, college professors, and students can have more interaction.

As Charles Silberman has pointed out, new teachers are often thrust into a situation fraught with anxiety and fear, and these fears and anxieties do not necessarily evaporate with experience. The techniques most frequently used to help teachers overcome their problems are in-service training and graduate courses given in colleges and universities. In-service programs often include workshops, guest speakers, and seminars but vary from one district or system to another. Some schools have no in-service education for teachers, and the programs in others are inadequate for real professional growth.

The American Association of Colleges for Teacher Education devoted much of its energy in 1989 to identifying a common knowledge base all teachers should share. This proved a difficult task, especially for elementary teachers. There is still much disagreement concerning the makeup of a common knowledge base. Graduate courses in education for teachers are popular because many schools require teachers to obtain a master's degree within a few years from the time of employment, and salary increases are often tied to the acquisition of graduate credit hours or advanced degrees. Graduate work in psychology, administration, statistics, and educational philosophy is certainly of value, but there is a minimum of clinical experience or training designed to aid teachers in procedures of instruction and curriculum development. Of course, many teachers use graduate schools of education as a means of preparing themselves for positions as administrators, college teachers, or research workers.

The fact that large numbers of teachers believe that they are poorly prepared and the learning problems of so many students illustrated by failure in achievement are helping to support the development of new programs. With more certified teachers than jobs available, administrators can be more selective if they know what kinds of skills and what type of teacher training is most effective. Currently there is a teacher shortage in several fields including special education. Many persons now entering the field of education are serious about becoming as skilled and professional as possible. They are demanding clinical training of the sort provided in professional fields such as medicine. Pressures are building for college faculty members to become more directly involved with students and teachers in actual learning situations.

Illich has suggested that teachers should have easy access to learning Webs—centers in which teaching, learning, and communication skills can be developed. Centers where teachers can voluntarily meet to exchange experiences, thoughts, feelings, and suggestions for improving practice are now being suggested nationwide. Such a center was created in Bay Shore, New York, in 1972, and pilot programs have been established for teacher centers in Vermont and Florida.

In 1993, the National Council for Accreditation of Teacher Education (NCATE) approved outcomes-based standards for the preparation of teachers based upon standards developed by professional subject matter associations such as the National Science Teachers Association. According to Karen Diegmueller's article entitled

"NCATE Moves Forward in Approving Outcomes for Preparation of Teachers," several states have entered into partnership agreements with NCATE to conduct joint reviews of teacher training institutions. Some teachers in the mid-1990s were working toward National Teacher Certification. Public school and university, school and community, and school and workplace partnerships continue to be advocated by NCATE. Supporting various alternatives in assessment including portfolios and a balance of measures are also a trend. The goal of the American Federation of Teachers, the National Education Association, NCATE, and other professional organizations was to utilize all avenues possible to improve the teaching–learning environment, maintain safe schools, raise standards, and improve achievement levels.

The philosophy behind such efforts is that all children can learn with adequate facilities and support systems. Arthur J. Wise, president of the NCATE, noted that forty-five states and the District of Columbia had integrated NCATE's professional review of teachers colleges with their own review. Seventeen states required NCATE accreditation by 2001. NCATE is aligning teacher preparation standards with national standards for advanced certification and quality assurance. Nell Noddings and other authors focus on creating a homelike, nurturing environment in schools to meet the needs of students without such an atmosphere in their homes and communities.

Most states have set up assessment instruments to measure student performance. Political candidates responding to voters' concerns are focusing on measurement of student progress in schools. Recently there has been a backlash against rating schools against one another. Teachers are crying foul since there is a divergence between well-funded schools and underfunded schools, between students with strong parental involvement and those with little, between English- and non-English-speaking students in their achievement levels.

Title II of the Higher Education Act of 1998 was an effort to make teacher preparation programs more accountable. Blair, in an *Education Week* (2001) article entitled "Education Schools Strain to File Report Cards," noted that the nation's 1,300 colleges of education and alternative teacher preparation programs are required to submit data on passing rates on state tests, numbers of students in each program, together with faculty to student ratios. The report cards will also document whether a program has been approved by the state or has been labeled "low performing." Although the information was due by April 9, 2001, there has been difficulty gathering the data, finding some degree of uniformity in the information obtained, and organizing the data for state and federal reporting agencies. Reporting deadlines may continue to be extended.

While there has been criticism over the complexity of the process, others find it assists in developing collaboration among teacher education schools. The end result may be a better understanding of the unique challenges in educating teachers in the various states and, in time, more uniformity in process and outcome of teacher preparation programs. Ranking teacher education programs in the states and submitting the data to the Federal Education Department and then to Congress may result in an unintended bureaucratic nightmare.

New Methods.   An effort is being made to introduce students to methods such as the use of programmed learning, distance learning, team teaching, individualized instruction, laboratory techniques, and methods of research. Most states now require student teachers to be competent in the use of instructional techn can be certified. A better understanding of remedial reading and le is sometimes demanded. The knowledge explosion, the way leart mass media, social problems of students, and the development c. ... . require that teachers continue their training as long as they work. An example is the new mathematics of the 1960s; new mathematics required arithmetic teachers to re-learn teaching concepts through graduate courses or workshops. Current trends stress mathematics that deals with real-life work problems.

A variety of programs have been developed to deal with cross-cultural language and academic development (CLAD), as is the case in California. With an increasingly diverse limited English proficient population, teacher education programs are being developed for specialized credentials in working with bilingual student populations (BCLAD). Bilingual education has been controversial, and English immersion in California and Arizona is being implemented. Bilingual advocates continue to defend their programs often on the basis of respecting the language and culture of diversity. Arkansas has an English as a second language emphasis in a master's degree secondary education program and is expanding the program to include K through 12 to meet demands of an expanding Hispanic population. The California and Arkansas programs are a microcosm of expanding teacher credentialing programs to meet multicultural population needs. Florida Atlantic University, Boca Raton, as well as other universities have developed special programs for speakers of languages other than English.

Several critics who had never worked in professional education nor made a study of teacher-training institutions argued that good teachers are made through mastering subject matter. Admiral Hyman Rickover, American history professor Arthur Bestor Jr., business tycoon Albert Lynd, and columnist Dorothy Thompson were among the enemies of professional education. They argued that a knowledge of subject matter and a good liberal education could replace a knowledge of child psychology in the training of teachers. This same point of view was expressed earlier by perennialists, the Great Books advocates, and the Council for Basic Education. The Carnegie Corporation provided funds for a study of teacher education conducted by James B. Conant, former president of Harvard University. Conant published his conclusions in 1963, making the colleges primarily responsible for selecting courses for teachers. This study negates the role of the states in certification of teachers. In the late 1980s, California began selecting master teachers and giving them extra pay to coach newly certified teachers. This mentor project worked well, but as educational reformer John Goodlad pointed out, it was limited to the techniques of the model master teachers at a time when more revolutionary changes were needed.

Recent Growth.   In recent years, there has been an unprecedented growth in school enrollments at all levels from elementary school through college. Some 53 million students, a record number, enrolled in public school in the fall of 2000. Vast numbers of new developments that affect education have accompanied this growth. Technological advances have given rise to educational television, robots, filmstrips, VCRs, motion pictures, overhead projectors, computers for assisting instruction, Powerpoint presentations, a variety of wireless information access devices, and so forth. Boys and girls who enter the first grade after years of exposure to television and other mass media bring new vocabularies and new experiences into the classroom. The teaching machine (computer-assisted instruction), in both its simple and complicated forms, is now a subject of conversation in schools and homes. Few informed educators doubt that these technologies will have a growing role in the educational future of America. Self-instructing machines, team teaching projects, individual assignments, and nongraded organization are now being tested in schools and by research and development centers in colleges of education. Language laboratories, developed by the Army Specialized Training Program, have made a considerable impact on the teaching of foreign languages.

The knowledge explosion has encouraged thinking about a year-round school and the lengthening of the school week through longer hours or Saturday classes. If this is not done, we may still expect the average school year to lengthen from 185 days to more than 200 days within a decade. The proliferation of subjects seems only to have begun as the scientific explosion continues to gain momentum. There is still the task of providing adequate challenge for the gifted child, appropriate work for the child with mental retardation, and adequate guidance for all. Even with the work of modern psychologists Jean Piaget and Jerome Bruner, we still have much to find out about the learning process.

The history of American education can never be finished. As this book goes to press, new innovations in education and cultural changes in the society continue to make new demands. We can only expect that past traditions and trends of development will provide some indication of the future paths of our schools.

A NEW CENTURY—THE TWENTY-FIRST

Globalization and immigration, legal and illegal, have challenged policy makers in their efforts to improve educational achievement levels. This is partly due to language and cultural differences. Although historically there have been fifty varying educational policies as each state determines curriculum content, and local governance, a competitive economic environment requires some way of uniformly evaluating student performance. Although local control has been an article of faith in American education from colonial times, a trend has been toward state centralization of school/student achievement information. Blouin (2000) reported on a U.S. Department of Education funded model program to provide high-quality data to improve decision making at the school district and state levels. The information gathered includes performance on standardized achievement tests, data on school lunches, special student services received, as well as race and gender. Administrators and teachers can access the database to improve their educational efforts. Teachers can track individual students' test scores over time to determine achievement levels. The Data Delivery system provides information that is easily accessible through Web sites. Researchers Ronna Turner and Sean Mulvenon of the University of Arkansas, Fayetteville, plan to include millage rates, funding levels, as well as other variables to expand the databased decision making.

Although there continue to be unforeseen negative effects of performance assessment, the trend toward standardized measurement of student and school achievement levels is increasing nationwide. Savoye (2000) reported on Cincinnati's legislation to pay teachers on the basis of their performance. A commission, with two-thirds of its members teachers, developed an evaluation system. The scale was built around sixteen categories. Teachers will be identified as distinguished, proficient, basic, or unsatisfactory. The score will be used to place teachers in pay levels of accomplished, advanced, career, novice, and apprentice. New teachers need to pass the apprentice level by the second year and novices by the fifth year or face nonrenewal of contracts. Savoye continued by noting that concerns about objectivity are dealt with by use of peer reviews. Provisions are included in the plan to eliminate it if the costs are too high or by 70 percent vote by teachers. With teacher shortages, it remains to be seen how effective the plan will be over time.

Marshall (2000) reported on teacher, parental, student, and administrator division, discord, confusion, low morale, and chaos created by Florida's distribution of some $152 million, most of which was earmarked for schools with improved student test scores on the Florida Comprehensive Assessment Tests. Schools are graded mainly on FCAT test scores.

Often schools with students at risk, English deficient and physically and mentally challenged students, and low-income families are rated low, either D or F. Since outstanding teachers in these schools often received limited or no funds due to the difficulty of identifying and measuring outstanding performance for merit increases, the state provided $1.3 million to the Palm Beach County School district to attract and retain teachers at low-performing schools (Travis, 2001). Tanner (2000) noted that teachers often spend weeks teaching to standardized tests that frequently emphasize mechanics while the regular curriculum is put on hold. Tanner wrote, however, that performance assessments can be useful when used as an instructional approach to teach reasoning and problem solving as Dewey did in the late 1890s. There are no easy answers or shortcuts to improving student achievement, and a multitude of initiatives will continue to be deployed to seek increased accountability for results. Authentic testing, portfolio, and other forms of measuring student achievement are being utilized in some school systems. The National Conference of State Legislatures reported on continuing struggles for adequate school funding to meet new state assessment standards. The major concern among state legislatures is what to do about students who will not pass tougher tests. Michigan has a lawsuit challenging their tests especially in regard to special needs students. Poor performance schools are being taken over by states, closed, or turned over to corporations to manage.

The Individuals With Disabilities Education Act (IDEA 1997) provided for Individualized Education Programs (IEPs) for special education students. An IEP team determines whether or not it is appropriate for a student to take state mandated standardized tests under a philosophy of inclusion in classroom activities. If it is appropriate, the IEP team determines any modifications that may be needed for measuring student achievement. If it is not appropriate, each state is developing special examinations appropriate for the exceptional student. The 106th Congress and the president provided the highest funding in the history of IDEA. The federal contribution to IDEA was raised from 12 percent in 2000 to 15 percent in 2001. The 107th Congress is working to include special education funding as a permanent part of the budget.

THEN TO NOW

One of the great tragedies of American education is that we keep inventing the wheel. Often, ideas that hold great promise for improving teaching and learning are discarded with the movement that brought them about. For example, the psychological concepts of Herbart were rejected by the progressives and by John Dewey himself. This happened because of Dewey's reaction against lock-step programs and rigid systems that developed from the followers of Herbart in America such as Charles DeGarmo. Actually, the ideas of Herbart were well ahead of their time and might have been retained by those who sought to reform teacher-centered methods and formal steps of instruction. Herbart taught that the mind is a unitary organism, and therefore he could not support mental discipline or faculty psychology. He understood the need for relating one subject to another and so developed a core curriculum. Long before psychoanalysis, Herbart studied the relationship of the conscious to the subconscious mind and suggested a logical means by which new ideas from experience may be assimilated and stored by the learner. These ideas were not in conflict with the basic theories of the progressives. Indeed, they might have proved very helpful to the same progressive educators who scorned them because they were identified with the American Herbartian movement. Progressives turned to Gestalt psychology, but many current notions about educational psychology were anticipated by Herbart and might have been used to improve the educational environment for generations.

Exactly the same thing happened with progressive education in its period of decline. As we have seen, progressives ruled education in the 1930s, but by 1940 there was much criticism of their child-centered programs and permissive practices. The movement ceased to exert much influence after the conservative reaction in education triggered by World War II. Beyond question, many progressives were extreme in their views, and their schools were by no means perfect. Nevertheless, progressive education brought about numerous experiments that are of great pedagogical value today. The fact that most American teachers are not well versed in their own professional history means that they must begin from scratch in order to create new methods and programs. Progressives anticipated and worked with numerous plans and ideas that today are called educational innovations. This point is well made by Judith Ford in an unpublished doctoral dissertation called "Innovative Methods in Elementary Education: A Description and Analysis of Individualized Instruction in the Progressive Movement in Comparison with the Innovative Modern Elementary School" (1977).

The progressive educators tried, in some form, most of the current practices designed to improve instruction. An exception is computer-assisted instruction, since computers and teaching machines were not available in the 1930s. Following are some of the most obvious parallels:

❑ *Inquiry based instruction.*   This method is often associated with Piaget and science teaching. John Dewey was a strong advocate of laboratory instruction and discovery learning. Almost all of the progressive schools used inquiry as a major method, and records exist of their success.

❑ *Mastery learning.*   Modern mastery learning is usually associated with Benjamin Bloom. Recall and application of learning to a problem-solving situation were a mainstay of progressive schools. Ellsworth Collings best demonstrated it in the McDonald County Rural School in 1905.

❑ *Individual contracting.*   Using individual contracts with students to stimulate specific learning is now a practice in many schools. The formal writing of contracts with specific behavioral goals is current, but the idea of students participating in choosing what and when they would learn goes back to Helen Parkhurst and the Dalton Contract Plan of 1919.

❑ *Differentiated staffing.*   Many professional educators now support differentiated staffing. Having all teachers trained in the same way seems inefficient and wasteful. Master teachers, general teachers, learning specialists, teaching assistants, instructional materials specialists, clerks, and nonprofessional staff members might make up a better team for instruction. The progressives used community resource people in their schools. They did not hesitate to bring in people with different training for various school-related tasks. J. Lloyd Trump, who first urged differentiated staffing in schools, was influenced by the progressive experiments.

❑ *Flexible scheduling.*   The Gary Platoon Plan organized by William Wirt in 1915 used flexible scheduling. Most of the progressive schools were not tied to the clock or the calendar. They pioneered programs that used whatever time was necessary to accomplish learning without regard to filling days with even blocks of time or earning units of credit. Numerous modern schools use computers to program flexible individualized schedules.

❑ *Individualized instruction.*   Today, a body of literature supports the idea that individualized instruction may be superior for many students. Carleton Washburne experimented with such a plan at Winnetka in 1919. Most progressives allowed students to progress at their own speed, a practice that required special individual assignments and evaluation. The history of progressive education shows that individual instruction worked better than group instruction for some learning but that it required more time of teachers. Progressives supported the social interaction of groups for certain subjects (such as social studies) but used individualized projects as well. They understood that each child is unique and that there are many styles of learning. In some ways, the progressive schools were similar to modern alternative schools, almost all of which use individualized instruction.

❑ *Open classrooms.*   In spite of all the modern literature on the subject, the progressives pioneered open classrooms. Marietta Johnson's School of Organic Education at Fairhope, Alabama, was an early example. Freedom for students to move about, small group activities, an informal atmosphere, inquiry, and freedom of expression were characteristics of progressive education. The best of open classroom instruction is described in progressive literature.

❑ *Team teaching and nongraded schools.*   John Dewey himself created teams of teachers to work with students in the laboratory school at the University of Chicago. Like the progressives who followed him, Dewey was aware that several teachers working together can provide a richer educational environment and better evaluation. Although the progressives did not establish nongraded schools in name, they did allow students to learn at their own rate of speed and were not bound by any external standards. Progressives wrote about the perils of self-contained classrooms and rigid programs that require all children to achieve the same goals within a given span of time.

If American education is to meet the great challenges of the future, it must be efficient, flexible, professional, and stimulating. Schools cannot afford to re-invent and test programs or methods that were tried and tested in the past. Educators need to learn about both the success and the failure of earlier educational experiments and to use those experiments as guides in making a better quality learning environment. The educational reforms of the late 1980s, responding to *A Nation at Risk* and other critical reports, seemed to ignore history. Former Secretary of Education William Bennett wanted to restore a classical curriculum with intellectual rigor for the college-bound elite. Wide support for this by conservative groups and authors like Diane Ravitch and Allen Bloom obscured the goal of progressive education for all. Secretary Laura Cavazos, during the George Bush administration, stressed greater equality. Education Secretary Richard W. Riley sought more equality for students who were at risk due to poverty and disadvantaged community conditions. George W. Bush's education secretary Rod Paige continues the effort to raise academic achievement levels of at-risk students. In addition, government, businesses, and the community worked to increase computer availability and access to the Internet in all of the nation's schools.

Providing mentoring resources to assist elementary children in reading and mathematics is another major initiative. Teachers, students, faculty, administrators, and parents are increasingly communicating through e-mail systems and accessing knowledge bases through the Internet. Goals 2000 efforts will continue the search for excellence called for in the reform reports of the 1980s while expanding opportunities for at-risk students. History of education assists students in analyzing the appropriateness and effectiveness of innovations in education. Behavioral engineering has become more refined than in the days of John B. Watson. State and nationwide behavioral change efforts designed to motivate students at all educational levels to avoid lifestyle risk behaviors illustrate the continued application of the work of Watson and Skinner.

The history of education reveals a continuing effort to include ever more of the population in accessing equitable opportunities in education and the workforce. From the Olde Deluder Satan Acts of 1642 and 1647 to the nation's latest appropriations and budget, Congress, the executive branch, and state legislatures work to provide more opportunities for upward mobility through education as well as caring for the welfare of youth. An example is the Children's Internet Protection Act, requiring all schools that receive technology funds under the Elementary and Secondary Education Act (ESEA) to use filtering software and have an acceptable use policy that has been developed with public input. Other initiatives include substance abuse prevention, mental health, maternal and child health, and twenty-first-century community learning programs. Many federal, state, corporate, and volunteer programs are working to provide special assistance programs for the nation's poor and marginalized population.

GAINING PERSPECTIVE THROUGH CRITICAL ANALYSIS

1. Analyze the contributions of the Committee of Fifteen to the development of education programs.
2. Compare early educational surveys with today's school report cards. What are similarities, differences, and purposes driving each reporting mechanism?
3. Trace the conflict between state and local control of schools and funding sources. Who is winning the battle? Use current research from recent periodicals and/or the Internet to support your opinions.
4. List the major contributions of the federal government to education policy making between 1918 and 2001. In your opinion, which contributions had the greatest impact? What actions have been taken in the past year by the federal government to impact education policies and practices? Suggested sites *http://www.ed.gov; http://www.loc.gov.*
5. Identify trends for the National Council for Accreditation of Teacher Education. Examine your state's education standards and professional competencies from the Internet and give four examples of how the standards improve education. (Florida's Professional Competencies for Teachers of the 21st Century as well as professional standards of other states are available online. Florida e-mail is *odutoln@mail.doe.state.fl.us.*)

HISTORY IN ACTION IN TODAY'S CLASSROOMS

1. Use your journal to record the major events in the history of academic freedom. Have there been changes in the way teachers are viewed by the public over time?
2. Check periodicals and the Internet to discover at least one case where a teacher has been dismissed for lack of academic freedom protections. Discuss the issues involved. Are teachers professional educators or servants of the state?
3. Send a request by fax or e-mail to your state legislative representative asking him or her to discuss their perceptions of recent developments in education. Try to determine if he or she views teachers as professionals or as servants of the state. Add the findings to your journal.
4. Visit a child welfare services agency in your community. What psychological interventions are being utilized to deal with children and their families?
5. The Internet would influence which phase of Dewey's act of thought process?
6. Find a copy of national standards for your particular content area of interest by using the library, contacting the professional association, or using the Internet. Analyze the standards in terms of current literature dealing with pros and cons of such standards. Identify pros and cons of high-stakes testing. Suggested sites *http://www.ncate.org/; http://www.aypf.org.*
7. In your journal, list at least three reasons supporting separate programs for gifted and talented students and at least three reasons against such programs. Suggestions *http://www.cec.sped.org; http://www.ericec.sped.org.*

INCREASED UNDERSTANDING THROUGH ONLINE RESEARCH

Visit the Prentice Hall Foundations Web site (*http://www. prenhall.com/foundations-cluster*) and examine Topics 2, 3, and 4. Using the resources available in these topics, give three reasons supporting your opinion as to whether the following statement is true or false: John Dewey would advocate assessing students' critical think-ing skills through holistic methods of evaluation. Use the chapter's opening quotation to help with your response. Write and submit your response to your instructor using the Electronic Bluebook module also in any of these three topics of the Web site.

BIBLIOGRAPHY

Appropriations and Budget 106th Congress. National Governors' Association. *http://www.nga.org/106congress/budget.asp* (2000, December 28).

Blair, Julie. "Education Schools Strain to File Report Cards." *Education Week* (March 28, 2001): 1, 30.

Blouin, Melissa. "Measuring Performance in the Schools." Fayetteville, AR: *University of Arkansas Research Frontiers* (Fall 2000): 28–29.

Brown, Ellsworth. *The Making of Our Middle Schools*. New York: Littlefield, 1970.

Burton, Warren. *The District School as It Was*. New York: Arno Press, 1969 (reprint of 1928 edition).

Butts, Freeman. *Public Education in the United States: From Revolution to Reform*. New York: Holt, Rinehart and Winston, 1978.

"Clinton Signs Record Education Increase." *AASA Leadership News* (December 22, 2000). Available *http://www.aasa.org/publications/In/00-12-22billsign.htm*.

Cremin, Lawrence. *The Transformation of the School*. New York: Alfred A. Knopf, 1961.

Cubberley, Elwood. *Public Education in the United States*. New York: Houghton Mifflin, 1934.

Dewey, John. "America—By Formula" in *Individualism—Old and New*. New York: Capricorn Press (1962): 24.

Diegmueller, Karen. "NCATE Moves Forward in Approving Outcomes for Preparation of Teachers." *Education Week* (October 13, 1993): 4.

"Dollars to Students, Not Districts." *Wall Street Journal Editorial* (January 12, 2001): A 18.

Feistritzer, Emily. *Profiles of Teachers in the U.S.* Washington, DC: National Center for Educational Information, 1986.

Ford, Judith. "Innovative Methods in Elementary Education: A Description and Analysis of Individualized Instruction in the Progressive Movement in Comparison with the Innovative Modern Elementary School." Unpublished doctoral dissertation, University of Oklahoma, 1977.

Gutek, Gerald. *An Historical Introduction to American Education*. New York: Thomas Crowell, 1970.

Health, Education, and Human Services Division. *School Facilities: America's Schools Report Differing Conditions*. Washington, DC: Health, Education, and Human Services Division, June 1996.

Hohn, Robert L. *Classroom Learning and Teaching*. New York: Longman, 1995, 275–76.

Hurd, Nancy K. Personal conversation and site tour. Delray Beach, FL: Community Child Care Center (December 2000).

Jeffry, R. "Kentucky's Virtual University Creates Fund to Spur Other On-Line-Education Programs." *The Chronicle of Higher Education* (November 24, 2000): A 54.

Karier, Clarence. *Shaping the American Educational State: 1900 to the Present*. New York: Free Press, 1975.

Katz, Michael. *Class, Bureaucracy, and Schools*. New York: Praeger, 1971.

"Legislators' Group Opens Clearinghouse to Track School Finance." *Education Week* (February 28, 2001): 19.

Lewis, Laurie, Cyle Snow, Elizabeth Farris, Becky Smerdon, Stephanie Cronen, Jessica Kaplan, and Bernie Green, Project Officer. "The Condition of America's Public School Facilities." Washington, DC: U.S. Department of Education, National Center for Educational Statistics, 1999: iii, iv.

Manzo Kathleen Kennedy. "Study Offers new Insights on State lotteries," *Education Week* (November 1, 2000) *http://www.edweek.org/ew/ewstory.cfm?slug~09lottery.h20&keywords~state%20lotteries*1/26/2002.

Marshall, Toni. "School Bonuses Fuel Strife and Confusion." *South Florida Sun Sentinel* (2000, December 3): 1, 4 A.

McKissack, Patricia and Frederick. *The Civil Rights Movement in America*. Chicago: Childrens Press, 1987.

McLaughlin, Milbery. *Evaluation and Reform: The Elementary and Secondary Education Act of 1965*. Cambridge, MA: Harvard University Press, 1975.

Moorefield, Story. "The G.I. Bill." *American Education* (August–September 1974): 25.

Pitsch, Mark. "E.D. Officials Begin Task of Marketing Their Proposal to 'Reinvent' the Elementary and Secondary Education Act." *Education Week* (September 29, 1993): 22.

Prosser, Charles. *Secondary Education and Life*. Cambridge, MA: Harvard University Press, 1939.

Pully, Brett. "Rites of Passage." *New York Times* (June 16, 1998).

Rainie, Lee, and Dan Packel. "Sixteen Million Newcomers Gain Internet Access in the Last Half of 2000 as Women, Minorities, and Families with Modest Incomes Continue to Surge Online." Washington, DC: *The Pew Internet and American Life Project* (2001, February 18). Available *http://www.pewinternet.org*.

Rippa, Alexander. *Education in a Free Society*. 2d ed. New York: David McKay, 1971.

Savoye, Craig. "City Tries Paying Teachers for Results." *The Christian Science Monitor* (2000, December 5): 1, 4.

Smith, Elaine M. *Mary McLeod Bethune Papers*. New York: University Publications of America, 1995 *http://www.usnet/upa/guides/bethune.htm*.

Snyder, Thomas D. *Digest of Educational Statistics*. Washington, DC: U.S. Office of Education, Office of Educational Research and Improvement, 1999: 1–5. (One Room Schools Table 97).

Snyder, Thomas D. *National Center for Educational Statistics, Encyclopedia of Educational Statistics, Projections of Educational Statistics*. Washington DC: U.S. Office of Education, 1999, 2000. Available *http://nces. ed.gov*.

Tanner, Laurel N. "Critical Issues in Curriculum Revisited." *The Educational Forum* (Fall 2000): 16–21.

The National Conference of School Legislatures. Available *http://www.ncsl.org/programs/press/2000/pr001212h tml#education* (2000).

Travis, Scott (2001, February 9). "Bonus Checks for Some Teachers Create Tension." *Sun-Sentinel South Florida* (February 9, 2001) 3B.

Tyack, David. *The One Best System: A History of American Urban Education*. Cambridge, MA: Harvard University Press, 1974.

Watson, John B. *Behaviorism*. New York: W. W. Norton and Company, 1924.

Wise, Arthur J. "Creating a High Quality Teaching Force." *Educational Leadership* (2000 December/2001 January): 18–21.

Vygotsky, Lev S. *Thought and Language*. Cambridge, England: Cambridge University Press, 1962.

CHAPTER EIGHT

ISSUES IN MODERN AMERICAN EDUCATION

Even if only one child in ten could gain in intellectual effectiveness through a more favorable environment, we would still be bound to make the effort. . . . Individuals do differ greatly in their capacities, and each must be enabled to develop the talent that is in him (her). We believe that every person should be enabled to achieve the best that is in him (her), and we are the declared enemies of all conditions, such as disease, ignorance or poverty, which stunt the individual and prevent such fulfillment.

John W. Gardner

School Desegregation	Civil Rights Movement	Campus Rebellion
1954 Brown case issue	1960s Martin Luther King, Jr.	1961–1968 Kennedy-Johnson legislation
1957 *Sputnik* issue	1961 John Gardner's *Can We Be Equal and* *Excellent Too?*	1966 Coleman Report
Criticisms of Arthur Bestor, James Conant, and Hyman Rickover	1963 Michael Harrington's *The Other America*	

Figure 8.1   Time Line of Issues in Modern American Education

Anything that has already happened *is* history even if it happened only a moment ago. Making a good historical analysis of events just past is often more difficult than making one for those that occurred in an earlier period. Recent occurrences in educational history are often surrounded by controversy. Very few modern events are free from criticism, and even the educational community often finds itself taking sides. Political groups get involved quite often in current educational concerns, and public opinion plays a vital role in numerous decisions. Although it was once rare for problems over the schools to result in litigation, it is now very common. Books that are critical of many aspects of education now become best-sellers while past critics write for much smaller audiences. Since education touches all of the American people and since the means of communication are expanding so rapidly, the current history of education is very much the history of controversial issues. Although judgments about current events are hard to make, an understanding of history could provide us with the best foundation possible for placing such events in perspective.

In Chapter 2, various positions in the philosophy of education are discussed. Philosophy is seldom universally accepted, so conflicting ideas and contradictory views are common. Pragmatists and idealists did not agree in the early twentieth century, and they do not agree today. The same can be said for schools of psychology like Gestalt and behaviorism. The fight over the legal status of private schools that led to the Oregon case of 1925 provides background for the issue of tax support to parochial schools and the legality of tuition tax credits for nonpublic education.

In the past few decades, critical issues that pose serious questions for the future of education have appeared in the schools. There are also controversies in the general society that translate into problems for education. Members of the educational

Equal Opportunity	Accountability	Return to Basics
1968 Issues over bilingual and multicultural education	1969 Arthur Jensen studied IQ and race	1973 Only 2,500 black doctorates in all fields
Accountability tests	1969 Theodore Roszak's *The Making of a Counterculture*	1979 John Goodlad's *What Are Schools For?*
Compensatory education for the disadvantaged	1970 Charles Reich's *The Greening of America*	1980s National critical reports, *A Nation at Risk, Action for Excellence, Making the Grade*
	Ivan Illich's *Deschooling Society*	

profession, with the help of sound scientific research, must solve some of these issues. Other issues can be solved only by cooperation between the general public and those in the profession. Still other issues continue to exist for the reason that no solution is obvious or certain, even if the best possible interaction between educators and the public takes place. Altering the curriculum of the public schools to prepare children to cope successfully with future conditions is always uncertain precisely because techniques for future prediction are inexact.

Issues involving the purposes or goals of education concern both the layperson and the professional educator in a society that is, to some degree, democratic. This kind of problem is the subject of philosophy of education, but it also involves values, norms, and attitudes that can be understood through sociology, economics, history, social psychology, and political science. Although various groups such as realists and pragmatists have clear-cut educational goals, the educational philosophy of the whole American people is not fixed and certain. In a fluid culture, the aims of education in one period of time are often altered considerably by the next generation. Specific aims, goals, and purposes are hotly debated not only among educators but also by the whole of the body politic. The purpose of education promises to be the object of much disagreement and discussion in the future, as it has been in the past.

The role of the teacher and that of the profession in addressing a problem or an issue concerning schools often consists of communication and clarification. The public may be unaware of the existence of problems, or there may be a misunderstanding of the exact nature of those problems. Difficulties concerning poverty, crime, taxation, employment, equal rights, academic freedom, racial integration, discipline, and so forth, often have educational significance that is not clear to the casual observer. Explaining what the issues really mean and outlining possible consequences of various plans of action must often fall to educators. Analysis and clarification of hidden issues or underlying problems must often be undertaken before a solution can be reached. Obviously, past experience including a knowledge of history can provide clues to the probable success or failure of alternatives.

A number of approaches can be taken to the history and understanding of current issues and challenges in American education. This chapter focuses on a number of well-known educational conflicts that have reached the courts. Litigation has always been important for educational policy, as in the Dartmouth College case of 1819 and the Kalamazoo high school decision of 1874. In contemporary society, many cases handled by the state and federal courts are vital to understanding recent educational history. Although each case is decided on its own merits, recent state and federal court education cases appear to reflect a trend toward conservatism. Current rulings give educators more support in creating and maintaining a safe school environment, controlling disruptive or threatening student behavior, and maintaining a proper learning environment. Many school districts have a zero tolerance policy for student misbehavior, especially for drug abuse. Earlier chapters examined the ideas of well-known philosophers, psychologists, and public officials who influenced education. This chapter deals with important modern educational critics and spokespersons for major organizations. Critics often serve as guides to significant educational problems. This chapter also focuses on a number of current educational issues for which educational institutions and teachers are accountable.

LITIGATION: THE COURTS AND PROBLEMS OF EDUCATION

Religion and Public Schools.   Religion was the major subject in colonial schools, but with the separation of church and state, public schools could teach only interdenominational or nonsectarian religious principles. Still, the curriculum remained heavily influenced by religious writings, prayer, and Christian morality. Bible reading was considered nonsectarian in most communities. The fact that a Protestant Bible was not acceptable to Catholics carried little weight, and Jews were also discriminated against in school programs. Before the twentieth century, minority groups often chose not to make an issue of religion in the public schools. If Catholic, Jewish, or other minority religious groups were unable to support their own schools, they normally accepted the rules of the public schools even when the requirements went counter to their own beliefs.

In the past few years, however, there have been a great number of court cases over the religious requirements or practices in public schools. Although the majority of the cases have decided against the inclusion of religious practices, a large number of Americans have felt that the schools are responsible for moral training that could hardly be given without reference to religion. Religious liberals and nonbelievers have attacked the practice of beginning the school day with prayer, and Jehovah's Witnesses have claimed that saluting the flag constitutes worship of a "graven image." There is no clear-cut division between patriotic and religious exercises; even the Pledge of Allegiance has contained the words *under God* since 1954. Furthermore, chaplains have been assigned to military units. And *in God we trust* has been stamped on coins. The major educational problem, however, concerns Christian Christmas programs, religious exercises, and the reading of Scripture as part of the public school program.

In 1996, and in an 1998 update, President Bill Clinton instructed the Office of the Attorney General and the Department of Education to issue a bulletin outlining protected religious activity, including saying grace before meals, debating religious topics with classmates, expressing religious beliefs in school assignments, and wearing clothing with religious messages to the same extent that students are permitted to wear clothing containing other comparable messages. A number of professional organizations including the American Association of School Administrators, American Federation of Teachers, and Association for Supervision and Curriculum Development have endorsed *The Bible and the Public Schools* published by the nonpartisan National Bible Association, which provides guidelines for teaching about the Bible. A 1995 article in *Educational Leadership* included the concepts that religious liberty is an inalienable right of every person, and religious liberty and public schools include the concept that they can neither inculcate nor inhibit religion. The article further noted that public schools must be places where religion and religious convictions are treated in fairness and respect.

In *Abington School District v. Schempp* (1963), the court outlawed a 1959 Pennsylvania legislative rule requiring the reading every day in schools of ten verses from the Bible. In *Murray v. Curlett* (1963), the Baltimore school commissioners were prevented from requiring the reading of a chapter from the Bible or the reciting of the Lord's Prayer as an opening exercise in schools. These cases led to the publication in 1964 by the American Association of School Administrators of policy guidelines entitled *Religion in the Public Schools*. Conservatives called for restoring religion to the public schools and even proposed a constitutional amendment, sponsored by Senator Everett Dirksen of Illinois, to allow voluntary prayer in schools. Nevertheless, the First Amendment statement that Congress shall make no law respecting an establishment of religion remains the basis for preventing schools from requiring prayer or religious activities.

In *Lee v. Weisman* (1992), the court ruled that the inclusion by public officials of a prayer, even one that is nondenominational, in an elementary or secondary school graduation ceremony constitutes a violation of the First Amendment. Nonetheless, the Supreme Court declined to review *Jones v. Clear Creek Independent School District Texas* (1992), a U.S. Court of Appeals ruling that held that a senior class could vote on whether to include school prayer at graduation as long as the prayers were nonsectarian and nonproselytizing in nature.

In a Texas school district case, *Santa Fe v. Doe* (2000), the Supreme Court ruled that school-sponsored student-led prayer at football games violates the First Amendment establishment clause. In a California case, *Cole v. Oroville High School* (2000), the Ninth U.S. Circuit Appeals Court held that a district policy authorizing a student to deliver a prayer prior to football games constituted an impermissible government entanglement in religion. Other federal courts, in other states, have held that overt expressions of devotion are in violation of the establishment. However, in *Adler v. Duval County Florida School Board* (2000) a federal circuit court held that a student could choose to deliver a prayer at graduation if she or he wishes. The issue will be revisited by the Supreme Court in the future as it has been in the past. However, there has never been a rule prohibiting the study of religion. Indeed, American history cannot be understood without studying the impact of religion on the development of this nation. George W. Bush, as one of his first acts as the forty-third president, declared January 21, 2001, as a national day of prayer. "For Goodness' Sake: Why So Many Want Religion to Play a Greater Role in American Life," a report of the *Public Agenda Research Studies,* found a majority of Americans believe religion has a place in the public schools, but tend to support a moment of silent prayer over nondenominational or overtly Christian prayers. The report finds most Americans are reluctant to isolate students whose faiths are different.

The issue of the role of religion in education is centered on two quite controversial issues: the promotion of religious instruction in public schools and the use of public tax money to aid nonpublic schools. In 1919, Nebraska passed a law prohibiting private or parochial schools from teaching any subject in any language other than English. However, four years later, in *Meyer v. Nebraska,* the Supreme Court ruled that law unconstitutional. Although holding that the state can require attendance at some school, the Supreme Court stated that parents could send their children to private schools at which some subjects need not be taught in English. This was a landmark case concerning both religion and the language of instruction.

Two years later the Supreme Court reinforced in *Pierce v. Society of Sisters* the right of parents to choose nonpublic schools. This case made unconstitutional a 1922 Oregon law that required all children between the ages of eight and sixteen to attend *public* schools. There has been no effort to outlaw private or parochial schools since 1925, and the Pierce doctrine remains in force.

The right of the student to be protected from rules that violate his or her religious freedom was at issue in the Gobitis case of 1938. The Gobitis family members were Jehovah's Witnesses who objected to the school requirement that all students must say the Pledge of Allegiance to the American flag. The court upheld the school board in this case, but in 1943, it reversed its position in *West Virginia v. Barnett.* Religious freedom thereafter became a valid reason for children to be excused from school activities that violate their religious beliefs.

In 1947, approximately 2 million public school students were released to attend religious classes during some part of the school week. In *McCollum v. Board of Education of Champaign, Illinois,* in 1948, the Supreme Court held that releasing students to attend religious classes held in public school buildings was illegal. A later case in New York ended with a ruling that release time does not violate separation of church and state if religious classes are held outside the schools.

Lawsuits have sometimes resulted in changing educational practices, as in the New York Regents' prayer case of 1962. Using the coercive power of the school to make children participate in religious activities has been held to violate the First

Amendment. Although a 1976 Gallup Poll found that 70 percent of parents favored compulsory attendance, the Supreme Court has held that Amish parents can use the First Amendment as a basis for keeping their children out of high school. In the 1972 case of *Wisconsin v. Yoder,* the compulsory attendance law of the state was set aside to protect the free exercise of the religious views of parents. The 1993 Phi Delta Kappa/Gallup Poll of public attitudes toward public schools found that some two out of three Americans (67 percent) support choice in public schools, but some 74 percent oppose allowing parents to send their children to private schools at public expense. The 2000 thirty-second Phi Delta Kappa Gallup poll found that 52 percent of the public (based on a standard national telephone sample) was opposed to allowing parents to send their children to a public, private, or church-related school with the government paying part or all of the tuition.

Cases involving public aid to parochial schools have created major concerns in educational circles. In the 1950s, the NEA and the American Association of School Administrators adopted resolutions opposing all efforts to use public funds for nonpublic education. NEA 2000–2001 resolutions reaffirmed the belief that voucher plans, tuition tax credits, or other funding arrangements to subsidize pre-K through 12 private school education can undermine public education. Furthermore the resolutions include the statement that the NEA finds that federally or state-mandated parental option or choice plans compromise a commitment to free, equitable, universal, and quality education for every student. Federal legislation provided school lunches for parochial schools in 1948, and the government allowed GI Bill and NDEA funds to be used for scholarships to nonpublic schools. The National Science Foundation made grants to private universities, and the Higher Education Act of 1965 gave money to church-related colleges for nonreligious purposes. Private schools also got libraries and instructional materials under the Elementary and Secondary Education Act of 1965.

In the Cochran case of 1930, the Supreme Court held that although direct aid to private and parochial schools was illegal, the state could use public funds to pay for transportation, lunches, textbooks, and health services that were of benefit to all children. This "child benefit" theory was also the basis in the Everson case for the use of taxes to pay for the transportation of students to Catholic schools. Everson upheld Cochran; however, the Supreme Court was split, and the issue has not cooled.

Many advocates of the public schools fear that any aid to private and parochial schools will weaken public education. They point out that equality of educational opportunity and integration suffer in nonpublic programs. For them, any aid to private education is a violation of the separation of church and state. They illustrate the difficulty Americans had in obtaining tax support for public schools in the era of Horace Mann, and quote Thomas Jefferson on the necessity of keeping religion segregated from government. Several states now prohibit the use of tax money for any kind of aid to parochial schools, whether for child benefit or not. This issue is also tied to the question of tuition tax credits for parents who choose to send their children to private schools and to federal aid to nonpublic education. The arguments were especially heated in the early 1980s. In 2001 while centrists from both political parties supported President George W. Bush's efforts to improve educational achievement in all schools, including low performing ones, the use of federal funds for private school attendance was controversial. The Bush administration's educational theme is *No Child Will Be Left Behind.* Criticism of public schools caused many parents to demand tuition tax credits; spokespersons for public education held that such credits would weaken the very foundation of public schools. The NEA in general continues to oppose using federal funds for religious schools.

Although Bible reading, nonsectarian prayers, and released time for religious instruction are illegal in public schools, the issue is not resolved. There is considerable pressure to "restore religion" to the public classroom, which may increase with the George W. Bush administration faith-based initiatives and educational agenda.

About the same time that Ronald Reagan became a candidate for president, the new religious and political right represented by evangelists like Jerry Falwell began to gain strength. Carrying their message on television, as well as in churches and publications, they became a major voice for the "moral majority." This group objects to banning prayer in schools, demands that creationism be taught in place of the theory of evolution, and attacks "liberal" teachings such as values clarification, sexual preferences, abortion rights, and alternative lifestyles. The moral conservatives favor banning books that they feel do not support their definition of good child behavior. Since members of this group often send their children to private schools, they support vouchers or the deduction of tuition from income tax returns, as provided by law in Minnesota. Other states including Florida are moving toward vouchers, although California and Michigan defeated voucher proposals. Religious and other conservatives often oppose what they call "secular humanism"; they believe secular humanism has corrupted educational practices and the whole culture and have formed parents' groups to rid the schools of "humanist" books. Well-organized and well-funded, the religious conservatives have taken their efforts into the courts. They have also put great pressure on Congress to "restore prayer" to the public schools with limited success. Various conservative and liberal groups representing special interests are entering the political arena to elect individuals at the grassroots level to influence educational decisions. Pat Robertson's television programs tend to reflect those interests. However, it is important to note that the "moral majority" and the Christian Coalition are not monolithic organizations. Conservative Christians hold a variety of views. In "Christian Right Falls Out of Unison on School Prayer," Felsenthal (1997) finds a diversity of opinions on the subject, with some believing religion is best left to the home and church. As the population grows more diverse, many other religions, such as the Muslim and Hindu faiths, are expanding their membership.

In *Epperson v. Arkansas* (1968), the court ruled that an antievolution statute is unconstitutional because evolution is a science rather than a secular religion, and students cannot be restricted from such information. Thirteen years later, on March 19, 1981, Governor Frank White signed the Arkansas Legislative Act 590 or The Balanced Treatment for Creation Science and Evolution Science Act into law. In *McLean v. Board of Education of Arkansas* (1982), a federal court ruled the act unconstitutional on the grounds that it had been passed to advance religion, that it had as a major effect the advancement of particular religious beliefs, and that it created for the state of Arkansas excessive and prohibited entanglement with religion. In *Edwards v. Aguillard* (1987), a Louisiana statute was rejected on similar grounds. The court ruled that giving equal time to creation science and evolution was designed to discredit scientific knowledge and to prevent educators from disseminating such information, in violation of the First Amendment establishment clause.

The courts have generally not gone along with book banning. For example, in *Pico v. Board of Education, Island Trees Union Free School District No. 26,* in 1980, the board's decision to ban *Soul on Ice, Slaughterhouse Five,* and *Black Boy* was not upheld. More successful have been efforts to control books by influencing the list of approved books for public schools in states like Texas.

Control of the school curriculum through the selection or rejection of materials is an activity in which many groups are now engaged. Conservative groups putting pressure on school systems to reject certain textbooks include the Liberty Foundation, the Stop Textbook Censorship Committee, and the Educational Research Analysis. The last organization, headed by Mel and Norma Gabler, has had much visibility and influence. Some censorship advocates like Phyllis Schlafly provide checklists for parents who are looking for what some consider to be morally or politically offensive materials in books. On the liberal side are the American Civil Liberties Union, the Council for Democratic and Secular Humanism, People for the American Way, and the National Association for the Advancement of Colored People; in general, these groups support academic freedom and reject censorship. The National Organization for Women has recently become active in gender issues in textbooks. Conservative and liberal groups have influenced textbook and curriculum content throughout our educational history. Prominent radio personalities such as Dr. Laura and Rush Limbaugh espouse traditional educational and personal ethics.

In the 1960s, the Supreme Court barred state-sanctioned prayer and Bible reading in public schools, in support of Jefferson's separation of church and state. The Supreme Court was silent on such issues for nearly two decades but indicated a new willingness to address First Amendment issues in the 1980s. In 1985, the Court ruled in *Wallace v. Jaffree* that an Alabama law allowing silent prayer in schools violated the establishment clause. The Court reviewed *Bender v. Williamsport,* a case that involves the legality of student-initiated devotional meetings held during noninstructional time in a public school. Lower courts barred the meetings, but a district court upheld students and the high court denied an appeal. A number of cases dealing with school prayer are being heard in federal courts, and some could end up in the Supreme Court. *Lemon v. Kurtzman* (1971) provided the Lemon test. The ruling found that governmental enactments must have a secular purpose, the effects of which neither advance nor prohibit religion and do not involve excessive entanglement with religion. The Lemon test may be challenged in the future. In *Bown v. Gwinnett* (1995), federal courts upheld a Georgia legislative act allowing for a moment of quiet reflection in schools, as long as it is not over sixty seconds and not intended as a religious exercise. In *Herdahl v. Pontotoc* (1995), on agreement with parties in a lawsuit, the court held that seventh- through twelfth-grade students in a Mississippi school district could hold voluntary devotional meetings prior to school hours in the school gym.

Darden (2000), of the National School Boards Association, finds that while the Supreme Court and lower federal courts have been more willing to allow a relationship between schools and religion in general, they draw the line on outright prayer (particularly when it seems publicly sponsored, endorsed, religiously motivated, or unduly coercive). *Mitchell v. Helmes* (2000) illustrates the current trend toward permitting computers and other technology equipment that are federally funded under various federal education acts to be used by private schools, including religious schools, on the basis of the child benefit theory.

In 1984, President Reagan signed into law the Equal Access Act, which made it illegal to deny access to students who wish to conduct a meeting, on the basis of religious, political, philosophical, or other content of the speech at such meetings. There is confusion over the intent of this legislation since it appears to conflict with cases like *Lubbock Civil Liberties Union v. Lubbock Independent School District* (1983), which prohibited policies designed to encourage religious meetings. On the other hand, *Widmar v. Vincent* (1981) stated that permitting college students to engage in voluntary religious activities on campus would not violate the establishment clause. Schools that allow a "limited open forum" in which special interests are dealt with on public school property face both equal access and separation issues.

The Supreme Court has addressed this conflict during the administration of President Clinton. In *Lamb's Chapel v. Center Moriches Union Free School District* (1993), the Supreme Court ruled that if schools provide school facilities for some uses permitted by state law, religious groups must have the same access to these facilities.

On February 28, 2001, the U.S. Supreme Court heard a case, *Good News Club v. Milford Central School,* that denied use of school facilities to a religious youth group. It is expected that the high court will rule that school districts may not discriminate against religious groups who wish to use school facilities while secular groups can use such facilities. Critics of letting religious groups use public schools for club meetings fear these facilities will be used for religious proselytizing, while advocates of such use of school facilities after school hours believe it is a constitutional right. As Richey (2001) noted, the court for over forty years has decided such cases on the basis of the crucial difference between government speech endorsing religion, which the establishment clause forbids, and private speech endorsing religion, which the free speech and free exercise clauses protect. On June 11, 2001, the high court ruled that the Milford School District violated the free-speech rights of the Good News Club.

Additional cases focused on support of nonpublic schools and tax relief for tuition. With current interest in the voucher system, it is noteworthy that in *Mueller v. Allen* (1983) the Supreme Court found no violation of the Constitution in tax deductions benefiting parents of parochial school students. The 1977 case of *Wolman v. Walter* supported providing nonpublic school pupils with books, tests, and remedial services. The Court objected to parts of the Ohio law providing field trips and instructional services to nonpublic school students, since these advanced a sectarian purpose instead of general child benefit. In *Zobrest v. Catalina Foothills School District* (1993), the Supreme Court ruled that public funds could be used for services for a deaf student in a parochial school. The ruling may encourage advocates of public support for some aspects of religious education.

In *Aguilar v. Felton* (1985), the Supreme Court ruled that utilization of Title I funds for public school teachers working in parochial schools to teach remedial work to low-income and low-achievement students led to an unacceptable level of entanglement between church and state. Since Title I funds were designated to be used for public and private school children, school districts after Felton (1985) provided needed remedial education in mobile vans parked just outside private school grounds. Others bused children to public schools or to other facilities off private school grounds. Funds for the vans came out of Title I funds and did not violate the separation of church and state, according to *Walker v. San Francisco Unified School District* (1995), *Pulio v. Cavazos* (1991), and *Barnes v. Cavazos* (1992). The Supreme Court on an appeal of *Agostini v. Felton* (1997) overturned *Aguilar v. Felton* (1985). The Court found that use of public school instructors in private parochial schools to teach remedial classes for low-income and low-achievement students under Title I funds does not advance or create excessive entanglement with religion. New York City had spent over $100 million since 1985 to provide vans that served as classrooms. The vans were parked on public streets near parochial schools.

Support of teaching creationism, attacks on textbooks thought to reflect secular humanism, and demands by conservatives for a more restrictive curriculum will likely be tested in future court cases, as will the Lemon test.

Vouchers. Bowman (2001) notes that national teachers' unions and a number of congressional Democrats helped defeat citizen initiative voucher plans in California and Michigan. Some twenty states are considering voucher plans. In *Simmons-Harris v. Zelman* (2002), a Cleveland voucher plan providing funding for disadvantaged children to attend private schools including those with religious affiliations was found constitutional. The high court ruling may lead to increased private or private religious school enrollment.

The Bush administration and Education Secretary Rod Paige are seeking to find other terms such as school choice, student opportunities, or scholarships to allow students in overcrowded or low-performing schools to transfer to private schools or other public schools. Currently Florida has the only statewide voucher program in the nation. In *Holmes v. Bush* (2000) a state appeals court found the state constitution allows the use of public funds for private schools in some circumstances. With Vermont Senator James Jeffords switching to the Democratic party in 2001, the George W. Bush education agenda will be modified. Vouchers were eliminated from the education budget of 2002, but the Bush proposal of tying federal aid to improvement in students' test scores was approved. Provisions for low-income, disadvantaged students to transfer to other public schools remained in the legislation. Transfer would be permitted if at-risk students are victims of violence, or in low-performance schools. Tutorial services could be provided by parochial schools. The issues will be revisited by the high court and be a subject of controversy and litigation in the future (Toppo, 2001).

In June 2001, Congress passed an education bill that increased federal funding for education and required states to assess students in grades three through eight annually in math and reading. Low-scoring schools would receive additional aid and low-income students could transfer to other public schools after two years. After three years low-income students in low-performing schools would be eligible for federal funds for tutoring or transferring to another public school.

Involuntary Segregation.   Involuntary segregation refers to excluding certain children from schools, usually on the basis of race. The problem of segregation is clearly linked to the period following the American Civil War and to the freeing of the slaves. Public schools for blacks and whites established during the period of Reconstruction in the South were quickly eliminated in the 1880s. Thereafter, Southern states made laws that required that schools could not admit children from both races to the same classes, and segregation began.

As we have seen, federal attempts to provide support to the South for education (as with the Hoar Bill and the Blair Bill) failed. This failure left a large part of the nation in a condition of poverty and without the resources to provide adequate schooling for its children. The problem was made even more acute by the requirement of a dual school system that was expensive and inefficient. Schools in the South lacked resources from the 1880s to the 1950s, but the black schools were a cut below all the others.

Northern states did not usually have laws prohibiting racially integrated schools, but many Northern schools were segregated because of population patterns. White students did not attend schools with a majority of black pupils until after the Brown case. Many schools in Northern cities were all black or all white according to their location and the demography of the area. As Jonathan Kozol points out, inner-city schools in the Bronx, New York, and other communities continue to have segregated pockets of racial poverty and crime.

The prospect for social equality in the South at the time was so dubious that Booker T. Washington (1858–1915) thought blacks should accept segregation in return for some access to education. The *Plessy v. Ferguson* case of 1896 affirmed the principle that separate but equal facilities were legal. In 1906, W. E. B. Du Bois started the Niagara movement. It led to the organization in 1909 of the National Association for the Advancement of Colored People (NAACP). In the 1930s, the NAACP began to challenge segregation laws on the grounds that facilities provided to black students were not even remotely equal to those of whites.

While not attacking the segregation laws on principle, the Supreme Court began to require admission of black students to Southern professional schools, unless the states could prove that they had equal facilities for blacks within their borders. Finally in 1950, a direct challenge to segregated education was presented to the Court in *Sweatt v. Painter*. In this case, an applicant who had been denied admission to the University of Texas Law School solely on the basis of color claimed that the instruction available in the newly established state law school for blacks was markedly inferior to the instruction at the university; thus, equal protection of the law was denied. In a unanimous decision, the Supreme Court ordered the student's admission to the white school, indicating that it was virtually impossible in practice, at least in professional education, for a state to comply with the separate-but-equal formula.

Following the decision in the Sweatt case, the NAACP and other organizations advanced the fight against segregation in public schools. This pressure resulted in several public school segregation cases. The Court proceeded with a great deal of circumspection and required an unusual amount of investigation by the counsels. Their deliberation was understandable; if segregation in public schools was determined to be a denial of equal protection of laws, it would in all likelihood be impossible to defend segregation in other sectors of public life. The legal foundation of the social structure of a great part of the nation was under attack. By 1954, it had become obvious to the public that black children in segregated states received a much poorer schooling than white students. In 1952, for example, Arkansas spent $102 for the education of each white child compared with $67 for each black child. Black colleges were often substandard, and few jobs were open to black students who had graduated from Northern universities. Integration in the armed forces after World War II and the success of blacks who sued for entry into Southern universities led to the Supreme Court decision of 1954, *Brown v. Board of Education.*

In this famous case, NAACP lawyer Thurgood Marshall argued that equality of educational facilities was not the question. Marshall claimed that prestige, teaching standards, the academic surroundings, and the inference of inferiority were important in educational equality. The Court agreed, saying that segregation was construed to deprive minority group children of equal educational opportunity. By its decision, the Supreme Court held that all laws concerning or permitting school segregation were in conflict with the Fourteenth Amendment and ordered involuntary segregation to cease within a "reasonable time." Several major cities like Baltimore, Washington, DC, and St. Louis made a complete transition to integrated schools on the basis of the 1954 decision.

This decision met with much opposition, especially in the South, as did most decisions involving integration. One of the frequent arguments against forced integration is illustrated by an article reprinted from the *American Bar Association Journal.* Eugene Cook, attorney general of Georgia, and William J. Potter (1956) criticized the Brown decision severely. The opinion of the Court, said these critics, "did not hold that the old 'separate but equal' doctrine, laid down in *Plessy v. Ferguson,* was a bad law. It held that it was bad sociology."

Considerable progress toward desegregation was made in border states, but in the Deep South various measures designed to frustrate desegregation were tried. Boycotting or nonsupport of integrated schools, student assignment plans to minimize integration, and the temporary abolition of public schools, as in Prince Edward County, Virginia, took place. Integration of the teaching staff and token integration through bringing in a few minority-group students to all-white schools were common attempts to meet legal requirements without basic change. Private academies were established in parts of the South in an effort to escape court-ordered integration, especially in areas where black people were in the majority.

A serious problem in many areas has been de facto segregation, or segregation based upon school district boundaries that encompass children from only one race. The problem of de facto segregation is by no means confined to the South; blacks, Mexican Americans, and other minority groups have been forced to live (often for economic reasons) in a single part or section of most cities. Racial boundaries tend to move rapidly so that schools that are planned to serve students from different races or ethnic backgrounds often end up being built in areas where only one race is present. Often some sort of educational park, cluster of school buildings, or central administration assignment of students has been used as an instrument for integration.

Heavy opposition to such efforts is often encountered. Many parents object to having their elementary school children attend schools other than those in their own neighborhoods or within walking distance of their homes. Some fear that integration will have a negative effect on children, such as introducing them to foul language, crime, and drugs. Many school districts have experienced a loss of enrollment as a result of court-ordered desegregation plans. Parents move their families into suburban areas in order to avoid what they believe to be unfortunate aspects of school integration. Perhaps the greatest opposition has occurred when cities have attempted to solve the integration problem by busing students from one school to another in order to achieve some degree of racial balance. Los Angeles and Orlando, among other cities, now have a majority-minority population. Latinos and blacks are in the majority of formerly minority populations. However, these populations are not monolithic and have notable differences within them. A major problem for education has been the mandate given to schools to foster integration while the general public in many communities was unwilling to cooperate. Nevertheless, research indicates that whenever black, Hispanic, and white students can be placed together in positive and meaningful educational experiences at an early age, racial tension is reduced and human relations are improved.

Delays and circumventions in desegregation have not been confined to public schools. The attempt of Authurine Lucy to enter the University of Alabama in 1956 and the violence created by James Meredith's admission to the University of Mississippi in 1962 are illustrative of the problems of integration in higher education. Nevertheless, colleges and universities have been racially integrated with much less conflict than in public schools.

As the black movement for freedom and integration reached revolutionary levels, plans for school integration were set into motion throughout the United States. Some plans found general acceptance, but most efforts to move large numbers of children from one area of a city to another for integration of schools were bitterly opposed. With the assassination of Martin Luther King Jr. in 1968 and the passage of the Civil Rights Act in 1964, desegregation entered a new phase. The Civil Rights Act specified that no person could be discriminated against on the basis of race, color, sex, or national origin in any program that received federal assistance. This meant that federal funding could be withheld from school districts or states that failed to adopt reasonable and acceptable plans for integration.

Some of the Southern school districts with the greatest need for financial help have been the least willing to integrate. Plans involving the mass busing of children have drawn fire from parents, politicians, and the public. Federal courts and the Department of Health, Education, and Welfare have insisted upon prompt compliance with the law, but the struggle goes on in many communities. School buses were attacked and burned in Michigan. Riots over busing black students to South Boston

High School in 1974 caused the closing of the school. Many state legislatures have issued laws against busing for racial balance, and Congress has come close to considering such a law. Meanwhile, schools attempt to follow legal guidelines and carry on the task of public education as best they can.

Although the Supreme Court has continued to uphold the Brown decision, militant resistance to busing has not died out, and many school districts still reflect segregation. Sometimes this situation occurs when the population of a city changes dramatically as in the case of Newark, New Jersey, or the Bronx, New York. The Court has held that school boards may not intentionally gerrymander a school district to encourage segregation (*Keyes v. Denver*), but some American cities are entirely white or black. In *Milliken v. Bradley,* the Supreme Court reversed the lower federal court ruling, which said Detroit should adopt a metropolitan desegregation plan to include its suburbs. On the other hand, the Court in 1977 refused to review the decision of Judge Garrity in *Morgan v. Hennigan.* The Court let stand the placing of the school system in federal receivership because the Boston school board had intentionally increased segregation. Numerous other cases are still pending, and the mood of the nation seems to be swinging away from support for court-ordered busing plans. Los Angeles was allowed to discontinue busing for racial integration in 1981. Nevertheless, desegregation reflects the multiracial society of the 2000s in the country, and America will not go back to conditions that existed before 1954.

Although future deliberations may result in different conclusions, the Supreme Court in *Missouri v. Jenkins* in 1995, after asserting that states cannot deny an access in education due to race, noted that we must forever put aside the notion that simply because a school district today is black, it must be educationally inferior. A Kansas City school district request to continue and expand an eighteen-year-old continuing court order requiring the state to fund "remedial quality" programs because student achievement levels stand at or below national norms was reviewed. The court noted that at some point we must recognize that the judiciary is not omniscient and that all problems do not require a remedy of constitutional proportions. The court continued by stating that usurpation of the traditionally local control over education not only takes the judiciary beyond its proper sphere but also deprives the states and their elected officials of their constitutional powers. The Eighth Circuit Court of Appeals in *Missouri v. Jenkins* (2000) recommended reinstatement of the court supervision of the Kansas City, Missouri, school district. On July 28, 2000, a federal judge named another monitor for the Kansas City school district. After nearly three decades of court supervision, and some nineteen school superintendents in the last thirty years, the current superintendent plans on concentrating on improving the performance of all students on the Missouri Assessment Program Tests. Some fifteen charter schools with additional ones under development are serving an increasing number of schools within the Kansas City school district, with Central Missouri State University.

Following close upon the efforts to end involuntary segregation came attempts to make college education and jobs accessible to a larger number of disadvantaged minorities and to women. Affirmative action plans were established in institutions of higher education to accomplish these goals in recruiting faculty and students. Federal guidelines intended to increase minority enrollment led to some institutions setting up a quota for minority students, frequently about 10 percent of the total. Some colleges allowed admission officers to require lower aptitude scores from minorities because research showed many tests were culturally biased.

Opposition to affirmative action appeared in the form of the Committee on Academic Nondiscrimination and Integrity in 1972. This committee charged that policies favoring minority and female candidates over others better qualified hurt professional performance. Although it recognized the evils of past discrimination, it objected to preferential admission standards for minorities.

In 1978, the Supreme Court agreed to hear arguments in the case of *Regents of the University of California v. Allan Bakke*. Bakke contended that the quota for minorities at the medical campus at Davis had caused him to be rejected for admission, although his scores were much higher than those of minority candidates who were admitted. The Court ordered that Bakke be admitted on the basis that his rights under the Fourteenth Amendment had been violated. However, it was also stated in the opinion that race and background factors may be considered by institutions making decisions on admissions. In the case of *Steelworkers v. Weber* in 1979, a challenge similar to that of Bakke, the Court upheld the legality of an affirmative action plan worked out by the United Steelworkers.

Affirmative action was addressed in *Adarand Constructors v. Penna* (1995) by Sandra Day O'Connor writing for the majority. She wrote that affirmative action should be narrowly tailored and not broadly interpreted. Several federal cases have rejected the concept of affirmative action on the basis of race-neutral policies. In *Hopwood v. Texas* (1996), the Supreme Court turned back a 1994 decision in a federal court of appeals that held that law school admissions at the University of Texas must be race neutral. Advocates of affirmative action programs noted that moving to race-neutral policies would severely limit minority enrollment in higher education. This has been the case in both the University of Texas and the University of California where minority enrollment in 1997 fell since affirmative action based on race was phased out. Recently, however, minority enrollment has increased as the focus has shifted to recruiting low-income students. The University of Michigan at Ann Arbor and the University of Nevada currently face litigation similar to the Hopwood case.

Another challenge to affirmative action involved two public school teachers, one white and one black. The teachers were hired at the same time; they had the same experience and education (except that the minority teacher had a master's degree). The white teacher was laid off for the purpose of maintaining diversity in the school. Taxman sued and won over $400,000 and reinstatement in the job. *Piscataway v. Taxman* (1997) was withdrawn from the Supreme Court docket after civil rights groups raised enough money, some $300,000, to settle the case out of court. Civil rights groups may have feared a court decision that would be unfavorable to affirmative action; by settling out of court, they may have sought to buy time—with the expectation of an appointment by President Clinton of another judge who supported affirmative action. After one of the narrowest elections in history, George W. Bush's federal court appointments will be under scrutiny by civil rights groups. The district court in *Tuttle v. Arlington County School Board* (1999) held that diversity could not be a compelling school interest and enjoined Arlington from initiating a race-based admissions policy. Alexander and Alexander (2001) point out that the courts continue to use narrow focus and strict scrutiny in dealing with diversity and race-based policies.

Whatever the future of affirmative action legal decisions, the concept has been an instrument of national policy for over forty years. Schools and educators at all levels tend to remain committed to the goals of supporting and enlarging minority student and faculty numbers. Other avenues of meeting these goals—such as needs-based, class-based, or socioeconomic background affirmative action programs—are being explored. Florida's governor Jeb Bush has implemented a program to increase minority enrollment without the use of affirmative action in order to avoid litigation similar to *Tuttle v. Arlington.* His One Florida Plan was vigorously debated by civil rights groups. Affirmative action continues to be debated and subject to continued litigation with emotions running high on both sides of the issue.

Litigation and Equality of Opportunity.
Although some part of the educational budget for most school districts is federally collected and distributed, American school support is largely a state and local matter. Traditionally, the federal government has had no role in school finance except where federal funds were involved. This changed dramatically in 1971 with a case brought on behalf of Mexican-American children in Los Angeles. Using the equal protection guarantee of the Fourteenth Amendment, the California Supreme Court ruled, in *Serrano v. Priest,* that the state's system of financing public schools was discriminatory. The basis of the argument was that the quality of education provided was a function of the wealth of each district and therefore discriminated against poor children. Following the Serrano case, more than fifty suits in thirty states were filed against the local property tax systems. Minnesota, Texas, New Jersey, and Connecticut had their property taxes struck down by the courts. Disparities among school districts' tax bases within states will continue to be litigated in the future.

The impact of *Serrano v. Priest* might have been even more dramatic if the Supreme Court had not taken a different stand in *San Antonio Independent School District v. Rodriguez.* A Texas federal district court had ruled the Texas system of local property taxation illegal, as in the Serrano case. In 1973, however, the Supreme Court in a five to four decision reversed the district court decision and held that the system in Texas did not absolutely deprive poor people of education, nor did it discriminate against any definable category of the "poor." In spite of this support for the property tax, attention was brought to the inequality of educational opportunity in various districts within states. Many state legislatures have taken a hard look at their system of school funding since the Serrano and Rodriguez cases. Recent state and federal court rulings require equity provisions for financially burdened school districts. A Texas Supreme Court decision in *Edgewood v. Kirby* (1989) required the state legislature to correct inequities in funding between financially burdened and affluent school districts. In *Rose v. Council for Better Education, Inc.* (1988), a Kentucky Supreme Court decision upheld a lower court ruling that the state had failed to provide an efficient system of common schools. The ruling led to the Kentucky Educational Reform Act of 1990, which provided for more effective schools together with equity in taxation to ensure a guaranteed minimum level of financial support per pupil for all school districts. In a democratic society, it is hard to justify unequal financial support for education; thus, new laws have been proposed and others probably will be.

Changing educational practices and the characteristics of students have influenced modern litigation. An example is the need many school officials have to search for illegal drugs in schools or on the persons of students. In *New Jersey v. T.L.O.* (1985), the Supreme Court held that the Fourth Amendment does apply to searches conducted by public school officials. However, school officials need not obtain warrants before searching a student, nor must they have probable cause before searching. The validity of a school search depends on its reasonableness under the circumstances. The clause in the Fourteenth Amendment pertaining to equal protection under the law applies also to the rights of students. Older practices of dismissing students from school because they marry, are pregnant, or commit a crime are no longer legal, although recent federal court decisions are giving school authorities more power and control of student behavior. Zero tolerance policies, although being modified in many school districts, continue to be implemented to eliminate or reduce school violence. Federal courts support educators in their quest to maintain an environment conducive to learning and rediscover loco parentis (the teacher and administrator stand in relation to the student as does a parent), although careful provision is made for students' civil rights.

Following the demand for accountability, schools were tested on the legality of new requirements for students. Some cases had to do with whether a diploma could be withheld from a student who had passed required courses but who was below par in performance. In *Debra v. Turlington* (1983), the Court ruled that functional literacy tests may be required as a prerequisite for a high school diploma, but the tests must be a valid measure of instruction. The Court also prevented statewide use of tests in Florida, until the state showed that discrepancies in passing rates of white and black students were not due to educational deprivations suffered by blacks before integration. In *Debra v. Turlington* (1984), Florida's high school exit exams were upheld, and by 1996 at least sixteen states required students to pass competency tests in order to receive diplomas. Exit tests for graduation are becoming more common throughout the country as increased attention is paid to standards.

Other Significant Court Cases.   Although the most important influence of the courts has been directed toward desegregation, religion, and equality, there have been several other areas of educational importance. A common practice in many American cities was to test children and then to place them in a fixed curriculum according to the ability group into which they fell. This practice, called the "tracking system," was found unconstitutional in 1967 in *Hobson v. Hansen*. The tracking system tended to promote segregation within schools and make it impossible for students to get out of the track once they had been placed in it.

The right to privacy and to due process under the law has been extended to children in the United States. In 1971, students in Columbus, Ohio, who were suspended for ten days from school without a hearing, brought suit. In this case, *Goss v. Lopez,* the Court held that high school students must be granted due process including notice of the charges against them and an opportunity must be provided for them to present their side of the story. Similar cases have protected children suspended for wearing long hair or violating school codes of dress. The Family Educational Rights and Privacy Act of 1974 (also called the Buckley Amendment) requires schools to provide access to records to students over the age of eighteen and to parents of younger students. Another landmark case on children's rights was *Tinker v. Des Moines* in 1969. Quaker students in the Des Moines public schools were suspended for wearing black armbands to protest the war in Vietnam. The Supreme Court found that wearing armbands was a symbolic case of expression, and therefore it was protected under the First Amendment, like freedom of speech. Modern courts have also been active in matters concerning loyalty oaths, violations of civil liberties, and academic freedom. As a general rule, schools are prohibited from making any rule or regulation that impinges upon rights that students would enjoy if they were adults.

New challenges to public school finances could emerge from *Franklin v. Gwinnette County Public Schools* (1992). The case allowed a student, who alleged that she was sexually harassed by a teacher, to seek money damages from the school district under a federal law prohibiting gender bias. The ruling was based on Title IX of the Education Amendments of 1972 and could open school districts to suits dealing with race, ethnicity, age, and disability. All school districts distribute policy handbooks to parents, students, teachers, and administrators; the handbooks define and explain permissible behavior in regard to issues of sex, race, and crime. The handbooks also identify procedures for reporting incidents of impermissible behavior while maintaining confidentiality. Student to student sexual harassment could be subject to money damages whenever school authorities knew or should have known of such behavior. In the *School Law Reporter,* Rossow and Parkinson (1997) note, however, that the court found, in *David v. Monroe County Board of Education* (1996), that a school could be held liable for student to student harassment. Other federal court rulings have found schools not liable for peer harassment. The U.S. Office of Civil Rights continues to develop guidelines for peer harassment policies in education. The issue will be revisited in the future in federal court decisions.

With large numbers of children who are not citizens of the United States seeking to enter the schools, especially along the border with Mexico, litigation has emerged. In *Doe v. Plyler* in 1978, a school district's exclusionary policy regarding alien children was struck down. The Fifth Circuit Court of Appeals upheld the decision in 1980. In 1982, the Supreme Court permanently enjoined the state of Texas from excluding undocumented alien children from tuition-free public schools. All children must be served, whether or not they hold citizenship. Congressional legislation to limit public services for legal and illegal aliens is being discussed, but one would suspect continued support for the child benefit theory of assisting youngsters in need.

Just as compulsory attendance was tested in the courts at an earlier time, so home schooling has more recently become an issue. For a multitude of reasons including control of the values to which children are exposed, some parents are educating their children at home. In *Stephens v. Bongart* in 1937, the court found that home instruction was not equivalent to that provided in public schools partly because of a lack of opportunity for socialization. However, in the Massa case of 1967, it was held that socialization and social development had no place in determining whether home schooling was equivalent to public education. In a recent case, *Mazanec v. North Judson-San Pierre School Corporation* (1985), parents were found entitled to educate their children at home if those parents made a good faith effort to meet certain minimum requirements. However, in *West Virginia v. Riddle* (1981), the court held that the state's interest in protecting children extends to home schools. With growing numbers of home and small religious schools, educators have expressed concern about the role of the public school in carrying the culture to all. This is a major theme in John Goodlad's *What Are Schools For?*

Other recent cases have involved the treatment of people with disabilities, discrimination in staff employment, and the use of federal funds for state programs. In *Bennett v. Kentucky Department of Education* (1985), the Court held that neither substantial compliance nor lack of bad faith excused a state from repaying federal funds misspent for readiness classes. Reinforcing the right of due process in *Cleveland Board of Education v. Loudermill* (1985), the Court held that termination must be only for cause and that an employee must have an opportunity to respond to the charges motivating discharge. In another 1985 case, *School Committee of Burlington v. Department of Education of Massachusetts,* the Supreme Court ruled that where a local education agency's proposed placement for a child with a disability is inappropriate, the school authority must pay for a private placement in which the parents unilaterally enrolled their child.

Martha L. Thurlow and David R. Johnson in a *Journal of Teacher Education* article noted that the Individuals with Disabilities Education Act Amendments of 1997 (public law 105-17) require states and districts to have students with disabilities participate in state and district assessments and to report on their performance. To avoid unintended multiplier effects, educators need to know about the role of participation in individualized education plan teams, how to make good decisions about accommodations and alternative assessments knowledge about diploma options and related issues can help special education students benefit from high-stakes testing. The challenges to students with disabilities lie in alternative diplomas, watered-down curriculum, and lowered expectations that create a challenge for teachers. Students graduating with alternative diplomas may have limited job access.

In Loco Parentis.   In the seventeenth, eighteenth, and nineteenth centuries, school administrators, staff, and teachers held the power to discipline and set rules and regulations for students in the same manner as parents. Although state and federal court decisions depend on the facts of each case, in loco parentis may be revisited by the courts. The Supreme Court in *Vernonia School District v. Acton* (1995) upheld drug testing in schools, noting that subjects of the policy are children who have been committed to the temporary custody of the state as schoolmaster. The Court continued by finding that in that capacity the state could exercise a degree of supervision and control greater than it could exercise over free adults. Further, the Court found that there are substantial needs of teachers and administrators for the freedom to maintain order in schools to have a safe and proper environment for learning.

Whatever the future holds for educational litigation, decisions will be influenced by the composition of the courts. If there are a few Supreme Court and federal judge retirements during the George W. Bush administration, a conservative swing might occur. Congress and the courts shifted to the right under the previous Bush administration, and there may be an effort to maintain a conservative court, although both political parties are moving toward the middle of the spectrum. With increased political activism any Supreme Court appointment will be subject to intense scrutiny. With the U.S. Senate almost evenly divided between the two parties and with recent razor-thin Democratic control, bipartisanship will be necessary to prevent gridlock. Each party will continue to get congresspersons to switch parties.

A case that illustrates the interplay between Congress and the courts is *Grove City College v. Bell* (1984). Here, the Court held that affirmative action applies only to programs specifically receiving federal funds. The proposed Civil Rights Act of 1984, stipulating that the whole school is subject to affirmative action even if only one program is receiving federal funds, did not pass. Congress subsequently changed the City College decision to include all university programs in affirmative action, not just those that receive federal funding.

Single-Sex Schools. In *United States v. Virginia Military Institute* (1996), the Supreme Court found that an exclusively male admission policy violated the equal protection clause of the Fourteenth Amendment. It found that women have a right to full citizenship stature—equal opportunity to aspire, achieve, participate in, and contribute to society based on their individual talents and capacities. The Court in its decision reviewed the history of sexual discrimination citing *Bradwell v. Illinois* (1873). In that nineteenth-century case, the Court denied a woman the right to practice law: "In view of the peculiar characteristics, destiny and mission of woman, it is within the province of the legislature to ordain what offices, positions and callings shall be filled and discharged by men, and shall receive the benefit of those energies and responsibilities, and that decision and firmness which are presumed to predominate in the sterner sex." In the Virginia Military case, the court found that women seeking a VMI quality education cannot be offered anything less to afford them genuinely equal protection.

MORE RECENT EDUCATIONAL CRITICS

Clashing views on controversial issues have characterized writing in the educational field for many years. Historically, institutionalized education has been characteristically rigid, and that rigidity has led to criticism by progressives and other liberal writers. On the other hand, business leaders and political conservatives have often attacked the schools for promoting socialistic ideas or for teaching about social issues. Liberal versus conservative arguments over the curriculum, moral training, and the rights of children have been present in the educational literature for generations.

Curriculum matters often tie in with methods and with psychology. When Charles Eliot chaired the Committee of Ten in 1892, specific subjects were prescribed for the high schools. Latin, Greek, English, German, French, Spanish, algebra, geometry, trigonometry, astronomy, meteorology, botany, zoology, physiology, geology, physics, chemistry, history, and physical geography were the subjects that received support. Critics soon pointed out that the high school curriculum lacked vocational subjects, sociology, psychology, and the humanities. The committee was also highly influenced by the then popular educational psychology that stressed mental discipline. Later psychologists were quick to take issue with subjects chosen because of their alleged ability to train the mind. Others argued that the subjects chosen were all intended for college preparatory students, even though the majority of the high school population was not college bound.

Critics of education in modern America provide a means by which issues in contemporary schooling may be studied. Some critics find philosophical fault with the aims and purposes of education. Others attack teacher education, the curriculum, or the methods used in schools. Many are concerned about the quality of programs and the products produced by schools. In addition to being numerous and verbal, critics are also well established in staunch positions with considerable public support. Some people think that modern critics perform a service by isolating problems and illuminating inadequate aspects of the educational system. Others say that responsible criticism requires offering attainable solutions and working within the system to achieve them. Clearly there are many more critics ready to focus on the shortcomings rather than offer reasonable answers or alternatives. Several critics do have a talent for providing poignant insight into the teaching–learning process and the total school environment. Many critics reach professionals within the educational system who take them seriously enough to attempt change. Colleges of education have been especially sensitive to the charges of critics. Of course, critics also create anger, frustration, disgust, and other negative reactions both inside and outside the system.

During the 1950s, the nation enjoyed a period of relative prosperity and tranquility. The hysterical fear of communism that had caused attacks on academic freedom began to subside. Various social and legal movements toward the achievement of racial equality began to alter the educational system.

The reaction to the successful launching of *Sputnik* brought this tranquil period to an end. In the wake of fear and criticisms of American educational failures, European schools were compared favorably with those in the United States. James B. Conant, former president of Harvard, called for the reorganization of high schools with more emphasis on excellence. Admiral Hyman Rickover insisted that the major purpose of education is to produce the experts who create the technology and science upon which a modern nation depends for winning wars, hot or cold. These views carried the day, and through such programs as the National Defense Education Act (NDEA), emphasis was placed upon science, technology, mathematics, foreign languages, and high standards.

In the 1960s, a new wave of criticism arose following the politically, socially, and emotionally turbulent decade marked by civil rights activity at home and war in Vietnam. Critics proclaimed that recent academic reforms had failed or at least were not meeting prevalent needs. Although College Board scores indicated that the public schools of the 1960s produced students with comparatively better skills in science and mathematics, questions were raised about the relevance of the curriculum, attitudes produced, individual needs of students, and the role of schools in social change.

In the 1970s, dissatisfaction permeated the social order, and the grim realities facing the nation created a diversity of new educational criticisms. Fear that a lasting peace might not be achieved in the world, loss of faith in government following the Watergate affair, and the prospects of unemployment in an economy marked by inflation and recession added to uncertainty about the future. People began to ask how children should be educated to cope with the energy crisis, ecology problems, the depletion of natural resources, urban congestion, rising crime, a world population explosion, and a changing job market. Others focused less on problem solving and economic survival and more on the developmental, creative, and human needs of individual students. One group of critics concerned themselves with the way schools mold or shape students. They were sensitive and sympathetic to groups of children who to one degree or another are "victims" of society and therefore of the school system.

By 1980, the focus of criticism had taken a conservative turn. Distrust of big government and bureaucracy caused dissatisfaction with programs for social engineering, school integration, and efforts to aid the poor. Inflation fueled a demand for more job-related training, more efficient use of school time, and less busing for desegregation. A new wave of attacks on teaching the theory of evolution, sex education, and values clarification came from the "moral majority." Multicultural studies and bilingual education became less popular, and there were new demands for accountability. The reputation of education declined as ACT scores continued to slide and many high school graduates proved unable to read beyond an elementary level. "Excellence" and a "return to basics" were the most popular slogans of the times.

During the 1990s, SAT and ACT scores stabilized, educational reform and restructuring continued unabated, and cultural diversity was stressed. **Political correctness** was a term widely used to refer to the influence of various liberal groups. There was great national concern over the AIDS virus and the cancer-causing effects of cigarettes.

During the 2000s, as in the past, public schools and universities will be engaged in a wide variety of initiatives to provide an environment of educational excellence where all belong, all learn, and all succeed. (Mission statement of Rogers, Arkansas, Public Schools.) For every initiative there will be counteracting forces. High-stakes testing is being rethought with some states curbing the movement; the American Bar Association has recommended ending the policy of one-size-fits-all solutions to problems confronting public schools, such as zero tolerance school discipline policies. The bar association finds that zero tolerance policies may redefine students as criminals with unfortunate consequences. Vouchers and charter schools have their advocates and opponents; for-profit educational corporations that manage schools are being utilized and debated by educators, professional associations, and unions; bilingual education has supporters and detractors; affirmative action and diversity policies have been influenced by recent federal court decisions; and lawsuits in several states have been initiated to redistribute tax dollars more equitably among rich and poor school districts. There will be continued efforts to deal with a multitude of issues confronting public school populations into the foreseeable future.

Samuel Bowles and Herbert Gintis.   Among those who advocate radical school reform or argue that education cannot be improved without a far-reaching social revolution are Bowles and Gintis. Their 1976 book, *Schooling in Capitalist America,* called attention to hostility of the school toward the need of the individual for personal development. Like Paul Goodman, Edgar Friedenberg, John Holt, Everett Reimer, and Paolo Freire, these authors call for radical school reform. Bowles has questioned whether education has been of any real economic benefit to minority people, showing that the relative incomes of blacks declined even when the absolute incomes improved. He has also been very critical of the way James Coleman analyzed his data in the Coleman Report. Like Ivan Illich, Bowles and Gintis take an extreme antischool position. They do not think the schools can be reformed without drastic alteration of the underlying social and economic forces.

George Dennison.   George Dennison established the first "street school," an alternative educational program for minority children from low-income families on New York's Lower East Side. Half of his students came from public schools in which they had been given labels such as "severe learning and behavior problems." In his 1969 *The Lives of Children,* Dennison tells about his experiences with these children, including the violence and obscenity inherent in the daily routines of the pupils. Relating his work with disturbed children to the views of A. S. Neill, John Dewey, Paul Goodman, and Leo Tolstoy, Dennison discusses the needs of those who have been cast off by society or parents. His writings have gained the attention of educators and social reformers sensitive to the depth of individual problems that plague the lives and experiences of many children in the modern world.

John Holt.   An experienced teacher on both the elementary and secondary levels, Holt began expressing himself to other educators in 1964 when he wrote *How Children Fail*. He urged teachers to focus on children and their individual needs rather than on the formal ingestion of a rigid curriculum. Calling attention to the ominous relationship between the fear and expectation of failing and actual failure, Holt showed how teachers often contribute to a self-fulfilling prophecy. He supported a child-centered approach in which each pupil can develop his or her own activities and abilities at his or her own speed. In two other books, *What Do I Do Monday?* (1970) and *Freedom and Beyond* (1972), Holt offered practical suggestions to teachers about how to keep interest alive in schools and what can be done to encourage each student to reach his or her maximum potential.

Ivan Illich.   Any educator who has not heard of Ivan Illich is isolated indeed! In *Deschooling Society* (1971), Illich not only denounced compulsory education but also called upon modern nations like the United States to give up their public systems of education. Illich's background is somewhat different from that of most other educational critics. He was a Catholic priest in New York City, Puerto Rico, and South America until he resigned in 1961 to found the Intercultural Center for Documentation in Cuernavaca, Mexico. As a result of his experiences in Latin America, Illich concluded that mass education has detrimental effects upon poor people. For example, he says that to go to school in Mexico for two or three years and then drop out is worse than not attending school at all. Dropping out makes one a failure in the eyes of society, and the learning gained probably is of no use to a poor laboring man.

Illich believes that the right of the individual to learn is actually hindered by compulsory attendance and mass education. Schools are used as screening devices to sift out the gifted few or justify the existence of high schools and colleges for the children of the wealthy and powerful. Illich thinks it is not feasible to create schools that will actually meet the educational needs of the masses. Education is the responsibility of society and must not be delegated to schools that are operated by governments for the benefit of the few. He contends that the disadvantaged would have a better chance if the bond between education and schooling were completely severed. By deschooling society, there would no longer be power or prestige associated with staying in school a long time or acquiring a degree.

Probably no one, including Illich, really expects that the United States will abandon its public schools. His criticism is important because it calls attention to the fact that education may benefit one class of society at the expense of others and that the values fostered by public schools are not necessarily those of greatest use for the survival of the individual and the well-being of the people.

Herbert Kohl.   As a result of his first teaching experience with black sixth graders in East Harlem, Herbert Kohl wrote *36 Children* (1967); it tells about how he created a curriculum from his students' experiences and his own imagination. Holding that the standard school curriculum prevents communication between teacher and student, Kohl claimed success in combining creativity and relevant experiences with academic achievement. A more recent book, *The Open Classroom,* is presented as a "handbook for teachers who want to work in an open environment." Kohl has become a leader among teachers and parents who want to foster better community participation in education, and he has worked with various systems in the creation of alternative schools. *The Discipline of Hope: Learning from a Lifetime of Teaching* (2000) focuses on how every child can learn and how teachers need to find creative ways to facilitate learning.

Jonathan Kozol.   Unlike Kohl, Jonathan Kozol was dismissed as a substitute teacher in a Boston elementary school for deviation from the established curriculum. Concerned about his sincere efforts to communicate with lower-class black students, Kozol shocked the nation with his book *Death at an Early Age: The Destruction of the Hearts and Minds of Negro Children in the Boston Public Schools* (1967). More than a critic of school programs, Kozol is politically sensitive to problems such as minority rights, bureaucratic manipulation by school boards, and the insensitivity of the public to the needs of some groups of children. In 1972, he wrote *Free Schools* and became interested in the efforts to develop meaningful learning programs for children with backgrounds culturally different from those of the majority. Kozol currently writes for educational journals and gives speeches, such as his highly publicized 1973 NEA Convention speech that called attention to the inadequate programs he sees in American schools.

Kozol produced another very strong criticism of education in his 1985 book entitled *Illiterate America*. In it, he states that 25 million Americans cannot read the front page of a newspaper or the poison warnings on a can of pesticide and that another 35 million people in this nation read below the level necessary for success in society. Kozol finds that the United States ranks forty-ninth among the 158 member nations of the United Nations in literacy. He makes a passionate call for educational reform at all levels. In *Savage Inequalities: Children in America's Schools* (1992), Kozol reported on the at-risk school populations in inner cities and found the gap widening between the have and have-not populations. In *Amazing Grace, the Lives of Children and the Conscience of a Nation,* (1996) and *Ordinary Resurrections, Children in the Years of Hope* (2000), Kozol explores the world of poverty, crime, and discrimination through the heart, soul, eyes, and words of children. His narration through the words of children in at-risk communities provides a ray of hope for the future in areas of poverty created by greed, neglect, racism, and expedience.

Theodore Roszak.   It may be fairly said that Theodore Roszak is spokesman for the counterculture that pugnaciously criticizes establishment ways of conducting society and its agencies. Roszak came to the attention of the public with *The Making of a Counter Culture* (1969), *Where the Wastelands End* (1972), and *A Man for Tomorrow's World* (1970). A history professor, Roszak has had a considerable effect on curriculum development and has addressed groups such as the Association for Supervision and Curriculum Development. He totally rejects compulsory education, which he considers "a product of the rigid social orthodoxy of industrial society." *The Cult of Information* (1994) analyzes the data glut of a culture of computer technology that may obscure basic questions of justice. He represents a considerable number of social critics who are disenchanted with modern industrial society and its institutions. Roszak advised students to escape from the restrictions and conformity of modern public schools.

Charles Silberman.   Charles Silberman is among those educational critics who do not take extreme positions but promote their own ideas while taking issue with both existing school practices and the views of other critics. Silberman believes the school system has some merit. At the same time he opposes the views of those who wish to eliminate schools entirely and those who advocate a child-centered theme. Silberman believes that there is a need for centrality of purpose and a clear educational philosophy in American schools. He attributes failure in recent curriculum reform movements to the fact that educators have not understood the issues that perplexed the progressive education movement or the problems of educating the child for the modern society. Like Paul Goodman, Silberman is an established journalist and a respected scholar. *Crisis in the Classroom* is the best-known statement of his educational criticism, and it has been widely read since its publication in 1970. Both Silberman and Kozol warn educators to be wary of past errors. They suggest that we use history as a guide to sift through past experience and eliminate what is obsolete and ineffective and retain what is beneficial.

Gerald W. Bracey, the Sandia Report, and David Berliner.

In "Why Can't They Be Like We Were" (1991), Bracey discussed an alternative view of education. He suggested that reform report conclusions about mediocrity and decline, from *A Nation at Risk* forward, were often based on faulty data collection and interpretation. Bracey pointed to ambiguity of terms used in the reform reports and found that various linkages discussed, such as that between education and international competitiveness, were as tenuous as that between education and economic well-being. In "The Third Bracey Report on the Condition of Public Education," Bracey noted that we need to look at the interpretation of the data about schools afresh, freed from the chronic perception that schools have failed.

In "Perspectives on Education in America," Robert Huelskamp summarized the findings of a 1991 national study of education by the Strategic Studies Center, Sandia National Laboratories. He reported surprising results that indicated that on nearly every measure investigated there were steady or slightly improving trends. Areas for educational improvement were identified: the need for national agreement on essential changes plus strong leadership to make such modifications; the continuing need to improve the performance of minority, urban, and immigrant students; efforts to enhance the status of elementary and secondary schools; and, most importantly, the need to upgrade the quality of the data available on education.

The Bracey and Sandia research efforts suggest that many reform reports were issued without careful analysis of available data on education. Authors of both reports looked for data to support success stories in school achievement that were contrary to popular literature. In "The Third Bracey Report on the Condition of Public Education" (1993), Bracey reiterated his earlier conclusion that although there are horrific challenges facing American schools, we need to interpret the data more objectively, disregarding the belief that schools have failed. "The Tenth Bracey Report on the Condition of Public Education" (2000) analyzed standards and high-stakes testing in historical perspective through the intervening years and continued to find methodological flaws in school research. Bracey found that testing and standards imposed by legislatures, boards, and governors fail to measure what teachers teach. In addition, Bracey found widespread manipulation of test scores including setting low standards to be met and choosing low reading difficulty questions. Some states focused on intense remediation for low-scoring students and steering students to GED programs and special education to avoid having to report their test results. Bracey noted that in some cases claims of significant improvement in test scores are based on mirages, smoke, and mirrors. In a humorous note, Bracey found that the focus on higher standards has led to an explosion in pediatric practice due to heavy student backpacks. The positive and negative aspects of media educational reporting are also explored. Some Goals 2000 were seen as unrealistic; others required more resources than were made available.

In *The Manufactured Crisis,* Berliner refutes critics of American education through research demonstrating the effectiveness of the nation's education effort when reviewed in terms of the egalitarian mission to serve all students regardless of social or economic backgrounds. In *The Manufactured Crisis: Myths, Fraud and the Attack on America's Public Schools* (1995), Berliner and Biddle find that American public school students are doing as well or slightly better on standardized tests than in the past and that student intelligence is steady or rising slowly regardless of increased enrollment.

He noted that critics railing against increased educational costs due to bureaucracy were wrong. Higher costs are due to expanding services for special needs students and keeping schools open. America's schools are not generating unproductive workers but rather its workforce leads the world in productivity and the nation has a surplus of educated and technically able workers. In reviewing Bracey, Sandia, and Berliner's work, one cannot help but find Sissela Bok's book *Lying: Moral Choice in Public and Private Life* a timely resource illustrating how misinformation is disseminated as part of public policy. All authors cited however find that schools and educators are continually challenged by poverty pockets, lack of parental involvement, underachievers, student motivation, and growing numbers of English as a second language students.

David Mathews.   In *Is There a Public for Public Schools,* Mathews, president of the Kettering Foundation, finds a feeling of a lack of ownership in public schools by community members. In "The Lack of a Public for Public Schools" (1997), Mathews calls for rewriting a compact with the public through which a diverse array of citizens' voices can be heard. According to Mathews, since public schools have lost their legitimacy, alternatives such as vouchers, charter schools (currently Manno and his colleagues report that there are over 1,700 charter schools in operation in thirty-six states and the District of Columbia enrolling over 350,000 students), home schools, private schools, and site-based management systems have developed. Rather than emphasizing test scores, Mathews calls for engaging the public in a dialogue for helping communities decide what serves their interests. Colonial New England had town meetings in which members of the townships could air their concerns about schooling and education. A renewal of partnerships for active and reflective listening among all populaces involved in education at all levels is required. Mathews believes that a genuine public voice should be found to offset the voices of special interests, each one convinced that its concerns are separate from the concerns of others.

Over a decade ago, at a Southern Futures Society meeting, Mathews discussed a fragmented society whose governmental leaders faced gridlock while special interest groups pushed their own agendas. Mathews renewed a call for a sense of shared purpose and direction. He stated that education in its broadest sense is the key to shaping the future in positive directions.

Critics with Other Viewpoints.   Although no complete enumeration of modern educational critics is possible here, some of those with special interests or points of view should be mentioned. Sylvia Ashton-Warner, in *Teacher* (1963) and *Spearpoint: Teacher in America* (1972), is concerned with the meaning of equality and authority in education. Joseph Featherstone's *Schools Where Children Learn* (1971) warns about "faddishness" and raises the question of whether schools can build a more equal society. The problem of relevance is of concern to George Leonard in *Education and Ecstasy. Teaching as a Subversive Activity* by Neil Postman and Charles Weingartner deals with relevance and with communication. William Glasser's *Schools Without Failure* and Sunny Decker's *An Empty Spoon* are other examples of the same theme. Glasser's *The Quality School: Managing Students Without Coercion* (1998) stresses the need for a humane people-centered approach to all aspects of education in an age of conflict. Alfie Kohn in *The Schools Our Children Deserve: Moving Beyond Traditional Classrooms* and *Tougher Standards* (2000) discusses the excesses of a competitive high-stakes testing school environment and its effect on the quality of the learning environment. He finds schools are doing much better than they are given credit for and negative reporting tends to feed on itself.

Those who claim the schools have not been interested in humanistic psychology include Abraham Maslow and Carl Rogers. Another psychologist, Jerome S. Bruner, believes that too much emphasis has been placed upon the structure of knowledge within the disciplines and not enough concern has been given to structure in the context of learning and problem solving. Jean Piaget holds that learning takes place at various levels or stages of development that depend upon both maturation and experience. He believes that too little attention has been given to the process of learning and too much to the content.

The wide range of criticisms of American education is not surprising in a rapidly changing, pluralistic, dynamic, and democratic culture. Some critics operate from a scholarly base within the profession, some represent philosophical causes, some are concerned about the role of the school in social change, and others attack education for its support of social values. As long as education is not an exact science and the American society is dynamic and open, criticism may be expected to continue. The problem for the professional educator is understanding exactly what the critics are saying and selecting the best ideas from a host of suggested alternatives.

The School as Agency for Social Action. The role of the school in social change is a philosophical issue, as Theodore Brameld and his critics are quick to point out. In recent years, so many programs have developed that seem to use education as a social institution for cultural change that the problem of purpose and function of schools has received new attention.

As James S. Coleman and Edgar Z. Friedenberg have insisted, demands and challenges for the adolescent members of modern society are very great. The impact of social change on the adolescent, pressures on middle-class teenagers, and the problem of youth values in an open society are major concerns for schools. Superimposed on these concerns are the special problems of low-income students, the children of the urban poor, and the youth from African-American, Native-American, or Latino families. These students have more than their share of educational difficulties and are more apt to drop out of school. Various attempts to compensate for cultural disadvantages and meet the needs of all children and adolescents have been tried. Rod Paige, former school superintendent of Houston public schools and Bush administration education secretary, believes in making intense efforts to raise achievement levels of all children and leave no child behind.

Ever since the Wechsler Scales for measuring adult intelligence were invented and the Army Alpha and Beta tests were given in World War I, mass testing to establish norms has been used in the United States. Many educators fear that both individual and group intelligence tests are misused in schools, but the first great objection to grouping or categorizing students by test scores came from those who charged cultural bias. It was argued that merely being from a middle-class white environment gave students an unfair advantage on instruments for measuring ability. Efforts to construct culture-fair tests were followed by attempts to remove racism and sexism from textbooks. Most American public school textbooks before 1960 made black and other minority people "invisible" and fostered definite sex roles for youngsters.

Project Head Start, Vista, Job Corps, Talent Search, Teacher Corps, and Upward Bound are federally funded projects to help disadvantaged students. Job Corps centers were established to teach vocational skills to high school dropouts. Upward Bound attempted to prepare disadvantaged youth for success in college. Other programs used federal funds for more teachers, buildings, and equipment in areas with concentrations of low-income or minority children.

The issue of federal projects is still undecided. Supporters of the programs say that the disadvantaged as a result of their development made gains and that no harm was done to other students. They call for more money and an extension of the programs on all levels. Others claim that the schools should not be involved in attempts to equalize differences or to change society through social action programs. The Coleman Report, Illich's *Deschooling Society,* and the work of Christopher Jenks indicate that these programs made very little lasting difference. Illich does not believe that it is possible for government-sponsored school programs to compensate for cultural differences. The George W. Bush administration is focusing on flexibility in providing states and districts with more freedom in how federal funds are spent to encourage better student performance, according to *Education Week*'s Erik Robelen. He further reported on Bush's plan for creating new programs for reading, charter schools, mathematics, and science education, coupled with new demands including annual testing in grades three through eight. Continued efforts to increase funding for a variety of programs for at-risk children will be undertaken to ensure equal access. Increased remedial assistance through state and federal funding is also being sought.

Superimposed upon the issues concerning the role of the government in aiding the culturally different were more emotional ones concerning race, heredity, and intelligence. In 1969, psychologist Arthur Jensen published an article in the *Harvard Educational Review* that suggested that black students average about fifteen points below whites on IQ tests. The writings of William Shockley also supported an inferior position for blacks. Jensen tried to point out that his data were not a basis for judging the intellectual capacity of any individual, but there were strong criticisms of his work. Charges of racism and the use of Jensen's studies to prove that integration must fail only further clouded the issue. Authors on both sides allowed their emotions to rule their logic, and controversial articles continue to appear in the early 2000s.

Both the number of critics and the depth of concern they expressed increased dramatically in the 1980s. The political and religious "new right" expresses an increasingly popular position. It eschews any concern for developing moral autonomy in children and supports the teaching of what its supporters deem to be right. People of this persuasion have formed groups to purge the schools of "humanist" books and to restrict the teaching of sex education and values clarification. In practice, these conservative moralists defend educational programs that they believe will create moral character, patriotism, strict discipline, deference to authority, and opposition to secular humanism. They have no problem with the idea that schools should indoctrinate "truth" and ethical behavior patterns in children. They see the current schools corrupted with humanistic values and liberalism and often support home schooling, vouchers, and charter schools.

Another set of critics emerged with the 1983 and 1984 national reports that were critical of education. Many of these reports came from fields such as business, engineering, economics, and government. A number of critics offered their own plans for achieving excellence in education. Intense pressure is being placed on educators to demonstrate improved academic achievement in all the states. A primary political and social issue in the 2000s is improved school performance. While criticism of public schools continues, Linda Jacobson in *Education Week* noted areas of progress. Clinton's "early learning fund" was put into effect quietly as part of the 2001 federal budget passed by Congress. Local governments and community leaders can apply for funding of parenting programs, literacy promotion, and improved access to early childhood programs for children with special needs. The 2001 budget also provided for financial aid loan forgiveness for child-care providers, early childhood programs for high poverty areas, as well as child-care assistance for low-income families. Chapter 9 deals with the movement toward excellence, including the plans of critics like Boyer, Goodlad, Sizer, and Adler.

ASSESSMENT AND ACCOUNTABILITY

The idea that schools and educators should be responsible for their actions is not new in American education. Annual reports of Horace Mann and the journal articles of Henry Barnard carried criticisms of inadequate or mistaken pedagogical efforts. The means by which teachers are trained has been under fire since the development of normal schools and university departments of education. As early as 1898, the American Association of Manufacturers charged the schools with "repressive brain stuffing," "dulling the intellect," and failing to provide youth with the skills needed to enter the job market. The business community ever since has taken issue with educators over the curriculum and the degree of concentration on courses needed for preparing an effective workforce. Educators have also attacked each other, as in the rejection of the Herbartian lock-step methods by the progressives and the subsequent rejection of the progressive program by William Bagley and the essentialists. Perhaps the main difference between the past and the present is that today attacks are more widespread and rapid, due to modern communications and the mass media.

American public schools experience periods of ebb and flow both in the interest expressed by the public and in public pressure. Following 1970, criticism of schools and teaching was linked to demands for accountability. The basic concept comes from the field of management, and it is intended to hold someone responsible for performing according to terms previously agreed upon. While serving as Secretary of Defense, Robert McNamara brought the unrelenting evaluative practices of business to government through his program planning and budgeting system. In education, the founding of the accountability movement is usually credited to the works of Leon Lessinger (*Every Kid a Winner: Accountability in Education,* 1970).

The sudden popularity of the concept of accountability can be traced to growing dissatisfaction with the quality of schools, a feeling that educators were closing ranks against public criticism, and the ever-increasing pressure for more tax dollars to finance education. Many educators have been quite negative about accountability, and the issues surrounding it continue to be argued in the twenty-first century. Total Quality Management and Effective Schools were popular themes in the mid-1990s, as the influence of business and industry efforts toward continuous product improvement as well as customer satisfaction were emphasized in education. Typical of the popular books on effective schools through empowerment was William Byham's *Zapp In Education,* 1992.

As a theoretical concept, few would quarrel with accountability. Teachers obviously need to be responsible for what they do, and the educational profession does not object to evaluation. However, teachers do object to the idea that they are guilty of something and must be punished and to the negative presumption that legislation is needed to make them do their jobs. More significant, questions occur to which no one seems to have the answers. Who is accountable? If the student fails to learn, is that always to be blamed on the teacher and not on the student or the parents? There is massive evidence that schools are responsible for only a part of the child's learning and teachers for an even smaller part. For what are teachers accountable? Information and skills that can be examined on tests surely do not represent total learning. Incidental, collateral, and attitudinal learnings are not capable of being organized into objective sequences and are hard to test. Most accountability tests measure only a very limited part of what the student actually learns. John Goodlad pointed out that timeworn instruments of assessment and archaic criteria for evaluation are poor means for measuring pupil achievement. To whom are educators accountable? The answer to this would seem to be the clients (students, parents, and employers), but if teachers have had no role in determining educational policy, accountability is unfair. Often state or federal officials determine the criteria for accountability with no input from the local community. If teachers are treated as mere employees and not consulted about issues or practices in the schools, they can hardly be held accountable as professionals.

The complexity of teaching is seldom fully understood by those seeking performance accountability. Student language deficiencies, violence, variable motivation, discipline, dysfunctional behavior, harassment, and discrimination are part of the culture of schools in the 2000s as was true in the 1990s. Although there have always been these challenges in our educational history, the degree of severity of such issues is much greater now.

In the past, reputations of teachers were built on some estimate of what constituted "good" teacher behavior. Keeping order in the classroom and grading each student fairly were examples of such behavior. In recent years, the measure of good teaching has shifted to the ability of the teacher to produce specific behavioral changes in learners. California's Stull Act requires that the competence of teachers be measured at least in part by the performance of students. The implication is that when students do not learn, for whatever reason, the fault is to be placed on certified personnel. Some critics see this idea as analogous to the ancient practice of paying physicians only if the patient recovers. Accountability has also been tested in the courts. In 1976, a student who had been allowed to graduate from high school, although he was unable to read at sixth-grade level, sued the San Francisco Unified School District. Lawyers for the plaintiff argued that the school personnel were negligent in failing to detect and correct his learning problem. In *Donohue v. Copiague* (1979), a student charged a New York school with failure to cope with his learning disabilities. The plaintiffs were not successful in these two cases, but the idea of holding teachers accountable to society for the quality and quantity of educational results has clearly been established. Courts in New York and Iowa have reaffirmed that teachers cannot be held liable for poor student performance, but the public demand for accountability has not diminished. McCarthy and Cambron-McCabe (1992) found that although no educational malpractice claim has yet been successful, some courts have found instances in which plaintiffs might recover damages in an instructional tort action. In general, courts have been loathe to interfere with the administration of public schools.

In the 1970s, many states passed laws for accountability. Some require the assessment of students on specific tests; others are broad and vague. Seven states involved in the Cooperative Accountability Project require some sort of evaluation, but specific measures are determined locally. Some educators fear that business-industrial models of accountability threaten teachers with punitive and often inoperable directives. Others see the schools becoming more rigid and authoritarian, with emphasis placed on improvement of test performance and nothing else. Sociologist Robert Havinghurst cautions against a simple form of accountability that makes teachers totally responsible while taking no account of other forces in the learning environment. Both the NEA and the National Commission on Teacher Education and Professional Standards have called accountability unprofessional, inhumane, and arbitrary unless the profession develops the standards and methods of measurement itself. These organizations are especially opposed to laws that require the application of business and commercial instruments to education. The American Federation of Teachers (AFT) has taken an even stronger stand, linking accountability laws to "school-haters" who are looking for scapegoats to blame for social failures. Both organizations support high standards and excellence in education. Nevertheless, today most states require some form of assessment and accountability for public schools. The most common means of assessment is a standardized achievement test, and failure often results in the loss of state funds. There is a trend toward measuring and publishing public school achievement results; this trend motivates teachers to teach "to the test."

The Learning First Alliance—comprised of a number of organizations including the National PTA, American Association of School Administrators, American Federation of Teachers, and American Association of Colleges of Teacher Education, among others—issued a report in 2001 calling for mid-course corrections on standards and accountability. The report raises questions about how states and school districts are implementing standards and accountability and concluded that in any large-scale effort to improve a complex system, there must be continuous reviews of progress and unintended consequences. There are dangers of excessive reliance on standardized test scores especially for at-risk students. Student appraisal should use a variety of relevant information about student achievement.

Competency Tests for Teachers.

Along with accountability, the public has become concerned with weeding out teachers who are poorly prepared or incompetent. Colleges of education often require standardized test assessment for certification. These tests provide external evidence of skills and knowledge of subject matter and are used with other performance data for teacher certification. Prior to 1978, when Florida passed a bill requiring a comprehensive written examination before certification, three states required beginning teachers to pass the National Teacher Examination (NTE) (currently the Educational Testing Services Praxis Series). Georgia, New York, Oklahoma, and Wisconsin had plans for some form of competency testing by 1981, and several other states were considering such requirements. After 1978 when the Supreme Court ruled that the NTE was not discriminatory (although more black teachers than white failed it), other states began to use it. It seems likely that some form of minimum competency test will be required for all beginning teachers in the nation in the near future.

Some school districts administer their own tests to new teachers before hiring them. The Dallas Independent School District had high failure rates (about 50 percent) when tenth-grade verbal and quantitative ability tests were given as a prerequisite to teaching. This alarming rate has done little to enhance the public view of institutions that train teachers. It should be pointed out, however, that these tests measure knowledge of subject matter and not skills in teaching. If colleges and universities are to be held accountable, the academic departments that teach mathematics and geography are more vulnerable than colleges or departments of education. Although superior knowledge of subject matter does not necessarily make a superior teacher, the public has a right to demand that teachers are minimally competent in basic subjects.

President Sandra Feldman of the American Federation of Teachers (AFT) favors entry-level testing of teacher candidates on the grounds that an improved profession will result. She also calls for national standards for teacher tests. Both the AFT and the NEA oppose tests for teachers who are already in service. There is a national trend toward upgrading and improving standards for teachers at all educational levels. Most states require some form of teacher testing at the entry level. Ohio has a licensing plan to require all new teachers to be evaluated on their performance as well as on courses they take and scores on paper-and-pencil tests. Their on-the-job performance will be based on interviews and observations of their instruction (Archer and Blair, 2001). Test pressures have led to some instances of teachers being dismissed for cheating on tests.

Accountability tests are inadequate if they measure only limited aspects of education such as skill in mathematics, and more comprehensive tests are difficult to construct. It has not been determined if tests should be criterion-referenced, norm-referenced, or both. Teacher candidates are now required to pass minimum competency tests in many states before they can be certified. There are questions about the effectiveness of such tests in predicting success in the classroom and some concerns about the effect on the projected future shortage of teachers. With a record public school enrollment of more than 50 million in 2002, the demand for teachers could well exceed the supply. Some states already have a teacher shortage and are using a variety of perks to recruit them including bonuses, housing allowances, and continuing efforts to increase salaries.

In the 2000s, many communities throughout the nation have overcrowded classes. In Florida, many classes have over thirty pupils, and there is a shortage of school facilities. In some instances, major corporations have built school buildings on their grounds to serve their employees and the surrounding community elementary-age children. Partnerships are being formed with communities, businesses, and service organizations to purchase needed computers and printers. Florida's school districts have been expanding school facilities and building new schools to serve a growing student population. In Palm Beach County fifty-four schools were at more than 120 percent of their capacity in the spring of 2001, but major school expansion programs were under way to alleviate the congestion. Meanwhile portable classrooms are used to house the influx of students due to migration from other counties, states, and countries.

The Carnegie Foundation in 1987 founded the National Board for Professional Teacher Standards. Chaired by Governor James B. Hunt of North Carolina the organization provides national teacher certification through portfolios developed by teachers and attendance at one of 200 assessment centers nationwide. The program is designed to improve teacher competency. The first teachers to receive certificates of advanced competency completed the program in 1995. Assessment includes teacher commitment to students and student learning, knowledge of subject matter, managing and monitoring student learning, thinking systematically about their practice, and learning from experience and service as members of a learning community. Teachers provide videos of their teaching and participate in two days of performance-based assessment. By 2001 over a thousand teachers were participating in the program, and state departments of education as in Florida were issuing Professional Competencies for Teachers of the Twenty-First Century. Topics included in the Florida guidelines were assessment, communication, continuous improvement, critical thinking, diversity, ethics, human development and learning, knowledge of subject matter, learning environments, planning, the role of the teacher, and technology.

Curriculum Concerns.   The entire body of subjects or courses offered in the program of a school is the curriculum. Historically, one of the best ways to understand what a school system tried to accomplish is to study its curriculum. District schools in colonial New England taught religion, reading, and writing; the Latin grammar schools concentrated on Latin, Greek, and theology. The use of a core curriculum and the involvement of students in the selection of courses from a wide spectrum of possibilities were characteristic of progressive schools. In the 1950s, *Sputnik* and the NDEA produced a discipline-centered curriculum stressing science, mathematics, and foreign languages. With the civil rights movement and a demand for equal educational opportunity came a child-centered program with emphasis placed on ethical, social, and multicultural subjects. This program was followed by a "back to basics" movement with more formalized instruction and strict accountability. Within a period of only thirty years, popularity has shifted from Deweyan progressives to strict academicians to social reconstructionists to conservative essentialists. The future promises to be filled with conflicting demands for different curricular choices.

While the debate goes on, teachers and administrators are faced with making curriculum choices and building appropriate programs. Given some basic assumptions about purposes, it is possible to develop a logical and consistent curriculum. In the past, such tasks were undertaken by the central administration or by local or state boards, but now many schools and individual teachers have considerable freedom in curriculum matters. The selection of materials and the stress placed upon certain concepts or examples have a profound effect on the school curriculum. A teacher who feels that ecology should be included in the work of the student can provide ecological materials in a variety of related subjects ranging from biology to civics.

A vast body of literature has grown up around the problem of curriculum development. Curriculum choices can never be made in isolation, and the needs and wishes of the public must always be weighed against the teacher's perception of the needs of the child.

Since the mid-1960s, two schools of thought have dominated the controversy over curriculum organization and content. One of these is the free, open, child-centered, humanistic, and socially oriented movement. The theory behind this movement is grounded in the work of John Dewey, A. S. Neill, the social reconstructionists, and humanistic-existential authors. The other school of thought calls for standardized subject matter, no-nonsense basic education, high academic standards, and discipline-oriented schools. The philosophical foundation for this position reaches back to Plato and has been supported by twentieth-century perennialists and essentialists.

Modern spokespeople for the first movement include Edgar Friedenberg, Paul Goodman, John Holt, Herbert Kohl, and Charles Silberman. They oppose the conformity and docility characteristic of the subject-centered school. Accusing traditional schools of indifference to social issues and a meaningless curriculum, these authors demand relevant programs geared to the actual needs and desires of students. For them, the content of the curriculum is less important than the process used and the degree to which the learner is able to relate to the school activities. This means that much of the content of the curriculum must be taken from experiences in the life of the student. The school should deal with social issues, materials drawn from the mass media, and problems of the local community. Sex education and drug education are included in the curriculum along with human relations and programs designed to help students understand the racially and culturally different. Calling for free and open education, these authors emphasize the development of self-concept, problem solving, the ability to make reasonable choices, and humanistic attitudes. They understand the need for basic skills like reading, but they have no interest in filling the mind of the student with lots of facts or in "mastering" specific subjects. They wish to foster a positive attitude toward learning and practical skills for dealing with other people and the outside world.

Holding the opposite position are authors like Jacques Barzun, Arthur Bestor, Mortimer Adler, Robert Hutchins, and James Koerner. Similar to the belief expressed by James Conant and Admiral Rickover after *Sputnik*, their point of view is that the schools must concentrate on producing subject matter experts and superior scholars to lead the technological society. Koerner, as spokesperson for the Council for Basic Education, opposes the "soft" pedagogy of progressive education and demands a return to "solid" academic subjects. The council argues against student input into the curriculum, saying that the adults know best what children should study. This is also the position of Hutchins, who wants a curriculum composed of those aspects of the culture that have been subjected to the greatest amount of sophistication and refinement (the classics, mathematics, and science). Bestor believes that the function of the school is the teaching of intellectual disciplines, not teaching about current social problems or different cultural groups. This group opposes social engineering in education and bending the curriculum to make it relevant to the student.

By 1980, the Council for Basic Education and the "back to basics" movement had gained vast public support, partly from parents who are disappointed with the level of information and skills learned by their children in public schools and partly from the "moral majority," who question some of the assumptions of an open, humanistic, child-centered, life-adjustment program. The Council for Basic Education and Education Planet Web sites provide information on national standards guidelines for curriulum. In calling for a return to fundamentals and a curriculum of basic studies, Barzun has said, "Nonsense is at the heart of those proposals that would replace definable subject matter with vague activities copied from life or with courses organized around problems or attitudes." In our twenty-first century, advocates of the normal curve of probability based on standardized test scores are supporting school districts in requiring students with low test scores to repeat grade levels. Others are supportive of authentic assessment or a variety of measures of achievement including portfolios and projects chosen by students. The former see high test scores as indicative of success in a competitive environment; the latter see them as lowering self-esteem and self-worth of students who are not good test takers and as culturally biased.

Curriculum Innovations and Methods.
A number of emergent trends have provided persuasive arguments to broaden the public school curriculum. It is not the case that all schools have adopted new subjects, but sufficient demand has been expressed to make new subjects important in the field of curriculum development.

New curriculum trends reflect an interest in interdisciplinary approaches to schooling as well as a thrust toward individualization and relevance.

❑   Career education is an expression of discontent with the old division between vocational and academic programs. With emphasis on the functional value of career planning for all students, this program claims to be part of general education. On the theory that almost all students will enter some sort of work in the future, career education emphasizes occupational training, career information and guidance, and the involvement of business and community groups. The aim is to make career education available to all students and not just to those in vocational or industrial programs. Tech-prep and work-study programs link school and business.

❑   Consumer education is now part of the social studies curriculum in many schools. The pressures of inflation and the need of all people to make wise choices in purchasing make consumer education valuable. Courses are often included as part of economics or career education, but sometimes consumer education is taught as a separate course.

❑   Environmental education reflects a public concern with energy, pollution, ecology, and depletion of natural resources. Population pressures on the natural environment have created a demand for better understanding of environmental issues. Most schools attempt to build environmental content into standard courses in geography and the sciences. Many of these concerns are multicultural ones and have created a new demand for global education.

❑   Ethnic and multicultural educational offerings have grown rapidly since the "black revolution" and the emergence of interest in ethnic identity. Some states require schools to include courses in ethnic studies or cultural pluralism, and most have policy statements on the subject. The need for identity and recognition of minorities and ethnic groups is clear. Ethnic education is designed to enhance self-esteem of culturally different students and to promote understanding by majority students.

❑   Education dealing with drug and alcohol abuse is an expanding program. Because of the widespread problem of abuse and addiction, public demand for such education has been strong. Coordinated programs with law enforcement agencies, community health projects, and former drug abusers are often found. The major criticism of these programs comes from those who do not feel that they are well taught and effective. The transfer of the former education secretary, William Bennett, to the position of chief drug control officer in the Bush administration and fear of the AIDS virus among drug abusers gave new support to this program in schools.

❑   Sex education was placed in the school curriculum because of high rates of illegitimacy, venereal disease among students, the national increase in divorce, and massive evidence that students are sexually active. The sensitive nature of the subject and the belief by many that the school has no business dealing with matters of sex have created considerable controversy over this subject. Yet the evidence is clear that students are not getting appropriate information about sex from their parents, religious institutions, or peers. The number of unwed teenage mothers is increasing at an alarming rate, and very few sexually active students use contraceptives. The traditional units on reproduction in biology classes are hopelessly inadequate and now are supplemented with programs on dating, marriage, parenthood, child care, health, and social responsibility. Expanded sex education classes and programs are addressing the problem more adequately in the 2000s. Sexual abuse and harassment are dealt with through policy handbooks, lectures, and systems for defining inappropriate behavior. Procedures are provided for reporting incidents to authorities as well as maintaining confidentiality. All states have reporting procedures for teachers who suspect a child has been physically, emotionally, or sexually abused.

❑ Character education, conflict resolution, and partnerships between public schools and universities, public schools and the community, and public schools and businesses are being developed. Conflict resolution programs designed to deal with student conflicts and preserve a safe school environment are expanding in public schools. Character education programs are in operation in a growing number of public elementary and secondary schools.

❑ Authentic assessment was explored to improve the quality of student projects, enhance communication between teachers and students, encourage students to engage in discovery learning on an individual basis, and bring theory into practice. In *The Culture of Education* (1996), Jerome S. Bruner states that reform begins when one focuses on how learning takes place and how children are acculturated into society. He believes we need to move toward how we interpret and understand the ambiguities we face in life and utilize a collaborative school culture. Bruner stresses holistic learning to more effectively relate school to community. Another way of enhancing student assessment is looping, or having the same teacher stay with students two or more years and then start over again with another group. It is being implemented in a number of school systems.

❑ Programs are assisting teachers in learning how to observe for characteristics of behavioral dysfunction in students, and teachers are encouraging students to report on others who make threats of violence. Law enforcement agency profiles to identify students with violent aggressive behavior potential are being implemented in some school systems, along with peace and aggression-control curriculum to address student violence.

❑ School programs are being designed to address bullying. It has been estimated that over 160,000 students are afraid to go to school due to fear of harm from bullies. Helping administrators, teachers, and children develop strategies for dealing with bullying and increasing parental involvement in the education of their children by assisting them in dealing with behavioral aggressiveness are goals of these programs.

❑   Service learning is explored as a hands-on experience in using schools as an agency for social action. As part of the curriculum, service learning engages students in networking, outreach, and becoming contributing members of society as was noted earlier in the 1918 Cardinal Principles of Secondary Education.

Although not strictly adding to the curriculum, numerous modifications have been undertaken that alter certain subjects. Courses in mathematics have been changed to allow for metric conversion. Although using the metric system is voluntary, it is expected that mathematical skill in metrics will be needed in the future. Handheld calculators are now part of the equipment of many students and are as common as the slates of the nineteenth century. Teachers have had to adjust to giving less time to practice in manual calculation and more to problems in which electronic calculators are used. Computers are rapidly becoming available in classrooms across the nation. Language and techniques for using microcomputers are included in many courses in science and mathematics at all levels. Students are introduced to computers in kindergarten and have basic computer skills by the time they complete first grade. In Arkansas and many other states, teachers and administrators utilize computers to record daily school attendance and other reporting requirements as well as for data-based information to improve student achievement. Many reports are sent directly over computer networks to the state departments of education, and schools not meeting state standards are quickly identified and corrective measures implemented.

The curriculum can never be totally divorced from methods. The same subject matter used for a lecture and in discovery learning will produce very different results in students. As a general rule, conservatives are more comfortable with time-honored methods such as lecture, textbook assignments, homework, standardized tests, and library reports. Liberals tend to promote laboratory methods such as discovery learning, problem solving, and inquiry learning. The activity curriculum and the child-centered curriculum are not popular with the "back to basics" movement, although both liberals and conservatives use individualized instruction. Computer-assisted instruction is acceptable to the subject-matter curriculum advocates so long as it does not stray from the subject. Team teaching, block scheduling, and flexible scheduling are most often found in schools with a progressive orientation. The activity-centered curriculum that began with William H. Kilpatrick in the 1920s centers on life experiences such as field trips, group projects, social enterprises, and local centers of interest. Some modern schools support an activity curriculum by working with community groups, social agencies, and governmental institutions. The activity curriculum requires extensive student and community participation. Businesses and communities often "adopt a school" providing funds and volunteers for enrichment programs.

Competency-Based Training and Performance Contracting.   Just as competency-based teacher education has become popular, there is a demand that public school students show evidence of mastery of fundamental subjects. The move to place greater emphasis on reading, writing, and mathematics in elementary schools and on English, science, history, and mathematics in secondary schools sup-

ports minimum competency testing. Some schools have contracted with private firms to produce specific behavior in specified areas of learning. Such performance contracting (as in Texarkana in 1972) has produced disappointing results, but it is clear that the public demands improvement in the informational levels and skills of students. The pros and cons of testing for minimum competency are much the same as the arguments over accountability.

Demands for stress on basic education and an end to "frills" call for testing students to make sure that they have at least the minimum requirements for each course. Those favoring competency testing want an end to social promotion. They believe no student should graduate from high school without demonstrating proficiency in reading, oral and written communication, and mathematics. Part of the interest in private education comes from the belief that public schools are soft on the fundamentals and try to provide a curriculum that is too broad. Project 81 in Pennsylvania is an example of a statewide attempt to ensure that all students meet graduation requirements as measured by competency tests. Florida also is a leader in adopting tests for minimum competency. It is argued that merely accumulating the necessary credits is not enough and that testing for knowledge of course content must be universal. Those favoring minimum competency testing usually stress patriotism, strict discipline, homework, dress codes, and teacher-directed activities. They are against innovations in the curriculum, electives, and such "frills" as sex education. As in the past, so current educators and the courts focus on "in loco parentis" or having teachers and administrators stand in relation to students as do their parents. Maintaining an environment conducive to serious learning is a goal of the public and educators.

Arguments against competency testing are both theoretical and practical. Many educators oppose a narrow curriculum with no electives. They feel that such programs lack interest and relevance to the needs of students. Those who favor problem solving and inquiry as methods doubt that the tests used are adequate. They say that eliminating the new math, linguistic approaches to grammar, and humanistic studies means a return to the nineteenth century. There are also charges that tests are culturally biased against minorities and ethnic groups. Some believe that it is unfair to prevent a student from graduating because the school has been unable to develop his or her skills. Use of standardized test scores for admission to higher education institutions is currently being debated as in California where elimination of SAT scores for college admission is being reexamined. Many argue that the minimum competency tests are directed toward mechanical skills and the memorization of information. They say that competency programs detract from higher skills such as reading for comprehension and logical thinking and that only those things that can be easily tested are given emphasis, making the curriculum rigid, narrow, unimaginative, and dull.

Of course, some schools and teachers use contracting with individual students as an instructional method. Giving a grade for specific performance is most often used in schools with a progressive orientation, but it is not different in concept from requiring specific competency for graduation. Whatever the arguments, minimum competency testing seemed to be winning public support in the early 1980s and is a widespread trend in the 2000s.

Educating the Exceptional Child.   In the eighteenth and nineteenth centuries special education children were often excluded from schools, and even in the early twentieth century parents often kept their disabled children at home. Alexander and Alexander in *American Public School Law* (2001) cited cases in which student behavior resulting from imbecility was grounds for expulsion, and academically disabled students were excluded from regular classes due to the depressing and nauseating effect on teachers and schoolchildren.

In the twentieth century, vast gains were made in the diagnosis and treatment of students with special problems. Starting with programs for children who are deaf or blind, educational institutions developed a variety of effective methods for educating the exceptional child. New facilities for children with disabilities were built, including ramps and rest rooms to accommodate students in wheelchairs. The Rehabilitation Act of 1973 prohibits discrimination by failure to provide access and reasonable facilities for people with disabilities. Obvious physical and mental disabilities have been understood and dealt with in education for many years, although with varying degrees of success. Learning specialists trained to work with various learning disabilities have been in the schools only for a little over a decade. Programs for students with mental retardation and students with trainable mental disabilities were developed to identify and help students with less pronounced difficulties. The gifted and talented were ignored by many schools on the grounds that they would learn in spite of the system. Even today, numerous school systems are just starting special programs for the gifted, and restricted finances remain a challenge in many school districts. In the early 2000s, litigation in the area of special education continues to proliferate. In some cases, students and parents are suing school systems for providing special learning education services to disabled students and excluding regular students from the learning assistance.

A major issue concerning special students centers on Public Law 94-142. In hearings for this law (passed in 1975), it was pointed out that 1.75 million children with disabilities were excluded from school and another 4 million were not receiving full educational services. The law required that each exceptional learner be placed in the least restrictive environment in which his or her educational needs could be satisfactorily served. This meant that children who previously spent their entire in-school time in special classes would be mainstreamed. Children with disabilities must spend at least part of the day in classes with nondisabled students. The intent of Public Law 94-142 was to remove the stigma attached to students with disabilities, to improve social relationships, to provide nondisabled learning models, to allow for a richer and more competitive environment, and to learn to live in the real world outside of the school. Other reasons included allowing more students to be served, providing more cost-effective education, and decentralizing services to reduce transportation costs.

The Individuals with Disabilities Education Act Amendments of 1997 (IDEA) bases the formula for allotments to the states through 2006 on demographics: How many children live in a state, and what percentage of those children are living in poverty? The amendments also seek to ensure that a portion of the IDEA funds are used to provide outreach and technical assistance to historically black colleges and universities and to institutions with a minority enrollment of at least 25 percent.

The 1997 amendments also address the challenge of dealing with children whose violence-prone behavior is identified as part of their disability. Now school personnel can order removal of a child with a disability from the classroom and place him or her in an alternative educational setting for forty-five days, if there is the possibility of injury to the child or others. During this period, with appropriate provision for parental appeal, consideration of moving the child to an alternative educational setting is undertaken. Educational administrators continue to have difficulty interpreting the IDEA act in terms of what special services are to be provided as well as how to fund these programs.

Funding special education is another problem. If it is determined to be in the child's best interests, students have to be provided air transportation to attend. Originally, the federal government was to fund some 40 percent of the costs of these special education programs; however, the federal government's legal contribution decreased to 7 percent, and states and local school districts are required to fund the rest. As Berliner notes in his *Manufactured Crisis,* expenditures for education continue to rise, but most of the funds are allocated for special education. These programs provide a good illustration of how the American educational system continues to reflect an expanded social consciousness. From the early days of the republic, philanthropy has served the nation well. John Harvard gave a library and 300 pounds for Harvard; Horace Mann wrote of the stewardship theory of wealth whereby those who attained wealth had an obligation to provide for others in need. The Bill and Melinda Gates Foundation has provided funds for worthy causes throughout the nation. The Kennedy Foundation provided funds for special education. Peabody College of Vanderbilt was a major recipient of the funding. In 2001 William T. Coleman and his wife Claudia gave $250 million for a cognitive-disabilities center at the University of Colorado. Coleman, founder of BEA Systems, a builder of Internet platforms, saw how a six-years-old niece with physical and mental disabilities responded by using a computer, and he wanted to make a difference in the lives of others in the field of assistive technology.

An Individualized Education Program (IEP) is required for all mainstreamed exceptional children. This is a plan for education cooperatively prepared by parents, teachers, and school officials. It covers the content, objectives, means of implementation, and evaluation of each student's program. Usually this plan is drafted by the classroom teachers and modified by parents and learning specialists. An IEP cannot be altered without the consent of the child's review committee.

There is no question about the benefit of mainstreaming to the exceptional child. If all children were in small classes and if good cooperation always existed between the learning specialist and the regular teacher, there might be no controversy. This is not the case. Regular classroom teachers often feel that they are not prepared and do not have the time to work well with children with disabilities. Making and reviewing an IEP for each child requires much time and energy that might be devoted to other tasks. The teachers often feel that they must give most of their time to the special learners while they are present in the classroom. Parents of nondisabled children often complain that their children are getting less attention as a result of mainstreaming. Others say that the presence of students with disabilities for a large portion of the day reduces the level of expectation and takes away from excellence. Sometimes the classroom teacher feels that he or she must work harder than the learning specialist, and as a result, negative feelings result. Although colleges of education usually require a course in special education, many classroom teachers do not feel able to meet the needs of children with disabilities. It is not always clear just what responsibilities belong to the learning specialist and which ones to the classroom teacher, especially when the specialist is functioning as an observer to review the effectiveness of the program. Mainstreaming seems to be working well in a number of school systems; however, there is a good deal of criticism, and public acceptance is mixed.

The Council for Exceptional Children, in its 1993 spring meeting, noted that full inclusion is a step on a continuum of services for all students with disabilities. The council further noted that inclusion of students with mental or physical disabilities in regular classrooms throughout the school day is a meaningful goal to be pursued by schools and communities. There are supporters and detractors of the inclusion concept, including special education teachers, administrators, parents, and students.

The Council for Exceptional Children worked in 2001 to increase federal special education funds to 40 percent of the full amount needed by 2007. Efforts are under way to helping children succeed by fully funding the Individuals with Disabilities Act. Although the 106th Congress appropriated $6.3 billion for special education in 2001, triple the funding of five years ago, it still accounts for only 15 percent of total average per pupil expenditure, rather than the 40 percent promised, according to Joetta Sack of *Education Week.* A number of special education political action groups are working to increase funding for the area. Meanwhile the number of students diagnosed with specific learning disabilities rose some 45 percent from the 1987–1988 school year to over 2.8 million in 1998–1999. Coeyman (2001) in "When Special Education?" reported that racial minorities make up a disproportionate number of students involved due to intentional or unintentional racial bias. Coeyman went on to note that many special education classes involve lower expectations and less demanding curricula, and in a high-stakes testing environment they are especially destructive for special education students, according to a report by the Civil Rights Project at Harvard University cited by Coeyman.

The percentage of disabled students taught in regular classrooms in the United States has risen significantly since 1985. Students with the most severe disabilities are placed more often in special classes or resource rooms, which are still favored over separate facilities.

Classroom Placement of Students with Disabilities

Percentage of Students with Disabilities, Age 6 to 21

	1985–86	1989–90	1992–93	1993–94	1994–95	1995–96
Regular class	25.5	31.5	39.8	43.4	44.5	45.4
Resource room	43.1	37.6	31.7	29.5	28.8	28.7
Separate class	24.4	24.9	23.4	22.7	22.4	21.7
Separate facilities	6.9	6.1	5.1	4.4	4.3	4.3

Source: Cited in Marjorie Coeyman, *The Christian Science Monitor.* March 13, 2001:20. National Center for Education Statistics, 1999 report, "The Condition of Education."

There is concern among some educators that more funding could lead to misdiagnosis of students being placed in special education because they could not receive services through other means.

Along with increased attention to inclusion, there are several current studies, including Mary Wagner and her colleagues' *What Happens Next? Trends in Postschool Outcomes of Youths with Disabilities* (1992), that are designed to survey postschool outcomes. These studies indicate significant movement toward social independence and economic improvement within five years of completing high school even though most jobs held are low-skill, low-wage positions.

The Americans with Disabilities Act of 1990 mandated full availability to special telecommunications systems by July 1993 for over 26 million citizens with hearing and speech impairments. As our history demonstrates, an expanded social consciousness continually reaches toward including more of the American populace of all ages, races, genders, and exceptionalities in the nation's educational and social services.

Some of those who oppose mainstreaming of students with disabilities support programs for gifted and talented youngsters. Demands for academic rigor, excellence, and intellectual development were loud in the era of the cold war and *Sputnik*. James Conant argued in *The American High School Today* that the academically talented student was not being sufficiently challenged. In *Excellence: Can We Be Equal and Excellent Too?* John Gardner pointed out that excellence is needed not only in scientists and engineers but also in teachers, scholars, professional people, and social leaders. The White House Conference of 1955 stressed the development of the abilities of especially bright children. Science, mathematics, and foreign languages were considered the major areas of needed excellence. In *The Shopping Mall High School*, Arthur Powell and his colleagues treated almost all of the seemingly antithetical goals of making serious educational demands on students and graduating almost all of them.

Following the NDEA, interest in the gifted began to shift toward a better understanding of the exceptionally bright student. It was pointed out that many of the most able students found school boring and a waste of time. Tests of intelligence failed to reveal special qualities such as creative ability. It was found that gifted and talented students often felt socially isolated from other students and sometimes had difficulty in adjusting to group norms. By the 1970s, demands were growing for special programs for all gifted and talented students. Limitations of money slowed the development of these programs, but legislation was passed that required that special offerings be made available for the gifted. Gifted and talented students must also be mainstreamed, but there is less controversy over this. Most teachers find having the gifted in their classes part of the day much less stressful than dealing with students with disabilities. All schools provided some type of program for the gifted and talented by the end of the 1990s and early 2000s. Interest in the academically talented has increased since former U.S. Commissioner Sidney Marland submitted to Congress in 1972 a report that recommended better education for the capable student. Nevertheless, low funding and a lack of trained teachers for the gifted have caused programs to lag far behind the level provided for students with disabilities.

The Civil Rights Act of 1991 provides regulations for companies with twenty-five or more employees and after 1994 for companies with fifteen or more workers that compel them to provide accommodations for people with disabilities, including auxiliary aids, removal of structural barriers, and new construction and alteration standards. By 1993, universities and businesses had worked to remove barriers to equal access to facilities. Elevators, sidewalk modification, easy access, and door-to-door transportation for people with disabilities have been provided in most major institutions. All institutions will be required to provide equal access in the future. Old buildings do not have to be upgraded for disability access, but once renovation or remodeling starts, buildings have to be compliant with disability access regulations.

In *University of Alabama v. Garrett* (2001), by a five to four decision, the Supreme Court ruled that lawsuits in federal court by state employees to recover money damages for alleged discrimination under the Americans with Disabilities Act are barred by the Eleventh Amendment (sovereign immunity). The majority ruled that a state employee must rely on state law and state courts for discrimination remedies. Although individuals with disabilities continue to have federal access for state employment discrimination, the Alabama decision has been widely criticized by disability civil rights groups fearing loss of federal power in lawsuits under the Americans with Disabilities Act in the states. There will be future lawsuits over state versus federal powers, and each case will be decided on its individual merits as well as future changes in the composition of the Supreme Court. Special education lawsuits may be affected by this ruling.

In 1990, Congress passed the Older Workers Protection Act, barring age discrimination in employment and in employee benefits coverage. Early studies on removal of the age seventy retirement requirement for institutions including schools and universities will have little effect, since most individuals prefer to retire well before that age. Some of these programs may be passed to the states under the Bush administration and with a five to four often conservative Supreme Court as noted in the *University of Alabama v. Garrett* case.

Voucher Plans.   The voucher system is a plan for financing schools with tax money but with parents in control of that money. A voucher is a certificate issued to parents. The parents give the voucher to a school of their choice, and the school exchanges the voucher for payment by the government. The system was studied at Harvard University in the 1960s. Voucher plans were tried in the South after 1954 as a means of supporting segregated schools but were found unconstitutional. Some states have attempted to use a voucher system for supporting parochial schools, and cases are still pending on their legal status. Modern proposals for voucher plans guard against racial discrimination or the use of taxes to supplement tuition at expensive private schools.

Proponents argue that parents should have a choice as to which schools their children attend. They say the schools would become more competitive and establish many alternatives in curriculum and methods. They point out that without the voucher system only those wealthy enough to pay tuition can select schools for their children; the poor must accept whatever the local public schools offer. Properly regulated, a voucher system could bring innovation and reform to schools and give parents much more control over the education of their children. These arguments are especially strong in California, where a large segment of the population is supporting a law requiring that the state adopt the voucher system. Although the California and Michigan voters defeated voucher proposals in 2000, efforts to expand school choice continue. President George W. Bush has proposed that states offer vouchers if no improvements are made in public schools after three years.

Many public school people and organizations such as the AFT and NEA are opposed to the voucher system. They believe that the schools would become more segregated, with middle-class parents selecting one type and the poor and minorities concentrated in others. Competition between schools would foster publicity seeking, and teachers would opt to be popular rather than professional. Many believe that the system would be unworkable and that it might destroy public education in the United States.

Although research reports differ on the effectiveness of voucher programs, Jay P. Greene, senior fellow at the Manhattan Institute for Policy Research, in a report entitled "An Evaluation of the Florida A-Plus Accountability and School Choice Program," noted that the performance of students on academic tests improves when public schools are faced with the prospect that their students will receive vouchers. The Florida plan provides for students to choose a different public or private school if their school receives two failing grades on state standards during a four-year period. Whether improvement is due to the voucher arrangement or intense efforts to raise student achievement, governors and state departments of education are committed to school improvement.

Multicultural and Bilingual Education.

Issues over including multicultural studies in the curriculum and providing primary instruction in a language other than English developed in the 1970s and continued into the 2000s. The United States is made up of a large number of people with diverse cultural backgrounds. Blacks and Hispanics are the largest minorities with approximately 35 million each, although Hispanics are the largest minority in 2001. Native Americans, certain European minorities, Arabians, and Asian Americans are a growing part of the American population. Asian Americans are one of the fastest growing minorities in the country. Some members of these groups have been assimilated into the mainstream of the culture, but others maintain an ethnic identification and can be regarded as subcultures. In many large cities there is a majority-minority population with minorities as the majority of the population in Los Angeles, Orlando, and other urban centers.

Multiculturalism and diversity are major areas of concern throughout the educational system from the National Council for the Accreditation of Teacher Education standards to public school and university administration. Colleges of education, following NCATE standards, encompass multiculturalism and diversity within their education courses as well as having a number of courses and degree programs specifically targeting the topic. In the future, as the nation becomes ever more multiracial and multiethnic, tolerance for diversity in accepting, appreciating, and understanding the benefits of the rich human resources of multiple cultures in a holistic frame of reference will be essential.

Historically, education has been used as an instrument for bringing foreigners into the national culture. Early arguments for public schools stressed the need to Americanize the immigrants and to make sure that all children learned to speak English. Although this "melting pot ideal" did not result in uniform cultural patterns, the dominant Anglo-Protestant group managed to require conformity to its language, cultural preferences, and value orientation. Schools not only reflected middle-class interests but also showed a decided preference for white, Anglo-Saxon establishment norms. Of course, assimilation did not include African Americans, Native Americans, and Hispanics, who were segregated and not allowed to fully participate in the majority society. In their cases, they were told to assimilate in the mainstream culture. In the early 2000s, movements toward total English immersion emerged with California and Arizona implementing such programs while New York chose to provide English immersion with bilingual education as an option. Although controversial among bilingual, English as a second language advocates, preliminary results indicate positive results with total English immersion programs.

The civil rights movement called attention to discrimination against minority and ethnic groups. African Americans were the first to demand equality of opportunity, with Hispanics and Native Americans soon following. As part of the minority revolution, pride in ethnic culture and ethnic identification increased. The unique contributions of minorities to language, art, food, entertainment, and sports were emphasized, together with ethnic histories and distinctive cultural patterns. This increasing ethnic identification led to the concept of cultural pluralism and a growing respect for the contributions made by each ethnic group and minority. Schools began offering programs in cultural awareness and specialized courses like black history and Hispanic studies. Multicultural education was also seen as a means of reducing prejudice through better understanding.

Many schools in America have incorporated elements of multiculturalism into existing programs. Units dealing with Eskimos and Native Americans have been part of the curriculum for years. Textbooks have been rewritten so that black and Hispanic role models are taught along with those from the dominant culture. Attention is given to special events such as Native-American Week or Hispanic Heritage Week. A growing interest in international social and economic issues has fostered interest in global education. Where large numbers of minority children are in attendance, courses in ethnic studies or cultural pluralism are sometimes offered. Colleges that train teachers encourage the teaching of values that support cultural diversity, ethnic awareness, the exploration of alternative lifestyles, and an understanding of cultural pluralism. Professional groups, state departments of education, and local curriculum committees are developing methods and programs for multicultural emphasis in all public school classrooms.

Bilingual and bicultural education grew out of the problems non-English-speaking and limited-English-speaking children were having in schools where primary instruction was in English. Before the civil rights movement, most states required that public school instruction be given only in English. In the 1960s, attention was called to the large number of students who failed or who dropped out of school because the instruction was in a language foreign to them. This was especially the case in Texas, where many Spanish-speaking students entered schools in which teachers spoke no Spanish. In 1968, the Bilingual Education Act was passed, and appropriations of nearly $160 million for bilingual programs were made by 1979. This act calls for instruction in two languages for children whose native tongue is other than English. Projects using various Native-American and Asian languages were created, but most bilingual instruction is in English and Spanish. Support for bilingual education also came from a Supreme Court case in 1974.

In *Lau v. Nichols,* the Court held that schools must take steps to aid students who find the educational experiences "wholly incomprehensible" because they do not understand English. The Court stated that the San Francisco Unified School District's failure to provide remedial language instruction to Chinese-speaking students constituted a violation of their civil rights under the Civil Rights Act of 1964. This case stands, even though federal funding for bilingual programs was reduced in the budget cuts of the Reagan administration. The ground is shifting as total English immersion grew during the Clinton and George W. Bush periods.

Minority and culturally different students often suffer from educational disabilities related to their cultural backgrounds. Studies of Native-American children have shown that some Indian youngsters are taught to be quiet in the presence of elders and that their primary learning patterns are very different from those used in most classrooms. Although Black English is not one of the bilingual programs, students used to speaking a black dialect often have trouble acquiring language skills in standard English. Educators are beginning to understand that different instructional approaches are needed with different racial and ethnic groups.

Opposition to bilingual and multicultural education is widespread. Obviously the "back to basics" people are against spending time in pluralistic or multicultural studies when that time might be used for fundamental courses. Conservatives regard such studies as another "frill" that should be eliminated from the basic curriculum. Others argue that the multicultural movement tends to promote cultural, social, and economic separation. They want the schools to emphasize the core values of the dominant culture and to assimilate the culturally different into the American mainstream. Some feel that bilingual programs allow children to maintain their first language and discourage the use of English by allowing them to function in school with another language. The idea of a large region of the United States where Spanish is the primary language is considered harmful to national unity by this group. It is feared that the curriculum will be fragmented by attempts to include cultural diversity and cultural pluralism. Educators like Harry Broudy believe that large amounts of material on ethnic diversity tend to "trivialize" the curriculum and can be used to justify a poor quality education for disadvantaged students. They believe that stress on ethnic and cultural differences can lead to cultural separation, social fragmentation, and have a disunifying effect on the body politic. This seems especially important when educators are trying to find ways to support the values at the core of the democratic society. Americans generally are beginning to doubt that the goals of equal educational opportunity can be achieved through schooling, and there is now much opposition to spending money for social engineering or for ethnic studies.

Yet educators realize the American society is based on the principle of equality and that it is improper to force every child into a mode of behavior determined by the norms of the majority. It is important to recognize the unique contributions of the cultures of others, including African Americans, Native Americans, women, Hispanics, and Asian Americans. Recognizing and appreciating the contributions of diverse cultures bridges gaps in communication and mutual interaction.

As Dewey noted, schools are miniature societies. Forms of discrimination—such as sexism, racism, and classism—and cultural and linguistic conflicts infecting society are reflected in our schools. Americans' historical treatment of Hispanics, Asian Americans, and Native Americans has left wounds that often still require healing efforts. In *The Ethical, Legal, and Multicultural Foundations of Teaching* (1993), Fred Kierstead and Paul Wagner call for transcultural education designed to provide for an interchange of cultural ideas for human improvement. In this sense, multicultural education's divisive components would be replaced by the study of cultures because of their contribution to humanity as a whole. Rather than dividing ethnic and culturally diverse groups within a macroculture like America, transcultural education would study cultures for their unifying themes. Multicultural education in its present form stresses differences rather than commonalities, and Kierstead suggests that a new phase of multicultural education, a transcultural phase, would promote more tolerance, interdependence, and respect for human dignity. This is particularly important in a time when our nation faces hate crimes and militant groups. The intolerance that has been exhibited by militia and freemen in the late 1990s and 2000s is incompatible with a pluralistic society. In addition, in a number of areas of the country, one in four children live in abject poverty as pointed out by many authors and illustrated by the work of Jonathan Kozol. This threatens the nation's social fabric and stability.

The Changing Role of Women in Education.   The struggle for equal rights for women has a history as long as that for minorities. Vast change has occurred since Emma Hart Willard began a boarding school for girls in her home in 1814 and Mary Lyon opened Mount Holyoke Seminary in 1837. Elizabeth Blackwell became the first American woman to earn the Doctor of Medicine degree, and astronomer Maria Mitchell was appointed the first female science professor at Vassar in 1862. Florence Bascom became a geologist with the U.S. Geological Survey in 1896 and a fellow of the Geological Society of America in 1894. In 1920, Florence Sabin, who took one of the first medical degrees from Johns Hopkins University, was the first woman to be elected to the National Academy of Sciences. Alice Evans was elected the first female president of the Society of American Bacteriologists in 1928, and Maria Mayer won the Nobel Prize in 1963 for physics research. Other prizes went to Rosalyn

Yalow for medicine in 1977 and to Barbara McClintock in physiology and medicine in 1983.

Historian Darlene Clark Hine, in *Black Women in America: An Historical Encyclopedia* (1993), provided a reference book that described the role of black women in American history from the seventeenth century to the present. From an account of Africans put ashore from a Dutch ship at Jamestown in 1619 to the 1992 election of Senator Moseley Braun of Illinois, detailed accounts of the struggles for progress and survival are provided.

Edward Stevens and George Wood, in *Justice, Ideology, and Education* (1992), note that the civil rights movement of the 1950s, antiwar protests, and counterculture groups helped create a climate of liberation. Currently, sexual harassment programs and seminars are held for employees in most of society's institutions. Sexual discrimination has been addressed in Title IX of the Educational Amendments of 1972. Currently the *Educational Law Reporter* contains an increased number of cases dealing with sex discrimination and harassment.

The Civil Rights Act of 1991 includes a section dealing with civil rights and women's equity in employment, and the Glass Ceiling Act or Women's Equal Opportunity Act provides awards for firms that demonstrate extensive efforts not only to create opportunities for women and minorities but also to assist them in advancing to upper management positions. Major corporations, leading universities, and other institutions provide valuing-diversity workshops, seminars, and training sessions that deal with retaining and promoting culturally diverse employees. Sensitivity sessions are utilized to deal with issues of sexual harassment, hate crimes, and subtle forms of discrimination against women and minorities.

In "Effective Sexual Harassment Policies: Focus on the Harasser and the Campus Culture" (1993), Melora Sundt refers to a federal court decision in *Ellison v. Brady* (1991) to illustrate increased awareness of harassment issues for educators. The Ellison case developed the "reasonable woman standard" to deal with harassing behavior that creates a hostile work environment. In *Davis v. Monroe* (1999) the Supreme Court ruled that a school district may be held liable for student-to-student sexual harassment only where the behavior is so severe, pervasive, and objectively offensive that it denies its victims the equal access to education that Tile IX is designed to protect. The Court noted that damages are not available for simple acts of teasing, shoving, pushing, and name-calling among schoolchildren even when comments may target differences in gender. Administrators and teachers generally, however, have sexual harassment policy guidelines for all schoolchildren and employees with provision for student reporting and confidentiality on reporting incidents of inappropriate behavior.

Since the early national period, a majority of the nation's teachers have been women. Traditionally, the work of women has been viewed as less valuable than that of men, a view that has helped to keep status and salaries low. Prestige for women in education was enhanced by the selection of social studies teacher Christa McAuliffe for the ill-fated *Challenger* space flight in 1986. Nonetheless, men still hold the majority of high-paying administrative positions in the schools. In spite of decades of work to eradicate sexual stereotypes from textbooks and the call for gender equity by the

National Organization for Women, discrimination still exists. Research shows that girls are still discouraged from seeking careers in science and mathematics. In "Glass Ceiling Restricts Women" (1996), Shea finds the "glass ceiling" in public education; although 75 percent of elementary and secondary schoolteachers are women, they constitute only 10 percent of the superintendents nationwide. This situation will change in the future due to the increased number of women in educational administration graduate and doctoral programs. Successful women have been at the forefront of providing models for girls. Jane Fonda donated $12.5 million for the establishment of an interdisciplinary research center at Harvard University's Graduate School of Education. The Harvard Center on Gender and Education will specialize in exploring the effect that gender has on the learning and development of children.

Modeling and mentoring help expand networking to improve the status of women within society and the workforce. Rimon and Kaufman in *How Jane Won: 55 Successful Women Share How They Grew* (2001) provide narrative accounts of how women overcome challenges to move from ordinary girls to extraordinary women. Goldberg in a *Kappan* interview with Carol Gilligan, "Restoring Lost Voices," notes Gilligan's research with adolescent girls in search of connection with others. Gilligan calls for amplifying the voices of children by creating engaging curriculum to help them understand what they are saying and seeing. The National Women's Studies Association also works to provide networking to change the lives of women through feminist education with research at the pre-kindergarten through postsecondary levels.

A large number of American women, especially single mothers, live in poverty. In *Women and Children Last,* Hunter College Professor Ruth Sidell calls for a more humane set of social policies to deal with poverty, work and welfare, and the rights of women and children. Although much progress has been made, equality for women in education will continue to be an issue in our twenty-first century.

TAKING SIDES TODAY AND TOMORROW

In this chapter, we have discussed issues, court cases, and contemporary critics. In every controversy, there is a connection to earlier arguments, writers, or litigation. Nothing that is at issue in modern American education is without historical foundation. The current question of the proper role for the federal government in educational matters relates to the land grants of the Northwest Ordinance and the Morrill acts. The caustic criticism of schools in *Deschooling Society* is not far removed from the attack on society and education in *Emile.* Rousseau and Illich are separated by centuries, but the positions they represent are much the same.

The relationship between the schools and the wider society is still debated. The appeal made by citizens of Kalamazoo to the courts in the 1870s is an illustration of using litigation for resolving educational conflicts. This was true for the desegregation cases of the 1950s, the equal opportunity cases of the 1970s, and litigation over financial support of schools that continues in the twenty-first century. Some aspects of the social and educational milieu stir up public emotion and debate at an extreme level. An example is the *Roe v. Wade* case, which legalized abortion, and the strongly held opinions about whether it should be upheld or reversed. Another is the question of whether small school districts with scarce resources must bear the whole cost of educating students with severe disabilities. Few object in principle to Public Law 94-142, which requires local educational agencies to ensure an education in the least restrictive environment for children with disabilities. However, McCay Vernon cites a situation in New Jersey in which the cost of educating one child with extreme hyperactivity places an added tax burden of $1,500 per year on each citizen of the county. This problem has not been solved for the future, and it is sure to be an issue for years to come.

Sometimes, a local reaction to a wider controversy can so divide a community that education is affected for a long period of time. We have seen that there is national strife over the selection and adoption of school textbooks and book censorship. In Kanawha County, West Virginia, textbook selection by two committees (from state approved textbook lists) was sent forward to the board. The board unanimously voted to accept the recommendations and made the collection available for public review. By the winter of 1975, many of the books were labeled as "dirty, anti-Christian, or anti-American" by some parents and local groups. Local ministers were divided on the issue, but the flames were fanned by organizations as diverse as the NEA, the Council of Parents and Teachers, the NAACP, the National Library Association, the Ku Klux Klan, and the John Birch Society. The board ended up by banning books that depicted racial strife, demeaned patriotism, supported alien forms of government, debased religious or ethnic groups, encouraged sedition, or used offensive language. The judgment about these themes was very broad so that a great many books were removed from the schools.

Underlying this turbulent issue over textbooks were social conflicts of a more basic kind. Kanawha County was made up of about 200,000 people, of which two-thirds were relatively affluent. The remainder were rural poor, who made a living in the coalfields of Appalachia. This group was denied an adequate standard of living and felt exploited. Another problem was that the schools, including the textbook committees, allowed them little or no involvement in the decisions. In the aftermath of the Kanawha County controversy, it is clear that conflict over textbook selection was triggered by a much deeper community conflict. We can anticipate future educational arguments whenever there is a serious value conflict within the culture. For example, in communities containing both fundamentalists and religious liberals, it is to be expected that creationists will pose arguments against evolution as the only credible theory of the origin of life. The conflict illustrates values promoted by a dominant group resulting in variation in the quality of education different groups of children receive.

Many of the results of taking sides on issues such as involuntary segregation are now history. Heated debate continues over the unfavorable comparisons of American and foreign students on standardized tests of achievement. Decades of federal support for equalization, illustrated by programs like Head Start and Upward Bound, did not support high levels of achievement. The "Nation at Risk" report triggered emphasis on competition, excellence, and high academic standards. In the Reagan administration, education secretary William Bennett gave his support to programs like the Great

Books of the Western world and the Paideia Proposal of Mortimer Adler. The classical-perennialist curriculum of James Madison High School and the highly general liberal arts program became the rage of the 1980s as a model of quality secondary education. Regardless of the merits of this kind of schooling, critics say that it is not for everyone. Floretta McKenzie, school superintendent in Washington, DC, argues that the perennial approach fails to provide vocational training, specific skills needed for employment, and comprehensive instructional strategies to accommodate different learning styles of poorly motivated students. Dr. McKenzie is not only a prominent practicing educator but also a leading advocate of minority education and equality. She feels that the Great Books program or the Paideia Proposal will lead to a dual system of education and an increase in the dropout rate. The problem is especially central to states like Texas, where half of the 3.5 million school-age children are black or Hispanic. Education secretaries Lauro Cavazos, Richard Riley, and current secretary Rod Paige are keenly interested in equality of opportunity as well as learning outcomes for all of the nation's students and propose to fight for a lower dropout rate and higher achievement levels. This issue will not be easily resolved in the near future and will be of concern throughout the early 2000s. John Gardner may have put it best when he asked, "Can we be equal and excellent too?" *No Child Will Be Left Behind* is the slogan of the George W. Bush administration. Access, achievement, and equity will be the challenge of the future in a multiracial society with persistent pockets of poverty, crime, and violence.

With the fifty separate state educational systems, the problems of funding American schools and providing equality of opportunity by eliminating differences between the number of dollars supporting each child within states are continuing issues. Courts have recently ruled that Arkansas, Texas, and Montana are in violation of required equalization rules. The fundamental problem is that of securing adequate taxation to support schools, especially in areas where the economy is weak or where other priorities such as roads get more support. Finding creative, innovative ways to finance schools as well as to cope with increased expensive litigation in a litigious society will continue to be a challenge.

Attitudes of the public are critical and could be affected by activities such as teacher strikes. After a sixteen-month labor dispute culminating in an eleven-day strike that closed the schools, Los Angeles teachers won a 24 percent pay raise over three years. This strike in the nation's second largest school district put half a million students out of school. In addition to the $600 million pay plan, teachers won more authority (empowerment) over curriculum and methods. This was an impressive gain, but it remains to be seen what the effect on the attitude of the public in California will be. Teachers' salaries improved in the late 1990s, and there is renewed interest in teaching as a career both for service to youth and for a profession growing in esteem. In the spring of 2001, Hawaii's schools were closed as teachers went on strike for better salaries. The closure affected 183,000 public school students from nursery through high school and over 40,000 university students. About 13,000 public school teachers and over 3,000 university faculty were involved. Teachers' salaries in Hawaii currently range from $29,000 to $58,000 a year.

Governors, legislatures, businesses, and community groups are seeking to recruit and retain teachers through increased salaries and improved working conditions. Florida, like other states with increased immigration, is finding it difficult to keep up with a burgeoning student population. Large class sizes, temporary buildings, and pockets of poverty (with one in five children living in poverty) are the challenges of the state legislature.

Other ongoing controversies center on bilingual versus total English immersion programs and education for children with disabilities. Bilingual instruction was widespread in states like Florida, California, and Texas, where instruction was only in English and Hispanic children were seen at great disadvantage. George Sanchez found that students in Texas with Spanish family names received an average of only one-fourth the years of formal education of those with Anglo family names. Well over 5 million children now come from homes in which English is not the primary language. Federal help comes from Title VII of the Elementary and Secondary Education Act and Chapter 1 of the Education Consolidation and Improvement Act. State and local funds are also needed. There are strong arguments against bilingual education beyond the costs of providing it. Some think time and energy spent on instruction in two languages rob students of resources that should be spent on basic education. This argument is also used by those who believe that mainstreaming of students with disabilities focuses attention on special students to the detriment of nondisabled children. Zirkel in a *Phi Delta Kappan* article, "Sorting Out Which Students Have Learning Disabilities," notes the rapid increase in the category of learning disability while the percentage of students with more traditional and visible disabilities has declined. Zirkel suggests using multiple measures in addition to standardized, multiple choice tests for high-stakes accountability such as portfolios, essays, and structured interviews. Zirkel also finds a need to preclude students who are not really learning disabled from receiving special accommodations and, as a result, unfair advantages.

Another criticism is historical. Formerly, when minority groups came to the United States, they were assimilated into the culture and became English speaking. Assimilation was the theory behind the Lau decision, which required the San Francisco schools to provide language instruction for its Chinese-speaking students. The rapidly growing Spanish-speaking minority, however, continues to use Spanish after receiving bilingual instruction. For this reason, some states have passed legislation that makes English the official language. Still other critics like Diane Ravitch say that bilingual programs grew out of the civil rights movement and ethnic political pressure and that there is no proof that they work. Limited English proficiency programs, however, are expanding in many teacher education programs, especially in areas such as northwest Arkansas and Florida, which have a rapidly growing Latino population.

Ever larger numbers of American children are assessed to need some sort of special education. With a growing number of minority children and new global awareness, it is unlikely that the Bilingual Education Act of 1968 will be repealed, although total English immersion seems to have achieved notable positive results. Multiethnic education, an approach to making schools pluralistic, attempts to integrate education and to avoid reliance on English and Anglo-Saxon values. Equalizing school financing to improve school facilities and educational programs between rich and poor school districts will continue to be a focus of state budgets. These factors will continue to be addressed and debated in the future.

Because of the dynamic nature of society and the fact that education is an enterprise that involves our most important resource, children, we can expect a high level of controversy in the future. Only a few issues are fully resolved. Most of the arguments over educational issues will continue into the future, and new ones are almost certain to emerge.

GAINING PERSPECTIVE THROUGH CRITICAL ANALYSIS

1. Name at least two ways educational controversies can arise. How have controversies been dealt with in the past, and what strategies do past actions suggest for the present?
2. Identify at least three events that demonstrate the continuing problems of separation of church and state as it relates to religion in the public schools. What historical court decisions led to the *Agostini v. Felton* (1997) decision.
3. It has now been over forty years since *Brown v. Board of Education*. Give your opinion regarding the effects of the 1954 decisions on education to-

day. Do you think we have unity within diversity or a more fragmented society? Give reasons for your answers.
4. Choose two court cases that you think made the greatest contribution toward improving the equality of opportunity in educational programs. List two reasons why you selected each of the cases.
5. Name three critics of educational systems and practices in America, and identify their major criticisms (high-stakes testing, total English immersion versus bilingual education, school financing, poverty and crime, gender issues, role of service learning).

HISTORY IN ACTION IN TODAY'S CLASSROOM

1. Set up and carry out a telephone interview (or an e-mail correspondence) with a schoolteacher or administrator to determine his or her perceptions of the role of law in major controversies affecting their schools. Add these findings to your journal, and compare your findings with those of your classmates.

2. In your opinion, is the primary purpose of school to be an agency for social action or to impart basic knowledge through a planned curriculum, or both? Support your opinion with examples from the current literature in your field. Add the information to your journal.

INCREASED UNDERSTANDING THROUGH ONLINE RESEARCH

Visit the Prentice Hall Foundations Web site (*http://www.prenhall.com/foundations-cluster*) and examine Topics 5, 10, and 16. Using the resources available in these topics, write a detailed essay response to the following question: How have federal courts including the Supreme Court affected educators and curriculum in the areas of diversity, ethnicity, race, gender, and social consciousness? Write and submit your response to your instructor using the Electronic Bluebook module also in any of these three topics of the Web site.

BIBLIOGRAPHY

Adams, James Truslow. *Frontiers of American Culture.* New York: Scribner's, 1944.

Alexander, Kern, and M. David Alexander. *American Public School Law.* Belmont, CA: Wadsworth, 2001: 539; 440. Cases cited: *Watson v. City of Cambridge,* 157 Mass.561, 32 N.E. 864 (1893) and State ex.rel. *Beattie v. Board of Education,* 169 Wis.231, 172 N.S. 153 (1919).

Archer, Jeff, and Julie Blair. "Performance Testing Being Readied for Ohio Teachers." *Education Week* (January 17, 2001): 14.

Ashton-Warner, Sylvia. *Teacher.* New York: Simon and Schuster, 1963.

———. *Spearpoint: Teacher in America.* New York: Knopf, 1972.

Ballantine, Jenne. *Schools and Society: A Unified Reader,* 2d. ed. Mountain View, CA: Mayfield Publishing, 1989.

Barzun, Jacques. *Teacher in America.* Boston: Little, Brown, 1945.

Bender v. Williamsport, 475 U.S. 534, 106 S.Ct. 1326 (1986).

Berliner, David C. "Educational Psychology Meets the Christian Right: Differing Views of Children, Schooling, Teaching and Learning." *Teachers College Record* (Spring 1997):381–416.

Berliner, David C., and Bruce J. Biddle. *The Manufactured Crisis: Myths, Fraud and the Attack on America's Public Schools.* New York: Addison Wesley, 1995.

Bloom, Benjamin. *All Our Children Learning.* New York: McGraw-Hill, 1980.

Bok, Sissela. *Lying: Moral Choice in Public and Private Life.* New York: Alfred A. Knopf, 1999.

Bowles, Samuel, and Herbert Gintis. *Schooling in Capitalist America.* New York: Basic Books, 1976.

Bowman, Darcia Harris. "Republicans Prefer to Back Vouchers by Any Other Name." *Education Week* (2001 January 31): 22.

Bracey, Gerald W. "Why Can't They Be Like We Were?" *Phi Delta Kappan* (October 1991):104–17.

———. "The Third Bracey Report on the Condition of Public Education." *Phi Delta Kappan* (October 1993):105–17.

———. "The Tenth Bracey Report on the Condition of Education." *Phi Delta Kappan* (October 2000): 133–44.

Bradwell v. Illinois (1873): 16 Wall 130:142.

Bruner, Jerome S. *The Culture of Education.* Cambridge, MA: Harvard University Press, 1996.

Byham, William C. *Zapp in Education.* New York: Fawcett Columbine, 1992.

Coeyman, Marjorie. "When Special Education?" *The Christian Science Monitor* (March 13, 2001): 15, 18.

Conant, James. *The American High School Today.* New York: McGraw-Hill, 1959.

Cook, Eugene, and William I. Potter. "The School Segregation Cases: Opposing the Opinion of the Supreme Court." *American Bar Association Journal* (April 1956) 42:313.

Cordasco, Francesco. *Bilingual Schooling in the United States: A Sourcebook for Educational Personnel.* New York: McGraw-Hill, 1976.

Council of Basic Education. Available: *http://www.c-b-e.org/*

D'Amico, R., C. Marder, L. Newman, and Mary Wagner. *What Happens Next?: Trends in Post School Outcomes of Youth with Disabilities.* Menlo Park, CA: SRI International, 1992.

Darden, Edwin C. "Prayer Falls on Hard Times." In *Legal Issues in Education Practice: Challenges and Opportunities in the 21st Century.* Education Law Association 2000 Conference Papers. (2000): 6–10.

Davis v. Monroe County Board of Education, 526 U.S. 629, 119 S.Ct. 1662 (1999).

Decker, Sunny. *An Empty Spoon.* New York: Harper and Row, 1969.

Dennison, George. *The Lives of Children: The Story of First Street School.* New York: Random House, 1969.

Education Planet. Available: *http://www.educationplanet.com/search/Education/General/National Education Standard.*

Elam, Stanley M., Lowell C. Rose, and Alec M. Gallup. "The 25th Annual Phi Delta Kappa Gallup Poll of Public's Attitudes Toward the Public Schools." *Phi Delta Kappan* (October 1993):138, 150.

Ellis, Arthur, John Cogan, and Kenneth Howey. *Introduction to the Foundations of Education.* Englewood Cliffs, NJ: Prentice-Hall, 1981.

Estes, Nolan, and Donald Waldrip. *Magnet Schools: Legal and Practical Implications.* NJ: New Century Education Corporation, 1978.

Featherstone, Joseph. *Schools Where Children Learn.* New York: Liveright Press, 1968.

Felsenthal, Edward. "Christian Right Falls Out of Unison on School Prayer." *Wall Street Journal* (February 24, 1997): A 24.

"For Goodness Sake: Why So Many Want Religion to Play a Greater Role in American Life." *Public Agenda Research Studies* (2001) Available: *http://www.publicagenda. org/specials/religion/religion.htm*

Gardner, John W. *Excellence: Can We Be Equal and Excellent Too?* New York: Harper and Row, 1961.

Gatti, Richard, and Daniel Gatti. *New Encyclopedia Dictionary of School Law*. West Nyack, NY: Parker Publishing Company, 1983.

Gewertz, Catherine. "Internet Tycoon Gives $250 Million for Cognitive-Disabilities Project." *Education Week* (January 24, 2001): 7.

Glasser, William. *Schools Without Failure*. New York: Harper and Row, 1968.

———. *The Quality School: Managing Students Without Coercion*. New York: Harper, 1998.

Goldberg, Mark E. "Restoring Lost Voices." *Phi Delta Kappan* (May 2000): 701–704.

Greene, Jay P. "An Evaluation of the Florida A-Plus Accountability and School Choice Program." New York: The Manhattan Institute for Policy Research. (2001, February). Available: *www.manhattan-institute.org*

"Guidance on Religion in Schools Is Available." *Your School and the Law* (July 1996) 26(7):4.

Hewett, Frank, and Steven Forness. *Education of Exceptional Learners*. Boston: Allyn and Bacon, 1977.

Hine, Darlene Clark. *Black Women in America: An Historical Encyclopedia*. Brooklyn, NY: Carlson Publishing Co., 1993.

Holt, John. *How Children Fail*. New York: Pitman, 1964.

———. *What Do I Do Monday?* New York: Dutton, 1970.

———. *Freedom and Beyond*. New York: Dutton, 1972.

Huelskamp, Robert M. "Perspectives on Education in America." *Phi Delta Kappan* (May 1993):718–21.

Hurst, Marianne. "Fonda Gives Harvard Education School $12 Million." *Education Week* (March 7, 2001): 10.

Illich, Ivan. *Deschooling Society*. New York: Harper, 1971.

Jacobson, Linda. "Clinton's Early-Learning Fund Quietly Becomes Reality." *Education Week* (January 24, 2001): 22.

Jensen, Arthur R. "How Much Can We Boost I.Q. and Scholastic Achievement?" *Harvard Educational Review* (Winter 1969) 39(1):1–123.

———. "Reducing the Heredity-Environment Uncertainty." *Harvard Educational Review* (Summer 1969) 39(3):449–83.

Jones, R. L., ed. *Mainstreaming and the Minority Child*. Reston, VA: Council for Exceptional Children, 1976.

"Kansas City School District Loses Accreditation." *2000 Cable News Network* (2000, September 15): Available: *http://www.cnn.com/2000/fyi/teachers/education. news/05/03/kansas.city/*

Kierstead, Fred, and Paul A. Wagner. *The Ethical, Legal and Multicultural Foundations of Teaching*. Madison, WI: W. C. Brown and Benchmark, 1993.

Kohl, Herbert. *36 Children*. New York: New American Library, 1967.

———. *The Open Classroom*. New York: Vintage Books, 1970.

Kohn, Alfie. *The Schools Our Children Deserve: Moving Beyond Tradtional Classrooms and Tougher Standards*. New York: Houghton Mifflin, 2000.

Kozol, Jonathan. *Death at an Early Age: The Destruction of the Hearts and Minds of Negro Children in the Boston Public Schools (New York Review)*. Boston: Houghton Mifflin, 1967.

———. *Free Schools*. Boston: Houghton Mifflin, 1972.

———. *Illiterate America*. Garden City, NY: Anchor Press/Doubleday, 1985.

———. *Savage Inequalities*. New York: Harper, 1992.

———. *Amazing Grace: The Lives of Children and the Conscience of Nation*. New York: Harper, 1996.

———. *Ordinary Resurrections Children in the Years of Hope*. New York: Crown Publishing Group, 2000.

La Follette, Marcel Chotkowski. *Creationism, Science, and the Law: The Arkansas Case*. Cambridge, MA: MIT Press, 1993.

Leonard, George Burr. *Education and Ecstasy*. New York: Delacorte Press, 1968.

Manno, Bruno V., Chester Finn, Jr., and Gregg Vanourek. "Beyond the Schoolhouse Door: How Charter Schools Are Transforming U.S. Public Education." *Phi Delta Kappan* (June 2000): 737.

Mathews, David. *Is There a Public for Public Schools?* Dayton, OH: Kettering Foundation Press, 1996.

———. "The Lack of a Public for Public Schools." *Kappan* (June 1997): 741–43.

McCarthy, Martha M., and Nelda H. Cambron-McCabe. *Public School Law: Teachers' and Students' Rights*. Boston: Allyn and Bacon, 1992.

Missouri v. Jenkins, 216 F.3d 720 (2000).

Mitchell v. Helms, (98–1648) 151 F 3d 347 reversed (2000).

"NEA 2000–2001 Resolutions." National Education Association. Washington, DC (2000): Available: *http://www. nea.org/resolutions/00/00a-30.html*

Nieto, Sonia. *Affirming Diversity.* New York: Longman, 1992.

Noll, James. *Taking Sides: Clashing Views on Controversial Educational Issues.* Guilford, CT: Duskin, 1980.

Ormstein, Allan, and Daniel Levine. *An Introduction to the Foundations of Education.* 2d ed. Boston: Houghton Mifflin, 1981.

Postman, Neil, and Charles Weingartner. *Teaching as a Subversive Activity.* New York: Delacorte Press, 1969.

Powell, Arthur, Eleanor Farrar, and David Cohen. *The Shopping Mall High School.* Boston: Houghton Mifflin, 1985.

Pratte, Richard. *Pluralism in Education.* Springfield, IL: Charles C. Thomas, 1979.

Proctor, Samuel B., ed. *A Man for Tomorrow's World: Addresses by Theodore Roszak and Alexander Frazier.* Washington, DC: Association for Supervision and Curriculum Development, 1970.

Prosser, Charles. *Secondary Education and Life.* Cambridge, MA: Harvard University Press, 1939.

Ravitch, Diane. *The Schools We Deserve: Reflections on the Educational Crisis of Our Times.* New York: Basic Books, 1985.

————. *The Revisionists Revised: A Critique of the Radical Attack on the Schools.* New York: Basic Books, 1995.

"Religious Liberty, Public Education, and the Future of American Democracy." *Educational Leadership* (May 1995):92–93.

Richey, Warren. "Can Religious Groups Hold Meetings in Public Schools?" *The Christian Science Monitor* (February 28, 2001): 1, 4.

Rimon, Sylvia B., and Sara Rimon Kaufman. *How Jane Won: 55 Successful Women Share How They Grew.* New York: Crown Publishing, 2001.

Robelen, Erik W. "Flexibility May Be Sticking Point for K–12 Budget." *Education Week:* 1, 24.

Rose, Lowell, and Alec M. Gallup. "The 32nd Annual Phi Delta Kappa/Gallup Poll of the Public's Attitudes Toward the Public Schools." *Phi Delta Kappan* (2000, September): 42.

Rossow, Lawrence F., and Jerry Parkinson. "U.S. Department of Education, Office of Civil Rights, Sexual Harassment Guidance: Harassment of Students by School Employees, Other Students, or Third Parties." *School Law Reporter* (May 1997) 39(5):49–50.

Roszak, Theodore. *Where the Wasteland Ends: Politics and Transcendence in Postindustrial Society.* Garden City, NJ: Doubleday, 1972.

————. *The Making of a Counter Culture.* Berkeley, CA: University of California Press, 1995.

Russo, Charles J. and Mawdsley. "U.S. Supreme Court Reviews Issue On School Access by Religious Groups." *Your School and the Law* (March 14, 2001):1, 6.

Sack, Joetta L. "Special Education Costs Can Be Taxing for Districts." *Education Week* (March 14, 2001): 1, 32, 33.

Sanchez, George. *Forgotten People: A Study of New Mexicans.* Albuquerque, NM: University of New Mexico Press, 1940.

Shea, Linda. "Glass Ceiling Restricts Women." *Collegiate Times* (1996): *http://ct.ufp.org/-pagan/ctarchives/news/960426/restricts.htlm.*

Sidel, Ruth. *Women and Children Last: The Plight of Poor Women in Affluent America.* New York: Viking, 1986.

"Standards and Accountability." Learning First Alliance, Washington, DC: 2001. Available: *http://www.learningfirst.org/news/standards-exec.html*

Stevens, Edwards, and George H. Woods. *Justice, Ideology, and Education.* New York: McGraw Hill, 1992.

Sundt, Melora. "Effective Sexual Harassment Policies: Focus on the Harasser and the Campus Culture." In *Synthesis: Law and Policy* (1993) 4(4):333.

Taylor, Bonnie B. *Contemporary Legal Issues.* Denver, CO: ABC-CLIO, 1996, 91.

"The Bible & Public Schools." The National Bible Association and First Amendment Center (1999). Available: *http://www.teachaboutthebible.org/bps/bpsfaguide01.htm*

Thurlow, Martha L., and David R. Johnson. "High-Stakes Testing of Students with Disabilities." *Journal of Teacher Education* (Vol. 51, No. 4, September/October 2000): 305–314.

Toppo, Greg. "House OKs Bush Education Aims but Keeps Vouchers Out." *Arkansas Democrat Gazette* (May 24, 2001): 5 A.

Travis, Scott. "Crowding to Ease, School District Says." *Sun Sentinel South Florida* (March 24, 2001): 1 A, 12 A.

Tuttle v. Arlington Country School Board, 195 F3d.698 (4th Circuit 1999).

Tyack, David. *The One Best System.* Cambridge, MA: Harvard University Press, 1974.

"U.S. Circuit Court of Appeals Strikes Down Cleveland's Voucher Program." *Your School and the Law* (2001, Janaury 3): 1, 5.

Wagner, Mary, Ronald D'Amico, Camille Marder, Lynn Newman, and Jose Blackorby. *What Happens Next? Trends in Postschool Outcomes of Youth with Disabilities.* Washington, DC: Office of Special Education Program, U.S. Office of Education, 1992.

Walsh, Mark. "Public Sees Role for Religion in Schools." *Education Week* (January 17, 2001): 13.

Webb, Rodman, and Robert Sherman. *Schooling and Society.* 2d ed. New York: Macmillan, 1989.

Wise, Arthur. *The Bureaucratization of the American Classroom.* Berkeley, CA: University of California Press, 1979.

Zirkel, Perry A. "Sorting Out Which Students Have Learning Disabilities." *Phi Delta Kappa* (April 2001): 639–41. (Most of the controversial issues in education are well covered in electronic databases such as ERIC and through search engines of the Internet.)

CHAPTER NINE

EDUCATIONAL REFORM: 1980s, 1990s, 2000s, AND THE SEARCH FOR EXCELLENCE

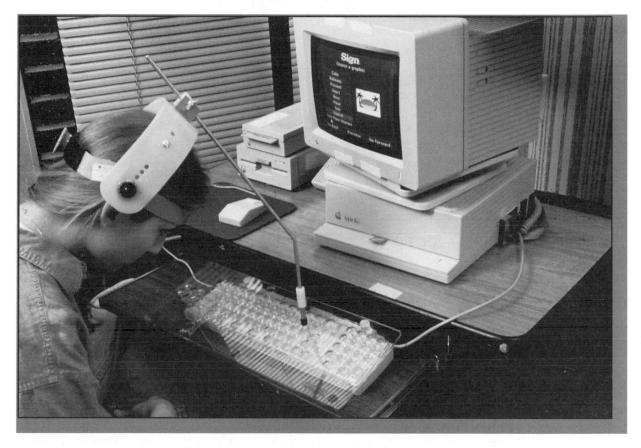

Tomorrow's systems of education will evolve if present arrangements are dynamic . . . [and] schooling and education are not synonymous. . . . Hope for the future rests with our ability to use and relate effectively all those educative and potentially educative institutions and agencies in our society—home, school, church, media, museums, workplace and more.

John I. Goodlad

Nixon	Ford	Carter	Reagan
1974 Watergate scandal, loss of respect for government	1976 Bicentennial NEA politically active	Continuation of social engineering in education	Stress on basics
High inflation, revolt of taxpayers	1979 Separate Department of Education	Bilingual programs for growing Hispanic minority	New power of political and religious right
			Conservative social and fiscal policies and rise of the fundamentalist "New Right"

Figure 9.1   Time Line of Educational Reform

THE GREAT AMERICAN EDUCATIONAL REFORM MOVEMENT

As demonstrated in previous chapters, the period of American history from the Kennedy and Johnson administrations to the Reagan, Bush, Clinton, and George W. Bush administrations was dominated by the social reform movement. Rejecting the old Darwinian concept of survival of the fittest, social engineers and educators joined forces in an effort to attain equality of opportunity and "create the great society" as well as "build a bridge to the twenty-first century."

Aside from school lunch programs and health measures, the first such programs concentrated on racial desegregation of the schools. Egalitarian programs focusing on the culturally deprived, the urban poor, the at-risk students, and the disadvantaged soon followed these efforts. Thus, Project Head Start, Talent Search, magnet schools, child care centers, Upward Bound, and mainstreaming were superimposed on integration plans such as busing to achieve racial balance. The influx of vast numbers of Spanish-speaking children (currently moving toward the largest minority population in the United States) fostered bilingual programs, and federally sponsored enrichment agendas were followed in the cities. In the early twenty-first century bilingual education has been subject to review. There is a trend toward total English immersion in several states, and bilingual education is an option in others.

Progress was made toward an equal and democratic society in the 1960s and 1970s, although not at a rate that satisfied critics like Illich and Kozol. Almost all of the federal money for education was earmarked for these projects, and virtually

Bush		Clinton		G.W. Bush
1980s *A Nation at Risk*	1986 Gramm- Rudman	2001 IDEA Inclusion full funding for learning disabled	2002 High-stakes testing teacher shortage	2002 Leave no child behind
Other national reform reports	1986 Holmes Group	2000 Effort to impeach President Clinton	1993 National Service Trust Fund	
	1984 Responses by Ernest Boyer, John Goodlad, and Theodore Sizer	1994 Whitewatergate	1988 Shortage of teachers	

every school district was affected to some degree. When new ideas for the improvement of education appeared in the early 1980s, such as those espoused in B. Othanel Smith's *A Design for a School of Pedagogy* (1980), there was insufficient public support for implementation.

It should have come as no surprise that concentration on access to schooling and equity would have a leveling effect on overall achievement. After all, when the population of students expanded to include minorities, the disadvantaged, and those with exceptional needs, some regression might have been expected. College Boards, for example, once taken only by elite college-bound high school students, declined as the numbers of pupils taking them expanded. John Gardner, among others, had previously raised the question of whether the public schools could be both equal and excellent. The two goals are not mutually exclusive, but sterling success in scholarship requires effort and money, as does equality.

Reform Reports. More than thirty examinations of public education in the United States followed closely on the publication of *A Nation at Risk*. Some of these were sponsored by special interest groups, several emerged from the work of commissions and professional organizations, and a few represented individual efforts (see Figure 9.2). By 2001, calls for educational reform had become part of the social, economic, and educational culture. The public, educators at all levels, the corporate sector, and politicians vied with each other to present a variety of strategies for improving educational delivery systems and student achievement across income levels. Understanding and respecting diverse cultures and populations will continue to be

The Paideia Proposal: An Educational Manifesto, Mortimer J. Adler, on behalf of the members of the Paideia Group, 1982.

The Troubled Crusade: American Education 1945–1980, Diane Ravitch, 1983.

A Place Called School: Prospects for the Future, John Goodlad, 1983.

Academic Preparation for College: What Students Need to Know and Be Able to Do, Educational Equality Project, The College Board, 1983.

Action for Excellence: A Comprehensive Plan to Improve Our Nation's Schools, Task Force on Education for Economic Growth, Education Commission of the States, 1983.

High School: A Report on Secondary Education in America, Ernest L. Boyer, The Carnegie Foundation for the Advancement of Teaching, 1983.

Making the Grade, Report of the Twentieth Century Fund Task Force on Federal Elementary and Secondary Education Policy, 1983.

Horace's Compromise: The Dilemma of the American High School, Theodore R. Sizer, 1984.

A Study of High Schools, Theodore Sizer, cosponsored by the National Association of Secondary School Principals and the National Association of Independent Schools, 1984.

In Search of Excellence: Lessons from America's Best Run Companies, Thomas Peters and Robert Waterman, 1984.

Investing in Our Children, Report of the Committee for Economic Development, 1985.

A Nation Prepared: Teachers for the 21st Century, Report of the Carnegie Task Force on Teaching as a Profession, 1986.

Time for Results, National Governors' Association, 1986.

Cultural Literacy: What Every American Needs to Know, E. D. Hirsch Jr., 1987.

The Forgotten Half: Non-College Youth in America: An Interim Report on the School-to-Work Transition, Report of William T. Grant Foundation's Commission on Work, Family and Citizenship, 1988.

Teachers for Our Nation's Schools, John Goodlad, 1990.

Horace's School: Redesigning the American High School, Theodore, R. Sizer, 1991.

Results in Education: 1990, Report of the National Governor's Association, 1991.

Savage Inequalities: Children in America's Schools, Jonathan Kozol, 1991.

Shared Vision: Policy Recommendations for Linking Teacher Education to School Reform, Calvin Frazier, 1993.

The Basic School, Ernest Boyer, 1995.

The Schools We Need and Why We Don't Have Them, E. D. Hirsch Jr., 1996.

What Matters Most: Teaching for America's Future. National Commission on Teaching and America's Future, 1996.

Horace's Hope: The Future of the American High School, Theodore Sizer, 1996.

The Public Purpose of Education and Schooling, Edited by John I. Goodlad and Timothy J. McMannon, 1997.

Knowing What Students Know: The Science and Design of Educational Assessment, The National Resarch Council, 2001.

Would School Choice Change the Teaching Profession? Caroline Hoxby, 2000.

Left Back, A Century of Failed School Reforms. Diane Ravitch, 2000.

Figure 9.2 Major Educational Reform Reports

emphasized in the corporate sector as well as in education as legal and illegal immigration continues to expand a multiracial society. For the first time, the 2000 census provided an opportunity for respondents to identify more than one racial background. Over time this will require cooperation among racial groups to have access to federal funding for disadvantaged, at-risk, and poverty pockets. African Americans will join Hispanics (Latinos) and other cultural and racial groups in seeking assistance at federal, state, and local levels. With increasing majority-minority demographics the challenge for the future will be a search for unity within diversity to prevent social fragmentation.

A Nation at Risk.

A Nation at Risk, issued by the National Commission on Excellence in Education, had an impact similar to that of *Sputnik* in 1957. The report has been criticized by educators for focusing too much on high schools, using too narrow a sample and dated information, being biased in favor of a business model, and comparing comprehensive American schools with limited-population elite schools in Germany and Japan. Nevertheless, *A Nation at Risk* caught the attention of the public and educators alike. The report made a strong case for the urgency of reform if the nation was to retain its place in the modern world. It was followed by a myriad of other studies and reports, but there is no question that *A Nation at Risk* had the most influence.

In international comparisons, the report showed that American students never were first or second and often were dead last as ranked against other industrial nations on nineteen academic tests. About 13 percent of the nation's seventeen-year-olds and 40 percent of minority youth were functionally illiterate. Some 23 million adults could not pass simple tests of reading, writing, and comprehension. Half of the population of gifted students failed to match their tested ability in school performance. The average achievement of secondary students was lower than in 1957. Nearly 40 percent of the high school seniors could not draw inferences from written material, and only a third could solve a mathematical problem requiring several steps.

The report pointed out that College Boards (SAT test scores) declined steadily from 1963 to 1980. On the average, verbal scores dropped 50 points and scores in mathematics 40 points. Achievement in English and science had dropped, and the proportion of students demonstrating superior achievement had also declined dramatically. Between 1975 and 1980, remedial courses in mathematics offered by four-year colleges increased by 72 percent, so that they came to make up a fourth of the mathematics curriculum. Average achievement scores of college graduates also fell between 1975 and 1980. Business and military leaders were cited as saying that high school graduates were so deficient in such basic skills as reading, writing, spelling, and computation that they were forced to spend millions of dollars for remedial training courses just to bring workers and trainees up to ninth grade level.

A Nation at Risk was credited with creating the momentum for educational reform, but it did not offer a model for high-quality education. Almost nothing in the report deals with pedagogy; concentration was on mechanical solutions, regarded by the profession as bureaucratic and simplistic. No means of implementing excellence while maintaining equality was suggested. The report asked for more of the same, more basic courses, more homework, longer school years, more required courses, and better pay for teachers. Most educators saw this as a Band-Aid solution when a major new direction was needed. They saw little help for improving schools, such as Eastside High School in Paterson, New Jersey, where principal Joe Clark won both admiration and blame for maintaining discipline with a bullhorn and a baseball bat. The report had little to say about how to reform schools with significant problems. As discussed in Chapter 8, Gerald W. Bracey, David C. Berliner, and Bruce J. Biddle found research flaws in the various reform reports that seriously understated student performance and achievement.

After nearly twenty years of neglect except for social measures, education again became a top national priority in the 1980s, 1990s, and 2000s. It was a major agenda item for the presidential elections of 1984, 1992, 1996, and 2000. In 1984, thirty governors organized task forces on schooling, as did hundreds of school boards. Universities made efforts to strengthen relationships with schools, and the private sector offered its own reform package. The National Governors' Association report, *Time for Results,* advocated a national board to certify teachers, performance and pay links, school choice, school buildings open all year, and academic bankruptcy for schools and school districts not meeting standards. In 1991, the same group issued *Results in Education: 1990,* a report evaluating the results of earlier proposals for sweeping educational reforms. The report concluded that there was uneven and slow implementation of the proposals. In "Verbal, Math Scores on S.A.T. Up for Second Straight Year" (1993), Millicent Lawton, however, found thirty-two states reporting efforts toward developing higher education standards and/or new or improved assessment measures. Although some view the educational efforts of the governors to be political public relations endeavors, progress is being made in developing a technological base for sharing results of educational reform throughout the nation.

In *A Shared Vision: Policy Recommendations for Linking Teacher Education to School Reform* (1993), Calvin Frazier noted few results from the reform reports of the 1980s and suggested part of the fault was in teacher training institutions. Frazier called for more input from lawmakers, clear assignments for everyone involved in school reform, clear standards for teacher education programs, licensure of new teachers, and additional funds for effective school reform. In *Horace's School: Redesigning the American High School* (1992), Sizer discussed his eight years of managing the Coalition of Essential Schools. He also found the reform movement of the 1980s to have little effect on the lives of his fictional English teacher or his students. *Horace's Hope: The Future of the American High School* (1996) provides Sizer's views of the potentially positive effects of the current debate raging in education. Out of the debate over charter schools, vouchers, standards, and visions, Sizer finds a foundation being built, from the bottom up, for a more effective educational system that will serve well in the next century. Sizer finds an emerging community of individuals committed to education change and effectiveness. Based on the energy and idealism of youth and on teachers who challenge youth to be the best they can be, he views the future with hope. And he believes that some of the most salient ideas can be gleaned from an examination of the most influential publications.

Diane Ravitch in *Left Back: A Century of Failed School Reforms* examines educational history concluding that there continues to be a need to emphasize the liberal arts in education and to avoid dumbing down the curriculum through a variety of educational tracks. Although polemic in her account, Ravitch pinpoints the failure of a policy of expecting public schools to be all things to all people and emphasizes the role of high expectations and academic excellence as a route to effective educational reform. Her account continues the call for liberal arts education of the Yale Report of 1819, the Harvard Report of 1945, as well as *A Nation At Risk*.

Caroline Hoxby (2000) in *Would School Choice Change the Teaching Profession?*, finds school choice policies would lead to improved teacher and student effectiveness and achievement. The National Research Council's report *Knowing What Students Know: The Science and Design of Educational Assessment* (2000) stresses that school assessments should be available in usable forms for multiple constituencies as a route to more fair and valid inferences about student achievement. The report stressed the importance of developing measurement instruments based on increased knowledge of how students learn and how such learning can be more effectively measured. In addition to calling for increased funding for assessment research, the assessment committee members recommended training teachers in more effective use of tests that measure individual student progress and competence. Recent reform reports reflect increased understanding of the complexity of educational issues and challenges in the twenty-first century.

The Business Model.

A Nation at Risk took economic competition as its cause for being. *Action for Excellence* (1983), by the Task Force on Education for Economic Growth, stressed America's position in a changing world market. It argued that public education must prepare students with greater scientific and economic knowledge and provide them with computer literacy. It suggested a partnership of state and corporate support while delegating the needs of specialized groups and minorities to state and corporate leaders. "America's Competitive Challenge" (1983), a report by the Business-Higher Education Forum, argued that federal funding should upgrade university facilities, but it also argued that industry should invest more in the education of its workers. It suggested that industry and the universities work together for better utilization of all educational resources.

As Naisbitt pointed out in *Re-inventing the Corporation* (1985), American corporations spend $60 billion annually on education and training. Their programs are so vast that they offer an alternative to traditional university training; of course, these corporations apply business measures of efficiency and cost effectiveness to their programs. Much of this corporate support is similar to that described in Raymond E. Callahan's *The Cult of Efficiency: A Study of the Social Forces That Have Shaped the Administration of the Public Schools* (1962). The book describes how schools came under the influence of efficiency experts at the turn of the century.

Henry A. Giroux (1999) finds the corporatizing of American education reflects a crisis of vision regarding the meaning and purpose of "democracy" when market cultures, market moralities, and market mentalities may be shattering community, eroding civic society, and undermining the nurturing system for children. Deron Boyles in *American Education and Corporations* (2000) analyzed the growing use of schools as sites for consumer materialism. Waddell (2001) notes the problem of using school Web sites for advertising, and that some ads contain information inappropriate for children. Some school districts and states are getting into online advertising to help pay for laptop computers. Waddell notes that even when school districts seek to prohibit online advertising, the Internet is so expansive that school officials find it difficult to enforce restrictions.

Although there continue to be challenges in a cyclical economic system, with pockets of poverty and periodic corporate downsizing as market shifts require new goods and strategies, the American social network provides needed protection for the at-risk population. The corporate sector through philanthropic foundations often provides additional support for at-risk children, although efforts need to be made to assist Third World nations in addressing health and poverty challenges. The American economic model, although frequently subject to employment fluctuations, provides an efficient distribution of goods and services that attracts immigrants from throughout the world seeking a better life.

There should be little surprise in the discovery that business corporations feel they have the best models for educational reform. Successful commercial enterprises have been able to compete in a changing world market and have their own measures of efficiency. The most popular book of the period dealing with the ways in which business and industry have tried to recapture excellence is *In Search of Excellence: Lessons from America's Best Run Companies,* written by Thomas J. Peters and Robert H. Waterman in 1982. Their belief is that what works for the private sector can also be used by public institutions, such as schools. Their ideas included the following:

- A bias for action: doing something—anything—is better than the status quo
- Learning the preferences of the customers and catering to them
- Breaking up the corporation into small units and encouraging independent thinking
- Productivity through people: making all workers responsible and allowing them to share in rewards
- Insisting that executives keep in touch with essential business and have direct involvement with workers
- Concentration on the business at hand rather than pursuing secondary goals
- Simple structure with authority at lower levels and few top administrators
- Fostering a climate that stresses dedication to the central values of the company combined with tolerance for the activities of all who accept those values

Clearly these concepts were acceptable to educational institutions. The question remains, however, of applying the incentives of a profit-making corporation to schools. The difference in the 1980s, 1990s, and 2000s was that reform was demanded, and successful corporations provided a pattern with much public support. Forty-four business leaders and forty governors attended a National Education Summit in 1996 calling for tougher standards with accountability, workforce skills, and the improvement of education for global competition. An earlier summit called for the creation of a nonprofit resource center, Achieve, to provide assistance in improving academic and student assessments as well as the use of technology in schools. Robert B. Schwartz, former head of educational programs for Pew Charitable Trusts, was chosen to head Achieve. President Bill Clinton, who addressed the summit meeting, noted that school populations are diverse in terms of race, income, ethnicity, and background. Schools, he noted, have fractured authority and financing and are burdened by social problems. He identified these areas of challenge: (1) having standards accompanied by accountability; (2) rewarding and demanding higher standards of teachers; (3) holding schools accountable for results; (4) seeking business/community help in school district re-invention of their budgets; (5) having more options including charter schools; (6) making school safety a priority; (7) keeping schools open longer; and (8) getting the business community involved in expanding technology in classrooms. Clearly, partnerships between school districts and business are occurring more frequently throughout the nation.

The George W. Bush administration is closely tied to the business/corporate sector. The president's early cabinet appointments reflect the influence of the business community. In the corporate and educational sector, the concept of diversity views multiculturalism in education and the workforce as a strong tree with many different yet equally important branches (Kleiman, 2001). Multiculturalism and diversity is a work in progress as demographic changes occur. Schmitt (2001) reported on an increase in majority-minority populations revealed by the 2000 census. Bruce Katz, director of the Brookings Institute Center on Urban and Metropolitan Policy (2001), reported that for the first time nearly half of the nation's 100 largest cities are home to more Hispanics, blacks, Asians, and other minorities than whites. The vast majority (71 of 100) of American cities lost white residents. Immigration and higher birthrates among foreign-born are changing the complexion of U.S. cities. Although a small part of the population shifts may have occurred as people who identified themselves as white in the 1990 census listed themselves as multiracial, the population shift shows the volatility and complexity of change in the United States in the twenty-first century. These demographic shifts will lead educators to continue their work in progress on dealing with diversity issues and challenges.

The Paideia Proposal.   Mortimer Adler, longtime advocate of the Great Books curriculum and philosophical companion to Robert Hutchins, wrote the *Paideia Proposal: An Educational Manifesto* in 1982. His plan advocates giving the same quality of schooling to all. It requires a program of study that is both liberal and general. All sidetracks, specialized courses, and vocational training are eliminated. The basic course of study to be followed in twelve years of schooling allows only one choice, that of a second language.

Adler identifies three distinct modes of teaching and learning, rising in successive gradations of complexity and difficulty from the first to the twelfth year. All three modes are essential to the overall course of study. Mode One represents the acquisition of organized knowledge by means of didactic instruction, lectures, and responses, using textbooks and other aids in these subject areas: language, literature and the fine arts, math, natural science, history, geography, and social studies. Mode Two represents the development of intellectual skills (skill of learning)—by means of coaching, exercises, and supervised practice—in operations of reading, writing, speaking, listening, calculating, problem solving, observing, measuring, estimating, and exercising critical judgment. Mode Three represents enlarging the understanding of ideas and values by means of Socratic questioning and interaction with major contributions to literature.

In addition to these three main modes of learning, the required course of study includes physical education, care of the body, computer skills, manual arts, and an introduction to various careers. Adler was convinced that children judged unable to pursue his curriculum simply had not yet had their minds challenged by such requirements.

The Paideia plan gained advocates among those favoring liberal education and thinking skills. It was almost the exact opposite of the models proposed by *A Nation at Risk* and the business sector. Although no powerful organizations or political groups embraced the Paideia Proposal, it has influenced the movement away from early specialization in the high schools and the strengthening of general education requirements in colleges and universities.

Tanner (1991) in his book *Progressive Education at the Crossroads: Crusade for Democracy* discussed in historical perspective Dewey's experimentalism. Experimentalism had been viewed in an adverse light in the 1960s through the 1980s by radical revisionists, critical theorists, and neo-Marxists. Tanner noted that Dewey and his followers fought to uphold the democratic-liberal traditions in popular education in the face of great opposition. While Adler stressed the liberating influence of the liberal arts tradition, Dewey viewed the problems of public education as interconnected with social, political, economic, and cultural problems. Dewey saw the school and society as intertwined. The school was a miniature society. "The saint sits in his tower while the burly sinners rule the world" was a call for interaction between schools and the larger community from which they drew their students and to which they returned as participating and contributing citizens. Progressivism and traditionalism have their strong advocates in the twenty-first century as they did in the nineteenth and twentieth.

Boyer, Goodlad, and Sizer.   Three names that appeared constantly in the reform literature of the mid-1980s were Ernest Boyer, John Goodlad, and Theodore Sizer. The three had been associated with studies of education long before the critical reports emerged, and each had developed a plan for improving schools. Boyer's most important contribution was a report for the Carnegie Foundation for the Advancement of Teaching in 1983 entitled *High School: A Report on Secondary Education in America*. In a tribute to Ernest Boyer (1928–1995) in *Educational Leadership,* Vito Perrone noted that Boyer always encouraged educators to maintain a human face in schools as well as to create an integrated curriculum and to integrate classrooms and neighborhoods.

Goodlad, a recognized expert in curriculum, made a major contribution to the reform literature in *A Place Called School: Prospects for the Future* (1984). Goodlad and

McMannon's edited book entitled *The Public Purpose of Education and Schooling* (1997) continues the conversations about improving education, recognizing the complexity of the educational process. Goodlad, as Dewey, noted that democracy and the nation's educational infrastructure are inextricably entwined and sensitively interdependent.

Sizer published *Horace's Compromise: The Dilemma of the American High School* (1984). In *Horace's Hope: The Future of the American High School* (1996), Sizer reiterates the continuing need for educational reform and notes the progress that has been made toward an improved educational system for the twenty-first century. In a *Kappan* article called "The Rising Tide of School Reform Reports," Patricia Cross of Harvard credited Boyer, Goodlad, and Sizer with the most influential reform books from within the educational profession.

Boyer's detailed studies of secondary education tend to support some of the disturbing accounts of teaching conditions described earlier by sociologists like Dan Lortie in *Schoolteacher*. Boyer thinks that the teaching profession is in deep crisis in this nation, and he says teachers are fully aware of their situation. Teachers are deeply troubled not only about low salaries but also about loss of status, bureaucratic pressures, lack of recognition, and a poor public image. Boyer believes that it makes no sense to talk about recruiting better teachers for the future unless the conditions of teaching are improved. The professional ethos that attracted many teachers in the first place has withered under public criticism and an outmoded school structure. He argues that the push for excellence must begin by improving the conditions that drive out good teachers. Fewer students choose to enter teaching as a profession, and those who do are not the best students. Boyer is also critical of college programs for the preparation of teaching and the methods by which states handle certification.

Flexibility and freedom are keys to Boyer's ideas of reform. He sought a comprehensive modernization process that would free teachers to innovate on the individual school level. He states that the average high school teacher with six classes a day and only fifty-four minutes of preparation time is hard pressed to pursue excellence. Reviewing subject matter, preparing lesson plans, grading papers, advising students, and making out report cards also take time that might be given to improving teaching techniques. He believes that the nature of the classroom and working conditions must change for excellence to be achieved. Flexibility and decentralization need to replace top-down decision making and bureaucratic standardization. Involving parents and integrating classrooms and neighborhoods so that students can learn by interacting with adults are essential in developing a human face in schools. According to Boyer, reforms will fail unless teachers at the local level are supported by the public and given real professional status.

Goodlad's *A Place Called School: Prospects for the Future* (1984) also calls attention to the plight of the profession and the crisis of schooling. In fact, Goodlad thinks that the problems of schooling are of such crippling proportions that the entire system of public education could collapse. Monetary solutions are not sufficient to regain excellence. He states that nonproductivity, low achievement, high dropout rates, poor attendance, low teacher morale, and loss of public confidence are symptoms of severe problems. Mere application of business practices or piecemeal measures like higher standards for high school graduation will not do. According to Goodlad, there is, however, a mandate for change that legitimizes drastic action. Thus, he finds an opportunity in the crisis of the 1980s.

In his plan for educational renewal, Goodlad does not abandon the quest for social equality that dominated schooling in the 1960s and 1970s. He is keenly aware of the denial of access to knowledge and access to effective teaching for racial minorities and those relegated to lower tracks through testing. The disadvantaged students are those who might gain most from varied pedagogical techniques and individualized instruction. They are the least likely to benefit from those reforms that pursue excellence by increasing the proportion of failures.

Goodlad's concept of educational reform requires that we focus on entire schools as opposed to "tinkering" with structure and curriculum. To do this, the community must be involved, and Goodlad has even suggested that the community be the major educator of the child. Colleges and universities should be linked in partnerships aimed at improving both public schools and teacher education. Not content merely to write about renewal, Goodlad announced his sponsorship of twelve such school–university partnerships at the American Association of Colleges of Teacher Education (AACTE) meeting in Chicago in 1986. His *Teacher's for Our Nation's Schools* (1990) called for autonomous centers of pedagogy in colleges and universities in order to have the same authority exhibited by medical and law schools.

Theodore Sizer also supports more experimentation on the local school level as a means for altering the high degree of standardization and sameness common to educational institutions. A decentralized model with school-based management and delegation of authority to district or school building levels is preferable to the line-staff model in vogue. By designating certain schools as experimental units with license to try innovative approaches, better techniques of instruction can be developed. The school principal must have authority for allocation of resources and must act as instructional leader. In *Horace's Compromise* (1984), Sizer recommends that individual schools be relieved of mandated curriculum, allowing experimentation based on the unique conditions of each community. Schools within schools should be set up as laboratories. School-based management should be used to move more authority to individual units and provide more instructional options. The involvement of teachers, parents, students, community leaders, and representatives of business and industry should be encouraged.

Sizer is very much concerned about the inability of high school teachers to get to know their students well enough to coach them toward excellence. For example, in learning to write well, students need a lengthy interaction with one teacher who goes over each theme, makes corrections, suggests improvements, and gives encouragement. This is impossible for an English teacher who has five different classes of thirty students. In order for the teacher to know the mind of the child well and to serve as a mentor or coach, the ratio of teachers to students must be reduced. Sizer suggests having secondary teachers offer more than one subject to the same students. English teachers might have the same students for English, sociology, and American history. This would require broader teacher training, but it would allow for better results.

Boyer, Goodlad, and Sizer set the scene for continued examination of the process and product of education. The balance between child-centered and subject-centered education that Dewey wrote about in *The Child and the Curriculum* (1902) confronts twenty-first-century educators. While the pendulum is currently swinging toward intellectual discipline through high-stakes testing policies, parental voices are increasingly calling for alternative methods of evaluation for students at risk.

Michael Apple (2001) views the current push for standards and tests as running the risk of affixing labels on children at risk and their teachers. Apple notes that although there are increasing calls for more flexible forms of assessment, declining state resources tend to result in more traditional standards and testing to the detriment of minority and culturally diverse populations of students.

Comment and Criticism. *Action for Excellence, Making the Grade,* and *A Nation at Risk* were political documents. They gave vivid accounts of American education in decline with little regard for accuracy. Their aim was to get action from state and federal policy makers and from the public. The practical school administrator got very little guidance from these reports as means for actual school improvement.

The drive for educational excellence should also include at-risk children, as noted in the Committee for Economic Development's *Investing in Our Children, Savage Inequalities: Children in America's Schools* (1985) and the William T. Grant Foundation's *The Forgotten Half: Non-College Youth in America: An Interim Report on the School-to-Work Transition* (1988). These works call for greater recognition of the education, social and economic needs, and aspirations of these children. Non-college-bound students deserve the same opportunities to excel in society and in the workplace. The drive for excellence should not be excessively focused on college-bound students.

In *Cultural Literacy* (1987), E.D. Hirsch suggested that all educated persons should have knowledge of the best ideals of humankind. Lack of such knowledge, Hirsch noted, is at the base of our literacy challenge. Hirsch reiterated this theme in *The Schools We Need and Why We Don't Have Them* (1996). He again emphasizes the importance of content, commonality, and coherence in the curriculum, as well as the importance of rediscovery of a sense of community in our culture as a route to preserving the fragile fabric of our society. Hirsch seeks an educational system designed to provide universal competence in our children to lessen the us-versus-them mentality in society and education.

Academic Preparation for College (1983) synthesized the judgment of hundreds of high school teachers and college professors concerning the knowledge and skills students should bring from high school to college. It set high standards and a rigorous course of study for such subjects as English, mathematics, science, social studies, foreign languages, and the arts. There was also the requirement for students to master competencies in reading, writing, speaking, reasoning, mathematics, and study skills. On the negative side, many educators felt that the report was idealistic and far-fetched. It appealed mostly to elite schools, where most students are college-bound and where resources are adequate. Many who are concerned about dropouts and teaching minimum competencies to average children saw the report as unrealistic.

Nevertheless, *Academic Preparation for College* provided a comprehensive curriculum model and a specific plan for reform.

What Matters Most: Teaching for America's Future (1996) reflects the continued search for higher standards in education. The report calls for a crusade to improve student achievement levels through a comprehensive approach to redesigning, restructuring, monitoring, and licensing schools and educators to reach higher standards throughout the system. Special emphasis is placed on a National Board for Professional Teaching Standards.

Zollers, Albert, and Cochran-Smith (2000) reported on a multiyear collaborative self-study designed to teach social justice. Zollers and her colleagues found that social justice involves faculty recruitment/retention/mentoring, student admissions/advising, and review of frameworks and knowledge that guide coursework and curriculum. The authors' study was a response to changing demographics as diversity permeates all levels of the educational system.

A number of common points run through most of the reports. Although in trouble, public schools are a mainstay of American society. In spite of vouchers, tax rebates for private school tuition, and alternative schools with tax support, no serious proposals for ending public school education have been made. Education is correlated with economic growth, and high-quality schooling is essential to the national well-being. Neither the individual nor the nation can prosper without high-quality education. Education is the universal right of all people in a free society. Education is a lifelong process, and the foundation for it must be laid in elementary schools. Access to postsecondary education is dependent on the quality of high school programs for all. It is not satisfactory to push one segment of the population through a low-achievement secondary education and into the workforce. This implies that the process of learning is as important as content.

Education must be accountable. No sector of society is without responsibility for teaching and learning. It is in the national interest for the federal government to regulate, legislate, and fund national school programs. Local districts are responsible for implementing programs, the delivery of educational priorities, legislation, regulations, and funding. The fundamental building block of educational renewal consists in the recruitment and training of high-quality teachers.

The reform reports and studies of the 1980s through the early 2000s had many points in common. They called for revised curriculums and the strengthening of requirements in English, mathematics, social studies, physical education, art, music, computer sciences, and foreign languages. All called for higher student efforts including tests for promotion and graduation, better discipline, and more homework. Some suggested beginning education earlier and extending the school day and year. Most asked for additional programs to benefit the gifted and talented and other programs to give special help to slow learners. There were several calls for upgrading textbooks, establishing a core curriculum, and eliminating tracking. At least eight studies demanded a revision of vocational courses. Most required incorporating outside learning experiences into the curriculum, and several emphasized the need to improve reasoning skills. Almost every study said something about higher college admission standards.

The reports disagreed about how all of this was to be accomplished and who would pay for it. It is always easier to call attention to a problem than it is to provide a viable solution. Many school leaders were dismayed to find the national reports gave them very little practical advice about how to achieve the excellence demanded. Much of the state-level activity that followed the reports was directed toward regulations such as teacher and pupil testing, stronger academic standards, and mandated curriculum requirements. A student of history might wonder if the twenty-first century will be spent correcting the overregulation of the 1980s, 1990s, and early 2000s. These decades were spent addressing the permissiveness and neglect of earlier decades but will possibly be part of the problem rather than the solution for the rest of our twenty-first century.

School Effectiveness.   The dismal statistics that pointed to failure and mediocrity in American education in the 1980s were by no means descriptive of all institutions. Averages ignore data that falls at the upper or lower ends of the scale. Many have drowned in rivers that average only three feet in depth. Numerous communities know very well that their schools are outstanding and that they have achieved the excellence demanded in the national reports. The educational profession by 1984 was identifying characteristics of effective schools that could be used as tools of evaluation and for ascertaining which schools could serve as models of superiority.

Older studies of school effectiveness have been used as the basis for new research. Weber's 1970 study of reading achievement in inner-city schools found that strong leadership, high student expectations, a good atmosphere for learning, use of phonics, individualization of instruction, careful evaluation, and adequate numbers of trained reading teachers made an outstanding program. In 1981, Zerchykov cited administrative leadership, an orderly school, frequent monitoring of student progress, redirection of resources toward basic instruction, a good atmosphere, stress on basic skills, and realistic instructional expectations as factors creating school effectiveness.

By 1985, studies of school effectiveness were in progress throughout the nation by school districts, state departments of education, professional organizations, and universities. Two critical factors emerged from these studies to be added to those previously identified. Effective schools must have the support and involvement of the community, and school principals must be dynamic instructional leaders. Boyer also addressed this question and found that effective schools have the following characteristics:

- Effective schools have clear goals and a commitment to public education.
- They identify a core of learning common to all students.
- They attract the best teachers in the area.
- They promote mastery of communication skills and language use.
- They prepare students for work and for further education.
- They use flexible patterns of instruction.
- They have ties with business, college, and community leaders.
- They use technology effectively.
- They develop strong administrative leadership.

National leaders involved in *A Nation at Risk* had their own agendas for bringing about effective schools. In 1983, Education Secretary Bell called for high schools to require four years of English, three years each of mathematics, social studies, and science, and passing of examinations in all of these areas. He also said that by 1989, SAT and ACT scores should surpass the 1965 levels, dropout rates should be cut by 10 percent, and entry-level teachers' salaries should be competitive with those of business and engineering. Neither Bell nor Secretary William Bennett, who followed him in office, provided a specific plan for how these things might be accomplished or how they would be financed.

Two other terms were widely used in the school effectiveness literature of the mid-1980s. *Time-on-task* dealt with the actual part of each day spent on instruction, as opposed to time used for announcements, passing through halls, taking attendance, and the like. *Efficiency* focused on the most cost-effective means of accomplishing educational goals in order to maximize scarce resources. Defined as academic learning time or engaged learning time, time-on-task did allow for a higher part of each day to be spent by students in paying attention to their studies. Students are on-task when they are actively engaged in activities that match their abilities and interests and that they succeed in most of the time.

However, the California Beginning Teacher Evaluation Study of 1977, which studied this topic in detail, showed that only rather small gains could be made by cutting down wasted time. Current research shows that sizable increases in achievement require sizable increases in time, if time is the only variable modified. Better use of time is essential, but it might not be sufficient to achieve excellence. Likewise, the effective school research shows that, as efficiency increases, there is little room for additional improvement through more efficient methods. For example, in January 1983, 85 percent of high schools, 68 percent of middle schools, and 42 percent of elementary schools had microcomputers in use for instruction. The amount of idle time was so small that better efficiency in the utilization of computers would accomplish very little. Real improvement in computer-linked instruction must come from buying more and newer machines or making existing computers available during hours when school is not in session, because they are already nearing maximum use during the regular school day. Studies also show that regardless of the numbers of computers in classrooms, adequate instructional software and the instructor's ability to teach students effective computer skills are essential.

Other research indicates there is not a strong or consistent relationship between student performance and school resources, at least after variations in family input are taken into account (Hanushek, 1997). However, in reviewing school finance reform in Kentucky, Adams and White (1997) found increased equal opportunity resulted as funds were distributed more uniformly throughout the state's school districts. Court decisions requiring more equitable distribution of resources between school districts are essential for equal access and opportunity. The task is not easy as witness the number of states under court orders to improve school funding formulas.

The Bush and Clinton administrations, reacting to the 1990 work of the National Governors' meetings on education, adopted six national education goals for the year 2000 designed to encourage more effective schools through focusing on learner outcomes. Subsequently, three additional national education goals were added to include teacher improvement, adult education, and parental involvement in education. The nine goals are as follows:

1. All children will start school ready to learn.
2. The high school graduation rate will increase to at least 90 percent.
3. Students completing grades four, eight, and twelve will have competency in academic subject matter including English, mathematics, science, history, and geography.
4. Students in the United States will be first in the world in mathematics and science achievement.
5. Every school will be free of drugs and violence.
6. Schools will offer an environment conducive to learning.
7. Every school will promote partnerships to increase parental involvement.
8. The nation's teaching force will have access to programs for continuous improvement of their professional skills and knowledge.
9. Every American adult will be literate and possess knowledge and skills to compete in the world economy.

In his 1997 State of the Union Address, President Clinton once again made education a national priority. He stressed improving access to higher education, rewarding academic achievement, and utilizing federal work-study funds in colleges that encourage students to work as mentors to elementary children in the areas of reading and math skills.

Although the goals were widely heralded as a base for educational excellence, few professional educators believed they would be achieved by 2000, because of restricted financial resources as well as potential social and political roadblocks to reform. *What Matters Most: Teaching for America's Future*, a 1996 report by the National Commission on Teaching and America's Future, reiterated Goals 2000. It was another call for action to move toward higher standards, toward modeling best practices for teaching and learning, and toward greater cooperation between schools and the business community. Chaired by North Carolina Governor James B. Hunt and comprised of a large spectrum of education and corporate leaders, the commission called for, among other things, the following:

❑   Establishing a professional standards board, accreditation for all schools of education, and licensing teachers based on demonstrated performance including tests of subject matter and teaching knowledge
❑   Organizing teacher education and professional development programs around standards for students and teachers and developing extended graduate-level teacher preparation programs that provide a yearlong internship in a professional development school
❑   Putting qualified teachers in every classroom, providing incentives for teaching in teacher-shortage areas, eliminating barriers to teacher mobility, and increasing the ability of low-wealth districts to pay for qualified teachers

❑   Encouraging and rewarding teacher knowledge and skill, developing a career continuum for teaching linked to assessments and compensation systems that reward knowledge and skill, setting goals and enacting incentives for National Board Certification in every state and district, and seeking to certify 105,000 teachers in this decade, one for every school in the United States

❑   Creating schools that are organized for student and teacher success, investing more in teachers and technology and less in nonteaching personnel, providing venture capital for challenge grants, and selecting, preparing, and retaining principals who understand teaching and learning and who can lead high-performing schools

As with other reform efforts, *What Matters Most: Teaching for America's Future* called for a national effort based on models of best practices. It served as a guide to educational improvement for a new millennium.

In *A Framework for Appraising Educational Reforms* (1996), Ernest R. House states that the best educational reforms would focus on greatly reducing the administrative hierarchy, transforming the purpose and structure of the central staff to a small strategic staff, reducing the size of schools to 300 to 400 students, making schools relatively autonomous and unregulated, and providing opportunity for schools of choice. House identified items encompassed within recent reform proposals such as national goals and standards, decentralization, open markets, performance assessment, and self-assessment. Many of these factors reflect a corporate/industrial model. Raising funds to implement these reform reports will continue to be a challenge in the future. That roadblock (fund-raising) seems universal in school reform proposals. A trend in reform reports is to move toward national certification and evaluation of entry-level educators on a voluntary basis at first.

In *The Principalship: A Reflective Practice Perspective,* Thomas J. Sergiovanni stresses the importance of the moral aspect of leadership for the future. He notes that moral leadership re-centers people as centers of action, not merely as recipients of action. Carr and Harris (2001) in *Succeeding with Standards: Linking Curriculum, Assessment, and Action Planning* wrote of the need for celebrating milestones such as completing assignments, developing comprehensive assessment systems, and completing standard-based action plans for reform to enhance student learning. Making achievement an adventure in success experience through graduation challenges, inquiry fairs, and other activities to showcase student performance together with community-wide celebration of student success is a powerful, positive tool for effective learning and improved student achievement.

Early congressional work on George W. Bush's educational initiatives included concurrence by both parties on defining school failure. Failure would mean lack of academic progress by any group of disadvantaged students in schools receiving federal funds meant to close achievement gaps. A school would not be given a passing grade if most students show progress in proficiency tests but a specific minority group of students or limited-English-skills students were not showing improvement

(Anderson, 2001). The 2002 educational reform bill is a work in progress as the president and both political parties seek to provide funding for education. Early budget work included an increase of $2.5 billion annually over the next six years, in addition to the $6.3 billion already allocated, for students with disabilities. Focus on accountability, results, and continued testing, especially in grades three through eight, will be included in the final version of the educational reform budget.

Reform Initiatives in States and Cities.

The pursuit of excellence in the several states did not begin with *A Nation at Risk,* but the national reports certainly stimulated renewed activity. According to *Action in the States* (1984) by the Education Commission of the States, school reform was a high-priority item everywhere. All but five states had legislatively enacted initiatives or were awaiting action by the legislature or the state board. The states have generally followed the public demand to cut down on curriculum offerings not considered basic—such as art, music, and physical education—and to require more "solid" courses. Most states have chosen to mandate the basic curriculum with emphasis given to courses such as English, mathematics, science, and social studies. Governors, legislatures, and state and local boards usually collaboratively develop action plans for renewal. Hearings for the public have been conducted in most of the states with comprehensive action plans. Educators and business leaders have been invited to participate.

State educational reform plans are diverse because of demographic factors, the existing level of educational achievement, and the economic conditions. Nevertheless, all the states share some of the same concerns. In addition to upgrading the curriculum, they wish to strengthen standards for high school graduation, raise teacher certification requirements, improve salaries for teachers, promote business involvement in education, and integrate technology into instruction. Competency testing for promotion and especially for high school graduation is part of the plan in most states. Some states also call for continuous staff development, school-based accountability, and curriculum updating through re-accreditation.

As a rule, state efforts aimed at educational excellence in the mid-1980s were conservative. Economic and political forces caused the states to opt for strengthening existing schools rather than designing a new approach to education. State plans tended to call for more testing, more homework, more hours in the school day and school year, and emphasis on basics in the curriculum. Foreign language requirements and computer literacy also received attention in many state programs. Career education and preparing for the world of work were addressed because of the strong expressions of concern by business leaders. With the increase of single-parent families and latchkey children, state plans dealt with school responsibility for health and nutrition. In "The Socratic Approach to Character Education" (1996), Elkind and Sweet address character education increasingly being incorporated into the curriculum at all educational levels in response to vandalism and crime in the nation's schools. Some curriculum changes reflected public interest in environmental, nuclear war, and energy issues as well as international and multicultural concerns.

The 1980s, 1990s, and 2000s witnessed several state and city school administration reforms and fiscal restructuring. All the changes dealt with what Linda Darling-Hammond, director of the National Center for Restructuring Education at Columbia University, referred to as a new school reform model designed to develop communities of learning, grounded in grassroots of democratic discourse. She saw these reforms as a way to empowerment and educational freedom for educators of students in a learning community.

The Chicago School Reform Act of 1988 required basic changes in Chicago public school governance. The act sought more involvement and input of local stakeholders in school governance and policy making. By 2001 Chicago had implemented annual testing from kindergarten through eighth grade, mandated improvement plans, placed penalties on low-performing schools that failed to improve, and allowed parents to transfer children to any school in the system that would accept them. Anne Lewis (2001) in a *Kappan* commentary continued by noting that Chicago schools have improved but only minimally. She added that The Consortium on Chicago School Research in reports for the Annenberg Challenge found that children do better on skills tests when challenged to think by teachers. In *City Schools Leading the Way* (1993), Forsyth and Tallerico noted that the Illinois state law provided for increases in parental input in Chicago's school policy. Forsyth and Tallerico also added that Boston was another city school system that moved toward decentralization, accountability, and increased input from parents, teachers, and administrators.

The widely watched 1990 Kentucky Educational Reform Act has been positive to date. Under a state supreme court order (*Rose v. Council for Better Education,* 1988), the state moved toward equal opportunity and an efficient system of education for all school districts. The school districts were re-evaluated and reconstructed to meet the court order. An independent research group, the Kentucky Institute for Educational Research, evaluates the progress of state reforms. Their research findings indicated over 90 percent of entry-level teachers reported being moderately to extremely well prepared to establish a positive learning environment, communicate high expectations, design instruction that is developmentally appropriate, use different teaching strategies for different instructional purposes, and communicate the core concepts of their discipline (NCATE, *Quality Teaching,* 1997).

A variety of strategies have been undertaken by states and cities to improve educational achievement levels. Gehring (2001) reported that teachers in a school district in Washington State have started giving student grades on employability to prepare them for workplace success. Work habits, commitment to quality, attendance, punctuality, communication, and interpersonal skills are graded in addition to the regular academic achievement. In Oakland, California, an affiliate of the California Teachers Association opposed the plan, but the superintendent and the school board voted to give administrators bonuses for higher student test scores on annual state tests (Stricherz, 2001). Low-performing school districts in Pennsylvania are subject to improvement plans including proposals for private contractors to run the schools, management and fiscal reviews, and teacher training programs that include parents. Schools that do not improve by 2003 will be taken over by a three-person control board named by the state (Johnston, 2000). States are pushing for higher education standards, taking over the administration of problem schools, focusing on improving at-risk student achievement levels, implementing innovative experimental programs, addressing high dropout rates, and seeking to increase school funding.

The trend toward increased decision making at the school site level, although spreading, is yielding mixed results. Further restructuring, modification, and experimentation are to be expected in the years ahead. Collective bargaining, restricted finances, and teacher strikes will require continued work in conflict resolution to achieve effective schools.

The concept emerging in the state and city school reforms responded to Arthur Wirth's (1992) call for more democratic participation in public school policy making. Yet, as McKersie (1993) noted, pitfalls exist in implementing reform when there is failure to recognize that the educational enterprise is complex, that there are many voices representing many interests, and that politics involves compromise and consensus to achieve necessary funding for implementing innovative educational reforms. Impediments to educational reform in addition to funding limitations include increased costly litigation as various interest groups seek to implement their own agendas often to the detriment of the overall school programs.

Local Reform Initiatives.

Historically, some of the most impressive efforts to achieve excellence in education have been initiated at the local or district levels. Examples include the Dalton Plan of the Progressive Era and the Philadelphia Parkway Program of the 1960s and 1970s. Urban school reform in Atlanta in the 1970s under the leadership of Superintendent Alonzo Crim also showed how a failing district could be made into an outstanding one with local effort. Most of the alternative schools in the United States were developed without state or national leadership.

Laboratory schools, schools-without-walls, and magnet schools intended to draw students to a superior and specialized program were created by school districts. Larger school districts with considerable resources, a highly professional staff, and active community leaders have been able to establish models of excellence in education. Sometimes the leadership has come from the superintendent and sometimes from the school board, the parent-teacher organization, or reform-minded citizens. John Dewey insisted that the school and the community work as a unit for high-quality education. John Goodlad stated many times that the community should be the major educator of the child. Educational historian Lawrence Cremin argued that the community should serve to interlock all educative agencies within and outside of the school.

Following *A Nation at Risk,* most local school districts in the United States began to evaluate performance standards and accountability. Student outcomes were evaluated in terms of behavior and competence. While state boards focused on learner achievement, many individual schools looked at the relationship between the curriculum and student performance.

Wolf, Borko, Elliott and McIver (2000) reported on four schools that sought to meet the standards of the Kentucky Reform Act of 1990. Each of the four exemplary schools, their administrators, and faculty took local control of the statewide initiative. They worked diligently on connections and relationships, built a foundation of trust in one another, and engaged in constant dialogue that supported and provided the foundation for professional and personal growth that enriched their lives and led to improved achievement levels for pupils. Internalizing the spirit of the reform—being the best one can be and maintaining high expectations of students—led to involvement, commitment, nurturing, and caring, all of which contributed to positive results. In the end, all school success is local requiring total commitment of administration, faculty, and staff.

Financial Crunch.   The Reagan administration created the National Commission on Excellence but made it plain that the federal government would not fund its recommendations. According to the NEA, it would cost almost $24 billion to implement the recommendations, and if the school year were lengthened, it would cost about $40 billion. Even decreasing class size by one or two students would require millions of dollars. And increasing teachers' salaries across the nation would carry a staggering bill. President Reagan maintained that schools need more discipline, not more money; his educational leaders (T. H. Bell and W. Bennett) said that states and local districts would have to finance the reforms.

This, of course, was more realistic for some states than for others. California was in better shape to finance reform than states that had suffered recession, such as Michigan, Oregon, and the industrial Northeast. Sun Belt states that were doing well before the decline in oil prices were hit with major cutbacks in 1984. The decline was most dramatic in Louisiana, Oklahoma, and Texas. None of the states that depend on agriculture for revenue were able to adequately fund reforms or salary increases for teachers. In every state, education must compete with demands for prisons, bridges, roads, and sewer systems. Educational reform also bumps up against needs to repair physical plants or meet safety requirements. In 1983, it was estimated that $25 billion was needed by local school districts just to repair buildings, replace defective equipment, and eliminate hazardous asbestos. By 1994, many states including California and Florida had difficulty funding the educational effort due to a sluggish economy. By 1997, budget surpluses, the result of a strong economy, were widespread.

Much of the money for excellence in education needed to be raised at the local district level, but this was becoming increasingly difficult in the mid-1980s. Arkansas, for example, traditionally a poor state and one ranked low in educational achievement, passed tough new standards for schools, to be implemented in 1987. It was estimated that the cost of these standards would be $298 million. Part of the funding was to come from state revenues, but local districts were required to bear the costs of employing new teachers for subjects not formerly offered. A shortfall in the collection of state taxes in 1985 reduced the school fund by $25 million. Local millage elections were held in 120 districts in 1984 and 242 districts in 1985. In 70 percent of these elections, higher millages were passed, indicating strong local support for high-quality education. Nevertheless, the local efforts were not enough, and Arkansas trailed the national average per pupil expenditure in 1986 by $1,136. It is not realistic to expect local districts and state governments to fund reforms without federal help. By 1986, most states were experiencing great difficulty in paying for better educational programs.

States are being asked to assume most of the costs for educational excellence at a difficult time. The taxpayers' revolt characterized by California's Proposition 13, which limited spending in that state, was followed by balanced budget legislation in seventeen states between 1977 and 1981. States like Idaho, Montana, California, and Michigan are unlikely to pass new taxes without significant improvement in their economies.

In *Nordlinger v. Hahn* (1992) the Court upheld the constitutionality of California's Proposition 13, which protected the rights of existing homeowners. By mid-1993, six state supreme courts had ordered legislatures to fund schools more equitably. Most states in 1993 faced severe financial restrictions with increased demands for educational staff and facilities in the face of growing enrollments and decreased finances.

By late summer 1997, Baldauf noted that many states had large budget surpluses, squirreling away some $20 billion in reserve funds. There is, however, caution in expenditures because in a cyclical economy this year's surplus can be next year's deficit. Regardless of the caution, school districts in many states received increased funding.

At the end of the Clinton administration, although there was a national budget surplus, the new economy with overvalued high-tech dot.coms went into a tailspin. The Federal Reserve chairman–Alan Greenspan, President George W. Bush, and Congress worked to lower interest rates, implement tax cuts, and called on Europe and Asia to help support efforts to avoid or limit a global recession. State, community, and local surpluses were at risk as tax revenues declined with plant closures and growing employee layoffs. The 2001 and 2002 national budget greatly increased the amount of funds destined for education with provision for special education and for children at risk.

The Committee for Education Funding, a nonpartisan school advocacy coalition of 100 organizations, hailed the congressional efforts to increase education funding for the future. Although political machinations could change the outcome, a budget resolution to increase education funding by over $350 billion over ten years was passed by the Senate. The resolution included full funding of IDEA, increasing Pell Grants, Head Start, increases in TRIO and college work-study funding, and funding toward hiring 100,000 new teachers. Congress and the George W. Bush administration made education a budget priority for 2001 and beyond. Educational funding varies from state to state, and among urban and rural communities, depending on the tax base between rich and poor communities, equity funding programs, desegregation litigation and federal monitors, inflation, and cost of living adjustments.

Gramm-Rudman Amendment. Congress passed the Gramm-Rudman Bill in 1985. The bill, a response to President Ronald Reagan's supply-side economics, slashed the federal deficit by reducing federal expenditures for social and welfare programs. National defense, social security, and interest on the national debt were exempt, so that all cuts aimed at reducing the deficit had to come from programs like education, highways, and welfare. The Reagan administration opposed new taxes and threatened to veto any that were passed. The immediate impact of Gramm-Rudman was to cut programs such as Title 1, a program that undeniably helped raise the reading and mathematics scores of disadvantaged youngsters.

Many of those advocating educational reform, especially the spokespersons for national commissions and the federal government, say the way to improve schools is not to spend more money. Most educators agree that "throwing" money at a problem will not make it go away, but they are convinced that many vital reform programs are expensive. Both educators and economists dispute the theory that economic growth will be sufficient to offset federal cuts. There was considerable national feeling that Gramm-Rudman would not achieve a balanced budget and that the cost to society was too high. Several constitutional challenges to the bill were made in late 1986. By 1997, both political parties supported increased funding for education, although there were often different priorities.

The Clinton administration's national service program, envisioned in President Clinton's book *Putting People First* (1992), was designed to have a National Service Trust Fund that guaranteed every American who wanted a college education the means to obtain one. The National and Community Service Trust Act, passed by Congress in 1993, provided jobs for over 20,000 young people in 1994 and for over 33,000 by 1996. Under the plan, students would receive $4,725 a year for full-time service (1,700 hours) and $2,362 for part-time service (900 hours), for postsecondary education or training tuition. The jobs would be in the areas of environmental, educational safety programs and would provide a wage, child care, and health insurance. Based on his work with educational apprenticeship programs while governor of Arkansas, President Clinton also sought a national school–job link to be funded based on states' willingness to engage in a systematic school-to-work program.

Funding worthwhile educational programs remained conservative in an era of administration and congressional efforts to balance the budget. By the end of the Clinton administration, with a large budget surplus, there was increased spending on education. At the opening of the George W. Bush administration, both political parties vied for increased educational spending. With the surplus and a declining economy, the president and Congress passed a large tax cut bill. By the spring of 2002, the national budget projections predicted deficit spending in the future. In recent years only the John Kennedy and Ronald Reagan administrations had passed tax cuts prior to the Bush administration.

Meanwhile, the price of keeping the existing system in operation continues to climb. NEA figures show that Americans raised their spending for K through 12 programs by $9.1 billion in 1985–1986. Enrollments increased nationwide by an estimated 109,000 to a total of 44.6 million students by 1995. Secondary enrollment declined slightly but was more than offset by elementary gains. In the fall of 1997, public schools had a record enrollment with a projection of 54.6 million students by 2006. The nation's teaching force was some 3 million in 1996. Although the per student expenditure varied considerably from state to state, schools spent an average of $3,677 per pupil in 1985–1986 and $5,652 in 1995–1996. New Jersey spent the most with $9,318 per child, and Utah spent the least with $3,670 per pupil in 1995–1996. Average salaries for teachers rose by 7.3 percent nationally to $25,257 in 1985–1986 and to $36,900 in 1995. Federal revenues increased by 0.2 percent from a 6.9 percent average in 1994–1995 to 7.1 percent in 1995–1996. Average revenues from states increased from 47.6 percent in 1994–1995 to 47.9 percent in 1995–1996. It is obvious that state and local efforts are hard pressed to meet basic needs and to increase teachers' salaries with the additional burdens of new programs for excellence, special education, and replacing programs lost through federal budget cutting. According to Berliner (1995), although expenditures for education have increased, much of the increase has gone to programs for special education.

By 2001 there were efforts to raise teachers' salaries in most states. Burgeoning enrollment approaching 54 million public school students due to immigration and increased birthrates among low-income families had led to overcrowded classrooms in Florida and other states. Many school districts were engaged in school building and upgrading programs to meet needs of a growing student population. *Education Week*'s 2001 report "A Better Balance: Quality Counts" (with support by the Pew Foundation) found that 1999 unadjusted average state expenditure per pupil was $6,408. The average teacher salary was over $39,000 while beginning teacher salaries were reported to be $26,639 in 1998. Beginning state salaries in 2001 varied from region to region and from state to state with over $31,000 in many states and much higher in some of the wealthy districts. The American Federation of Teachers reported that the average teacher salary in 1999–2000 was $41,820. Florida and a number of other states reported teacher shortages across the spectrum and a severe shortage of substitute teachers. Many school districts are turning to temporary employment agencies to fill the substitute teacher need.

Rebuilding Versus Restructuring.   The American school system was designed in the early national period under the leadership of school reformers like Horace Mann. It reflected the influence of the old New England colonial district and catered to the needs of a new democracy. The nation then was dominated by agriculture, making a common school with summer vacations and local control quite acceptable. With the rise of industry, standardization of the curriculum and a delivery system based on a Newtonian mechanistic model were adopted. The school system became a closed machine with top-down administration, predetermined standards, lock-step definitions of content by grade, and fixed rules of behavior. Obviously the system worked well to prepare students for the factory or the office. With its emphasis on assimilation, conformity, and traditional values, it was able to handle the masses of European immigrants and the growing American population. Mass production philosophy and assembly-line concepts lent themselves to efficiency in the production of trained workers at low cost.

New needs began to emerge with the world wars, the Great Depression of the 1930s, social unrest, the rising affluence of the middle class, the human rights movement, and the demands of minorities for status. Superimposed upon these changes were the new requirements of the information age, a service economy, and a global culture. New programs were tried in an effort to cope with changing life conditions, social mobility, and new expectations. These included open classrooms, individualized instruction, alternative schools, nongraded schools, team teaching, and magnet schools. In general, these innovations were added to the existing system, but they did not become the dominant pattern. Many were simply tried for a time and then withdrawn, allowing the old system to emerge again.

Most of the current reform movement is aimed at modifying the basic traditional schools. There are those who think a piecemeal approach is not adequate and that it is now time for a holistic redesign of the whole structure. Some of those who would restructure education have moved their children outside the system. The home school movement of the mid-1980s is an example. With individual computers, communications networks, and many parents working at home, it became possible to give children a basic education without recourse to the schools. Although parents for religious or cultural reasons keep many students at home, the home school movement is growing among well-educated citizens who prefer to provide their own educational programs for their children. States have initiated testing programs to evaluate the learning of home-educated children when they wish to transfer to public schools.

Private education in the United States represents another alternative that has not lost its popularity. Many private and parochial schools are very traditional. They often have high achievement because of a select student body and/or rigorous discipline and conduct standards, strong parental support, high-quality teachers, and a demanding curriculum. Nevertheless, private schools are not subject to state regulations and controls (unless they request state accreditation). They are therefore free to pursue innovative programs and alternative learning techniques. Very few private schools had adopted radical or innovative programs by 1986. The growth in private education has been among religious fundamentalists and others dissatisfied with the quality of public education. Evangelical fundamentalists such as Jerry Falwell and other conservative groups gave support to private religious schools in the 1980s. Some parents in cities like Seattle choose to send their students to private schools deemed to be of high quality. Both groups support the Reagan administration's plan to provide vouchers for schooling. Both parties, along with the Clinton and George W. Bush administrations, support privatization programs, charter schools, parental choice, and involvement in education. Vouchers that give parents the option of moving their children from low-performing, low-standard public schools to other high-performing public schools or private schools with federal funds are subject to intense controversy and debate between the Democrats and Republicans in Congress.

At best, federal responses to the reform demands of the 1980s, 1990s, and 2000s must be described as piecemeal. One thrust is the policy of deregulation, first applied to the airlines. Deregulation attempts to remove federal controls from business and industry in keeping with the free market theory and competition. Of course, most of the federal regulations concerning schools were applied to the use of federal money. As fewer dollars flow from the national treasury into school programs, the question of federal control becomes less significant. However, Milton and Rose Friedman argued in *Free to Choose* that governmental rules and regulations restrict the freedom of citizens in educational matters. Of course, most laws regulating education are made by the states, and it is unlikely that those laws will be repealed. The free market concept also supports funding plans that would allow parents to spend their vouchers at a school of their choice, public or private. Many educators believe that vouchers would dismantle the public school system, especially in the large cities where there are many disadvantaged and minority children. Deregulation advocates want choice and options for parents, while others believe that federal funds for the nation's poverty, at-risk, special needs, limited-English-proficiency students are necessary and threatened by deregulation proposals.

The Clinton administration proposed programs to vaccinate all children, to create pilot enterprise schools with empowerment zones, and to create year-round community centers in urban and rural communities for the disadvantaged. Another proposal was the Goals 2000: Educate America Act; it was intended to increase equity among schools without federal mandates. Early George W. Bush administration efforts to roll back many Clinton proposals have been controversial and scaled back. There have been some modifications in Clinton's education initiatives but in general mainly a change in direction, not a rollback.

Barn raising, or helping neighbors replace farm buildings destroyed by fire or weather, was a community effort in colonial days through the twentieth century. Efforts to rekindle a spirit of service and helping others have been spreading through America's school districts. The Reagan, Bush, Clinton, and George W. Bush administrations stressed the importance of volunteerism in America. The first African-American Secretary of State Colin L. Powell helped found American Promise—The Alliance for Youth and is an ardent advocate of volunteerism to improve the quality of life for youth in America. Several states by 1997 were implementing mandatory community service as part of high school graduation requirements. Maryland was one of the first states to make student service mandatory for graduation. Students were given opportunities to choose things they were interested in and later to use their experiences for class papers. Community volunteer agencies were receptive to student assistance. Federal court decisions, although subject to reappraisal, have upheld mandatory community service for graduation. There will be increased volunteerism in the twenty-first century as school districts expand options in the curriculum for service learning.

Goodlad's call for focus on entire schools—not just teachers, curriculums, or organization—is a more holistic approach. The Rand Corporation's study of school effectiveness argued that increased expenditures on traditional practices would do little good. Patricia Cross of Harvard called attention to the mechanical solutions to the crisis of the 1980s and suggested that the old educational structures may be inadequate to cope with modern diversity. Others describe current reforms as ordinary and conventional. In "As Schools Start Up: Reform Shifts from Spending to Seeing Results" (1993), Henderson noted that the 1990s saw improvements in teachers' salaries to an average of over $36,000. Year-round schools and strengthened academic requirements together with a focus more on achievement and performance outcomes than on increased spending reflect future trends. In "Verbal, Math Scores on S.A.T. Up for the Second Straight Year" (1993), Lawton found that although SAT scores were up, verbal scores were still a point below the 1983 average. Improvements in SAT scores were attributed to increased nationwide demands for more rigorous academic studies. In the late 1990s and early 2000s, reform efforts continue to yield results as international comparisons show that American students have improved in math and science, although international studies vary in their conclusions. Some studies show that U.S. schools have islands of excellence together with underfunded poorly performing ones. Gehring in an *Education Week* (2001) summary of an Organization for Economic Cooperation and Development Report found the United States lagging seventeen other countries in secondary school graduate literacy.

Meanwhile some parents choose alternatives to public schools. Home schooling is a parental option with a new trend toward having groups of children taught by mothers who have expertise in individual academic fields. A current example of an update of Bertrand Russell's 1927–1939 experimental Beacon Hill School at Telegraph House near Petersfield is Cedarwood Sudbury School in Santa Clara, California. Some eighteen schools are modeled on the Sudbury system. Students, ages five through nineteen, are chosen on the basis of their ability to function as self-directed, autonomous members of the school community and may enroll through open admissions any time in the school year. Sudbury students mix freely with students and staff members of all ages, move around freely, choose things that interest them, vote in school meetings and for maintaining or dismissing teachers. As with Russell's 1927 Beacon Hill School, so Sudbury encourages independent student inquiry and permissiveness.

ACHIEVING EXCELLENCE IN TEACHER EDUCATION

As the public system of education experiences change in America, there have been major consequences for teachers and teacher educators. In periods of teacher shortages, colleges and universities with teacher education programs were under great pressure to admit more students in order to feed the market. This caused officials to pay slight attention to standards, especially when the funding for the institutions of higher education was enrollment driven. The shortage ended with the matriculation of the baby boom generation, but it is likely to return with heavy competition for skilled workers, improving salaries, better working conditions, and the retirement of a major segment of the teachers in service. At this writing, most states face a large shortage of teachers and substitute teachers in certain areas, and the problem is expected to become nationwide in the future. Already some states, such as Arkansas, are meeting the teacher shortage by making it easier to hire uncertified teachers with strong credentials as well as providing avenues to become certified.

Status of Teachers.   The 1980s may be characterized as a period of professional decline at the very time when better professional performance was demanded. Teaching was one of the first professions open to women in the United States. As more men entered the teaching field, the low salaries of teachers became unacceptable, and teachers began to organize in order to improve their situation. Such organizations as the NEA and the AFT eventually became powerful enough to influence federal policy. The creation of the Office of Secretary of Education in 1978 was at least partly a response to the growing power of teachers' organizations; and the reduction of the scope of that office in the Reagan administration cannot be separated from what President Reagan viewed as political opposition by teachers. Strike and work stoppages have not improved the image of teachers in the public mind, nor have the professional organizations. Although able women now have the choice of many professions outside teaching, traditional lower salaries for teachers have contributed to inequality for women, since the teaching force remains heavily female.

The difficulty of attracting and retaining high-quality teachers remains in part because salaries are still not competitive with those of college graduates working in other fields, although there has been improvement. The 1990s and early 2000s represent a period of attempts to re-create and renew education through a variety of reform proposals. Efforts to increase faculty, staff, and administrative salaries continue as states and communities vie for teachers. In many states, restricted finances limited progress toward salary increases. Oregon faced a limited tax base created by a voter-mandated restriction on property tax increases. By cutting other programs, the legislature found the money for adequate funding of schools, but it also revoked the teacher tenure law at the same time. Starting in 1998, Oregon teachers were all on two-year contracts. This tenure change reflected a demand for greater accountability, but it lowered the prestige of teaching. The current trend is to eliminate all tenure for public school teachers and administrators. Tenure is under attack in higher education, although it is a highly valued and desired recruiting tool and will remain in higher education institutions together with provisions for frequent post-tenure review.

In 1984, for example, Marvin Cetron found that the average starting salary of an American teacher was $14,500. He compared this with $19,344 for a librarian, $20,484 for an economist, $24,864 for a computer analyst, $26,844 for an engineer, and $42,978 for a personnel director. Even workers with no college degrees were paid better than teachers, with sanitation workers starting at $20,290 and city bus drivers at $22,906. Collective efforts to increase salaries are certainly one reason why many noneducators view professional organizations in education as militant. This is due to misunderstanding by the public about teacher workloads and professional job requirements. It is unfortunate that so much of the effort of teachers through their organizations has been used to fight for better wages and working conditions instead of for better standards and a stronger curriculum, because this has hurt the professional image.

Still, by 1985, the low pay and low status of American teachers had gained the attention of state legislatures. Most states at that time were examining ways to improve teachers' salaries through career ladder plans, incentives for master teachers, or state salary schedules. Unfortunately, at the very time when states were realizing that higher salaries for teachers are imperative if excellence in education is to be achieved, federal cutbacks in funding under the Gramm-Rudman legislation and a sluggish economy, due to factors such as the decline in oil and agricultural prices, limited the power of many governing bodies to address the situation. Many local educational authorities (LEAs) also have reached their limits of raising money through higher millage elections. Although there is room for improvement, educators' salaries have increased markedly in recent years due to a vastly improved economy. There is still wide variation in teachers' salaries and school facilities, however, between rural and urban, rich and poor school districts. In a cyclical economy there will continue to be peaks and valleys in educational funding. The tax base shrinks during economic downturns with large worker layoffs leaving schools with restricted financing.

The National Education Association Ranking and Estimates for 1999–2000 show that the average salary for teachers in the United States for 1998–1999 was $37,405. All states are seeking to raise teachers' salaries, and after the NEA report was issued the Rhode Island State Department of Education revised its average teacher salary for 1998–1999 to $45,650 and for 1999–2000 to $45,650. The *Occupational Outlook Handbook,* 2000–2001, notes that the national average salary of public school teachers in 1998 ranged from $33,590 to $37,890. The American Federation of Teachers reported beginning teachers with a bachelor's degree earning an average of $25,700 in 1997–1998 with an estimated average salary of elementary and secondary public school teachers as $39,300. The *Occupational Handbook,* 2000–2001, reported average salaries were $38,470 for accredited librarians in 1998; from $26,540 to $45,330 for entry-level economists; from $32,470 to $52,150 for computer systems analysts; from $36,100 to $58,600 for starting engineers; from $29,800 to $49,500 for human resource managers; and an average of $36,820 and up for inspectors and compliance officers, depending on educational degree level.

Although there are variations among school districts, an entry-level Florida teacher salary with a bachelor's degree was $30,000 to $31,000 and the average teacher salary was $36,700 in the 1999–2000 school year. Connecticut, New York, Michigan, Pennsylvania, and New Jersey had the highest teacher salaries, between $48,300 and $52,400 on average in 2000. In many areas of the country, even during cyclical economic downturns, bonuses are paid to recruit teachers. Teacher salaries are increasing due to a tight job market and a national education agenda. Although the states and the federal government were facing cyclical ups and downs in educational finances from 1993 to 2001, many efforts were under way to increase teachers' salaries through various state and local tax increases as well as through lotteries. The Arkansas legislature like some other states moved to increase teachers' salaries. The legislature approved a bill to increase teachers' salaries up to a $3,000 raise in 2001 depending on the availability of state revenues.

Georgia implemented an innovative model program to provide free tuition through lottery funding to any higher education institution in the state for motivated and prepared students. This has provided unique opportunities for students at risk but with good academic records to continue in higher education.

A Trend of Negative to Positive Factors.

Low salaries were by no means the only problem facing teachers in the 2000s. In *High School* (1984), Ernest Boyer reported that teachers are deeply concerned about the loss of status, a negative public image, little recognition for their work, and heavily bureaucratic pressures imposed by the board or the administration. Recruiting better students to become teachers is difficult when many teachers in service feel frustrated or are seeking to leave the profession. Traditionally, teachers have been the best recruiters, suggesting that their better pupils consider the teaching field. This trend was definitely in decline by 1986 when numerous teachers, along with parents, advised students not to become teachers. In May 1985, the Corporate Forum on Education and the Economy created a Task Force on Teaching as a Profession to study the declining ability of the profession to attract promising future teachers. Boyer, reflecting an earlier study by Emily Feistritzer on the teaching profession, stated that students preparing to teach have lower SAT scores than other college students and that the standards in colleges of education are low.

As departments, colleges, and schools of education began to strengthen entrance requirements in response to the national criticism, state departments were slow to deny teaching positions to unqualified people. Feistritzer reported in 1983 that all but two states made provision for issuing an emergency or other substandard teaching credential. The same boards that directed their departments to license only teachers who passed tests such as the NTE failed to shut the door on temporary certificates. As the predicted shortage of teachers materializes, state departments will come under increasing pressure from local superintendents to allow them to fill teaching positions with any available warm body. Recruiting high-quality teachers or enforcing higher professional standards will be very hard if state departments bend to this pressure. Education is the only field in which unqualified persons may be hired in the place of professionals. Certainly this does not occur in medicine, law, or engineering.

Albert (1997) reports that although there are continuing problems—such as critics questioning public school teacher competence, violent kids, crime in schools, and one in six public school teachers leaving the profession within the first year—teaching is gaining in prestige. Salaries are better, teachers feel more respected, individuals are leaving jobs to become teachers, and more college freshmen are interested in teaching than at any other time since the mid-1970s. This trend is timely, since the Department of Education reports that some 2 million teachers will be needed in the next decade to replace retiring teachers. Individuals in the late 1990s and early 2000s show interest in the teaching profession because they want to make a difference in society.

Challenges to the education profession also include that of increasing crime on school campuses. In "Fear Stalks the Hallways" (1993), James Hellegaard noted that according to former Secretary of Education Richard Riley there were over 3 million thefts and violent crimes on or near school campuses every year and that in many school districts student absenteeism was growing due to fear of being victimized on school grounds. He noted that over 160,000 children nationwide skip classes daily for fear of physical harm and bullying. And in Florida, one of the nation's most populous states, criminal offenses ranging from thefts to assaults and homicides rose over 34 percent in one year, from over 46,000 incidents in the 1990–1991 school year to over 61,000 in 1991–1992. The 1998 U.S. Department of Justice, Bureau of Justice Statistics, National Crime Victimization Survey showed 1,582,300 cases of theft; 1,153,200 acts of violence; and 252,700 acts of serious violence against students twelve to eighteen occurring at school or on the way to and from school.

Teachers and administrators are not immune to the rapid increase in school crime. According to the Florida Educational Coalition Crime and Violence Survey, pupils physically attack over 6,000 teachers nationwide each school day. In Palm Beach

County, one of the largest school districts in the nation, many schools have a variety of surveillance systems including x-ray and television cameras in classrooms and halls. Students must be fingerprinted prior to entering public schools for observing, participating, and practice teaching with supervision. Some students report that public schools feel like a prison with control of the inmate population. Public school monitoring of everyone who enters the facility is a nationwide practice.

In "The Art of Undoing Violence Is Finding Its Own Place in Classrooms and Streets" (1993), Holmstrom reported that 100,000 children take guns to school every day, and many schools and school districts have initiated antiviolence and conflict resolution programs from kindergarten through high school. The education department reported that for the 1995–1996 school year over 6,000 students in twenty-nine states and the District of Columbia were expelled for carrying weapons, including guns, to school. Such reporting is required under the 1994 Gun Free Schools Act. In our twenty-first century, a major goal of governmental, parental, and educator organizations is to provide safe schools. Character education and conflict resolution are being incorporated into the curriculum to address the issues of school violence and vandalism. Despite the criticism of zero tolerance policy, school administrators tend to support such policies to maintain a proper learning environment. Although there is a record of declining crime and violence in schools, the degree of severity of violence has increased.

Educators believe that the causes of increased school crime include social fragmentation, single-parent families, latchkey children, easy access to drugs, finding a sense of belonging through gang membership, easy access to weapons, poverty, and intolerance. Hate crimes are growing on the campuses of our public schools and colleges. Workshops and seminars on conflict resolution and sensitivity training are being developed to address the issue. In 1993, Secretary of Education Richard W. Riley sought legislation for a safe school program targeted to assist poor districts in high-crime areas, and by late 1997 such programs were expanding throughout the nation. President Clinton started a major initiative to deal with hate crimes, bigotry, and intolerance.

Rose and Gallup's "The 32nd Annual Phi Delta Kappa/Gallup Poll of the Public's Attitudes Toward the Public Schools" (2000) found violence, fighting, gangs, drugs, and dope ranked in the top five problems faced by schools. While typical responses to student violence are increased restrictions and increased law enforcement personnel on school grounds, Raywid and Oshiyama (2000) called for smaller classes and mutual respect among all the school's constituents, reciprocity among students and between them and adults, responsibility to self and the greater community, and a reverence for place and its connections. Teachers and administrators have an obligation to treat students with respect and kindness and a duty to encourage civility and comity among pupils. This can be done by example, through high expectations, and by genuine care and nurturing of students. Socrates over 2,000 years ago believed the only evil is ignorance. Students who knew better would conduct themselves more appropriately. Thus knowledge of appropriate behavior is a key to helping youngsters reach mature decisions and aggression control. There are no easy answers to the complex factors behind school violence, but Raywid and Oshiyama believe viewing students as multidimensional not exclusively academic creatures will be helpful in building a more humane school environment.

Changes in Teacher Education.

The National Commission on Excellence and other groups created awareness for the need to improve education. At first the focus was on secondary schools, but the focus soon spread to colleges that prepare teachers, since not much progress toward excellence can be made unless the quality of teacher education programs is addressed.

One of the first reactions by SCDEs (schools, colleges, and departments of education) was that although teacher education needed improvement, the criticism should not fall exclusively on them. When teachers fail in basic skills—such as reading, writing, and mathematics—it is important to note that the SCDEs are not the ones who teach those skills. Likewise, when a teacher is weak in his or her subject matter, it should be noted that the teacher did not study the discipline in an SCDE. The general public was slow to understand that teachers take only one-fourth to one-third of their work in the area of professional education. Professors of education argued that the entire university faculty has responsibility for preparing teachers, including professors in arts and sciences. Nevertheless, there was a clear mandate for SCDEs to revise their programs in order to achieve excellence. Organizations like the National Council for Accreditation of Teacher Education (NCATE) had started this process long before the national reports appeared. More stringent NCATE standards were adopted in 1984. Not all SCDEs are NCATE accredited, but many states also adopted the standards of the organization as a model for quality teacher education programs.

A survey undertaken by the American Council on Education in 1984 showed that nine of ten colleges with teacher education programs had minimum requirements, but eight of ten had initiated higher admission standards. Most were requiring some exit test for certification, such as a satisfactory score on the NTE. Graduation and certification requirements are not always the same, but colleges were attempting to conform to the state testing requirements. Curriculum changes included a larger general education component, heavier concentration on a subject matter discipline, a familiarity with computers, extended practice teaching, and more concentration on communication skills. The SCDEs were already requiring tests and measurement, educational technology, a course in the exceptional learner, child and adolescent psychology, social foundations of education, diversity and multiculturalism, and appropriate methods courses. Several institutions required two courses in reading for all teachers. Virtually all SCDEs had educational practice as a requirement, and most also expected candidates to have field-based laboratories before the practice teaching experience. University–public school collaboration has increased with many teacher education courses currently being taught in public schools. Public school teachers occasionally serve as visiting teachers in education colleges.

A 1985 survey funded by the National Science Foundation, the U.S. Department of Education, and the National Endowment for the Humanities was based on a sample of 1,040 colleges with teacher education programs. Here is what they found:

- SCDEs admit students after the freshman year or at the start of the junior year.
- Seven of ten institutions require a minimum GPA in university-wide courses for entry. The average GPA requirement was 2.4 (NCATE now recommends a 2.5 to 2.7 GPA for entrance).
- Two in five programs require exit testing. Most others plan to initiate exit testing. The NTE is the most used exit test.
- The average number of credit hours required for graduation was 127. Of these, the average number in education was 43 for elementary majors and 30 for secondary majors. This included practice teaching for which an average of 10 credit hours is allowed.
- Secondary students spend an average of 85 clock hours in practice teaching, and elementary students spend an average of 113.
- Most SCDEs require mathematics, science, and communications of all candidates; about half require computer science. Speech, hearing, and writing tests, together with personal interviews and recommendations, are becoming common for entry. About half the institutions also require standardized or proficiency tests. Almost all have a special requirement in English.

In the 1990s and 2000s, SCDEs raised standards, required higher GPAs, and implemented five-year programs. Exit testing was required in more states. In 1994, the AACTE issued a report on the status of multiculturalism; it identified a continuing need to meet the demand for teachers of color. Women, minority faculty, and student recruitment continues to be a mission of SCDEs. Student populations increasingly reflected a dramatic growth in African-American, Hispanic, Asian-American, and Native-American races.

The teacher education programs satisfied state and NCATE standards and conformed to the major suggestions found in the national reports of 1983. However, many professional educators argued that a four-year college program was not adequate to prepare candidates for the new demands of the teaching field. At the very least, it was suggested that an entry-level teacher with a bachelor's degree needed further education along with experience in order to become a master teacher. In-service programs for teachers were therefore stressed as a means of continuing the education of new professionals and upgrading the skills of teachers with longer service. By 1986, it was agreed that a four-year college commitment and an equal or longer commitment by a school district to continue the education of teachers were needed for a competent profession. In our twenty-first century, there is much discussion of exactly what knowledge base is essential to the preparation of every American teacher. The Yale Report of 1828 and the Harvard Report of 1945 raised the same question about "what is ultimately worth knowing." Traditionalists call for the liberating liberal arts, the best ideas of humankind; the progressives call for problem solving, critical thinking, and a process of inquiry that is not memorization or restricted by limits of the past; revisionists of various persuasions call for teaching Third World philosophies, narratives of oppressed persons, and writings through the lenses of minorities and those from diverse cultural and ethnic backgrounds.

In the late 1990s and 2000s, NCATE stresses expanding its accreditation program to cover more of the 1,314 state-approved teacher preparation schools. Jeanne Ponessa in *Education Week* (1997) notes that the National Commission on Teaching and America's Future, a privately organized panel, calls for NCATE accreditation together with licensing under the Interstate New Teacher Assessment and Support Consortium and master certification by the National Board for Professional Teaching Standards. An alternative accreditation group, the Teacher Accreditation Council, was formed in 1997. However, NCATE remains the nation's major education accreditation agency. NCATE's standards are followed in twenty-eight states, whether or not those states seek national accreditation. A 2001 article "Accrediting Body Changing the Status Quo in Teacher Preparation" shows teacher accreditation and preparation standards have been raised for colleges of education in all areas. The article also referred to A National Council of State Legislatures report that shows NCATE to be a cost-effective means to upgrade teacher preparation in the states, and the National Alliance of Business with the Business Roundtable called for all colleges of education to be accredited. In 2001 NCATE enforced new, rigorous standards of professional preparation, licensing, and advanced certification on the 600 institutions it accredits. The organization currently is using state–NCATE partnerships in over forty-six states to reduce costs and to eliminate duplication of effort. NCATE, seeking continuous review of its accreditation procedure, has implemented a policy for third-party testimony to include the various populaces—faculty, administrators, students, alumni, and cooperating K–12 teachers, as well as other interested community organizations.

In "Groundbreaking Teacher Preparation Standards to Be Used Beginning Next Year" (2000), Arthur Wise, NCATE president, said it is not enough for a faculty member to say "I taught the material." The 2001 standards include performance-based accreditation based on results that the teacher education candidate knows the subject matter and can teach it effectively in a real classroom. Diversity, faculty performance and development, unit governance and resources, together with field experiences, program assessment, unit evaluation, and clinical practice are focuses of twenty-first-century NCATE standards.

NCATE and other educational organizations are committed to improving teacher preparation programs in terms of both process and product. Having been involved in preparing for NCATE visits at several institutions, it is clear to these author that such preparation is time-consuming, expensive, and a difficult challenge for faculty, administration, and staff. NCATE, however, helps the profession police itself and, through a cooperative effort with state departments of education and other professional education associations, provides channels and models for improving teacher effectiveness and student achievement levels.

Five-Year Programs and the Holmes Group.   Long before *A Nation at Risk* was published, some major universities like Stanford had given up undergraduate teacher education to concentrate on graduate studies. They argued that the research based in education has grown so large that teachers and administrators need high-quality graduate work and that many now wish to enter the profession after having completed an undergraduate degree in another field. Certainly it is true that growing numbers of teachers take advanced courses and most expect to earn a master's or specialist degree during their careers. By the mid-1980s, numerous universities were offering graduate-level courses for certification to accommodate degree holders and transfer students from other fields, even if they continued to offer the basic four-year teacher education program. Some states like New Jersey allowed local districts to provide the training for certification to prospective teachers with degrees in subject fields.

A similar approach was taken by a subset of the National Association of State Universities and Land Grant Colleges called the Holmes Partnership, after former Dean Henry Holmes of Harvard's Graduate School of Education. Under the leadership of Deans Judith Lanier of Michigan State and John Palmer of the University of Wisconsin, the organization is committed to a broad strategy of reform for teacher education. The Holmes Group intends to make the education of teachers intellectually sound, to create relevant and defensible standards of entry into the profession, to connect schools of education with public schools, and to base teacher education on state-of-the-art research. Some of the fourteen original member universities insist that a five-year teacher education program is a minimum for these goals.

In 1986, the Holmes Group invited 123 leading research universities with colleges or departments of education to join the coalition. The Holmes Group is another major organization of professional leaders in education that could influence the course of teacher education as has occurred with NCATE, AACTE, ASCD, and AERA. *A Nation Prepared: Teachers for the 21st Century* (1986) tied giving teachers more control over schools to increased accountability; it also recommended phasing out undergraduate education programs. By 1993, several colleges and universities had moved to a five-year education major program, thus eliminating the undergraduate program. Some educators view this controversial move to five- and six-year programs as detrimental to future educators, in part due to the added cost and training time. However, many SCDEs that implemented five-year programs retain a number of undergraduate programs.

Most professional educators and teacher educators in the universities believe that the real key to excellence, which is absolutely vital to the future well-being of the nation, rests upon our ability to recruit, educate, and retain high-quality teachers. The criticism of the national reports could offer an opportunity to make education a real profession on a par with law and medicine. Certainly the knowledge and research are adequate if resources can be found to strengthen and extend professional training. All critics agree that a well-founded general education and in-depth knowledge of the subject matter discipline are essential for teachers. The field experience and pedagogical parts of teacher education must be vastly improved to develop a true teaching professional committed to lifelong teaching and learning. School to university/business/community partnerships are part of many five-year programs.

The Holmes Partnership argues that education for teachers must not only be improved but also be restructured. A Holmes Group report, "Tomorrow's Schools of Education" (1995), stressed the need for teamwork and interdependence in teacher preparation as well as contributing to the development of state and local policies that give all children the opportunity to learn from highly qualified educators.

Boyer (1984, 1995) and Goodlad (1990, 1997) hold that the entire school community must be involved in a partnership with the universities to create a professional climate in which teacher candidates may learn to be professionals. A fifth-year internship with continued formal education has been used in an increasing number of states. College of education faculty in research universities assigned to teach in off-campus programs in public schools often find it difficult to engage in research and publication necessary for tenure and promotion. Many university administrators are working to provide alternative avenues for promotion and tenure for those engaged in university to public school cooperative ventures.

Nancy Faust Sizer and Theodore R. Sizer in "A School Built for Horace" (2001) discussed the challenges and opportunities of developing a charter experimental school designed to implement the best of educational reform ideas. In the 340-student-body school, children ages twelve and up have a personal learning plan with a contract among student, school, and the family. Students are promoted through three divisions, regardless of age, by public presentation of portfolios and exhibitions for older students. The school had a waiting list for the academic 2001 year. School admission is open on a lottery basis to any child wherever he or she lives. The worry for Horace's administrators and teachers is that too many policy makers and citizens will assume that "standards" by definition require standardization; that reform can be achieved by jawboning, regulation, and low-cost testing; and that humiliation is a necessary part of competition. The founders hope that their experimental charter school will be a model for others interested in school reform in both theory and practice.

A detailed Rand Institute study, "Improving Student Achievement," showed variations among the states in effectiveness of school reform measures, with more rural northern states having the highest average achievement scores and southern states usually among the lowest. The more urban northern states generally fell in the middle of the score distribution. The level of expenditures per pupil and its allocation affected student achievement particularly for states with disproportionately higher numbers of minority and disadvantaged students. The authors Grissmer, Flanagan, Kawata, and Williamson (2000) found higher achievement scores with lower pupil–teacher ratios, higher public pre-kindergarten participation, lower teacher turnover, and higher levels of teacher resources. Hanushek (2001) analyzed the Rand study and suggested a larger database would yield more in-depth analysis.

Much greater stress is now placed on continuous in-service education for teachers after they begin teaching. Continuous updating of methods and the application of the latest research to teaching situations will be part of the professional activity of all future teachers. The United States demands and deserves the best possible teachers for the information age. There are still arguments about how to design and support a teacher education that will produce such professionals. Meanwhile, the teacher shortage has caused many states to provide some sort of alternative certification for would-be teachers with college degrees but no preparation in pedagogy. Distance learning teacher education degrees will require new monitoring systems to ensure adequate preparation for working in ever more complex teaching–learning environments.

REFORM IN EDUCATIONAL ADMINISTRATION

Educational administration underwent major changes in the 1980s and 1990s, both in the universities where administrators are prepared and in the field. Doctoral programs in school administration have become much more research oriented, and management skills taken from business administration have been added. Many educational administrators seek more practitioner-oriented doctoral programs and question the applicability of research-oriented programs to their ongoing careers. On the other hand, there is a national trend toward requiring more faculty and student research in institutions with doctoral programs. More efficient methods of operating the schools have been developed. Superintendents learn more about school law, school finance, personnel management, conflict resolution, inclusion, information technology, university to school collaboration, managing change, human rights, accountability, assessment, litigation, and site-based management. Principals devote more time to evaluation of teachers, planning in-service training, and serving as instructional leaders. *Accountability, safe schools, gender equity, diversity,* and *effective schools* have become key words in the administration field.

Educational administrators traditionally were successful teachers who were promoted and then learned management skills on the job or with continued graduate training. This pattern still exists to some extent in America, but the level of required training has increased to the point where administrators must expect to spend additional years in the graduate classroom taking advanced coursework before assuming a principalship or a superintendency. State requirements for administrative certification have also been strengthened, demanding a specific course of study as well as experience. Alternative certification programs designed to encourage managers from industry and business to become school administrators have been implemented in some states. Some school board chairpersons believe there should be a school administrator for operations and management and one for the academic affairs. Competition for the better jobs is keen, and the salaries are high by educational standards. Administrators who can articulate goals, inspire workers to work harmoniously toward those goals, maintain good relations with the public and school board, and demonstrate leadership are in demand.

Nevertheless, the pressures in urban school districts are such that the average longevity of superintendents in large urban areas is less than three years. High turnover and early burnout continued to plague the field of school administration in the closing years of the 1980s, 1990s, and early 2000s. Divided school boards, single-interest groups, and managing budgets are continuing challenges for administrators. Pros and cons of databased decision making also create administrative pressures since statistics and research often do not take into account the necessary people-centered rationale for the schools' existence.

Professional improvement and information sharing have been greatly enhanced by the major organizations in administration. These provide a forum in which administrators can discuss problems and evaluate possible solutions with peers from similar school districts. Administrator organizations publish journals, maintain links to professors in the leading universities, and apprise administrators of changing regulations. The National Association of Secondary School Principals is one of the oldest and best-respected professional organizations. The American Association of School Administrators holds major conventions and attracts superintendents as well as political and academic leaders from across the nation. The National Council of Professors of School Administration and the University Council for Educational Administration serve the needs of those who train administrators and foster the dissemination of research. Elementary principals have their own organization, and all major associations have local and state affiliates. Much of the debate over the best responses to the reports demanding school reform has taken place in these organizations and on their useful and valuable Web sites.

Most of the educational reform reports of the 1980s, 1990s, and early 2000s stressed the role of the principal and superintendent in exercising leadership for improving instruction. Administrators were expected to develop a positive organizational climate to facilitate staff development and improve learning processes. Reports urging increased mandated standards, more testing of students and teachers, more discipline, an end to "soft" subjects, and strict control of the educational process clearly called for a firm hand. By 1985, however, educators began to stress the importance of the human element in the schooling process. Education is a complex process, and caution must be used in implementing massive changes envisioned by the reports. Literature in administration began to reflect the impact of "unintended multipliers" of reform reports such as elitism, teacher flight, lower morale, loss of creativity, and high dropout rates when oversimplified solutions are applied. Currently there is a backlash against high-stakes testing by students and teachers in many states.

A Nation at Risk said little about the principal as instructional leader. In the early national period, it was intended that principals perform that role, but in the twentieth century they became managers. School principals in the 1960s often gave most of their attention to discipline, scheduling, the physical plant, reports, busing, extracurricular activities, and other functions not directly related to instruction. Research shows that administrative leadership at the school-building level is critical. The Connecticut School Effectiveness Project of 1982 cited instructional leadership by a principal who understands and applies the characteristics of instructional effectiveness as one of seven measures of good schools. (The others were a safe, orderly environment; a clear school mission; a climate of high student expectation; time-on-task; frequent monitoring of student progress; and positive home– school relations.) School administrators' commitment to professionalism includes creating and maintaining an atmosphere of comity; mutual respect for students, faculty, and staff; human decency and recognition of the importance of self-esteem; self-worth for everyone within the public school environment; and encouraging teachers to help students gain a sense of ownership in their school, their learning, and their future prospects in employment and life.

Other studies have found that principals in effective schools spend time in classrooms to identify problems and to help teachers develop strategies for dealing with them. A school principal who can achieve balance between strong leadership and maximum autonomy for teachers will help to achieve excellence. Some of the critics say that the studies of principals as instructional leaders conducted in inner-city schools may not apply to others. Goodlad (1990) doubts that principals can maintain a higher level of teaching expertise than the teachers can. Not all principals have the ability to become the exceptional, charismatic leaders that researchers describe. It is clear, however, that principals must devote much of their time and energy to instructional improvement if excellence is to be achieved. Maintaining effective relations with funding agencies, state and national governmental funding processes, and community organizations is vital to ensure adequate resources for schools. School administrators' organizations maintain links with legislative bodies to influence budget decisions as they affect education.

Educational administrators in the 1980s accepted many ideas from business, such as the Peters and Waterman (1982) conclusion that excellent organizations have profound respect for individual workers and stimulate unusual effort by ordinary people. They sought university programs to help them deal effectively with multiple changes in a democratic system of education. To the themes of accountability, organizational climate, and managing change for excellence were added collective negotiation with teachers and fact finding for bargaining. Other trends for educational administrators were increased emphasis on ethical values, maintaining order and discipline in schools, and dealing with federal disengagement from the schools.

The American Association of School Administrators is seeking to make Individuals with Disability Act funding mandatory. Rather than be subjected to the political budget process, advocates for full funding of inclusion and special education for physically, mentally, and emotionally challenged citizens seek to have mandatory ongoing resource allocation. Pressure is being placed on Congress for mandatory funding for IDEA by a number of professional education organizations including the National Education Association, the American Federation of Teachers, the National School Boards Association, the National Association of Secondary School Principals, the National PTA, and the American Speech and Hearing Association. According to the Council for Exceptional Children organization, Congress has promised for twenty-five years to fully fund IDEA, yet funding is at 14.8 percent. Full funding or 40 percent of the average per special education student is the goal of special education advocates. In 2001 the average per pupil expenditure was estimated to be $7,066. With 6,138,000 students served under IDEA, schools are qualified to receive $17.35 billion in federal funds. Schools, however, are receiving $6.34 billion.

From the early days of the republic our nation has been committed to expanding the nation's social network to cover an ever larger portion of at-risk special needs citizens. That efforts are made to do so at local, state, and national levels is a historical record. Members of Congress are committed to expanding services to those in need and at the same time maintain fiscal responsibility. School administrators' organizations work to ensure they present justification for educational funding at all governmental levels.

Zirkel (2001) in "Sorting Out Which Students Have Learning Disabilities" points to the challenge of parents shopping around for psychologists and physicians who will diagnose their children as learning disabled in order to get special help to excel in school. Zirkel in his *Phi Delta Kappa* article notes that parents may bring attorneys or disability advocates to a school and threaten legal action. School administrators who believe that an accommodation is unwarranted may have difficulty making tough decisions in the face of such pressure. Zirkel noted that 41 percent of the college freshmen who reported in 1998 that they had a disability came from the "learning disability" category, compared with 15 percent in 1988. Meanwhile the percentage of students with more traditional and visible disabilities had declined significantly. For instance, the proportion of visually impaired students went from 32 to 13 percent, and that of orthopedically impaired students went from 14 to 9 percent.

In *Educating for a New Millennium,* Shane and Tabler (1981) stipulated the importance of basing the organization and administration of education on local control so that those most familiar with community needs would make priorities and deploy resources. They also called for an alternative to the bureaucratic model of administrative structure common to schooling and business. A diversified concept of organizational life in which individuals have flexibility and freedom is supported also by both Goodlad (1990) and Boyer (1984, 1995). Former University Counsel for Educational Administration (UCEA) director Jack Culbertson argues that administrators will have to become more effective in utilizing computer data in decision making as well as in coping with exploding information and rapid expansion of technology. He also stresses good management training in a period of declining resources for schools. Good working relations with school boards, state officials, departments of education, and political leaders are critical to the modern administrator. Fenwick W. English (2001) fears that total reliance on using hard data as the only reliable source of information may drive out and replace the value of other forms of information that are crucial to understanding human interaction and affective learning and teaching.

In *New Schools for a New Century* (1995), Kenneth J. Tewel views the administrator's role as building new relationships with teachers through listening and problem solving in order to expedite the change process. By building staff and teacher support for change through improving communication, administrators can eliminate barriers to school restructuring designed to improve achievement outcomes. Getting teachers involved in the change processes is seen in the current interest in experimentation with flexible scheduling designed to reform the traditional seven or eight-period day. Block scheduling is designed to increase time available for students to learn in a changed classroom environment.

Since the responsibility of enforcing laws rests on school administrators, they must be especially sensitive to the legal aspects of reform. Following the lead of the Supreme Court in the Brown decision of 1954, education has become recognized as a legal right for all citizens. By the 1970s, this right was extended to those with special needs. The 1975 Education for All Handicapped Children Act made it incumbent on all districts to provide, to children with special needs, education in the "least restrictive environment." Superimposed on this law were the various state regulations concerning excellence. Every state in the nation made some effort to improve education through legislation in the 1980s. Laws mandated curriculum reform, graduation requirements, student evaluation, longer school days and years, and plans to reward teachers through career ladders or master teacher programs. Another responsibility was responding to the increased number of lawsuits brought against schools. Lawsuits have increased dramatically since 1980 and range from cases involving accidents to those accusing schools of failing to provide equal access to education. Litigation in the field of special education inclusion has increased exponentially in the past few years, and recently special education is being dealt with in some areas by parents in home schooling. Funding for home schooling special education is currently under review.

Goodlad (1990, 1997) has argued that principals and superintendents are self-selected. He means that those interested in administrative positions have pursued the necessary training and entered the job market. He suggests that future schools would be better served if the system chose teachers who had good administrative potential, determined by some testing procedure. Goodlad believes that the profession should determine which of its members ought to pursue administrative careers.

Partly in response to the national demands for reform, vast improvement in administrative training and practice occurred in the 1980s, 1990s, and 2000s. Accountability, quality control, the principal as instructional leader, effective schools, and standards for graduation were concepts that ruled the decades. Nevertheless, the criticism directed toward education in general focused on administrators in particular. In 1986, Assistant Secretary of Education Chester Finn called for throwing out school administrators and replacing them with businessmen or retired military officers. Even high officials had no concept of the professional role of the administrator or the sophisticated scholarly discipline upon which it rests. Various views of the role and function of school administrators will continue to be debated. Outsourcing school administration through for-profit organizations has been explored in some areas of the country with varying results.

In our twenty-first century, administrator concerns reflect key components of the reform reports. These concerns include empowering teachers for change, emphasizing gender and diversity, leadership skills for learner-centered schools and communities, collaborative and partnership preparation and leadership, site-based management, and multidimensional connections with professional development schools. In our future as in our past, educational administrators have been and will be committed to the highest ideals of professionalism in education. Challenges will continue to be opportunities to improve more effective educational delivery systems in our schools and communities.

THE SEARCH FOR EXCELLENCE CONTINUES

Throughout our educational history, educators whether by design or unintentionally served as conduits for an expanded social consciousness. From the early days of the republic, education was seen as vital for future generations. Though many efforts such as the Old Deluder Satan Act of 1647 were honored more in the breach than in the observance, a foundation for an educational system was laid.

The reforms of the 1980s, 1990s, and 2000s continue to expand opportunities for gender equity, equal opportunity and access for minorities, inclusion, safe schools, and ethnic diversity. Debate and controversy over innovations and progress will continue in the future as in the past. Demands for higher standards are met with concerns for students at risk, students with special learning needs, and limited English proficiency pupils. Aristotle's *Golden Mean* or a sense of balance to deal with excellence and support for the "best one can be" for those with special challenges will be forthcoming through reasoned inquiry and analysis. There are voices for redesigning teacher preparation programs through systemic change; there are also voices that recognize much reform hype is for public relations and political purposes. However, educators are doing an excellent job in terms of student outcomes, a fact often underreported by the media.

Meanwhile administrators, teachers, and staff will have to avoid hardening of the categories and prepare for emerging instructional delivery systems such as distance learning from ever-changing technology. History of education teaches us that there will be "new wine in old bottles," as old models are wrapped in new language. However, continued change in society and education is the story of our text.

GAINING PERSPECTIVE THROUGH CRITICAL ANALYSIS

1. Compare and contrast areas of agreement and disagreement among major educational reform reports. What impact have the reform reports had on educational effectiveness?
2. Do you agree with John I. Goodlad that schooling and education should not be synonymous (see chapter opening quotation)?
3. What role has the business community had on educational reform? What can educators do to monitor advertising on the Internet that may be inappropriate for students when search engines are provided free by companies?
4. Name three ways in which *A Nation at Risk* has impacted educational policies and practices. Share your list with your classmates, and add all of the findings to your journal.
5. Use the Internet and the library to find articles dealing with the effectiveness of two educational reform movements of the past on education practice today. Identify the pros and cons of high-stakes testing.
6. Analyze the constraints teachers face when entering the profession. Discuss the social, political, and financial challenges.
7. Compare and contrast the strategies for improving both the teaching and the learning environments in Horace Mann's time with those of the current National Council for Teacher Education, NCATE, the National Education Association, and Phi Delta Kappa.

HISTORY IN ACTION IN TODAY'S CLASSROOMS

1. Attend a parent-teacher conference. Identify suggestions for achieving excellence in student performance and teacher delivery systems. What (if any) major themes were discussed? If no suggestions were apparent, discuss your impressions of the purpose and outcome of the meeting. Add the findings to your journal.
2. Visit a temporary-help firm in your area to discuss the training programs offered to temporary workers today. What are the reasons for offering this training? Compare these programs with classes offered in the business education department of your local high school. Does the agency provide substitute teachers for public schools?

INCREASED UNDERSTANDING THROUGH ONLINE RESEARCH

Visit the Companion Web site that accompanies this text (*http://www.prenhall.com/pulliam*) and examine Topics 1, 6, and 8. Using the resources available in these topics, identify two areas in each of the topics as contributing to educational reform, standards, and best practices. Write and submit your response to your instructor using the Electronic Bluebook module also in any of these three topics of the Web site.

BIBLIOGRAPHY

"A Better Balance: Standards, Tests, and the Tools to Succeed, Quality Counts." *Education Week* (January 11, 2001):103.

Abraham, Katharine G. *Occupational Outlook Handbook*. Washington, DC: Bureau of Labor Statistics, Government Printing Office, 2000–2001:4, 57, 65, 90, 112, 179–197.

"Accrediting Body Changing the Status Quo in Teacher Preparation." *NCATE Newsbriefs* (February 21, 2001). Available: *http://www.ncate.org/newsbrfs/dec_rept_release.htm*

Action for Excellence. Task Force on Education for Economic Growth. Education Commission of the States, 1983.

Adams, Jacob E., and William E. White. "The Equity Consequence of School Finance Reform in Kentucky." *Educational Evaluation and Policy Analysis* (Summer 1997):165–84.

Adler, Mortimer. *The Paideia Proposal: An Educational Manifesto*. New York: Macmillan, 1982.

Albert, Tanya. "Common Theme Is Behind New Popularity: Service." *USA Today* (February 25, 1997):1A–2A.

Alexander, Lamar. *Time for Results*. New York: Report on Education by the National Governor's Association, 1986.

American Association of Colleges for Teacher Education. *Teacher Education Pipeline: Schools, Colleges, and Departments of Education Enrollments by Race, Ethnicity, and Gender*. Washington, DC: Author, 1994.

"America's Competitive Challenge: The Need for a National Response." Washington, DC: American Council on Education, Business-Higher Education Forum, 1983.

Anderson, Nick. "Senate Defines a Failing School in Education Bill." *South Florida Sun-Sentinel* (May 4, 2001):7A.

Apple, Michael. "Markets, Standards, Teaching and Teacher Education." *Journal of Teacher Education* (May/June 2001):194–195.

Ashton, Patricia, and Rodman Webb. *Making a Difference: Teacher's Sense of Efficacy and Student Achievement*. New York: Longman, 1986.

"Average Salary of Arkansas Teachers 9th Lowest in the Nation, Union Surveys Say." *The Arkansas Democrat Gazette* (May 19, 2001):1B, 3B.

Baldauf, Scott. "States Weigh Whether to Save or Spend Surpluses." *Christian Science Monitor* (June 19, 1997):4.

Berliner, David C., and Bruce J. Biddle. *The Manufactured Crisis: Myths, Fraud and the Attack on America's Public Schools*. New York: Addison Wesley, 1995.

Boyer, Ernest. *High School: A Report on Secondary Education in America*. Boston: Houghton Mifflin, 1984.

———. "The Basic School: A Community for Learning a New Beginning," (April 1995): *http: www.jmu.edu/basicschool/BASIC2.html*

Bracey, Gerald W. "The Sixth Bracey Report on the Condition of Public Education." *Phi Delta Kappa* (1996): *http://www.pdkintl.org*.

Callahan, Raymond E. *Education and the Cult of Efficiency: A Study of the Social Forces That Have Shaped the Administration of the Public Schools*. Chicago: University of Chicago Press, 1962.

Cardman, Michael. "Establishment Puts Weight Behind Full Funding Bill." *Education Daily* (2001):3–4.

Carnegie Forum on Education and the Economy. *A Nation Prepared: Teachers for the 21st Century*. New York: Carnegie Corp., 1986.

Carr, Judy F., and Douglas E. Harris. *Succeeding with Standards: Linking Curriculum, Assessment, and Action Planning*. Alexandria, VA: The Association for Supervision and Curriculum Development (2001): 155–156.

"Cedarwood Sudbury School." Available: *http://www.cedarwoodsudbury.org/admissions.html http://www.cedarwoodsudbury.org/aboutus.html*

Cetron, Marvin. *Schools of the Future: How American Business and Education Can Cooperate to Save Our Schools.* New York: McGraw-Hill, 1985.

Cheng, Yen Cheng. *Effectiveness and School Based Management: A Mechanism for Development.* London: Falmer Press, 1996.

Committee for Economic Development. *Investing in Our Children.* New York: Author, 1985.

Committee for Education Funding. "Committee for Education Funding Hails Major Victory for Education: Senate Votes to Increase Education Funding by $250 Billion Over Ten Years." Available: *http:/www.cef.org/view.cfm?id=490*

Cross, Patricia. "The Rising Tide of School Reform Reports." *Phi Delta Kappan* (November 1984) 66(3):167–72.

Darling-Hammond, Linda. "Reframing the School Reform Agenda." *Phi Delta Kappan* (June 1993):753–61.

Dewey, John. *The Child and the Curriculum.* Chicago: University of Chicago Press, 1902.

Editorial Projects in Education. *From Risk to Renewal: Charting a Course for Reform.* Washington, DC: Author, 1993.

Education Commission of the States. *Action in the States: Progress Toward Educational Renewal.* A Report of the Task Force on Education for Economic Growth, July 1984.

Elkind, David H., and Freddy Sweet. "The Socratic Approach to Character Education." *Educational Leadership* (May 1996):56–59.

English, Fenwick. "Dumbing Schools Down with Data Driven Decision Making: A Deconstructive Reading of a Popular Educational Leitmotif." *National Forum of Educational Administration and Supervision Journal* (2001):3–11.

Fantini, Mario. *Regaining Excellence in Education.* New York: Merrill/Macmillan, 1986.

Feistritzer, Emily. *The Condition of Teaching: A State by State Analysis.* Princeton, NJ: The Carnegie Foundation for the Advancement of Teaching, 1985.

Forsyth, Patrick B., and Marilyn Tallerico. *City Schools Leading the Way.* Newbury Park, CA: Corwin Press, 1993.

Frazier, Calvin. *A Shared Vision: Policy Recommendations for Linking Teacher Education to School Reform.* Denver, CO: Education Commission of the States, 1993.

Friedman, Milton and Rose. *Free to Choose a Personal Statement.* New York: Harcourt, Brace and Jovanovich, 1980.

Gardner, Howard. *Frames of Mind: The Theory of Multiple Intelligence.* New York: Basic Books, 1983.

Gehring, John. "Washington State Districts Issue Grades for Employability." *Education Week* (January 17, 2001):12.

———. "U.S. Seen Losing Edge on Education Measures." *Education Week* (April 4, 2001):3.

Giroux, Henry A. *Corporate Culture and the Attack on Higher Education and Public School.* Bloomington, IN: Phi Delta Kappa Educational Foundation Fastback Series (1999):46.

Goodlad, John I. *A Place Called School: Prospects for the Future.* New York: McGraw-Hill, 1984.

———. *Teachers for Our Nation's Schools.* San Francisco: Jossey-Bass, 1990.

Goodlad, John I., and Timothy J. McMannon, eds. *The Public Purpose of Education and Schooling.* San Francisco: Jossey-Bass, 1997.

Grissmer, David W., Ann Flanagan, Jennifer Kawata, and Stephanie Williamson. *Improving Student Achievement: What State NAEP Test Scores Tell Us?"* Rand Institute (2000). Available: *http://www.rand.org/publications/mr/mr/9241*

"Groundbreaking Teacher Preparation Standards to Be Used Beginning Next Year." *NCATE Accreditation* (May 15, 2000). Available: *http://www.ncate.org/2000/pressrelease.htm*

Hanushek, Eric A. "Assessing the Effects of School Resources on Student Performance: An Update." *Educational Evaluation and Policy Analysis* (Summer 1997):141–64.

———. "Have We Learned Anything New? The Rand Study of NAEP Performance." *Education Matters More* (2001). Available: *http://www.edmattersmore.org/2001sp/hanushek.html*

Hellegaard, James. "Fear Stalks the Hallways." *Gainesville Sun* (Sunday, June 6, 1993):1A.

Henderson, Keith. "As Schools Start Up, Reform Shifts from Spending to Seeing Results." *Christian Science Monitor* (August 30, 1993):1, 14.

Hirsch, E. D., Jr. *Cultural Literacy.* Boston: Houghton-Mifflin, 1987.

———. *The Schools We Need and Why We Don't Have Them.* New York: Doubleday, 1996, 237–38.

Holmes Group Consortium. *New Standards for Quality Teacher Education,* Washington, DC: U.S. Department of Education, 1984.

Holmstrom, David. "The Art of Undoing Violence Is Finding Its Own Place in Classrooms and Streets." *Christian Science Monitor* (September 1, 1993):1, 4.

Holt, John. *Teach Your Own: A Hopeful Path for Education*. New York: Delacorte Press/Seymour Lawrence, 1981.

House, Ernest R. "A Framework for Appraising Educational Reforms." *Educational Researcher* (October 1996):13.

Hoxby, Caroline M. "Would School Choice Change the Teaching Profession?" 2000. Available: *http://www.theconnection.org/archive/2000/10/1023a.shtml*

Hunt, James B., Jr. *What Matters Most: Teaching for America's Future*. New York: Teachers College, Columbia University, 1996.

Johnston, Robert C. "Troubled Pennsylvania Districts Eye Dramatic Changes." *Education Week* (November 22, 2000):18, 20.

"IDEA Funding: Time for a New Approach." Council for Exceptional Children (February 20, 2001):2–10. Available: *http://www.aasa.org/government_relations/IDEA%20Proposal.pdf*

Katz, Bruce, and Alan Berube. "Racial Change in the Nation's Largest Cities: Evidence from the 2000 Census." *The Brookings Center on Urban and Metropolitan Policy* (2001) Survey Released April 2001.

Kleiman, Carol. "Diversity Heads for the Next Level." *Sun-Sentinel South Florida:* Your Business, 2001:13.

Kozol, Jonathan. *Savage Inequalities: Children in America's Schools*. New York: Crown Publishing Company, 1991.

Lawton, Millicent. "Verbal, Math Scores on S.A.T. Up for Second Straight Year." *Education Week* (September 8, 1993):10.

Leary, James. *Educators on Trial*. Farmington, MI: Action Inservice, 1981.

Lewis, Anne C. "Washington Commentary." *Phi Delta Kappan* (April 2001):567.

Lyons, Kathleen, and Melinda Anderson. "U.S. Teacher Pay Rises Slightly: NEA Study Shows Salaries Declined in Some States." Washington, DC: *NEA News Release* (February 20, 1997): *http://www.nea.org/nr/nr.html*.

McKersie, William S. "Philanthropy's Paradox: Chicago School Reform." *Educational Evaluation and Policy Analysis* (1993 Summer) 15(2):109–28.

Naisbitt, John. *Re-inventing the Corporation*. London: Guild Publishing, 1985.

National Coalition of Advocates for Students. *Barriers to Excellence: Our Children at Risk*. Boston: Author, 1985.

National Commission on Excellence in Education. *A Nation at Risk: The Imperative for Educational Reform*. Washington, DC: U.S. Government Printing Office, 1983.

National Council for Accreditation of Teacher Education (NCATE). "New Teachers Say They Are Well Prepared." *Quality Teaching* (Spring 1997):1–2.

National Governors' Association 1991 Report on Education. *Time for Results*. Washington, DC: Author, 1990.

National Research Council. "Knowing What Students Know: The Science and Design of Educational Assessment." 2001. Available: *http://books.nap.edu/books/0309072727/html/12.html*

Owen, David. *None of the Above: Behind the Myth of Scholastic Aptitude*. Boston: Houghton Mifflin, 1985.

Perrone, Vito. "The Life and Career of Ernest Boyer (1928–1995)." *Educational Leadership* (March 1996) 53(6):80–82.

Peters, Thomas J., and Robert H. Waterman. *In Search of Excellence: Lessons from America's Best Run Companies*. New York: Harper & Row, 1982, 134–325.

Ponessa, Jeanne. "Despite Rocky Road, Ed. School Accreditation Effort on a Roll." *Education Week* (June 18, 1997):8.

"Rankings and Estimates: Rankings of the States 1999 and Estimates of School Statistics 2000." Washington, DC: National Education Association (NEA) Research, 2000.

Ravitch, Diane. *Left Back: A Century of Failed School Reforms*. New York: Simon and Schuster, 2000.

Raywid, Mary Anne, and Libby Oshiyama. "Musings in the Wake of Columbine." *Phi Delta Kappan* (February 2000):449.

Rose, Lowell C., and Alec M. Gallup. "The 32nd Annual Phi Delta Kappa/Gallup Poll of the Public's Attitudes Toward the Public Schools." *Phi Delta Kappan* (September 2000):46.

Rosenthal, Neal H., and Ronald E. Kirtscher. *The Occupational Outlook Handbook 1992–1993*. Washington, DC: Bureau of Labor Statistics, 1992–1993.

Russell, Bertrand Arthur William Russell, 3d Earl (1872–1970). *British Philosopher, Mathematician, and Social Reformer*. Available: *http://www. encyclopedia. com/printable/11228.html*

Sarason, Seymour B. *The Predictable Failure of Educational Reform*. San Francisco: Jossey-Bass, 1990.

Schmitt, Eric. "Urban Racial Makeup Shifting." *Sun-Sentinel South Florida:*3 A.

Sergiovanni, Thomas J. *The Principalship: A Reflective Practice Perspective*. Boston: Allyn and Bacon, 1991.

Shane, Harold Gray, and M. Bernadine Tabler. *Educating for a New Millennium: Views of 132 International Scholars*. Bloomington, IN: Phi Beta Kappa, 1981.

Sizer, Nancy Faust, and Theodore Sizer. "A School Build for Horace" (2001). Available: *http://www.edmatters.-org/2001sp/26.html*

Sizer, Theodore R. *Horace's Compromise: The Dilemma of the American High School*. Boston: Houghton Mifflin, 1984.

———. *Horace's Hope: The Future of the American High School*. Boston: Houghton Mifflin, 1996.

———. *Horace's School: Redesigning the American High School*. Boston: Houghton Mifflin, 1992.

Smith, B. Othanel. *A Design for a School of Pedagogy*. Washington, DC: U.S. Department of Education, 1980.

"Special Education Inclusion." *Teaching and Learning* (2001): 1–10. Available:*http://www.weac.org/resource/june96/speced.htm*

Stricherz, Mark. "Top Oakland Administrators to Receive Bonuses Tied to Test Scores." *Education Week* (January 24, 2001):5.

Synder, Thomas D. *Digest of Educational Statistics*. Washington, DC: U.S. Department of Education, 1996.

Tallerico, Marilyn. "Governing Urban Schools," in *City Schools Leading the Way*. Marilyn Tallerico and Patrick B. Forsyth, eds. Newbury Park, CA: Corwin Press, 1993, 239–40.

Tanner, Daniel. *Progressive Education at the Crossroads: Crusade for Democracy*. Albany, NY: State University of New York Press, 1991:xiii, xiv.

Tewel, Kenneth J. *New Schools for a New Century*. Delray Beach, FL: St. Lucie Press, 1995.

"Tomorrow's Schools of Education." *A Report of the Holmes Group* (1995). Available: *http://www.baylor.edu/SOE/SCHOLMES/TSOE.HTML*

Waddell, Lynn. "Flap Erupts over Ads on School Websites." *Christian Science Monitor* (May 2, 2001):2.

Weber, James R. *Instructional Leadership: A Corporate Working Model*. Eugene, OR: ERIC Clearinghouse on Educational Management (June 1987):55.

Weber, R. M. "The Study of Oral Reading Errors: A Review of the Literature," *Reading Research Quarterly 4* (1970):96–119.

William T. Grant Foundation. *The Forgotten Half: Non-College Youth in America: An Interim Report on the School-to-Work Transition*. New York: William T. Grant Foundation Commission on Work, Family and Citizenship, 1988.

Wirth, Arthur. *Education and Work for the Year 2000: Choices We Make*. San Francisco: Jossey-Bass, 1992.

Wolf, Shelby, Hilda Borko, Rebekah L. Elliott, and Monette C. McIver. "That Dog Won't Hunt!": Exemplary School Change Efforts within the Kentucky Reform. *American Educational Research Journal* (Summer 2000):349–393.

Woods, Peter. *Inside Schools*. Boston: Routledge & Kagan Paul, 1986.

Zerchykov, Ross. *School Boards and the Communities They Represent*. Boston, MA: Institute for Responsive Education, 1981.

Zirkel, Perry A. "Sorting Out Which Students Have Learning Disabilities." *Phi Delta Kappan* (April 2001): 639–641.

Zollers, Nancy J., Albert, R. Lille, and Cochran-Smith, Marilyn. "In Pursuit of Social Justice: Collaborative Research and Practice in Teacher Education." *Action in Teacher Education* (Summer 2000):1–11.

CHAPTER TEN

EDUCATION IN THE FUTURE: FROM NOW TO THEN

Societies ... are not machines and they are not computers. They cannot be reduced so simply into hardware and software, base and superstructure. A more apt model would picture them as consisting of many more elements, all connected in immensely complex and continually changing feedback loops. As their complexity rises, knowledge becomes more central to their economic and ecological survival.

Alvin Toffler

Industrial Era	Computer Age	Information Age	Post-Industrial Age
1969 *Apollo* moon landing	1970 Toffler's *Future Shock*	1980 Worldwide telecommunications networks	Socialization and basic learning through home computers and TV
	Transistor computer		
First generation vacuum tube computer	*Explorer* launched	1982 Naisbitt's *Megatrends* 1990 Naisbitt's *Megatrends* II *2000*	
	Toffler's *Powershift*	Microcomputer in homes	

Figure 10.1   Time Line of Contemporary and Future Education

American teachers have always attempted to prepare their students for the future, even when they expected that future to be exactly like the present. What distinguishes the current teacher from those in the past is the accelerating rate of change and uncertainty about what the future world will be like. For example, with most of the nation's schools connected to the Internet, what will be the most effective way of helping students monitor the quality of information accessed? In our information age, how can we prepare students to cope with computer crashes, glitches, utility company blackouts, intellectual property rights, and issues of privacy? In an interdependent connected world, how can educators address an increased backlash against globalization and its effect on poorer countries? We know that we must deal with lifelong learning, an exploding information environment, and a global economy, but knowledge of the future remains obscure while change occurs at an ever more rapid rate.

When the authors of this book were boys growing up in different parts of America, there was no television and only limited radio. Warm summer nights were often spent gazing in wonder at the stars and planets. The Big Dipper was easily recognized, we knew the red planet was Mars, and we had a vague notion that the Milky Way was a galaxy. But we did not know and could not have known what every child with access to the Internet, the World Wide Web, and instant information available anywhere through smaller, portable, wireless systems and television knows today. *Voyager* has produced close-up pictures of distant planets, deep-space probes by the Hubble telescope have revealed some 50 billion galaxies, astronomers debate the meaning of black holes, and astronauts spin around the globe, serving a permanent and growing space station. More has been learned about our universe since the landing on the moon than had been discovered in all prior human history.

2000			Communications Era	
2000 Genetic engineering common	2001 International terrorism strikes U.S.	2005 Automated highways	2015 Human travel by light beam	2030 Mind to mind communication
		2012 Drugs for raising intelligence		Nanotechnology
Microengineering			Computers with human thought ability	
2000 All students skilled in computer languages		Eight billion humans on Earth	2020 Worldwide guaranteed minimum income and world peace	Cheap energy from fusion

Perhaps nothing better illustrates the explosion of information than the landing of *Pathfinder* on the surface of Mars on July 4, 1997. Within hours of that event, pictures were being returned to Earth, placed on the World Wide Web, and viewed by tens of thousands of people at hundreds of Web sites. Gone were the speculation that there were canals on Mars and the question of beings such as those described in Wells' *War of the Worlds* (1898). Descriptions of Mars in reference books and texts became obsolete as fact replaced misinformation.

Building a permanent spaceship with international collaboration, expanding its parameters, and providing an opportunity for the first paying private citizen to travel to the spaceship for $20 million reflect a commitment to future exploration with ever expanding possibilities.

Whether or not teachers choose to call themselves futurists, they cannot afford merely to pass along past knowledge to new generations. They must prepare for the unknown, the unexpected, the continuing explosions of information, and a world in constant flux. It is a world in which we all seem to be drowning in the volume of new data, but making data into information and refining that into knowledge and wisdom is a vital skill. Snider (2000) noted that the Web was expected to double in size by 2001, growing by 7.3 million pages a day with 84 percent of the pages in the United States. He added that the percentage of information relevant to users is approximately 0.01 percent, and it will be up to technocrats to keep the Web relevant.

By the year 2007 it is anticipated that Chinese will be the language most used on the World Wide Web. Modern teachers must develop problem-solving skills, teach how to evaluate information, and make a foundation for lifelong learning. Future survival depends upon it. We are facing a virtual reality technological age where a machine-generated reality offers new learning experiences in which students can participate. Computer games, holographs, and simulation activities can serve as a created learning experience as opposed to an actual experience. As Royal Van Horn reported in a *Phi Delta Kappan* article (2000), one can find in nearly every classroom children writing, communicating, illustrating. They are using word processors, sending e-mail letters to friends, illustrating their writing, critiquing stories they have read, creating class and club newsletters, and so on. Kindergartners and first graders are growing up in a connected world.

History has its own intrinsic value, but most of us are interested in the past because of its practical value in understanding the present and its ability to suggest the probable course of future events. Out of necessity, teachers must be oriented toward the future. Children now entering kindergarten can reasonably expect to be alive and active well into the end of the twenty-first century. Colleges that train teachers are currently working with teacher candidates who will directly influence the citizens of the twenty-second century.

In a period of very slow cultural change such as the Middle Ages, significant spans of time were not critical. Today, with accelerating invention in many fields, the explosion of research and knowledge, careening technology, electronic communications networks, and computers, the rate of change does indeed approach *Future Shock*. The twenty-first century may well be as different from the twentieth as the twentieth was from the nineteenth. Children entrusted to the care of educators may expect changes that stagger the imagination. All indications point to an even faster rate of change, and not even an economic depression could reverse the trend. Because we cannot know the future in advance, it is necessary that we prepare future citizens for as wide a variety of alternatives as possible. It is extremely difficult to give future generations the skills and information (to say nothing of the attitudes and values) they will require for future survival, but anticipation of events to come seems fundamental to the attempt. The worst we can do is to send students into our twenty-first century armed only with an education based on the ideals and needs of nineteenth-century agrarian America. It is said that education always looks to the past and that invention in the schools comes slowly, but it is imperative that teachers become students of the future and that they do their utmost to give students the best tools possible for coping with a variety of probable futures.

On first reflection, history may seem an odd means for approaching the future. Further analysis will show that past recorded events do shed light on how human beings expected things to go, how things actually did go, and what consequences followed. The television series *Connections* is an example of the way one scientific discovery led to another until the whole shape of technology and even of human society was drastically altered in unexpected ways. An illustration is the invention in the twelfth century of the chimney, an invention that made it possible to heat numerous rooms on more than one floor. One result was a dramatic change in architecture, because buildings no longer had to be built around one fireplace, and with a hole in the roof for smoke ventilation.

An educational example is furnished by the social revolution that took place in Athens during the fifth century B.C. A new class of rich people emerged; they made their money from banking, shipping, and the manufacture of goods for export. These men wanted to obtain an education for their sons similar to that provided for the young men from the old aristocratic families. For this purpose, they hired migrant teachers called sophists, such as Protagoras, Gorgias, and Antiphon. The sophists were skilled at teaching oratory and grammar, but they also criticized conventional morality, religion, and law. They taught practical ways of getting ahead in the world and clever means for evading rules. The sophists drastically changed the values and norms of Athenian society and eventually altered the entire social order.

History can also be used as an instrument for analyzing and evaluating major forces or trends in the culture with the purpose of anticipating the future. Robert Heilbroner has done exactly that in his books *The Future As History* (1959), *An Inquiry into the Human Prospect* (1975), *21ˢᵗ Century Capitalism* (1993), and *Visions of the Future* (1995). In the first book, Heilbroner looked at long-standing trends in American culture as a means of defining the crucial problems that must be resolved if a viable future is to be achieved. He made no effort to play the role of prophet but gave detailed accounts of the revolutions in the twentieth century to show what must occur if liberal society is to survive. The second book treats the global situation in a similar way. Heilbroner looks at world economic trends, the challenges to political democracy, the exploding population, environmental destruction, and obliterative weaponry. His third book suggests that capitalism relies on a mechanism for its economic coordination that is inadequate to meet the needs of our emerging world— namely, of globalization of production and an ecological encounter. The end result will be major changes in our institutions. Heilbroner's fourth book entails a search for unity within diversity for building a civilization more humane and decent than our own. His conclusion is that neither industrial capitalism nor Marxist socialism in their present forms has the necessary strength to avoid global catastrophe.

Although he is pessimistic about what is happening in the modern world, Heilbroner uses history as a tool to spell out exactly what we must do if the consequences of our past activities are not to result in disaster. Thus, as do many futuristic writers, Heilbroner uses history as an instrument for examining societal propensities and suggesting alternatives.

Jeremy Rifkin in *The End of Work: The Decline of the Global Labor Force and the Dawn of the Post-Market Era* (1996) views a third industrial revolution in the information age as fraught with challenges. Either growing unemployment and displacement of workers will lead to a global economic calamity with increased social fragmentation or a civilization will exist where people will be paid for volunteer work to keep them occupied in a world with increased leisure time. In the early 2000s, corporate mergers and downsizing led to increased employee layoffs as labor is the first line of cost cutting when businesses seek to cope with a rapidly changing global marketplace. The Federal Reserve tried to maintain a prosperous economic cycle through managing interest rate increases and decreases in an ever more difficult global economy beset by political one-upmanship as growing polarization takes place in national legislative bodies between political parties.

Paul M. Kennedy, historian at Yale University, finds that the forces of technology, demography, political disintegration, cultural animosities, and ecological damage challenge our human condition. He notes that if these forces are to be contained, we will have to rely on human beings, educated and intelligent women and men who can offer creative responses to these challenges. Kennedy states that our ultimate tools for coping with the awesome task of preparing for the next century are knowledge, understanding, and critical analysis—or, in a word, *education*. He further notes that what today's young people do over the next few decades, particularly those who graduate from our universities and colleges, will vitally affect our future.

History is filled with examples of attempts to foretell the future. Some of the earliest legends and artifacts deal with predicting things to come and rationalizing the plausibility of those predictions. The difficulty is that forecasting the future has seldom proved accurate, and predictions that did come true were rarely accepted more widely than those that failed. One of the major difficulties is a human tendency to assume that the future will only be an extension of the present. Those without an appreciation of history believe that the future will consist of a massive dose of today. This is a serious error in a period of dramatic and accelerating change, as futurists are fond of pointing out. In general, the record of forecasting future events is not a good one, partly because changes in the behavior and values of people are not as easy to predict as weather patterns or oil production. As Harry Broudy puts it, "Human behavior cannot be extrapolated in any simple linear fashion." We can extrapolate the increasing need for energy by using the current rates of consumption as a base. But we cannot predict that the demand for energy—as measured by the demand for air conditioning, electrical heating, and household appliances—will increase at the same rate as it has in the last decade. The California energy debacle of 2001 demonstrates the lack of foresight in planning for the future as one of the world's largest economies teeters on the edge of a recession due to rising costs of power.

Many of those who claim to be futurists draw an analogy between well-established scientific or materialistic trends and what they believe will be the life conditions of the future. These extrapolists usually have the support of those in control of wealth and power who desire and expect that known general tendencies will merely accelerate. They ignore the possibility of radical changes in values, social behaviors, or attitudes. Herbert Spencer's doctrine of inevitable progress and the steady advance of technology leading to a utopian world for man was so popular and so widely accepted that few took seriously the dystopian predictions of H. G. Wells. Yet Wells—in such books as *The Time Machine* (1895), *War of the Worlds* (1898), and *The Shape of Things to Come* (1933)—anticipated world war, space travel, and the breakdown of the social order. Like Jules Verne before him, Wells made predictions that turned out to be far more accurate than those of his more "respectable" contemporaries. The same can be said for Huxley in *Brave New World* (1932) and Orwell in *1984* (1949).

In *The Evolution of Progress* (1993), C. Owen Paepke envisions an emerging concept of progress that will make human traits and abilities the subject rather than the source of change as the agenda of the next century. Paepke finds the lengthening of the life span and the discovery of genetic sources of exceptional mental abilities and other favorable traits to be a present and future possibility.

Joseph F. Coates identified twelve transforming issues for the future at the 1993 meeting of the Society for Human Resource Management (see Figure 10.2). In the early 2000s, modifications to the transforming issues include the following:

1. In a cyclical economy employee layoffs, corporate downsizing, mergers, buyouts, early retirement incentives, bankruptcies, and business losses are always a possibility. Employees and managers need to plan for such contingencies by recycling, retraining, and preparing for jobs in growth areas.
2. Majority-minority populations including Latino, Asian, and African-American populations continue to expand in major urban areas as the white population becomes a minority.
3. A vocal antiglobalization group will protest World Trade Organization initiatives and call for increased wealth distribution to have-not populations throughout the world.
4. Congress and the president will continue to focus on improving education through a variety of strategies including tokenism (paying students for learning results) and assessment and testing. There will be growing protests by parents and students against excessive reliance on standardized test scores, and alternative assessment measures will be explored.
5. Federal courts will order states to equalize school funding between rich and poor school districts. These issues provide guidelines to building scenarios about our future.

We must conclude from a historical perspective that science and the most sober human reasoning are conditioned to look only at the immediate past for causes of human problems. Human intellect and judgment are not well adapted to interpreting the behavior of social systems, anticipating radical changes in values, or understanding that existing governments are inadequate to manage the affairs of people in the modern world. One reason for this is that training has become so sophisticated and therefore so specialized that very few are educated broadly enough to see the whole picture. Futurism centers upon the interrelationship of human activities, the wide range of possible alternatives for human action, and the opportunities for consciously altering or inventing the future.

Intellectual activity does not always merely follow change in the materialistic and technological spheres. Ideas, such as those of the world's great religious leaders, have the power to change not only values but also priorities and views of the good life. Those who have really changed the world are the thinkers who have challenged basic theories, beliefs, values, and myths. Rousseau, Marx, Darwin, and Freud are examples of such thinkers.

Educators must be students of the future if they are to make any real progress in meeting the needs of students in the world of tomorrow. Scholars in many fields are speculating about the future and examining trends in the current world. Although much of the futuristic writing sounds a warning about what could happen, some of

1. Labor, seeking to overcome management power on the rise since the 1950s, will organize, sue, strike, sabotage employment, and seek legislation to enhance its power.

2. With the information fiber optic superhighways, more work will be done away from offices due to people wanting flexible schedules and for cost effectiveness.

3. African-Americans have made "enormous progress" in corporate America in the last 50 years. Coates estimates more than two-thirds have a "handhold on the upper mobility ladder." Because of this, the issue is no longer one of equal access but of performance. Hispanics and Latinos are one of the nation's largest minorities and will affect all aspects of American culture. Blacks, Hispanics and other minorities are now the majority in most of America's largest cities. Thus we have a minority-majority population expanding in major population areas.

4. There will be increased business cooperation and coordination on research and development for minimal individual company risk. Efforts will be made to develop a corporate culture and equity among groups from different organizations. Entrepreneurship will be more closely scrutinized as the bankruptcy of Enron, one of the nation's largest corporations, spreads its tentacles throughout the corporate and governmental sector. Employees' pension and job loss will result in careful examination of deregulation in the energy and other sectors. Educators will need to address moral and ethical conduct in a technological, cyber age where new financial models manipulated by free wheelers and dealers may damage the nation's social, economic, political and legal safety nets.

5. The future will hold widespread genetic testing, personality tests, and skill level tests so that employers can evaluate their investments.

6. Automation, training, and teamwork will be increasingly utilized to enhance productivity.

7. Global networking for increased world markets will be used to improve quality and exports. Globalization is essential to an overproducing economic system but the spread of worldwide terrorism threatens financial and economic systems. Educators will increasingly need to work toward full-service schools to pick up the slack of underemployed and unemployed families. In addition, there is an increasing movement of have-not nation's populations to industrialized society leading to overcrowded schools and increased costs of dealing with at-risk student populations. Florida, California, and New York face challenges of building enough facilities to house an ever expanding student population. With a low birthrate, newcomers to the United States are essential to provide the human energy to fuel the nation's industrial and agricultural base.

8. Due to increased employee costs, there will be exponential growth in part-time, contract, and temporary employees, doubling in the next decade from 25 percent to 50 percent of workers. There will be an increased use of substitute, part-time, and temporary teachers in public and private schools as well as expanded use of adjuncts in all levels of post secondary education.

Figure 10.2   Twelve Transforming Issues for the Future

Source: Joseph Coates, Futurist Consultant. Personal communication with author, Washington, DC, December 18, 1997. Modified by the authors 2002.

9. There will be an increase in women executives, who will push for flexible work schedules as well as a new corporate culture.

10. Education will increasingly be under scrutiny to find ways of improving product quality. School reform will be a perpetual activity in the foreseeable future as massive federal and state efforts are undertaken to improve academic achievement levels of minority, culturally and ethnically diverse populations and at-risk students. Increased federal spending will be directed to these reform efforts as well as toward serving special education populations.

11. Future work life will encompass more attention to quality of life cycle including child and elderly care.

12. Increased attention will be given to improving the quality of executive leadership.

13. There will be an increased focus on ethics, morality and character building in schools, the business community and society.

14. Efforts to improve school safety and societal security will be a major thrust for the foreseeable future.

Figure 10.2   Continued

the work is optimistic in tone. The ancient Chinese wrote the word *crisis* as a combination of the symbols for danger and opportunity.

TRENDS IN EDUCATION IN THE TWENTY-FIRST CENTURY

It is difficult to predict with any certainty how long emerging trends will last. But we will venture a few projections based on what is happening in the real world of the public schools in the dawn of our twenty-first century. We see the emergence of outsourcing, or the practice of subcontracting work that was formerly performed by school districts. For example, sanitation, food service, school janitorial services, and school administration are being turned over to outsource specialists such as Edison Schools with varying results and often strong educator organization protests. Trends in the future of education include safe schools; aggression control and peace curriculum, curriculum modifications to include character building, tolerance for difference and diversity, and civility; knowledge and sensitivity training sessions related to gender, culture, ethnicity, AIDS, English as a second language or total English immersion, age, and people who are physically, emotionally, and mentally challenged; empowerment of students and teachers; distance learning at all educational levels, high-stakes testing, alternative assessment strategies for poor test takers, changes in school scheduling; and suicide and teenage pregnancy prevention programs.

Faculty, administration, and student handbooks will grow in complexity as efforts are made to prevent excessive litigation, for example, in areas of hate crimes, hate language, as well as racial and sexual harassment. Zero tolerance for deviant behavior, no matter how minor, will be designed to prevent crime and violence in schools, although there will be a growing backlash against excesses in the program. Educational administration preparation will be oriented toward visions of organizations designed to facilitate change, empower people, and structure reform and modification, with principals as instructional leaders, developing networks and partnerships with universities, community groups, businesses, and civic organizations. Engaging teachers and administrators as instructional leaders in discourses of reform and change will be increasingly important.

Efforts to increase teachers' salaries will be countered by financial restraints as taxpayers seek to cut taxes. Litigation will increase exponentially as federal courts rule for equitable distributions of resources between have and have-not school districts. Court-ordered inner-city desegregation rulings will continue to place districts under federal court supervision in the future as in the past forty years.

The Internet and World Wide Web continue to have tremendous impact on our society. In a *Forbes* magazine interview (March 1997), writer Peter Drucker noted that thirty years from now large university campuses will be relics partially due to the high cost and the ability to deliver more lectures and classes off campus by satellite or two-way video at a fraction of the cost. Drucker continued by noting that today's buildings are hopelessly unsuited and totally unnecessary.

Computers will be more reliable and dependable in the future as efforts are made to make them capable of self-correcting software glitches. Smaller, more mobile wireless devices will permeate schools and society making access to information available everywhere. High-speed access with broadband connecting ever more devices to the Internet will expand exponentially. The Internet will need common platforms available like the nation's mail, phone, and rail system for maximum effectiveness. In order to provide energy for the information age, the use of alternative energy sources and conservation will be a necessity.

Means (2001) in an *Educational Leadership* article on "Technology Use in Tomorrow's Schools" finds students building Web pages and developing multimedia presentations, while educators are using network technology to support collaborations locally and at great distances. Means sees a move toward lower-cost, portable, handheld devices, often connected through global networks and equipment manufacturers investing in wireless technology. Students in the future can access information everywhere, at any time, and communicate with teachers and other students through notepads. Technology is in our future. Its use enhances information retrieval and dissemination. The downside of a growing emphasis on technology is lack of reliability, uneven accuracy and quality of information, pornography and other information potentially harmful to students and society, energy blackouts, overlooking the human element in learning and possible student obsession with chat lines and Web searches that require higher education counseling facilities to assist students who otherwise might drop out of school, and physical injury due to computer use. Whatever the downside of technology in our schools, there will be no turning back. Critical thinking, judicious use of our rapidly exploding technology, will benefit students, teachers, administrators, and society.

THE FUTURES MOVEMENT

Ever since Alvin Toffler wrote *Future Shock* (1970) and Alvin and Heidi Toffler wrote *Creating a New Civilization: Politics of the Third Wave* (1995), people in America have been more aware of what experts in certain fields have known for decades—that the rate of change in modern society is rapidly accelerating. A new group of scientists and authors, known generally as futurists, have taken issue with the standard assumptions implicit and explicit in modern civilization. They question the idea of progress leading to ever-greater production of goods, the expenditures of enormous quantities of energy, the rapid depletion of the nonrenewable natural resources, and the development of a worldwide market for materialistic consumer goods. Futurists build on the social theories of Karl Marx, Karl Mannheim, Pitirim Sorokin, Oswald Spengler, and Arnold Toynbee, among others. They are aware of the culture lag theory, which suggests that human beings cannot cope with the shattering stress and disorganization that result when materialistic invention comes too rapidly for social adjustment. Problems such as the exploding world population, the threat of nuclear war, pollution, runaway technology, the knowledge explosion, and environmental destruction cause many futurists to doubt the survival of civilization and its institutions, unless radical adjustments can be quickly made.

In *Cybernation: The Silent Revolution* (1962), Donald N. Michael shows how poorly prepared modern people are for the revolution now in progress. Kenneth Boulding refers to the automation-biological revolution as "The Great Transition" and considers it to be as significant in human growth and development as the discovery of agriculture or the Industrial Revolution. In *The Coming of Post-Industrial Society* (1976), Daniel Bell forecasts the most radical changes that have ever faced the human race. In *Overskill* (1972), Eugene Schwartz argues that the present trend toward increased technological and materialistic expansion cannot be maintained.

Lester Brown illustrates the growing economic gap between the rich and poor in *World Without Borders* (1972). He points out that the whole world is becoming poverty stricken in terms of Earth's total ability to sustain life and predicts that a stable world order depends on meeting the basic needs of all people. Radical economists like John Kenneth Galbraith and Robert Theobald maintain that the present socioeconomic system in the industrial nations like Japan, West Germany, and the United States cannot ensure survival. In *The Prometheus Project* (1969), Gerald Fineberg calls for a new and revolutionary set of long-range social goals. In *Beyond the Limits* (1991), Donella Meadows insists that for future survival there must be limits to growth. John R. Platt believes that a science for human survival is needed to examine social and individual priorities. He believes that greater care must be taken to avoid ecological disasters such as the Exxon oil spill off the coast of Alaska in 1989.

In *Education Work for the Year 2000* (1992), Arthur Wirth finds the United States facing two alternatives. One would entail adhering to our current course of education while ignoring the social disarray among the disadvantaged and the increasing segregation of Americans by income or while making a major shift in national priorities. The second option would require ensuring that all children regardless of race or class have equal access to the best education possible.

Some futurists see humanity as an endangered species clinging precariously to a life-support system that its own actions might destroy. Others are concerned about efforts to maintain wealth and privilege in an overpopulated world, where equality of distribution of resources is badly needed. Barry Commoner believes that our technology is responsible for deterioration in the quality of the environment and that a new and better technology is needed to prevent massive biological degradation. Almost all see overgrowth, increased industrialization, urbanization, unemployment, psychological alienation, environmental destruction, polarization of rich and poor, expansion of the population, and demands for resources beyond the capacity of Earth to provide them as major problems of the present and the future.

Most futurists are painfully aware of the danger of prediction and the terrible record that intellectuals have had of forecasting human events. Still, most of our basic institutions and beliefs depend on the assumption that things will remain pretty much as they are, an assumption that plainly runs contrary to fact. Electronic media and the invention of the computer have joined to produce an explosion of information unlike anything previously experienced. New knowledge can be quickly disseminated and applied to tasks that stagger the imagination, such as landing human beings safely on the moon. Each new technical development creates new possibilities for invention and the rapid exchange of ideas, plans, and programs that grow at an exponential rate. Linking information systems and machines creates cybernation. The possibility of a highly refined, automated cybernated system of production is now very real. There are also very great breakthroughs in areas of science such as biology and genetics, the results of which are not yet clear but are certainly highly significant. Every day much more is learned about human behavior and the learning process.

Bill Gates, founder of Microsoft, believes that the Internet will provide opportunities for multicast, better video compression, security technologies, 3-D browsing, personalization servers, server development, and site tracking. He sees speech recognition, natural language understanding, automatic learning, flat-screen displays, optic fiber, and Moore's law (doubling the storage capacity of transistors every eighteen months) as the technologies having the most impact over the next decade and a half. Intel's Gordon Moore also sees computer voice recognition as changing the way computing is done (Gates, 1997). This technology will have a great impact by opening up computing to the 50 percent of the population who are currently nonparticipants. In the future, students will be able to ask their computers to go out on the Net to find the information they want. Bill Gates and Collins Hemingway in *Business@ The Speed of Thought: Succeeding in the Digital Economy* (1999) discussed the possibilities and challenges of making management decisions through managing electronic information in a digital age. Gates supporters and detractors tend to agree with him that the Internet age is a work in progress. The future of our digital age remains to be discovered, but the changes will affect society and its educational institutions as much as any discovery in human history. Educators and students are internalizing daily the quantum leaps in our information age.

Futurists use different terms to refer to the transformation now taking place. The unknown state into which we are passing is termed *post-industrial, post-civilized, automated, cybernated, super-industrial, information-era, communications-era, digital-era, electronic-era,* and the like. Futuristic writers do not agree on exactly what form the great revolution will take, but they agree that it is already in process. The transformation offers great hope for achieving a higher level of human potential and "inventing the future"; however, it also poses the danger that people will be unable to adjust rapidly enough to change. Obviously, futurists have little faith that education can be guided by ideas of the past, for example, by the collection of classics known as the Great Books of the Western World.

In a recent interview, Alvin Toffler stated that the factory model of education is passé. He noted that the single most important educational gain in the last twenty years has been the fact that 20 to 40 million Americans learned how to use the PC. Through an information process of people-to-people learning, an enormous bank of skills was distributed throughout our society. Toffler concluded that if we understood people-to-people learning and distributed intelligence, we could transform and accelerate the learning process in ways that have nothing to do with classrooms and seats.

Alvin and Heidi Toffler (2001) in "New Economy? You Ain't Seen Nothing Yet" place the Internet in larger perspective. They report that with 3 million digital switches for every human being alive on the planet and half a billion PCs, one for every thirteen human beings as well as a burgeoning wireless usage, the new frontier will be intellectual property rights for Internet contributors. With a dot-com shakeout, with investor losses in technology and an economic down cycle in late 2000 and 2001, there were predictions of the demise of the new economy. The Tofflers, however, viewed the technological down cycle as a mere spike in the history of the new economy in the twenty-first century. Currently as in the past, the United States economic system depends on built-in obsolescence and foreign markets. Such a dependence on global markets and resources involves risk, as witness the fluctuations in energy and financial markets. However, the Tofflers find that innovation, creativity, and quantum leaps of technology are the open door to the future. The Internet has changed our future and will continue to shape our future in ways as yet unknown.

The Tofflers and other futurists see the digital revolution eventually converging and being modified by the biological revolution. Belsie (2001) discussed the publicly funded Human Genome Sequencing Consortium and the privately funded Celera Genomics Corporation's work in identifying genes in the genetic code. The possibilities for stem cell advances to regenerate human organs create a vision of improving the quality of life for young and old in the future.

Students in the future will need to learn maximum flexibility to respond to the unexpected and unforeseen. Computer glitches, uncertain energy supplies, the need for more reliable and dependable software and hardware—all require individuals to be able to function effectively when faced with occasional energy shutdowns. These problems will be resolved in the distant future, but being able to adjust to an unwired wireless society will continue to be vital. World and regional conflicts continue to plague humanity. The unpredictability of human behavior remains a fly in the ointment of the information age.

METHODS OF FUTURES RESEARCH

Futures research is concerned with collecting information and developing the processes by which alternatives are determined and policy is made in a variety of disciplines. It concentrates on anticipated developments, the probability that various events will occur in a given time period, and the consequences of alternatives. Much attention is given to the impact of one event upon another and the way two or more events might interact to change future conditions. Futures research is action-oriented and realistic rather than utopian. It assumes that human action can and should make a difference in increasing or decreasing the probability of various possible futures. Futures research concerns itself with conceptualizing and inventing the future by examining the consequences of various plans of action before they become tomorrow's reality.

Delphi.   The delphi technique is a means of forecasting based on the consensus of a group of specialists or experts. Delphi methodology involves first the selection of knowledgeable people in a given field or problem area. Each member of the group is asked to render forecasts individually. After all forecasts are collected, the results of the total survey are returned to each member of the group. Members can then revise their earlier forecasts or explain their reasons for not being in consensus with the other members. The process of collecting and distributing the survey results is carried out until each member understands all other positions and all have reached final conclusions on their individual positions.

Cross-Impact Matrix.   This is a refinement of the delphi technique, which purports to determine the impact of future events upon each other. A delphi procedure can be used to measure the relationships between forecasted events. A computer analysis of the matrix can also be used to develop a set of probabilities for a complex set of events.

Digital computers, which have the capability of solving hundreds of equations within short periods of time, provide the researcher with the means for dynamic systems modeling. Mathematical simulation through computer analysis can facilitate knowledge about inherent lags between normative and exploratory forecasts. The computer, however, can only simulate a system to the extent that operating equations accurately describe behaviors in the real system. Theobald stresses that "the computer is a very good servant and a very bad master."

Simulation and Gaming.   Simulation and gaming processes encompass a broad range of methodologies. They usually involve an analysis of alternative future systems. They can be confined to particular fields of futurist interests using the computer (as described previously), or they can involve more simplistic models such as three-dimensional (pencil and paper) games and experience compression techniques (brainstorming). The simulation can also involve a cross-impact analysis such as George Koehier's Futuribles—a game that provides participants with 288 possible futures in areas such as education, religion, energy, government, transportation, and so forth.

Perspective Trees.   In this process, the researcher first examines the forces of change (rather than solutions to problems) within a given parameter. Second, a list is devised containing broad categories (poverty, health, war) as well as specific categories (government regulations, subcultures). Next, numerous relations or perspective trees are produced. Although perspective trees do not provide a whole method for forecasting, they are instrumental in the planning process. They are especially helpful when used in conjunction with the delphi technique, trend extrapolation, or computerized cross-impact analysis.

Trend Extrapolation.   This technique entails an analysis of past and present trends in order to predict future trends. The central thesis is one of continuity; future trends will resemble past behaviors. A major problem in trend extrapolation is the selection of parameters. First, parameters are quantifiable at best. A subjective analysis of trends does not satisfy this methodology. Second, parameters must be selected that provide sufficient historical data. Third, regularity of patterns must be established. Fourth, the researcher should determine the interaction of past trends and changes in relationships between past and present parameters. Trend extrapolation can be used as a method itself, or it can be incorporated into other methods. Extrapolation assumes no discontinuity with the past and is widely used by business, industry, and government.

Scenario Concepts.   A scenario is usually a study of possible futures. Scenario conceptualization of the future is often limited by its subjective, nonquantitative format. It does provide, however, a creative means for analyzing futuribles without dependence upon past projections. This method is particularly important in the realm of social values. It is extremely difficult to model a hierarchical social system and to forecast value changes. Scenario conceptualizing facilitates a profile of social thresholds and provides descriptions of possible alternatives that oblige an individual to examine goals and priorities. The writing of scenarios is not only a research method but also one of the best ways for students to learn how to deal with the future. The construction and evaluation of scenarios has become one of the most common classroom activities.

Ethnographic Futures.   In *Foundations of Futures Studies* (1996), Wendell Bell describes the research as involving lengthy and detailed interviewing of respondents, often repeated interviewing of the same respondents, over a period of time. Bell notes that the role of the researcher is that of an active, sensitive, and sympathetic listener; a nondirective stimulator; and a careful recorder who moves the interview along by showing interest, offering encouragement, and posing questions as needed. This qualitative research often involves analyzing the text and context of respondents to gain holistic insights into their work lives and work worlds.

SCHOOLS OF FUTURISTIC THOUGHT

Because of the diversity of futures theories, it is helpful to divide them into groups according to general principles and shared beliefs. Just as in philosophy, there is some overlap, and a few individuals do not fit any given category. Nevertheless, some system of classification is essential for treating assumptions and selecting the positions from which a futuristic philosophy of education may be constructed.

Kahn

Briggs

Optimistic Extrapolists or Technological Enthusiasts.   As the name implies, optimistic extrapolists are hopeful about the future and often accuse critical theorists (like Robert Heilbroner) of crying "wolf." One of the best known representatives of this group is the late Herman Kahn of the Hudson Institute. Kahn predicts a future society where technology has provided people with all possible comforts and leisure time. Support for Kahn and the Hudson Institute comes from business and government. Optimistic extrapolists analyze existing trends and attempt to forecast future needs and markets. Kahn and his colleague Bruce Briggs say that there is no such thing as pollution, only resources that we have not yet learned to recycle. Extrapolists use think tanks to study trends and to propose alternative courses of action related to specific problems in industry. They have pioneered new methods of research such as delphi, computer-assisted trend analysis, and the cross-impact matrix.

Optimistic extrapolists or technological enthusiasts see growth and technological development as natural and good for the whole world. They believe that we will discover new resources and learn how to better utilize existing ones so that there will be ample support for a high quality of life, even for people in underdeveloped nations. This optimism is reflected in Daniel Bell's *The Coming of Post-Industrial Society* (1976). Other examples of the position are found in Olaf Helmer-Hirschberg's *Social Technology* (1966) and Fred Polak's *The Image of the Future* (1973). The educational need of the future will be for more and better-trained scientists, engineers, and planners.

Naisbitt

John Naisbitt's *Megatrends* (1982), *Megatrends II* (1990), and *Global Paradox* (1994) define the pervasive directions in which modern society is moving. Based on the analysis of national newspapers in the United States, he attempted to extrapolate the major trends that shape our world. Naisbitt is a cautious optimist, pointing out that a bright future is likely only if we understand the trends and alter our lives in order to take advantage of opportunities and avoid serious technological or societal traps. Naisbitt's megatrends include shifts in the following areas:

- ❑   From an industrial society to an information-based society
- ❑   From a forced technology to a high-tech mode
- ❑   From a national economy to a truly global economy
- ❑   From short-term planning to long-term planning
- ❑   From centralization to decentralization
- ❑   From institutional help to self-help in fields like health

❑ From representative democracy to participatory democracy
❑ From authority dominated hierarchies to networking
❑ From dominance of the North, in America, to dominance of the South
❑ From single option choices to multiple option choices
❑ From current sources of revenue to services and products that have not yet been invented

Some concepts in *Megatrends* fit a systems model or a participatory democratic model, but the book is mainly directed at understanding the most important existing trends that shape our lives.

Future Constructors.   Future constructors often have experience and training in science or engineering. They use laboratory experiments and empirical data for proving the points they wish to make. Future constructors plan to control the future; education will play a major role in bringing about the society they prescribe. One of the best statements of how this might be accomplished is found in B. F. Skinner's *Walden II* (1976). Future constructors believe that people can be educated to cooperate with planners and to make whatever adjustments are required for survival. They feel that future events cannot be left to mere chance or to individual wishes but must be designed for optimum benefit of all people. They say we must make better use of technology and do more with fewer resources. The future will most certainly not take care of itself; but planning, limiting growth, and social engineering can lead to the construction of a better future for all. Many writers in this group feel that very little progress has been made toward planning the future and that time is running out. As R. Buckminster Fuller put it, we must choose either utopia or oblivion.

In *The Unprepared Society* (1970), Donald N. Michael warns that people are not ready for the onslaught of the future but that utopia is possible through careful planning. He understands that a complete break with the past is impossible; however, he argues that human activities can be controlled and that the future can be altered in a positive way. Constructors wish to produce a future that provides human satisfaction, some degree of choice, and well-adjusted individuals. Of course, this implies that major social, economic, and environmental problems can be resolved. This is possible only if the best-trained planners and engineers are given the power to alter many of the priorities of the present industrial era. This point is very well made in John R. Platt's *The Step to Man* (1966) and in one of his articles entitled "Science for Human Survival."

Systems Futurists.   The popularity of general systems theory is reflected by those futurists who see the world as a series of interrelated systems. They point out that change in one area will often create vast and unexpected results in another. Systems futurists believe that our resources are finite on the "spaceship" Earth and that we must use them carefully. Members of this group use computer models to study the interaction of such variables as population growth, resource allocation, food supply, land use, and industrial growth. They believe that human survival depends upon a change of attitude among the peoples of the planet, who must now recognize the necessity of living within certain constraints. These futurists want to work closely with leaders in government and business to make them aware of thinking globally and adopting a systems approach to planning the social and economic future. Systems futurists are opposed to what Thorstein Veblen called "conspicuous consumption." They believe that education must provide experiences in holistic problem solving and stress the need to limit demand for scarce resources.

Lester R. Brown's *World Without Borders* (1972), *The Twenty-Ninth Day* (1978), and his yearly *State of the World Reports* treat demography, agriculture, and economics on a global scale. The "limits to growth" theory of Dennis and Donella Meadows reflects systems thinking. Jan Tinbergen is typical of the systems theorists associated with the Club of Rome. Hazel Henderson's *Creating Alternative Futures: The End of Economics* (1978) and *Building a Win-Win World: Life Beyond Global Economic Warfare* (1996) and Ervin Laszlo's *The Systems View of the World* (1972) are statements of the position of systems futurists.

Participatory Futurists or Transformationists.

Theobald

Numerous futurists, especially those with backgrounds in the social sciences and economics, fall into the category of participatory futurists. They agree with John Dewey that all mature human beings should participate in the decisions that affect them. In *An Alternatives Future for America II* (1970), Robert Theobald stresses the need for free access to unbiased information, open communication, dialogue, and authority based on use rather than status. Participatory futurists want to examine all available alternatives in order to bring about consensus on plans of action. This might require the altering of the economic system, educating for problem solving, more cooperative styles of life, and abandoning values of the industrial era.

Toffler

In *The Everyman Project* (1976), Robert Jungk speaks of forming communication networks to foster social responsibility. Alvin Toffler pointed out in *Future Shock* (1970) that the accelerating rate of change makes it dangerous to rely on past experience or modes of thought. In *The Third Wave* (1980), Toffler calls for decentralizing authority and solving most problems at the local or community level. Like other participatory futurists, Toffler recognizes the existence of tremendous problems, but he is convinced that all the people working together can resolve them.

Participatory futurists have recently addressed the need for a hands-on humanistic approach to the management of business and industry. In 1985, Toffler wrote *The Adaptive Corporation,* which called for a new kind of administrative leadership. Managers now need nonlinear skills that will enable them to understand and adapt to swiftly changing conditions. The key to this ability is found both in superior knowledge of what is going on in the world and in creating a work environment in which all employees participate.

Peters and Waterman strike a similar note in their analysis of the best-run companies. They argue for a participatory leadership style in which all workers pull together for excellence in the unit. Although these concepts are intended to apply to business organizations, they also can be adopted to education and government.

Evolutionary Futurists.

Emphasis on moral and spiritual values rather than on technological growth is characteristic of evolutionary futurists. They view the future with optimism because they believe that a new consciousness and more humane lifestyles will replace materialism and the rapid consumption of vital resources. Evolutionary futurists have roots in the past, especially in classical literature. Some of the concepts fostered by this group can be found in Maria Montessori's *The Absorbent Mind* (1967). These futurists envision a world in which human beings undergo a transformation to a higher form of spiritual awareness and achieve integration of body, mind, and spirit. Living in harmony with themselves and the universe is their goal. They believe that leadership should be in the hands of those people who demonstrate a strong sense of moral and ethical responsibility.

Willis Harman's *An Incomplete Guide to the Future* (1979) and E. F. Schumacher's *A Guide for the Perplexed* (1977) are typical of the works of these futurists. They are concerned about improving the quality of human life on Earth. They believe that natural and human resources are gifts that must be used with wisdom. Education should foster a strong sense of moral and ethical responsibility. Education is the means by which wisdom and spiritual values are acquired. Schools should be used to discipline the mind and aid understanding of the broad range of alternatives open to everyone. Mass media values, keeping up with the Joneses, and specialized job training are just the opposite of what the evolutionary futurists want. They are interested in general education for moral development that would include the classical wisdom of ages past.

Leonard   ### Humanistic Futurists.

George Leonard's classic *Education and Ecstasy* (1968) is a statement of many of the beliefs of the humanistic futurists. These people believe that the actions we undertake now create or invent the future. Humanistic futurists believe that modern society places too much emphasis on role playing, competition, status, and materialistic success. They believe that this emphasis has distorted human nature and made it difficult to pass from the industrial era into an age of awareness. People must remove their masks, become more sensitive to others, and learn compassion. Leonard feels that until people are more aware of their own bodies, feelings, and intellects, they cannot live fully in the present or create an adequate future. All of us need to deal honestly with our own emotions and discover what is of real value in life.

Transpersonal Education: A Curriculum for Feeling and Being (1976), edited by Gay Hendricks and James Fadiman, suggests the kind of schooling humanistic futurists desire. They want to see the planet kept beautiful and safe to stimulate joy in living. This requires better protection of the environment and limits to economic growth. Teachers should be co-learners and role models in a learning situation that is open, trusting, and sensitive. Learning must be an integral part of the total human experience, and students must get in touch with their own emotional being. In addition to creating sensitive and compassionate human beings, this group wants to challenge the values of the current industrial age. Humanists believe we have moved too far toward the kind of world described in Orwell's *1984* and Huxley's *Brave New World*. In order for each person to achieve his or her full potential, the highly technological structured world of business and industry must be abandoned. Affective learning is as important as cognitive learning. The study of alternative lifestyles, dream sharing, and sensory awareness activities should be part of the curriculum. This is the theme of Bob Samples' *The Metamorphic Mind: A Celebration of Creative Consciousness* (1976).

Visionaries and Radicals.   Two smaller groups with quite different conceptions of the future are the visionary futurists and the radical futurists. Those who fall into the visionary category refuse to be bound by the constraints of commonsense reality. They stress imagination for freeing people from the shackles of the past and enabling them to leap into a new era. They envision a future in which a complete transformation of human nature will occur and universal consciousness will develop. They believe Jules Verne and H. G. Wells were able to anticipate future events because their imaginations were unlimited. The idea that intelligence and awareness may transcend known human capacity is used in television programs like *Star Trek* and in the books of Arthur Clarke, Harlan Ellison, and Kurt Vonnegut Jr.

A leading visionary spokesperson is F. M. Esfandiary. In *Optimism One* (1970) and *Up-Wingers* (1977), he argues that such problems as resource allocation, energy, world peace, and pollution are irrelevant. He believes that by attaining cosmic awareness, new generations will have the whole universe at their disposal, and decisions will be made by all humanity through an instantaneous universal referendum. In *The Next Ten Thousand Years: A Vision of Man's Future in the Universe* (1974), Adrian Berry speaks of electronic brain stimulation and expanding human horizons through linking the brain to computers. Those who do not share these optimistic views are not considered futurists at all by the visionary futurists.

The best-known book by a radical futurist is Illich's *Deschooling Society* (1971). Illich—like Paul Goodman, Arthur Waskow, and Everett Reimer—believes schools foster bad social values and that they cannot be reformed. Radicals want to overthrow the existing power structure and drastically alter society to gain personal freedom and ensure the well-being of future generations. They think the past is repressive and should be forgotten. Distrusting all forms of authority, radical futurists view economic growth as just another form of exploitation. They say individuals must be freed from the burdens of economic and governmental oppression. For them, technology is to be feared when it is in the hands of a power elite.

IMPLICATIONS FOR EDUCATIONAL THEORY

A great deal of the history of American education is the history of conflict over future aims and goals. When Comenius wrote about his concept of pansophia and his belief that human beings could better themselves through schooling, he was preparing for a better future. Locke, Rousseau, Pestalozzi, and Herbart concerned themselves with the kind of education that they thought would bring about a utopian society. Most speculative plans for educational reform have been directed toward the kind of world that would be free of the problems and weaknesses of the present.

Those who wrote plans for a national system of education in 1795 and Jefferson's plan for public education in Virginia were also futuristic in the sense that they aimed at producing a better society and a more democratic one in years to come.

It is easy to trace elements of futurism in the educational theory of John Dewey. His pragmatic philosophy centered on the question of how we can know and control the world. Dewey created an educational theory to meet the needs of a growing, dynamic, urban, industrial society that was in constant flux. His principle of the continuous reconstruction of human experience in the light of new learning is one commonly found among futuristic writers. The idea of making a better society through the schools is central to social reconstructionists who followed Dewey.

Economics and sociology have heavily influenced the futures field, but it is interdisciplinary and broadly based. No adequate theory of education for the future can ignore the wide range of forces that influence the human condition. Marshall McLuhan has attacked the "fragmented unrelation" of the industrial era school curricula and pointed out that any subject studied in depth at once relates to other subjects. A futuristic educational philosophy must be global, open, synergetic, interdisciplinary, and oriented toward cultural synthesis.

Americans and citizens of the other industrial nations appear to be caught up in the pursuit of hedonism and what Veblen called "conspicuous consumption." Little effort is made to understand the past or to trace roots of the culture, so that people seldom appreciate their cultural heritage. Looking with apprehension at the future, many opt for a life centered in the present and pursue the immediate gratification of desires. Following the crowd to materialistic values and situational ethics as fostered by the mass media and commercial advertising is a poor approach to the future. Those with no sense of the past cannot locate themselves in historical perspective or live vicariously through their posterity.

This is not to say that the future should be approached by way of a rearview mirror image of the past. A traditional mind-set and the uncritical acceptance of earlier values could prevent us from accepting change or making the best choices among alternatives. Values of the Puritan ethic are not helpful in guiding the use of leisure time, nor can we expect an optimum future to be shaped by the ideals of the industrial era. Education must encourage the study and the use of the past to take maximum advantage of collective human experience, but it must not allow the future to be subsumed under the values of the past or the present.

As we saw in the opening chapter of this book, an accelerating rate of technological change together with the emergence of new problems in the adaptive nonmaterial culture is accepted as a fact of life by most futurists. There are disagreements about limiting technological growth and about the kinds of technology that might be most important for the good life of the future, but very few advocate a "back to nature" movement or a smashing of machines as the Luddites tried to do in the nineteenth century. Rapid change and invention will almost certainly continue unless there is a total breakdown of civilization resulting in a new dark age or total annihilation. Certainly, the knowledge explosion and the growth of electronic communications networks will have a major impact on education. If learning is to be an instrument for survival, it must prepare people to understand and control technological change. Change for its own sake or for mere economic growth is not necessarily healthy; however, many of the most important problems require a technological solution, and little progress can be expected unless people have access to new information and the tools for using it. The great task for educational theory is clearing the way for social inventions that will match expansion in technology and keep up with rapid change.

This change continues to occur at a rate that staggers the imagination. In 1986, it was estimated that the world contained some 5 billion computers. Granted, many of these were mere chips small enough to fit into credit cards; nevertheless computers outnumbered people on this planet. In the same year, 7,000 new articles in the scientific fields appeared every day, and new fiber optic communications cables made a quantum leap in the capacity to carry information. By 1990, interactive television made distance learning a viable option, vastly increasing the opportunity to carry formal learning to remote sites. The Internet and the World Wide Web expanded this service to the entire globe by the year 2000.

Many serious scholars including Robert Heilbroner and Christopher Lasch are not at all convinced that a Malthusian apocalypse or a nuclear holocaust can be prevented. Nevertheless, any hope for inventing the future by human action is predicated upon the assumption that people can understand and control the forces that shape their world. In the past, people beset by obscure problems and difficulties often adopted the "whatever will be will be" attitude and abandoned faith in human capability. This "failure of nerve" that has occurred periodically in human history makes planning impossible and abandons reason for fate. Even when problems appear to be insurmountable, educators must have faith in the ability of human intelligence to comprehend the world and to control the destiny of humanity. The belief that wisdom and rational action cannot alter the future is a self-fulfilling prophecy that education must combat.

There is a tendency for writers in futurism, especially science fiction authors and utopian novelists, to suggest desirable goals without saying how these goals are to be achieved. Futurism in educational theory will do well to consider John Dewey's argument that means and ends can never be separated and that the ends do not justify the means. Goals, ends, and aims in future education must be evaluated not only on the basis of their desirability but also on the criterion of the possibilities for implementation. Simple solutions to complex problems often have side effects that are as bad or worse than the original problems. It must be remembered that nothing is done in a vacuum and that what is involved in reaching a goal is just as important as the goal itself. In society and education, as in ecology and economics, any change or alteration will have widespread and often unpredicted effects beyond the primary area in which the change takes place.

Maximum realization of the human potential cannot be achieved unless people work together to resolve the really crucial problems, such as preventing nuclear war, protecting the natural environment, and meeting with scarce resources the basic needs of all people. Solving basic problems is necessary but not sufficient for realization of the human potential. There must also be the opportunity to achieve the good life, the life of greatest value. This, in turn, implies the availability of alternatives and the ability to choose. Schools often set arbitrary limits to choice and inhibit creativity. Limits are also set by society in that models are taken from the industrial era with its emphasis on materialism, production, exploitation, and growth. It is incumbent upon future educators to make sure that education clearly delineates the problems, provides learners with necessary tools and information, and encourages the selection of sane alternatives. Every educational plan for the future must show that it enhances the chances for human survival and the quality of life.

CHARACTERISTICS OF FUTURISTIC EDUCATION

Some leading educational futurists have suggested specific changes in order to help bring about a viable future for the citizens of tomorrow. Although these alternatives are speculative, they do address the problem of the inadequacy of existing bureaucratic schools to meet the needs of the next century. Their purpose is to criticize certain characteristics and practices in current educational institutions and to offer possible substitute practices more likely to meet future requirements.

Replacing Linear with Synergetic Processes.   Institutions are established to meet certain human needs. However, they are apt to become self-sustaining bureaucracies with goals of self-aggrandizement and immortality. The school, like most bureaucracies, has a dominant nonhuman priority: its own survival. The objectives of the institution are necessarily more important than individual objectives. It is possible to change this aim of permanence by changing two other essential characteristics of the bureaucracy: its linear design and the division of labor.

American institutions have been, by Theobald's (1970) analysis, successful in the recent past by concentrating on major goals while ignoring secondary and tertiary consequences. Theobald specifies that this is a consequence of linear design. He cites seven inherent weaknesses that are characteristic of linear organizations. They are most applicable to the school.

1. Linear institutions can only receive information that they are designed to receive. This requires that information must be adjusted to the classification system. Schools are primarily designed to receive state-approved textbooks. Information must conform to specialized courses. Teachers cannot easily provide new materials because of the cost and time involved.
2. Linear organizations can make only linear decisions. This implies that educators must extend existing patterns. Administrators cannot make decisions from the perspective of students or teachers.
3. Linear institutions are easily overloaded. Teachers often have too many students, activities, and information to process in short periods of time. Decisions become difficult to administer properly.
4. Linear organization people tend to be promoted until they reach a level of incompetence. In education, upward mobility requires many teachers to become administrators.

5. Linear organizations are capable of reproducing. This is especially true in higher education as departments attempt to gain strength through numbers.

6. Linear organizations tend to repress unfavorable information. Educators rarely pass unfavorable information up or down the organizational hierarchy, because it may reflect upon an individual's competence.

7. Linear organizations are only capable of controlling people who wish to be controlled.

A synergetic system is proposed as an alternative to linear organization. In its early stages, it is perceived as an "ad-hocracy"—Toffler's term for the creation of task forces that move within bureaucracies to complete temporary tasks. In a more advanced stage, ad-hocracy would be replaced by what Theobald calls "consentives." Consentives already exist in the form of buyers' cooperatives, community ecology groups, and Ralph Nader's Raiders. In education, the alternative of a synergetic, process-oriented organization first requires a distinction between training and education.

Education Is More Than Training.

The educational system is designed to carry out a process of training. Training perpetuates existing information and reinforces current trends. It is usually a memorization/regurgitation, short-term method of learning. For example, whenever students are expected to memorize the presidents of the United States, they are being trained. The true purpose of education, however, is to study the principles operant within an activity in order to facilitate new questions and new answers. In essence, education requires an environment in which students are not asked questions for which the answers are known; if the questions involve predetermined conclusions, the process is training.

Both education and training should be provided in the school. There are, obviously, skills such as keyboard usage and welding in which many students would choose to be trained. The problem is that training has dominated the curriculum. It is suggested that many school problems are attributable to students' growing resistance to training. Even on college campuses, many students are questioning the assumptions inherent in the present system. For them, learning through training is not "relevant" because it does not provide an atmosphere for re-examination of society's priorities, classifications, habits, and values. Although training was an asset to the Industrial Revolution, the emerging communications era requires an educational system that will enhance the development of new values and behavior patterns. It will also add to the ability to solve problems and to communicate in a meaningful way.

Education for the Unknown.

Throughout the history of education, students attended schools to learn what they did not know, from teachers who were presumed to know. A grave error in traditional education was that it gave insufficient attention to fielding problems for which there was no known answer. Learners emerged from the schools with little skill in inquiry or in probing for new answers. Now, however, focus must be on working together to deal with probabilities and uncertainties. Experts can be used to clarify aspects of problems, but they alone cannot resolve the most important human and societal difficulties. Students need to think of learning as a technique of cooperative problem analysis and sharing of sources of information. Information must become knowledge and knowledge must become wisdom before unknown issues can be resolved. At this point in time, we do not have the answer to many of the most important problems, such as controlling nuclear arms, ending international terrorism, and providing basic human services to all the people of the world. Unless it moves away from exclusive treatment of what is well understood and toward helping students cope with the unknown, future education will fail. Problem solving, communication skills, and willingness to risk making mistakes are critical to such efforts. As George Leonard has argued, real learning means that the student must be prepared to change and to risk having his or her prejudices altered. It is very clear that survival depends on learning how to cope with major problems that are as yet unresolved.

Structural Authority Versus Sapiential Authority.   Structural authority provided an important rationale in the industrial-era worldview. Railroads were built, assembly lines were developed, and warfare was accomplished through the principle of structural authority. This authority, which is derived from one's position or rank, is the dominant pattern in educational institutions. The organizing prerequisite of the school is one whereby professors "teach" and the students "learn." Under the auspices of structural authority, the student is expected to accept the information, assume that it is correct, ingurgitate it as accurately as possible, and regurgitate all information deemed significant by the teacher. The critical factor is that position rather than competency establishes the authority of the teacher.

Sapiential authority, a term developed by Robert Theobald and Tom Paterson, is proposed as a future alternative form of authority. Sapiential authority is not based upon title or rank. It depends upon no sanctions from governments, schools, or other institutions. Rather, sapiential authority is based upon the possession of information, knowledge, or ideas that find support among others. A model for this exists today in the learned societies and professions. When a paper is read or a thesis is presented, it is accepted or rejected by those most knowledgeable about the field; one's institutional position does not protect one's words from peers' scrutiny. A major qualification of sapiential authority is that all participants have the opportunity for critical analysis of any given piece of information. Structural top-down authority models would be replaced with horizontal models for cooperative sharing of work and information in the future. Engaging students in meaningful and purposeful learning in authentic assessment models in the future would replace standardized factory model examinations. Emerging models of educational administration seek to empower teachers in having an ownership stake in reform and change processes for improving educational outcomes.

Many people fear that the breakdown of traditional authority will result in chaos. This is particularly true of the new religious and political conservatives who became powerful in the 1980s. They want to return to earlier conditions as a psychological rejection of uncomfortable change. They urge schools to "return to traditional values" with stress on basic, noncontroversial curriculum materials, and reliance on the authority of the teacher. The new "right" appears to be moving education far back into the past at exactly the time it needs to look to the future.

There are those in every organization who have been promoted beyond their level of competence and fear any attack on structural authority because it threatens their security. Schools, like other bureaucratic institutions, use structural authority to protect incompetent individuals and useless regulations. Even though sapiential authority has not yet received serious attention, it is a necessary part of education for future survival. One qualification is necessary: This authority should not be interpreted as license or made to support the belief that one idea is just as valid as any other idea. But the problems of the present and the future are so vast and so difficult that every individual's best contributions are needed. Education must, therefore, provide conditions that allow for perception of sapiential authority by each individual and for development of each individual's full potential.

School Learning Versus Lifelong Learning.

The schools of the industrial age have become so specialized that there is no longer room in the curriculum for developing a broad understanding of the world. In *Overskill* (1972), Eugene Schwartz shows that specialization is self-defeating. Civilization cannot be saved by a group of highly trained specialists who do not understand other fields.

Technology for the information age requires experts, but in modern society there are many places—for example, the Internet—where specialized information and skills can be obtained. Likewise, one would not care to visit a doctor who had learned nothing since graduating from medical school many years ago. In order to facilitate lifelong learning, the school must focus on more education (rather than training) and sapiential authority instead of rigid structure. There must be an atmosphere conducive to interdisciplinary studies and humanistic values. Modern world problems are interrelated, and their solutions depend upon what Fuller calls a concept of synergy. He means that the unique behavior of whole systems cannot be predicted by any behaviors of their component functions taken separately.

Dewey often pointed out that the school should not be separate from the community and that the child need not be in conflict with the curriculum. Dichotomies between theory and practice or between idealistic and technical subjects could become academic as learning is understood to be a lifelong practice. The mass media is already engaged in education. Xerox has an educational program that is almost of university status, and many corporations train their own computer operators. Adult and continuing education will surely grow. So long as the concept of reaching a certain educational plateau (such as high school graduation) and then ending education to enter the workforce remains in vogue, specialized training will remain paramount. However, we are entering a learning society and an age of information. People must now expect that they will go on learning throughout life not only as preparation for earning a living but also for avocations and leisure activities. Preparation for a life of learning should replace the idea of terminal schooling in the theory and practice of education.

Replacing Games with Cooperation.

Educational institutions rely primarily upon the use of positive and negative sanctions that result in an "I win–you lose" competitive structure. Grading practices often lead to sorting children into success groups and failure groups. Educators talk about cooperation but enforce competition between students. As John Goodlad has pointed out, grades in school are good predictors of further success in school but not good predictors of success in jobs or in life. Winning high grades in a competitive school environment does not make good workers, compassionate human beings, caring parents, and concerned citizens. Winners tend to be disproportionately middle class, white, and affluent. However, because they have been taught to perpetuate competition in work and in world affairs, winners are also losers. This is a zero sum game in which everyone eventually will lose. The ecological crisis is one physical representation of this problem. Competitive attitudes put stress on limited natural resources and endanger wildlife. As giant industrial corporations downsize and become more efficient in a global market, their workers need cooperative skills.

Learning how to cooperate is a future survival skill that educational institutions must now begin to practice and to teach. Students trained as passive, noninvolved spectators in the classrooms are not apt to be involved in cooperative activities outside. The mass media (especially the medium of television) also tend to promote isolation, noninvolvement, and spectatorism. School activities need to be made more cooperative and action-oriented, with all students emotionally involved. Education involves change, and the school situation must promote change in the learner. A passive attitude does not promote change, and neither does competition. At the very least, students must be prepared to risk their prejudices if learning is to take place. Because education is the process that changes the learner, the traditional school environment will simply not do. Within the existing school system, the competitive environment has precluded all efforts of teaching cooperation. In the future, it may be possible for educators to teach a healthy competitive perspective within a cooperative framework. At present, schools pick up competitive attitudes to control and manipulate children.

Skill in Evaluation. Students in the twenty-first century will regard it as curious that learners once thought teachers and textbooks were unquestioned authorities. In the information age, so many sources of knowledge exist that a constant examination of what is true and what is useful must be made. Literacy exercises like checking one written account against another and the comparison of various interpretations will be supplemented by Internet checks of validity of facts. Priority must be given to critical viewing at a time when vast amounts of information are transmitted by the medium of television. No person in the future will be educated unless he or she has learned to detect subtle psychological persuasion, false logic, emotional appeals, and similar tricks used to make people believe what is not true. If unbiased information and the ability to apply that information to problems are critical to future well-being, all students must be good at evaluation. The argument of Postman and Weingartner that all students need a built-in "crap detector" will become even more valid as the information age develops. The ability to analyze and evaluate information was not stressed in many of the industrial age schools, and it is not a part of many of the reform plans that followed *A Nation at Risk*. Nevertheless, the lifelong learner and problem solver of tomorrow must be an expert at critical evaluation. Since our information becomes obsolete rapidly, Alvin Toffler argues that in the future, the illiterate person will be one who has not learned how to "learn, unlearn, and relearn" (Toffler, 1970).

The Future School: A Problem Analysis/Resource Distribution Center. In the future, educational institutions at all levels must become resource centers for the distribution and creation of unbiased information. Universities have long been expected to achieve this goal on a national and international basis. The linking of telecommunications and computers makes vast quantities of information available to any group or individual. Data banks for information can now be found in schools and even in many homes. Obviously schools will need to stop concentrating on the memorization of bits of information and start stressing how to find and use information. The process of comparing conflicting accounts of events and evaluating the validity of available data must take a much more important role in education. The research function of determining whether or not information can be trusted can no longer be left to universities alone. Each future citizen must have unbiased data upon which to make vital decisions, and the skills of judging information must be taught early in life.

Because a great deal of our knowledge about the world comes to us through television, critical viewing is also a survival skill. Raw data and unorganized information are not very useful in solving problems. Knowing how to quickly find and systematize information will surely become a vital part of tomorrow's education. Even when it is identified and organized, information is not knowledge, and knowledge is not wisdom. Students must learn to make evaluative judgments, analyze, clarify, generalize, and understand. Many futurists have said that we are drowning in data and information. Thus, it is knowledge and wisdom that must be developed through the process of education.

Much that passes for education today is of little value in helping students learn to solve problems. Giving information to the pupil is an inadequate means of producing self-directed scholars and future citizens. The questions for which answers are unknown are the most significant ones. Theobald's contention that everything already discovered should be called training and that the term **education** should be used only for unresolved issues has implications for problem analysis centers. Future problems will certainly require input from individuals with different backgrounds and training; therefore, students need to learn how to cooperate to reach consensus. Inquiry, discovery, and scientific methods of learning must take precedence over lectures, reading texts, and selecting answers from multiple choice tests. The problem analysis/resource distribution centers can be modeled on some of the best of existing practices and earlier experiments such as those of the progressives. It is not necessary to invent a totally new process but merely to change the focus of education from the acquisition of information to the application of data to problem situations in a cooperative and action-oriented environment.

FUTURES CURRICULUM

Professional educators are not waiting for futures programs to gain acceptance in all schools before taking action. The popularity of the annual meeting of the Education Section of the World Futures Society, attended by hundreds of classroom teachers, attests to the interest many have in futurism. Although formal courses in futurism are most often found only at the university level, thousands of teachers incorporate elements of futures studies into the classes they normally offer. Communications networks and publications exist to promote various methods and materials used in the futures education movement. Some universities such as the University of Massachusetts and the University of Houston at Clear Lake offer degree programs in futurism. Such universities also conduct courses and workshops for teachers interested in giving a future focus to the subjects they teach.

In *Preparing Students for the 21ˢᵗ Century* (1996), Uchida, Cetron, and McKenzie identified what schools can do to prepare students for the twenty-first century. The list was based on responses of a council of fifty-five advisers from fields such as education, business, government, psychology, sociology, anthropology, and demography. The council members were asked to name the most important knowledge, skills, and behaviors students will need for the future. Here are some of the suggestions:

❑ Incorporate "marketplace" technology in learning and as part of graduation requirements, and ensure that new and emerging technologies are incorporated in the school program.
❑ Respect all students' abilities to learn by promoting active versus passive learning.
❑ Commit greater time for professional development for teachers.
❑ Develop world-class standards, redefine the basics, and clarify what is expected of students.
❑ Provide more time for students and teachers to work on "real world" projects.
❑ Increase parental and community involvement in schools.
❑ Strengthen authority and control of schools and teachers.
❑ Create new systems that strengthen the connections among the school, the home, and the workplace in order to complement school learning.
❑ Reflect an international perspective in the curriculum.

Transnationalism and a global economy require students who have a perspective of history and its role in understanding our new millennium. To function effectively in the future, students must have an understanding of our global interdependent world.

Interdisciplinary Approach. Futurism in education is not confined to any single discipline or subject area. Indeed, the overarching feature of treating the future in the curriculum is the interdisciplinary focus. The idea of a core curriculum as invented by Herbart and used by the progressives is central to futurism. Relating history to sociology and economics or stressing the connections between biology, psychology, and ecology is common practice. A characteristic of futures is that the impact of one field of human endeavor on another is studied. The symbiotic relationship of plants and animals living in the same environments or the impact economic development might have on natural ecological balance is analyzed. The word **synergy** describes the change that altering one aspect of the world might have on another. Synergetic, symbiotic, integrated, holistic, core, interdisciplinary studies are found in the futures curriculum. It is believed that the narrow boundaries of disciplines and narrow specialization could interfere with the complete understanding of an issue. Future problem solvers must be able to bring together information from a variety of subject areas if their solutions are to be viable. Innovative methods need not be for the elite only. A 1989 study in Orange County, California, found that poor achievers gained most by problem solving and creative classroom activities.

Problem Analysis Focus.

Futuristic teachers attempt to help students analyze the problems around them. To say that things cost more because of inflation or that food is scarce in Africa because the soil is thin represents inadequate understanding. In order to solve problems and to select wisely between alternative futures, it is necessary to distinguish between probable causes and glib explanations. Futures courses are known for probing deeply to find the underlying causes of difficulties, especially social ones. When the reasons for failure in some human endeavors are understood, students are in a better position to evaluate possible, probable, and preferable futures. The study of trends and probable projections is strengthened if students have learned to be critical and to search for reasons when things do not go as expected. Inventing the future is not mere speculation about personal and societal preferences; it involves being realistic, critical, analytic, and careful. Futures also stress the power of the individual and the group to alter the future. The notion that "whatever will be will be" and the belief that human action can make no difference in the course of human events are not accepted. Fatalism is replaced with a proactive orientation and a belief that many alternative futures are possible. Participation, involvement, creativity, and choosing are stressed by futurists as ways of getting people to take the initiative instead of waiting for the future to shock them.

Faith in Human Ability to Control the Future.

In spite of the critical and analytic aspects of futurism, the field is generally optimistic. Obviously, the world is in crisis, and the possibility of such a catastrophe as thermonuclear war or new terrorist attacks is real; however, futurists believe that the major dilemmas with which societies are faced are capable of being solved. There is considerable skepticism about the viability of current technological solutions to global problems, but futuristic literature is not highly pessimistic. Futurism stresses the power that well-educated citizens have in controlling their own lives and tends to support the belief that human action can prevent the apocalyptic end of civilization. Stress is placed on the notion that what we do today will determine the shape of the future.

Open-Ended, Inquiry-Based Methodology.

Futurists attempt to avoid the mere imposing of facts and information on students. Much of the curricula are hypothetical, especially where possible and probable alternative futures are concerned. Evaluation of student written scenarios and classroom delphi polling are often used. Schools usually do not have access to sophisticated instruments such as the computer-based cross-impact matrix, but students can be involved in trend extrapolation, modeling, and various kinds of futures games through virtual reality. Teachers attempt to avoid authority relationships or any attempt to dictate the right answer, but they try to promote logical thinking and careful analysis by students. The teacher as facilitator promotes problem solving, informed speculation, creative imagination, and systematic thinking. Student involvement does not mean that one future alternative is just as good as another or that the courses have no intellectual rigor. Students are encouraged to project themselves into a variety of probable future situations and to think logically about the problems and opportunities such situations might create. The use of science fiction literature, exploratory predictions, attitude surveys, and brainstorming techniques is common. A major goal is creating individuals who will be more likely to manage their own future in a pro-active way.

Value Teaching in Futuristics.
A strong value component is found in most futures courses. Values usually emerge whenever alternative futures are considered, because of the nature of the choices students must make. For example, continued economic growth produces pollution, the destruction of natural resources, urban congestion, and materialism. If these by-products of expansion are to be avoided, future citizens must be willing to live on a lower standard or to adopt other styles of life. The question of whether or not affluence brings about the good life can hardly be considered without challenging cherished values. Futurism requires students to constantly re-examine adherence to the values of the current industrial era. Concepts like simple living, appropriate technology, environmental protection, zero population growth, and world political stability imply serious reconstruction of personal and societal values. Most futurists think that the present trend toward preparing for higher grades and better scores on College Board examinations does not support values education or treat ethical issues.

FUTURE TRENDS

Although we cannot be certain about what will take place in the immediate future and long-range forecasts are always risky, there are certain trends in American education that seem likely to continue, and some worldwide forecasts can be made with a high degree of probability that they will occur. The sneak attack by terrorists that destroyed New York's World Trade Center and part of the Pentagon will affect teachers, students, parents, administrators and the public for the foreseeable future. Bioterrorism further threatens the commonweal and creates new fears and psychological disruptions. For the first time in American history the national safety of school children and the public will challenge educators to deal with fear, emotion, anxiety, anger, trust, suspicion of others, and constant vigilance. If some degree of stability continues in the next decades, the following events seem likely to occur:

1. Education will continue throughout life. The present nine-month school year will be replaced by learning opportunities available at any time

anywhere. Mass media, the Internet, wireless cell phones, online degrees and courses, and information access systems will be used as educational aids at all educational levels. Adults will continue to learn throughout life to prepare for workplace and job changes. It will be necessary to retrain constantly in order to keep up with changes in various fields. Cycles of learning and work will replace the present pattern of school first and work later. Learning for life and leisure will be more important than job training. Corporate downsizing, reinvention, reorganization, mergers, and employee layoffs will lead to less organizational loyalty. America's cyclical economic system will require continual job recycling.

2. As alternative educational delivery systems expand, the old system of semester terms and units of credit will be altered. Means will be found to certify that the learner has the necessary level of skill and information to enter a new learning environment without showing academic credentials. Since much of the learning will be fostered by industry or given in courses, transcripts will be less significant. There will be a variety of educational delivery systems, including independent study degree programs, variable place and time classes, and degrees through e-mail and World Wide Web networks, as witness Phoenix University with some 60,000 students taking degrees through the master's level in a variety of delivery formats. Peter Drucker and others foresee the demise of large traditional university campuses. He sees them as relics in the next century and notes that with the delivery of "more lectures and classes off campus via satellite or two-way video at a fraction of the cost (of today's universities) ... [t]he college won't survive as a residential institution." Colleges and universities in response to market pressures are implementing a variety of distance learning degree programs. Distance learning systems will become more reliable, dependable, and will include ever more academic degree programs, such as Concord University's online law degree. Traditional college education will continue to exist in the future but with a trend toward Saturday, evening, and weekend classes to meet the needs of place-bound students (those who have well-paid professional jobs and families to support and cannot leave their jobs for school during the day).

Joseph F. Coates believes more emphasis ought to be placed on the possibility of radical change in the location and attendance at educational institutions. He believes no one will be "going to" a college or university with an intent to stay there for an extended period of time. Exceptions might occur in relation to laboratory work, or dance or art, or other areas that require hands-on experience. Coates finds that information technology, low-cost telecommunications networking, and the improved quality of material available will make it attractive for whole curricula to be conducted remotely and ad lib perhaps starting with the junior year of high school or before. Both Drucker and Coates find college costs excessive; they could be cut through remote learning by 75 or 80 percent, although higher education administrators are finding the implementation of distance learning to be costly.

3. The curriculum will be very much enlarged to include new discoveries, leisure and avocational skills, travel, human values, group therapy, sensitivity training, and psychological guidance. The idea of a curriculum as broad as life itself, as Comenius suggested, will finally become a reality. There will be nothing that cannot be formally studied if the students are interested. The seamless curriculum of the future will continue to be influenced by an increasingly diverse, multiracial, multicultural population and lifelong learning. English deficient and English as a second language students will require a teaching force and a curriculum based on understanding their unique needs in cultural transformation, acceptance, and understanding. At-risk students will receive national focus under the philosophy "leave no child behind."

4. Fewer classroom teachers will be needed, but there will be an increase in the number of people engaged in teaching and learning as retirements lead to a national teaching shortage. Long years of training may be required before a person is allowed to manage a future learning environment. However, much learning will be informal and lifelong, so that the distinction between the teacher and the taught will erode away. Learning facilitators will perform a variety of functions, and educational centers will have differentiated staffing as well as complete service schools offering learning and childcare. Computers, the Internet, the World Wide Web, Web sites, and wireless access will carry on many teaching tasks, but specialists will be available to help with any learning disability and to stimulate students. Distance learning course and degree programs will tend to require more student collaboration, team work, and group work.

5. Ideally there will be less competition, less standardization, less grouping by ability, and less pressure on the student. More attention will be given to growing, developing, problem solving, communication, and personal goals. Since learning will be an activity for life, knowing how to learn in an efficient and joyful way will be a very highly prized future skill. In a transnational, highly competitive global economy, students will be expected to cope with a need for flexibility and lifelong learning. Standardized national high-stakes testing of student achievement levels is incorporated in federal funding for education. Although some criticize the factory model of education so prevalent in the past, high-stakes testing is part of the twenty-first-century educational scene. There is growing protest about excesses in the use of standardized test scores to rate and rank students, teachers, schools, and school districts.

6. Age-specific compulsory learning institutions (called schools) will be replaced by a variety of diversified learning environments. Young people will be able to take responsibility for their own learning at a much earlier age. It will be common to find children and senior citizens in the same learning situations. A learning society will emerge, one in which most people will spend a great deal of every day of their lives in some kind of learning environment of their own choice. Vouchers, charter schools, and a

variety of alternative educational systems will be in the future surrounded by supporters and detractors. With a divided electorate and an almost evenly divided Senate, both political parties are trying to encourage members to switch loyalties as was demonstrated by the recent Senator Jeffries' defection. The possibility of governmental gridlock rather than necessary bipartisanship is present. Each party currently has a razor-thin vote margin in the Senate.

7. An emerging contingent workforce with an ever-increasing number of part-time workers who have little job security and few health benefits will require flexibility in educational aims, educational content, and length of schooling. The National Association of Temporary and Staffing Services, based on a recent DRI/McGraw-Hill survey of 200 temporary-help employment firms, revealed explosive expansion of part-time, temporary work for the foreseeable future. The number of temporary employees increased some 17.3 percent in 1992 to 1.3 million. At the start of the twenty-first-century, this form of outsourcing will continue to increase ("Temps Getting More Work," 1993).

   Senator Howard Metzenbaum of Ohio sees the possibility of 50 percent part-time workers in the near future. He finds such a possibility alarming for the nation's standard of living. With corporate downsizing, overtime work is used instead of new hires. When additional employees are needed, part-time and temporary workers are used to keep costs down. The challenge for education is to prepare individuals for job market reality.

8. Technology will make possible many new educational possibilities. Telecommunications and computers, the Internet, wireless systems, e-mail, and broadband accessing will make information available to everyone. People will be able to link themselves electronically with others who share the same subject interests and to contact the best-known experts in the field. Chemical and electronic learning aids including brain stimulation will be used to help concentration and eliminate learning blocks. The skill required to quickly find and evaluate any information on any subject will become as common as reading is today. New companies will produce and market educational materials as well as entertainment computers and a myriad of new communication networks. An example is Achieve Communications, a company committed to bringing families and schools together online (*http://www.webAdemic.com*).

9. Education will stress the understanding of the forces in the environment that must be controlled in order to ensure the maximum realization of human potential and the good life. Problem-solving centers will emerge, and students will become skilled at finding alternative solutions to all major difficulties. Greater attention will be given to world understanding and to the issues that involve all of the people on Earth, although protests against globalization will continue. All major new developments in the world (and perhaps in space) will immediately take a place in the curriculum. At the same time, much educational activity will occur with small interest groups, or it will be directed toward the solution of community problems. The

ability to analyze data, to think in a systematic way, and to be realistic about the possibilities of the future will be skills everyone will need to develop. Those skills include teaching tolerance for a multiracial, multicultural, multiethnic, and multiage society. Respecting the rights of others—age, gender, culture—is a responsibility due from past to future generations.

10. As reported in *Education Week*'s "The New Divides" (2001), although the nation's schools have growing access to computers, there is a need to increase technical support services; computer assistance for boys and girls of all economic, racial, and cultural backgrounds; updating classroom and school computers; rapid access to information through broadband connections; and integrating the human element in computer training. There remain additional computer training needs for special needs students—those with diverse racial and cultural backgrounds, gender and language barriers—and more effective technology use. As of May 2001, thirty-five states include technology in state standards for students, and other states are in the process of implementing such standards.

The past, present, and future are always related. A real understanding of what has happened in American education and why it happened is essential for guiding action now and for inventing the future. As Lasch argued in *The Culture of Narcissism* (1978), those without an appreciation of history have no interest in the future because they live only for the present. Our hedonistic culture stresses the importance of living now and letting tomorrow take care of itself; such an attitude is devastating to the teaching profession. In *Powershift* (1990), Toffler noted that for over 300 years the world was perceived as a great clock or machine, in which knowable causes led to predictable results. He believes we are witnessing one of the most important changes in the history of power. Toffler stated that it is clear that knowledge, a source of the highest quality of power, is gaining importance in our society and world. He projects that the most important power shift will occur in the hidden relationship between violence, wealth, and knowledge. In *War and Anti-War* (1993), Toffler calls for an understanding of the linkage between knowledge, wealth, and war.

In December 2000, a report entitled "The Power of the Internet for Learning: Moving from Promise to Practice" was published. Senator Bob Kerrey chaired a commission studying Web-based education. The commission's conclusion was that learning should be student centered, focusing on strengths and needs of individual learners and making lifelong learning a practical reality. Additional recommendations included making Internet resources and broadband access widely available and affordable for all learners; providing continuous training and support for all educators and administrators at all educational levels; expanding Internet research; disseminating high-quality online educational content that meets the highest standards of educational excellence; revising outdated regulations that impede innovations; protecting online learners and ensuring their privacy, including addresses and advertising that can interfere with student learning; and sustaining funding for "e-learning" as a centerpiece of the nation's federal education policy.

Dugger, Jr. (2001) in a *Kappan* article entitled "Standards for Technological Literacy" reported that the International Technological Education Association and its

Technology for All Americans Project have developed curriculum standards for technological literacy that pinpoint what students in grades K through 12 should know and be able to do. The standards provide a benchmark for defining technological literacy. The American Association of School Administrators is collaborating with a number of professional organizations to develop technology standards for educational administrators. All these efforts are designed to more effectively integrate technology in the administration, teaching, and learning process in the nation's schools.

The authors opine that students should view technology as a tool to enhance learning, not as an end in itself. Further, the move from data, to information, to knowledge, to wisdom requires persistent critical thinking and monitoring (filtering skills) to refine and evaluate information. Selecting data from the growing supply of information will be increasingly important in the future. The challenge for educators and society will be to resist the temptation to avoid viewing technology as a cheap, quick fix to complex problems. Educators must be future-oriented if they are to prepare students for a world of tomorrow that will be vastly different from today. The background of historical understanding and the appreciation of issues and conflicts of the past provide the best foundation we can have for predicting trends and preparing for a viable future. Perhaps the most important use of history is that it shows us how far short of our own traditions we have fallen and stimulates us to strive for a higher realization of our individual and collective potential in the world of the future.

GAINING PERSPECTIVE THROUGH CRITICAL ANALYSIS

1. What impact is the Internet and World Wide Web having on education instruction today? Give examples from your school experiences or current literature.
2. Analyze the contribution of futurists to educational thought.
3. Compare and contrast various methods of educational research. Give two examples of research projects that would be appropriate for each method.
4. Name two futurist thinkers, and discuss their contributions to educational policies and practices.
5. Identify gender, racial, demographic, special needs, and language gaps in educating students with technological skills needed in the future.

HISTORY IN ACTION IN TODAY'S CLASSROOMS

1. Visit a computer lab in your school. Discuss with those in charge of the lab how they are planning to keep up with the fast-changing field. Identify the problems they relate to you about adequate financing and quickly dated hardware and software.
2. In your journal, describe the classroom of the future. Use current literature in your field to support your ideas.
3. Review copies of the *Futurist* magazine to find at least two alternative scenarios for the future of American education.
4. Review the works of Wendell Bell, Alvin Toffler, Robert Heilbroner, and Paul Kennedy. Give four examples of the role of history in futures studies.
5. Identify the role of business/industry in futures studies.
6. Analyze strengths and weaknesses of a technologically based educational system. Include inequities in classrooms and school districts in access and distribution of computers and software.

INCREASED UNDERSTANDING THROUGH ONLINE RESEARCH

Visit the Companion Web site that accompanies this text (*http://www.prenhall.com/pulliam*) and examine Topics 12, 14, and 15. Using the resources available in these topics, identify frontiers of technology for improving instruction, finding a job, and meeting the educational challenges of the tragedy of September 11, 2001, as well as the bioterrorism in its aftermath. Write and submit your response to your instructor using the Electronic Bluebook module also in any of these three topics of the Web site.

BIBLIOGRAPHY

Academic Preparation for College: With Academic Preparation in English, the Arts, Mathematics, Science, Social Studies, and Foreign Languages. New York: The College Board, 1986.

Barzun, Jacques. *The American University.* New York: Harper and Row, 1968.

Bell, Daniel. *The Coming of Post-Industrial Society: A Venture in Local Forecasting.* New York: Basic Books, 1976.

Bell, Wendell. *Foundations for Futures Studies: Human Science for a New Era.* Volume I, "History, Purposes and Knowledge," and Volume II, "Values, Objectivity and Science." New Brunswick, NJ: Transaction Publisher, 1996.

Belsie, Laurent. "The Short, Simple Human Gene Map." *The Christian Science Monitor* (February 13, 2001): 1, 10.

Berry, Adrian. *The Next Ten Thousand Years: A Vision of Man's Future in the Universe.* New York: Saturday Review Press, E. P. Dutton, 1974.

Botkin, James, Mahdi Elmandjra, and Mircea Malitza. *No Limits to Learning: Bridging the Human Gap.* New York: Pergamon Press, 1979.

Boulding, Kenneth. *Equity and Efficiency in Economic Development.* Montreal: McGill-Queen's University Press, 1992.

————. *Evolution, Order and Complexity.* London: Routledge, 1996.

Bowman, Jim, Fred Kierstead, Chris Dede, and John Pulliam. *The Far Side of the Future: Social Problems and Educational Reconstruction.* Washington, DC: World Future Society, 1978.

Boyer, William. *America's Future: Transition to the 21st Century.* New York: Praeger, 1984.

Boyett, Joseph, and Henry Conn. *Workplace 2000.* New York: Plume-Penguin, 1992.

Bright, James. *Practical Technology Forecasting.* New York: Industrial Management Center, 1978.

Broudy, Harry. *Paradox or Promise: Essays on American Life.* Englewood Cliffs, NJ: Prentice-Hall, 1961.

————. *The Real World of the Public Schools.* New York: Harcourt, Brace and Jovanovich, 1972.

Brown, Lester Russell. *World Without Borders.* New York: Vintage Books, 1972.

————. *The Twenty-Ninth Day.* New York: W. W. Norton, 1978.

————. *Vital Signs 1997: The Environmental Trends That Are Shaping Our Future.* New York: Norton, 1997.

Bushwellere, Kevin, and Erik Faterni. "Technology Counts 2001: The New Divides." *Education Week* (May 10, 2001): 10, 11, 12, 62.

Cetron, Marvin. *Schools of the Future: How American Business and Education Can Cooperate to Save Our Schools.* New York: McGraw-Hill, 1985.

Cheng, Yin Cheng. *School Effectiveness and School Based Management: A Mechanism for Development.* London: Falmer Press, 1969.

Commoner, Barry. *The Closing Circle: Nature, Man and Technology.* New York: Bantam Books, 1974.

Cornish, Edward. *The Study of the Future: An Introduction to the Art and Science of Understanding and Shaping Tomorrow's World.* Washington, DC: World Future Society, 1978.

Didsbury, Howard, ed. *Challenges and Opportunities from Now to 2001.* Bethesda, MD: World Future Society, 1986.

————. *The Years Ahead: Perils, Problems and Promises.* Bethesda, MD: World Future Society, 1993.

Dillin, John. "As 'Good' Jobs Become 'Bad' Jobs, Congress Takes a Closer Look." *Christian Science Monitor* (June 18, 1993):1, 4.

Drucker, Peter. "Seeing Things as They Really Are." *Forbes* (March 10, 1997): 122–28.

Dugger, William E., Jr. "Standards for Technological Literacy." *Phi Delta Kappan* (March 2001): 513–17.

Dunn, Joe, and Howard Preston. *Future South—A Historical Perspective for the Twenty-First Century*. Urbana: University of Illinois Press, 1991.

Esfandiary, F. M. *Optimism One*. New York: Norton, 1970.

———. *Up-Wingers*. New York: Popular Library, 1977.

Feinberg, Gerald. *The Prometheus Project: Mankind's Search for Long-Range Goals*. Garden City, NY: Doubleday, 1969.

Fuller, R. Buckminster. *Utopia or Oblivion: The Prospects for Humanity*. New York: Overlook Press, 1969.

Gates, Bill. "Looking Beyond with Bill Gates and Gordon Moore." *PC Magazine, The PC of the Future* (March 25, 1997): 29–235.

Gates, Bill, and Collins Hemingway. *Business@The Speed of Thought: Succeeding in the Digital Economy*. New York: Warner Books, 1999/2000.

Glines, Don. "Can Schools of Today Survive Very Far into the 21st Century?" NASSP Bulletin (February 1989) 73(514).

Goodman, Paul. *Change in Organizations: New Perspectives on Theory, Research and Practice*. San Francisco: Jossey-Bass, 1982.

Harman, Willis W. *An Incomplete Guide to the Future*. New York: Norton, 1979.

Heilbroner, Robert. *The Future as History*. New York: Harper and Row, 1959.

———. *An Inquiry in the Human Prospect*. New York: W. W. Norton, 1975.

———. *21st Century Capitalism*. New York: W. W. Norton, 1993.

———. *Visions of the Future: The Distant Past, Yesterday, Today, Tomorrow*. New York: Oxford University Press, 1995.

Helmer-Hirschberg, Olaf. *Social Technology*. New York: Basic Books, 1966.

Henderson, Hazel. *Creating Alternative Futures: The End of Economics*. New York: Berkeley, 1978.

———. *Building a Win-Win World: Life Beyond Global Economic Warfare*. San Francisco, CA: Berrett-Koehler, 1996.

Hendricks, Gay, and James Fadiman, eds. *Transpersonal Education: A Curriculum for Feeling and Being*. Englewood Cliffs, NJ: Prentice-Hall, 1976.

Hipple, Theodore, ed. *The Futures of Education 1975–2000*. Santa Monica, CA: Goodyear, 1974.

Illich, Ivan. *Deschooling Society*. Harper and Row, 1971.

Judy, Richard W., and Carol D'Amico. *Workforce 2020*. Indianapolis, IN: Hudson Institute, 1997.

Jungk, Robert. *The Everyman Project: Resources for a Humane Future*. London: Thames and Hudson, 1976.

Kadaba, Lini S. "Futurist (Joseph Coates) Identified Issues That Will Transform Corporations." *Tulsa World* (June 13, 1993): 4G.

Kennedy, Paul M. "Preparing for the Twenty-First Century." *On the Horizon* (December 1993) 2(2): 1–2.

———. *Preparing for the Twenty-First Century*. New York: Random House, 1993.

Kerrey, Senator Bob. *The Power of the Internet for Learning: Moving from Promise to Practice*. Washington DC: Report of the Web-Based Education Commission to the President and the Congress of the United States (December 2000): iii, iv.

Kierstead, Fred, Jim Bowman, and Christopher Dede, eds. *Educational Futures: Sourcebook*. Washington, DC: World Future Society, 1979.

Kurian, George Thomas, and Graham T. T. Molitor, eds. *Encyclopedia of the Future*. Old Tappan, NJ: Simon & Shuster, 1995.

Lasch, Christopher. *The Culture of Narcissism: American Life in an Age of Diminishing Expectations*. New York: Norton, 1978.

Laszlo, Ervin. *The Systems View of the World: The Natural Philosophy of the New Developments in the Sciences*. New York: G. Braziller, 1972.

Leonard, George Burr. *Education and Ecstasy*. New York: Delacorte Press, 1968.

Meadows, Donella H. *Beyond the Limits: Confronting Global Collapse, Envisioning a Sustainable Future*. Post Mills, VT: Chelseas Green, 1991.

Means, Barbara. "Technology Use in Tomorrow's Schools." *Educational Leadership* (December 2000/January 2001): 57–61.

Michael, Donald N. *Cybernation: The Silent Conquest*. Santa Barbara, CA: Center for the Study of Democratic Institutions, 1962.

———. *The Unprepared Society: Planning for a Precarious Future*. New York: Harper and Row, 1970.

Montessori, Maria. *The Absorbent Mind*. Madras, India: Kalakshetra Publications, 1987.

Naisbitt, John. *Megatrends*. New York: Warner Books, 1982.

———. *Re-inventing the Corporation: Transforming Your Job and Your Company for the New Information Society*. London: Guild Publishing, 1985.

———. *Megatrends 2000: Ten New Directions for the 1990s*. New York: Morrow, 1990.

————. *Global Paradox*. New York: Avon Books, 1994.

Paepke, C. Owen. *The Evolution of Progress*. New York: Random House, 1993.

Peters, Thomas J. *In Search of Excellence: Lessons from America's Best-Run Companies*. Sydney, Australia: Harper and Row, 1984.

Peters, Thomas, and Robert Waterman. *In Search of Excellence: Lessons from America's Best Run Companies*. New York: Warren Books, 1982.

Platt, John R. *The Step to Man*. New York: John Wiley and Sons, 1966.

————. "What We Must Do." *Science* (November 1969):1115–22.

————. *Perception and Change: Projections for Survival*. Ann Arbor: University of Michigan Press, 1970.

————. *The Next Twenty Years of Change*. Washington, DC: American Educational Research Association, 1979.

Polak, Fred. *Image of the Future*. San Francisco: Jossey-Bass, 1973.

Postman, Neil. *Teaching as a Subversive Activity*. New York: Dell, 1987.

Pulliam, John, and Jim Bowman. *Educational Futurism: In Pursuance of Survival*. Norman, OK: University of Oklahoma Press, 1974.

Reimer, Everett W. *School Is Dead: Alternatives in Education*. Garden City, NJ: Doubleday, 1971.

Rubin, Louis, ed. *The Future of Education: Perspectives on Tomorrow's Schooling*. Boston: Allyn & Bacon, 1975.

Samples, Bob. *The Metaphoric Mind: A Celebration of Creative Consciousness*. Reading, MA: Addison-Wesley, 1976.

Schumacher, E. F. *A Guide for the Perplexed*. New York: Harper and Row, 1977.

Schwartz, Eugene S. *Overskill: The Decline of Technology in Modern Civilization*. New York: Ballantine Books, 1972.

Scileppi, John. *A Systems View of Education: A Model for Change*. Lanham, MD: University Press of America, 1984.

Skinner, B. F. *Walden Two*. Englewood Cliffs, NJ: Prentice-Hall, 1976.

Snider, Mike. "More Useless Information: 2 Billion Web Pages." *USA Today* (July 1, 2000): 3 D.

"Technology Standards for School Administrators." Available: *http://cnets.iste.org/tssa/*

"Temps Getting More Work." *Tulsa World* (June 27, 1993):2G.

Theobald, Robert. *An Alternative Future for America 2000*. Chicago: Swallow Press, 1970.

————. *Futures Conditional*. Indianapolis: Bobbs-Merrill, 1972.

————. *Turning the Century*. New York: Knowledge Systems, 1992.

Toffler, Alvin. *Future Shock*. New York: Random House, 1970.

————. *Learning for Tomorrow*. New York: Random House, 1974.

————. *The Third Wave*. New York: Morrow, 1980.

————. *The Adaptive Corporation*. New York: McGraw-Hill, 1985.

————. *Powershift: Wealth and Violence at the Edge of the 21st Century*. New York: Bantam, 1990.

————. *War and Anti-War*. New York: Little Brown, 1993.

————. *Creating a New Civilization: The Politics of the Third Wave*. Kansas City, MO: Turner Publishing, 1995.

Toffler, Alvin, and Heidi Toffler. *Creating a New Civilization: Politics of the Third Wave*. New York: Turner Publishers, 1995.

————. Interview. *StarTribune*, 1996: *http://www.startribune.com/stonline/html/digage/toffler4.htm, 1996.*

————. "New Economy? You Ain't Seen Nothing Yet." *Wall Street Journal* (March 28, 2001): A 14.

Uchida, Donna, Marvin Cetron, and Floretta McKenzie. *Preparing Students for the 21st Century*. Bethesda, MD: World Future Society, 1996.

Uldrich, Jack, "Why Nanotechnology Will Arrive Sooner Than Expected." *The Futurist* (March-April 2002) 16–22.

Van Horn, Royal. "Technology: Friendly Advice for Administrators." *Phi Delta Kappan* (May, 2000): 719.

Waskow, Arthur I. *Running Riot: A Journey Through the Official Disasters and Creative Disorder in American Society*. New York: Herder and Herder, 1970.

Wirth, Arthur. *Education and Work for the Year 2000: Choices We Face*. San Francisco: Jossey-Bass, 1992.

World Future Society, ed. *The Future, A Guide to Information Sources*. Washington, DC: World Future Society, 1979.

Zerchykov, Ross. *School Boards and the Communities They Represent*. Boston, MA: Institute for Responsive Education, 1981.

————. *School-Community Relations*. Tempe, AZ: Arizona State University, 1994.

GENERAL ANNOTATED BIBLIOGRAPHY

Alison, Clinton B., Ed. *Kellie McGarrh's Hangin' in Tough: Mildred E. Doyle, School Superintendent*. New York: Peter Lang Publishing, 2000, 160 pp. In Doyle's biography, McGarrh analyzes issues that interest educational historians and feminist scholars. These issues include women's struggles to acquire and keep administrative positions. Also analyzed are the differences in the way men and women operate in leadership positions and the impact of homophobia on those who are not stereotypically "masculine" or "feminine."

Bailyn, Bernard. *Education in Forming of American Society*. Chapel Hill, NC: University of North Carolina Press, 1960, 147 pp. This critical essay on American history of education from the cultural standpoint surveys the main themes of educational history yet to be written. It contains a useful evaluation of earlier movements in American cultural history, such as Puritanism, philanthropy, race relations, and the growth of sectarianism.

Bowen, William G., and Derek Bok. *The Shape of the River*. Princeton: Princeton University Press, 2000. An intensive research study and report on college persistence and success for minority students at the nation's elite institutions. Findings included recommendations for a consistent program of mentoring and support services to assist students-at-risk in study habits and skills needed for degree completion.

Boyles, Deron. *American Education & Corporations*. New York: Falmer/Taylor and Francis Group, 2000. A critical analysis of the role of corporate America in education with a focus on the power of advertising in a competitive marketplace economy.

Butts, Freeman. *The Education of the West: A Formative Chapter in the History of Civilization*. New York: McGraw-Hill, 1933. This work is a very sound general history by one of the best-known American educational historians.

_____. *Public Education in the United States: From Revolution to Reform*. New York: Holt, Rinehart and Winston, 1978. The work is outstanding for its detail and depth of study. It is the best account of legislation and court cases in recent years.

Caine, Renate Nummeal, and Geoffrey Caine. *Education on the Edge of Possibilities*. Alexandria, VA: ASCD, 1997. This overview of brain-based learning is designed to encourage teachers to move toward an information delivery approach that is flexible, creative, and open to students' search for meaning such as John Dewey introduced in the 1930s and 1940s.

Coates, Joseph, and Jennifer Jarratt. *What Futurists Believe*. Mt. Airy, MD: Lomond, 1989. This work profiles futures writings of leading authors in the field.

Cobb, Nina, Ed. *The Future of Education: Perspectives on National Standards in America*. New York: College Entrance Board, 1994. This series of articles on national standards includes the effect of standards on teachers, educational policy, and subject matter associations.

Commager, Henry Steele, Ed. *Documents of American History*. New York: Appleton-Century-Crofts, 1963, 739 pp., including index. This work contains 665 noteworthy documents that were significant in the shaping of American history. Documents pertinent to education are included.

Cremin, Lawrence. *The Wonderful World of Ellwood Patterson Cubberly: An Essay on the Historiography of American Education*. New York: Columbia University Teachers College, Bureau of Publications, 1965. This work is an interesting and delightful treatment of the first great American educational historian by a leading modern scholar in the same field.

_____. *American Education: The Colonial Experience 1607–1783*. New York: Harper & Row, 1970. This work offers an analysis and description of the formative period of American education during the drive for independence.

_____. *Public Education*. New York: Basic Books, 1976. This treatment of the history of American education gives attention to public policy, the emerging role of government, and the issues over control of schools.

_____. *American Education: The National Experience 1783–1876*. New York: Harper & Row, 1980. This work offers an analysis and description of American education during the period of building and unifying the nation.

_____. *American Education: The Metropolitan Experience 1876–1980*. New York: Harper & Row, 1988. This portrayal of American education as the nation achieved world power status identifies three persistent elements of American education: popularization, multitudinousness, and politicization.

_____. *Popular Education and Its Discontents*. New York: Harper & Row, 1990. This compilation of three essays explores increasing dissatisfaction with education, radical changes in society and education, and a continuing effort to solve social problems indirectly through education rather than through politics.

Curti, Merle. *The Social Ideas of American Educators*. Patterson, NJ: Pageant Books, 1959, 613 pp., including index. Contents include the following: Part I, (1) Colonial Survivals and Revolutionary Promises, 1620–1820; (2) New Conflicts and a New Solution 1800–1860; (3) Education and Social Reform: Horace Mann; (4) Henry Barnard; (5) The Education of Women; (6) The School and the Triumph of Business Enterprise, 1860–1914; (7) Education in the South; (8) The Black Man's Place: Booker T. Washington, 1856–1916; (9) William T. Harris, The Conservator, 1835–1908; (10) Bishop Spalding, Catholic Educator, 1840–1916; (11) Francis Wayland Parker, Democrat, 1837–1902; (12) G. Stanley Hall, Evolutionist, 1846–1924; (13) William James, Individualist, 1842–1910; (14) Edward Lee Thorndike, Scientist, 1874–1949; (15) John Dewey, 1859–1952; and (16) Post-War Patterns. A conclusion and bibliographical notes follow, and there is a treatment of recent educational history. This book provides an excellent social understanding of American educational development.

Also useful is Curti's *The Growth of American Thought*, New York: Harper & Row, 1951.

Curtis, Stanley J., and M. E. A. Boultwood. *A Short History of Educational Ideas*, 3d ed. London: University Tutorial Press Ltd., 1964. 615 pp., including index. This standard text in Western educational history pays considerable attention to American education and American educational leaders. Helpful bibliographical information is given at the end of each chapter.

Didsbury, Howard F., Jr., Ed. *Future Vision: Ideas, Insights and Strategies*. Bethesda, MD: World Future Society, 1996. These articles from the World Future Society 8th General Assembly explore a world of have and have-not nations and possibilities for a more equitable and humane future.

Dworkin, Martin. *Dewey on Education*. New York: Columbia University Teachers College Press, 1959. This best quick reference to the work of Dewey is for those who do not wish to use Dewey's own books. Also suggested is Dewey's own *Democracy and Education,* New York: Macmillan, 1916.

Epstein, Terrie. Adolescents Perspectives on Racial Diversity in U.S. History: Case Studies from an Urban Classroom. *American Educational Research Journal* (Spring 2000): 185–214. An analysis of the challenge and opportunity of incorporating the historical experience of racial diversity into traditional narratives of U.S. history. Perspectives of Eurocentricism, and Afrocentricism explored in depth.

Fantini, Mario. *Regaining Excellence in Education*. New York: Merrill/Macmillan,1986. This very good analysis of the reform movement in education results from *A Nation at Risk* and other reports of the 1980s. It deals with future trends as well as the responses of state and local groups to the demand for educational reform. Reports and sources are well documented and succinctly presented.

Gatti, Richard, and Daniel Gatti. *New Encyclopedic Dictionary of School Law*. West Nyack, NY: Parker Publishing, 1983. This complete analysis of laws and court cases that altered the shape of American education concentrates on the recent trends in the courts and the philosophical shifts that have created new trends in the relationship between schools and governing agencies.

Good, Harry, and James Teller. *A History of American Education,* 3d ed. New York: Macmillan, 1973. This detailed history of American education comes complete with index and extensive bibliography. It is especially useful for the period prior to the twentieth century.

Good, Thomas L., and Jere E. Brophy. *Contemporary Educational Psychology*. New York: Longman, 1995. This excellent overview of the field focuses on the integration of theory and practice.

Goodlad, John I., and Timothy J. McMannon, Eds. *The Public Purpose of Education and Schooling*. San Francisco, CA: Jossey-Bass, 1997. This work offers an overview of major themes of educational reform movement in theory and practice.

Gutek, Gerald L. *Historical and Philosophical Foundations of Education*. Columbus, Ohio: Merrill/Prentice Hall, 2000. This work covers three broad themes: major movements in world history, the biographies of leading educators, and philosophies and ideas that emerge from their ideas. Each chapter identifies and analyzes major contributions to educational theory and practice.

Hirsch, E. D., Jr. *The Schools We Need, Why We Don't Have Them*. New York: Doubleday, 1996. This work is a call for rediscovery of William Bagley's essentialism, which stresses the importance of common values and meanings essential to a democratic culture. Hirsch stresses bringing our children closer to universal competence in cultural literacy.

Johanningmeier, Erwin. *Americans and Their Schools*. Chicago: Rand McNally. This superior text is both very detailed and interesting. It would be an excellent choice for a text in a graduate-level history of American education course. Johanningmeier is an interesting author to read, and he puts to rest a number of common myths about education in this nation.

Judy, Richard W., and Carol D'Amico. *Workforce 2020*. Indianapolis, IN: Hudson Institute, 1997. This work is an analysis of changing demographics in the composition of the future workforce.

Karier, Clarence J. *Shaping the American Educational State, 1900 to the Present*. New York: Free Press, 1975. This collection of essays and documents on the most important forces at work in developing the modern American educational system deals with issues and problems as well as ideas and movements.

Knight, Edgar W. *Fifty Years of American Education*. New York: Ronald Press, 1952, 484 pp., including index. Other standard works on the subject by the same author include *A Documentary History of Education in the South Before 1860,* Chapel Hill: University of North Carolina Press, 1949, and *Education in the United States,* Boston: Ginn, 1951.

Kohn, Alfie. *No Contest: The Case Against Competition*. New York: Houghton-Mifflin, 1992. This work stresses the importance of cooperation to improve student motivation in education and enrich society.

Kurian, George Thomas, and Graham T. T. Molitor, Eds. *Encyclopedia of the Future*. Old Tappan, NJ: Simon & Schuster, 1995. The forty-two articles explore the future from a variety of perspectives with forecasts and projections about possible, probable, and preferable futures from H. G. Wells to Alvin Toffler.

Levine, Daniel, and Robert Havinghurst. *Society and Education,* 6th ed. Boston: Allyn and Bacon, 1984. This very complete sociology of education calls attention to the social forces in American education that have shaped modern conditions. It provides the student of history with an in-depth understanding of modern social attitudes and trends.

Lozer, Steven E., Paul C. Violas, and Guy Senese. School and Society New York: McGraw-Hill, 2002. Historical & contemporary perspectives on the evolution of American Education.

Lucas, Christopher J. *Teacher Education in America: Reform Agendas for the Twenty-First Century*. New York: St. Martin's Press, 1997. This work offers an analysis of trends in education through historical background, teacher surveys, and proposals for the teaching profession.

Mayer, Frederic. *American Ideas and Education*. New York: Merrill/Macmillan, 1964. This intellectual and social history of American education is especially useful for the student of ideas, attitudes, movements, and people. Mayer includes a large number of quotations from the leaders with whom he deals.

McCown, Rick, Marcy Driscoll, and Peter Geiger Roop. *Educational Psychology: A Learning-Centered Approach to Classroom Practice*. New York: Allyn and Bacon, 1996. This detailed analysis and record of the field focuses on cultural diversity and gender issues.

Meyer, Adolphe E. *The Educational History of the American People,* 2d ed. New York: McGraw-Hill, 1967. This very readable text presents the material in a refreshing way. It does assume some basic knowledge of American history on the part of the student.

Monroe, Paul, Ed. *A Cyclopedia of Education*. New York: Macmillan, 1911–1913. This monumental five-volume work includes illustrations, charts, diagrams, and references. The work is dated but still the only one of its kind and a valuable source of information. A revised edition that will include modern material is in progress.

Morgan, Gordon D. *Toward An American Sociology.* Westport, CT: Praeger, 1997. This work offers an interesting and informative analysis of sociology in light of its evolution throughout history.

Mulhern, James. *A History of Education,* 2d ed. New York: Ronald Press, 1959. Parts W and V of this work contain a wealth of material pertaining to the growth of and the changes in the American educational system.

Naisbitt, John. *Megatrends.* New York: Warner Books, 1982. The student of history interested in the future will find in this book a very interesting presentation of the major forces operating to shape our world. Naisbitt describes the most important trends and suggests alternative courses of action to cope with them.

Noddings, Nel. *Philosophy of Education.* Boulder, CO: Westview Press, 1996. This survey of contemporary trends and problems in philosophy of education includes a final chapter, "Feminism, Philosophy and Education," that summarizes the text from a feminist perspective in which Nel Noddings gives her personal convictions on the subject.

Perkinson, Henry. *Two Hundred Years of American Educational Thought.* New York: McKay, 1976. This book contains one of the best accounts of the critics of education to be found anywhere in the literature.

_____. *Since Socrates: Studies in the History of Western Educational Thought.* New York: Longman, 1980. Perkinson gives a fresh account of the development of educational thought in the Western world, with stress placed on intellectual and cultural history.

Potter, Robert E. *The Stream of American Education.* New York: American Book, 1967, 522 pp., including a list of sources and an index. Potter's book is one of the most complete single-volume treatments of American education available. It is especially useful for the study of current educational issues and problems.

Power, Edward J. *Main Currents in the History of Education,* 2d ed. New York: McGraw-Hill, 1969. This work offers a useful general treatment of major American educational ideas.

_____. *Transit of Learning: A Social and Cultural Interpretation of American Educational History.* 1979. This work offers a contextual treatment of curriculum development in the United States.

_____. *Legacy of Learning: A History of Western Education.* Albany, NY: State University of New York Press, 1991. This work contributes to understanding the evolution of curriculum development in American education.

Pratte, Richard. *Ideology and Education.* New York: Wiley, 1977. This useful account of the theories and philosophies of education treats individual thinkers and the social conditions that contributed to their ideas.

Ravitch, Diane. *Left Back: A Century of Failed School Reforms.* New York: Simon and Schuster, 2000. From a historical, traditional, academic, intellectual perspective, Diane Ravitch examines the progress movement. She finds the movement became a source of anti-intellectualism. Her models of educational excellence were William Torrey Harris, William C. Bagley, and Charles H. Judd among others.

Rippa, S. Alexander. *Education in a Free Society.* New York: Longman, 1997. This well-developed comprehensive approach to American educational history focuses on education in a free society.

Rusk, Robert, and James Scotland. *Doctrines of the Great Educators.* New York: St. Martin's Press, 1979. This work offers a new account of the contributions to education made by those who really changed the basic conceptions about education.

Smith, L. Glenn, and Joan K. Smith, Eds. *Lives in a Narrative of People and Ideas.* New York: St. Martin's Press, 1994. This work offers an overview of Western education through biographies of individuals who influenced educational theory and practice.

Talbott, Stephen L. *The Future Does Not Compute: Transcending the Machines in Our Midst.* Sebastopol, CA: O'Reilly and Associates, 1995. This book offers an analysis of the potential adverse effects of a computer driven society on human values.

Thayer, V. T. *Formative Ideas in American Education.* New York: Dodd, Mead, 1965. Professor Thayer presents the philosophic views and changing theories held by leading educators in the United States. The detail in which significant ideas are presented makes Thayer very good reading for serious educators.

Toffler, Alvin. *War and Anti-War.* New York: Little Brown, 1993. This work offers viewpoints of a futurist on the impact of technology on the individual, society, and the world community.

Travers, Paul, and Ronald Rebore. *Foundations of Education: Becoming a Teacher,* 4d ed. New York: Allyn and Bacon, 2000. A university professor and a public school superintendent author of a textbook for prospective teachers that combines historical, philosophical, and social perspectives on education. Dialogues between the two authors precedes each chapter.

Tyack, David B., Ed. *Turning Points in American Educational History*. Waltham, MA: Blaisdell, 1967. Some of the most significant writings and documents in the history of American education are presented, with introductions by the author. This work is a well-selected collection of the most significant material relating to the subject of schooling in America.

Tyack, David B., and Larry Cuban. *Tinkering Toward Utopia: A Century of School Reform*. Cambridge: Harvard University Press, 1995. This critical analysis of educational reform movements is unlike the historical nature of most current reform arguments that result in both a magnification of present defects in relation to the past and an understatement of the difficulty of changing the system.

Urban, Wayne, and Wagoner, Jennings. *American Education: A History*. New York: McGraw-Hill, 1999. Analysis and integration of historical events including coverage of Native American traditions and Southern education.

Warren, Donald, Ed. *History, Education, and Public Policy*. Berkeley, CA: McCutchan, 1978. This collection of essays and documents gives a clear account of the way education and public policy in the United States are related.

Webb, Rodman, and Robert Sherman. *Schooling and Society*, 2d ed. New York: Macmillan, 1989. This work offers an overview of education and its relation to society.

Wirth, Arthur. *Education and Work for the Year 2000: Choices We Make*. San Francisco, CA: Jossey-Bass, 1992. This work offers an analysis of choices facing American society. Choices are offered between the status quo and the need for changing priorities to provide for increasing numbers of individuals at risk.

GLOSSARY

Academic Freedom. The liberty of teachers and scholars to pursue scholarly questions without fear of control or chastisement by administrative personnel of educational or governmental institutions.

Academy. An American secondary school of the colonial and early national era that stressed practical subjects like bookkeeping rather than the classics.

Accountability. The requirement that schools be responsible to the public for how well students do. This requirement is met through student testing.

Acculturation. Integrating into the dominant society through acclimating to its culture, mores, and folkways.

Activity Curriculum. A school program or curriculum chosen by the students themselves with the guidance from the teacher. The activity curriculum was used in some schools associated with progressive education.

Apperceptive Mass. The term used by the philosopher–psychologist Herbart to describe interlocking related or associated ideas in the subconscious part of the mind.

Assessment. Efforts to measure through quantitative and qualitative devices the effectiveness and achievement levels of teachers, students, and administrators.

Associationism. The school of psychology that holds that learning should emphasize the relationships of concepts or ideas. Herbart was an associationist in this sense.

Authentic Assessment. Student assessment balanced among a variety of evaluation measures designed to relate educational theory to real-life issues.

Axiology. The study of moral ethical standards, and judgments.

Bargaining, Collective. A provision for negotiating with a school board by which teachers are represented not as individuals but as a group. A union or a professional organization may be the bargaining agency.

Behaviorism. A school of psychology started by John B. Watson in 1912 that assumes nothing about people or animals and bases its conclusions entirely upon the observed reactions or "behavior" of subjects when they are exposed to a given stimulus.

Block Scheduling. Flexible scheduling designed to improve educational outcomes. Designed to expand time allocated for specific subjects.

Chaos Theory. Human history once viewed as having some rational base of predictability and now viewed as continuing epochs of change, disturbance, flux, and flow. Unpredictability of complex phenomena as paradigm shifts occur creating less stability and more intellectual upheavals.

Charter Schools. Public schools formed by parents, teachers, administrators, or other interested parties to provide innovative learning environments with reduced bureaucratic regulations. There are over 700 charter schools operating in twenty-five states with charter school laws, and the numbers continue to rise.

Child-Centered School. A school in which the primary concern is with developing the whole child rather than with subject matter. John Dewey and the progressive educators developed child-centered schools in which they tried to follow the natural needs, interests, and abilities of children.

Child Study Movement. The scientific study of the nature of children and learning. It began around 1900 by G. Stanley Hall.

Coeducational Colleges. Coeducation was given an impetus by Oberlin College in 1833. By the 1860s, women gained more support for college entrance by Cornell University's Andrew D. White. Prior to 1833, there were female academies and colleges.

Common School.   A school for all of the people. In the United States, free, public, elementary schools were the first "common" schools, but the term is now applied also to public high schools.

Compensatory Education.   Systematic efforts to overcome problems of the culturally different student as with Head Start or bilingual teaching.

Competency-Based Teacher Education.   A requirement that teachers demonstrate, before they are certified, minimum competency in the subjects they will teach. Competency testing of students to see how well they can perform is now often required before graduation.

Comprehensive High School.   A secondary school that attempts to cater to the needs of all students by offering more than one course of specialization in its program. Comprehensive high schools usually have a college preparatory course and one or more scientific or vocational courses that are terminal.

Compulsory Education.   School attendance that is required by law on the theory that it is for the benefit of the commonwealth to educate all the people. Today, the practice is under attack by critics.

Constructivism.   Similar to Jerome Bruner's discovery learning. Encouragement of multidimensional learning environments to assist students in developing critical thinking skills that can be transferred from theory into practice.

Core Curriculum.   A program in which the different subjects of the curriculum are related to a central group of studies. History and geography are combined into the social studies core. Model core curricula often relate foreign languages with other subjects.

Cultural Assimilation.   Integration through language or culture of the dominant society.

Dame School.   A low-level primary school in the colonial and early national periods usually conducted by an untrained woman in her own home. Dame school teachers taught only the bare fundamentals, for which they received small fees or presents.

De Facto Segregation.   A condition of segregation or separation of races into different schools caused by district boundaries that include children from only one race in a given school. This differs from segregation de jure, which is a legal requirement for segregated schools (illegal since 1954).

Deism.   The belief, held by many liberal colonial leaders, that God created the world and then withdrew to let it operate according to natural law. This means that man is on his own because God does not interfere with the affairs of men.

Developmental Stage.   The theory that learning depends upon the maturity of the learner and that it is necessary to reach a certain level of development (physical or mental or both) before certain kinds of learning can take place.

District System.   A scheme of school organization, originating in Massachusetts, in which the local geographical unit or district is the legal authority for a school or schools. Modern districts, within state systems, are the legal areas covered by the services of a given school or schools.

Diversity.   Cultural, ethnic, physical and mentally challenged uniqueness in student learning styles, coping strategies and multiple intelligences.

Early Childhood Education.   Any systematic effort to teach a child before the normal period of schooling begins. Froebel and Montessori were pioneers in the field. Project Head Start is a modern example of early childhood education.

Education.   As used by futurists refers to that for which there are no known answers, as opposed to training.

Empirical Principle.   The belief, as expressed by John Locke, that the measure of the truth of an idea is its comparison with commonsense reality. Many nonempirical theories hold that logic, revelation, or innate feelings test truth.

The Enlightenment.   A pattern of thought that protested against authority in religious and secular life. The Enlightenment stressed science, reason, and the dignity of all men, and it helped to create the shift of thought that made the American Revolution possible.

Epistemology.   The study or theory of the nature and limits of knowledge.

Essentialism.   An educational theory that is a protest against progressive education and consists of an effort to identify the most important practical skills that are then taught to children as the basic or essential subjects.

Experimental Schools.   Schools in which new methods or materials are tried in an effort to select the best. Universities, school systems, or private groups can conduct experimental schools. Normally, careful records are kept in order to measure the progress of pupils using a new curriculum or technique against those using more established ones.

Faculty Psychology. The belief, which was the basic psychology of educators in the nineteenth century, that the mind is divided into separate faculties or powers like willing, memory, and reasoning. Exercise of the faculties was supposed to strengthen the mind; thus the study of Latin grammar would transfer to or improve the ability to use logic.

Formative Evaluation. Using evaluation methods including student feedback to improve instruction. Provides information to assist students throughout their learning process.

Futurism. A philosophical position and a movement in education designed to shift emphasis from the current era to the needs that will emerge in a period of rapid change.

General Education. Education that is not specialized and that is designed for general living or good citizenship rather than preparation for a vocation. There is an issue over just what should be included in general education as well as how many years should be devoted to it.

Goals 2000. Efforts to encourage more effective schools by stressing broad-based learning outcomes for all students in public schools.

Governmental Gridlock. Political infighting that blocks legislation or governmental action.

Graded School System. A division of schools into groups of students according to the curriculum or the ages of pupils, as in the six elementary grades. Early schools were not graded, and a substantial number of modern elementary schools are experimenting with nongraded systems, although grading is still the common practice.

Great Awakening. A religious revival in colonial America that was responsible for the creation of many schools and church-related colleges. Jonathan Edwards is credited with starting the Great Awakening among Puritans in about 1733.

Herbartian Method. The formal system of presenting subject matter to students by the American followers of Herbart, using the five formal steps of preparation, presentation, association, generalization, and application.

High School. High school emerged from the Latin grammar school and originally provided for college preparatory studies. They were given popular impetus by the Michigan supreme court Kalamazoo Case in 1874, which found that city high schools were part of the state public school system.

Hornbook. A single printed page—containing the alphabet, syllables, a prayer, and other simple words—that was used in colonial times as the beginner's first book or preprimer. Hornbooks were attached to a wooden paddle for ease in carrying and covered with a thin sheet of transparent horn for protection.

Humanism. A movement to attain knowledge of life and institutions through the study of the Latin and Greek classical authors. Humanism influenced the American colonies and had a profound effect on the development of American schools. Modern humanism is concerned with the needs and values of people.

Idealism. A major school of philosophy that holds that only ideas are real and that objects cannot exist outside the mind. Idealism was used by Berkeley to signify the opposite of realism. Jonathan Edwards and W. T. Harris were American idealists who influenced education.

Inclusion. Full inclusion of disabled students in regular classrooms.

Industrial Revolution. The transition from an agrarian to an industrial society and the machine age.

In-Service Training. Continuing education for teachers who are actually teaching or in service. Such training can be conducted in a school as a workshop or extension course, or teachers can attend classes in a university at night or during vacation periods.

Intelligence Quotient (IQ). A number that is obtained by dividing mental age (found by a standard or normal test) by chronological age. Intelligence quotients are widely used for placing children in school programs, although they are by no means perfect measurements.

Internet. Computer worldwide network. Formerly used by military and academic researchers on a limited basis.

Involuntary Segregation. Forced separation of students on the basis of race, color, or creed. Racial segregation cannot be required by law in the United States since the Supreme Court decision in the Brown case of 1954.

Kindergarten. A "garden of children" or an institution where small children can grow and develop. The term was coined by Froebel, who began the first schools for children aged four, five, and six years. Kindergartens appeared in America about the time of the Civil War and are now schools for five-year-olds.

Knowledge Revolution. The tremendous explosion of information in almost every field. The amount of information is so great that it is difficult for scholars to be aware of the new knowledge discovered in their own and related fields. The knowledge revolution is accompanied by a vast increase in sources of information, especially computers.

Laissez-Faire. The idea, based on Adam Smith's *Wealth of Nations,* that the government should not interfere in any way with the laws of supply and demand. *Laissez-faire* theory holds that the best government is one that governs least.

Land Grant College. Colleges or universities founded or supported by a gift of public land. The Morrill Land Grant Act of 1862 established many American agricultural and mechanical colleges.

Latin Grammar School. A classical secondary school with a curriculum consisting largely of Latin and Greek, the purpose of which was preparation for college.

Lock-Step. A rigid or uniform organization and curriculum in which each grade or course is the foundation for each higher grade or course and in which there is no flexibility. The influence of the American Herbartianists led to the lock-step in our public schools after 1890.

Logic. A science that deals with rules of valid critical thinking. Also, the analysis of common fallacies in language usage.

Looping. Teachers staying with students from first to second or higher grade levels and then repeating the cycle with other students. Similar to the one-room school concept of our educational history.

Lyceum. Associations for the dissemination of knowledge (arts, literature) and cultural advancement. First organized by Josiah Holbrook in 1862.

Mainstreaming. The process, required by Public Law 94–142, of placing exceptional learners in the least restrictive learning environment. This means that students with disabilities spend at least part of each day in a "regular" classroom.

Melting Pot. The assimilation of immigrants into mainstream culture and total immersion into the dominant language.

Mental Discipline. A theory, associated with faculty psychology and transfer of training, that holds that the mind must be disciplined or exercised through drill, memorization, and the study of difficult subjects.

Metaphysics. The search for reality, truth, and meaning of existence.

Middle School. A modern school organizational plan. Middle schools can be imposed between elementary and junior high schools, or they can replace junior high schools. A 4–4–4 plan uses the term *middle school* for the middle four years.

Modular System. Flexible schedule in a school, organized around modules of time (usually fifteen minutes each), to allow for different time periods for various subjects and individual needs.

Monitorial Schools. Schools developed by Joseph Lancaster and Andrew Bell in which one teacher taught a number of bright students or monitors who, in turn, taught other groups of children. Monitorial schools were brought to America in the early national period in an attempt to provide cheap charity education for poor students.

Multiculturalism. Appreciation and understanding of diverse populations—culture, race, ethnicity, gender, age, social class—and providing a climate for academic and social success.

Multi-Track System. The educational program, found in Europe and in the American colonies, that provided one kind of education for the wealthy elite and another kind for the ordinary people.

A Nation at Risk. One of a series of national reports in the early 1980s that were critical of American schooling. These reports created a demand for excellence and a movement for school reform.

Naturalism. In philosophy, the belief that the world contains only forces that require no supernatural explanation. In education, the belief that children should be free to follow their own interests, desires, and needs. Rousseau was a naturalist in education.

Nongraded School. A school that is not divided into specific grades for each age group. Nongraded schools can have children grouped according to social needs, ability, or progress, or not grouped at all.

Normal School. An American teacher-training school or college. Nineteenth-century normal schools were often two-year institutions on about the same level as high schools. Modern teacher-training colleges are four-year institutions, and many offer graduate training.

Object Lessons. Teaching by means of objects and activities rather than through abstract symbols and words. Edward Sheldon first introduced the object lesson of the Swiss educator Pestalozzi in America at the Oswego Normal School in 1850.

Old Field School. A colonial educational institution developed in Virginia by families who would cooperate to build an elementary school on one of the fallow "old fields." These schools were the counterparts of district schools in New England.

Open Classroom. A modern educational innovation in which self-contained classrooms are replaced with an open plan with individualized instruction and freedom for the child to move about the school.

Outsourcing. Using specialized expertise for school management needs—for example, using Marriott Food Services to provide school lunches. Sanitation, bookstores, school management, and the like, have been turned over to private organizations.

Parochialism. Limited, restricted view of individuals and society. Isolationistic tendency.

Parochial Schools. Denominational schools. An early founder of parochial schools was Elizabeth Seton.

Pedagogy. The scientific study of education, or the curriculum of teacher-training institutions with regard to how to teach.

Perennialism. A term used by Theodore Brameld to describe a position that opposes pragmatism and progressivism and that looks toward a restoration of the absolute or ultimate value system of ages past. Robert Hutchins and many Catholic educators can be described as perennialists.

Political Correctness. Sensitivity to needs, interests, and diversity of at-risk students and specific populations. Sometimes used to infer excessive single interest political groups and educational power blocks.

Pragmatism. The school of philosophy that holds that only the practical results of a belief give it meaning and that arguments that have no practical consequence are meaningless. Charles Peirce coined the term, and John Dewey is a good example of a pragmatist in education.

Programmed Learning. Any learning device that can be used by a student in such a way that a reaction to his or her activities is immediately supplied. These devices range from simple, printed notebooks to computer-assisted instruction, and the learner is not dependent upon a teacher in order to progress.

Progressive Educators. A term applied to a group of educators who objected to subject-centered schools, followed the philosophy of John Dewey, and applied the doctrines of Rousseau, Pestalozzi, and Froebel to education. Francis W. Parker was an early progressive, but the term is usually associated with members of the Progressive Education Association, which was founded in 1918.

Project Method. The method of William H. Kilpatrick and his followers. Any learning activities in which pupils have an opportunity to choose, direct, or plan their own work under conditions similar to those of real life.

Rate Bill. A scheme for supporting schools that was a transition from fees to tax support. Each child was charged a rate or graduated amount for schooling, according to what the parents were able to afford.

Sapiential Authority. A term used by futurists like Theobald to mean authority based in truth or use value of information rather than upon status or position.

Scientific or Sense Realism. An effort to relate education to the "real" or commonsense world. Scientific thinkers like Copernicus, Galileo, and Bacon started it. John Locke and Benjamin Franklin were scientific realists who influenced American schools.

Sectarianism. A term that refers to religious denominations. Early schools were under the control of particular church groups or sects until the Bill of Rights required that public schools be secular because of separation of church and state in America.

Secularism. The principle of religious freedom applied in such a way that the sphere of influence of religious groups or religious leaders does not extend to public institutions like the schools.

Single-Track System. An educational program in which all the students have the same kind of educational opportunity rather than one school system for the elite and another for the masses.

Social and Future Philosophy. The exploration of the accelerating world of change. Especially concerned with the study of the school as a social institution and concepts including freedom, human rights, leadership, ideology, power, equity, and justice. The exploration of possible, probable, and preferable futures and analysis of alternative scenarios for the future.

Social Darwinism. The theory of evolution applied to society rather than to biology. Sumner and Spencer used social evolution to justify the existing social conditions and the concentration of wealth in the hands of the few.

Social Fragmentation. Excessive focus on differences to the detriment of tolerance, comity, civility, and unity essential for democratic theory and practice.

Social Reconstruction. The belief that society can be made over or changed. Some social reconstructionists in education have held that the schools can reconstruct society. Theodore Brameld believes that schools should have some role in social change.

Special Education. A school program designed for the child who is exceptional, that is, either gifted or below normal in ability. The study of exceptional children is now well established, and most American school systems have special education classes.

Subject-Centered School or Curriculum. The traditional educational program that is organized around subject matter or around major concepts in the organized fields of knowledge or disciplines. It is in opposition to the child-centered curriculum, which emphasizes individual differences, needs, and interests of children.

Summative Evaluation. Judging student learning through examinations at the end of a program or course. There is less room for student learning throughout the course or program of study.

Sunday School. A movement started by Robert Raikes in England and transferred to the United States in the early 1800s. It attempted to teach the fundamentals to children who worked in factories during the week.

Synergy. The impact of change in one aspect of the culture on other seemingly unrelated aspects.

Tabula Rasa. As used by John Locke, the theory that children have no innate ideas at birth and that the mind comes to be furnished with ideas through the sense organs or sensation. All learning comes through experience, and the mind is blank at birth.

Team Teaching. A plan by which several teachers, organized into a team with a leader, provide the instruction for a larger group of children than would usually be found in a self-contained classroom. Team members can handle classes together, or one member can teach a large number of children while the others work with individuals.

Terminal Education. Education or schooling that is not designed to lead to further or higher schooling.

High school vocational programs that lead directly to jobs rather than to college are examples of terminal education.

Theocracy. Civil and political power vested in the same person or group. Separation of church and state in America is guaranteed by the Bill of Rights, but the early New England governments were theocracies.

Time-on-Task. An effort to improve schools by paying close attention to the time actually spent by students in paying attention to their subjects as opposed to time devoted to activities such as passing in halls or listening to announcements.

Transfer of Training. The theory, associated with faculty psychology and mental discipline, that learning one subject will aid or transfer to the study of another subject.

Utilitarianism. In education, the doctrine that the school curriculum should be governed by its usefulness for vocational success or public utility.

Vocational Education. Training that is intended to prepare the student for a particular job or to give a basic skill needed in several vocations.

Voluntary Segregation. The practice of establishing a school or other institution that is not for the use of the general public but that is under the control of a specific group. Parochial and private schools are examples of voluntary segregation.

Vouchers. Providing families with a voucher that can be used in public or private schools of their choice.

World Wide Web. Linkage of information channels worldwide. Assists in disseminating and organizing information.

Zero Tolerance. Infractions of school rules and regulations result in immediate disciplinary action regardless of whether the student act is a major or minor infringement of school policy.

INDEX

Ability grouping, 369
Abington School District v. Schempp, 233
Absenteeism, 319
Academic bankruptcy, 119
Academic freedom, 214–215, 383
Academician, 141
Academic Preparation for College,
    301–302
Academies, 91, 147, 383
Accidence (Cheever), 116
Accountability, 259–262
    competency tests, 262–263,
        268–269
    curriculum concerns, 264–265
    curriculum innovations and methods,
        265–268
    definition, 383
    exceptional children, 270–274
    multicultural and bilingual
        education, 275–278
    performance contracting, 268–269
    vouchers, 274–275
    women in education, 278–280
Accreditation, 166
"Accrediting Body Changing the Status
    Quo in Teacher Preparation," 323
Acculturation, 383
Achieve Communications, 297, 370
Action for Excellence (Task Force on
    Education for Economic Growth),
    295, 301
Action in the States (Education
    Commission of the States), 307
Activity curriculum, 383
Adams, Jacob E., 304
Adams, John, 106
Adams, John Quincy, 112
Adaptive Corporation, The (Toffler), 354
Adarand Constructors v. Penna, 244
Addison, Joseph, 105
Ad-hocracy, 360

Adler, Alfred, 66
Adler, Mortimer, 33, 37, 40, 49, 265, 282,
    297, 298
*Adler v. Duval County Florida School
    Board,* 234
Administrative reform, 326–330
Adolescent Society, The (Coleman), 72
Advanced Research Projects
    Administration, 194
Affirmative action, 243–245, 249
African Americans
    1812–1865, 150–151
    1865–1918, 159–160, 161, 172–173, 179
    1918–2002, 199–200
    educational difficulties, 257
    equal opportunity, 246
    multicultural education, 275–278
    segregation, 240–245
    See also Minorities
Agassiz, Louis, 170
Age of Reason (Paine), 109
Agostini v. Felton, 239
Agricultural changes, 1865–1918, 162–163
Aguilar v. Felton, 239
*Aims of Education and Other Essays,
    The* (Whitehead), 39
Albert, R. Little, 302
Albert, Tanya, 319
Albert the Great, 20
Alcohol abuse, 266
Alexander, Kern, 245, 270
Alexander, M. David, 245, 270
Alternatives Future for America II, An
    (Theobald), 354
*Amazing Grace, the Lives of Children
    and the Conscience of a Nation*
    (Kozol), 254
American Association of Colleges of
    Teacher Education (AACTE), 217,
    262, 300, 324
American Association of Manufacturers, 259

American Association of School
    Administrators, 205, 233, 235,
    262, 327, 328, 372
American Bar Association Journal, 241
American Civil Liberties Union, 237
American College and University, The
    (Rudolph), 142, 172
American Council on Education, 72, 321
American Education and Corporations
    (Boyles), 296
American Federation of Labor, 162
American Federation of Teachers,
    218, 233, 261, 262, 275, 316,
    318, 328
American Freedman's Union, 159
American frontier, 134–135
American Herbartian Association, 178
American Herbartianism, 178, 222
American High School Today, The
    (Conant), 273
American Journal of Education, 141,
    143
American Journal of Psychology, 71
American Missionary Association, 159,
    172
American Normal School Association,
    165
American Philosophical Society, 105,
    112
American Promise—The Alliance for
    Youth, 315
American Psychological Association, 63
American Public School Law (Alexander
    and Alexander), 270
American Revolution, 103–104
    educational environment, 110–111
    educational founders, 111–112
    educational leadership, 112–114
    educational movements, 115–116
    governmental proposals for
        education, 114–115

American Revolution—(*continued*)
school ideas and curriculum, 116–117
then to now, 117–123
American Speech and Hearing Association, 328
American Summerhill Association, 52
Americans with Disabilities Act, 273, 274
American Women's Education Association, 148
American Youth Commission, 72
"America's Competitive Challenge" (Business-Higher Education Forum), 295
Amish, 235
Amos, John, 33
Anabaptists, 22
Analytic philosophy, 49–50
Anderson, Nick, 306–307
Angell, James R., 63
Anglicans, 82, 88–89, 90, 92, 108
Annenberg Challenge, 308
Annual Report of the School Committee of Concord (1855), 149
Antioch College, 172, 173
Antiphon, 341
Apperceptive mass, 383
Apple, Michael, 54, 301
Application, 178
Apprenticeship/mentoring, 167, 224
Aquinas, Thomas, 20, 33, 38
Arabians, 275
Aristotle, 20, 32, 33, 331, 38, 49, 60
Arkansas Legislative Act, 590, 236
Armstrong, Samuel C., 172
Army Specialized Training Program, 220
ARPANET, 194
Art as Experience (Dewey), 44
"Art of Undoing Violence Is Finding Its Own Place in Classrooms and Streets, The" (Holmstrom), 320
Ashton-Warner, Sylvia, 257
Asian Americans, 173, 200, 275, 277, 278, 297
"As Schools Start Up" (Henderson), 315
Assessment, 259–262
competency tests, 262–263, 268–269
curriculum concerns, 264–265
curriculum innovations and methods, 265–268
definition, 383
exceptional children, 270–274
multicultural and bilingual education, 275–278
performance contracting, 268–269
vouchers, 274–275
women in education, 278–280
Assimilation, 283

Assistive Technology Act, 205
Association, 178
Association for Supervision and Curriculum Development, 233
Association of College and Preparatory Schools of the Southern States, 165
Associationism, 63–64, 177, 383
Associations
southern, 160–161
standardizing, 165
See also specific associations
Attendance, compulsory, 247
Attitudes, 282
Augustine, Saint, 36
Ausubel, David, 66, 67
Authentic assessment, 267, 383
Axiology, 31–32, 383
Ayer, A. J., 50

Bacon, Francis, 21, 24, 32, 39, 105
Bagley, William C., 47, 259
Bailey, Ebenezer, 138
Bailyn, Bernard, 19
Balanced Treatment for Creation Science and Evolution Science Act, 236
Baldauf, Scott, 182, 311
Baltimore, Lord, 89
Bandura, Albert, 69
Baptists, 92, 97
Bargaining, collective, 383
Barnard, Henry
assessment and accountability, 259
educational leadership, 141, 142, 143
normal schools, 141, 147, 148
social integration, 149–150, 187
state school systems, 119, 128
U.S. Office of Education, 120–121
university departments of education, 175
Barnes v. Cavazos, 239
Barr, Stringfellow, 33
Barzun, Jacques, 265
Bascom, Florence, 278
Basedow, Johann, 145–146
Beacon Hill School at Telegraph House, 316
BEA Systems, 271
Beecher, Catherine, 142, 148
Behavioral engineering, 224
Behaviorism, 50
definition, 383
educational philosophy and, 51–52
educational psychology and, 64–65
Bell, Andrew, 115
Bell, Daniel, 17, 75, 347, 352
Bell, T. H., 48, 310
Bell, Wendell, 57, 75, 351

Belsie, Laurent, 349
Bender v. Williamsport, 237
Bennett v. Kentucky Department of Education, 248
Bennett, William, 40, 47, 75, 224, 266, 281–282, 304, 310
Bergen, Timothy J., Jr., 33, 34, 35
Bergson, Henri-Louis, 34
Berkeley, George, 32, 37, 109
Berkeley, Sir William, 86
Berliner, David C., 255–256, 271, 294, 313
Berry, Adrian, 356
Bestor, Arthur, Jr., 47, 219, 265
Bethune, Mary McLeod, 199–200
Bethune-Cookman College, 199
Betsor, Arthur, 214
"Better Balance: Quality Counts," 313
Beyond Freedom and Dignity (Skinner), 51, 65
Beyond the Limits (Meadows), 347
Bible, 7, 22
curriculum and, 116
dame schools and, 88
King James Version, 169
public schools and, 232, 233, 237
Puritans and, 94, 95
southern colonies and, 85
Bible and the Public Schools, The (National Bible Association), 233
Biddle, Bruce J., 256, 294
Bilingual education, 219, 251, 275–278, 283
Bilingual Education Act, 277, 283–284
Bill and Melinda Gates Foundation, 194, 271
Bill for More General Diffusion of Knowledge (Jefferson), 113, 117
Bill of Rights, 111, 169. *See also specific Amendments*
Binet, Alfred, 70
Black English, 277
Blackwell, Elizabeth, 278
Black Women in America: An Historical Encyclopedia (Hine), 279
Blair, Bill, 160, 240
Blair, Henry, 160
Blair, James, 88
Blair, Julie, 218
Block scheduling, 196, 383
Bloom, Allan, 40, 45, 224
Bloom, Benjamin, 68–69
Blouin, Melissa, 220
Blount College, 139
Blow, Susan E., 144
Bode, Boyd, 33, 45, 213
Bogen, J. E., 69
Bohr, Niels, 13

Bok, Derek, 176
Bok, Sissela, 256
Book for Mothers (Pestalozzi), 146
Boston Latin Grammar School, 94
Boston News Letter, 105
Boston Primary School, 137
Boulding, Kenneth, 56, 75, 347
Bouvier, Leon, 151
Bowles, Samuel, 252
Bowman, Darcia Harris, 239
Bowman, Jim, 56
Bown v. Gwinnett, 237
Boyer, Ernest, 298–301, 303, 318, 319, 325, 329, 330
Boyle, Robert, 21, 105
Boyles, Deron, 296
Bracey, Gerald W., 255–256, 294
Bradwell v. Illinois, 249
Brameld, Theodore, 33, 45–46, 257
Braun, Moseley, 279
Brave New World (Huxley), 214, 342, 355
Bray, Thomas, 88
Brickman, William W., 19
Briggs, Bruce, 352
Brookings Institute Center on Urban and Metropolitan Policy, 297
Brooks, Charles, 120, 147
Broudy, Harry, 33, 39, 277, 342
Brown, Lester R., 347, 354
Brown University, 92, 139
Brown v. Board of Education, 241, 243, 329
Bruner, Jerome S., 51, 66, 67, 220, 257, 267
Bruno, Giordano, 21, 26
Bryan, William Jennings, 162
Bryn Mawr College, 172
Buber, Martin, 33, 52–53
Buchanan, James, 141
Building a Philosophy of Education (Broudy), 39
Building a Win-Win World: Life Beyond Global Economic Warfare (Henderson), 354
Bullying, 267, 319
Bush, George H. W., 46, 224, 290, 304
    drug education, 266
    educational goals, 224
    educational reform, 290
    volunteerism, 315
Bush, George W., 46, 224, 290, 315
    accountability, 121
    affirmative action, 244
    discrimination, 274
    diversity, 297
    educational funding, 203, 235–236, 258, 311, 312

educational goals, 205, 208, 224, 282
educational reform, 290, 306, 314
family values, 100
in loco parentis, 249
prayer in schools, 234
presidential election (2000), 14
social reconstructionism, 46–47
standardization, 214
taxes, 181–182
terrorism, 75
total English immersion, 277
volunteerism, 315
vouchers, 118, 119, 239, 275
Bush, Jeb, 245
Business@The Speed of Thought (Gates and Hemingway), 348
Business-Higher Education Forum, 295
Business model, 295–297
Business Roundtable, 323
Butler, J. Donald, 32, 37
Butler, Judith, 54
Butler, Nicholas Murray, 48, 175
Butts, R. Freeman, 164
Byham, William, 260
Byrd, William, 86

Caesar, Julius, 6
California Beginning Teacher Evaluation Study, 304
Callahan, Raymond E., 295
Calvin, John, 22, 93
Calvinists, 22, 90, 93
Cambron-McCabe, Nelda H., 261
Campbell, Kate, 55
Campe, J. H., 146
Camus, Albert, 32, 33, 53
Capper-Ketcham Act, 205
Cardinal Principles of Secondary Education, 166–167, 198, 268
Career education, 266
Carl D. Perkins Vocational and Applied Technology Education 1998 Amendments, 205
Carnap, Rudolph, 50
Carnegie Corporation, 219
Carnegie Foundation, 160, 166, 263, 298
Carr, Ezra, 164
Carr, Harvey, 63
Carr, Judy F., 306
Carroll, John, 169
Carter, James C., 128, 142, 152, 194
Carter, Jimmy, 121, 204, 209
Catechism, 94
Catherine of Aragon, 22
Catholic Counter-Reformation, 21–23, 24
Catholics, 22, 89, 91, 108, 136, 169, 232
Cattell, James M., 62, 63, 70

Cavazos, Laura, 224, 282
Cedarwood Sudbury School, 316
Celera Genomics Corporation, 349
Censorship, 237
Center on Gender and Education, 280
Central Missouri State University, 243
Cetron, Marvin, 317, 365
Chaining, 67
Change (periodical), 176
Chaos theory, 383
Character education, 267, 320
Charity education, 88–89
Charter schools, 383
Chavis, John, 149
Cheever, Ezekiel, 94, 109, 116
Chemical learning aids, 370
Cheney, Dick, 204
Cherryholmes Cleo, 57
Chicago School Reform Act, 308
Child and the Curriculum, The (Dewey), 301
Child-centered school, 383
Children's Internet Protection Act, 225
Childs, John, 45
Child study movement, 70–73, 383
Chinese Exclusion Act, 162
Chipman, Nathaniel, 112
Chomsky, Noam, 69
Christian Coalition, 236
"Christian Right Falls Out of Unison on School Prayer" (Felsenthal), 236
Christian Science Monitor, 82
Cicero, 20
Citadel, 17
City-level educational reforms, 307–310
City Schools Leading the Way (Forsyth and Tallerico), 308
Civilian Conservation Corps, 206
Civil Rights Act (1964), 242, 277
Civil Rights Act (1984), 249
Civil Rights Act (1991), 274, 279
Civil Rights Project, 272
Civil War, 132, 158–159, 179–180, 181, 240
Cixous, Helene, 54
Clark, Joe, 294
Clarke, Arthur, 356
Clement VII, 22
Cleveland Board of Education v. Loudermill, 248
Cleveland, Grover, 161
Clinic for Child Development, 72
Clinical psychology, 59
Clinton, De Witt, 110, 141
Clinton, William Jefferson
    affirmative action, 244
    educational funding, 120, 121, 205, 208

Clinton, William Jefferson—(*continued*)
    educational goals, 75, 118–119, 181, 304, 305
    educational reform, 290, 297
    hate crimes, 320
    national service program, 312
    private education, 314
    religious liberty, 233
    standardization, 214
    total English immersion, 277
    volunteerism, 315
Closing of the American Mind, The (Bloom), 40
Club of Rome, 354
Coates, Joseph F., 17, 343, 344–345, 368
Cobb, Stanwood, 210
Cochran case, 235
Cochran-Smith, 302
Coeducational colleges, 383–384
Coeyman, Marjorie, 272
Cognitive psychology, 59, 69
Cold war, 190
Coleman, Claudia, 271
Coleman, James S., 72, 252, 257
Coleman Report, 252, 258
Coleman, William T., 271
Coles, Edward, 113, 141
Cole v. Oroville High School, 233–234
Collective bargaining, 383
College Entrance Examination Board, 166
College of New Jersey, 92, 109, 110
College of Philadelphia, 92, 109, 110, 121, 138
College of Rhode Island, 92, 97, 109, 110
Colleges
    1865–1918, 170. *See also* Higher education
    minorities (1865–1918), 172–173
    See also Higher education; *specific colleges*
Collings, Ellsworth, 210, 223
Colonial America, 82–83
    cultural changes in, 105–106
    democratic ideals, 104–105
    educational changes in, 109–110
    liberalism, 108–109
    middle colonies, 89–92
    New England colonies, 92–97
    philosophical changes, 106–108
    religious sectarianism, 83–84
    social class in, 84–85
    southern colonies, 85–89
    then to now, 97–101
Columbia University, 92, 168, 175, 211
Comenius, John A., 6–7
    educational history, 123
    Enlightenment and, 55, 108

futures philosophy, 356, 369
general philosophy, 34
influence of, 35, 106–107
sense realism, 33, 39, 60
Coming of the Post-Industrial Society, The (Bell), 347, 352
Commission of Public School Personnel Policies, 216
Commission on the Reorganization of Secondary Education, 166, 198
Committee for Economic Development, 301
Committee for Education Funding, 311
Committee of Fifteen, 191
Committee of Ten, 61, 165–166, 198, 250
Committee on Academic Nondiscrimination and Integrity, 244
Committee on College Entrance Requirements, 166, 167
Committee on Unit Courses, 166
Common Faith, A (Dewey), 44
Common school, 92, 129, 384
Common School Journal. See Connecticut Common School Journal
Common school revival, 127–128
    age of, 135–137
    educational leadership, 141–143
    European influences, 143–149
    higher education, 138–141
    high schools, 137–138
    social, political, and economic trends, 128–135
    then to now, 149–152
Commoner, Barry, 348
Common Sense (Paine), 109
Communism, 190, 250
Community Child Care Center (Delray Beach, Florida), 191
Community colleges, 201–202
Compendious Dictionary (Webster), 112–113
Compendium on the Magnificence, Dignity, and Excellence of the University of Paris (Goulet), 18
Compensatory education, 384
Competency-based teacher education (CBTE), 216, 384
Competency-based training, 268–269
Competency tests, for teachers, 262–263
Competition, 362–363, 369
Comprehensive high schools, 198, 384
Compulsory education, 247–248, 384
Computer-assisted instruction, 193
Computers, 189, 193–194, 346, 348, 350, 364, 370, 371. *See also* Internet

Comte, Auguste, 11
Conant, James B., 48, 214, 219, 250, 265, 273
Concept learning, 67
Concept of Mind, The (Ryle), 50
Concord University, 368
"Condition of America's Public School Facilities, The" (Lewis), 195
Conference for Education, 160
Conflict resolution, 267, 320
Connecticut Common School Journal, 141, 142
Connecticut School Effectiveness Project, 327
Connectionism, 64
Connectionist psychology, 63–64
Connections (television program), 24, 340
Consciousness, 60–62
Consentives, 360
Conservative traditions, 22–23
Consolidation, 196
Consortium on Chicago School Research, 308
Conspicuous consumption, 354, 357
Constitutional Convention, 114
Constructivism, 384
Consumer education, 266
Contents of Children's Minds on Entering School, The (Hall), 72
Contracting
    individual, 223
    performance, 268–269
Cook County Normal School, 177, 209
Cook, Eugene, 241
Cookman Institute of Jacksonville, Florida, 199
Cooley, Thomas McIntyre, 164
Cooper, J. Arthur, 32
Cooper, Peter, 123
Cooperation, 362–363
Cooperative Accountability Project, 261
Copernicus, Nicolaus, 21, 26
Coram, Robert, 112, 117
Core curriculum, 365, 384
Core values, 14–16
Cornish, Edward, 56
Corporate Forum on Education and the Economy, 319
Cottage School (Riverside, Illinois), 210
Cotton, John, 93, 95
Council for Basic Education, 48, 219, 265
Council for Democratic and Secular Humanism, 237
Council for Exceptional Children, 272, 328
Council of Parents and Teachers, 281
Council of Philadelphia, 91

Counts, George S., 33, 45, 211, 212
Cousin, Victor, 128, 144
Crandall, Prudence, 149
Creating Alternative Futures: The End of Economics (Henderson), 354
Creating a New Civilization: Politics of the Third Wave (Toffler and Toffler), 347
Creationism, 236–237, 239
Cremin, Lawrence A., 164, 309
Crim, Alonzo, 309
Crime, 320, 346
Crime Awareness and Campus Security Act, 200
Crisis in the Classroom (Silberman), 254–255
Criticism
    educational reform, 301–303
    individual critics, 249–259
    progressive education, 212–214
Cross, Patricia, 299, 315
Cross-cultural language and academic development (CLAD), 219
Cross-impact matrix, 350
Cubberley, Ellwood P., 18
Culbertson, Jack, 329
Cult of Efficiency, The (Callahan), 295
Cult of Information, The (Roszak), 254
Cultural assimilation, 384
Cultural changes, in colonial America, 105–106
Cultural diversity. *See* Bilingual education; Minorities; Multicultural education; *specific minority groups*
Cultural lag, 13
Cultural Literacy (Hirsch), 301
Culture of Education, The (Bruner), 267
Culture of Narcissism, The (Lasch), 371
Curriculum, 250
    accountability and assessment, 264–268
    common school revival, 136–137
    core, 365, 384
    futures philosophy, 364–367, 369
    high schools (1865–1918), 164
    innovations and methods, 265–268
    religion and, 237
    Revolutionary period, 116–117
    subject-centered, 388
    universities (1865–1918), 171–172
Curry, J. L. M., 160
Curti, Merle, 12
Cyberlaw, 189
Cybernation: The Silent Revolution (Michael), 347

Dallas Independent School District, 262
Dalton Contract Plan, 223

Dalton Plan of the Progressive Era, 309
Dame schools, 88
Darden, Edwin C., 238
Dare the Schools Build a New Social Order? (Counts), 45
Darling-Hammond, Linda, 307–308
Dartmouth College, 96, 97, 109, 110, 121, 138–139, 232
Darwin, Charles, 26, 62, 70, 171, 179, 343
David v. Monroe County Board of Education, 247
Davis v. Monroe, 279
Day-care centers, 191, 202
Daytona-Cookman Collegiate Institute, 199
Daytona Educational and Industrial Training School for Negro Girls, 199
Death at an Early Age (Kozol), 253
Debra v. Turlington, 246
Decker, Sunny, 257
Declaration of Independence, 106, 112
Dede, Christopher, 56
De facto segregation, 241–242, 384
Defense of Common Sense, A (Moore), 49–50
DeGarmo, Charles, 178, 222
Deism, 384
Delphi technique, 350
Demiashkevich, Michael, 47
Democracy, 49, 104–105
Democracy and Education (Dewey), 44, 163, 209
Democratic Party, 162, 205
Dennison, George, 252
Denominations, in middle colonies, 91. *See also* Religious sectarianism; *specific religious denominations*
Deregulation, 314–315
Descartes, René, 21, 37, 53, 60
Deschooling, 252–253
Deschooling Society (Illich), 252, 258, 280, 356
Desegregation, 150–151, 242
Desert Storm. *See* Persian Gulf War
Design for a School of Pedagogy, A, 290
Determinism, 58
Developmental psychology, 59, 66–68
Developmental stage, 384
Dewey, Evelyn, 210
Dewey, John, 7, 9, 29, 30, 185
    analytic philosophy, 49
    behaviorism, 51
    curriculum, 264
    Dennison and, 252
    educational philosophy, 32, 73
    educational reform, 309
    essentialism, 47–48

experience, 75
experimentalism, 298
Froebel's influence on, 147
functionalism, 63
futures philosophy, 357, 358
Gestalt psychology, 65
inquiry based instruction, 223
life adjustment education, 213
multicultural and bilingual education, 278
Parker's influence and, 177, 209
participatory futurists, 354
postmodernism, 54, 55
pragmatism, 33, 40, 41, 42–45, 176
Progressive Education Association, 210–211, 212
progressivism, 209, 210, 214
psychoanalysis, 66
psychology, 62
public schools, 163
rigid systems, 178–179, 182, 222
Smith-Hughes Act, 168
social and futures philosophy, 55
team teaching, 224
Diegmueller, Karen, 217–218
Differentiated staffing, 223
Digest of Educational Statistics 1996, 198
Digest of Educational Statistics 1999, 196, 199, 205
Dirksen, Everett, 233
Discipline of Hope, The (Kohl), 253
Discovery learning, 66
Discrimination, 162, 169–170, 244, 249
Distance learning, 369
District system, 384
Diversified learning environments, 369–370
Diversity, 89, 384. *See also* Bilingual education; Minorities; Multicultural education; *specific minority groups*
Doe v. Plyler, 247
Donohue v. Copiague, 261
Door of the Languages Unlocked (Comenius), 107
Dostoyevsky, Fyodor, 53
Drucker, Peter, 346, 368
Drug education, 265, 266
Du Bois, W. E. B., 155, 173, 183, 200, 240
Due process, 246–247
Dugger, William E., Jr., 371–372
Dunkards, 90
Du Pont de Nemours, P. S., 112
Durkheim, Emile, 11, 72
Dutch Reformed church, 92
Dutch West India Company, 90
Dwight, Edmund, 147

Early childhood education, 384
Eastside High School (Paterson, New
    Jersey), 294
Eaton, John, 121
Eaton, Thomas, 86, 88
Ebbinghaus, Hermann, 62, 63
Ebonics, 99
Economic Opportunity Act (EOA), 206
Economic trends
    1812–1865, 128–135
    1918–2002, 189–190
Edelman, Marion Wright, 182
Edgewood v. Kirby, 245
Edison Schools, 345
Educating for a New Millennium (Shane
    and Tabler), 329
Education
    American Revolution, 110–117
    colonial America, 109–110
    definition, 384
    future of, 337–345
    society and, 8–11
    training versus, 360
    twenty-first century trends, 345–346
    unknown in, 360–361, 364
Education: A Beginning (Van Til), 38
Education Amendments, 120, 247
Education and Ecstasy (Leonard), 213,
    257, 355
*Education and Work for the Year 2000:
    Choices We Face* (Wirth), 74
Education as Power (Brameld), 45, 46
Education Commission of the
    States, 307
Education Consolidation and
    Improvement Act, 207, 283
Education departments, in universities
    (1865–1918), 175–176
Education for All Handicapped Children
    Act, 329–330
"Education for Economic Growth"
    (Hunt), 73, 74
Education of All Handicapped Children
    Act. *See* Public Law 94-142
Education of Man, The (Froebel), 146
Education Planet, 265
Education Professions Development
    Act, 208
"Education Schools Strain to File Report
    Cards" (Blair), 218
Education Section of the World Futures
    Society, 364–365
Education Week (periodical), 218, 258,
    259, 272, 313, 316, 323, 371
Education Work for the Year 2000
    (Wirth), 347
Educational administration, reform in,
    326–330

Educational Amendments, 279
Educational change, rate of, 11–16
Educational founders, 111–112
Educational funding
    1918–2002, 202–204
    educational administration, 328
    educational reform, 310–311
    futures philosophy, 369
    home schooling, 330
    public attitudes, 282–283
    state funds, 136
    See also Vouchers
Educational history, 1–8
    1865–1918, 155–183
    1918–2002, 185–225
    educational change, 11–16
    intellectual background, 20–23
    overview, 23–26
    purposes of, 16–20
    role of, 123
    society and education, 8–11
    See also American Revolution;
        Colonial America; Common
        school revival
Educational Issues in the Kindergarten
    (Blow), 144
Educational Law Reporter, 279
Educational Leadership (periodical),
    233, 346
Educational Leadership (Perrone), 298
Educational leadership
    American Revolution, 112–114
    common school revival, 141–143
Educational materials, in Revolutionary
    period, 116–117
Educational movements, 115–116
Educational philosophy, 29–36
    1865–1918, 176–179
    analytic philosophy, 49–50
    behaviorism, 51–52
    essentialism, 47–48
    existentialism, 52–54
    humanism, 48–49
    idealism, 36–38
    modern realism, 39
    overview, 73–76
    perennialism, 40
    postmodernism, 54–55
    pragmatism, 40–45
    protest philosophies, 50–55
    realism, 38–39
    social and futures philosophy,
        55–58
    social reconstructionism, 45–47
    technology and, 58–59
Educational psychology, 59–62
    behaviorism, 64–65
    cognitive psychology, 69

connectionist psychology
    (associationism), 63–64
functionalism, 63
Gestalt psychology, 65
humanistic and phenomenological
    psychology, 69–70
mastery learning, 68–69
modern developmental psychology
    and stage theory, 66–68
psychoanalysis, 66
structuralism, 62
Educational reform, 290–291, 330–331
    administrative reform, 326–330
    Boyer, Goodlad, and Sizer, 298–301
    business model, 295–297
    comment and criticism, 301–303
    financial limitations, 310–311
    Gramm-Rudman Amendment, 311–313
    initiatives, 307–310
    Nation at Risk, 293–295
    Paideia Proposal, 297–298
    rebuilding versus restructuring,
        313–316
    reports, 291–293
    school effectiveness, 303–307
    teacher education, 316–326
Educational Reform Act, 245–246
Educational Research Analysis, 237
Educational Statistics to 2008, 200
Educational Talent Search, 46
Educational theory
    European, 145
    futures philosophy and, 356–359
    See also Educational philosophy
Educational Wastelands (Bestor), 47
Educators. *See* Teachers
Edward VI, 22
Edwards, Jonathan, 93, 97, 105, 109
Edwards v. Aguillard, 237
Effective Schools, 260
"Effective Sexual Harassment Policies"
    (Sundt), 279
Eighth General Assembly of the World
    Future Society, 57
Eight-Year Study (Progressive Education
    Association), 47, 212, 214
Einstein, Albert, 59
Eisenhower, Dwight D., 190
Eisner, Eliot, 56
Electronic learning aids, 370
Elementary and Secondary Education
    Act (ESEA), 120, 202, 207–209,
    225, 235, 283
Elementary Education in Europe
    (Stowe), 145
Elementary schools
    1918–2002, 191–192
    during common school revival, 137

Elementary Work (Basedow), 145
Eleventh Amendment, 274
Eliot, Charles W., 165, 167, 171, 210, 211, 250
Elizabeth I, 22, 123
Elkind, David H., 307
Ellison, Harlan, 356
Ellison v. Brady, 279
Elmtown's Youth (Hollingshead), 72
E-mail, 194
Emerson, Ralph Waldo, 33, 37, 48, 140
Emile (Rousseau), 60, 74, 145, 146, 210, 280
Empirical principle, 60, 106, 384
Empty Spoon, An (Decker), 257
End of Work, The (Rifkin), 341
English Classical School, 138, 164
English, Fenwick W., 329
English Grammar (Murray), 116
English High School, 138
Enlightenment, 108, 139, 384
Environment, 370
Environmental education, 266
Episcopalians, 90
Epistemology, 31, 384
Epperson v. Arkansas, 236
Equal Access Act, 238
Equal Opportunity Act, 120
Equal opportunity, and litigation, 245–246
Erasmus, Desiderius, 20, 48
Erikson, Erik, 66
Erikson, Kai, 55
Esfandiary, F. M., 356
Eskimos, 276
Essay Concerning the Human Understanding (Locke), 60
Essentialism, 47–48, 259, 264, 384
"Essentialist's Platform for the Advancement of Education, An" (Bagley), 47
Ethical, Legal, and Multicultural Foundations of Teaching, The (Kierstead and Wagner), 278
Ethnicity. *See* Minorities; *specific minority groups*
Ethnographic futures, 351
European educational theory, 145
European heritage. *See* Colonial America
European influences, during common school revival, 143–149
European school model, 144–145
Evaluation, skill in, 363
"Evaluation of the Florida A-Plus Accountability and School Choice Program, An" (Greene), 275
Evangeline (Longfellow), 10
Evans, Alice, 278

Evening Hours of the Hermit (Pestalozzi), 146
Everson case, 235
Every Kid a Winner: Accountability in Education (Lessinger), 260
Everyman Project, The (Jungk), 354
Evolutionary futurists, 355
Evolution of Progress, The (Paepke), 342
Excellence: Can We Be Equal and Excellent Too? (Gardner), 273
Exceptional children, 270–274, 371
Exemplars in Educational Philosophy (Cooper), 32
Existentialism, 50, 52–54, 264
Experience and Education (Dewey), 43–44, 212
Experience, 60, 106
Experimentalism, 42, 298
Experimental psychology, 59
Experimental schools, 211–212, 384
Extrapolation
   optimistic, 352–353
   trend, 351

4-H clubs, 168
Faculty psychology, 385
Fadiman, James, 355
Falwell, Jerry, 49, 236, 314
Family Well-Ordered, A (Mather), 93
Farmer's Institutes, 168
Fatalism, 366
"Fear Stalks the Hallways" (Hellegaard), 319
Featherstone, Joseph, 257
Federal Board of Vocational Education, 205
Federal government. *See specific departments, offices, elected officials, and legislation*
Federal Security Agency, 204
Feinberg, Joel, 55
Feistritzer, Emily, 319
Feldman, Sandra, 262
Feldmann, Linda, 182
Fellenberg, Philipp Emanuel von, 167
Felsenthal, Edward, 236
Field experiences, 216
Finance. *See* Educational funding
Fineberg, Gerald, 347
Finn, 330
First Amendment, 111, 114, 233, 234–235, 237, 247
Fiske, John, 171
Fithian, Philip, 86
Five Formal Steps of Teaching and Learning, 178
Five-year programs, 324–326
Flanagan, Ann, 325
Flanders, Ned, 72

Fleury, Claude, 18
Flexible scheduling, 223
Flexner, Abraham, 48
Florida Atlantic University, 219
Florida Comprehensive Assessment Tests, 221
Florida Educational Coalition Crime and Violence Survey, 319
Florida in the 21st Century (Bouvier), 151
Florida Sunshine State Affiliate, 199
Fonda, Jane, 280
Forbes (magazine), 346
Ford, Judith, 222
Ford, Paul Leicester, 95
"For Goodness' Sake: Why So Many Want Religion to Play a Greater Role in American Life" (Public Agenda Research Studies), 234
Forgotten Half: Non-College Youth in America (William T. Grant Foundation), 301
Formative evaluation, 385
Forsyth, Patrick B., 308
Forum (journal), 70
Foucault, Michel, 54
Foundations of Futures Studies (Bell), 351
Founding of the American Public School Systems (Monroe), 18
Four Philosophies and Their Practice in Education and Religion (Butler), 32
Fourteenth Amendment, 150, 241, 244, 245, 246, 249
Framework for Appraising Educational Reforms, A (House), 306
Francis, David R., 182
Franklin, Benjamin, 40, 48, 58, 91, 105, 106, 109, 112, 188
Franklin v. Gwinnette County Public Schools, 247
Frazier, Calvin, 294
Free Schools (Kozol), 253–254
Free school societies, 115–116
Free to Choose (Friedman), 314
Freedmen's Bureau, 159
Freedom and Beyond (Holt), 252
Freedom of religion, 111–112, 169, 232–239
Freire, Paolo, 252
French Revolution, 113
Freud, Sigmund, 62, 66, 343
Friedenberg, Edgar Z., 252, 257, 264
Friedman, Milton, 314
Friedman, Rose, 314
Froebel, Friedrich, 35, 37, 42, 60, 70, 144, 145, 146–147, 176, 177, 178, 209
Frontier, 134–135

Fuller, R. Buckminster, 353, 363
Functionalism, 63
Functional psychology, 43
Funding. *See* Educational funding
Future As History, The (Heilbroner), 341
Future constructors, 353
Future Shock (Toffler), 4, 347, 354
Futuribles, 350–351
Futurism
  curriculum, 364–367
  definition, 385
  educational characteristics, 359–364
  educational theory and, 356–359
  overview, 347–349
  research methods, 350–351
  schools of, 352–356
  trends, 367–372

Gabler, Mel, 237
Gabler, Norma, 237
Gagné, Robert, 66–67
Galbraith, John Kenneth, 347
Galilei, Galileo, 21, 24
Gall, Franz Joseph, 60–61
Gallup, Alec M., 320
Galton, Francis, 70
Games, 362–363
Gaming, 350–351
Gardner, James, 273
Gardner, John W., 214, 229, 282, 290
Garvey, Marcus, 179
Gary Platoon Plan, 223
Gassendi, Pierre, 21
Gates, Bill, 348
Gazzaniga, Michael, 69
GEAR UP, 120, 208
Gehring, John, 308, 316
Gender bias, 247
Gender equity, 279–280
General education, 385
General Education Board, 160, 211
General Education in a Free Society,
  198–199
Generalization, 178
Geological Society of America, 278
George III, 80
George-Dean Act, 205
George Peabody College for
  Teachers, 160
George-Reed Act, 205
Gesell, Arnold, 72
Gestalt psychology, 65
GI Bill, 180, 189, 200, 206–207, 235
Gifted and talented students, 273
Gilbert, William, 21, 24
Gilligan, Carol, 280
Gilman, Daniel Coit, 170–171
Giroux, Henry A., 54, 295

Glass Ceiling Act, 279
"Glass Ceiling Restricts Women" (Shea), 280
Glasser, William, 257
Global paradox (Naisbitt), 352
Goals 2000, 255, 305, 315, 385
Gobitis case, 234
Goldberg, Mark E., 280
Good, Harry, 18
Goodlad, John, 289
  assessment and accountability, 260
  educational administration, 328, 329
  educational reform, 298–301, 309,
    315, 325
  home schooling, 248
  mentoring, 219
Goodman, Paul, 33, 252, 264, 356
Good News Club, 238
Goodrich, Samuel, 116
Gorgias, 341
Gospel, 93, 94
Goss v. Lopez, 247
Goulet, Robert, 18
Governmental gridlock, 385
Graded schools, 137, 385
*Grammatical Institute of the English
    Language* (Webster), 113, 116
Gramm-Rudman Amendment, 311–313,
  317
Great Awakening, 96, 97, 385
Great Books of the Western World, 40,
  219, 281–282, 297, 349
Great Depression, 180, 181, 189–190,
  215, 313
Great Didactic (Comenius), 107
Great School Wars (Ravitch), 169
Greenback Party, 162
Greene, Jay P., 275
Greene, Maxine, 74
Greenspan, Alan, 181
Grissmer, David W., 325
"Groundbreaking Teacher Preparation
    Standards to Be Used Beginning
    Next Year" (Wise), 323
Grove City College v. Bell, 249
Growth, 49
Guide for the Perplexed, A
    (Schumacher), 355
Gulf War. *See* Persian Gulf War
Gun Free Schools Act, 320
Gutenberg, Johannes, 2, 21, 24
Guts-Muths, Johann, 146

Habermas, Jurgen, 54, 58
Hall, G. Stanley, 62, 71–72, 167
Hall, Samuel, 141, 148
Hamilton, Alexander, 113, 114
Hampton Institute for Negro Higher
    Education, 172, 173

Hanushek, Eric A., 304, 325
Harman, Willis, 355
Harris, Douglas E., 306
Harris, William T., 37, 144, 165, 176–177
Harvard Center for Teaching
  Learning, 176
Harvard College, 40, 84, 94, 96, 109, 110
Harvard Educational Review, 258
Harvard, John, 271
Harvard Report, 295, 322
Harvard University, 139, 140, 171–172,
    173, 198, 219, 271, 272, 274, 280
Harvey, William, 21
Hatch Act, 168
Hate crime, 320
Havinghurst, Robert, 261
Hawley, Gideon, 141
Head Start, 46, 191, 206, 208, 213, 214,
  258, 281, 290, 311
Hegel, Georg W. F., 32, 34, 37, 176
Heidegger, Martin, 33, 53
Heilbroner, Robert, 17, 46, 341, 352, 358
Heisenberg, Werner, 58
Hekman, Susan, 55
Hellegaard, James, 319
Helmer-Hirschberg, Olaf, 352
Hemingway, Collings, 348
Henderson, Hazel, 354
Henderson, Keith, 315
Hendricks, Gay, 355
Henry VIII, 22
Henry, Patrick, 106, 111
Herbart, Johann F., 33, 35, 39, 61, 62,
    145, 177–178, 182, 222, 365
Herbartian method, 385
Herdahl v. Pontotoc, 237
Higher education
  1865–1918, 170–172
  1918–2002, 199–201
  colonial America, 88, 92
  common school revival, 138–141
Higher Education Act, 208, 218, 235
Higher Education Amendments of
  1998, 200
Higher Education Facilities
  Act, 207
High School (Boyer), 318
*High School: A Report on Secondary
    Education in America* (Carnegie
    Foundation for the Advancement
    of Teaching), 298
High schools
  1865–1918, 163–167
  1918–2002, 197–199
  birth of, 137–138
  definition, 385
  educational reform, 298–299
  See also Secondary education

Hill Academy, 170
Hindus, 236
Hine, Darlene Clark, 279
Hirsch, E. D., 301
Hispanic Heritage Week, 276
Hispanic/Latinos, 200, 245, 241, 242,
    257, 275, 276, 278, 297. *See also*
    Minorities
History. *See* Educational history
Hoar Bill, 160, 240
Hoar, George F., 160
Hobbes, Thomas, 21
Hobson v. Hansen, 246
Hocking, W. E., 47
Hodgkinson, Harold, 56
Hohn, Robert L., 70
Holbrook, Josiah, 140
Holland, Robert C., 57
Hollingshead, A. B., 72
Holmes, Henry, 324
Holmes Group, 324–326
Holmes Partnership, 324, 325
Holmes v. Bush, 239
Holmstrom, David, 320
Holt, G. T., 53
Holt, John, 33, 252, 264
Home and Colonial Training Institution
    of London, 174–175
Home schooling, 247–248, 316
Hooker, Thomas, 109
Hopwood v. Texas, 244
*Horace's Compromise: The Dilemma of
    the American High School* (Sizer),
    299, 300
*Horace's Hope: The Future of the
    American High School*
    (Sizer), 294
*Horace's School: Redesigning the
    American High School*
    (Sizer), 294
Hornbooks, 88, 385
Horne, Herman, 32, 33, 37, 45
Horney, Karen, 66
House, Ernest R., 306
Howard, O. O., 159
How Children Fail (Holt), 252
How Gertrude Teaches Her Children
    (Pestalozzi), 146
"How to Make Our Ideas Clear"
    (Peirce), 41
How We Think (Dewey), 43, 63
Hoxby, Caroline, 295
Hudson Institute, 151
Huelskamp, Robert, 255
Huguenots, 22, 90
Hullfish, Gordon, 45
Human Genome Sequencing
    Consortium, 349

Humanism, 48–49, 108, 215, 236, 237,
    239, 259, 264, 385. *See also*
    Renaissance
Humanistic futurists, 355–356
Humanistic psychology, 69–70, 257
Human Nature and Conduct (Dewey), 63
Hume, David, 32, 60, 105, 108
Hunt, James B., 73, 74, 75, 263, 305–306
Hus, John, 90
Husserl, Edmund, 53, 54
Hutchins, Robert M., 33, 40, 49, 265, 297
Hutchinson, Ann, 55
Huxley, Aldous, 214, 342, 355
Huxley, T. H., 171

I and Thou (Buber), 53
IBM, 194
Idealism, 36–38, 385
Ignatius of Loyola, Saint, 22
Illich, Ivan, 33, 53, 54, 216, 217,
    252–253, 258, 280, 290, 356
Illinois College, 158
Illinois State Normal, 174
Illiterate America (Kozol), 254
Image of the Future, The (Polak), 352
Immigration laws, 162–163
"Improving Student Achievement" (Rand
    Institute), 325
Inclusion, 385
Incomplete Guide to the Future, An
    (Harman), 355
Independence, sway of, 111
Individual contracting, 223
Individualized Education Program (IEP),
    221, 271
Individualized instruction, 193, 223
Individuals with Disabilities Education
    Act (IDEA), 120, 221–222, 272,
    311, 328
Individuals with Disabilities Education
    Act Amendments, 248, 270–271
Industrial education
    1865–1918, 167–168
    1918–2002, 205
Industrial exploitation, 161–162
Industrial Revolution, 11–12, 81, 116,
    129, 132–133, 161–162, 385
Infant schools, 144
Initiatives, reform, 307–310
In loco parentis, 248–249
"Innovative Methods in Elementary
    Education" (Ford), 222
Inquiry based instruction, 223
Inquiry-based methodology, 366–367
Inquiry into the Human Prospect, An
    (Heilbroner), 341
In Search of Excellence (Peters and
    Waterman), 296

In-service training, 385
Institutes, for teacher training, 147–148
Institutio Oratoria (Quintilian), 18
Institutional structure, evolution of,
    190–202
Institutions, linear, 359–360
Instrumentalism, 42
Integrated Services Digital Network, 194
Integration, 241, 242, 258
Intelligence, 60–61
Intelligence quotient (IQ), 385
Intercultural Center for
    Documentation, 253
Interdisciplinary curriculum, 365–366
Interests, 49
International Technological Education
    Association, 371–372
*International Yearbook of the
    International Institute of
    Teachers College* (Kandel), 18
Internet, 189, 193–194, 271, 346, 348,
    349, 358, 370, 385
Interstate New Teacher Assessment and
    Support Consortium, 323
*Investing in Our Children, Savage
    Inequalities* (Committee for
    Economic Development), 301
Involuntary segregation, 385
Ipswich Grammar School, 94
Is There a Public for Public Schools
    (Mathers), 256

Jacksonian Democracy, 128–129
Jacobson, Linda, 259
James, William, 33, 41–42, 51, 62, 63,
    176, 179
Jay, John, 112
Jefferson, Thomas, 103
    educational history, 123
    educational ideas, 117
    educational leadership of, 113–114
    Enlightenment and, 108
    freedom of religion, 111, 235, 237
    futures philosophy, 357
    humanism, 48
    Locke's influence on, 106
    national university, 112
    secondary schools and, 88
    state universities, 139
Jeffords, James, 239
Jehovah's Witnesses, 232–233, 234
Jenks, Christopher, 258
Jensen, Arthur, 258
Jews, 90, 169, 232
Jim Crow laws, 150
Job Corps, 206, 213, 258
John Birch Society, 281

John Dewey Society for the Study of Education and Culture, 45
Johns Hopkins University, 170–171, 278
Johnson, Andrew, 120, 159
Johnson, David R., 248
Johnson, Lyndon B., 46, 118, 121, 190, 207, 208, 209, 290
Johnson, Marietta, 209–210, 223
Johnson, Samuel, 58, 109
Johnston, Robert C., 308
Jones, Margaret E. M., 175
Jones v. Clear Creek Independent School District Texas, 233
Journal of Teacher Education, 248
Judd, Charles, 70
Jung, Carl, 66
Jungk, Robert, 354
Jungle, The (Sinclair), 182
Junior colleges, 201–202
Junior high schools, 197
Justice, Ideology, and Education (Stevens and Wood), 279

Kagan, Jerome, 68
Kahn, Herman, 352
Kalamazoo case, 163–164
Kandel, I. L., 18, 45
Kanpol, Barry, 54
Kant, Immanuel, 32, 33, 37, 108
Katz, Bruce, 297
Katz, Michael, 19
Kauffmann, Draper, 56
Kaufman, Polly Welts, 148, 149
Kaufman, Sara Rimon, 280
Kawata, Jennifer, 325
Kelper, Johannes, 16
Kendall, William, 194–195
Kennedy Foundation, 271
Kennedy, John F., 46, 118, 121, 190, 207, 209, 290, 312
Kennedy, Paul M., 341–342
Kentucky Educational Reform Act, 308
Kentucky Institute for Educational Research, 308
Kentucky Reform Act, 309
Kepler, Johannes, 21
Kerrey, Bob, 371
Kettering Foundation, 256
Keyes v. Denver, 243
Kidder, Rushworth, 57
Kierkegaard, Soren, 33, 53
Kierstead, Fred, 56, 278
Kilpatrick, William H., 33, 45, 210, 268
Kindergartens, 144, 146–147, 191, 202, 385
King James Bible, 169
King, Martin Luther, Jr., 46, 179, 180, 242
King's College, 92, 109
Klieman, Carol, 297

Knight, Edward, 172
Knights of Labor, 162
Knowing What Students Know (National Research Council), 295
Knowledge revolution, 385–386
Knox, John, 22
Knox, Samuel, 112, 114
Koehier, George, 350–351
Koerner, James, 265
Koffka, Kurt, 65
Kohl, Herbert, 193, 253, 264
Kohlberg, Lawrence, 53
Kohler, Wolfgang, 65
Kohn, Alfie, 257
Komensky, John A. *See* Comenius, John A.
Korean War, 180, 207
Kozol, Jonathan, 182, 240, 253–254, 278, 290
Ku Klux Klan, 281

Laboratory schools, 309
Labor, Health and Education Bill, 208
"Lack of a Public for Public Schools, The" (Mathers), 256
Lag theory, 13
Laissez-faire, 26, 386
Lamb's Chapel v. Center Moriches Union Free School District, 238
Lancaster, Joseph, 115, 128
Land grant college, 386
Language laboratories, 220
Lanier, Judith, 324
Laplace, Marquis de, 58
La Salle, Jean-Baptiste de, 22
Lasch, Christopher, 57, 358, 371
Lashley, Karl, 64
Laszlo, Ervin, 354
Latin grammar schools
    definition, 386
    middle colonies, 91
    New England colonies, 96
Latinos. *See* Hispanics/Latinos
Laud, William, 22
Lau v. Nichols, 277
Lawrence Scientific School, 140
Laws
    cyberlaw, 189
    immigration, 162–163
    Jim Crow laws, 150
    national education, 114
    school finance, 204
    state, 136
    See also Litigation; *specific legislation*
Lawton, Millicent, 294, 315
Leadership, educational, 112–114, 141–143
League of Nations, 189

Learning environments, diversified, 369–370
Learning First Alliance, 262
Lectures on Schoolkeeping (Hall), 148
Lectures to Young Ladies (Phelps), 148
Lee, Robert E., 132
Lee v. Weisman, 233
Left Back: A Century of Failed School Reforms (Ravitch), 295
Legislation. *See* Laws
Leibniz, Gottfried Wilhelm, 21
Lemon test, 237
Leonard and Gertrude (Pestalozzi), 146
Leonard, George, 53, 213, 257, 355, 361
Leonardo da Vinci, 21
Lessinger, Leon, 260
Lewin, Kurt, 65
Lewis, Anne, 308
Lewis, Laurie, 195
Liberalism, 108–109
Liberty Foundation, 237
Life adjustment education, 212–213
Lifelong learning, 362, 367–368
Lincoln, Abraham, 8, 123, 141, 150, 159, 188
Lincoln School, 211
Linear institutions, 359–360
Linton, Ralph, 14
Literary support, during common school revival, 141
Litigation, 330
    court cases, 246–248
    equal opportunity, 245–246
    future of, 346
    in loco parentis, 248–249
    involuntary segregation, 240–245
    religion and public schools, 232–239
    single-sex schools, 249
    vouchers, 239–240
    See also Laws
Little School in the Woods (Greenwich, Connecticut), 210
Lives of Children, The (Dennison), 252
Lives of the Noble Grecians and Romans, The (Plutarch), 17
Local funding, 202–203
Local-level educational reforms, 307–310
Locke, John
    academies and, 91
    educational history, 123
    empiricism, 32
    Enlightenment and, 108
    European educational theory, 145
    experience, 60
    futures philosophy, 356
    influence of, 35, 106
    realism, 33, 38
    social philosophy, 55
Lock-step, 386

Loeb, Penny, 151
Log College, 110
Logic, 32, 386
Longfellow, Henry Wadsworth, 10
Looping, 386
Lortie, Dan, 299
Loyal educational authorities (LEAs), 317
*Lubbock Civil Liberties Union v. Lubbock
    Independent School District,* 238
Lucy, Authurine, 242
Luddites, 357
Luther, Martin, 22, 26
Lutherans, 22, 90
Lyceum, 140, 386
*Lying: Moral Choice in Public and
    Private Life* (Bok), 256
Lynd, Albert, 45, 47, 219
Lyon, Mary, 142, 148, 278
Lyotard, Jean Francois, 54

MacIver, Robert, 13
Madison, James, 111, 112, 114
Magnet schools, 151, 290, 309
Mainstreaming, 271–272, 273, 290, 386
Making of a Counter Culture, The
    (Roszak), 254
Man for Tomorrow's World, A
    (Roszak), 254
Manhattan Institute for Policy
    Research, 275
Mann, Horace, 127, 128
    assessment and accountability, 259
    educational leadership, 141,
        142–143
    educational opportunities, 148,
        149–150, 152, 187
    educational reform, 313
    European school model, 145
    freedom of religion, 235
    normal schools, 147
    perennialism, 40
    philanthropy, 160, 271
    phrenology, 61
    school survey, 194
    social reconstructionism, 45
    standardization, 123
    state school systems, 119
Mannheim, Karl, 12, 46, 347
Manno, Bruno V., 256
Manufactured Crisis, The (Berliner and
    Biddle), 256, 271
Manzo, Kathleen Kennedy, 203
Marcel, Gabriel, 53
Maritain, Jacques, 33
Marland, Sidney, 273
Marshall, Ann S., 150–151
Marshall, John, 139
Marshall, Thurgood, 152, 241

Marshall, Toni, 221
Marx, Karl, 12, 343, 347
Mary I, 22
Maslow, Abraham, 49, 51, 53, 65, 69,
    188, 257
Massa case, 248
Massachusetts Institute of Technology
    (MIT), 171
Mastery learning, 68–69, 223
Materials. *See* Educational materials
Mather, Cotton, 18, 93, 107, 109
Mathews, David, 256
Maxcy, Spencer, 56
Mayer, Maria, 278
Mayflower Compact, 82
Mayhew, Jonathan, 109
Mayo, Charles, 175
Mayo, Elizabeth, 175
*Mazanec v. North Judson-San Pierre
    School Corporation,* 248
McAuliffe, Christa, 279
McCall, William, 71
McCarthy, Joseph, 48, 121, 215
McCarthy, Martha M., 261
McClintock, Barbara, 279
*McCollum v. Board of Education of
    Champaign, Illinois,* 234
McDonald County Rural School, 223
McGuffey, William Holmes, 137
McGuffey's Eclectic Readers, 137
McKenzie, Floretta, 282, 365
McKersie, William S., 162, 309
McKissack, Patricia, 200
McLaren, Peter, 19
*McLean v. Board of Education of
    Arkansas,* 236
McLuhan, Marshall, 357
McLuhan, Michael, 56
McMannon, Timothy J., 299
McMurry, Charles, 178
McMurry, Frank, 178
McNamara, Robert, 260
Mead, George H., 41
Meadows, Dennis, 354
Meadows, Donella, 347, 354
Meaning of the Twentieth Century, The
    (Boulding), 56
Means, Barbara, 346
Measurement, and child study, 70–73
"Measurement of Educational Products," 71
Mechanics' Free Press, 140
Medieval education, 20
Megatrends (Naisbitt), 352–353
Megatrends II (Naisbitt), 352
Meking, Thomas, 91
Melting pot, 386
Menendez, Pedro, 81
Mennonites, 90

Mental discipline, 386
Mental Tests and Measurement
    (Cattell), 70
Mentoring/apprenticeship, 167, 224
Meredith, James, 242
Meriam, Junius L., 210
*Metamorphic Mind: A Celebration of
    Creative Consciousness*
    (Samples), 356
Metaphysics, 31, 58, 386
Methodists, 115
Methods of Instruction (Neef), 146
Metzenbaum, Howard, 370
Mexican Americans, 241, 245. *See also*
    Hispanics/Latinos; Minorities
Meyer, Adolphe E., 164
Meyer v. Nebraska, 234
Michael, Donald N., 347
Microsoft, 348
Middle Atlantic States Association, 165
Middle colonies, 89–92
Middle schools, 197, 386
Milford School District, 238
Mill, John Stuart, 53, 86
Milliken v. Bradley, 243
Mills, Caleb, 142
Milton, John, 105, 107
Mind, 60–62
Mind, Self and Society (Mead), 41
Mini-courses, 196
Minimal Self, The (Lasch), 57
Minorities
    1865–1918, 162–163, 172–173
    business model, 297
    common school revival, 149, 152
    multicultural and bilingual
        education, 275–278, 283–284
    religion and, 232
    total English immersion, 283–284
    value teaching, 152
    See also specific minority groups
Missouri Assessment Program
    Tests, 243
Missouri v. Jenkins, 243
Mitchell, Maria, 278
Mitchell v. Helmes, 238
Modern developmental psychology and
    stage theory, 66–68
Modern realism, 39
Modular system, 386
Monitorial schools, 115, 386
Monroe, James, 112
Monroe, Paul, 18
Montesquieu, 108
Montessori, Maria, 147, 191, 211, 355
Montessori schools, 191, 202
Moody Bible Institute, 199
Moore, George E., 49–50

Moore, Gordon, 348
Moral Majority, 100, 236, 251, 265
Moravians, 90
Morgan, Lloyd, 63
Morgan v. Hennigan, 243
Morrill Act (1862), 120, 140–141, 162, 168, 170, 171, 205, 280
Morrill Act (1890), 150, 160, 162, 168, 170, 171, 173, 205, 280
Morrill, Justin, 140
Morse, Jedidiah, 116
Mt. Holyoke Female Seminary, 148
Mueller v. Allen, 238
Multicultural education, 251, 266, 275–278
Multiculturalism, 297, 386
Multidimensional values, 99–101
Multimedia systems, 194
Multiple discrimination, 67
Multi-track system, 386
Mulvenon, Sean, 220
Murphy, Archibald, 141
Murray, Lindley, 116
Murray v. Curlett, 233
Muslims, 236
Myrdal, Gunnar, 12

1984 (Orwell), 51, 342, 355
Nader, Ralph, 360
Naisbitt, John, 295, 352–353
National Academy of Early Childhood, 191
National Academy of Sciences, 278
National Advisory Council on Quality Teacher Education, 208
National Alliance of Business, 323
National and Community Service Trust Act, 120, 312
National Association for Colored Women, 199
National Association for the Advancement of Colored People (NAACP), 237, 240, 241, 281
National Association of School Superintendents, 120, 165
National Association of Secondary School Principals, 327, 328
National Association of State Universities and Land Grant Colleges, 324
National Association of Temporary and Staffing Services, 370
National Bible Association, 233
National Board Certification, 306
National Board for Professional Teacher Standards, 263
National Board for Professional Teaching Standards, 302, 323
National Board of Popular Education, 148

National Board of Professional Teaching Standards, 119
National Center for Educational Statistics, 195
National Center for Education Statistics 2000, 199
National Commission on Excellence in Education, 48, 293, 310, 321
National Commission on Teacher Education and Professional Standards, 261
National Commission on Teaching and America's Future, 305, 323
National Conference of State Legislatures, 203, 221
National Council for Accreditation of Teacher Education (NCATE), 217, 218, 275–276, 308, 321–323, 324
National Council of Professors of School Administration, 327
National Council of State Legislatures, 203, 323
National Crime Victimization Survey, 319
National Defense Education Act (NDEA), 120, 200, 205, 207, 208, 214, 250, 264, 273
National Defense Training Program, 205
National Education Association (NEA)
    1865–1918, 160, 165, 166, 177
    assessment and accountability, 261, 262, 275
    educational administration, 328
    educational psychology, 61, 71
    educational reform, 310, 312, 316, 318
    institutional structure, 191, 198
    Kozol, Jonathan, 254
    litigation, 235, 236
    textbooks, 281
National education legislation, 114
National Education Summit, 296–297
National education system, 112
National Endowment for the Humanities, 322
National Governors' Association, 294
National Herbart Society, 177
Nationalization, 134
National Library Association, 281
National Organization for Women (NOW), 237, 280
National PTA, 262, 328
National Research Council, 295
National School Boards Association, 238, 328
National School Lunch Act, 206
National Science Foundation, 235, 322
National Science Teachers Association, 217
National Service Legislation, 120

National Service Trust Fund, 312
National Society for the Study of Education, 195
National Teacher Certification, 218
National Teacher Examination (NTE), 262, 319, 321
National Teachers' Association, 165
National Teachers Corps, 208
National university, 112
National Women's Studies Association, 280
National Youth Administration, 200, 206
Nation at Risk, A (National Commission on Excellence in Education), 386
    criticism of, 224, 255
    educational administration, 327
    educational reform, 291, 293–295, 298, 301, 304, 307, 309, 324
    essentialism, 48
Nation Prepared: Teachers for the 21st Century, 324
Native Americans, 149, 173, 257, 275–278. *See also* Minorities
Native-American Week, 276
Naturalism, 386
"NCATE Moves Forward in Approving Outcomes for Preparation of Teachers" (Diegmueller), 218
Neef, Joseph, 146
Negro Affairs Division of the National Youth Administration, 200
Neill, A. S., 33, 52, 252, 264
Nelson, Henry, 72
New and Complete System of Arithmetic, A (Pike), 116
New Deal, 180, 189–190, 206
"New Divides, The," 371
"New Economy? You Ain't Seen Nothing Yet" (Toffler and Toffler), 349
New England Association of Colleges and Secondary Schools, 165
New England colonies, 92–97
New England Primer, 7, 94, 95, 116
New Jersey v. T.L.O., 246
New Schools for a New Century (Tewel), 329
Newton, Isaac, 21, 58, 105
New York Free School Society, 115–116
New York Regents' prayer case, 234–235
New York University, 175
New York Working Men's Advocate, 133
Next Ten Thousand Years, The (Berry), 356
Niagara movement, 240
Nietzsche, Friedrich, 53, 54
Nixon, Richard M., 181, 209
Noddings, Nel, 74, 218
Nongraded schools, 193, 224, 386
Nordlinger v. Hahn, 311

Normal schools, 147–148, 174, 215, 386
North Atlantic Treaty Organization (NATO), 183
North Central Association, 165, 166
Northwest Association of Secondary and Higher Schools, 165
Northwest Ordinance, 114, 120, 140, 160, 280
Novum Organum (Bacon), 21
Nussbaum, Martha, 54

Oberlin College, 148, 172
Object lesson, 175, 386
Occupational Handbook (2000–2001), 318
O'Connor, Sandra Day, 244
Ogburn, William F., 12, 55–56
Ogden, R. M., 65
Oglethorpe, James, 108
Old Deluder Satan Act, 24, 79, 94, 224, 331
Older Workers Protection Act, 274
Old field schools, 88, 386–387
One Florida Plan, 245
O'Neill, Robert, 130
On the Origin of Species (Darwin), 171, 179
On the Origins of the University of Paris (Goulet), 18
Open classroom, 193, 223–224
Open Classroom, The (Kohl), 253, 387
Open-ended methodology, 366–367
Optimism One (Esfandiary), 356
Optimistic extrapolists, 352–353
Orbis Sensualism Pictus (Comenius), 107
Ordinance of 1785, 114, 120, 140, 160
Ordinary Resurrections, Children in the Years of Hope (Kozol), 254
Oregon case, 169–170
Organization for Economic Cooperation and Development Report, 316
Orwell, George, 51, 342, 355
Oshiyama, Libby, 320–321
Oswego movement, 174–175
Outsourcing, 387
Overskill (Schwartz), 347, 362
Owen, Robert, 144

Paepke, C. Owen, 342
Page, David, 148
Paideia Proposal: An Educational Manifesto (Adler), 40, 282, 297–298
Paige, Rod, 182, 224, 258, 282
Paine, Thomas, 108, 109
Palm Beach County School, 221
Palmer, John, 324
Parental Rights and Responsibilities Act, 119
Parker, Francis W., 177, 209

Parkhurst, Helen, 211, 223
Parkinson, Jerry, 247
Parley, Peter, 116
Parochialism, 89, 387
Parochial schools, 169–170, 235, 239, 314, 387
Participatory futurists, 354
Part-time workers, 370
Pascal, Blaise, 53
Pastorius, Francis Daniel, 89–90, 91
Paterson, Tom, 361
Patterns of Educational Philosophy (Brameld), 45
Pavlov, Ivan, 51, 63
Payne, W. H., 175
Peabody College, 271
Peabody, Elizabeth, 144
Peabody Fund, 160
Peabody, George, 160
Pedagogy, 387
Peer harassment, 247
Peirce, Charles S., 33, 41, 49, 176, 179
Peirce, Cyrus, 141, 148
Pell grants, 120, 208, 311
Penn, William, 91
Pennsylvania Constitution, 114
People for the American Way, 237
Perennialism, 40, 219, 264, 387
Performance contracting, 268–269
Perkinson, Henry, 50
Perrone, Vito, 298
Persian Gulf War, 180, 207
"Perspectives on Education in America" (Huelskamp), 255
Perspective trees, 351
Pestalozzi, futures philosophy, 356
Pestalozzi, Johann H.
  educational leadership, 141–142
  educational philosophy, 34, 35, 39, 145, 176, 177, 178, 209
  educational psychology, 60, 67, 70
  influence of, 146
  manual training, 167
  teacher education, 175
Peters, R. S., 50
Peters, Thomas J., 296, 328, 354
Pew Charitable Trusts, 297
Pew Internet and American Life Project, 193
Phelps, Almira, 148
Phenomenological psychology, 69–70
Philadelphia Parkway Program, 309
Philanthropinum, 145
Philanthropy, 160
Philbrick, John D., 137
Philosophy, in colonial America, 106–108. *See also* Educational philosophy

Phoenix University, 201, 368
Piaget, Jean, 67–68, 72, 220, 223, 257
Pico v. Board of Education, Island Trees Union Free School District No. 26, 237
Pierce, Gilbert Ashville, 170
Pierce, John D., 142
Pierce v. Society of Sisters, 234
Pike, Nicholas, 116
Pilgrims, 94
Pinar, William, 56
Pinckney, Charles, 112
Piscataway v. Taxman, 244
Place Called School, A (Goodlad), 298, 299
Plagiarism, 189
Planck, Max, 58
Plato, 11, 20, 32, 33, 36, 37, 50, 54, 59–60, 264
Platt, John R., 75, 347, 353
Pledge of Allegiance, 233, 234
Plessy v. Ferguson, 150, 240
Plutarch, 1, 17, 26
Polak, Fred, 352
Political correctness, 251, 387
Political leaders, during common school revival, 141
Political parties, 161–162. *See also* *specific parties*
Political trends
  1812–1865, 128–135
  1918–2002, 189–190
Ponessa, Jane, 323
Poor Richard's Almanac (periodical), 105
Popular Science Quarterly, 41
Population changes, 1865–1918, 162–163
Populist Party, 162
Postman, Neil, 257, 361
Postmodernism, 50, 54–55
Potter, William J., 241
Poverty, 278, 283
Powell, Arthur, 273
Powell, Colin, 315
"Power of the Internet for Learning, The," 371
Powershift (Toffler), 371
Practice teaching, 216
Pragmatism, 40–45, 179, 387
Pragmatism: A New Name for Some Old Ways of Thinking (James), 41
Prayer, 232–235, 236, 237
Preparation, 178
Preparing Students for the 21ˢᵗ Century (Uchida, Cetron, and McKenzie), 365
Presbyterians, 22, 92
Preschools, 191, 202
Presentation, 178

Presley, Elvis, 180
Prickett, John, 141
Primary schools
    1918–2002, 191–192
    during common school revival, 137
Princeton, 92
Principalship: A Reflective Practice Perspective (Sergiovanni), 306
Principia Mathematica (Whitehead and Russell), 39
Principle learning, 67
Principles of Psychology (James), 62
Pring, Richard, 50
Privacy, 246–247
Private education
    1865–1918, 169–170
    educational reform, 314
    See also Parochial schools
Problem analysis, 360–361, 364, 366
Problem solving, 67
Professional Competencies for Teachers of the Twenty-First Century, 263
Professional educators, 141–142
Professional schools, 171
Programmed instruction, 196
Programmed learning, 193, 387
Progressive Education (journal), 210
Progressive education, 209–211, 212–214, 222–224, 387
Progressive Education Association (PEA), 72, 179, 209, 210–211, 212
Progressive Education at the Crossroads: Crusade for Democracy (Tanner), 298
Progressive Education Society, 45
Project 81, 269
Project method, 387
Prometheus Project, The (Fineberg), 347
Proposition 13 (California), 311
Prosser, Charles, 212
Protagoras, 341
Protestants, 22, 25, 169
Protestant Reformation, 21–23, 24
Protest philosophies, 50–55
Psalter, 7, 95, 116
Psychoanalysis, 66
Psychology (Dewey), 63
Psychology. *See* Educational psychology
Public Agenda Research Studies, 234
Public attitudes, 282
Public Education in the United States (Cubberley), 18
Public Law 94-142, 120, 270, 281
Public Law 105-17, 248
Public Purpose of Education and Schooling, The (McMannon), 299
Public schools
    1865–1918, 163–167

common school revival, 133–134
    partnerships with, 267
    religion and, 232–239
Public School Society of New York, 116
Public Works Administration, 206
Pulio v. Cavazos, 239
Puritans, 22, 24
    colonial liberalism and, 108–109
    New England colonies and, 92–97
    philosophy of, 93–94
    values, 98–99
Putting People First (Clinton), 312

Quackery in the Public Schools (Lynd), 47
Quakers, 22, 82, 89, 90, 91, 108, 149, 169, 247
Quality School, The (Glasser), 257
Quality Teaching (NCATE), 308
Quantum mechanics, 58–59
Queen's College, 92, 109
Quincy Grammar School, 137
Quintilian, M. F., 6, 18, 20, 70

Racism, 258
Radcliffe, 172
Radicals, 356
Rafferty, Max, 33, 45, 47
Raikes, Robert, 115
Rand Corporation, 315
Rand Institute, 325
Rate bill, 387
Raup, Bruce, 45
Ravitch, Diane, 169, 224, 283, 295
Raywid, Mary Anne, 320–321
Reagan, Ronald
    assessment and accountability, 277
    educational funding, 118, 121, 204
    educational philosophy, 46
    educational reform, 290, 310, 311, 312, 314, 316–317
    Elementary and Secondary Education Act, 208, 209
    Equal Access Act, 238
    volunteerism, 315
Realism, 38–39
Reasonable woman standard, 279
Reauthorization Act, 202
Rebuilding, 313–316
Reconstruction, 240
Reconstruction Finance Corporation, 206
Reform. *See* Educational reform
Reformation, 21–23, 24
Regents of the University of California v. Allan Bakke, 244
Rehabilitation Act, 270
Reimer, Everett, 252, 356
Re-inventing the Corporation (Naisbitt), 295

Religion, and public schools, 232–239.
    See also specific religions
Religious cycles, in New England colonies, 96–97
Religious freedom, 111–112, 169, 232–239
Religious revolutions, 21–23
"Religious Right Win Seats on School Boards Across the U.S." (Walters), 100–101
Religious sectarianism. *See* Sectarianism; *specific religions*
Renaissance, 20–21, 22–23, 24, 26
Rensselaer Polytechnic Institute, 140
Reorganization, 167
Reports, on educational reform, 291–293
Republic (Plato), 36, 59–60
Republican Party, 161, 205
Research, futures philosophy, 350–351
Resource distribution center, 364
"Restoring Lost Voices" (Gilligan), 280
Restructuring, 313–316
Results in Education: 1990 (National Governors' Association), 294
Revolutionary period. *See* American Revolution
Rhode Island State Department of Education, 318
Rice, Joseph, 70–71
Richardson, Joseph, 120
Richey, Warren, 238
Rickover, Hyman, 214, 219, 250, 265, 48
Rifkin, Jeremy, 341
Rigid systems, protest against, 178–179
Riley, Richard W., 208, 224, 282, 319, 320
Rimon, Sylvia B., 280
"Rising Tide of School Reform Reports, The" (Cross), 299
Robelen, Eric, 258
Roberts, Benjamin, 149
Robertson, Pat, 236
Rodriguez case, 208
Roe v. Wade, 281
Rogers, Carl, 33, 51, 65, 69, 257
Rogers, John, 95
Roosevelt, Franklin D., 180, 189–190, 200, 206
Rorty, Richard, 33, 54
Rose, Loweel C., 320
Rosenwald Fund, 160
Rose v. Council for Better Education, 245, 308
"Rosie the Riveters," 206
Rossow, Lawrence F., 247
Roszak, Theodore, 254
Rousseau, Jean Jacques
    colonial liberalism and, 109

educational philosophy, 32, 34, 35, 39, 42, 55, 74, 145
educational psychology, 60, 67, 70
Enlightenment, 108
futures philosophy, 343, 356
influence of, 106, 176
Pestalozzi and, 146
progressive education, 209, 210
Royal Society of London for Improving Natural Knowledge, 107
Royce, Josiah, 33, 37
Rudolph, Frederick, 142, 172
Rugg, Harold, 33, 45
Rural War Production Training Program, 205
Rush, Benjamin, 112, 117
Russell, Bertrand, 39, 49–50, 316
Russell, William, 141
Rutgers, 92
Rutherford, Ernest, 13
Ryle, Gilbert, 50

Sabin, Florence, 278
Sack, Joetta, 272
St. John's College, 143
Salaries, 203, 310, 313, 316–318, 319, 346
Salzmann, Christian, 145
Samples, Bob, 356
San Antonio Independent School District v. Rodriguez, 245
Sanchez, George, 283
Sandia National Laboratories, 255
Sandia Report, 255–256
Sandifer, Jawn A., 150
San Francisco Unified School District, 261, 277
Santa Fe v. Doe, 233
Sapiential authority, 361–362, 387
Sartre, Jean Paul, 33, 53, 54
Savage Inequalities: Children in America's Schools (Kozol), 254
Savoye, Craig, 221
SCDEs (schools, colleges, and departments of education), 321–322, 324
Scenario concepts, 351
Scheduling, flexible, 223
Scheffler, Israel, 50
Schlafly, Phyllis, 237
Schmitt, Eric, 297
Scholes, L. C., 157
School and Society (Bagley), 47
School and Society (Dewey), 168
"School Built for Horace, A" (Sizer), 325
School Committee of Burlington v. Department of Education of Massachusetts, 248

School effectiveness, 303–307
School finance. *See* Educational funding
School ideas, in Revolutionary period, 116–117
Schooling in Capitalist America (Bowles and Gintis), 252
School Law Reporter (Rossow and Parkinson), 247
School learning, 362
School of Organic Education (Fairhope, Alabama), 209, 223
School societies, 115–116
Schools of Tomorrow (Dewey and Dewey), 210, 213
Schools Our Children Deserve, The (Kohn), 257
School survey, 194–195
Schools We Need and Why We Don't Have Them, The (Hirsch), 301
Schools Where Children Learn (Featherstone), 257
Schools Without Failure (Glasser), 257
Schools-without-walls, 309
Schoolteacher (Lortie), 299
School use, extended, 211
School vouchers. *See* Vouchers
Schumacher, E. F., 355
Schurz, Margarethe Meyer, 128, 144
Schwartz, Edward, 361
Schwartz, Robert B., 297
Science and Human Behavior (Skinner), 65
Science, educational history and, 21
"Science for Human Survival" (Platt), 353
Scientific determinism, 58
Scientific realism, 39, 60, 107, 108, 387
Scotia Seminary, 199
Scott, Winfield, 132
Scwartz, Eugene, 347
Sears, Barnas, 160
Second Great Awakening, 137
Second Morrill Act. *See* Morrill Act (1890)
Secondary education
1812–1865, 137–138
1865–1918, 163–167
colonial America, 88
educational reform, 298–299
See also High schools
Sectarianism, 83–84, 387. *See also* specific religions
Secularism, 236, 237, 239, 259, 387
Segregation, 150, 240–245, 384, 385, 388
Sense realism, 39, 60, 107, 108, 387
Separate Baptists, 90
Separate-but-equal doctrine, 240–241
Separation of church and state, 112. *See* Freedom of religion

Separatists, 22
Sergiovanni, Thomas J., 306
Serra, Junipero, 81
Serrano v. Priest, 245
Service learning, 268
Servicemen's Readjustment Act. *See* GI Bill
Seventeenth Yearbook of the National Society for the Study of Education, 71
Seventh Annual Report to the Massachusetts Board of Education (Mann), 145
Sex education, 265, 266–267, 269
Sexism, 258
Sexual harassment, 247
Shane, Harold Gray, 56, 329
Shape of Things to Come, The (Wells), 342
Shaping Florida: The Effects of Immigration (Bouvier), 151
Shared Vision, A (Frazier), 294
Shea, Linda, 280
Sheffield Scientific School, 140
Sheldon, Edward, 141, 146, 148, 174–175
Shelton, Ian, 16
Shockley, William, 258
Shopping Mall High School, The (Powell), 273
Sidell, Ruth, 280
Signal learning, 67
Silberman, Charles, 217, 254–255, 264
Simmons-Harris v. Zelman, 239
Simon-Binet test, 70
Simon, Theodore, 70
Simulation, 350–351
Sinclair, Upton, 182
"Single Education Standard? States Are All Over the Map" (Baldauf), 182
Single-sex schools, 249
Single-track system, 387
Sizer, Nancy Faust, 325
Sizer, Theodore R., 294, 298–301, 325
Skinner, B. F., 33, 51–52, 64, 65, 66, 69, 224, 353
Smith, Adam, 108, 109, 129
Smith, B. Othaniel, 290
Smith College, 172
Smith, Elaine M., 200
Smith, Eugene R., 210
Smith-Hughes Act, 120, 168, 205
Smith, Huston, 57
Smith-Lever Act, 168, 205
Smith, Mortimer, 47–48
Smith, Samuel, 112
Smith, William, 121
Snider, Mike, 339

Social action, school as agent for, 257–259
Social and future philosophy, 55–58, 387
Social Change (Ogburn), 55–56
Social class, in colonial environment, 84–85
Social Contract (Rousseau), 145
Social Darwinism, 387
Social fragmentation, 387
Social Frontier (journal), 45
Social Frontier, 211
Social Ideas of American Educators, The (Curti), 12
Social philosophy, 55–58
Social reconstruction, 45–47, 264, 387–388
Social Technology (Helmer-Hirschberg), 352
Social trends
    1812–1865, 128–135
    1918–2002, 189–190
Society, and education, 8–11
Society for the Propagation of the Gospel in Foreign Parts (SPG), 82, 89, 90, 110, 135
Society of American Bacteriologists, 278
Society of Sisters of the Holy Names of Jesus and Mary, 170
Socrates, 20, 53, 320
"Socratic Approach to Character Education, The" (Elkind and Sweet), 307
Soltis, Jonas, 50
Sorokin, Pitirim, 13, 347
"Sorting Out Which Students Have Learning Disabilities" (Zirkel), 283, 329
South Boston High School, 242–243
Southern Association of Colleges and Schools, 160
Southern associations, 160–161
Southern colonies, 85–89
Southern Education Board, 160
Southern Futures Meeting, 256
Spearpoint: Teacher in America (Ashton-Warner), 257
Special education, 388
Special needs students, 270–274, 371
Spencer, Herbert, 171, 179
Spengler, Oswald, 347
Spiritual Milk for American Babes drawn from Both Brests of the Testements for their Souls' Nourshment (Cotton), 95
Spring, Joel, 19
Sputnik, 214, 250, 265
Staffing, differentiated, 223
Stage theory, 66–68

Standardization, 369
Standardizing associations, 165
"Standards for Technological Literacy" (Dugger, Jr.), 371–372
Stanford-Binet scales, 71
State constitutions, 114–115
State education systems, beginning of, 135
State funding, 136, 202–203
State laws, 136
State-level educational reforms, 307–309
State of the World Reports (Brown), 354
State universities, 139–140. *See also* Higher education; *specific universities*
Statistical Abstract of the United States, 198
Steelworkers v. Weber, 244
Stephenson, George, 123
Stephens v. Bongart, 247–248
Step to Man, The (Platt), 353
Stevens, Edward, 279
Stevens, Thaddeus, 136, 141
Stimulus–response learning, 67
Stone, Cliff, 71
Stop Textbook Censorship Committee, 237
Stowe, Calvin, 141, 145
Strategic Studies Center, 255
Stricherz, Mark, 308
Structural authority, 361–362
Structuralism, 62
Studebaker, John, 212
Students Right to Know, 200
Study of History, A (Toynbee), 56
Stull Act, 261
Subconsciousness, 61–62
Subject-centered school or curriculum, 388
Succeeding with Standards (Carr and Harris), 306
Suffer Little Children (Rafferty), 47
Sumner, William, 12, 14
Sunday schools, 115, 388
Sunday School Society, 115
Sundt, Melora, 279
Surveys, 194–195
Swaggart, Jimmy, 49
Swartz, James, 56
Sweatt v. Painter, 240, 241
Sweet, Freddy, 307
Swett, John, 142
Swift, Jonathan, 105
Syms, Benjamin, 86, 88
Synergistic processes, 359–360
Synergy, 366, 388
Syracuse University Research Institute, 207
Systems futurists, 353–354
Systems View of the World, The (Laszlo), 354

Tabler, M. Bernadine, 329
Tabula Rasa, 388

Talent Search, 258, 290
Talks to Teachers (James), 62
Tallerico, Marilyn, 308
Tanner, Daniel, 298
Tanner, Laurel N., 221
Tappan, Henry P., 170
Task Force on Education for Economic Growth, 295
Task Force on Teaching as a Profession, 319
Taxes, 281
    cyclical economy, 318
    equal opportunity, 245
    Gramm-Rudman Amendment, 312
    Hoar Bill, 160
    Mann, Horace, 143
    Puritans, 94
    religious freedom, 111, 234, 235, 236, 238
Teacher Accreditation Council, 323
Teacher (Ashton-Warner), 257
Teacher Corps, 258
Teacher education, 316
    1865–1918, 173–176
    1918–2002, 215–220
    changes in, 321–323
    five-year programs and Holmes Group, 324–326
    status of teachers, 316–318
    trends, 318–321
Teachers
    academic freedom, 214–215
    common school revival, 141–142, 147–148
    competency-based training and performance contracting, 268–269
    competency tests for, 262–263
    educational history and, 26
    futures philosophy and, 369
    progressive, 212–214
    salaries, 203, 310, 313, 316–318, 319, 346
    status of, 316–318
    training for, 147–148
Teachers Corps, 208, 216
Teachers of Our Nation's Schools (Goodlad), 300
Teachers of the Christian Religion, 111
Teaching as a Subversive Activity (Postman and Weingartner), 257
Team teaching, 192, 196, 224, 388
Teapot Dome Scandal, The (Sinclair), 182
Technological enthusiasts, 352–353
Technology, 58–59, 346, 348, 357–358, 361, 370. *See also* Industrial Revolution

Technology for All Americans Project, 372
"Technology Use in Tomorrow's Schools" (Means), 346
Telnet, 194
"Temps Getting More Work," 370
Tennant, William, 110
Tenth Amendment, 114, 118
"Tenth Bracey Report on the Condition of Public Education, The" (Bracey), 255
Terman, Lewis, 70, 72, 73
Terminal education, 388
Tewel, Kenneth J., 329
Textbooks, 160
Theobald, Robert, 347, 350, 354, 359–360, 361, 364
Theocracy, 388
Theory and Practice of Teaching (Page), 148
"Third Bracey Report on the Condition of Public Education, The" (Bracey), 255
Third Plenary Council of Baltimore, 169
Third Wave (Toffler), 11
Thirteenth Yearbook of the National Society for the Study of Education, 195
"32nd Annual Phi Delta Kappa/Gallup Poll of the Public's Attitudes Toward the Public Schools, The" (Rose and Gallup), 320
36 Children (Kohl), 253
Thompson, Dorothy, 219
Thoreau, Henry David, 37, 48
Thorndike, Edward L., 51, 62, 63–64, 71
Thought and Language (Vygotsky), 68
Thurlow, Martha L., 248
Ticknor, George, 139, 171
Time for Results (National Governors' Association), 294
Time Machine, The (Wells), 342
Time-on-task, 388
Tinbergen, Jan, 354
Titchener, Edward, 62
Title IX, 247, 279
Tocqueville, Alexis de, 1
Toffler, Alvin, 337
  educational change, 4, 11
  futures philosophy, 56, 347, 349, 354, 363, 371
  Wirth and, 75
Toffler, Heidi, 347, 349
Tolerance, 371
Tolstoy, Leo, 252
"To Make a Nation" (Loeb), 151
"Tomorrow's Schools of Education" (Holmes Group), 325

Toppo, Greg, 239
Total English immersion, 276, 283–284
Total Quality Management, 260
Tougher Standards (Kohn), 257
Toward a Reconstructed Philosophy of Education (Brameld), 45, 46
Toynbee, Arnold, 56, 347
Tracking system, 246
Traditions, conservative, 22–23
Training, versus education, 360
Transcendentalism, 140
Transfer of training, 388
Transformationists, 354
Transpersonal Education: A Curriculum for Feeling and Being (Hendricks and Fadiman), 355
Travis, Scott, 221
Treatise on the Selection and Methods of Studies (Fleury), 18
Trend extrapolation, 351
TRIO, 120, 311
Troy Female Seminary, 142, 148
True Reading, Spelling, and Writing of English, The (Pastorius), 90
Truman Commission, 201
Truman, Harry S., 190
Trump, J. Lloyd, 223
Turner, Frederick Jackson, 134
Turner, Nat, 149
Turner, Ronna, 220
Tuskegee Normal and Industrial Institute, 172–173
Tutorial schools, 87–88
Tuttle v. Arlington County School Board, 244–245
21st Century Capitalism (Heilbroner), 341
Twenty-Ninth Day, The (Brown), 354

Uchida, Donna, 365
Ulich, Robert, 47
Understanding Media (McLuhan), 56
Union College, 139
United Nations, 190
U.S. Bureau of Education, 174
U.S. Bureau of Justice Statistics, 319
U.S. Commissioner of Education, 160
U.S. Constitution, 111, 114, 118. *See also specific Amendments*
U.S. Department of Agriculture, 168
U.S. Department of Education, 120, 121, 220, 233, 319, 322
U.S. Department of Health, Education, and Welfare, 121, 204, 209, 242
U.S. Department of Justice, 319
U.S. Department of the Interior, 204
U.S. Geological Survey, 278

U.S. government. *See specific departments, offices, elected officials, and legislation*
U.S. Office of Education, 121, 204, 207, 212
U.S. Office of Indian Affairs, 173
U.S. Office of Secretary of Education, 316
U.S. Office of the Attorney General, 233
United States v. Virginia Military Institute, 249
Universal Geography (Morse), 116
Universities
  1865–1918, 170–172
  education departments, 175–176
  national, 112
  state, 139–140
  See also Higher education; *specific universities*
University Council for Educational Administration, 327
University of Alabama, 242
University of Alabama v. Garrett, 274
University of California, 244
University of Chicago, 209, 224
University of Colorado, 271
University of Houston at Clear Lake, 365
University of Iowa, 172, 175
University of Massachusetts, 365
University of Michigan, 175, 244
University of Mississippi, 242
University of Nevada, 244
University of Pennsylvania, 121
University of Tennessee, 139
University of Texas Law School, 240, 244
University of the State of Pennsylvania, 121
University of Virginia, 108, 113, 139
University of Wisconsin, 143
Unknown, education for, 360–361
Upward Bound, 46, 258, 281, 290
Up-Wingers (Esfandiary), 356
Utilitarianism, 388

Values
  core, 14–16
  multidimensional, 99–101
  Puritan, 98–99
Value teaching, 367
Vanderbilt University, 172, 271
Van Doren, Mark, 48
Van Horn, Royal, 339–340
Van Til, William, 38
Vassar College, 172
Veblen, Thorstein, 13, 354, 357
Verbal discrimination, 67
"Verbal, Math Scores on S.A.T. Up for Second Straight Year" (Lawton), 294, 315
Verne, Jules, 342, 356

Vernon, McCay, 281
Veronia School District v. Acton, 248
Victoria, Irwin, 81
Vienna Circle, 50
Vietnam War, 179–181, 182, 207, 247
Vinci. *See* Leonardo da Vinci
Violence, 267, 319, 346
Virginia Military Institute, 249
Visionaries, 356
Visions of the Future (Heilbroner), 341
Vista, 258
Vocational education
    1865–1918, 162–163, 164, 167–168
    1918–2002, 205
    definition, 388
Vocational Education Act, 205
Vocation Bureau and Breadwinner's
    Institute, 168
Voltaire, 105, 108
Voluntary segregation, 388
Volunteerism, 315
Vonnegut, Kurt, Jr., 356
Vouchers, 118, 236, 239–240, 274–275,
    388
Vygotsky, Lev, 68

Waddell, Lynn, 296
Wagner, Mary, 273
Wagner, Paul, 278
Wagschal, Peter, 57
Walden II (Skinner), 51, 65, 353
*Walker v. San Francisco Unified School
    District,* 239
Wallace v. Jaffree, 237
Walters, Laurel, 100–101
Walters, Richard, 69
War of the Worlds (Wells), 339, 342
Wars. *See specific wars*
Washburne, Carleton, 211, 223
Washington, Booker T., 172–173, 200, 240
Washington College, 175
Washington, George, 112
Waskow, Arthur, 356
Watergate, 181, 251
Waterman, Robert H., 296, 328, 354
Watson, John B., 51, 64, 224
Wealth of Nations (Smith), 109
Weber, Max, 11
Weber, R. M., 303
Webster, Noah, 112–113, 116, 117, 123, 152
Wechsler, David, 71
Wechsler Scales, 71, 258

Weingartner, Charles, 257, 363
Wellesley College, 172
Wells, H. G., 339, 342, 356
Wertheimer, Max, 65
Western Literary Institute, 141
Western Reserve, 136
Westminster Catechism, 116
Westminster Shorter Catechism, 95
West Point, 114
West Virginia v. Barnett, 234
West Virginia v. Riddle, 248
What Are Schools For? (Goodlad), 248
What Do I Do Monday? (Holt), 252
*What Happens Next? Trends in
    Postschool Outcomes of Youths
    with Disabilities* (Wagner), 273
*What Matters Most: Teaching for
    America's Future* (Hunt), 73, 302,
    305, 306
Wheeler, Raymond, 65
Wheelock, Eleazar, 138
Wheelock, John, 138
"When Special Education?" (Coeyman), 272
Where the Wastelands End (Roszak), 254
Whiskey Rebellion, 132
White, Frank, 236
White, William E., 304
Whitehead, Alfred North, 32, 33,
    34, 39
White House Conference of 1955, 273
Whitman, Walt, 140
Whitney, Eli, 132
"Why Can't They Be Like We Were"
    (Bracey), 255
Widmar v. Vincent, 238
Wieman v. Updegraff, 121
Wilderspin, Samuel, 144
Wiley, Calvin, 142
Willard, Emma Hart, 142, 148, 278
William and Mary College, 88, 109,
    110, 114
William Penn Charter School, 91
William T. Grant Foundation, 301
Williams, Roger, 84, 109
Williamson, Stephanie, 325
Wilson, Woodrow, 161, 189
Winthrop, John, 55
Wirt, William, 211, 223
Wirth, Arthur, 74–75, 309, 347
Wisconsin v. Yoder, 100, 235
Wise, Arthur J., 218, 323
Wise, John, 109

Wittgenstein, Ludwig, 50, 59
Wolf (Governor of Pennsylvania), 141
Wolman v. Walter, 238
Women
    accountability and assessment,
        278–280
    common school revival educational
        opportunities, 142, 148–149
    education (1918–2002), 200
    multicultural education, 278
    World War II and, 206
Women and Children Last (Sidell), 280
Women's Equal Opportunity Act, 279
Women Teachers on the Frontier
    (Kaufman), 148
Wood, George, 279
Worcester Polytechnic Institute, 167
Workforce 2020 (Hudson Institute), 151
Workforce Investment Act, 205
Works Progress Administration, 206
World Future Society. *See* Eighth
    General Assembly of the World
    Future Society
World Trade Center terrorist attack
    (2001), 180, 367
World Trade Organization (WTO), 343
World War I, 180, 189, 190, 205,
    206, 258
World War II, 180, 190, 205, 206,
    215, 222
World Wide Web (WWW), 193–194, 338,
    339, 346, 358, 371, 388
World Without Borders (Brown), 347, 354
*Would School Choice Change the
    Teaching Profession?*
    (Hoxby), 295
Wundt, Wilhelm Max, 62

Yale College, 72, 96–97, 109, 110
Yale Report of 1828, 139, 295, 322
Yale University, 139, 140, 341
Yalow, Rosalyn, 278–279

Zachery, Caroline, 72
Zapp in Education, 260
Zerchykov, Ross, 303
Zero tolerance, 246, 320, 388
Zirkel, Perry A., 283, 329
*Zobrest v. Catalina Foothills School
    District,* 238
Zollers, Nancy J., 302
Zwingli, Huldreich, 22